## THOMAS COOK

On 5 July 1841 Thomas Cook, a 33-year-old printer from Market Harborough, in Leicestershire, England, led a party of 570 temperance enthusiasts on a railway outing from Leicester to Loughborough which he had arranged down to the last detail. This proved to be the birth of the modern tourist industry. In the course of expanding his business Thomas Cook and his son John invented many of the features of organised travel which we now take for granted. Over the next 150 years the name Thomas Cook became synonymous with world travel.

Today the Thomas Cook Group employs over 10,000 people worldwide, with more than 1600 locations in over 100 countries. Its activities include travel retailing, tour operating and financial services – Thomas Cook is a world leader in traveller's cheques and foreign money services.

Thomas Cook believed in the value of the printed word as an accompaniment to travel. His publication *The Excursionist* was the equivalent of both a holiday brochure and a travel magazine. Today Thomas Cook Publishing continues to issue one of the world's oldest travel books, the *Thomas Cook European Timetable*, which has been in existence since 1873. Updated every month, it remains the only definitive compendium of European railway schedules.

The *Thomas Cook Touring Handbook* series, to which this volume belongs, is a range of comprehensive guides for travellers touring regions of the world by train, car and ship. Other titles include:
Touring by train
*On the Rails around Europe* (2nd edition December 1995)
*On the Rails around France* (Published 1995)
*On the Rails around Britain and Ireland* (Published 1995)
*On the Rails around the Alps* (Publication April 1996)
*On the Rails around Eastern Europe* (Publication April 1996)
Touring by car
*On the Road around California* (Published 1994)
*On the Road around New England* (Publication January 1996)
*On the Road around Normandy, Brittany and the Loire Valley* (Publication January 1996)
Touring by ship
*Greek Island Hopping* (Published annually in February)

For more details of these and other Thomas Cook publications, write to Passport Books at the address on the back of the title page.

# ON THE ROAD AROUND
# Florida

## A Comprehensive Guide to Florida by Car

Fred Gebhart & Maxine Cass
Eric & Ruth Bailey

A THOMAS COOK TOURING HANDBOOK

Published by Passport Books,
a division of NTC Publishing Group
4255 West Touhy Avenue,
Lincolnwood (Chicago),
Illinois 60646-1975 USA.

Text: © 1995 The Thomas Cook Group Ltd
Maps and diagrams:
© 1995 The Thomas Cook Group Ltd

ISBN 0-8442-9014-9
Library of Congress Catalog Card
   Number: on file

Published by Passport Books in conjunction
with The Thomas Cook Group Ltd.

Managing Editor: Stephen York
Project Editor: Deborah Parker
Map Editor: Bernard Horton
Maps drawn by Amanda Plant
Copy-editing by Martin Rosser
Cover illustration by Michael Bennallack-Hart
Text design by Darwell Holland
Text typeset in Bembo and Gill Sans using QuarkXPress
Maps and diagrams created using Aldus Freehand and GST Designworks
Text conversion by Riverhead Typesetters Ltd, Grimsby
Printed in Great Britain by Bell & Bain Ltd, Glasgow

All rights reserved. No part of this publication may be reproduced, stored in a retrieval system or transmitted, in any form or by any means electronic, mechanical, recording or otherwise, in any part of the world, without the prior permission of the publishers. All requests for permission should be addressed to the NTC Publishing Group at the above address.

*While every care has been taken in compiling this publication, using the most up-to-date information available at the time of going to press, all details are liable to change and cannot be guaranteed. The publishers cannot accept any liability whatsoever arising from errors or omissions, however caused. The views and opinions expressed in this book are not necessarily those of the publishers.*

**The Writing Team**
Written and researched by
**Fred Gebhart and Maxine Cass**
**Eric and Ruth Bailey**
Series and Book Editor: Melissa Shales

## About the Authors

**Fred Gebhart and Maxine Cass** are both photojournalists, who live in San Francisco. This is their second joint project: On the Road around California the first. Fred Gebhart contributes regularly to publications in Asia, Europe and the US. Tackling Florida gave him the chance to indulge his interest in scuba diving. Fred's earliest childhood memory of Florida is the looming walls of Castillo de San Marcos in St Augustine. Maxine Cass gardens and indulges a very fat cat in California between research trips around the world. Maxine studied Medieval European History at the University of California, Santa Barbara, and has lived in Greece and Senegal. The author of *A AAA Photo Journey to San Francisco*, her work is published in Europe, the US, Canada and Asia. Maxine loved the wild places and fauna of Florida.

**Eric and Ruth Bailey**, are experienced journalists who turned to free-lance travel writing some 15 years ago. Members of the British Guild of Travel Writers and The Society of Authors. both have traveled widely in Canada, Greece, Ireland, Mexico, the Philippines, South Africa, and the US. They have visited Florida more times that they can remember and have travelled thousands of miles, seeing the state from canoes, hot air balloons and on foot, as well as from the comfort of a car. The Baileys have written six travel guides on their own account – including *New York* and *Ireland* in the *Passport Illustrated Travel Guides* Series – and have contributed to others, including *On the Rails around Britain & Ireland*. They have a particular interest in inland waterways boating and are devoted dog lovers.

# CONTENTS

| | | | |
|---|---|---|---|
| Acnowledgements | 6 | Travel Essentials | 16 |
| Introduction | 7 | Driving in Florida | 46 |
| How to Use This Book | 9 | Background Florida | 55 |
| Route Map | 12 | Touring Itineraries | 59 |
| Driving Distances and Times | 14 | | |

## ROUTES AND CITIES

*In alphabetical order. Routes are listed in both directions – the reverse route is shown in italics. To look up towns and other places not listed here, see the Index, p. 348.*

| | | | |
|---|---|---|---|
| ATLANTA | 337 | LAKE CITY | 298 |
| *Atlanta to Tallahassee* | *328* | *Lake City to Orlando* | *261* |
| *Atlanta to Jacksonville* | *332* | | |
| | | LAKE OKEECHOBEE | 170 |
| COCOA | 157 | | |
| *Cocoa to Orlando* | *256* | MIAMI | 71 |
| | | Miami City tour | 81 |
| DAYTONA BEACH | 267 | Miami to Fort Lauderdale | 124 |
| *Daytona Beach to Orlando* | *257* | Miami to Fort Myers | 118 |
| | | Miami to Key West | 88 |
| EVERGLADES NATIONAL PARK | 112 | | |
| | | ORLANDO | 230 |
| FORT LAUDERDALE | 128 | *Orlando to Cocoa* | *256* |
| Fort Lauderdale to Fort Myers | 136 | *Orlando to Daytona Beach* | *257* |
| Fort Lauderdale to Palm Beach | 139 | *Orlando to Lake City* | *261* |
| *Fort Lauderdale to Miami* | *124* | *Orlando to Sebring* | *264* |
| | | *Orlando to Tampa* | *250* |
| FORT MYERS | 177 | | |
| Fort Myers to St Petersburg | 186 | THE PALM BEACHES | 144 |
| *Fort Myers to Fort Lauderdale* | *136* | West Palm Beach to Fort Myers | 174 |
| *Fort Myers to Miami* | *118* | West Palm Beach to Sebring | 167 |
| *Fort Myers to West Palm Beach* | *174* | West Palm Beach to Titusville | 149 |
| | | *West Palm Beach to Fort Lauderdale* | *139* |
| JACKSONVILLE | 278 | | |
| Jacksonville to Atlanta | 332 | PANAMA CITY | 308 |
| Jacksonville to Live Oak | 286 | Panama City to Pensacola | 313 |
| Jacksonville to Tallahassee | 297 | *Panama City to Tallahassee* | *304* |
| *Jacksonville to Titusville* | *266* | | |
| | | PENSACOLA | 317 |
| KEY WEST | 100 | Pensacola to Tallahassee | 325 |
| *Key West to Miami* | *88* | *Pensacola to Panama City* | *301* |

# CONTENTS

| | | | |
|---|---|---|---|
| PINELLAS PENINSULA | 202 | TALLAHASSEE | 299 |
| | | Tallahassee to Atlanta | 328 |
| ST AUGUSTINE | 272 | Tallahassee to Panama City | 304 |
| St Augustine to Tampa | 226 | Tallahassee to Jacksonville | 297 |
| | | Tallahassee to Pensacola | 325 |
| ST PETERSBURG | 194 | Tallahassee to St Petersburg | 292 |
| St Petersburg to Tallahassee | 292 | | |
| St Petersburg to Tampa | 213 | TAMPA | 216 |
| St Petersburg to Fort Myers | 186 | Tampa to St Augustine | 226 |
| | | Tampa to Orlando | 250 |
| SEBRING | 168 | Tampa to St Petersburg | 213 |
| Sebring to Orlando | 264 | | |
| Sebring to West Palm Beach | 167 | TITUSVILLE | 158 |
| | | Titusville to Jacksonville | 266 |
| SPACE COAST | 158 | Titusville to West Palm Beach | 149 |
| | | | |
| Hotel Codes and Central | | Index | 348 |
| Booking Numbers | 346 | Reader Survey | 351 |
| Conversion Tables | 347 | Colour Planning Maps | Facing back cover |

## ACKNOWLEDGEMENTS

Thomas Cook Publishing and the authors would like to thank the following individuals, businesses and organisations for their generous help during the research for this book:

Allison Blankenship; Betsy Dross; Rosalie, George & Marjory Leposky; Paul & Virginia McCarthy; Shannon Noble & Worth International Communications Corporation; Poi; Anne Hersley-Towler; GraceAnn Walden; Chelle Koster Walton; Gary Stogner and Dean Sullivan, Florida Division of Tourism, Tallahassee; The Zimmerman Agency, Tallahassee; Rona Hawkin, Wakulla Springs State Park; The Peabody, Orlando; Paul Steiner, Orlando/Orange County CVB; Sheraton Inn Tampa; The Hilton, Melbourne; Lori Campbell Baker, Daytona Beach Area CVB; Ivanhoe Beach Resort, Ormond Beach; Tica Walley, St Augustine/St John's County Chamber of Commerce; The Ponce de Leon Golf and Conference Resort, St. Augustine; Nicole Joseph, Jacksonville and the Beaches CVB; Marina Hotel, Jacksonville; John and Rita Kovacevich, The Hoyt House, Fernandina Beach; Amelia Island Plantation; Edgewater Beach Resort, Panama City Beach; Sheilah Bowman, Pensacola C & V Information Center; Clarion Resort and Convention Center, Pensacola Beach; Ramada Hotel, TallahasseeResidents Inn By Marriott, Gainesville; Port Paradise Resort, Crystal River; Fred Corrigan, Innisbrook Hilton Resort, Palm Harbor; Lakeside Inn, Mount Dora; Barbara Dannield, Georgia Department of Industry, Trade and Tourism; Renaissance Hotels International; Jenny Stacy, Savannah Area CVB; Ballastone Inn, Savannah, Georgia; Ruth Birch Sykes, Macon-Bibb County CVB; The 1842 Inn, Macon, Georgia.; J B Thompson; Niall Davison, Thomas Cook Own Label; Bob Clark and Elaine Taylor, Insurance Products Thomas Cook Group; . . . and all of the alligators, armadillos, birds, manatees, turtles and other creatures that have survived the human tide flowing into Florida.

# INTRODUCTION

People have been attracted to Florida as a holiday playground for well over a century. But it was a mouse that set it on course in 1971 to become the USA's top leisure destination. Not just any mouse: Mickey Mouse.

Few would have heard of the 28,000 acres of swampland west of Orlando if Walt Disney World had not developed it with the Magic Kingdom and other themed entertainments. The Central Florida area is now home to numerous theme parks, water parks and not-to-be-missed attractions which are constantly expanding or introducing new ideas to entice visitors to return again and again.

Known as the Sunshine State, Florida is noted for its year-round sunshine. It could also be considered the Schizophrenic State, the north and south being distinctly different in personality. Those who eschew the prospect of spending time amid cartoon characters or in a *Miami Vice* set would probably delight in the historic small towns, hiking trails, forests and wildlife of the north. Those same people, persuaded perhaps by their families to take in Miami and Walt Disney World in a Florida vacation, may find themselves thoroughly enjoying the experience.

There is a great deal more to Florida, north and south, than sunshine and hype. The distance between Pensacola, in the Panhandle near the state's border with Alabama, and Key West, the southernmost point, is 792 miles. Florida is larger than Greece. It is also larger than England and Wales combined.

It cannot claim to be the most beautiful state in the nation. The scenery is pleasant rather than stunning. Much of Florida is flat, with a few gentle hills in the central and far northern regions. Water provides the best views: the Intracoastal Waterway, the Atlantic Ocean and the Gulf of Mexico, and the crystal-clear springs, rivers and lakes beloved by anglers and birdwatchers.

Lesser-known aspects of the state show that Florida has many faces. The rodeos that reflect the early cattle-rearing days. The racehorse breeding and training region of Ocala. The groves of oranges, limes and grapefruit. The Salvador Dali Museum housing some of his most famous works. Places where you can hire a canoe and paddle silently through forests of palms and hardwood trees, sighting whitetail deer, raccoons, the ubiquitous alligator and possibly an armadillo. The plantation houses and Spanish moss which give Northern Florida its Deep South ambience...

Other aspects of Florida are world famous. Spaceport USA at the Kennedy Space Centre. The cruise ship ports — Miami is the world's busiest, with around three million passengers a year. The wide range of seafood. The golf courses — 1100 at the last count, and that's 200 more than any other American state. And the beaches.

You have a choice of golden beaches dotted with palm trees, beaches where collectors search for rare shells, beaches you can drive along as the tide ebbs, and beaches where the dazzling white sand is almost pure quartz.

With over 1800 miles of coastline,

## INTRODUCTION

12,000 miles of rivers and streams and three million acres of lakes, Florida can cope with any number of fishing enthusiasts. Freshwater fishing from boat or bank may yield a largemouth bass. Sea-going boat charters offer instruction and hire of all equipment if required. You could do battle with marlin, shark or the spectacular sailfish. Or you can sit in the sun on a public pier with rod and line. Anything you catch may be cadged off you by a posse of pelicans. Fishing comes easily to them, but why should they bother when you can land a beakful for them?

Watersports are a major activity. Snorkellers off Key West can explore the only living coral reef in the continental USA, watching colourful tropical fish flit by. More than 4000 wrecks provide adventure for scuba divers. Waterskiing, jetskiing, parasailing, surfing, dinghy sailing, speedboating, tubing, canoeing and kayaking can be enjoyed. Deep springs with extraordinarily clear water attract divers, and can also be surveyed from glass-bottomed boats.

It is no surprise that tourism is the state's biggest industry, providing employment for nearly 660,000 Floridians and attracting about 40 million visitors a year. Of these, around 83% are Americans. Of the international visitors, most (about 2.5 million) are from Canada. About a million visitors from the UK holiday in Florida each year, the vast majority of them making repeat visits.

Florida is the fourth most populated state in the USA, with about 13 million residents. (The state is only beaten by California with a population of 30 million, New York with 18.3 million and Texas with 17.5 million).

The state has more than 100,000 miles of roads. Car rental is the cheapest in the US, and all the major companies are represented in Florida. Generally, drivers have to be over 21.

You can drive great distances, especially through the forests of the north and north-west, without seeing a dwelling, let alone a filling station or restaurant. Although the weather here is still ideal for touring in winter, any café or gas station you encounter may be closed. Set off with a full tank and refreshments on board.

Atlanta, Georgia, is a convenient gateway for visitors planning a pre- or post-Olympics tour of Northern Florida during 1996. A taste of the beautiful Deep South is provided by a round trip to Savannah, Amelia Island, Jacksonville, then along Florida's Panhandle and the dazzling beaches of the Emerald Coast, returning to Atlanta through Tallahassee and Macon.

Accommodation in Florida is of a high standard, with more than one-third of a million rooms and suites in hotels, motels, inns and self-catering units. The state is well geared up for campers, with at least 700 campsites, the vast majority having facilities for RVs (recreational vehicles). More than five million people camp in Florida each year.

Are there any problems in paradise? Florida has suffered negative publicity in recent years after attacks on tourists. An infinitesimal proportion of visitors has been involved, but one incident is one too many, and in a state generally regarded as safe, international headlines have resulted. Don't let these put you off. Rental cars are now unidentifiable, highway rest centres have security patrols and a number of other steps taken to protect tourists are dealt with in this book. Take the precautions you practise on your home ground and you should find Florida a friendly and hospitable destination.

# HOW TO USE THIS BOOK

## ROUTES AND CITIES

On the Road around Florida provides you with an expert selection of 22 recommended routes between key cities and attractions of Florida (and the alternative gateway city of Atlanta in Georgia), each in its own chapter. Smaller cities, towns, attractions and points of interest along each route are described in the order in which you will encounter them. Additional chapters are devoted to the major places of interest which begin and end these routes. For large places such as Miami there may be several chapters – e.g. one for the downtown or city centre and one for the greater metropolitan area. These route and city chapters form the core of the book, from page 71 to page 343.

The routes have been chosen to take in as many places of interest as possible. Where applicable, an alternative route which is more direct is also provided at the beginning of each recommended route chapter. This will enable you to drive more quickly between the cities at the beginning and end of the route, if you do not intend to stop at any of the intermediate places. To save space, each route is described in only one direction, but of course you can follow it in the reverse direction, too.

The arrangement of the text consists of a chapter describing a large city or region of interest first, followed by chapters devoted to routes leading from that place to other major destinations; e.g. the first city to be covered is Miami (pp. 71–87, with two chapters beacuase of its size), followed by routes from Miami to Key West (pp. 88–99), Miami to Fort Myers (pp. 118–123), and Miami to Fort Lauderdale (pp. 124–127). Key West and the Everglades are described in chapters following the Miami to Key West route. After the Miami to Fort Lauderdale route comes the chapter on Fort Lauderdale, followed in turn by routes out of Fort Lauderdale to other places, and so on.

The order of chapters thus follows the pattern of your journey, beginning in the south of Florida and proceeding generally northwards, ending with routes to Atlanta. However, you can just as easily work backwards going south. To find the page number of any route or city chapter quickly, use either the alphabetical list on the **Contents** pages, pp. 5–6, or the master **Route Map** on pp. 12–13.

The routes are designed to be used as a kind of menu from which you can plan an itinerary, combining a number of routes which take you to the places you most want to visit.

## WITHIN EACH ROUTE

Each route chapter begins with a short introduction to the route, followed by driving directions from the beginning of the route to the end, and a sketch map of the route and all the places along it which are described in the chapter. This map, intended to be used in conjunction with the driving directions, summarises the route and shows the main intermediate distances and road numbers; for a key to the symbols used, see p. 11.

### DIRECT ROUTE

➡ This will be the fastest, most direct, and sometimes, predictably, least interesting drive between the beginning and end of the route, usually along major highways.

## HOW TO USE THIS BOOK

### SCENIC ROUTE

➡ This is the itinerary which takes in the most places of interest, usually using ordinary highways and minor roads. Road directions are specific; always be prepared for detours due to road construction, etc.

The driving directions are followed by sub-sections describing the main attractions and places of interest along the way. You can stop at them all or miss out the ones which do not appeal to you. Always ask at the local tourist information centre (usually the Convention & Visitors Bureau or Chamber of Commerce) for more information on sights, lodgings and places to eat at.

 **SIDE TRACK**

This heading is occasionally used to indicate departures from the main route, or out-of-town trips from a city, which detour to worthwhile sights, described in full or highlighted in a paragraph or two.

### CITY DESCRIPTIONS

Whether a place is given a half-page description within a route chapter or merits an entire chapter to itself, we have concentrated on practical details: local sources of tourist information; getting around in city centres (by car, by public transit or on foot as appropriate); accommodation and dining; post and phone communications; entertainment and shopping opportunities; and sightseeing, history and background interest. The largest cities have all this detail; in smaller places some categories of information are less relevant and have been omitted or summarised. Where there is a story to tell which would interrupt the flow of the main description, we have placed **feature boxes** on subjects as diverse as 'The Atlanta Olympics' and 'Railroad Barons'.

Although we mention good independently owned lodgings in many places, we always also list the hotel chains which have a property in the area, by means of code letters to save space. Many travellers prefer to stick to one or two chains with which they are familiar and which give a consistent standard of accommodation. The codes are explained on p. 346, and central booking numbers for the chains are also given there.

### MAPS

In addition to the sketch map which accompanies each route, we provide maps of major cities (usually the downtown area, but also the greater metropolitan area in places like Miami), smaller towns, regions, scenic trails, national parks, and so on. At the end of the book is a section of **colour road maps** covering the whole area described in this book, which is detailed enough to be used for trip planning and on the road. The **key to symbols** used on all the types of map in this book is shown on p. 11.

### THE REST OF THE BOOK

At the front of the book, **Driving Distances** is a tabulation of distances between main places, to help in trip planning. The use of the **Contents** and **Route Map** pages has already been mentioned above. **Travel Essentials** is an alphabetically arranged chapter of general advice for the tourist new to Florida or to the United States, covering a wide range subjects from accommodation and safety to facilities for disabled travellers and how much

# HOW TO USE THIS BOOK

to tip. **Driving in Florida** concentrates on advice for drivers on the law, rules of the road, and so on. **Background Florida** gives a concise briefing on the history and geography of this fascinating state. **Touring Itineraries** provides ideas and suggestions for putting together an itinerary of your own using the selection of routes in this book. At the end of the book, the **Conversion Tables** decode US sizes and measures for non-US citizens. Finally the **Index** is the quick way to look up any place or general subject. And please help us by completing and returning the **Reader Survey** at the very end of the text; we are grateful for both your views on the book and new information from your travels in Florida.

## KEY TO MAP SYMBOLS

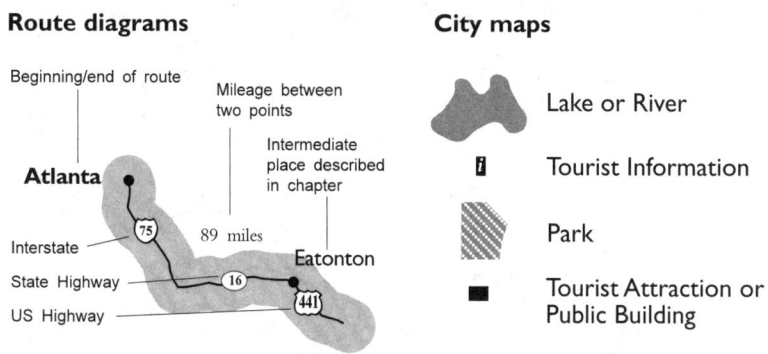

## KEY TO PRICE DESCRIPTIONS

It is impossible to keep up to date with specific tariffs for lodging and accommodation or restaurants, although we have given some general advice under 'Cost of Living' in the Travel Essentials chapter on p. 16). Instead, we have rated establishments in broad price categories throughout the book, as follows:

| *Accommodation (per room per night)* | | *Meal (for one person, excluding drinks, tip or tax)* | |
|---|---|---|---|
| Budget | Under $35 | Cheap | Under $5 |
| Moderate | Under $90 | Budget | Under $10 |
| Expensive | Under $150 | Moderate | Under $20 |
| Pricey | $150 and higher | Pricey | Over $20 |

## ABBREVIATIONS USED IN THE BOOK
*(For hotel chains, see p. 346)*

| | | | |
|---|---|---|---|
| Bldg | Building (in addresses) | Jan, Feb | January, February, etc. |
| Blvd | Boulevard | min(s) | minute(s) |
| Dr. | Drive (in addresses) | Mon, Tues | Monday, Tuesday, etc. |
| Fwy | Freeway | Rd | Road (in addresses) |
| hr(s) | hour(s) | Rte | Route, e.g. Rte 450 |
| Hwy | US or State Highway, e.g. Hwy 1 | St | Street (in addresses) |
| I- | Interstate Highway, e.g. I-95 | Ste | Suite (in addresses) |

# ROUTE MAP

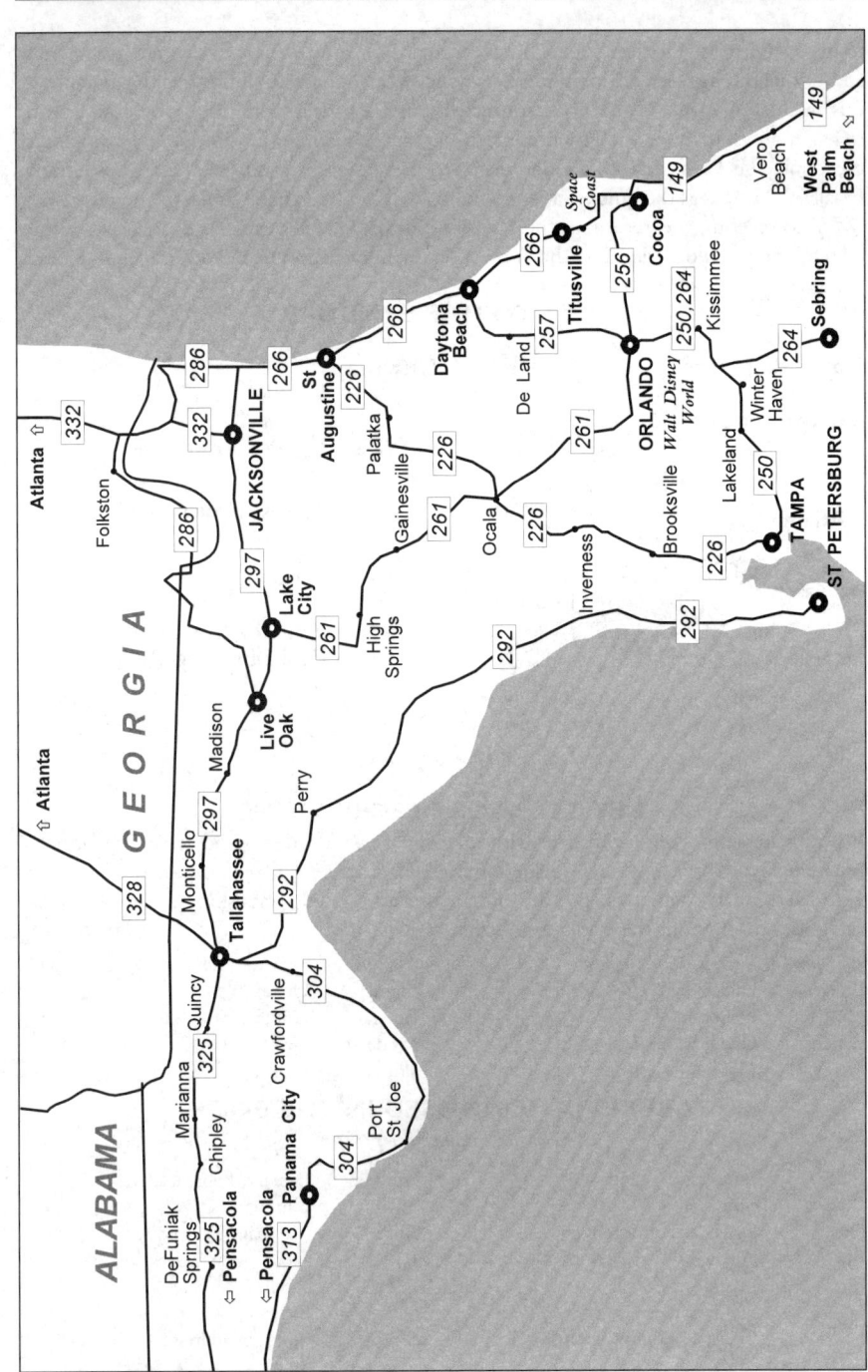

**KEY TO ROUTES**

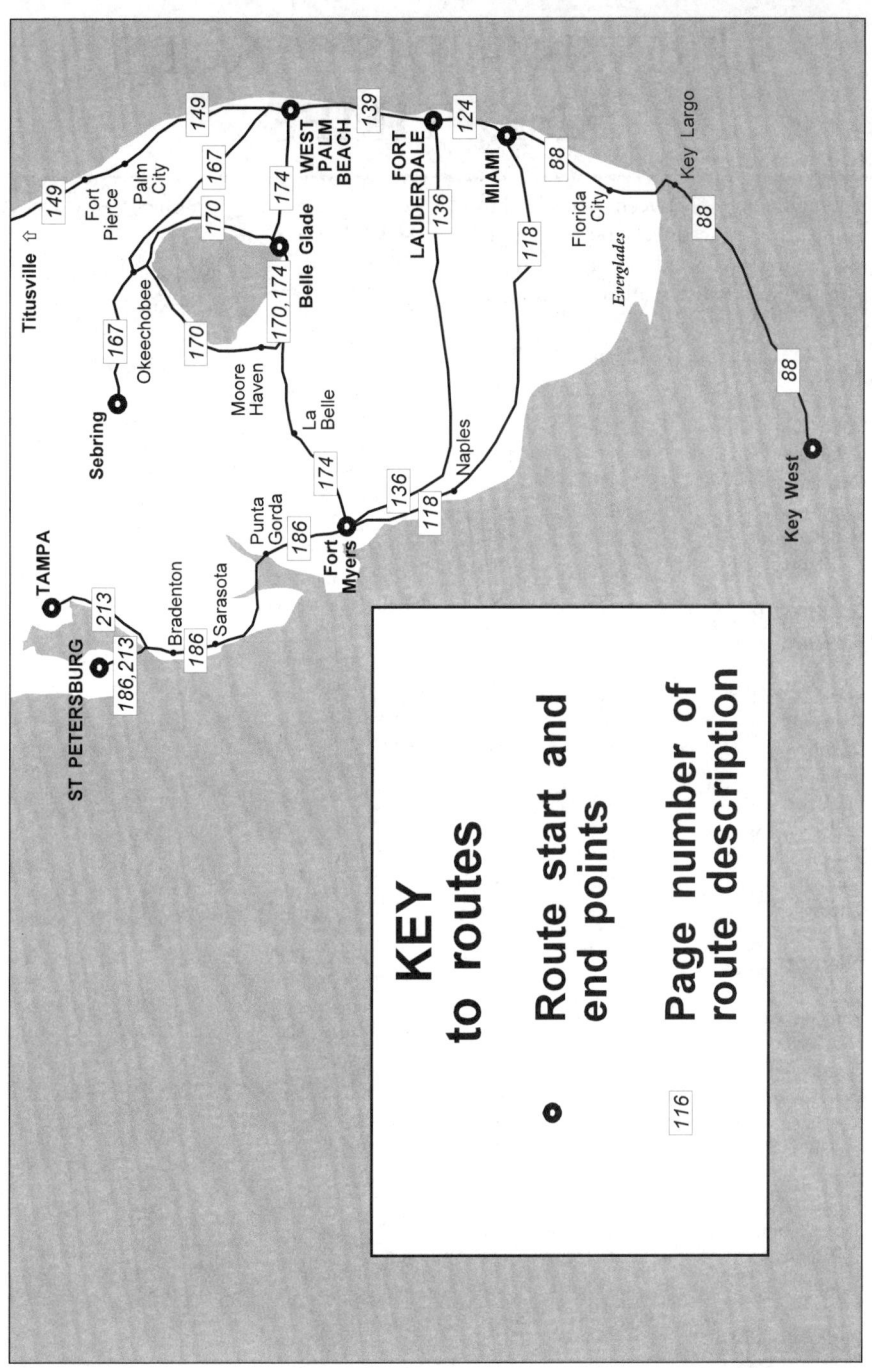

# Driving Distances and Times

These distances between major centres follow the most direct routes. Timings are approximate and do not allow for stops or for adverse traffic or road conditions.

|  | Miles | Hours |
|---|---|---|
| **Atlanta to . . .** | | |
| Fort Lauderdale | 653 | 13 |
| Jacksonville | 336 | 6¾ |
| Miami | 676 | 13½ |
| Orlando | 470 | 9½ |
| Pensacola | 457 | 9¼ |
| St Petersburg | 516 | 10¼ |
| Tallahassee | 266 | 5¼ |
| Tampa | 522 | 10½ |
| West Palm Beach | 610 | 12¼ |
| **Jacksonville to . . .** | | |
| Atlanta | 336 | 6¾ |
| Fort Lauderdale | 317 | 6¼ |
| Gainesville | 69 | 1½ |
| Miami | 340 | 6¾ |
| Orlando | 134 | 2¾ |
| Pensacola | 354 | 7 |
| St Petersburg | 208 | 4¼ |
| Tallahassee | 163 | 3¼ |
| Tampa | 186 | 3¾ |
| Titusville | 134 | 2¾ |
| West Palm Beach | 274 | 5½ |
| **Miami to . . .** | | |
| Atlanta | 676 | 13½ |
| Fort Lauderdale | 22 | ½ |
| Fort Myers | 141 | 2¾ |
| Gainesville | 331 | 6½ |
| Jacksonville | 338 | 6¾ |
| Key West | 155 | 3¼ |
| Orlando | 228 | 4½ |
| Pensacola | 649 | 13 |
| Sebring | 161 | 3¼ |
| St Petersburg | 302 | 6 |
| Tallahassee | 463 | 9¼ |
| Tampa | 245 | 5 |
| Titusville | 204 | 4 |
| West Palm Beach | 64 | 1¼ |

|  | Miles | Hours |
|---|---|---|
| **Orlando to . . .** | | |
| Atlanta | 470 | 9½ |
| Fort Lauderdale | 209 | 4¼ |
| Fort Myers | 153 | 3 |
| Gainesville | 109 | 2¼ |
| Jacksonville | 134 | 2¾ |
| Key West | 371 | 7½ |
| Pensacola | 428 | 8½ |
| Sebring | 86 | 1¾ |
| St Petersburg | 105 | 2¼ |
| Tallahassee | 242 | 4¾ |
| Tampa | 85 | 1¾ |
| Titusville | 40 | 1 |
| West Palm Beach | 166 | 3¼ |
| **Tallahassee to . . .** | | |
| Atlanta | 266 | 5¼ |
| Fort Lauderdale | 444 | 9 |
| Fort Myers | 356 | 7¼ |
| Gainesville | 144 | 3 |
| Jacksonville | 163 | 3¼ |
| Key West | 606 | 12¼ |
| Orlando | 242 | 4¾ |
| Pensacola | 191 | 3¾ |
| Sebring | 303 | 6 |
| St Petersburg | 250 | 5 |
| Tampa | 239 | 4¾ |
| Titusville | 275 | 5½ |
| West Palm Beach | 401 | 8 |
| **Tampa to . . .** | | |
| Atlanta | 522 | 10½ |
| Fort Lauderdale | 234 | 4½ |
| Fort Myers | 123 | 2½ |
| Gainesville | 128 | 2½ |
| Jacksonville | 202 | 4 |
| Key West | 387 | 7¾ |
| Miami | 245 | 5 |
| Orlando | 85 | 1¾ |
| Pensacola | 425 | 8½ |
| Sebring | 84 | 1¾ |
| St Petersburg | 20 | ½ |
| Titusville | 130 | 2½ |
| West Palm Beach | 193 | 3¾ |

# THOMAS COOK TOURING HANDBOOKS
## All the practical information you need to plan your holiday

Practical guides to help you plan and enjoy your fly-drive holiday. Unique route-based books with 352 pages containing over 40 driving routes designed to reveal the very best of your chosen region. Mix and match the routes to make up your ideal tour or use one of the ready-made itineraries.

### On the Road around California
**Price £10.95**
★ Covers the whole of California, including Los Angeles, San Francisco, San Diego and the Pacific Coast
★ Includes popular side-trips to Las Vegas and Mexico

### On the Road around New England
**Published February 1996 Price £10.95**
★ Covers all of New England, state by state, city by city
★ Includes details of side-trips to Quebec, Montreal, Niagara Falls and New York City

The above publications are available from bookshops and Thomas Cook UK retail shops, or direct by post from Thomas Cook Publishing, Dept (TPO/FLO), PO Box 227, Peterborough PE3 8BQ UK (Extra for p&p). Tel: 01733 268943/505821

# TRAVEL ESSENTIALS

An alphabetical listing of helpful tips and advice for those planning a Florida holiday.

## ACCOMMODATION

Florida offers accommodation on every price level imaginable, from five-star hotels and posh resorts to youth hostels and campsites. Local tourist offices can provide accommodation lists and telephone numbers, but generally can't make bookings. Where available, accommodation services are noted in the text.

Accommodation can be extremely hard to find in major tourist destinations during high season, which is usually mid-Dec–end-Mar, plus weekends and major public holidays. Resort areas on the Atlantic and Gulf (of Mexico) coasts must be booked several months in advance. From Apr–May and Sept–Nov, high season prices are halved. During the hot and humid summer, expect to book rooms at 20%–30% of high season rates.

Thomas Cook or any other travel agent can handle room bookings when purchasing air tickets and vehicle hire. All-inclusive fly-drive arrangements, and 'do it yourself packages' such as Thomas Cook's Florida and America programmes, can provide hotel vouchers, exchangeable at a range of hotel chains, which guarantee a pre-paid rate at participating chains, although they do not guarantee rooms – it's up to you to phone ahead as you go, or take a chance on availability. It's particularly important to pre-book the first and last nights' stay to avoid problems when connecting with international air flights.

Throughout the book we have indicated prices of accommodation in a comparative way by using terms such as 'moderate' and 'pricey'; see 'How to Use This Book', p. 9, for an explanation of what these descriptions mean in terms of dollars.

### Hotels and Motels

US hotel rates are quoted for single or double occupancy; children under the age of 18 usually stay cheaply or for free with parents. Florida's high season prices in Key West, Naples and Palm Beach rival those of New York City.

Most chain hotels and motels have toll-free reservation telephone numbers that can be reached from anywhere in North America. Many also have centralised world-wide reservations systems in other countries. On p. 346 there is a selection of these, along with the abbreviations used in the text of this book to indicate which chains are present in the town or city being described. Toll-free UK booking numbers for specific hotels are given in the text.

You will normally require a voucher or credit card number to guarantee any advance booking. Ask for discounts if you're disabled, a senior (over 55), a student, a motoring club member, in the military, or travelling in low season. When checking in, always ask if there's a cheaper room rate than the one you pre-booked. It's often cost-effective to find lodging day by day, especially in off-peak seasons.

**Motels** are often the best bet. Literally 'motor hotels', motels are one- to three-

ACCOMMODATION

storey buildings offering a modest version of hotel accommodation. Most belong to nation-wide chains which enforce service and safety standards.

Independent motels may not be quite as fancy, but offer even lower prices. Motels fill up fast during high season, but last-minute rooms are usually available in low season, especially during the week. The *AAA TourBook for Florida* and the *AAA TourBook for Georgia, North Carolina and South Carolina* list thousands of motels and hotels; thousands more are just as comfortable and affordable. Check the motels that line major highways entering most cities and towns. Special prices are often noted on a roadside sign, but apply to only a limited number of rooms. **Budget hotels**, especially in cities, tend to be dim, dirty and dangerous. Look for a motel or youth hostel instead.

If you are visiting one city or area for a few days to several months, a suite hotel or more modest kitchenette or efficiency apartment provides more space with complete or partial kitchen facilities for self-catering. Hotels and motels without dining rooms are usually happy for residents to order take-out deliveries and may have a selection of menus from restaurants that will deliver stashed in reception.

Many lodgings offer non-smoking rooms. Specify which you require when booking and verify your choice on arrival. Insecticide sprays are a way of life in the South, and Florida and Georgia are no exception. Request another room if fumes from either are a problem.

## Bed and Breakfast

Most areas of Florida and Georgia have at least one Bed and Breakfast. Key West and St Augustine have many. Prices range from budget to pricey; styles are basic to posh. Standard breakfast fare includes fruit juice, coffee, tea or iced tea, an egg dish, a porridge of oatmeal or grits, and bread, pancakes or waffles.

**Bed and Breakfast: The National Network (TNN)** has reservation services for both states: **The Bed & Breakfast Co./Tropical Florida**, Marcella Schaible, *PO Box 262, Miami, FL 33243-0262; tel: (305) 661-3270*, and **Bed & Breakfast Atlanta**, Madalyne Eplan/Paula Gris, *1801 Piedmont Ave N.E., Suite 208, Atlanta, GA 30324; tel: (404) 875-0525 or (800) 96-PEACH.*

## Camping

Camping means a tent or motorhome (recreational vehicle/RV) in a campsite. **KOA, Kampgrounds of America**, is a private chain of RV parks that also accept tents; *tel: (406) 248-7444* for details. Other private RV parks are plentiful, as RV travel is a permanent way of life for some Floridians and for visitors from colder climates, called 'snowbirds'. Some campsites are public, such as those in state parks. Overnight fees range from $3 to more than $20, depending on season, location, waterfront proximity, electricity hook-ups, number of persons and vehicle size. Standard facilities include a barbecue, tent site, nearby showers/toilets, and, during high season, daytime guided hikes and evening educational programmes around a large campfire.

State park campsite reservations may be made up to 60 days in advance of check-in, by contacting individual parks. Request a Florida State Parks brochure and price list from the **Dept of Environmental Protection**, *Florida Park Information, Mail Station #535, 3900 Commonwealth Blvd, Tallahassee, FL 32399-3000; tel: (904) 488-9872*. Private campsite information is available from

# TRAVEL ESSENTIALS

**Florida Association of RV Parks and Campgrounds**, *1340 Vickers Dr., Tallahassee, FL 32303-3041; tel: (904) 562-7151.*

## Youth Hostels

**Hostelling International (HI-American Youth Hostels)**, *733 15th St N.W., Suite 840, Washington, DC 20005; tel: (202) 783-6161* was created for those on tight budgets. There are HI-AYH hostels in Miami Beach, Orlando, Fort Lauderdale and Atlanta, Georgia. A dormitory-style room and shared bath is $12–14 per person per night. All have family rooms. **The Y's Way** (YMCA), *224 East 46th St, New York NY 10017; tel: (212) 308-2899* operates a hostel in Key West. *The Hostel Handbook, 722 St Nicholas Ave, New York, NY 10031; tel: (212) 926-7030* is an extensive list of cheap lodgings that loosely conform to the definition of a hostel. The down side: when more than two people are travelling together and can share a room, cheap motels may be even cheaper than hostels.

## Airports

The major Florida airports are Miami International (MIA), Orlando International (MCO) and Tampa International (TPA). Fort Lauderdale-Hollywood (FLL), West Palm Beach (PBI), Jacksonville (JAX) and Key West (EYW) all have smaller international airports. Fort Myers' Southwest Regional Airport (RSW) is one of Florida's busiest.

William B. Hartsfield-Atlanta International Airport (ATL), Georgia, usually known simply as 'Hartsfield' is the prime air hub for the South Eastern USA.

**Travelers Aid** desks provide tourist information; airport information booths cover airport facilities, airport-to-city transportation and local accommodation information, though no reservations are made.

All major airports have foreign exchange and banking services and car hire facilities. Public transport to the nearest city is usually available but not always practical in terms of routes, time or safety.

Luggage trolleys (baggage carts) are free for international arrivals at MIA. Porters, called 'sky caps', replace luggage carts at airports like MCO and TPA. Though some terminals connect with gates via a monorail or people-mover (moving walkway), many have distant concourses, a navigational disaster if flight connections are tight. Be prepared for long walks through terminals on arrival. Specific airport arrival information is given in the chapters dealing with the major airport cities.

## Bicycles

Cycling is popular in Florida's parks and recreation areas, where bike paths are well signed. Bikes can be hired by the hour, half day or whole day, from the park ranger (warden) or concessionaire. Urban drivers are not accustomed to sharing the street with cyclists, so try to avoid busy city streets.

For serious bikers (as cyclists are called in the US), Florida has developed three park-to-park trails. For information contact the **Office of Greenways and Trails,** *Dept of Environmental Protection, MS 795, 3900 Commonwealth Blvd, Tallahassee, FL 32399-3000; tel: (904) 487-4874* and **State Bicycle Office,** *Florida Dept of Transportation, 605 South Suwannee St, Tallahassee, FL 32399-0450.* There are also several regional bike trails. The 33-mile Pinellas Trail from St Petersburg to Tarpon Springs follows a converted rail route through urban areas

## TRAVEL ESSENTIALS

to shady suburbs. Orlando has the four-mile Orange County Trail, Gainesville boasts the 14-mile Hawthorne State Trail or consider pedalling the Boca Grande Trail (Fort Myers). On-your-own bike tours are also possible, but beware of many single-lane roads with no lay-bys in case of breakdown, and always be cautious about personal security.

Florida State law does not require bicyclists to wear protective helmets while riding, but law enforcement officials strongly recommend headgear. Police use bicycle patrols in some urban areas.

### Borders

**US Customs and Immigration** (C&I) has a reputation as one of the most unpleasant travel experiences the world has to offer. It can be, for citizens returning home as well as for first-time holidaymakers. Visitors who overstay tourist and student visas are the largest single source of illegal immigrants to the USA. The flow of migrants slipping into Florida from the Caribbean, Latin America and South America makes illegal immigration a hot political and social concern.

C&I officials have *carte blanche* to ask any question, search anyone or anything, and do it in any unpleasant manner they see fit. Most are polite to a fault, but the only defence against an inspector who got up on the wrong side of the bed is to have passport, visa or visa waiver, proof of support and return ticket in order, and to bring in only legal effects. Drug trafficking searches are frequent, as Miami and Florida's numerous ports are convenient for drug couriers.

The USA does not have diplomatic relations with Cuba, 90 miles from Key West. Cuban products like cigars are prohibited. Florida prices for alcohol, tobacco, perfume and other typical duty-free items beat most **duty free** shops. Follow the locals into chain supermarkets (Publix, Winn Dixie, Food Lion, and others) and discount stores (Target, Kmart and Wal-Mart are the most common).

**Agricultural inspection** is another matter. Unprocessed plant, meat and cheese products, especially fresh or raw fruits and vegetables, may not be brought into the US because of the danger of spreading agricultural pests and disease. Canine Agricultural Inspectors, also known as the Beagle Brigade (though other breeds are also used), may perform the check at airport arrival halls.

The importation of weapons, narcotics, or certain non-approved pharmaceutical products is prohibited. Carry prescription medicines with documentation (such as a doctor's letter) to prove they are legitimate.

### Buses

**Greyhound Bus Lines**, *Customer Service, 901 Main St, Dallas, TX 75202; tel: (800) 231-2222*, provides long distance bus services between major cities. There are discounts for seniors (over 65), disabled travellers, and children (under 12) riding with a full-fare adult. The **International Ameripass** offers special discounts for travellers not resident in North America, for seven, 15 or 30 days. Greyhound passes are obtainable through Thomas Cook travel shops in the UK.

If you're buying tickets locally and are able to reserve at least three days in advance, they should cost less than $70, depending on distance to be travelled. Local transport companies listed in the telephone directory under individual cities and towns provide local services.

Thomas Cook publishes bi-monthly timetables of US buses in the *Thomas Cook Overseas Timetable*. A special edition

**Bicycles • Buses**

devoted to US (and Canadian) buses and trains, containing much additional travel information, is published annually under the title *Thomas Cook North American Rail and Bus Guide* (full details of these and other publications are given under 'Useful Reading' on p. 44).

**CAMPERS AND RVS**

It's the freedom of the open road, housekeeping on wheels, a tinkerer's delight, a large machine cruising high above roadside scenery. The flat terrain of Florida and Georgia appeals to an RV crowd tired of hurtling down slopes and ploughing up grades in the wilder geographic areas of North America. An RV, caravan, or motorhome provides a kitchen, sleeping and bathroom facilities, all integrated atop a lorry chassis. For many in Florida, an RV offers year-round lodging and freedom to travel.

Fly-drive packages, such as Thomas Cook's America programme, usually offer the option of hiring an RV. The additional cost of hiring an RV can be offset by the economics of assured lodging for several people, space for meal preparation and eating, and the convenience of comfort items and souvenirs stored nearby. RVs are cramped, designed to stuff you and your belongings into limited space. The economics work only if advance planning assures that the pricey spur-of-the-moment allure of a hotel shower or unplanned restaurant meal won't overcome RV campers! Factor in the cost of petrol – an RV guzzles three–four times more than a medium-sized car.

Always get operating manuals for the vehicle and all appliances before leaving the RV hire lot, and get someone to demonstrate how *everything* works. Systems may be inter-dependent or more complex than anticipated. Be prepared to pre-plan menus and allow additional time each morning and afternoon/evening to level the RV (perfect levelling is essential for correct operation of refrigerators), hook up or disconnect electricity, water and sewer hoses, and cable television plugs. As at home, some basic housecleaning must be done; also allow time for laundry at RV parks.

Buy a pair of sturdy rubber washing gloves to handle daily sewer chores. Pack old clothes to wear while crawling under the vehicle to hook up and disconnect at each stop – many RVers carry a pair of overalls. Without hook-ups, water and electricity are limited to what you carry with you from the last fill-up or battery charge. If you camp in a park without hook-ups, locate the nearest toilets before dark. Using showers and toilets in RV parks or public campsites will save time cleaning up the RV shower space and emptying the toilet holding tank. Keep a strong torch (flashlight) handy.

When you move out on the road, expect anything that's not secured to go flying, or shake, rattle, and roll. Quickly get into a routine of allotted tasks and assign a quick-grab spot for maps, snacks, cameras and valuables. Do not leave valuables in sight. Carelessly strewn maps and brochures mark the occupants as visitors in any vehicle.

RV travel information: **Recreation Vehicle Industry Association (RVIA)**, *Dept RK, PO Box 2999, Reston, VA 22090-0999; tel: (703) 620-6003*. To plan RV camping, request: **Go Camping America** *Camping Vacation Planner, PO Box 2669, Reston, VA 22090-0669; tel: (800) 477-8669*.

**Camping clubs** offer RV information for members. Some like the **Good Sam Club**, *PO Box 6060, Camarillo, CA 93011; tel: (805) 389-0300*, offer roadside assistance for breakdowns and tyre changing. Many camping clubs publish magazines or newsletters with tips on operating and driving an RV. For an insight into RV travel, find a copy of *Heartland Highways, PO Box 23518, Fort Lauderdale, FL 33307-3518; tel: (305) 566-0713*, a periodic tabloid covering home-on-wheels travel in Florida and the Eastern US.

Campsite directories list private RV park locations, directions, size, number of pitches, hook-ups, laundry, on-site convenience stores and showers. Private campsite information is available in the *Official Florida Camping Directory* from the **Florida Association of RV Parks and Campgrounds,** *1340 Vickers Dr, Tallahassee, FL 32303-3041; tel: (904) 562-7151*. Popular guides are: *Trailer Life Campground & RV Services Directory, TL Enterprises, 29901 Agoura Rd, Agoura, CA 91301,* ($19.95); *Woodall's Campground Directory (Eastern Edition), 28167 N. Keith Dr., Lake Forest, IL 60045; tel: (708) 362-6700,* ($13.70); *Wheelers RV Resort & Campground Guide, 1310 Jarvis Ave, Elk Grove Village, IL 60007; tel: (708) 981-0100,* ($15.50); *Kampgrounds of America (KOA) Directory, PO Box 30558, Billings MT 59114-0558; tel: (406) 248-7444,* ($3 or free at KOA campsites). The **AAA** have the *AAA Southeastern CampBook* for public and private campsites. See 'Parks Information' on p. 35 for campsites on state or federal land.

## CHILDREN

Florida is theme park heaven for families with children. Mouse, movies, medieval, mermaids, multicultural: if it can be conceived of, the idea has been turned into a special effects extravaganza, a stomach-churning ride, or ersatz critter encounter. Orlando rates a place on the map as Theme Park Central, home to Walt Disney World's Magic Kingdom, Disney-MGM Studios Theme Park and EPCOT Center, Universal Studios Florida, Sea World of Florida, and Gatorland. Splendid China's miniature replicas and Medieval Life's village, dinner and tournament are in nearby Kissimmee. Cypress Gardens' evocation of the Antebellum South and Busch Gardens' (Tampa) Moroccan-African zoo park are within an hour's drive.

Arrive early, and start at the back of the theme park or ride the 'name' rides before the crowds appear. Weekdays outside holiday periods are least crowded. Many parks have water rides. Dress the children in cotton and buy cheap ponchos (rainwear) in a discount store, or pay plenty for a logo poncho in the park. Carry healthy snacks, ask for smaller-portion children's meals in restaurants, and enjoy the relief of air-conditioned attractions or theatres during the heat of the day.

Often ignored are the much less expensive natural areas like state park and reserve boardwalks where parents can take children to see *real* birds, alligators and other swamp denizens in natural habitats. The fine sand on Gulf of Mexico beaches makes brilliant white castles; children are champions at shell collecting.

From museums to transport, check for children's rates, often segmented by age, e.g. under three free, six–12 years $3, 12–18 years $4. A valid student card must be shown to claim student rates. Get an international ID card (ISIC) before leaving home.

Travelling with children is never easy, but preparation helps. *Travel with Children*, by Maureen Wheeler (Lonely Planet) is filled with useful tips. Kids get bored and cranky on long drives. Pack favourite games and books, and pick up a book of travel games. A traditional favourite is to count foreign, i.e., non-Florida or non-Georgia license plates. Another is to count gators, white herons, hawks, or birds with red feathers. The winner – always a child – gets a special treat later in the day. If the children are old enough, suggest that they keep a detailed travel diary. It will help them focus on Florida instead of what they might be missing back home. A diary also helps them remember details later to impress friends and teachers. Collecting anything, from postcards to admission tickets to plastic souvenir cups, also adds a whole new dimension to travel.

Any driving destination in Florida is equipped for children of all ages, from nappies to video games. Most hotels and motels can arrange for babysitters, though the price may be steep. Many motel chains allow children under 12, 14, sometimes 18, to stay free in their parents' room. A rollaway child's bed, often called a cot, usually comes at no or low cost. For a baby's cot, ask for a crib.

Suites or efficiencies with a refrigerator and stove make family meals easier and economical. Theme park meals are not inexpensive, and healthy snacks are lacking. For meals outside theme parks, picnic lunches offer flexibility. It's also a good idea to carry a small cooler filled with ice, cold drinks and snacks like Florida's renowned citrus, especially in hot weather. In central Florida, citrus product stores offer free samples of juice. Most towns and highway/interstate entrances have coffee shops with long hours, children's menus and familiar fast food names. If the children like McDonalds at home, they'll like Big Macs in Florida – and vice versa.

## CLIMATE

Sun and warmth draw visitors to Florida, the Sunshine State, from around the world. Both the Atlantic and the Gulf Coasts are subject to winds and high humidity in any season. Winter snows in Atlanta are juxtaposed with sweltering sunshine in Key West. Much of Georgia, the Panhandle, North and Central Florida receive wintertime frost. A 300-ft high ridge in the highlands, which extends from Lake Wales south to the west side of Lake Okeechobee, separates weather blowing east from the Gulf of Mexico from Atlantic breezes.

|  | MIAMI | ORLANDO | TALLAHASSEE | KEY WEST |
|---|---|---|---|---|
| **JANUARY** | | | | |
| Highest | 76°F/24°C | 70°F/21°C | 64°F/18°C | 76°F/24°C |
| Lowest | 59°F/15°C | 50°F/10°C | 41°F/5°C | 66°F/19°C |
| **APRIL** | | | | |
| Highest | 83°F/28°C | 81°F/27°C | 80°F/27°C | 82°F/28°C |
| Lowest | 67°F/19°C | 61°F/16°C | 56°F/13°C | 74°F/23°C |
| **JULY** | | | | |
| Highest | 89°F/32°C | 90°F/32°C | 91°F/33°C | 89°F/32°C |
| Lowest | 75°F/24°C | 73°F/23°C | 72°F/22°C | 80°F/27°C |
| **OCTOBER** | | | | |
| Highest | 85°F/29°C | 82°F/28°C | 81°F/27°C | 84°F/29°C |
| Lowest | 71°F/22°C | 66°F/19°C | 58°F/14°C | 75°F/24°C |

Rain falls year-round, but is usually much heavier during winter, Dec–Mar. Hurricane (cyclone) season is roughly the month of Sept, though tropical storms, the precursors to hurricanes, blow through for several months either side. Thunderstorms are awesome in power; lightning crackles for hours, often setting forests and swamps ablaze.

Semi-tropical temperatures reign. Spring and fall have the least extreme temperatures and shoulder season prices.

## Clothing

Florida is informal, with the preference for pastel or light-coloured clothing. Denim blue jeans are seldom seen; Bermuda shorts are worn by men and women. More practical are lightweight long trousers, sturdy walking shoes, and a cover-up shirt or blouse for daytime touring. Swamps and areas with mosquitoes, no-see-ums, poisonous snakes, poison ivy and poison sumac (see under 'Health', p. 29) demand long trousers, shoes and socks, and a long-sleeved shirt.

Miami, Fort Lauderdale, Palm Beach, St Augustine, Tampa Bay and Tallahassee favour casual but fashionable resort wear. Atlanta is quite formal. T-shirts or polo jerseys are accepted for day wear everywhere. At night, men may be required to wear a shirt and tie to dinner. Sandals and bare feet are the norm only at the beach. A pullover or medium-weight jacket protects against winter frost and occasional snow in northern Florida and Georgia. A compact umbrella, light raincoat, or windcheater which can be stored in a carrying bag can be useful all year. A sun hat or tennis visor protects against strong sun, and tennis shoes are good in wet weather or for beachwalking.

Resort wear is sold everywhere. Florida T-shirts and costume and shell jewellery are a bargain. Don't worry if you've forgotten something. Clothes are generally far cheaper that in Europe.

## Consulates

**Australia:** None in Florida. *Suite 2920, 1 Peachtree Center, 303 Peachtree St N.E., Atlanta, GA 30308; tel: (404) 880-1700.*
**Canada:** *First Union Financial Center, 200 South Biscayne Blvd, Suite 1600, Miami FL 33131-2310; tel: (305) 579-1600 or (305) 372-2352.*
*Suite 400, South Tower, One CNN Center, Atlanta, GA 30303-2705; tel: (404) 577-6810.*
**New Zealand:** *New Zealand Embassy, 37 Observatory Circle NW, Washington, D.C., 20008; tel: (202) 328-4800.*
**Republic of Ireland:** *Consulate General, Ireland House, 345 Park Ave, 17th Floor, New York, NY 10154-0037; tel: (212) 319-2550 or (212) 319-2555.*
**South Africa:** *Embassy Consular Section, 3051 Massachusetts Ave NW, Washington, D.C.; tel: (202) 966-1650.*
**UK:** *Brickell Bay Office Tower, Suite 2110, Miami, FL 33131; tel: (305) 374-1522 or (305) 374-8196.*
*Suite 2700, Marquis One Tower, 245 Peachtree Center Ave, Atlanta, GA 30303; tel: (404) 524-5856 or (404) 524-5858.*

## Cost of Living

While Florida and Georgia have local sales taxes and hotel/lodging taxes and surcharges, the combined levy is less than the VAT charged in most of Europe. Prices are marked or quoted *without tax*, which is added at the time of purchase (see 'Sales Taxes', p. 37). Petrol prices are a special bargain, with prices about $1.00–$1.20 per US gallon (4 litres), or about $0.25–$0.30 per litre. Motel rooms, depending on season, cost $25–$70 per night; hotels from $50 up.

# TRAVEL ESSENTIALS

Restaurant meals, including soup or salad, main course, dessert, beverage and tax are about $10–$20 per person for lunch; $15–$25 for dinner. Theme parks charge about $40 per adult entrance; national and state parks $3.25–$6.00 per car; most museums $2–$7 per person.

## Currency

US dollars are the only currency accepted in Florida and Georgia. Bill denominations are $1, $2 (very rare), $5, $10, $20, $50, $100, $1000 (rare), and $10,000 (rarer). All bills are the same colour, green and white, and size, so take great care not to mix them up. The only differences, apart from the denominations marked on them, are the US president pictured on the front and the designs on the back. There are 100 cents to the dollar: coins include the copper 1-cent piece, 5-cent nickel, 10-cent dime, 25-cent quarter, 50-cent half-dollar (rare), and an extremely rare Susan B. Anthony dollar.

Banks can exchange foreign currency or travellers' cheques, but expect interminable delays (and extraordinary fees) as they telephone the main office in search of exchange rates and procedures. Better to seek out one of the Thomas Cook locations noted in this book or ask at your local hotel. However, travellers' cheques denominated in US dollars, from well-known issuers such as Thomas Cook, are acceptable almost everywhere and can be used as cash or changed easily. To report Thomas Cook travellers' cheque losses and thefts, call 1-800-223-7373 (toll-free, 24-hr service).

For security reasons, avoid carrying large amounts of cash. The safest forms of money are US dollar travellers' cheques and credit or debit cards. Both can be used almost everywhere. If possible, bring at least one, preferably two, major credit cards such as **Access**, **MasterCard**, **American Express**, or **Visa**. (Thomas Cook locations will offer replacement and other emergency services if you lose a MasterCard.) Plastic is the only acceptable proof of fiscal responsibility. Car hire companies require either a credit card imprint or a substantial cash deposit before releasing a vehicle, even if the hire has been fully prepaid. Hotels and motels also require either a credit card imprint or a cash deposit, even if the bill has been prepaid or is to be settled in cash.

Some shops, cheaper motels, small local restaurants and low cost petrol stations require cash. If using a credit card, check with the merchant/proprietor, as many cash-only businesses do not post notice. There are numerous Automated Teller Machines (automatic cash dispensers), or **ATMs**, throughout the area and you will certainly be able to get a cash advance with a credit or debit card and may well be able to use your home cashcard. **Star** and **CIRRUS** are the most common international systems used in Florida, but check terms, availability and PIN (personal identification number) with the card issuer before leaving home.

## Customs Allowances

Personal duty-free allowances which can be taken into the USA by visitors are 1 US quart (approx. 0.9 litres) of spirits or wine, 300 cigarettes, or 50 (non-Cuban) cigars and up to $100 worth of gifts.

On your return home you will be allowed to take in the following:
**Australia:** goods to the value of A$400 (half for those under 18) plus 250 cigarettes or 250 g tobacco and 1 litre alcohol.
**Canada:** goods to the value of C$300, provided you have been away for over a week and have not already used up part of your allowance that year. You are also

allowed 50 cigars plus 200 cigarettes and 1 kg tobacco (if over 16) and 40 oz/1 litre alcohol.

**New Zealand:** goods to the value of NZ$700. Anyone over 17 may also take 200 cigarettes or 250 g of tobacco or 50 cigars or a combination of tobacco products not exceeding 250 g in all plus 4.5 litres of beer or wine and 1.125 litres spirits.

**South Africa:** goods to the total value of 500 Rand. Anyone over 18 may also take 400 cigarettes and 50 cigars and 250 g tobacco plus 2 litres wine and 1 litre spirits plus 50 ml perfume and 250 ml toilet water.

**UK:** The allowances for goods bought outside the EU and/or in EU duty-free shops are: 200 cigarettes or 50 cigars or 100 cigarillos or 250 g tobacco plus 2 litres still table wine plus 1 litre spirits or 2 litres sparkling wine plus 50 g/60 ml perfume plus 0.5 litre/250 ml toilet water.

Florida/Georgia prices for alcohol, tobacco, perfume and other typical duty-free items beat most **duty-free** shops. Follow the locals into chain supermarkets (Publix, Winn Dixie, Food Lion and others) and discount stores (Target, Kmart and Wal-Mart are the most common).

## DISABLED TRAVELLERS

Access is the key word. Physically challenged is synonymous with disabled. Physical disabilities should present less of a barrier in the United States than in much of the world. State and federal laws, particularly the Americans with Disabilities Act (ADA), require that all business, buildings and services used by the public be accessible by handicapped persons, including those using wheelchairs. Every hotel, restaurant, office, shop, cinema, museum, post office and other public building must have access ramps and toilets designed for wheelchairs. Most cities and towns have ramps built into street crossings and most city buses have some provision for wheelchair passengers. Even many parks have installed paved pathways so disabled visitors can get a sense of the natural world. Disabled parking spaces are enormous, numerous, and very close to entrances.

The bad news is that disabled facilities aren't always what they're meant to be. Museums, public buildings, restaurants, and lodging facilities are usually accessible, but special automobile controls for disabled drivers are seldom an option on hired vehicles, especially without an increased rate. And, while wooden boardwalks in parks may be *accessible*, the slat construction makes navigation a bumpy torture.

Airlines are particularly hard on disabled passengers. US carriers can prevent anyone who is not strong enough to open an emergency exit (which weighs about 45 lb, 20.5 kg) or has vision/hearing problems from sitting in that row of seats – even if it means bumping them from the flight. Commuter airlines sometimes deny boarding to passengers with mobility problems on the grounds that they may block the narrow aisle during an emergency.

Some public telephones have special access services for the deaf and disabled. Broadcast television may be closed-captioned for the hearing impaired, indicated by a rectangle around a double cc in a corner of the screen.

Ask before booking hotel or motel accommodation. Elevators for access above the ground floor level may not exist, or may be in an awkward place or too tiny to accommodate a wheelchair. Some are old-fashioned freight elevators and require an operator! Are fire alarms, and doorbells indicated visually as well as audibly? Will a wheelchair be able to use the fire escape route? Are nearby restaurants accessible?

A few miles south of Tallahassee is Trout Pond, set aside for disabled persons and senior citizens. The sense-involving, 700 ft-long **Discovery Trail**, specially-designed fishing pier and pool are open from Apr 1–Oct 31. **Wakulla District Ranger Station**, *US Forest Service, Route 6, Box 7860, Crawfordville, FL 32327; tel: (904) 926-3561.*

The **Florida Department of Commerce Division of Tourism and Florida Governor's Alliance**, *107 West Gaines St, Collins Bldg, Tallahassee, FL 32399-2000; tel: (904) 487-1462* publishes a *Planning Companion for Travelers With Disabilities,* in print, large print, Braille, audiotape and on computer disk electronic file. Tourism contacts and attractions accommodating the disabled are listed.

**US Information**: SATH (Society for the Advancement of Travel for the Handicapped), *347 5th Ave, Suite 610, New York, NY 10016; tel: (212) 447-7284.* The *Travelin' Talk Directory, PO Box 3534, Clarksville TN 37043-3534; tel: (615) 552-6670,* is a North America guidebook of services and emergency contact information for disabled travellers, with newsletter updates.

**UK Information**: RADAR, *12 City Forum, 250 City Road, London W1N 8AB; tel: (0171) 250 3222* publish a useful annual guide called *Holidays and Travel Abroad* which gives details of facilities for the disabled in different countries.

## Discounts

Reductions on entrance fees and public transport for senior citizens, children, students and military personnel are common. Some proof is eligibility is usually required. For age, a passport or driving licence is sufficient. Military personnel should carry an official identification card. Students will have better luck with an International Student Identity Card (ISIC), from their local student union than with a college ID.

The most common discount is for automobile club members. Tour guides from AAA (Automobile Association of America) affiliates (AAA Auto Club South and AAA Florida/Louisiana/Mississippi) list hundreds of member discounts for Florida and Georgia. The auto clubs publish a seasonal list of discounted local attractions. Always ask about 'Triple A discounts' at attractions, hotels, motels, and car hire counters. Most recognise reciprocal membership benefits.

Some cities will send high-season discount booklets on request, good for shops, restaurants or lodging. Motel discount coupons are published in *Travelers Discount Guides,* which cover a number of states including Florida and Georgia. These can be picked up free in the US or can be obtained in advance from **Exit Information Guide, Inc.** *4205 N.W. 6th St, Gainesville, FL 32609; tel: (904) 371 3948,* $7 for one guide.

## Drinking

You must be 21 years old to purchase or to drink any kind of alcoholic beverage in Florida and Georgia. Licensed establishments are called bars, lounges, saloons or pubs. Convenience stores sell beer, wine, and sometimes spirits, but prices are higher than at grocery stores.

Laws against drinking and driving are very strict, and strictly enforced with fines and imprisonment. If stopped under suspicion of Driving Under the Influence

(DUI), the police officer will ask you to choose between one of three tests: breath, blood, or urine. A sober, designated driver should take the wheel anytime a partying group imbibes.

Alcoholic beverages are prohibited on Florida beaches; public drinking is frowned upon. Any liquor, wine or beer container in a vehicle (RVs excepted) must be full, sealed and unopened – or in the boot.

## Electricity

Florida and Georgia (like the rest of the USA) use 110 volt 60 hertz current. Two- or three-pin electrical plugs are standard throughout the country. Electrical gadgets from outside North America require plug and power converters. Both are difficult to obtain in the USA because local travellers don't need them, but are widely available in travel shops, chemists and airports before leaving home.

Beware of buying electrical appliances in Florida and Georgia for the same reason. Few gadgets on the US market can run on 220 V 50 hertz power. Exceptions are battery-operated equipment such as radios, cameras and portable computers. Tape cassettes, CDs, computer programmes and CD-ROMs sold in the US can be used anywhere in the world.

US video equipment, which uses the NTSC format, is *not* compatible with the PAL and SECAM equipment used in most of the rest of the world. *Pre-recorded* video tapes sold in the USA will not work with other equipment unless specifically marked as compatible with PAL or SECAM. *Blank* video tapes purchased in America *can* be used with video recorders elsewhere in the world. Discount store prices on blank video cassettes are very reasonable.

## Emergencies

In case of emergency, ring 911, free from any telephone. Ambulance, paramedics, police, fire brigades, or other public safety personnel will be dispatched immediately. See also under 'Health' on p. 29.

If you lose your Thomas Cook travellers' cheques, call 1-800-223-7373 (toll-free, 24-hr service).

## Food

American pioneer traditions demand huge portions and endless refills of (weak) coffee. Most restaurants serve steak, chicken and seafood. Some eateries, especially those in Georgia, bow to the regional traditions of Southern cuisine: fried food, fried chicken, grits (white corn meal), hush puppies (fried cornbread), pecan pie, cream pies. Occasionally, Louisiana Cajun-style gumbo (spicy soup) and blackened fish will appear.

Good, wholesome food is really quite difficult to find, especially tasty, non-calorific snacks in an area of the USA that traditionally regarded sugar as a precious treat.

Florida's own culinary specialities include Key lime pie; stone crab (claws) with mayonnaise; conch (fritters, raw, or in spicy chowder); (alli)gator (no longer an endangered species); seafood from the Atlantic, Caribbean and Gulf of Mexico; hearts of palm (from the swamp cabbage which 'dies' when its centre is removed for this delicacy); and Cuban fare. Nuevo Cubano, with tropical Caribbean fruits and vegetables mixed with flavours from India and south-east Asia, became trendy a few years ago. During much of the year, dining is *al fresco*, though dining areas are often screened against insects.

Iced tea, served with a slice of lemon and traditionally candy-sweet, remains the ubiquitous thirst-quencher. Citrus

## TRAVEL ESSENTIALS

juice flavour changes seasonally with variations in the fruit crop, but is widely available in South Central Florida. The Hispanic population favours *batidos,* a tropical fruit shake. The world headquarters of Coca Cola is in Atlanta; lots of local partisans begin the day with cans of Coke in lieu of coffee! At least as fortifying is *café cubano*, a small portion of brew so thick and rich that it's doled out to guests by the ounce. Cuban *café con leche*, is sweet, milky and rich.

Conspicuous consumption begins with breakfast. Thinly-sliced bacon and eggs cooked to order (boiled, poached or most often fried) come with chips, grits (white cornmeal porridge), or hash browns (shredded fried potatoes). Toast, a flat 'English' muffin with butter or margarine and jam, or a bagel with cream cheese and lox (smoked salmon slices) may be served alongside. Variations or additions include pancakes, French toast (bread dipped in egg batter and lightly fried), waffles and oatmeal porridge. A 'continental breakfast' is juice, coffee or tea, and some sort of bread, usually a pastry. Some hotels and restaurants offer Sunday brunch, usually from 1130–1430, with all-you-can-eat self-service buffets heaped with hot and cold dishes. The economical Sunday brunch also includes coffee, tea, orange juice, and sometimes cheap 'champagne' (sparkling wine).

Menus offer similar choices for lunch and dinner, the evening meal. Dinner portions are larger and more costly. Most menus offer appetisers (starters), simple salads, soups, pastas, entrées (main courses) and desserts. Fried is the preferred preparation method; ice cream or sherbet (sorbet) is a lighter dessert choice. Soup and/or salad is often included in the price of the main course, so check before ordering.

Platters, available in most restaurants and many fast food places, include a quarter or half chicken or a huge portion of barbecue beef or pork ribs, a choice of several 'fixin's': salads, boiled vegetables, or starch, and a cornbread muffin. For equally hearty eating, try a steak house where salad, baked potato and beans accompany a thick steak, often produced on mid-state cattle ranches. Italian restaurants serve pizza, pasta, seafood and steaks, with heavy doses of tomato sauce.

Cuban food can be a simple plate of succulent boiled chicken and rice, a choice of black, red, or pink beans, and baguette-style Cuban bread. Miami's Little Havana, around Calle Ocho, and Tampa's Ybor City are the centres for *Cubano*; most towns have at least one cafeteria counter that's ethnically totally Cuban. Fried plantains garnish a plate of *palomilla*, thinly-sliced grilled steak, parsley and onions. *Masas de puerco* is pork with lime. *Picadillo* is minced meat on rice and beans. Try a warm *media noche*, a Cuban sandwich with ham, cheese and mayonnaise on a *pan* (baguette). Wash it down with expresso-strength *café cubano* or a *batido* shake made of mango, guava or even more exotic Caribbean tropical fruit.

Stone crabs, most famous at Miami Beach's hard-to-get-into Joe's Stone Crab Restaurant, are actually the crab's claws, soon regenerated. Stone crabs, though pricey, will be on most southeastern Florida and Keys menus from Oct–May. The delicacy is served cold with mayonnaise. Pompano, grouper, red snapper and shrimp are other local seafood specialities.

Tarpon Springs has Greek cuisine; other international choices include Nicaraguan (Miami), Thai, Chinese, and British or Irish pub food. Seminole and

**FOOD**

Miccosukee Native Americans near the Everglades serve fry bread, fried catfish, and grilled roasted corn with butter.

Perhaps *beignets* or Chinese finger food came first, but America made fast food an international dining experience. Fast food is quick and economical. Food is ordered, paid for, and picked up from a service counter, all within a few minutes. Some fast-food outlets have drive-through service, where the driver pulls up to a window, orders from a posted menu, pays, and gets the meal, all without leaving the vehicle. Hamburgers, hot dogs, tacos, fried chicken, barbecue beef, and 'sub' (submarine) sandwiches layered with meats, cheeses and pickles are common offerings. McDonalds' golden arches and KFC's grinning chubby colonel are easy to spot.

Other common fast food chains include Arby's Roast Beef, A & W, Burger King, Carl's Jr., Checkers, Dairy Queen, Domino's Pizza, Jack-in-the-Box, Pizza Hut, Subway and Taco Bell. All are cheap.

The budget rung of the price ladder includes chain restaurants such as Kenny Roger's Roasters (excellent wood-roasted chicken platters), Perkins (a regular menu and with bakery goods available anytime), Denny's (common along freeways and usually open 24 hrs), Miami Subs, Olive Garden (Italian), Red Lobster (seafood), and Sizzler. Perkins and Denny's are open for breakfast, the others for lunch and dinner only.

Picnic provisions are cheapest at stores like Publix, Food Lion, or Winn-Dixie; some have a make-it-yourself salad bar for light, nutritious meals. Keep a supply of potable water handy, and try the wide variety of exotic fruit-flavoured colas and sodas available from Mexico and the Caribbean.

## GAMBLING

Gambling is illegal. Sometimes. Florida has a highly advertised lottery, casinos on Indian Reservations, and bingo in Roman Catholic churches. Florida citizens have voted against legalised gambling, yet Native American-run casinos have full parking lots. A perennial issue is offshore gambling on cruise ships. The US government strictly forbids gaming and betting in territorial waters.

## HEALTH

In case of emergency, ring 911, free from any telephone. Ambulance, paramedics, police, fire brigades, or other public safety personnel will be dispatched immediately.

Hospital emergency rooms are the place to go in the event of life-threatening medical problems. If a life is truly at risk, treatment will be swift and top notch, with payment problems sorted out later. For more mundane problems, 24-hr walk-in health clinics are available in urban areas and many rural communities. The large retired population in Florida assures that there are many speciality medical institutions.

Payment, not care, is the problem. Some form of **health insurance** coverage is almost mandatory in order to ensure provision of health services. Coverage provided by non-US national health plans is *not* accepted by Florida medical providers. The only way to ensure provision of health services is to carry some proof of valid insurance cover. Most travel agents who deal with international travel will offer travel insurance policies that cover medical costs in Florida, Georgia and the rest of the USA – at least $1 million of cover is essential.

Bring enough prescription medication to last the entire trip, plus a few extra days. It's also a good idea to carry a copy of the prescription in case of emergency. Because trade names of drugs vary from country to country, be sure the prescription shows the generic (chemical) name and formulation of the drug, not just a brand name.

No inoculations are required and Florida and Georgia are basically healthy places to visit. Common sense is enough to avoid most health problems. Eat normally (or at least sensibly) and avoid drinking water that didn't come from the tap or a bottle.

Sunglasses, broad-brimmed sun hats, and sunscreen help prevent sunburn, sun stroke and heat prostration. Be sure to drink plenty of non-alcoholic liquids, especially in hot weather.

Shorts are foolish for walks through the Everglades or other natural areas. Wear long trousers, socks and closed shoes. A long-sleeve shirt discourages many insects. **Mosquitoes** are active most of the time, and have Everglades National Park rangers discouraging human visitation from June–Nov. **No-see-ums**, beachside midges or sand flies, nip fiercely at sunrise and sunset. **Fire ants** make mounds of loose dirt, and their formic acid has a fiery burn. Small mites called **chiggers** burrow under the skin of wrists, ankles and waists, causing burning and itching like an intense mosquito bite. Transmitted through the bite of tiny ticks, **Lyme Disease** is frequently misdiagnosed and is usually mistaken for rheumatoid arthritis. Typical symptoms include temporary paralysis, arthritic pains in the hand, arm, or leg joints, swollen hands, fever, fatigue, headaches, swollen glands, heart palpitations and a circular red rash around the bite up to 30 days later. Early treatment with tetracycline and other drugs is nearly 100% effective; late treatment often fails. Symptoms may not appear for three months or longer after the first infected tick bite, but the disease can be detected by a simple blood test.

Widely available mosquito repellents are Cutter's, Off!, and 3M Ultrathon non-greasy creme. Avon Skin-So-Soft hand lotion is widely recommended against mosquitoes and no-see-ums.

**AIDS** (Acquired Immune Deficiency Syndrome) and other sexually transmitted diseases are endemic in Florida as in the rest of the world. The best way to avoid sexually transmitted diseases (or STDs, as they're usually called) is to avoid promiscuous sex. In anything other than long term, strictly monogamous relationships, the key phrase is 'safe sex'. Use condoms in any kind of sexual intercourse. Condoms can be bought in drug stores, pharmacies and supermarkets, and from vending machines in some public toilets.

**Rabies** is another endemic problem in Florida. It's most likely to afflict those who try to get close to the racoons that haunt many parks, but end up being bitten instead. If bitten by an animal, try to capture it for observation of possible rabies, then go to the nearest emergency medical centre. You must seek *immediate* treatment – if left too late, the disease is untreatable and fatal.

## HIKING

Walking is a favourite outdoor activity, especially in park areas. With the highest point in Florida only 325 ft above sea level, the going is flat; the terrain generally accessible.

The same cautions that apply anywhere else are good in Florida and Georgia: know the route; have a map, a compass and basic safety gear; carry food and water. It's also wise to stay on marked trails and on boardwalks. Wandering off the trail adds to erosion damage, especially in fragile forest and swamp areas. Avoid hiking alone and never let small children run ahead or fall far behind.

## Hiking Safely

American **alligators** (and the much rarer American crocodile) respect no trail, can run 30 mph, and are unpredictable. A gator near a pond will generally defend its hole – making swimming hazardous. Always look ahead on a path or when moving through water for **snakes**. Florida boasts the USA's largest herpetology collection – including six species of poisonous snakes. The aggressive Eastern Diamondback Rattlesnake can fling its body at a victim to a distance of half its length. Canebrake and Pygmy Rattlesnakes and the Panhandle's Copperhead are dangerous, but not as aggressive. The Cottonmouth Water Moccasin lives in fresh water, along the water's edge, and even hangs in trees. Red and yellow Coral Snakes, related to mambas and cobras, are pretty, appealing to touch – and deadly. In shallow water, shuffling shoes discourages snakes.

Scorpions can crawl into boots at night. Fire ants will fiercely defend their hill if disturbed. Racoons carry rabies. Lyme Disease ticks, chiggers, mosquitoes, and no-see-ums can cause discomfort from itching to death in the case of Lyme Disease. (see also p. 30).

A common hiking problem is **Poison Ivy**, a three-leafed plant that twines bright red in winter through brushy areas and up tree trunks. Berries are white. Bushy **Poison Sumac** also has white berries and numerous small leaves. A rash of small blisters breaks out upon skin contact. The best way to avoid the problem is to avoid the plants. Second best is to immediately wash skin or clothing that has come into contact with the plant in hot, soapy water. Once afflicted, drying lotions such as calamine or products containing cortisone provide temporary relief, but time is the only cure. Two trees found in South Florida, the Manchineel and Poisonwood, also cause dramatic skin irritation. Don't touch the native flora, and above all, don't sample its fruits which can be fatal!

## Hitch-Hiking

In an earlier, more trustful era, hitch-hiking was the preferred mode of transport for budget travellers. Today, hitch-hiking or picking up hitch-hikers is asking for violent trouble, from theft to physical assault and murder. *Don't do it.*

## Hurricanes

When waves begin to pound slowly but heavily, and filmy, wispy cirrus clouds suddenly appear from a fixed point on the horizon, Florida's weather is turning serious. Heavy, ugly clouds thicken and begin to whip in straight lines across the sky. Rain starts to lash the shore and winds slash the sky. Cycles of rain and wind grow stronger until the tropical storm exceeds a velocity of 75 mph.

A hurricane has struck. Similar to the concept of a cyclone or an Asian typhoon, a hurricane can change course in an instant, rearranging rivers, deltas, beaches and landscape beneath it.

All coastal areas in hurricane-prone areas, particularly the coasts and barrier islands, have evacuation routes to the mainland, then inland towards higher ground. 'Evacuation Route' signs are a blue stylised drop of water on a white background, with an arrow below to indicate the safe evacuation direction. No evacuation route is foolproof, as no natural event involving wind is predictable.

Florida telephone directories contain instructions for hurricane preparation and evacuation. Most useful in the North Atlantic hurricane season (June 1–Nov 30) is a working radio, either battery-powered or in a vehicle. Emergency information is broadcast, in a series of increasingly serious advisories.

Moving series of thunderstorms are a **tropical disturbance**. Round cloud patterns, low pressure, and winds up to 38 mph form a **tropical depression**. When storm clouds swirl anticlockwise from 39–74 mph, a **tropical storm** is named. Above 75 mph, a tropical storm becomes a **hurricane**. Hurricane winds average 100–150 mph, but can exceed 200 mph, flattening and shattering anything unlucky enough to be caught in their force. Ironically, the **hurricane eye** is much calmer, averaging 14–25 miles in diameter, and giving a false sense of security. Because tropical storms can be tracked up to 500 miles away from landfall, warnings can be issued through public **advisories**. What isn't predictable is the turns a hurricane may take, nor its destructive path.

An **advisory** is issued every six hours when a problematic storm is spotted by meteorologists. **Intermediate advisories** can be given every two–three hours. **Special advisories** are issued when the force or path changes significantly, and a **hurricane watch** begins when an area could eventually be hit. A 24-hr **hurricane warning** is time to check on emergency evacuation.

Actual destruction lasts two–four hours, ripping up palm trees, tossing roofs from houses, and strewing about anything in its wake. **Storm surge** waves can submerge all in their path. Torrential rains soak damaged property. What falls from the fierce storm clouds is a small part of the estimated two thousand million tonnes of water absorbed daily by a hurricane.

Local emergency officials set up evacuation centres, generally at schools or other safe, central public buildings.

When travelling in a car, keep the petrol tank filled. Quickly move to safety as directed with valuables and, if practical, gather fresh water, jackets and pullovers, first aid kit and non-perishable foodstuffs.

### INSURANCE

Experienced travellers carry insurance that covers their belongings and holiday investment as well as their bodies. Travel insurance should include provision for cancelled or delayed flights and weather problems, as well as emergency evacuation home in case of medical emergency. Thomas Cook and other travel agencies offer comprehensive policies. Medical cover should be high – at least $1 million. Insurance for drivers is covered in more detail in the 'Driving in Florida' chapter, p. 53.

### LANGUAGE

English is the official language, but Spanish may seem like the primary language in parts of Southern Florida, particularly in Greater Miami (Dade County). It may be the Spanish of Cuba, Nicaragua, Colombia, or Mexico. The Haitian community in Miami speaks its unique Creole, broadcast over local radio stations. Tourist brochures are frequently multi-lingual in Spanish, German, French, Italian and Japanese.

Even English can cause non-US visitors a few difficulties. *The Traveler's Pictorial Communication Guide*, Dorrance Publishing Co., 643 Smithfield St, Pittsburgh, PA 15222; tel: (800) 788-7654, shows Marty Katz' icon-like line drawings for visitors' needs which can be shown to

## TRAVEL ESSENTIALS

local residents. A selection of commonly encountered terms which may be unfamiliar or have a different meaning in America are set out in the box on p. 34. The next chapter, 'Driving in Florida', also provides a glossary of motoring terms for the non-US driver.

### LUGGAGE

Less is more where luggage is concerned. Porters exist at some airports (skycaps) and at expensive hotels. Luggage trolleys (baggage carts) are rare. Luggage has to be light enough to carry, or have wheels. The normal transatlantic luggage allowance is 2 pieces, each of 70 lb (32 kg) maximum, per person.

Luggage must also fit in the car or other form of transport around Florida and Georgia. Americans buy the same cars as Europeans, Australians, Africans, and the rest of the world, not the enormous 'boats' of the 1960s. If it won't fit in the boot at home, don't count on cramming it into a car when you arrive in the States.

### MAPS

Florida is a state on a building spree, and roads, thoroughfares and street signs change constantly. Maps published six months ago may be woefully out of date for urban areas. Signs are poor, made more confusing by as many as three names or numbers for roads in some areas (particularly bad in South Dade County near Miami).

Look for recent maps. Detailed city and metropolitan area maps are produced by the **American Automobile Association** and distributed through its two regional affiliates, AAA Auto Club South and AAA Florida/Louisiana/Mississippi. Both are known simply as AAA ('Triple

# THOMAS COOK TRAVEL INSURANCE
## For a really relaxed holiday

*When travelling abroad, insurance is one of those things that should not be left to chance. At Thomas Cook, we have developed a unique Recommended Travel Insurance package\*, with sensible prices and the following excellent cover:*

| | |
|---|---|
| Loss or damage of personal baggage | Loss of personal money |
| Loss of passport expenses | Medical expenses |
| 24-hour medical emergency assistance | Personal accident cover |
| Personal public liability | Travel delay compensation |
| Failure of carrier | Loss of deposit or cancellation |
| Curtailment of holiday | Missed departure |
| Medical inconvenience benefit | Airport Assistance |
| Travel Assistance | Legal Advice and Expenses |
| Homecall | Top-up liability |

Call in at your local Thomas Cook branch, for full details of the cover available. To ensure that you benefit from the most advantageous premiums available, these will be advised to you at the time of your booking.

\* Only for sale to those departing from the UK only

LANGUAGE • MAPS

## How to Talk Floridian

*Air boat* skims the surface of swamps, lakes or estuaries, with platform seating, and an airplane propeller affixed to the rear.
*Alternate* means 'alternative' not 'every other' – sometimes a source of confusion when reading timetables.
*Antebellum* A gracious style of Southern life and plantation mansion architecture before the US Civil War.
*Bayou* The sluggish waterways snaking north of the rivers which empty into the Gulf of Mexico.
*Beach access* Florida beaches are public by law; however, the route, or access to reach the sand may be restricted by private landowners or cities.
*Bed & Breakfast* Overnight lodging in a private home, usually with private facilities and frequently more expensive than nearby hotels and motels.
*Buffalo wings* Chicken wings, usually fried and served with a spicy sauce as an appetiser or bar food.
*Chili dog* or *chili burger* Hot dog or hamburger disguised with chili, onions and cheese.
*Chips* Crisps, usually made from potatoes, but also from corn, rice or other starches.
*Corn dog* Hot dog dipped in corn meal and fried. Usually served hot on a stick.
*Cotton candy* Candy Floss. Coloured, spun sugar on a paper cylinder, sold at theme parks.
*Cracker* Sometimes used perjoratively to describe a poor person from rural Florida or Georgia; more recently a term of pride for ancestors who lived off the land and swamps, raising cattle and cracking whips to overpower snakes, gators and other threats.
*Cuban sandwich* Ham, pork and cheese on a warm baguette.
*Downtown* City or town centre.
*Efficiency* Apartment without walls between the sleeping area and kitchen, with the bath/toilet facility in a separate, adjacent room, similar to a bedsit or studio flat.
*Fajitas* A Mexican dish, strips of grilled meat (beef, pork or chicken).
*Floribbean* Some fish, some spice, some tropical fruit; the mixture of Florida produce and seafood and Caribbean dishes.
*Grits* White corn meal, served as breakfast porridge.
*Hill* Florida's very rare slope that blocks the view ahead in a state renowned for flatness.
*Holiday* A public holiday, such as Labor Day, not a private holiday, which is a vacation.
*Hush puppies* Fried corn meal balls, by tradition given to dogs by fishermen to ensure silence, now a meal garnish.
*Intracoastal Waterway* permits water transit down the Atlantic Coast, sheltered by barrier islands, to Key West; transit via water from the Atlantic to the Gulf of Mexico at Fort Myers; and access to Texas from the Gulf of Mexico.
*Lodging* The usual term for accommodation.
*Outlet shopping* Shopping at stores specialising in factory overruns at reduced prices. In many cases, factory outlets are simply low-priced retail stores selling direct from the factory.
*Palmetto bug* A large cockroach.
*Parrotheads* are Jimmy Buffett fans, especially in Key West.
*Resort* A fancy hotel which specialises in leisure activities such as golf, tennis and swimming.
*River of Grass* is writer Marjory Stoneman Douglas' depiction of Everglades sawgrass.
*Road kill* Literally, animals killed by passing cars, but usually used to describe bad restaurant food.
*Spa* treatments include exercise classes, massage, facials, steam room, sauna and swimming and beauty treatments, usually in conjunction with a hotel stay.

A'). State, regional, county and city maps are available free to members at all AAA offices, but may not be available for all areas. Fortunately, most automobile clubs around the world have reciprocal agreements with AAA to provide maps and other services. Be prepared to show a membership card to obtain service.

**Rand McNally** road maps and atlases are probably the best known of the ranges available outside the USA, in the travel section of bookshops and specialist outlets. For computerised planning, **Microsoft Corporation**, *One Microsoft Way, Redmond, WA 98052-6399; tel: (800) 426-9400,* publishes Automap® Road Atlas and Automap® Streets software to cover US destinations with labelled roads, parks, landmarks and distances.

The possibilities are more confusing for backcountry travel. **US Geological Survey** quadrangle (topographic) maps show terrain reliably, but **US Forest Service** maps, touted as the ultimate off-road guide, are often out of date because trails change with alarming frequency. Even with the best of maps in hand, getting lost in the wilderness is a possibility. Always carry a topographic map and compass in addition to any other maps and guides. **Sierra Club**, *100 Bush St, San Francisco, CA 94101; tel: (415) 291-1600.* and **Wilderness Press**, *2440 Bancroft Way, Berkeley CA 94704-1676; tel: (510) 843-8080,* publish the most up-to-date and reliable back country maps and guides. Outdoor supply shops and good booksellers carry maps.

Before leaving civilisation behind, compare every available map for discrepancies, then check with national forest or park personnel. Most are experienced backcountry enthusiasts themselves, and since they're responsible for rescuing lost hikers and campers, they have a vested interest in dispensing the best possible information and advice.

## MEETING PEOPLE

Americans are generally friendly, at least on the surface. Friendliness does not extend to inviting new acquaintances to their homes, however. Personal safety is a prime consideration. Sports events, casual restaurants and bars can be meeting places, but most local people are justifiably wary of approaches by strangers. Always meet new acquaintances where other people are around. Professional associations, sports groups, clubs and churches welcome visitors from abroad; contact well in advance for meeting times and venues.

## OPENING HOURS

Office hours are generally 0900–1700, Mon–Fri, although a few tourist offices also keep short Sat hours. Most banks and other financial institutions are open 1000–1600 Mon–Thur, 1000–1800 on Fri, and 0900–1300 Sat. ATMs (cashpoints) are open 24 hrs.

Small shops keep standard business hours. Large shops and shopping centres open at 0900 or 1000 Mon–Sat and close at 2000 or 2100. Opening hours are slightly shorter on Sun. Many restaurants, museums and legitimate theatres close on Mon, but most tourist attractions are open seven days a week. An exception is J.N. 'Ding' Darling Wildlife Refuge on Sanibel Island which is closed on Fri.

## PARKS INFORMATION

For specific national and state parks, monuments, and seashores, see the appropriate description among the recommended routes throughout this book. For general information on national parks, monuments, refuges and seashore information, contact the **National Parks**

Service, *Southeast Region, 75 Spring St S.W., Atlanta, GA 30303; tel: (404) 331-5187.* For **Florida State Parks** information, contact *Department of Environmental Protection, Office of Recreation & Parks, Mail Station 535, 3900 Commonwealth Blvd, Tallahassee, FL 32399-3000; tel: (904) 488-9872.*

There is a charge for entry to national, state, and some regional parks. State parks charge daily fees; national parks and monuments charge by the week. Campsite fees are almost always additional.

Senior citizens and disabled persons should ask if discounts apply. If visiting more than four or five national parks, monuments or historical sites for which entrance fees are charged, purchase a $25 Golden Eagle Passport, which covers the holder and one other person. Blind and disabled travellers can request a free Golden Access Passport upon arrival.

When entering a park, ask the ranger for the park's brochure. This has a map and a description of historical sites, flora, animals, birds, reptiles and poisonous animals and plants to be avoided. Campers should request the pitch diagram brochure. Most natural areas will have free birdwatching or shelling lists available on request.

## Passports and Visas

All non-US citizens must have a valid full passport (not a British Visitor's Passport) and, except for Canadians, a visa in order to enter the United States. Citizens of most countries must obtain a visa from the US Embassy in their country of residence in advance of arrival. In the UK, your local Thomas Cook branch can advise on and obtain US visas (which last the life of your passport).

British citizens and New Zealand citizens can complete a visa waiver form, which they generally receive with their air tickets if the airline is a 'participating carrier'. Provided nothing untoward is declared, such as a previous entry refusal or a criminal conviction, which would make applications for a full visa mandatory, the waiver exempts visitors from the need for a visa for stays of up to 90 days. It also allows a side-trip overland into Mexico or Canada and return.

*Note:* Documentation regulations change frequently and are complex for some nationalities; confirm your requirements with a good travel agent or the nearest US Embassy at least 90 days before you plan to depart for the USA.

## Police

To telephone police in an emergency, ring 911. There are many different police jurisdictions within Florida (and Georgia), each with its own force. The roads are patrolled by the Florida Highway Patrol (FHP). See also under 'Security' on p. 38 and 'Police' in 'Driving in Florida'.

## Postal Services

Every town has a least one post office. Hours vary, although all are open Mon–Fri, morning and afternoon. Postal Service branches may be open Sat or even Sun. Some big hotels sell stamps through the concierge; large department stores may have a post office; and some supermarkets and shops catering to tourists sell stamps at the checkout counter. Some stamp machines are installed in stores, but a surcharge may be included in the cost. For philatelic sales, check major city telephone directories under US Postal Service.

Mail everything going overseas Air Mail (surface mail takes weeks or even months). If posting letters near an urban area, mail should take about one week. Add a day or two if mailing from remote areas.

Poste Restante is available at any post office, without charge. Mail should be addressed in block lettering to your name, Poste Restante/General Delivery, city state, post office's zip (postal) code, and United States of America (do not abbreviate). Mail is held for 30 days at the post office branch that handles General Delivery for each town or city, usually the main office. General Delivery zip codes include:

> Miami: 33101
> Orlando: 33802
> Key West: 33040
> Fort Lauderdale: 33310
> Jacksonville: 32203
> St Augustine: 32084
> Tampa: 33602
> St Petersburg: 33733
> Tallahassee: 32301
> Atlanta: 30301

Identification is required for mail pickup.

## PUBLIC HOLIDAYS

America's love affair with the road extends to jumping in the automobile for holiday weekends. Local celebrations, festivals, parades or neighbourhood parties can disrupt some or all activities in town. Following is a list of public holidays:

New Year (1 Jan); Martin Luther King Jr Day (third Mon in Jan); Lincoln's Birthday (12 Feb); Presidents' Day (third Mon in Feb); Easter (Sun in Mar/Apr); (Georgia) Confederate Memorial Day (26 Apr); Memorial Day (last Mon in May); US Independence Day (4 July); Labor Day (first Mon in Sept); Columbus Day (second Mon in Oct); Veterans Day (11 Nov); Thanksgiving Day (last Thur in Nov); and Christmas (25 Dec).

Post offices and government offices close on public holidays; public transport schedules may change and parking meter enforcement varies. Some businesses take the day off, though department and discount stores use the opportunity to hold huge sales, well advertised in local newspapers. Petrol stations remain open. Small shops and some grocery stores close or curtail hours.

Call in advance before visiting an attraction on a public holiday as there are frequently special hours. National and state park campsites and lodging must be reserved in advance for the holidays, wherever possible. Easter, Thanksgiving and Christmas are family holidays, and discounts may be available (to fill hotels and motels in some areas). In resort areas, prices may be higher for the year-end holidays as colder-climate residents head for warmer climates. Other holidays are 'mobile' for Americans, so book early. The most festive holiday is 4 July, Independence Day, when most cities have public fireworks displays.

Florida has a phenomenon known as Spring Break, corresponding to school holidays six weeks before Easter. Traditionally, college and high school students descend on certain Florida beach resort areas, drink, party and become rowdy. Fort Lauderdale has discouraged Spring Break revelries, and its 1990s annual estimates of 100,000 partymakers are a fifth of the numbers of former years. Other Spring Break meccas are Daytona Beach and Panama City, and Destin and Fort Walton Beach along the Gulf of Mexico.

## SALES TAXES

There is no Value Added Tax or Goods

& Services Tax in Florida or Georgia. Both states charge sales tax for most products and services, itemised separately on bills. In Florida, food products are not sales taxable; most beverages are. Newspapers in a vending box are not taxed; shops will charge tax. Florida sales tax ranges from 6% up, depending on the location, and there are additional lodging and dining taxes. Georgia's general sales tax rate is 4%. Car hire is subject to taxes and a surcharge, which can increase costs by as much as 15% above the daily, weekly, or monthly booking rate.

## SECURITY

Throwing caution to the winds is foolhardy anytime, and even more so on holiday. The US, by history and inclination, permits guns to circulate, both legally and illegally. Dial 911 on any telephone for free emergency assistance from police, fire, and medical authorities. In Orlando, a Tourist Office Policing Unit can provide additional assistance to travellers in distress.

On the other hand, millions of people travel in perfect safety each year in the US. So can you if you take the following common-sense precautions.

### Travelling Safely

Never publicly discuss travel plans or money or valuables you are carrying. Use caution in large cities, towns and rural areas. Drive, park and walk only in well-lit areas. Try to arrive at your lodging before dark. If unsure of roads or weather ahead, stop for the evening and find secure lodging. Sightsee with a known companion, or in a group. Hotel staff can suggest safe jogging routes, which should be changed daily. Solo travel, in urban areas or in the countryside, is not recommended.

The best way to avoid becoming a victim of theft or bodily injury is to walk with assurance and try to give the impression that you are not worth robbing (e.g. do not wear or carry expensive jewellery or flash rolls of banknotes). Use a hidden money-belt for your valuables, travel documents and spare cash. Carrying a wallet in a back pocket or leaving a handbag or camera bag open is an invitation to every pickpocket in the vicinity. In all public places, take precautions with anything that is obviously worth stealing – use a handbag with a crossed shoulder strap and a zip, wind the strap of your camera case around your chair or place your handbag firmly between your feet under the table while you eat. A few dollar bills and phone/vending machine change in your pocket saves displaying a wallet's contents.

Never leave luggage unattended, and only surrender your luggage to a uniformed skycap (porter). At airports, security officials may confiscate unattended luggage as a possible bomb. In public toilets, handbags and small luggage have been snatched from hooks, or from under stalls. Airports, bus and train stations usually have lockers. Most work with keys; take care to guard the key and memorise the locker number. Hotel bell staff may keep luggage for one or more days on request, and for a fee – be sure to get receipts for left luggage before surrendering it. If using a taxi or limousine service, watch your luggage being loaded and unloaded. Guard against pickpockets.

While concealed weapons are not illegal in Florida, defensive products resembling tear gas are legal only for persons certified in their proper use. Mugging, by individuals or gangs, is a social problem in the USA. If you are attacked, it is safer to let go of your bag or hand over the small amount of obvious money – as you are more likely to be attacked physically if the thief meets with resistance. *Never resist.* Dial 911, free, from any phone. Report incidents immediately to local police, even if it is only to get a copy of their report for your insurance company.

At theme parks, watch children carefully, hold hands and accompany children to restrooms. Children should not speak to strangers. Most parks have a parent-child lost and found service which either one can use to locate the other.

### Driving Safely

The driver, other front seat occupant and children under five years legally must wear seat belts in Florida. Children up to three years of age must have a separate car seat. Florida law prohibits license plate or other indications that a car is a hired vehicle. Have car hire counter personnel recommend a safe, direct route on a clear map before you leave with the vehicle. Miami has a 'Tourist Route' brochure, available from car hire agencies, which takes visitors from Miami International Airport to Miami Beach or downtown via fast freeways. Make sure that all car door and window locks work and operation is clear. Lock all valuables and luggage in the boot or glove box so that nothing is visible to passers-by or other drivers. Don't leave maps, brochures or guidebooks in evidence and don't leave a hotel parking tag in the window – why advertise that you're a stranger in town? Some hire companies in Florida offer cellular phones with a car adaptor, charger and batteries.

Always keep car doors and windows locked. Do not venture into unlit areas, neighbourhoods that look seedy, or off paved roads. *Do not stop* if told by a passing motorist or pedestrian that something is wrong with your car, or if someone signals for help with a broken-down car. If you need to stop, do so only in well-lit or populated areas, even if your car is bumped from behind by another vehicle.

If your car breaks down, turn on the flashing emergency lights, and if it is safe to get out, raise the bonnet and return to the vehicle. Security is provided at all 71 of Florida's highway rest stops for 16 hrs a day. Do not split passengers up. Freeway (telephone) call boxes are normally spaced one mile apart. Lights on emergency vehicles are red or red and blue, so do not stop for flashing white lights or flashing headlights. Ask directions only from police, at a well-lit business area, or at a service station.

At night, have keys ready to unlock car doors before entering a parking lot. Check the surrounding area and underneath and inside the vehicle before entering. Never pick up hitch-hikers, and never leave the car with the engine running. Take all valuables with you. Fill the petrol tank during daylight hours, and keep it at least half full.

### Sleeping Safely

When sleeping rough, in any sort of dormitory, train, or open campsite, the safest place for your small valuables is at the bottom of your sleeping-bag. In train sleeping cars, padlock your luggage to the seat, and ask the attendant to show you how to lock the compartment door at night. If in doubt, it's best to take luggage with you. Be particularly conscious of your luggage and surroundings around airports and train and bus stations.

Do not accept a room if an employee says the room number out loud. Ground-floor rooms, while convenient, give easier access to those intent on breaking in. A room on the third to the sixth floor is safest: burglars find easier pickings on the lower floors, and fire equipment may not reach above the sixth. Especially at night, use the well-lit main entrance to the hotel, and be conscious of movement around you as you move from the parking area to the hotel lobby.

In a room, lock all door locks from the inside. Check that all windows are locked, including sliding glass doors. Never leave the room at night without leaving a light and television on and the 'Do Not disturb' sign on the door. Lights deter prowlers, and when you return, any disturbance to room contents will be visible. If you keep belongings in a particular place in the room and check them daily, missing articles will be obvious. Carry a small flashlight (torch) with you to brighten dark areas and in case of power failures (caused by lightning in Florida).

Use a door viewer to check before admitting anyone to your room. If someone claims to be on the hotel staff or a repair person, do not let the person in before phoning the office or front desk to verify to person's name and job. A lightweight plastic doorstop is an additional deterrent. It's safer to call housekeeping to make up the room than to use the 'Maid Please Make Up Room' sign on the door.

Money, cheques, credit cards, passports and keys should be kept with you, or secured in your hotel's safe deposit box. When checking in, find the most direct route from your room to fire escapes, elevators, stairwells and the nearest telephone. Room keys should be with you, not left on restaurant tables or by the swimming pool. Use a hotel fitness centre or workout area only if staffed.

### Documents
Take a few passport photos with you and photocopy the important pages and any visa stamps in your passport. Store these safely, together with a note of the numbers of your travellers cheques, credit cards, and insurance documents (keep them away from the documents themselves). If you are unfortunate enough to be robbed, you will at least have some identification, and replacing the documents will be much easier. Apply to your nearest consulate (see 'Consulates' on p. 23 for addresses and phone numbers).

### SHOPPING
Uniquely Florida souvenirs include Florida wines; shells; gator, manatee and Florida panther paraphernalia; Seminole (Native American) costumes and beadwork; honey and tropical fruit preserves; dried fruit; and the ubiquitous T-shirts. Clothing can be a bargain, particularly at discount or factory outlet stores. Cameras and other photo equipment can be a fraction of UK prices, but do your homework on prices before you go, and shop around when you arrive.

Tape cassettes, blank video tapes, CDs, computer programmes and CD-ROMs sold in the USA can be used anywhere in the world. For more information on electrical goods, see 'Electricity' on p. 27.

### SMOKING
Lighting up is out in public buildings and public transport. All plane flights in the USA are non-smoking, and some hire cars are designated as non-smoking. Most hotels/motels set aside non-smoking rooms or floors; Bed and Breakfast establishments are almost all non-smoking. Restaurant dining regulations vary by location: some have a percentage of the eatery devoted to smokers. Bars and lounges are smoking locales. Smoking is prohibited in many stores and shops.

Always ask before lighting a cigarette, cigar, or pipe. When in doubt, go outside to smoke.

## SOLO TRAVEL

It's always safer to travel with a companion. If on your own, never leave your luggage unattended and ensure you stay in well-lit areas. However, solo travel is an excellent way to meet new people.

## TELEPHONES

The US telephone system is divided into local and long distance carriers. Depending on the time of day and day of the week, it may be cheaper to call New York or California than to call 30 miles away. After 1700 Mon–Fri, and all weekend, rates are lower. Useful phone numbers are provided throughout this book.

Public telephones are everywhere, indicated by a sign with a white telephone receiver on a blue field. Enclosed booths, wall-mounted, or free-standing machines are all used. If possible, use public phones in well-lit, busy public areas like *inside* grocery or convenience stores.

Dialling instructions are in the front of the local white pages telephone directory. There is a charge for information calls.

To call:
    long distance: dial 1 before area code
    In emergency: 911 (police, fire or medical assistance)
    Operator: 0
    Local number information: 411
    Long distance information: 1-area code-555-1212
    International operator: 00
    International calls: 011-country code (omit the first 0 if there is one)-local number. For example, to call Great Britain, Inner London, from the USA, dial: 011-44-171-local number.

Some country codes:

**Australia** 61
**New Zealand** 64
**Republic of Ireland** 353
**South Africa** 27
**United Kingdom** 44

Pay phones take coins, and a local call costs from $0.20–$0.25 or more. An operator or computer voice will come on-line to ask for additional coins when needed. Most hotels and motels add a stiff surcharge (as much as 70%) to the basic cost of a call, and may charge even if the call isn't connected, so find a public telephone in the lobby, and be discreet with any personal information.

Prepaid phone cards are no longer a novelty in the US, and are widely sold in Florida. Before you travel, ask your local phone company if your phone card will work in America. Most do, and come with a list of contact numbers. However, remember that the USA has among the cheapest overseas phone rates in the world, which makes it cheaper to fill pay phones with quarters than to reverse charges. A credit card may be convenient, but only economical if you pay the bill immediately.

For comparison, local call rates:
    coin $0.20–$0.25
    direct dial, calling card $0.35
    operator assisted, calling card $0.95
    hotel connection charge (additional) $0.50–$3.00
    hotel surcharge up to 70% more than basic timed rate

800 numbers are toll-free. Like all long-distance numbers, the 800 area code must be preceded by a 1, e.g. 1-800-123-4567. Some US telephone numbers are given in

letters, i.e. 1-800-96-PEACH. Telephone keys have both numbers and letters, so find the corresponding letter and depress that key. A few numbers have more than seven letters to finish a business name. Not to worry, US or Canadian phone numbers never require more than seven numerals, plus three for the area code.

900 numbers, widely advertised on television for everything from at-home shopping to sex to religion, make money for the advertisers by charging for call placement and by each minute connected.

## TIME

Florida spreads over two time zones, Eastern Standard Time (EST), GMT-5 hrs, and, in the north-west, west of the Apalachicola River, Central Standard Time (CST), GMT-6 hours. Georgia follows Eastern Standard Time. From the first Sun in Apr until the last Sun in Oct, clocks in both time zones and states are pushed forward one hour to Daylight Time (EDT or CDT), GMT-4 hours and GMT- 5 hours.

| TIME IN MIAMI(EST) | 8 a.m. | 12 noon | 5 p.m. | 12 midnt |
|---|---|---|---|---|
| TIME IN |  |  |  |  |
| Auckland | 1 a.m. | 5 a.m. | 10 a.m. | 5 p.m. |
| Cape Town | 3 p.m. | 7 p.m. | midnt | 7 a.m. |
| Dublin | 1 p.m. | 5 p.m. | 10 p.m. | 5 a.m. |
| London | 1 p.m. | 5 p.m. | 10 p.m. | 5 a.m. |
| Perth | 9 p.m. | 1 a.m. | 6 p.m. | 1 p.m. |
| Sydney | 11 p.m. | 3 a.m. | 8 a.m. | 3 p.m. |
| Toronto | 8 a.m. | noon | 5 p.m. | midnt |

## TIPPING

Acknowledgement for good service should not be extorted. That said, tipping is a fact of life, to get, to repeat, or to thank someone for service.

Service charges are not customarily added to restaurant bills, but may be in tourist areas like Miami Beach and Key West. Waiters and waitresses expect a tip of 15% of the bill before taxes are added on. In luxury restaurants, also be prepared to tip the maitre d' and sommelier a few dollars up to 10% of the bill. Bartenders expect the change from a drink up to several dollars.

Hotel porters generally receive $1 per bag; a bellperson who shows you to the room expects several dollars; in luxury properties, tip more. Room service delivery staff should be tipped 10%–15% of the tariff before taxes, unless there's a service charge indicated on the bill. Expect to hand out dollars for most services that involve room delivery.

Some hotels will have a chambermaid name card placed in the room: it's a hint for a tip of a few dollars upon your departure, but never required.

Ushers in legitimate theatres, arenas and stadiums are not tipped; cinemas seldom have ushers, nor are tips expected. In a nightclub with entertainment and 'name' entertainer billing, unless holding reserved show seats, $5–$20 to the maitre d' should get better seats. Showroom waiters expect $5–$10 per couple or party for a cocktails show; $10–$20 for a dinner show.

In Seminole, Miccosukee, or other Native-American operated casinos, if you're successful, tip the dealer or croupier between hands, throws of the dice, or spins of the wheel with a few chips. A slot machine changeperson likes a small percentage of the pay-off.

## TOILET/WCs

There is nothing worse than not being

## TRAVEL ESSENTIALS

able to find one! *Restroom* or *bathroom* are the common terms; *toilet* is acceptable; few people recognise *washroom* or *WC*. Most are marked with a figure or a male or a female; *Men* and *women* are the most common terms, though *caballeros* (or *senors*) and *damas* may be used in Spanish-speaking areas. Occasionally, a restroom may be used by both sexes.

Facilities may be clean and well-equipped or filthy. Most businesses, including bars and restaurants, reserve restrooms for clients. Petrol stations provide keys for customers. Public toilets are sporadically placed, but well-marked. Most parks and all official roadside rest stops have toilet facilities.

### TOURISM INFORMATION

In the US, each state is responsible for its own tourism promotion. The US Tourism and Travel Administration (USTTA) maintains offices abroad, but serves the entire United States, and is often unresponsive to enquiries.

Florida plans to privatise its tourism agency. Address requests for information well in advance to the **Florida Department of Commerce, Division of Tourism,** *Direct Mail, 126 W. Van Buren St, Tallahassee, FL 32399-2000; tel: (904) 487-1462* or *(904) 487-1465*. In the UK, **Florida Division of Tourism,** *18–24 Westbourne Grove, 1st Floor, London W2 5R11; tel: (0171) 727-1661.* In Canada, **Florida Division of Tourism,** *121 Bloor St E., Suite 1003, Toronto ONT M4W 3M5; tel: (416) 928-3139.* In Germany, **Florida Division of Tourism,** *Schillerstrasse 10, 60313 Frankfurt/Main; tel: 49-69-131-0732.* The text lists tourism contacts for cities and attractions en route.

Motorists will find information and citrus juice samples at **Florida State Welcome Centers** in Tallahassee, off I-10 at Pensacola, off I-95 at Yulee, off I-75 by Jennings, and by Hwy 231 at Campbellton. Several companies operate private welcome centre/lodging booking services, well-touted by billboards as cars approach. Sodas and coffee are cheap; information is free.

For Georgia, contact the **Georgia Department of Industry, Trade and Tourism,** *PO Box 1776, Atlanta GA 30301; tel: (404) 656-3590* or *(800) VISIT-GA*. Georgia operates **State Information Centers** daily from 0830–1730, in Augusta, Columbus, Kingsland, Lavonia, Plains, Ringgold, Savannah, Sylvania, Tallapoosa, Valdosta and West Point.

### TRAINS

**AMTRAK** is the official passenger train transportation company in the United States; *tel: (800)-872-7245*. Unfortunately, AMTRAK only covers a few areas of Florida, so request an *American Travel Planner* brochure. From Miami, trains run north to West Palm Beach, north-west to Okeechobee and Sebring, then north to Kissimmee, Orlando and Jacksonville. Another route connects Jacksonville to Tampa. Take the Sunset Limited service west from Jacksonville through Tallahassee and Pensacola to New Orleans and Los Angeles. There are no AMTRAK connections between Atlanta and Florida. Trains do not stop at each town en route, so check if there is a stop at your destination. AMTRAK operates charter buses south of Tampa to service Bradenton, Sarasota and Fort Myers. The 'All About America' programme permits three stopovers within 45 days at a highly discounted rate, from early Jan–mid-Jun. Expect to pay a supplement for sleeper compartments.

# TRAVEL ESSENTIALS

## Travel Arrangements

Given the fact that many of the world's international airlines fly into either Miami or Atlanta, and the ease of hiring cars at airports, Florida and Atlanta are ideal destinations for independently-minded travellers. However, the many types of air ticket and the range of temporary deals available on the busy routes make it advisable to talk to your travel agent before booking, to find the best bargain.

In fact, taking a fly-drive package such as one of Thomas Cook's own, or one of the many others offered by airlines and tour operators, is usually more economical than making all your own arrangements. All include the air ticket and car/RV hire element; some also follow set itineraries which enables them to offer guaranteed and pre-paid accommodation at selected hotels en route. Programmes such as Thomas Cook's America allow the flexibility of booking the airline ticket at an advantageous rate and then choosing from a 'menu' of other items, often at a discounted price, such as car hire, hotel coupons (which pre-pay accommodation but do not guarantee room availability) and other extras such as excursions.

## Useful Reading

Many British and international guidebook series feature a volume on Florida; local area guides are valuable once you've chosen a base and route. *Thomas Cook Travellers: Florida* (price £6.99) is available from bookshops in the UK and in Ireland, Canada, Australia, New Zealand and South Africa. Also in the *Thomas Cook Travellers* colour-illustrated guidebook series are *Orlando* and *Caribbean Cruising including Miami* (both priced at £7.99). In the USA the same titles are available in the *Passport's Illustrated Guides* series, priced $12.95 each.

Another colour-illustrated guide to the state is *Discover Florida* by Eric and Ruth Bailey, 1993, Berlitz.

Useful Thomas Cook publications, if you are considering using trains or buses for any part of your trip, are the *Thomas Cook Overseas Timetable* (published every two months, £7.90 per issue) and the annual *Thomas Cook North American Rail and Bus Guide* (£6.95). (For more details of Thomas Cook publications see pp. 15 and 70.)

If you are arranging your own accommodation as you travel, a comprehensive guide like the *AAA TourBook for Florida* and the *AAA TourBook for Georgia, North Carolina and South Carolina* or one of the *Mobil Regional Guides* can often be obtained through specialist travel bookshops outside the USA, or may be available from your own auto club.

Books you can buy in Florida include:

*Adventuring in Florida, The Sierra Club Travel Guide to the Sunshine State*, by Allen de Hart, 1991, Sierra Club Books, San Francisco CA.

*Audubon Society Field Guide to North American Birds*, Eastern Edition, Alfred A. Knopf, New York.

*Audubon Society Nature Guides: Atlantic & Gulf Coast Wetlands*, William A. Niering, Alfred A. Knopf, New York.

*Diving & Snorkeling Guide to Florida's East Coast*, Susanne & Stuart Cummings, 1993, Pisces Books, Miami FL.

*Everglades Wildguide*, Handbook 143, by Jean Craighead George, 1972, U.S. Dept of the Interior, Washington, D.C.

*Florida Off the Beaten Path*, by Bill and Diana Gleasner, 1993, Globe Pequot, Old Saybrook CT.

*Exploring Wild South Florida*, by Susan D. Jewell, 1993, Pineapple Press Inc., Sarasota FL.

*The Green Guide to Florida*, by Marty

Klinkenberg and Elizabeth Leach, 1993, Country Roads Press, Castine ME.

*A Guide to Everglades National Park and the Nearby Florida Keys*, by Herbert S. Zim, 1992, Western Publishing Co., Racine WI.

*Hidden® Florida*, by Stacy Ritz et. al., 1995, Ulysses Press, Berkeley CA.

*Hidden® Florida Keys and Everglades*, by Candace Leslie, 1994, Ulysses Press, Berkeley CA.

*The Hiker's Guide to Florida*, by M. Timothy O'Keefe, 1993, Falcon Press Publishing Co., Inc., Helena MT.

*Historic Places of St Augustine and St Johns County*, by William R. Adams and Paul L. Weaver, III, 1993, Southern Heritage Press, St Augustine FL.

*Hurricanes*, Sally Lee, 1993, Franklin Watts, New York NY.

*A Key West Companion*, Christopher Cox, 1983, St Martin's Press, NY.

*Miami & South Florida ACCESS®*, by Marilyn A, Moore and Karen Feldman Smith, 1993, HarperCollins Publishers, Dunmore PA.

*Mini-Day Trips for the Panhandle, Tampa-Big Bend, Southwest, Southeast, Orlando and Northeast*, by Joan Lundquist Scalpone, Punta Gorda FL.

*National Geographic Society Field Guide to Birds of North America*, National Geographic Society, Washington, D.C.

*Official Guide Book to Sarasota, Bradenton and Venice*, by Steve Rabow, 1994, Rabow Communications Arts, Sarasota FL.

*Unique Florida: A Guide to the State's Quirks, charisma, and Character*, by Sarah Lovett, 1993, John Muir Publications, Santa Fe NM.

*A Visitor's Guide to the Everglades*, by Jeff Weber, 1986, Florida Flair Books, Miami FL.

Two Florida authors wrote evocative classics: *The Everglades: River of Grass*, by Marjorie Stoneman Douglas, 1947. Marjorie Kinnan Rawlings won the 1939 Pulitzer Prize for Literature for *The Yearling*, about her experiences living on the land and with its people.

## WEIGHTS & MEASURES

Officially, the USA is converting to the metric system. In truth, few people have changed. (A few road signs show both miles and kilometres). The non-metric US measures are the same as Imperial measures except for fluids, where US gallons and quarts are five-sixths of their Imperial equivalents.

Conversions of weights and measures and temperatures are given on p. 347.

## WHAT TO TAKE

Absolutely everything you could ever need is available, so don't worry if you've left anything behind. In fact most US prices will seem low: competition and oversupply keeps them that way. Pharmacies (chemists), also called drug stores, carry a range of products, from medicine to cosmetics to beach balls. Prepare a small first aid kit before you leave home with tried and tested insect repellent, sun cream, and soothing, moisturising lotion. Carry all medicines, glasses, and contraceptives with you, and keep duplicate prescriptions or a letter from your doctor to verify your need for a particular medication.

Other useful items to bring or buy immediately upon arrival are a water-bottle, sunglasses, a hat or visor with a rim, a plastic folding chair, a Swiss Army pocket knife, a torch (flashlight), a padlock for anchoring luggage, a money belt, a travel adapter, string for a washing line, an alarm clock and a camera. Allow a little extra space in luggage for souvenirs.

# Driving in Florida

This chapter provides hints and practical advice for those taking to the state's roads, whether in a hire car or RV, or in their own vehicle.

## Accidents and Breakdowns

Holidays should be trouble-free, yet **breakdowns** can occur. Pull off to the side of the road where visibility is good and you are out of the way of traffic. Turn on hazard flashers or indicators, and, if it is safe for traffic flow and personal security, get out and raise the bonnet. Change a tyre only when out of traffic flow.

Dial 911 on any telephone to reach highway patrol, police, fire or medical services. Emergency call boxes are placed about every mile on freeways. Report your phone number, location, problem and need for first aid.

Hurricanes are a rare but potentially devastating driving hazard – see p. 31 for specific advice.

If involved in a **collision**, stop. Call the Florida Highway Patrol (FHP), local police or the county sheriff's office if there are injuries, death or physical damage to either vehicle. Show the police and involved driver(s) your driving licence, car registration, car insurance documentation, address and contact information. Other drivers should provide you with the same information.

Collisions have to be reported to your car hire company. Injuries or death must be reported to the police or FHP. Property damage valued over $100 must be reported in writing within five days of the incident to the Florida Department of Highway Safety and Motor Vehicles (offices are listed in phone directories).

Fly-drive travellers should bear in mind the effects of **jet-lag** on driver safety. This can be a very real problem. The best way to minimise it is to spend the first night after arrival in a hotel at the airport or in the city and pick up your hire vehicle the next day, rather than take the car on the road within hours of getting off the plane.

## Car Hire

Hiring a car or RV (camper van) gives you the freedom of the road with a vehicle you can leave behind after a few weeks. Whether booking a fly-drive package with an agency or making independent arrangements, plan well in advance to ensure you get the type and size of vehicle your heart desires. Ask about discounts for weekend or long-term rental, auto club membership, proximity to the airport or destination hotel, and a frequent renter programme. Enquire about free pick up and delivery of the vehicle. Free, unlimited mileage is common with cars, less so with RVs.

Sheer volume in airport hire car turnover means that in the USA it's usually cheaper to pick up the vehicle from an airport than from a downtown site, and to return it to the airport. A surcharge (called a drop fee) may be levied if you drop the car off in a different location from the place of hire. When considering an RV, ask about one-way and low-season rates.

You will need a valid credit card as

## DRIVING IN FLORIDA

security for the vehicle's value. Before you leave the hire agency, ensure that you have all the documentation for the hire, that the car registration is in the glove compartment, and that you understand how to operate the vehicle. For RVs, also get instruction books and a complete demonstration of all systems and appliances and how they interconnect. Because it advertises for criminal attention, Florida law prohibits a car that exhibits a hire company name on a window decal, on the fender (bumper), or on licence plate frames. Check the vehicle to verify that there are no hire indications.

Car size terminology varies, but general categories range from small and basic to all-frills posh: sub-compact, compact, economy, mid-size or intermediate, full-size or standard, and luxury. Sub-compacts are rarely available. Expect to choose between two- or four-door models. The larger the car, the faster it accelerates and consumes petrol. Some vehicles are equipped with four-wheel drive (4WD), unnecessary except for off-road driving (not covered in this book).

Standard features on US hire cars usually include automatic transmission, air conditioning (a necessity for summer and warm weather driving) and cruise control, which sets speed for long-distance highway driving, allowing the driver to take their foot off the accelerator.

### DIFFICULT DRIVING

Mountains don't exist in Florida; but the challenge of a slope is offset by the flatness of a landscape which easily mesmerises drivers. Occasional fog rises from the swamps, thunderstorms send vehicles careening across the roads under onslaughts of water, and a rare hurricane can make driving hazardous to impossible.

Florida's roads are well-surfaced, but lay-bys and verges are rare on non-urban roads. Country roads are usually built on a sort of dike, higher than the wetlands or the swamps on either side. What may appear solid may give way quickly, landing your vehicle in muck or worse. For vehicular and personal safety, don't attempt to pull off any road outside an urban area unless there is a sign indicating a public rest area. On the interstate highways, Florida's public rest stops have a security patrols for 16 hrs each day.

Be cautious during summer when cars can overheat and air conditioner use depletes petrol quickly. On some stretches of road, particularly the back roads of Northern Florida, filling stations, restaurants and shops are few and far between. Check oil and water frequently,

---

### Car and RV hire

Toll-free (in the US) telephone numbers for car hire companies:

| | |
|---|---|
| Advantage | (800) 777-5500 |
| Alamo | (800) 327-9633 |
| Avis | (800) 831-2847 |
| Budget | (800) 527-0770 |
| Dollar | (800) 800-4000 |
| Enterprise | (800) 325-8007 |
| Hertz | (800) 654-3131 |
| National | (800) 227-7368 |
| Thrifty | (800) 367-2277 |

Toll-free (in the US) telephone numbers for RV hire companies:

| | |
|---|---|
| Cruise America | (800) 327-7799 |
| Go Vacations, Inc. | (800) 487-4652 |
| Recreation Vehicle Rental Association (RVRA) | (800) 336-0355 |
| Rental Management Systems | (818) 960-1884 |

make sure the petrol tank is full, and pack a picnic lunch. Basic precautions include making sure that the car's engine and cooling system are in good working order, the tyres are properly inflated, and the petrol tank filled.

All travellers should carry extra fresh water, snacks, a torch (flashlight), a pullover and raingear/umbrella in case of trouble.

If using the car's cruise control on the swift interstates, expressways, or toll roads, beware of any sudden slowing of vehicles ahead – especially lorries (trucks). If there are two or more lanes moving in the same direction, drivers can overtake on either the left or the right, and do. In rural areas, prepare for farm equipment travelling at speeds as slow as 20 mph, which may block traffic for miles – with no place for the farmer to leave the road.

Traffic signals are strung on wires above the road and may not be visible if the vehicle in front of yours is high and wide. In that case, watch the movement of the other drivers around you for cues to continue driving. Many road signs are strung on the same wires, and require careful co-ordination with maps to verify location and direction. Watch for school buses stopping suddenly. When a school bus stops, a red stop sign is extended from the side of the vehicle. On a two-lane road, both lanes of traffic are required to stop behind it. If you're driving in the same lane as the bus, you must stop until the stop sign is withdrawn.

Floridian folklore holds that older drivers and visitors from out of state slow traffic down. No matter the driver's origin, traffic *can* slow to a crawl on any road or highway, especially at rush hour or when there's a special event or festival nearby.

Parts of main thoroughfares like the Tamiami Trail (Hwy 41) have stretches with only a single lane in either direction. One lorry in front can delay a whole string of cars. Plan on driving during the day, to enjoy the scenery along the route, and to allow for extra time if trapped in slow traffic.

Posted speed limits are honoured more in the breach than reality. The two extremes range from far exceeding the 65 mph maximum/40 mph minimum set for 'rural' interstate highways, to vehicles in all lanes driving for miles at half the 40 mph legal limit. Horn use is not customary, and has no effect on the speed of traffic.

Police and the Florida Highway Patrol (FHP) chase 'speeders' and issue tickets. Patrol cars will frequently await violators under a tree or in a driveway near a popular route like the Tamiami Trail or the Overseas Highway (US Hwy 1) down the Florida Keys. No quarter is given; it's safest to avoid driving as if you're trying to catch the proverbial last boat out before the island sinks into the sea!

Turns must be anticipated well in advance in order to change lanes to make, for example, a left turn at a busy intersection. The centre lane of a three-lane road is used for left turns. If two vehicles arrive at an intersection at the same moment, the one to the right proceeds forward first.

A driver is legally required to turn on headlights at dusk, or in fog or rain. By custom, long-time Floridians will drive with lights on at all times, a boon for spotting traffic approaching from up the road. Animals have the right-of way at all times; pedestrians have that right in marked crossing zones.

Peruse current maps before setting off in a car or an RV. Construction in many areas of Florida has rendered many maps so inaccurate as to be useless. Signs are posted *at* the entrance or turnoff to an attraction, so there may be little or no warning before you arrive at your destination.

## DISTANCES

Point-to-point distances are reasonable in Florida and Georgia, but may take some time if traffic is slow or weather conditions interfere. Plan on about three hours to cross Florida from the Atlantic to the Gulf of Mexico; Orlando is half way between the coasts. It's four hours from Miami to Key West or to Flamingo at the end of the road in the Everglades. Allow four hours between Tampa and Naples. Toll roads and the interstate highways should be used for fast movement between areas or be prepared for a slow crawl from town to town on Hwy A1A (on the Atlantic Coast) and Hwy 41 (Tamiami Trail up the Gulf Coast).

Plan on an average driving time of 40 mph, without stops. Use the sample driving distances and times on p. 14 as guidelines but allow for delays and stops.

## DOCUMENTATION

In Florida and Georgia, your home country's driving licence is valid if you are at least 16 years old. Car hire companies may have higher age requirements, typically 21 or older (with additional charges for under-25 drivers).

## INFORMATION

Auto club membership in your home country can be invaluable. AAA (Automobile Association of America) clubs provide members of corresponding foreign clubs travelling to North America the reciprocal services that AAA members are eligible to receive abroad. Auto club services include emergency road service and towing; maps, tour guide books and specialist publications; touring services; road and camping information; and discounts to attractions and hotels. The rule of thumb is, if it's free at home, it should be free in the USA, too. The AAA may charge for some services, like maps and tour books.

Emergency breakdown road service may not be available to some non-North American club members. For information on reciprocal clubs and services, contact your own club or request *Offices to Serve You Abroad*, American Automobile Association, 1000 AAA Drive, Heathrow, FL 32746-5063; tel: (407) 444-7700. Carry your own club membership card with you at all times.

## MOTORCYCLES

If *Easy Rider* is still your idea of America, so be it. Motorcycles provide great mobility and a sense of freedom. Luggage will be limited; the open road can make for long days in the saddle, and remember that potholes, gravel, poor roads, dust, smog and sun are a motorcyclist's touring companions.

Hire motorcycles locally by finding a telephone directory listing. Helmets are required by law for both driver and passenger in Florida and Georgia. Most motorcyclists turn on the headlight even in the daytime to increase their visibility. Cars can share lanes with motorcycles, though it's unsafe.

## PARKING

Public parking garages are well marked; in beach areas and kerbside in many cities, coin-operated parking meters are ubiquitous. Most meters require quarters ($0.25) for increments of one hour. Enforcement is vigilant, especially in beach areas. Alternatively, search for *beach*

# DRIVING IN FLORIDA

*access* signs, then park several blocks away and walk to the sand via the public access. On weekends, especially in winter or during Spring Break, beach parking will be scarce.

If you park in violation of times and areas posted on poles, or let the parking meter expire, expect to be issued a citation – a ticket that states the violation, amount of a fine, and how to pay it. If you do not pay it, the car hire company may charge the ticket amount (and any penalties) against your credit card. Fines range from a few dollars to several hundred dollars, depending on the violation and the location.

Valet parking at hotels, restaurants, and events may be pricey, and the parking attendant will expect an additional tip of a few dollars when returning the car. Leave the car keys with the valet attendant, who will return them with the car. Restaurants may 'validate' (include) parking if you patronise the establishment. Some hotels include valet parking as a part of the 'services' charge that is automatically added onto a bill. Be sure to check, or be prepared to tip – twice.

## PETROL

Petrol (gas) is sold in US gallons (roughly four litres per gallon). Posted prices including tax are shown in cents – as, for instance, 121.9 (= $1 and 21.9 cents) per gallon. Prices can vary from 96 to 155 cents per gallon, depending on location. Some areas with many stations will have enough competition to lower prices; others will not. Near urban areas, prices tend to be lower. Some stations will only accept cash in payment for petrol or require advance payment; others accept cash, credit cards and travellers' cheques. Check with the station attendant before trying to pump petrol, as many stations do not indicate what form of payment is acceptable.

Some stations offer full service, filling the petrol tank, washing the windscreen and checking motor oil, usually for about $0.35 extra per gallon. Most motorists use the more economical self-service.

Most US cars require unleaded petrol; diesel is widely available. The three fuel grades are regular, super and premium; use regular petrol unless the car company indicates otherwise.

When filling stations are more than a few miles apart, normally a road sign will state the distance to the next services. Open petrol stations are well-lit at night; many chains stay open 24 hrs, and have maps, snack foods, beverages and coffee.

Drivers of hired cars should carry a tyre pressure gauge. In Florida, many filling stations have air lines, but few have a gauge; guessing tyre pressure is a bit like playing Russian Roulette.

## POLICE

Police cars signal drivers with flashing red or red and blue lights, and sometimes a siren. Respond quickly, but safely, by moving to the side of the road. At night, you must reduce headlights to the parking, not driving, position. Roll the driver's side window down enough to converse with the police officer, but stay in the vehicle unless asked to get out. You have the right to ask an officer – politely – for identification, though it should be shown immediately. Have your driver's licence and car registration papers ready for inspection when requested. Officers normally check computer records for vehicle registration irregularities and the driver for theft, criminal record or other driving violations. If cited, do not argue with the officer, as a bad situation can only get worse.

## ROAD SIGNS

International symbols are used for directional and warning signs, but many are different from European versions; all language signs are in English, or occasionally in Spanish. Signs may be white, yellow, green, brown, or blue. (A selection of road signs is included in the Planning Maps colour section at the back of this book.)

Stop, yield, do not enter and wrong-way signs are *red* and *white*. *Yellow* is for warning or direction indicators. *Orange* is for roadworks or temporary diversions. *Green* indicates freeway directions and street names. *Brown* is an alert for parks, campsites, hiking, historic sites, etc. *Blue* gives non-driving information, such as radio station frequency for traffic or park information, services in a nearby town, and disabled facilities. Speed limits and distance are primarily shown in miles, not kilometres. Speed limit signs are *white* with black letters.

Traffic lights are red, yellow and green. Yellow indicates that the light will turn red; stop, if possible, before entering the intersection.

By custom, cars stop well behind street corners and pedestrian crosswalks. It is permitted to turn right at a red traffic light if there is no traffic coming from the left, i.e. as if it were a 'give way' sign, unless there is a sign specifically forbidding it.

A flashing yellow light, or hazard warning, requires drivers to slow down; flashing red means stop briefly, then proceed when safe.

## ROAD SYSTEM

The US Interstate Highway System was built in the 1950s to streamline the transportation of cargo across the country. Federal funds maintain the interstates, which are usually the smoothest roads available. The **interstate** highways, designated I-(number) in the text, are the straightest route from point to point. Florida's portions of the interstates are lined with forested woodland, and offer a verdant alternative to the scenic routes described in this book.

**Expressway** is a term for the interstate highways, **freeways** and **turnpikes**, devoid of traffic lights, stop signs or railroad crossings. They are similar to motorways but access is controlled. The Florida Turnpike, Sawgrass Expressway, and part of I-75 (Alligator Alley) are toll roads. Toll takers give change and can give receipts. Unfortunately, once on a toll roadway, the driver is committed. Refunds are seldom given for mistaken access to toll roads, though some toll takers will issue a chit and refund for a turnaround and exit. It may be miles before the next exit, so plan routes thoroughly before venturing in the vicinity of a toll road. Other roads parallel the toll roads, but will normally take much longer to traverse.

**Highways** have cross traffic interrupting the flow. East–west roads have even numbers, e.g., I-10; north–south roads are given odd numbers, e.g. I-95, I-75, Hwy 1, Hwy 41.1.

Rest areas, commonly along interstates, have restrooms with toilets and public telephones, and are usually landscaped. Picnic tables are provided, many sheltered from the sun. Though Florida has instituted a security guard system at the rest areas, use caution when leaving your vehicle, especially at night, and carry a powerful torch (flashlight).

Local roads range from satin-smooth to well-packed dirt. Dirt roads can mean ruts, especially if subjected to a recent rain. Ask at a local petrol station about

# DRIVING IN FLORIDA

road conditions before venturing on. Car hirers may prohibit driving on unpaved roads.

## RULES OF THE ROAD

### Lanes and Overtaking

Drive on the right. Vehicles are left-hand drive. The lane on the left, the *Number 1 Lane* is fast; the right is slowest, and cars enter or leave traffic from the right (unless otherwise indicated by signs). Overtake other vehicles on the left side. A solid white line at least 4 ft (1.2 m) from the kerb is a special lane for bicycles, and should be labelled *Bike Lane*.

Cars may and will pass you on both sides in a multi-lane road. For many drivers from the UK, this is the most unexpected and confusing feature of US roads. Use direction indicators, but don't be surprised if other drivers don't bother. Never turn against a red arrow.

Make right turns from the right-hand lane after stopping at stop signs or traffic lights unless there are signs to the contrary. Turn left from the most left-hand of lanes going in your direction, unless the turn is prohibited by a no-turn sign. Enter bike lanes only if making a right turn. Do not drive in areas marked for public transportation or for pedestrians (crosswalks).

Overtaking on a two-way road is permitted if the yellow line down the centre is broken. Tap the horn or blink headlights at night to alert the driver(s) being overtaken. If there are two or more lanes going in your direction, you may legally overtake from either the left or right. Signal your intentions, and only make a move when oncoming traffic is completely visible. Two solid yellow lines means no overtaking, and no turning – unless into a private driveway or for a legal U-turn. Driving or parking on sidewalks (pavements) or verges is illegal.

Main road drivers have the right of way over cars on lesser roads, but at the junction of two minor roads, cars to your right have the right of way when arriving at the same time you do.

Lorries carry Florida's agricultural produce (e.g. citrus, sugar, and strawberries) to market. Woe to the driver who gets caught behind a wedge of lorries which prevents overtaking. Remember to stay far enough behind that the lorry driver can spot you in the mirror.

### Freeway Driving

Lanes are numbered from left to right: number one is the extreme left-hand lane, number two the next lane to the right, and so on. An 'exit' or 'off ramp' is the ramp (slip road) leading off the freeway; an 'entrance' or 'on ramp' leads onto the freeway. 'Metering lights' are traffic lights controlling ramp access.

When freeway traffic does flow, it usually flows smoothly and quickly. 55 mph, the normal posted speed limit, or 65 mph on rural interstates, is widely ignored; 70–85 mph is common in the fast (left) lane, though subject to citation. The safest speed: match the general traffic flow in your lane, no matter how fast or slow.

When entering an expressway, *don't stop* on the ramp, but accelerate and merge into the freeway flow. Cars that stop on the ramp are likely to be hit from the rear.

Freeways may have **car-pool lanes**, for vehicles carrying a certain number of passengers. Signs will specify the number of passengers required to access those speedier lanes, and the effective hours. Car-pool lanes, also known as diamond lanes or HOV (high occupancy vehicle) lanes, are marked on the roadbed with a white diamond symbol. Special bus lanes, access or parking are also marked.

## Horns
Horns should be sounded only as a safety warning, never in anger. Be cautious around hospital quiet zones.

## Pedestrians
Traffic must stop for a pedestrian on a crosswalk (pedestrian crossing). Holidaymakers from all over the world may dart out into traffic, so be prepared. If a vehicle is involved in an accident with a pedestrian, the presumption of error will always lie with the driver.

## Speed Limits
The standard speed limit on freeways is 55 mph (88 kph) but 65 mph (104 kph) is allowed on the rural sections of interstate. The minimum is 40 mph (64 kph). Traffic may flow faster or slower than those limits, but the state highway patrols can ticket anyone going faster than the limit.

Regardless of posted speed limits, police can invoke the *Basic Speed Law* that holds that no one can drive faster than it is safe. The speed limit is 25 mph (40 kph) around schools and 30 mph (48 kph) in residential districts. At a railway crossing, approach at a constant speed, fast enough, the rules say, to coast across the tracks if the car engine stalls, but slow enough to stop behind lorries and buses which must stop.

## Seat Belts
In Florida and Georgia, seat belts must be worn by the driver, and passengers in the front seat. Even front seat passengers over age 15 can be cited and given a ticket if found without a fastened seatbelt!

Children under six years old must have restraints: infant carrier to age nine months or 20 lb; child car seat from nine months–four years (20–50 lb); lap belt from four years if over 40 lb; and both lap and shoulder belts if the child is at least 55 inches (1.39 m) tall. RV passengers behind the driver's area are not required to wear belts, but children should be safely seated while the vehicle is moving.

## VEHICLE INSURANCE
In 1995 a number of states, including Florida, abolished the minimum level of third party liability that US car hire firms had previously been obliged to provide. American drivers can extend their own vehicle insurance to cover third party liability, but it is now even more important for overseas visitors to make sure that they have adequate third party insurance.

Visitors hiring a car or RV are therefore very strongly recommended to take out top-up liability cover, such as the Topguard Insurance sold by Thomas Cook in the UK, which covers liability up to $1 million. (This is not to be confused with travel insurance, which provides cover for your own medical expenses – see p. 32).

Car rental agencies will ask the driver to take out various kinds of auto and personal property insurance, including collision damage waiver or CDW (sometimes called loss damage waiver, LDW). Refusing CDW makes the renter personally liable for damage to the vehicle, property, and any legal actions stemming from an accident. CDW is strongly recommended for drivers from outside the USA and often insisted upon as part of a fly-drive package. Sometimes it is paid for when booking the car hire abroad, sometimes it is payable locally on picking up the car. Occasionally, special hire rates

# DRIVING IN FLORIDA

will include CDW. US and Canadian drivers using their own cars should ask their insurance company or auto club if their coverage extends to Florida and Georgia. If not, arrange for insurance before signing the car hire contract.

## Vehicle Security

Florida has instituted armed security patrols in official rest stops. Nevertheless, wherever you are, lock it when you leave, lock it when you're inside, and don't forget about the windows. Never leave keys, documents, maps, guidebooks and other tourist paraphernalia in sight. Be mindful of anyone lurking in the back seat of the car or the accommodation part of the RV, especially at night. Watch other drivers for strange behaviour, especially if you're consistently followed. Never leave an engine running when you're not in the vehicle. Keep car keys with you at all times. And always park in well-lit areas.

### Some Florida Driving Terms

*big rig* a large lorry, usually a tractor, pulling one or more trailers.
*FHP* Florida Highway Patrol, the state road police force.
*citation* ticket (to be avoided).
*crosswalk* pedestrian crossing.
*connector* a minor road connecting two freeways or expressways.
*curve* bend.
*divided highway* dual carriageway.
*DUI* Driving Under the Influence of alcohol or drugs, aka Drunk Driving. The blood alcohol limit in Florida is 0.08% and very strictly enforced.
*evacuation route* a driving route from barrier islands, coastlines or lowlands to higher areas when a hurricane evacuation advisory is given. A white sign with a stylised blue water drop and directional arrow marks the route.
*expressway* The general term for interstate highway, freeway and turnpike, for a fast motorway without stop signs, traffic lights or railroad crossings.
*fender* bumper.
*freeway* motorway.
*garage* or *parking garage* car park.
*gas(oline)* petrol.

*grade* gradient, hill.
*highway* trunk road.
*hood* bonnet.
*LNG* Liquified petroleum gas used as fuel.
*motor home* motor caravan.
*pavement* road surface. A UK 'pavement' is a sidewalk.
*ramp* slip road.
*rent* hire.
*rubberneck(er)* slowing down to peer while driving past the scene of an accident or some unusual event.
*RV (recreational vehicle)* motor caravan.
*shoulder* verge.
*shift (stick)* gear lever.
*tailgate* driving too closely to the vehicle immediately in front.
*toll road* a multi-lane expressway where you pay to use it.
*tow truck* breakdown lorry.
*traffic cop* traffic warden.
*trailer* caravan.
*truck* lorry.
*trunk* boot.
*turnpike* a motorway for which a toll is charged (Florida Turnpike).
*windshield* windscreen.
*yield* give way.

# Background Florida

## Geography

Compact – yet covering a lot more ground than you might expect – and enjoying a largely subtropical climate, Florida was made for tourism. No place within its 58,167 square miles is more than 60 miles from a stunning beach.

Sand beaches, from brilliant white to golden, take up 1100 of the state's 1800 miles of coastline. Twelve of them are listed among the nation's top 20, rated on such virtues as water quality, temperature, cleanliness and beauty.

Geologically one of the youngest parts of the continental US, Florida could justifiably be called the 'Waterway State' rather than the 'Sunshine State'. It is sprinkled with 10,000 lakes ranging in size from one acre to the 450,000-acre **Lake Okeechobee**, the second largest stretch of fresh water in the country. A third of the state's lakes are in four Central Florida counties – **Lake, Orange, Osceola** and **Polk**.

The best known of Florida's 166 rivers is unquestionably the **Suwanee**, made famous by the songwriter **Stephen Foster** and flowing into the **Gulf of Mexico** after a 177-mile journey from the north. The rivers are fed by more than 300 springs, 27 of which are classified as 'first magnitude', which means they pump out at least 100 cubic ft of water per second.

Florida's topography is rather more diverse than the image of palm trees and beaches conjured up by most people. In the south are the **Everglades**, a 100-mile long 'Sea of Grass'. In the north are upland hardwood forests and the state's highest point, a dizzying 345 ft above sea level at **Lakewood**, near the Alabama border. Between those modest extremes are rolling hills, swamps, dunes and large areas as flat as a billiard table.

## Climate

Located 100 miles north of the Tropic of Cancer, Florida lists the climate as a valuable resource. Certainly the sun has been luring holidaymakers to the state for more than a century. Average summer temperatures range from 80.5°F in the north to 82.7°F in the south. In winter the average ranges from 53–68.5°F.

Rainfall averages 53 inches a year. Summer rainstorms can be surprisingly violent, but are mercifully short-lived. If you are outdoors at the time you will be soaked to the skin. However, the sun will soon have you dry again. Lightning can be a deadly hazard, so move fast when a lifeguard shouts 'Clear the beach!' June to October is the hurricane season in the Gulf of Mexico, but holidaymakers are more likely to encounter sunshine than raging storms.

## History

### The First Floridians

The living has always been easy in Florida. The area escaped the ravages of the Ice Age, and its warmer climate brought migrations of game, wildfowl and sea creatures from the north. Humans appeared on the scene some 10,000 years ago and found an abundant supply of food in generally pleasant surroundings.

Archaeologists believe early Floridians

may have been Central and South American peoples, rather than descendants of Asian migrants from the Siberia/Alaska land bridge. Strong cultural links have been established between Florida's ancient tribes and those further south.

Evidence unearthed from different parts of the state points to an enterprising people who kept themselves busy hunting and fishing. They used conch and other shells as tools, utensils and jewellery. They were making – and smashing – pottery 800 years before anyone else in North America. And they began growing crops a thousand years before the birth of Christ.

## The Explorers

Florida seems always to have attracted those with a keen sense of fantasy. The first Europeans were drawn by legends of a fountain of eternal youth. The search was led by **Don Juan Ponce de Leon**, a Spaniard who had been with **Christopher Columbus** on his second voyage to the New World.

After sailing among the Bahamas in March 1513, Ponce waded ashore near the St. John's River, in north-east Florida, and named the new territory in honour of *Pascua Florida*, Spain's Eastertime Festival of Flowers.

Ponce sailed south to the Florida Keys, then travelled up the west coast. But his search for the fountain of eternal youth was abandoned when he attempted to land near Charlotte Harbor, north of the present city of Fort Myers. The local natives, who may have close encountered European slave traders in the past, sent him packing.

In 1521 Ponce returned to Florida on a more pragmatic mission: to establish a settlement and convert the Indians to Christianity. This time he turned up at Charlotte Harbor with two ships, 200 men and 50 horses. He still failed to daunt the natives. The Spaniards had hardly stepped ashore before the air was thick with arrows. Wounded, Ponce was among the survivors who managed to scramble back to one of the ships, but he died shortly after reaching Cuba.

Ponce was one of an estimated 2000 Spaniards who died in a 40-year effort to colonise Florida and convert the Indians. On Good Friday, 1528, **Panfilo de Narvaez** landed in Tampa Bay with 400 men and started to get tough with the natives. He decided to leave when they told him there was gold at a place called Apalachee, in the north.

Narvaez led a party of his men overland to Apalachee, where they were to meet up with the ships. Weakened by disease and injuries from Indian attacks, they made it to the head of the Gulf of Mexico, but the ships didn't turn up. Narvaez spurred his men to build six makeshift boats and sail off in search of Mexico, but his luck had run out. He was one of many who perished when the boats capsized in a storm. Their fate remained a mystery until four survivors turned up in Mexico eight years later.

**Hernando de Soto** landed in Tampa Bay in May, 1539. With 1000 men, he had little trouble with the Indians, but soon found himself pushing northward in another fruitless and fatal search for gold. After three years of trudging through Alabama, Georgia and North Carolina, de Soto died of fever.

In 1559 **Tristan de Luna y Arellano**, a nobleman who had served with de Soto, led a force of 1500 to establish a settlement in Pensacola Bay. After two years of hardship, a hurricane put paid to their efforts and the settlement was abandoned.

A group of French Huguenots was the next to attempt settlement. Led by **Jean Ribaut**, the group set up a fortified community in north-east Florida in 1562. Now known as Fort Matanzas, the settlement lasted only three years.

Spurred on by the audacious French, the Spaniards – who despite repeated failure had come to regard Florida as their own – set up a heavily-manned base a few miles to the north. They landed in 1565, on the Feast of St Augustine.

To this day, the cities of Pensacola and St Augustine quibble over seniority. Pensacola says it is the oldest *established* European settlement in the United States. St Augustine claims to be the oldest such settlement *continuously occupied*.

The Matanzas settlement soon lost any claim of any kind. Shortly after the founding of St Augustine, the Spaniards launched an attack on the French, whose ships had been rendered useless by a hurricane. Jean Ribaut and his men were put to death. Matanzas is the Spanish for slaughter.

## The British

With a network of colonies elsewhere in North America and among the islands of the Caribbean, the British coveted Florida. British privateers and pirates had been plundering Spanish galleons for decades, but booty was not the same as territory. Repeatedly, British forces attacked St Augustine, but the fortifications were too strong.

Finally, Britain acquired the territory through diplomacy. In 1763, under the terms of the First Treaty of Paris, Havana, which had fallen into British hands during the Seven Years War, was exchanged for Florida.

The British enjoyed reasonable relations with the Indians and established settlements by introducing immigrants from Ireland and mainland Britain. Prosperous and content, Florida remained loyal to the crown when the American War of Independence began in 1776.

## Towards Statehood

Spain took advantage of Britain's war with its colony by sneaking into Pensacola and taking over west Florida, and in 1783 the whole lot was handed back to them under the Second Treaty of Paris. But Florida proved too much of a handful as a result of trouble from the Seminole Indians and incursions from neighbouring American states.

In 1821 the United States wrote off Spain's $5 million debt and took control of Florida. White settlers who arrived hungry for land soon stirred up more trouble with the Indians, and in 1835 the Second Seminole War began. The first occurred during Spanish sovereignty.

Led by young **Chief Osceola**, 4000 Seminole warriors kept an army of 10,000 Americans occupied among the Everglades and swamps and marshes elsewhere. In 1837 Osceola was arrested while riding into St Augustine under a flag of truce. He died in captivity a year later. All but 300 of Osceola's followers were rounded up and packed off to Oklahoma in 1842.

Under the leadership of **Chief Billy Bowlegs**, the 300 who remained took to the Everglades and the Big Cypress swamps. Skirmishes with the whites led in 1855 to the Third Seminole War, which officially lasted 79 years. Sporadic fighting went on for about three years, but eventually everyone lost interest. The treaty ending hostilities was finally signed in 1934.

Florida became the 27th member of the United States in March 1845.

Tallahassee was chosen as the capital because its central location was a compromise between the rival claims of Pensacola and St Augustine.

The young state began to flourish as agriculture expanded. Sugar, cotton, tobacco, rice and indigo were soon being shipped to markets at home and abroad. New settlers were drawn south, attracted by the climate and the prospect of prosperity. The Civil War ended their hopes.

Florida, the most southerly of the Southern states and committed to slavery, seceded from the Union and joined the Confederacy. When the war ended in 1865 the state was poorer by 5000 lost lives and $20 million in damage to commerce, industry and homes.

Recovery, however, was swift as peace brought shoals of sun-seeking settlers. By 1880 the state's population had reached 270,000 – almost double its 1860 total.

## The Boom Begins

Steamboat trips along the St John's River had brought tourism to northern Florida as early as the 1870s. But the leisure trade really began to open up when two rail tycoons called Henry pushed south along the east and west coasts, building luxury hotels as they went.

**Henry B. Plant** built the Atlantic Coast Railroad from Richmond Virginia, to Tampa, where his luxurious Tampa Bay Hotel is still a landmark. At Clearwater, the Belleview Biltmore Hotel (now the Belleview Mido) opened in 1897. It is still said to be the world's largest occupied wooden structure.

**Henry Morrison Flagler**, who founded Standard Oil with John D. Rockefeller, formed the Florida East Coast Railway in 1886. Among the chain of resort hotels he built along the line of the railway was The Breakers at Palm Beach, still a peak of poshness.

Flagler pushed on to Miami, where he opened steamship lines to the Bahamas and Key West, then extended his line to Homestead on the edge of the Everglades. His final triumph was to take the railway to Key West, soaring down the Florida Keys across a series of bridges. The aptly named Overseas Railway was completed in 1912. Flagler died a year later. In 1935 a hurricane wrecked the railway, but its line and many of its bridges were used to form the Overseas Highway.

Innovation became commonplace. In 1911 a pilot named **Lincoln Beachey** made the world's first night flight, soaring in the darkness above Tampa. New Year's Day 1914 saw the start of the first scheduled airline service in aviation history – from St Petersburg to Tampa, a distance of 21 miles.

Between the two World Wars Florida's population doubled to two million. During World War II tens of thousands of servicemen and women were sent to Florida for training, and when the war ended many of them returned to settle down in the sunshine – just as soldiers had done after the Spanish-American War of 1898.

In 1958 the National Aeronautics and Space Administration (NASA) began operations at Cape Canaveral, and from Florida's Atlantic coast the first communications satellite, mankind's first trip to the moon and the first Space Shuttles were launched.

And on 1 Oct 1971 the Magic Kingdom at Walt Disney World opened its gates to mark the beginning of another era of Florida fantasy.

**TOURING ITINERARIES**

# TOURING ITINERARIES

Much of the pleasure of a driving holiday lies in matching your itinerary to interests. By dividing Florida into recommended routes, this book makes it easy to plan your ideal tour. By linking several of our routes you can create a trip which will suit your tastes and you can be confident of following a tried and tested path which introduces you to the best that the route has to offer.

This chapter begins with some practical advice on tour planning, followed by four ready-made itineraries designed to show you as much as possible of Florida's variety during trips of 14 or 21 days. Feel free to vary our suggestions, using information in the route descriptions.

The remaining pages list features of Florida which you can use to create a self-planned 'themed' tour using the routes noted.

## PRACTICAL HINTS

Here are a few tips to make practicable routes easier to plan and fun to follow:

1. Use the most detailed maps available. The colour map section at the end of this book is useful for planning itineraries and will enable you to follow the routes while driving, but a more detailed road map will be invaluable to mix routes. The Florida Official Transportation Map, published by the Florida Department of Transportation, is free of charge from tourist information centres and Chambers of Commerce throughout the state. It is an excellent road map, with attractions, city maps and information about the state park system.

2. Don't schedule too much driving each day. Assume 50 mph of freeway driving, 40 mph on secondary roads, to allow for breaks and unplanned stops. Each route description in this book gives information about mileage and also likely driving times.

3. Unless accommodation is pre-booked, plan to arrive at each destination with enough time to find a place to sleep. In the north, west of Tallahassee, communities are few and far between and it would be wise to have accommodation reserved. The same applies to the Tamiami Trail and Alligator Alley in the south.

4. If you have a flight home at the end of your Florida holiday, remember to build in time to get to your airport city without having to rush.

5. Give serendipity a chance by not planning in too much detail. Allow time to spend an extra few hours or an extra day in some unexpected gem of a place.

## THE BEST OF FLORIDA

Apart from its size – its roads cover some 100,000 miles – Florida offers such a diversity of attractions and historic sites that it is unlikely the whole state could be covered sensibly in much less than three months.

## TOURING ITINERARIES

We have suggested four circular routes covering different areas, all interlocking within the overall network. Each route can be shortened or lengthened. After all, you can always come back. The tours combine recommended routes, with a few digressions and short cuts. Suggested overnight stops are in **bold type**. Feel free to adapt the tours to suit your own interests.

### SOUTHERN FLORIDA – 14 DAYS

Day 1: **Miami** (pp. 71–80).
Day 2: **Miami**.
Day 3: Miami to **Naples** (p. 119).
Day 4: **Naples**.
Day 5: Naples to **Sanibel/Captiva** (p. 181).
Day 6: **Sanibel/Captiva**.
Day 7: **Sanibel/Captiva**.
Day 8: **Sanibel/Captiva**.
Day 9: Sanibel/Captiva to **Fort Myers** (p. 177).
Day 10: **Fort Myers**.
Day 11: Fort Myers to **West Palm Beach** (pp. 144–148).
Day 12: **West Palm Beach**.
Day 13: West Palm Beach to **Fort Lauderdale** (pp. 128–135).
Day 14: Fort Lauderdale to **Miami**.

### SOUTHERN FLORIDA – 21 DAYS

Day 1: **Tampa** (pp. 216–225)
Day 2: Tampa to **Orlando** (pp. 230–249).
Day 3: **Orlando**.
Day 4: **Orlando**.
Day 5: **Orlando**.
Day 6: Orlando to Titusville, Spaceport USA and **Cocoa Beach** (route p. 256) Spaceport USA (p. 158).
Day 7: **Cocoa Beach**.
Day 8: Cocoa Beach to **Stuart** (p. 153).
Day 9: Stuart to **West Palm Beach** (pp. 144–148).
Day 10: **West Palm Beach**.
Day 11: West Palm Beach to **Fort Lauderdale** (pp. 128–135).
Day 12: **Fort Lauderdale**.
Day 13: Fort Lauderdale to **Naples** (p. 119).
Day 14: **Naples**.
Day 15: Naples to **Fort Myers** (p.177).
Day 16: Fort Myers to Sanibel/Captiva and back to **Fort Myers**.
Day 17: Fort Myers to **Sarasota** (p. 189).
Day 18: Sarasota to **St Petersburg** (pp. 194–201).
Day 19: **St Petersburg**.
Day 20: **St Petersburg**.
Day 21: St Petersburg to **Tampa**.

### NORTHERN FLORIDA – 21 DAYS

Day 1: Jacksonville to **Fernandina Beach** (p. 286).
Day 2: **Fernandina Beach**.
Day 3: Fernandina Beach to **St Augustine** (p. 272).
Day 4: St Augustine.
Day 5: St Augustine.
Day 6: St Augustine to **Gainesville** (p. 262).
Day 7: Gainesville to **Apalachicola** (p. 307).
Day 8: Apalachicola to **Panama City Beach** (p. 308).
Day 9: **Panama City Beach**.
Day 10: **Panama City Beach**.
Day 11: Panama City Beach to **Pensacola** (route pp. 313–316; Pensacola pp. 317–324).
Day 12: **Pensacola**.
Day 13: **Pensacola**.
Day 14: Pensacola to **Tallahassee** (route pp. 325–327, Tallahassee pp. 299–303).
Day 15: **Tallahassee**.
Day 16: **Tallahassee**.
Day 17: Tallahassee to **Lake City** (p. 263).
Day 18: Lake City to **Jacksonville** (pp. 278–285).

Day 19: **Jacksonville**.
Day 20: **Jacksonville**.
Day 21: **Jacksonville**.

## CENTRAL FLORIDA – 14 DAYS

Day 1: **Orlando** (pp. 230–249).
Day 2: Orlando to **Tarpon Springs** (p. 293).
Day 3: **Tarpon Springs**.
Day 4: Tarpon Springs to **Cedar Key** (p. 295).
Day 5: Cedar Key to **Ocala** (p. 228).
Day 6: **Ocala**.
Day 7: Ocala to **DeLand** (p. 258).
Day 8: Deland to **Daytona Beach** (p. 267).
Day 9: **Daytona Beach**.
Day 10: Daytona Beach to **Cocoa Beach** (p. 157)
Day 11: Cocoa Beach to **Orlando**.
Day 12: **Orlando**.
Day 13: **Orlando**.
Day 14: **Orlando**.

## THE MAJOR CITIES

### KEY WEST

'Laid back' is the term everybody uses to describe this southernmost tip of Florida. Key West (pp. 100–111) has Victorian architecture, a strong affinity with former resident Ernest Hemingway and a nightly assignment with the sunset attended by massed celebrants.

### MIAMI

Because of a history of violence, drug abuse and rioting in recent decades, cosmopolitan Miami (p. 71) is still regarded by some as the black sheep of the Florida family, with a street percussion of gunshots and police sirens. But the fine architecture, tropical vegetation cascading over tiers of balconies, sleek yachts, a highly efficient public transport system and fascinating spots like Little Havana, Coconut Grove and Coral Gables, remain a source of delight.

### FORT LAUDERDALE

Criss-crossed by hundreds of miles of canals, Fort Lauderdale (p. 128) is known as the Venice of America. Residents are as likely to have a boat moored as a car parked alongside the house and cocktail cruising is as popular as fishing. Boatless visitors can get afloat on *Jungle Queen*, a Mississippi-style riverboat. Fort Lauderdale also has a 6.5 mile stretch of wide beach and attractions like Butterfly World and Ocean World, to say nothing of a plethora of shopping malls, boutiques and galleries.

### PALM BEACH

This is Florida's Poshville – a place that drew the likes of the Astors, Rockefellers and Vanderbilts when Henry Flagler built a sumptuous hotel to go with the railway he brought here in 1894. With a resident historian, croquet lawn and 36-hole golf course, The Breakers is still in business, one of many top class hotels in Palm Beach (p. 144). Worth Ave, a kind of sub-tropical Fifth Ave, proves that wealth is still alive and well among the palm trees.

### FORT MYERS

Small but stately, Fort Myers (p. 177) elegantly straddles the Caloosahatchee River. The royal palms that line its wide main street were introduced by the inventor Thomas Edison, who lived in the city from 1886 until his death in 1931. Edison's neighbour from 1916 was the car pioneer, Henry Ford. Both homes are now open to the public. Fort Myers claims to be the gladiolus capital of the world. The blooms were first brought to the area by growers from Belgium, Holland and Luxembourg who settled in the area.

### ST PETERSBURG

Set on the west coast of Central Florida, St Petersburg (p. 194) is a cultural centre as well as a beach and resort playground. Its pier, jutting out into Tampa Bay, is a lively place with entertainment, shops and cafés. Open to visitors are a hospital for seabirds and more than a dozen museums and galleries, one of which has the world's largest collection of surrealist paintings by Salvador Dali. St Pete holds a sunshine record of 768 consecutive sunny days.

### TAMPA

Florida's third largest city is the home of Busch Gardens, the family entertainment centre and one of the top four zoos in the US. Another big attraction is Adventure Island, a family splash park. Tampa (p. 216) is also a major cruise port and an important commercial centre and university city. Ybor City is Tampa's Cuban quarter where you can watch cigars being made. Tampa International Airport is repeatedly voted the best in the country.

### ORLANDO

Once a small town surrounded by the citrus-growing industry, Orlando (p. 230), in Orange County, grew and grew with the arrival of the theme parks and attractions. It has a population of 165,000 and thousands of hotel rooms. Orlando International Airport claims to be the world's fastest-growing major hub. Winter Park is a village-style haven within Orlando's urban sprawl, with boutiques, small restaurants, a gallery displaying Tiffany glass and boat trips among smart properties. But Orlando does not live by tourism alone. It is, among other things, a major centre for high-tech, blue chip industries.

### ST AUGUSTINE

It's a world-weary traveller who can resist the charm of historic St Augustine (p. 272), with its ancient Spanish Quarter, open bay views, splendid architecture and fleet of horse-drawn carriages. and you get a colourful commentary with most of your sightseeing. The city has a growing reputation for its historic Bed and Breakfast properties.

### JACKSONVILLE

The St John's River flows through Jacksonville (p. 278), which is 12 miles inland from Jacksonville Beach and neighbouring beach communities. An important industrial and commercial centre, it makes good use of the river, developing Jacksonville Landing on one side and Riverwalk on the other.

### TALLAHASSEE

Florida's capital city is well worth the drive to the far north to see its canopy roads, where trees form a green archway and the imposing State Capitols, old and new. The home of two universities, Tallahassee (p. 299) has a student population of about 50,000, representing two-fifths of the total population. As well as its own attractions, Tallahassee has some delightful excursions on its doorstep.

### PENSACOLA

Pensacola (p. 317) vies with St Augustine for the title of oldest city. However, if you're travelling west it's certainly Florida's last city because you're not far from Alabama. The National Museum of Naval Aviation is an exciting must-see. Historic Pensacola Village has a mix of

# TOURING ITINERARIES

museums and historic homes. Anglers can fish Pensacola Bay from a bridge more than three miles long.

## ATLANTA, GEORGIA

You get two for the price of one here. Underground Atlanta presents the city's original streets transformed into six blocks of speciality shops, restaurants, street traders and entertainment places. Above ground: domes and spires, gleaming skyscrapers, museums galore and a strong African-American culture. The state was home to the late Martin Luther King, who was born in Atlanta (p. 337).

## SAVANNAH, GEORGIA

Preservation and restoration work since the 1960s has ensured that Savannah (p. 333) has retained its 18th and 19th century character. It has more than two square miles of National Historic Landmark District, a Victorian District in process of preservation and the Riverfront Plaza beside the Savannah River, with cobblestone streets and former cotton warehouses containing galleries, craft studios, boutiques and restaurants.

## THE TOP TEN SIGHTS

What you want to see in Florida seems to depend on how you get there. The Florida Department of Commerce keeps two sets of statistics on the major attractions – one set covering people who arrive by car and another for those who turn up by air. Here are both lists.

**Top Ten by Car:**
1. **Walt Disney World's Magic Kingdom:** Mickey Mouse draws the crowds to seven fantasy 'lands'. (Orlando chapter, p. 230–249).
2. **Epcot Center:** The science fact and fiction section of Walt Disney World, dominated by the geosphere, a giant golf ball. (Orlando chapter, p. 241).
3. **Disney-MGM Studios:** Another Walt Disney World winner – this time it's Tinseltown in Florida. (Orlando chapter, p.241–243).
4. **Universal Studios:** at last a rival to WDW! Universal Studios has an authentic film-making ambience and some great white-knuckle rides. (Orlando chapter, p. 245–246).
5. **Sea World:** Killer whales, gentle manatees, penguins, sea lions, and from 1995, polar bears and other Arctic creatures – all in awesome close-up. (Orlando chapter, p. 243).
6. **Busch Gardens:** A move away from Orlando. Now we're on the west coast for the family entertainment centre and zoo with an African theme. (Tampa chapter, p. 224).
7. **Spaceport USA:** Over to the east coast for the world of NASA. (Space Coast chapter, p. 160).
8. **Parks/Preserves:** Across the state.
9. **Cypress Gardens:** Florida's first theme park, opened in 1936, is a 200-acre botanical garden with spectacular water-ski shows, Southern Belles and much more. (Orlando to Tampa route, p.250).
10. **Church Street Station:** Back to Orlando for a swinging street full of night-time dining, shopping and entertainment attractions. (Orlando chapter, p. 230).

**Top Ten for air travellers**
1. Epcot Center.
2. Walt Disney World's Magic Kingdom.
3. Disney-MGM Studios.
4. Universal Studios.
5. Sea World.

THE MAJOR CITIES • THE TOP TEN SIGHTS

## TOURING ITINERARIES

6. **Parks/Preserves.**
7. **Busch Gardens.**
8. **Spaceport USA.**
9. **Typhoon Lagoon:** Walt Disney World's splash park, with raft rides, speed slides, body surfing and real sharks. (Orlando chapter, p. 230).
10. **Lake Buena Vista Village:** This is the Disney Village Resort area, a complex of major hotels and the Disney Village Marketplace, where there are shops and restaurants. Nearby is Pleasure Island, a nightclub theme park where New Year's Eve is celebrated every night of the year, (Orlando chapter, p. 230).

## TOP PARKS AND MONUMENTS

Florida's 11 areas operated by the National Parks Service are listed first, followed by state parks, preserves, shores and recreational areas administered by Federal or State authorities.

**Big Cypress National Preserve**, *30 miles west of Miami on Hwy 41; tel: (813) 695-4111*. This 716,000-acre preserve adjoining the north-west section of Everglades National Park covers parts of Collier, Dade and Monroe Counties. It sustains much subtropical plant and animal life and is the ancestral home of the Seminole and Miccosukee Indians.

**Biscayne National Park**, *9 miles east of Homestead on SW 328th Street (North Florida Dr.); tel: (305) 247-7275*. Of the 181,500 acreage, 95 per cent is water and includes part of a living coral reef. The park is accessible by boat from the Intracoastal Waterway. Tour boat services are available for island picnics and diving. Glass-bottomed boats provide trips on the reef tract.

**Canaveral National Seashore**, *midway between Jacksonville and West Palm Beach, the Seashore is accessible via Hwy 1 and I-95, I-4 and I-75. Access at New Smyrna Beach is via Hwy A1A near Turtle Mound, and at Titusville via Hwy 402 to Playalinda Beach; tel: (407) 267-1110*. More than 280 bird species are among the varied wildlife on this preserved part of Florida's Atlantic coast. The largely undeveloped wetlands cover nearly 58,000 acres. Access to the South District (Playalinda Beach) is restricted when a Space Shuttle launch is planned at the Kennedy Space Centre.

**Castillo de San Marcos National Monument**, *1 Castillo Dr., St Augustine; tel: (904) 829-6505*. This is the well-preserved main fortification, built from 1672–95, of the defences of St Augustine, the first permanent European settlement in the continental US. Self-guided tours, talks by rangers and living history demonstrations take place.

**De Soto National Memorial**, *five miles west of Bradenton on 75th Street; tel: (813) 792-0458*. The landing of Spanish explorer Hernando de Soto in 1539 is commemorated at the 25-acre Tampa Bay site. Interpretive films are shown at the Visitor Centre. There is a short self-guided nature trail.

**Dry Tortugas National Park**, *68 miles west of Key West; tel: (305) 242-7700*. The group of seven coral islands can be reached only by boat or seaplane. Trips go from Key West and parts of south-west Florida. **Fort Jefferson**, which served as a military prison before and after the Civil War, is on one of the islands. Bird and marine life is diverse in the 100 square miles of the park, which includes coral reefs and seagrass beds. Limited primitive camping is permitted on a first-come first-served basis.

**Everglades National Park**, *12 miles south-west of Homestead on Hwy 9336; tel: (305) 242-7700*. With nearly 1.4 million acres, Florida's largest national park is a subtropical fragile wilderness with extensive freshwater and saltwater areas, open 'Everglades prairies' and mangrove swamps. The range of wild creatures includes rare birds. There is backcountry canoeing, boat trips, tram trips from Shark Valley, fishing and environmental studies. An entrance fee is charged.

**Fort Caroline National Monument**, *13 miles east of downtown Jacksonville. Take Hwy 10 to either Monument or St John's Bluff Road north to Fort Caroline Road then east to the memorial entrance; tel: (904) 641-7155.* The memorial, which marks the first major attempt of the French to settle in what is now the US, overlooks the original site of the French Huguenot colony of 1564–65.

**Fort Matanza National Monument**, *14 miles south of St Augustine. Take Hwy A1A on Anastasia Island; tel (904) 471-0116.* A free ferry ride to Rattlesnake Island provides access for visitors to this Spanish fort dating from the early 1740s. The site of nearly 300 acres is in an area where 250 French soldiers challenged the Spaniards' supremacy in the New World in 1565 and were slain for their efforts. The English for *Matanzas* is slaughter.

**Gulf Islands National Seashore**, *stretching 150 miles from Santa Rosa Island, Florida to West Ship Island, Mississippi, the Seashore has a number of accesses, including Johnson Beach (Perdido Key) on Hwy 292, southwest of Pensacola. Take Hwy 292 west from Pensacola or Hwy 98 south from downtown Pensacola across Pensacola Bay Bridge;*

## The Intracoastal Waterway

Floridians are proud of the Intracoastal Waterway and many of them use it for cruising and other leisure boating. But few seem to realise that it extends far beyond their own state. The waterway, which crops up at many points around the coast of Florida, is part of a navigable, toll-free shipping route which extends some 3000 miles along the Gulf of Mexico and Atlantic coasts in the southern and eastern U.S.

Sounds, bays, lagoons, rivers and canals were utilised to form the waterway which is navigable in many parts by deep-draft vessels, although the lowest controlling depth is just over six ft.

The waterway is maintained by federal authority and the original intention was to construct a continuous channel from Brownsville, Texas, to New York City, but the link across Northern Florida – the Cross-Florida Barge Canal – was never completed. The western end of the canal, still navigable, is crossed on Hwy 19/98, about 11 miles north of Crystal River.

The Gulf section of the waterway serves ports for more than 1100 miles between Apalachee Bay and Brownsville, Texas. The Atlantic section serves ports between Key West and Boston, Massachusetts.

Florida can be crossed between the Gulf and Atlantic sections by entering the Caloosahatchee River at Fort Myers, crossing Lake Okeechobee and navigating along the St Lucie Canal to Stuart.

The best places to see the Intracoastal Waterway are along the Panhandle between Pensacola and Apalachicola, on the west coast between Clearwater and St. Petersburg Beach and also between Venice and Fort Myers Beach, and almost anywhere on the Atlantic side between Fort Lauderdale and Fernandina Beach.

*tel: (904) 934-2600*. The ruins of historic military forts are preserved at this site, which includes mainland terrain and some offshore islands, two of which have been designated wilderness.

**Timucuan Ecological and Historic Preserve**, *encompassing most of the northeast section of Jacksonville; tel: (904) 641-7155*. The preserve covers 35,000 acres of wetlands and historic sites and protects the fragile St John's and Nassau River coastal systems. It also holds the history of Timucuan Indian culture and four centuries of European/US settlement.

**Apalachicola National Forest**, *south and west of Tallahassee (Hwy 319 South from the capital); tel: (904) 942-9300*. The forest covers more than half a million acres. Sixty miles of the National Scenic Trail go through it. Hundreds of miles of dirt roads can be hiked or biked. Wild pigs and black bears live in the forest.

**Bahia Honda State Park**, *12 miles south of Marathon at Big Pine Key in the Florida Keys; tel: (305) 872-2353*. Florida's southernmost state park, with beach dunes, mangrove forest, tropical hardwood hammock and some rare plant species, the park offers fishing, diving, boat trips, camping and good swimming.

**Blackwater River State Park**, *15 miles north-east of Milton, off Hwy 90 at Holt; tel (904) 623-2363*. Known for its sandy bottom, the park's shallow waterway is ideal for tubing and canoeing. The park, rich in wildlife, has nature trails and camping facilities.

**Collier-Seminole State Park**, *17 miles south of Naples on Hwy 41; tel: (813) 394-3397*. The park's tropical hardwood hammock is characteristic of that found in the West Indies and the Yucatan Peninsula. Rare Florida royal palms flourish. The state is known for its alligators, but crocodiles are also natives of the park.

**Dade Battlefield State Historic Site**, *Bushnell, off I-75 and Hwy 48, west of Hwy 301; tel (904) 793-4781*. The scene of much bloodshed in Dec 1835, when only three soldiers survived out of more than 100 who fought in a battle that marked the start of the Second Seminole Indian War. The full story unfolds at the Visitor Centre.

**Falling Waters State Recreation Area**, *3 miles south of Chipley, west of Marrianna, off Hwy 77A; tel: (904) 638-6130*. In a park of geological formations, the big attraction is a 100-ft deep, 20-ft wide cylindrical pit into which a small stream drops 67 ft. Nobody knows where it goes from there. Nature trails, picnic tables and full camping facilities are in the park.

**Florida Caverns State Park**, *3 miles north of Marrianna on Hwy 167; tel: (904) 482-9598*. One of the most fascinating state parks, this has guided tours in a series of caverns with a variety of calcite formations. Activities in the park include swimming, canoeing, horse riding, fishing, nature study and camping.

**Fort Clinch State Park**, *off Hwy A1A, Fernandina Beach; tel:.(904) 277-7274*. Tours of the fort by candlelight and swimming in the Atlantic are among the activities at this fort, where both Union and Confederate troops spent time in the Civil War. 'Soldiers' in the authentic uniforms of the day man the fort and answer questions about the buildings and the war. The park has a fishing pier.

**Fort Zachary Taylor State Historic Site**, *Southard St, Key West; tel: (305) 292-6713*. Construction of the fort took 21 years. Work was hampered by hurricanes, yellow fever, manpower shortages and slow delivery of materials. Its strategic position and powerful armaments enabled the troops to hold ships hostage and shorten the Civil War. Some cannons and ammunition are encased in the walls. Others have been taken out and make a formidable display. Twice-daily guided tours are given.

**Homosassa Springs State Wildlife Park**, *West Fishbowl Drive, Homosassa, on Hwy 19; tel: (904) 628-5343*. This major attraction has a 45-ft deep natural spring where the water is a constant 72ºF year round – perfect for the injured or orphaned manatees rehabilitated there. A floating observatory enables visitors to watch the manatees and 34 species of fish. Also displayed in the park are animals, birds and reptiles indigenous to Florida, including bobcat, black bear, river otter, turtles, snakes and owls. Boats carry visitors from the park entrance, along a creek rich in wildlife, to the spring.

**Hontoon Island State Park**, *six miles west of Deland off Hwy 44; tel: (904) 736-5309*. Accessible only by private boat or free ferry service, the 1650-acre park has two large shell mounds, a legacy from the Timucuan Indians who inhabited the island. They ate snails gathered from the shallows of the St John's River, which, with the Hontoon Dead River, borders the island. An 80-ft observation tower and a replica of a 600-year-old owl totem discovered in 1955 are in the park.

**J.D. MacArthur Beach State Park**, *nearly three miles south of the intersection of Hwy 1 and PGA Blvd on Hwy A1A, northern Palm Beach County; tel: (407) 624-6950*. This barrier island is a prime example of subtropical coastal habitat remaining in south-east Florida. The **William T. Kirby Nature Centre** is within the park.

**J.N. 'Ding' Darling National Wildlife Preserve**, *1 Wildlife Drive, Sanibel Island; tel: (813) 472-1100*. Collect a self-guiding booklet at the Visitor centre and follow the five-mile Wildlife Drive by car through swampy mangrove forest, observing basking alligators, raccoons, anhingas, flamingoes and other creatures. There are boardwalks and canoe trails in the 5000-acre park.

**John Pennekamp Coral Reef State Park**, *Mile Marker 102.5, north of Key Largo, Florida Keys; tel: (305) 451-1202*. The park covers 70 nautical square miles of coral reefs, seagrass beds and mangrove swamps, much of it under water, and protects the only living coral reef in the continental US. Glass-bottomed boat tours, snorkelling and scuba diving tours, scuba diving lessons and boat rentals are available.

**Jonathan Dickinson State Park**, *12 miles south of Stuart on Hwy 1; tel: (407) 546-2771*. Ranger-guided tours and self-guided tours of the Loxahatchee River and cabin and canoe rentals are available.

**National Key Deer Wildlife Refuge**, *Big Pine Key, Florida Keys, park headquarters at western end of Watson Blvd; tel: (307) 872-2239*. Set up in 1954 to save the small and remarkably tame Key deer from extinction, the refuge is now home to several hundred of them.

**Kingsley Plantation**, *Fort George Island, north of Jacksonville Beach on Hwy A1A, then by Mayport toll ferry; tel: (904) 251-3122*. The plantation is within the Timucuan Ecological and Historic Preserve (see p. 66). Once the home of a slave trader who married one of his slaves, the 1792 plantation house is reached through the 2.5-mile Avenue of Palms amid thick vegetation. There are guided tours of the house and slave quarters.

**Lower Wekiva River State Reserve**, *nine miles west of Sanford on Hwy 46; tel: (407) 884-2009*. The systems of streams and wetlands provide an ideal habitat for black bears, otters, alligators,

# TOURING ITINERARIES

wood storks and sandhill cranes. Primitive backpack camping, hiking and canoeing are allowed in the 4600-acre preserve, which borders the St John's and Wekiva Rivers and Blackwater Creek.

## The Florida National Scenic Trail

If you grow tired of driving you can always get out and walk. About 1000 miles of prime hiking is available along the Florida National Scenic Trail, which traverses almost the entire state – 'almost' because a few sections have yet to be added.

Development of the trail was started by volunteers more than 25 years ago. When completed it will meander more than 1300 miles from the Big Cypress Preserve, about an hour's drive west of Miami, to Gulf Islands National Seashore near Pensacola. Volunteers and state and federal agencies are working to fill in the gaps.

In the south-east the trail wanders through a semi-tropical ecosystem featuring orchid-draped cypress trees. It crosses a terrain of rolling pinelands, palm hammocks, lakes and oaks in Central Florida. In the north there are rivers and woods. Deer, turkey, migrating birds and other wildlife are abundant in the many wilderness areas crossed by the trail.

The trail is freely accessible to walkers year-round, with opportunities for bird-watching, fishing, photography and camping. The winter and spring months are best for hiking in Florida.

Information: **The Florida Trail Association**, PO Box 13708, Gainesville, Florida 32604; tel: (904) 378-8823; toll-free 1-800-343-1882.

**Merritt Island National Wildlife Refuge**, *seven miles east of Titusville on Hwy 402; tel: (407) 861-0667*. Giant sea turtles clamber ashore to the wetlands of the refuge. This 40-mile haven adjacent to the Kennedy Space Centre is home to some 300 bird species.

**Myakka River State Park**, *nine miles east of Sarasota on Hwy 72; tel: (813) 361-6511*. Within the 29,000-acre park are 12 miles of the Myakka River, a diversity of habitats and a varied wildlife population. A range of activities can be enjoyed. Log cabins and camping facilities are available.

**Ocala National Forest**, *Visitor Centre is five miles east of Silver Springs on Hwy 40; tel: (904) 625-2520*. This is the world's largest sand pine forest. Its springs and rivers provide canoeing through tropical vegetation and open shallows. Exploration can also be made on foot or horseback. There are 100 miles of horse trails and 67 miles of the **Florida National Scenic Trail** (see box, left) within the forest's diverse ecology.

**Osceola National Forest**, *Olustee, east of Lake City on Hwy 90; tel: (904) 752-2577*. A 20-mile section of the National Scenic Trail goes through this north-eastern forest. Countless dirt roads are used for hiking, cycling and horse-riding. In the hunting season (Nov–Jan) visitors are confined to numbered roads, and bright orange jackets must be worn.

**St Andrew's State Recreation Area**, *three miles east of Panama City Beach off Hwy 392 (Thomas Dr.); tel: (904) 233-5140*. Waterside camping attracts many people to the park, where the dunes are covered with sea oats. Further inland, sand pines, scrub oaks and other hardy plants grow on the dunes. Alligators and wading birds may be seen in the freshwater areas. For sea anglers there are two piers. A boat park and ramp are available.

TOP PARKS AND MONUMENTS

## TOURING ITINERARIES

**Stephen Foster State Folk Culture Centre**, *off Hwy 41 North, White Springs; tel: (904) 397-2733.* On the Suwannee River, which composer Stephen Foster honoured in song – though he probably never saw the river. The centre is a venue for cultural events, and work can be bought at the craft village.

**Suwannee River State Park**, *13 miles west of Live Oak, off Hwy 90; tel: (904) 362-2746.* Wild turkeys, great horned owls and red tailed hawks are among the birds here. An overlook provides a view of the Suwannee and the Withlacoochee Rivers, which converge in the Park. There is a Civil War earthworks site and an old steamboat jetty.

**Tomoka State Park**, *three miles north of Ormond Beach on North Bridge Street; tel: (904) 676-4050.* The Tomoka and Halifax Rivers run through the woodland park. A sculpture of an Indian group dominates one corner. Canoes can be hired from the Visitor Centre.

**Wakulla Springs State Park**, *14 miles south of Tallahassee on Hwy 267 at Hwy 61; tel: (904) 922-3633.* Glass-bottomed boats provide trips around the clear water of one of the world's largest and deepest freshwater springs, and 30-min narrated river cruises provide a view of birds and other wildlife. Swimming and snorkelling are permitted in a designated area near the head of the spring.

---

### KOA - A GREAT PLACE TO CHECK INTO

**KOA** — **Kamping Kabins**

In 1996, why not rent a motorhome and let KOA take the worry away by pre-booking your campgrounds before you leave home? Choose from a selection of 'off the shelf' tours or let KOA tailor make the trip for you. If you are touring by car or motorcycle, check out KOA Kamping Kabins. One and two bedroom cabins sleep 4 or 6 and all you need to take along is your sleeping bag! An eleven night Kabin tour can cost under £250 for the whole family. All KOA's have hot showers and clean restrooms. Most have swimming pool, general store, laundry, BBQ's at each site and often a restaurant or cafe.

Call today for your KOA Directory and Atlas of North America
(£5 to cover postage and packing please)

KOA - KAMPGROUNDS OF AMERICA
Sales Agent UK - Project Tourism
The Old House, Balcombe Forest
West Sussex RH17 6JZ
Tel: 01444 811027
Fax: 01444 811744

MAKE MEMORIES TODAY

TOP PARKS AND MONUMENTS • ADVERTISEMENT

**ADVERTISEMENT**

# THOMAS COOK TRAVELLERS

With 42 titles in the range, and more being added each year, you are sure to find a guide to the destination of your choice. This is a comprehensive series of 192-page compact (192mm x 130mm) guides, created for the holidaymaker of the 1990s by Thomas Cook Publishing and leading guidebook publishers AA Publishing. Each guide is fully illustrated in colour with completely new research and mapping

### FEATURES INCLUDE:

★ Facts at your fingertips
★ Background information on history, politics and culture
★ Descriptions of major sights and lesser-known places
★ A 'Getting-Away-from-it-all' section
★ A street-by-street shopping and entertainment guide
★ An A-Z help-list packed with practical information
★ Tips on 'Finding your Feet'
★ Up to 10 city walks or excursions with full-colour maps

The above publications are available from bookshops and Thomas Cook UK retail shops price £6.99/£7.99, or direct by post from Thomas Cook Publishing, Dept (TPO/FLO), PO Box 227, Peterborough PE3 8BQ UK (Price £7.99/£8.99). Tel: 01733 268943/505821

**Thomas Cook**

**ADVERTISEMENT**

# MIAMI

The city of Miami writhes in a continual dance of clashing sensitivities and sensibilities, more attuned to the Caribbean and to Latin America than it is to Europe or the rest of North America. Nearly everyone who lives in Miami was born somewhere else, often outside the United States. Every political or economic crisis in the Caribbean or Latin America brings a new wave of refugees. Some have little more than the clothes on their backs. Others arrive with bank accounts that were once the national budgets of entire nations.

Half of Greater Miami is Hispanic, mostly from Cuba, plus others from Columbia, El Salvador, Nicaragua, Panama and Peru. There are more Haitians in Miami than in most cities in Haiti, not to mention Argentineans, Brazilians, Chileans, Greeks, Jamaicans, Iranians, Italians, Lebanese, Russians, Thais, Venezuelans, Vietnamese and almost any other ethnic, cultural, or religious group imaginable. Miamians have kept many of the customs they brought, much to the dismay of other Miamians who brought their own, sometimes radically different customs.

Geography contributes other instabilities. Miami perches atop a narrow strip of semi-dry land between the Everglades and the Atlantic. Mosquitoes and floods are perennial problems made worse by urban expansion into what was once marsh. Hurricane season brings an annual spectre of impending disaster that can be outrun or repaired, but never defeated.

## TOURIST INFORMATION

The **Greater Miami Convention & Visitors Bureau (GMCVB)**, *701 Brickell Ave, Suite 2700, Miami, FL 33131; tel: (800) 283-2707* (including Canada) or *(305) 539-3063*, open Mon–Fri 0830–1800, covers Miami, Miami Beach, Coconut Grove, Coral Gables and the rest of the Greater Miami and Metro-Dade County area. The **GMCVB at Bayside**, *Bayside Marketplace, 401 Biscayne Blvd* (downtown), *Miami; tel: (800) 283-2707* (including Canada) or *(305) 539-2980*, is open daily 1000–1830.

The **Art Deco Welcome Center**, *1001 Ocean Dr., Miami Beach, FL 33139; tel: (305) 672-2014*, is open daily 1100–1800. **Coconut Grove Chamber of Commerce**, *2820 McFarlane Rd, Coconut Grove, FL 33133; tel: (305) 444-7270*, and the **Coral Gables Chamber of Commerce**, *50 Aragon Ave, Coral Gables, FL 33134; tel: (305) 446-1657*, cover their respective cities.

The **Greater Homestead/Florida City Chamber of Commerce**, *160 US Hwy 1, Florida City, FL 33034; tel: (800) 388-9669* or *(305) 245-9180*, is open daily 0800–1600. **Miami Beach Chamber of Commerce (MBCoC)**, *1920 Meridian Ave, Miami Beach, FL 33139; tel: (305) 672-1270*, is open Mon–Fri 0830–1800 and Sat 1000–1600. **MBCoC kiosk**, *Washington Ave and Lincoln Rd,*

Miami Beach; tel: (305) 672-6222, is open Mon–Fri 0930–1600. **Activity Line**, *1680 Meridian Ave, Suite 616, Miami Beach, FL 33139; tel: (305) 620-2787*, offers multilingual information and travel directions for attractions, restaurants and night-clubs.

## Weather

Miami is subtropical by geography, but its summers are as steamy as any jungle. Temperatures and humidity climb to 90°F and over. Air conditioning is ubiquitous and assertive; a lightweight jumper or jacket helps ward off indoor chills. Winter temperatures occasionally dip to 40–50°F, but 70–80°F is more common. Nights are 10–15°F cooler than daytime year round.

Aug and Sept are the peak hurricane months, but they are *not* an annual occurrence in Miami. When hurricanes do strike, they come with several days warning and plenty of time for evacuation (see p. 31). Visitors are far more likely to be inconvenienced by summer thunderstorms which pass in a few hours.

Sunblock and hats are essential all year to avoid the leathery, wrinkled prune-like appearance of older sun worshippers. Strong sun and plentiful outdoor activities also makes skin cancer more common in Florida than in most of the US.

## Safety

Like any major US city, Miami has its share of crime and violence, but the pervasive lawlessness of tabloid headlines and *Miami Vice* reruns is a myth that sells advertising. Drug running is a major source of income throughout South Florida, but the merchandise is kept well out of sight. Visitors rarely glimpse the city's seamy underside of drugs, prostitution and violence unless they go looking for it. Areas to avoid after dark include Biscayne Blvd north of downtown; Overtown and Liberty City, also north of downtown; and unlit parks or beaches anywhere.

The city has marked preferred routes between the airport, downtown, Miami Beach, Coconut Grove, and other popular areas with blue signs carrying a bright orange sun. Hired vehicles no longer display logos, special number plates or other identifying markings which once made visitors obvious targets. The usual cautions remain in order: don't show off cash or expensive jewellery, don't leave anything in sight in a parked vehicle, keep vehicle doors locked at all times and plot out routes in advance. If lost, ask for directions at a police or brightly lit petrol station. Police, fire and other emergency vehicles in Florida use flashing blue and red lamps to get motorists' attention.

## ARRIVING AND DEPARTING

### Airport

**Miami International Airport (MIA)**; *tel: (305) 876-7077*, is seven miles, about 20 mins drive, from downtown. Flight information should be requested from individual airlines. Taxis and shuttle buses depart from the ground floor baggage claim areas. Taxis are $15 to downtown and $20 to Miami Beach, shuttles are $8 and $15. Public transport connections are slow and inconvenient.

MIA is the primary hub for flights in and out of the Caribbean and Latin America as well as one of the busiest airports in the world. The terminal is under permanent reconstruction. Most international flights arrive at Concourses B, D, E and F or the International Satellite Terminal. There are few moving walkways, so expect long walks to and from all

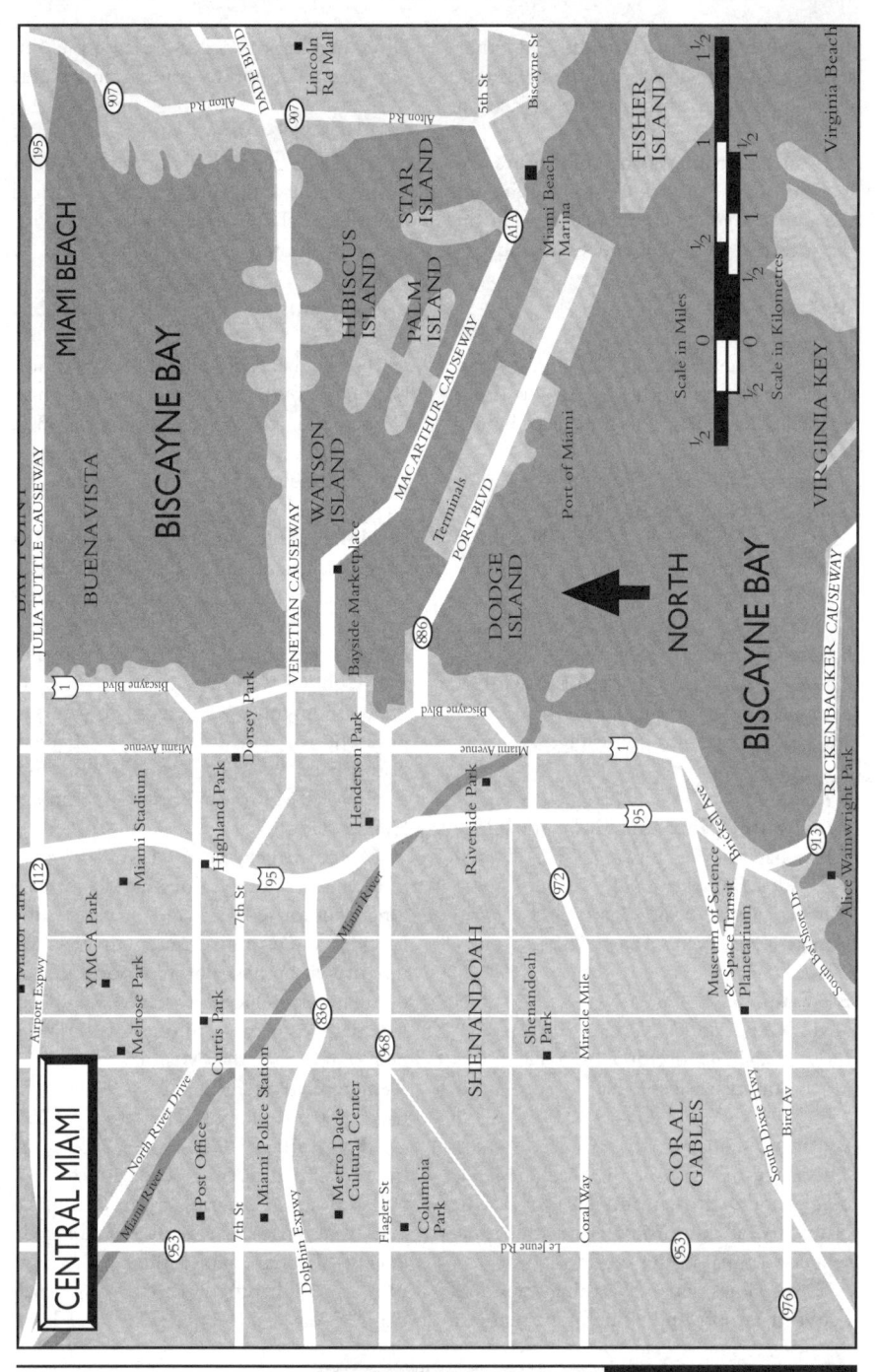

# MIAMI

## CENTRAL MIAMI MAP

gates. Most shops, restaurants and other services are concentrated in the main terminal hub. Concourses have few places to eat, drink or shop.

**Tourist Information Counters** are located outside all US Customs exits, on the upper level at Concourse E, and on the lower level of Concourses D and G.

## By Car

Car hire counters are located on MIA's lower level near baggage claim areas. Free shuttles connect with car hire parking lots. Get clear directions and maps before leaving the counter.

I-95 and Florida's Turnpike, Miami's main land links with the rest of Florida, pass within sight of MIA. The safest routes in and out of the airport are marked by large blue signs with an orange sunburst and the destination (Miami Beach, downtown, Key West, Coconut Grove, airport, etc.) marked below. The many secondary routes into the airport are badly signed and confusing.

## By Bus

**Greyhound Lines Inc.**; *tel: (800) 231-2222*, has stations at *411 N.W. 27th St and 700 Biscayne Blvd, Miami; 7101 Harding Ave, Miami Beach;* and *16250 Biscayne Blvd, North Miami Beach*.

## By Train

**AMTRAK**, *8303 N.W. 37th Ave; tel: (800) 872-7245* or *(305) 835-1221*, has north bound services.

## By Sea

The **Port of Miami**, on Dodge Island, between downtown and Miami Beach, claims to be the busiest cruise ship passenger terminal in the world.

Cruise lines generally arrange transfers between airport and ship for passengers. Disembarking passengers can also pick up hire cars at the port by prior arrangement.

## GETTING AROUND

Miami has a good public transport system – good for commuters that is. Most routes funnel into the city centre, with the very limited services of little use to visitors.

**Metrobus**, *6601 N.W. 72nd Ave, Miami, FL 33166; tel: (305) 638-6700*, serves the beaches, Miami Seaquarium, Orange Bowl Stadium, the Cultural Center and Metrozoo, Mon–Fri 0430–0200. Weekend and holiday schedules are limited. Fares are $1.25 each way; bus-to-rail transfers are $0.25.

**Metrorail**; *tel: (305) 638-6700*, is a 21-mile elevated rail system from Hialeah to downtown and Kendall, with stops approximately every mile. Tourist stops include the Miami Arena, Vizcaya and the Cultural Center. Trains run daily 0600–midnight, every eight mins during peak hours, every 20 mins off-peak hours. Fares are $1.25 each way with free transfer to Metromover at Government Center station.

**Metromover**; *tel: (305) 638-6700*, is indispensable for visiting the city centre. Small motorised carriages connect the Brickell and Omni business districts via downtown on two elevated loops. Visitor destinations include Bayside Marketplace, Miami Arena, the Cultural Center, several hotels and the Miami Convention Center. Carriages run every 90 seconds daily, 0600–midnight. The fare is $0.25.

**Tri-Rail**; *tel: (800) 874-7245*, commuter railroad serves Dade, Broward and Palm Beach Counties from Miami to West Palm Beach. Trains operate daily except Thanksgiving (third Thurs in Nov) and Christmas. Fares are $3 each way, $5 daily, $18.50 weekly or $22.50

for a FAST TRACK 12 PAK coupon book for 12 single journeys. Transfers to Metrorail and downtown Miami are free. All transit systems add frequencies and hours for major sporting, cultural and other public events.

## Driving in Miami

Constant construction in Miami makes accurate street maps rare, but **American Automobile Association** maps are more current than GMCVB publications. Apply in person, checking the telephone directory for addresses.

Miami is divided into four quadrants, Northeast, Northwest, Southeast and Southwest. **Flagler St** divides addresses north–south; **Miami Ave** is the east–west division. The sector designation, N.E., N.W., S.E, S.W., is a crucial part of addresses. **Avenues**, **Courts** and **Places** run north and south; **Streets**, **Terraces** and **Ways** run east and west. **Roads** run diagonally. All numbers start at Flagler St and Miami Ave *except* in Coral Gables and Hialeah, which have their own numbering systems. Miami Beach does not use sector designations, e.g. N.W. 3rd St is in Miami but 3rd St is in Miami Beach.

Traffic is a problem in Miami, and congestion is exacerbated by uniformly poor road signs. Streets are poorly marked and often change names without warning. S.W. 22nd St, for example, is also known as Miracle Mile, Coral Way, and S.W. 24th St as it runs from Biscayne Bay toward the Everglades. Driving habits vary wildly because so many Miamians have recently arrived from somewhere else. Expect anything from high speed weaving through slow-moving traffic to slow lorries lined up three abreast to block what is supposed to be a high speed artery.

Try to avoid rush hour, 0700–0930 and 1600–1800. Traffic is particularly slow in and out of Miami Beach because access is restricted to five causeways. The **MacArthur Causeway**, which connects downtown Miami and South Beach (southern Miami Beach), is usually the most crowded. The **Venetian Causeway**, a toll road, is faster at peak hours.

Biscayne Bay is an easy reference. Its shockingly blue waters are on the right when headed north, on the left when driving south and impossible to miss when driving east.

In **Miami Beach**, an island, the main reference point is **Collins Ave** (SR A1A), the only street which runs the length of the island. All of the beaches and most of the hotels lie between Collins Ave and the Atlantic Ocean; most residential areas lie between Collins and Biscayne Bay.

Miami and Miami Beach have metered street parking as well as car parks. Parking is sparse in central Miami and all of Miami Beach. So are lanes and traffic signals for left turns. Plan routes to avoid left turns where possible. The alternative is to wait for a traffic break, usually as the light turns from green to red, leaving just enough time for two or three cars to slip through as cross traffic thunders into the intersection.

## Staying in Miami

### Accommodation

**Miami** has more than 50,000 hotel rooms, but space can be extremely tight during major sporting events and the winter season (early Nov–late Apr). If winter weather is particularly nasty in the American North-east, rooms will be even tighter than normal in Miami. Rooms are 15–20% more expensive in Miami Beach than in Miami. There are fewer hotels on the island even though Miami Beach is one of America's hottest East Coast tourist attractions. **Central Reservations Service**, *11420 N. Kendall Dr., Suite 108, Miami, FL 33176; tel: (800) 950-0232*, offers free bookings. **Greater Miami & The Beaches Hotel Association**, *407 Lincoln Rd, Suite 10G, Miami Beach, FL 33139; tel: (800) 733-6426*, can book more than 100 area hotels. **Bed & Breakfast Tropical Florida**, *PO Box 262, Miami, FL 33243; tel: (305) 661-3270*, books Miami-area Bed and Breakfasts.

**Airport Area** chains include *CM, DI, Hd, Hn, QI, Rd, Rm* and *Sh*.

Most **Art Deco District** hotels were built in the 1920s and 1930s, allowed to fall into ruin and recently rebuilt. In keeping with the original style, they tend to be small, often with 40 or fewer small rooms. Atmosphere can be more important than amenities. But the Art Deco hotels are also the heart of the revitalisation that turned South Beach from a mouldering eyesore into an ultra-fashionable neighbourhood that appears on fashion pages worldwide.

Most of the Art Deco hotels are on **Ocean Dr.**, facing the ocean across a broad park, or on Collins Ave, one block inland. South Beach is compact, noisy, and lively until early morning, so don't expect much tropical tranquillity. Chains include *DI* and *Hd*; all are expensive–pricey.

The **Cavalier Hotel**, *1320 Ocean Dr., Miami Beach, FL 33139; tel: (800) 338-9076* or *(305) 543-2135*, favours photographers, models and art directors. The same toll-free number takes bookings for **Casa Grande**, *834 Ocean Dr; tel: (305) 672-7003*, **The Leslie Hotel**, *1244 Ocean Dr.; tel: (305) 534-2135*, and **The Marlin**, *1200 Collins Ave; tel: (305) 673-8770*. The only budget choices are the

**Miami Beach International HI-AYH Hostel**, *Clay Hotel, 1438 Washington Ave; tel: (305) 534-2988*, and the **Miami Beach International Travellers Hostel**, *236 9th St; tel: (305) 534-0268*.

**Turnberry Isle**, *19999 W. Country Club Dr., Aventura, FL 33180; tel: (800) 327-7028* or *(305) 932-6200*, is pricey and somewhat remote in **Aventura**, an up-market enclave at the north-eastern edge of Dade County, but has some of the best rooms and food in Miami.

Coconut Grove has three very pricey and popular hotels: **Grand Bay Hotel**, *2669 S. Bayshore Dr., Coconut Grove, FL 33133; tel: (800) 327-2788* or *(305) 858-9600*, may be the most elegant hotel in Miami. **The Grove Isle Resort**, *4 Grove Isle Dr., Coconut Grove, FL 33133; tel: (800) 884-7683* or *(305) 858-8300*, is on a private island. **Mayfair House Hotel**, *3000 Florida Ave, Coconut Grove, FL 33133; tel: (800) 433-4555* or *(305) 441-0000*, has only luxury suites.

**Coral Gables** has *Hd, HJ* and *Hy* as well as the pricey **Biltmore Hotel**, *1200 Anastasia Ave, Coral Gables, FL 33134; tel: (305) 445-1926*, the most opulent hotel in South Florida.

**Downtown** is expensive–pricey, with *BW, Ma, DI, Hd, HR* and *Sh*. More moderate motels are located nearer the airport. **The Fisher Island Club**, *One Fisher Island Dr., Fisher Island, FL 33109; tel: (800) 537-3708* or *(305) 535-6020*, is the restored winter estate of William Vanderbilt; very pricey, very posh, and very private – the only way on or off the island is by the club's yacht.

**Miami Beach** is dominated by famous names such as the **Eden Roc Resort**, *4525 Collins Ave, Miami Beach, FL 33140; tel: (800) 327-8337* or *(305) 531-0000*, and the **Fontainebleau Hilton**, *4441 Collins Ave, Miami Beach,*

FL 33140; tel: (800) 548-8886 or (305) 538-2000. Chains include DI, HJ, QI and Rm. Prices drop toward the north end of town.

## Eating and Drinking

Big-name restaurants are as expensive here as anywhere in the world, and as mercurial. For the latest and the hippest, check *South Florida* magazine and the *Miami Herald* food section. At the very least, splurge on a drink at the Biltmore Hotel in Coral Gables to sample the 1920s splendour of Miami's Golden Age.

For more realistic eating, check *Entertainment News & Views* and *New Times*, free newspapers in street corner racks. Best value for money are ethnic and local restaurants. **El Chalán**, 7971 S.W. 40th St, Miami, FL 33155; tel: (305) 266-0212, budget, serves enormous portions of Peruvian dishes and its seafood is outstanding. **Fishbone Grill**, 650 S. Miami Ave; Miami, FL 33130; tel: (305) 530-1915, moderate, has absolutely fresh fish. **Gertrude's**, 826 Lincoln Rd, Miami Beach, FL 33139; tel: (305) 538-6929, budget, has outstanding desserts and light meals on the Lincoln Mall in South Beach. **Monty's**, 2550 S. Bayshore Dr., Coconut Grove, FL 33133; tel: (305) 858-1413, budget–moderate, is a local and very relaxed favourite for stone crabs and other seafood as the sun sets behind the marina. **Mykonos**, 1201 Coral Way, Miami, FL 33145; tel: (305) 856-3140, budget, still tastes of Greece. **ShaBeen Cookshack**, Hotel Marlin, 1200 Collins Ave; tel: (305) 673-8770, moderate, has very bland Jamaican dishes but great people watching. **Taquerias el Mexicano**, 1961 S.W. 8th St (Calle Ocho), Miami, FL 33135; tel: (305) 858-1160, cheap–budget, is 100% Mexican and worth any translation problems. **Tap Tap**, 819 5th St, Miami Beach, FL 33139; tel: (305) 672-2989, is Haitian, toned down for American tastes.

## Communications

Address **Poste Restante** to *Main Post Office, Miami, FL 33101*. Mail can also be addressed to hotels.

## Money

**Thomas Cook Foreign Exchange**, *155 S.E. Third Ave, Miami, FL 33131*; tel: (305) 381-9252.

## ENTERTAINMENT

**South Beach**, the Art Deco district in southern Miami Beach, is the heartbeat of Miami nightlife. The best seat is any Ocean Dr. sidewalk café or restaurant between 7th and 13th Sts. Off duty models of both sexes prowl in outfits that will step out of tomorrow's fashion pages, mingling with pleasure seekers of all ages and proclivities.

Celebrity spotters can spend hours queueing at the hottest clubs waiting to catch a glimpse of Madonna, Sylvester Stallone, and other stars who have settled in Miami. *Entertainment News & Views* and *New Times* have the most complete listings, *ENV* for middle of the road to wild and *NT* for the farther fringes. Doormen reign supreme during the season; anyone without a famous face or a soon-to-be-famous body can expect to pass the night on the wrong side of the velvet rope. Admission standards slip in summer when the glitterati move to cooler climes.

**Tobacco Road**, 626 S. Miami Ave; tel: (305) 374-1198, is one of the oldest bars in Miami and one of the best Blues venues. **CocoWalk**, *Main and Grand, Coconut Grove*, is a block-long entertainment and shopping complex with bars,

# MIAMI

night-clubs, restaurants and cinemas that stays busy until well after midnight.

Miami has several dance companies, including three ballet companies and the **Ballet Flamenco La Rosa**, *1008 Lincoln Rd, Miami Beach, FL 33139; tel: (305) 672-0552*. The **Concert Association of Florida**, *555 17th St, Miami Beach, FL 33139; tel: (305) 532-3491*, brings dance and music superstars to Miami. Michael Tilson Thomas' **New World Symphony**, *541 Lincoln Rd, Miami Beach, FL 33139; tel: (305) 673-3331*, is one of three classical orchestras. The **Greater Miami Opera**, *1200 Coral Way, Miami, FL 33145; tel: (305) 854-1643*, performs Jan–Apr.

**Actor's Playhouse**, *8851 S.W. 107th Ave, Miami, FL 33176; tel: (305) 595-0010*, is one of Florida's largest professional theatre companies. **Coconut Grove Playhouse**, *3500 Main Hwy, Coconut Grove, FL 33133; tel: (305) 442-2662*, has a tradition of world premiere performances.

Miami has teams in every major professional sport: **Miami Dolphins** football, **Miami Heat** basketball, **Florida Marlins** baseball, **Florida Panthers** hockey and **Miami Hooters** indoor football. The Dolphins and the Marlins are both based at **Joe Robbie Stadium**, *2269 N.W. 199th St, Miami, FL 33056; tel: (305) 452-7000*. **Miami Arena**, *701 Arena Blvd, Miami, FL 33131*, a venue for concerts as well as sporting events, is home to both Miami Heat, *tel: (305) 577-4328*, and the Panthers, *tel: (305) 530-4444*.

The city also hosts professional tournaments in golf and tennis as well as a late Feb Grand Prix run on downtown streets.

On-track betting is legal on dog racing, horse racing, and jai-alai, a derivative of basque handball where players whip hard rubber balls off the walls at well over 100 mph.

## SHOPPING

**Flagler St** in Downtown Miami is heaven for tens of thousands of serious shoppers from around the world, for everything from cars to consumer electronics. Shopping is also recreation. **Bayside Marketplace**, *401 Biscayne Blvd, Miami, FL 33132; tel: (305) 577-3344*, and **CocoWalk**, *3015 Grand Ave, Coconut Grove, FL 33133; tel: (305) 444-0777*, combine shopping with eating, drinking and entertainment. **Caribbean Marketplace**, in Little Haiti, *5925-27 N.E. 2nd Ave, Miami, FL 33137; tel: (305) 751-2251*, modelled on the now-destroyed Iron Market in Port au Prince, Haiti, specialises in goods and flavours from the Caribbean. **Aventura Mall**, *19501 Biscayne Blvd, Aventura, FL 33180; tel: (305) 935-4222*, and **Bal Harbour Shops**, *9700 Collins Ave, Bal Harbour, FL 33154; tel: (305) 866-0311*, claim the expensive end of the shopping market, but shoppers who believe in truly conspicuous consumption should hold their credit cards for Worth Ave in Palm Beach (see pp. 144–148).

## SIGHTSEEING

**Downtown** Miami is home to hundreds of international banks and corporate offices, most of them focused on Latin America. Parking is scarce; use an outlying car park near a Metrorail or Metromover station and ride to Government Center Station. **Metro-Dade Cultural Center**, *101 W. Flagler St*, houses **The Center for the Fine Arts**; *tel: (305) 375-1700*, (admission $5) including travelling art exhibitions, **The Historical Museum of Southern Florida**; *tel:*

**ENTERTAINMENT • SIGHTSEEING**

*(305) 375-1492*, the finest museum on South Florida (admission $3), **The Main Public Library**; *tel: (305) 375-2665*, and a first floor plaza isolated from the import-export bustle of Flagler St below.

**Bayside Marketplace**, *401 Biscayne Blvd*, is brimming with buskers and food stands as well as more conventional shopping and entertainment. **Freedom Tower**, the Art Deco tower on Biscayne Blvd north of Bayside Marketplace, was once the home of the *Miami Herald*, then it became a processing centre for Cuban refugees in the early 1960s. The building is now empty.

In 1959, the blocks surrounding S.W. 8th St were an older working class neighbourhood that might have preferred to ignore Fidel Castro's revolution in Cuba. But low rents attracted some of the first Cubans who fled Castro's new government. What began as a trickle became a flood of refugees, welcomed with open arms by a succession of American governments dedicated to Castro's overthrow. Castro survived, and the neighbourhood chosen by those first refugees became **Little Havana**, the largest Cuban community outside Cuba.

The Cuban community, more than 500,000 strong, remains a potent political and economic force, but most Cubans have long since dispersed into Greater Miami. Little Havana remains the centre of Hispanic culture in South Florida, but today's residents are more likely to have come from Argentina, El Salvador, Mexico, Nicaragua or Peru. The language of Eighth St, universally called *Calle Ocho*, is Spanish. Many residents and shopkeepers speak little or no English, but smiles and patience overcome most language barriers.

South of Little Havana is **Coral Gables**, one of America's first planned communities, founded in 1923. The Gables has wide avenues, stately trees, and white street signs at ground level. East from Coral Gables is **Coconut Grove**, South Florida's oldest settlement. The Grove began as a hideaway for New England intellectuals and Key West refugees, then it grew into a winter retreat for the wealthy and politically powerful who shunned the ostentation of the Flaglers, Vanderbilts, and other habitués of Miami Beach. It became Miami's bohemian neighbourhood, then a centre for the drug trade, and is now home to some of Miami's most powerful families as well as **Vizcaya**, *3251 S. Miami Ave, Miami, FL 33129; tel: (305) 579-2708*, a sprawling Italianate country estate built in 1916. Admission $8.

**Key Biscayne**, at the end of a five-mile causeway just north of Vizcaya, was a favoured retreat for US President Richard Nixon. **Miami Beach** was named for its beaches, 15 miles of sand stretching from Bal Harbour to South Beach and the trendy **Art Deco Historical District**. The Art Deco district runs from Third St to 23rd St, but the most stunning restorations are concentrated along Collins and Ocean Aves between Fifth and 15th Sts.

## Museums and attractions
**American Police Hall of Fame and Museum**, *3801 Biscayne Blvd, Miami, FL 33137; tel: (305) 573-0070*, has a jail cell, an electric chair, and 10,000 other police-related items for lovers of law enforcement. Admission $6. **The Barnacle State Historic Site**, *3485 Main Hwy, Coconut Grove, FL 33133; tel: (305) 448-9445*, is one of Coconut Grove's early pioneer homes. Entrance: $1. **Biscayne National Park**, *PO Box 1270, Homestead, FL 33030; tel: (305) 247-*

2400, has glass-bottomed boat tours, snorkel and scuba dive trips from mangroves to living coral reefs. **Fruit and Spice Park**, *24801 S.W. 187th Ave, Homestead, FL 33031; tel: (305) 247-5727*, entrance $1, grows more than 200 different fruits and spices in an outdoor museum. **Miami Metrozoo**, *12400 S.W. 152nd Ave, Miami, FL 33177; tel: (305) 251-0403*, is one of the largest cageless zoos in America. Admission $8.25.

**Miami Seaquarium**, *4000 Rickenbacker Causeway, Miami, FL 33149; tel: (305) 361-5705*, admission $17.95, has dolphins, a killer whale and hundreds of other sea creatures. **Miami Museum of Science & Space Transit Planetarium**, *3280 S. Miami Ave, Miami, FL 33129; tel: (305) 854-4247*, explores space and science with more than 150 exhibits and one of the largest planetariums in the US.

Admission $9. **Venetian Pool**, *2701 DeSoto Blvd, Coral Gables, FL 33134; tel: (305) 460-5356*, is a historic Venetian-style swimming pool with waterfalls, caves and a beach. Admission $4. **Weeks Air Museum**, *14710 S.W. 128th St, Miami, FL 33196; tel: (305) 233-5197*, has a collection of World War I and II aircraft, many in flying condition. Admission $5.

### Tours

**Miami Design Preservation League**, *1001 Ocean Ave, Miami, FL 33139; tel: (305) 672-2014*, offers weekend walking and cycling tours of the Art Deco Historic District in Miami Beach. **Nature Connection**, *PO Box 330582, Miami, FL 33233; tel: (305) 556-7320*, sponsors guided walks and cycling trips through historic and natural areas, including hammocks and coral reefs.

---

# FOUR COOL HOSTELS IN THREE HOT LOCATIONS

Florida hostels offer everything under the sun for only $10-13 per night!

Go snorkeling, stroll the beaches, enjoy a mocha at an outdoor cafe, and of course, visit Mickey!

For reservations call Hostelling International -American Youth Hostels at 202/783-6161. In the USA and Canada, call toll free 1/800/444-6111

▲**HI-Fort Lauderdale** - swimming pool, across the street from the beach, 24-hour access, 305/568-1615

▲**HI-Miami Beach** - in the exciting South Beach area, two blocks from the beach, 24-hour access, 305/534-2988

▲**HI-Orlando Downtown** - on Lake Eola, near Church Street Station, shuttle service to the attractions, 407/843-8888

▲**HI-Orlando Resort** - swimming pool, 5 miles from WALT DISNEY WORLD®, 24-hour access, 407/396-8282.

**HOSTELLING INTERNATIONAL** *The seal of approval of the International Youth Hostel Federation*

# MIAMI CITY TOUR

Allow the better part of a day for this 70-mile tour of Greater Miami. Visiting all of the museums and attractions could stretch into several days.

## BAYSIDE MARKETPLACE TO LITTLE HAVANA

The route begins and ends at Bayside Marketplace, or can be picked up at any point. The route can be taken in either direction, but reversing it requires adjustments for one-way streets and misses several sights.

From **Bayside Marketplace**, drive four blocks south on Biscayne Blvd to E. Flagler St. On the left is **Bayside Park**. Turn right onto E. Flagler and then left onto S. Miami Ave. Traffic is usually heavy and the pavements crowded with business people, fruit sellers and shoppers. Spanish is the predominant language.

Cross the **Miami River**, home to fleets of small cargo ships and barges that carry everything from fresh produce to used cars throughout the Caribbean. **Tobacco Road** bar and **Fishbone Grill** restaurant (see p. 77) are on the right just beyond the river. Turn right at S.W. 7th St, a residential street, toward **Little Havana**. Continue three miles to S.W. 27th Ave, turn left, and left again onto S.W. 8th Ave, **Calle Ocho**.

Calle Ocho is a riot of colour and motion, although traffic moves slowly. The easiest area to explore on foot is S.W. 14th–S.W. 11th Aves, with parking on most side streets. The park at the north corner of S.W. 14th Ave, usually filled with men playing draughts, has a fine mural facing Calle Ocho. An Eternal Flame at S.W. 13th (Memorial Blvd) marks the **Brigade 2506 Memorial**, commemorating the abortive 1961 Bay of Pigs invasion of Cuba. A string of Cuban memorials, including a statue of Jose Martí, who led Cuba's 19th century fight against Spain, stretches three blocks along S.W. 13th Ave.

Turn right at S.W. 12th Ave (Ronald Reagan Blvd) to the **Cuban Museum of Arts and Culture**, *1300 S.W. 12th Ave; tel: (305) 858-8006*, open Tues–Fri 1000–1500 and Sat 1300–1600. Return to Calle Ocho and continue 2.5 miles east to Brickell Ave. One long block later, turn left onto S.W. 13th St (Coral Way), which turns left beneath I-95 to become S.W. 3rd Ave, shaded by stately banyan trees planted in the 1920s. One mile later, the avenue bears right to become S.W. 22nd St, known for a fine and constantly changing selection of ethnic stores and restaurants.

## CORAL GABLES

The banyans end abruptly at S.W. 37th Ave (Douglas Rd), the boundary with **Coral Gables**. S.W. 22nd St. becomes the **Miracle Mile**, running half a mile to LeJeune Rd (S.W. 42nd Ave). Walking up one side and down the other makes the mile. Shops span the gamut from chain restaurants to pricey boutiques. Prices, quality and street numbers climb toward the west.

Coral Gables still calls itself 'The City Beautiful', a phrase coined by developer George Merrick. Merrick laid out a planned community of broad boulevards

# MIAMI CITY TOUR

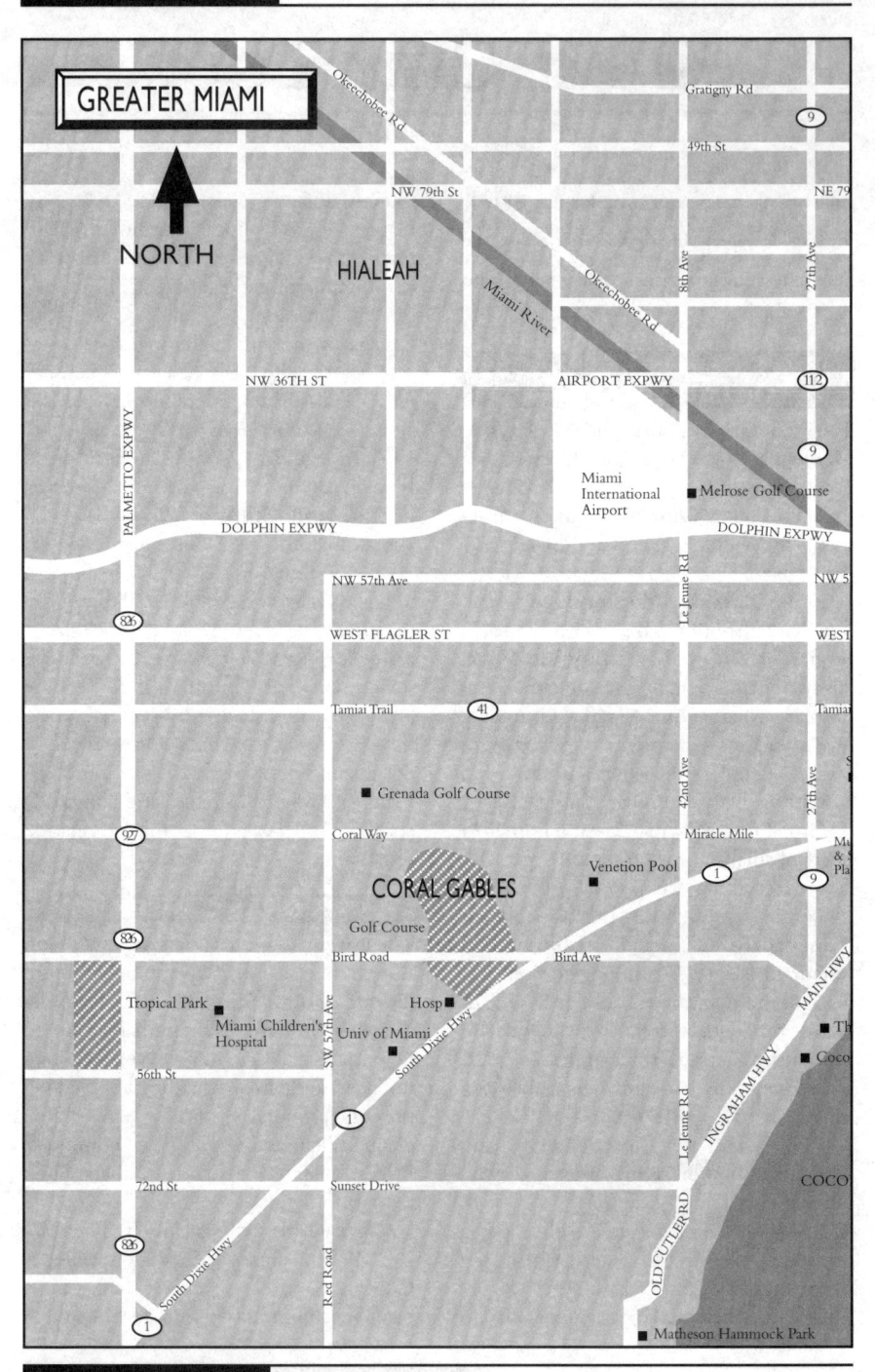

**GREATER MIAMI MAP**

# MIAMI CITY TOUR

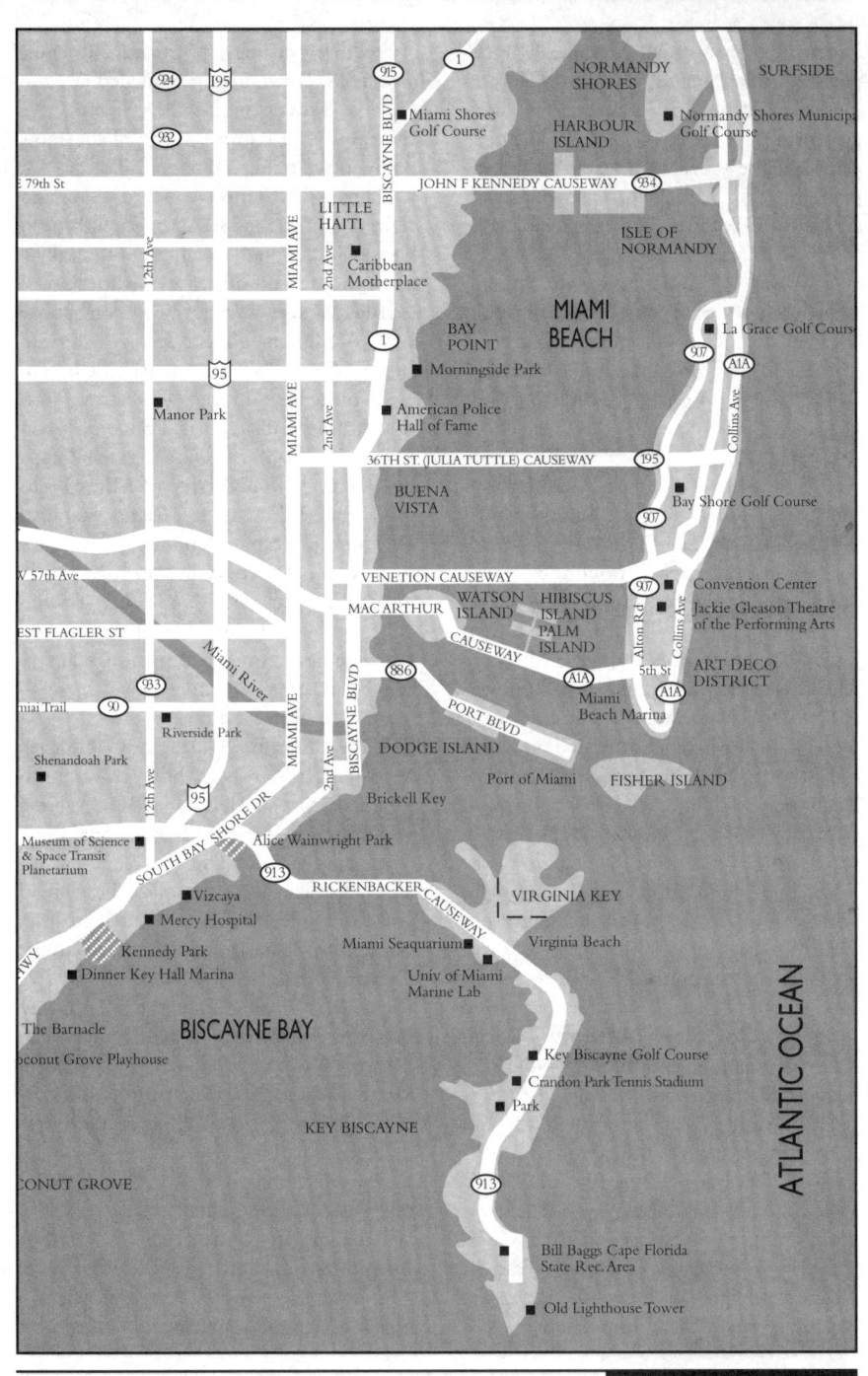

## GREATER MIAMI MAP

and typical Spanish Mediterranean architecture, began selling lots in 1921, and incorporated the city (gained legal self-governing status) in 1925. A 1926 hurricane and the Great Depression stalled his plans, but the Gables began growing again after World War II.

The Miracle Mile becomes Coral Way at LeJeune Rd and the ornate Spanish Renaissance **Coral Gables City Hall**. The Sat-only City Hall market is a good stop for locally grown fruit and produce. Ahead to the right is **Grenada Golf Course**, *2001 Granada Blvd; tel: (305) 442-6484*. One block beyond the course, turn right onto Toledo St, then left into the first driveway to park behind **Coral Gables House**, *907 Coral Way; tel: (305) 442-6593*, Merrick's boyhood home filled with family furnishings.

Turn right back onto Coral Way, then left at the first traffic signal, Granada Blvd. Ahead is a classical fountain and roundabout, **DeSoto Plaza**. Go almost completely around to DeSoto Blvd and turn right (north-east) one block to **Venetian Pool**, on the right, *2701 DeSoto Blvd; tel: (305) 442-6483*. Merrick's rock quarry was transformed into a Venetian fantasy municipal swimming pool, complete with red-striped poles, waterfalls, grottoes and a beach.

Turn right around the pool to return to DeSoto Plaza. Take DeSoto Blvd south-east to **The Biltmore Hotel**, *1200 Anastasia Ave; tel: (305) 445-1926*. The hotel opened in 1926 as the centrepiece of Merrick's community, but fell on hard times during the Depression. It became a hospital during World War II and stood vacant during 1968–86. Two multi-million dollar renovations later, The Biltmore looks much as it did in 1926, complete with polished marble, gleaming chandeliers, intricately carved and painted ceilings, courtyard fountains, and a 26-storey tower modelled on the Giralda Tower in Seville, Spain. The Biltmore Golf Course is one of the most competitive public courses in Florida.

Turn right onto Anastasia Ave and right onto Granada Blvd, lined with posh houses and enough stately trees to make a royal forest. The small canal is the **Coral Gables Waterway**, leading to Biscayne Bay. Venetian gondolas once ferried Biltmore guests to a private bayside beach. One mile beyond the Waterway, turn right at the traffic signal, Ponce de Leon Blvd. The stark concrete on the left is Metrorail; the **University of Miami** is to the right. Take the first right, Stanford Dr., onto the campus and the 'V' car park next to the **Lowe Art Museum**, *1301 Stanford Dr.; tel: (305) 284-3535*. Lowe's collection includes Renaissance and Baroque art, American paintings, Latin American art and Native American textiles and basketry; admission is $4.

Take Stanford Dr. out beneath Metrorail and cross S. Dixie Hwy onto Maynada St, just left of a Burger King restaurant. At the next traffic signal, turn right onto Sunset Dr. (S.W. 72nd St). The 'historic and scenic road' is lined with fine old homes and ancient trees laced with Spanish moss. At the **Bakery Centre**, on the right, *Sunset Dr. & Red Rd (S.W. 57th Ave)*, watch for the *trompe l'oeil* mural of an alligator and a man. The **Miami Youth Museum**, *5701 Sunset Dr., Miami; tel: (305) 661-3046*, is a cultural arts museum for children and their older companions.

Turn left onto Red Rd. Continue 2.5 miles past modest homes to Killian Dr. (S.W. 111th St). Turn right to **Parrot Jungle & Gardens**, *11000 S.W. 57th Ave; tel: (305) 666-7834*, one of Miami's oldest and most popular attractions with more than 1000 parrots, macaws, cockatoos, flamingos and other colourful birds, many flying freely. There are trained bird shows, photo opportunities with tropical birds, and a carefully tended 'jungle' of orchids, ferns, bald cypress trees, palms and live oaks. Admission is $10.95. Return to Red Rd, turn right, and continue 0.3 miles. Turn left onto Old Cutler Rd, which follows the Biscayne Bay north toward Miami. **Fairchild Tropical Garden**, *10901 Old Cutler Rd; tel: (305) 667-1651*, admission $11, is the largest tropical botanical garden in North America. Fairchild was heavily damaged by Hurricane Andrew in 1992, but replanting and regrowth has been rapid. A low, moss-covered stone wall follows the road on both sides, with stately homes half-hidden by the trees. Fairchild merges into **Matheson Hammock Park**, *9610 Old Cutler Rd; tel: (305) 666-6979*, 100 acres of upland forests and mangroves. The popular park has a marina and a saltwater pool, surrounded by sand and palms, that is flushed by the tides.

## COCONUT GROVE

From the park, go right on Old Cutler Rd two miles north to **Cartagena Plaza**. Continue through the roundabout, cross the bridge, and turn right into Ingraham Hwy and **Coconut Grove**. Ingraham jogs left to become Douglas St, then right at a traffic signal to become Main Hwy. Most of Coconut Grove's narrow roads were tunnelling beneath leafy canopies as pioneer trails long before Miami began. The 'village' begins 0.5 miles north on Main Hwy. To the left is **Coconut Grove Playhouse**, *3500 Main Hwy; tel: (305) 442-2662*, a cinema-become-theatre specialising in premiere performances. The sheltered benches opposite are the entrance to **The Barnacle State Historic Site**, *3485 Main Hwy; tel: (305) 448-9445*, an 1891 bayside house and one of the largest tracts of untouched hammock in South Florida. Many of the furnishings are original. Turn right at McFarlane Rd, putting **CocoWalk** on your left. Traffic begins to clog in late afternoon as CocoWalk bars and restaurants fill. Straight ahead is **Dinner Key Marina**, *3400 Pan American Dr.; tel: (305) 579-6980*, named after an early picnic spot.

McFarlane turns left into S. Bay Shore Dr. Continue through the first traffic signal to Pan American Blvd and turn right. At the end of the road is **Miami City Hall**, *3500 Pan American Dr; tel: (305) 579-6040*, built in the 1930s as a Pan American Airways terminal. Return to S. Bayshore Dr. at the pyramidal Grand Bay Hotel; turn right. **Kennedy Park**'s expansive lawns, walking paths and a wooden bridge overlooking Biscayne Bay are on the right. A catering truck usually parked in the north car park sells excellent frozen lemonade.

Fair Isle St and **Grove Isle** are 0.5 miles north of the park. S. Bay Shore becomes S. Miami Blvd at Mercy Hospital. One-half mile beyond, **Vizcaya**, *3251 S. Miami Blvd; tel: (305) 579-2813*, has 34 rooms filled with antique furniture, paintings, sculpture, textiles, and other decorative arts from the 16th–19th centuries. The Italian Renaissance-style villa was the winter estate of Chicago industrialist Charles Deering. Entrance fee is $8. Across the street is **Miami Museum of Science and Space Transit Planetarium**, *3280 S. Miami Blvd; tel: (305) 854-4521*, a hands-on science museum and wildlife centre. Admission $9.

Turn right just beyond Vizcaya onto S.E. 32nd St. and **Millionaire's Row**, Brickell Ave. Sylvester Stallone lives

# MIAMI CITY TOUR

behind the first gate on the right, guarded by stone lions. The 19th Amendment to the US Constitution, granting women the right to vote, was drafted and shepherded to enactment in 1919 from **Casa Serena**, 3115. Madonna lives at 3029, behind the only gate not offering a glimpse into the estate beyond. **Alice Wainright Park** has a pleasant expanse of grass and trees running down to the bay. Brickell Ave comes to a dead end beyond the park.

## SOUTH MIAMI AND KEY BISCAYNE

Return to S. Miami Ave and turn right, then right again onto the Rickenbacker Causeway. The return trip offers excellent views of the Miami skyline. **Virginia Key** and **Key Biscayne**, Miami's playground islands, are largely parks with beaches and facilities for golf, tennis, baseball, boating, fishing and picnicking. Former US President Richard Nixon had a home on Key Biscayne, but a later owner changed the building. Windsurfing equipment can be rented most days on **Hobie Island**, just beyond the toll plaza. The toll is $1. **Miami Marine Stadium**, *3601 Rickenbacker Causeway; tel: (305) 361-6732*, hosts concerts throughout the year, including a 4th of July fireworks spectacular. **Miami Seaquarium**, *4400 Rickenbacker Causeway; tel: (305) 361-5705*, admission $17.95, has a performing killer whale, dolphins, sea lions and more. **Virginia Key Beach**, a city park, is across the causeway from Seaquarium with two miles of beach and recreational facilities.

Continue on to Key Biscayne, the **Key Biscayne Golf Course**, **International Tennis Center** and **Bill Baggs Cape Florida State Recreation Area**, *1200 S. Crandon Blvd; tel: (305) 361-5811*. The 95-ft lighthouse is closed, but the surrounding park and beaches are open all year.

Returning via the causeway, turn right onto Brickell Ave, which is lined with the skyscrapers that appear in the opening credits of the *Miami Vice* TV series. Immediately after crossing the Miami River, turn right, then left, onto Biscayne Blvd and Bayfront Park to the right. Port Blvd and the **Port of Miami** are 0.5 miles north, on the right. Freedom Tower rises on the left just ahead. The approaches to the MacArthur Causeway are being rebuilt until 1996; follow signs for **Miami Beach**.

## MIAMI BEACH

**Watson Island**, two miles offshore, has a large park and Chalk's Seaplane base to the right. The park gives a close up of marine traffic in and out of Miami. Most cruise ships arrive in the early morning and depart late afternoon.

Promoter Carl Graham Fisher, the man behind the Indianapolis Speedway and the annual Indianapolis 500 auto race, spent much of his considerable fortune creating Miami Beach. By the 1920s, America's rich and famous flocked south to escape the icy blasts of winter. Boom turned to bust with a devastating 1926 hurricane, the 1929 stock market crash and World War II travel restrictions. Prosperity returned after the war, then disappeared as newer beachside playgrounds developed. By the early 1980s, much of Miami Beach had become a slum, the graceful Art Deco buildings disfigured by steel bars, broken glass and gaping roofs. The revival and rebuilding that began in the 1980s is still spreading.

The first Miami Beach roads lead left to **Palm** and **Hibiscus Islands** and **Star Island**, private residential enclaves. The obelisk beyond Star Island honours Henry Flagler, whose Florida East Coast Railway opened South Florida to the world. At the end of the causeway, turn right onto Alton Rd, passing the **Miami Beach Marina**. At the end of Alton Rd, turn left onto Biscayne St, then right at Washington St to enter **South Pointe Park**, a good place to watch passing ship traffic and fish.

Exit the park on Washington to 5th St, turn right, move to the middle lane, and turn left onto Ocean Dr. To the right lies a broad park opening onto the beach. On the left is the heart of **South Beach**, a line of restored Art Deco hotels and restaurants stretching to 15th St. Parking is scarce from mid-morning until well after midnight, thanks in part to RVs and lorries supporting the photo, video and cinema crews that have popularised South Beach. Try the public car park at Ocean Dr. and 13th St.

Turn left onto 15th St at the end of Ocean, then left again onto Collins Ave. The restored buildings may be treasures, but drivers need to watch for pedestrians and skaters darting into traffic. Turn right onto 5th St and right again onto Washington St. Turn left onto Espanola Way at the **Clay Hotel**, now Miami's HI-AYH Youth Hostel. Espanola is lined with outdoor cafés, galleries and hip boutiques that come alive in late afternoon.

Turn right onto Jefferson Ave at the foot of Espanola to continue north through blocks of flats or 'villas'. **Lincoln Road** is a pedestrian mall, home to Miami Beach's artistic community. An electric tram provides a daytime service up and down the road; there are ample car parks one-half block north. At 17th St (Hank Meyer Blvd), turn right toward Collins and the ocean. **Miami Beach City Hall** and the **Jackie Gleason Theater of the Performing Arts** are ahead on the left, with the **Miami Beach Convention Center** behind. Go left onto Collins Ave, usually crowded with beach goers. The **Bass Museum of Art**, *2121 Park Ave; tel: (305) 673-7533*, is two blocks to the left on 21st St.

The **Sans Souci Resort and Spa** is near 31st St. From 33rd St, the *trompe l'oeil* mural at the **Fontainebleau Hilton** can be seen. Collins Ave makes a sharp left at 44th St to avoid running through the mural. Continue three miles to 71st St and the John F. Kennedy Causeway. The causeway crosses **Treasure Island**, then **Harbor Island**, before launching across Biscayne Bay and a panoramic view south to central Miami.

## MIAMI BEACH TO BAYSIDE MARKETPLACE

Move into the right lane at the end of the causeway and take 82nd St westbound. Cross Biscayne Blvd and the railroad tracks, then turn left onto N.E. 2nd Ave and **Little Haiti**, where buildings and businesses sport French names and vibrant colours. On the left near 59th St is the heart of Little Haiti, the **Caribbean Marketplace**. Traffic moves more quickly and erratically here than in most of Miami, mimicking Haitian driving customs.

The **Design District**, a concentration of interior designers and accessory makers begins at N.E. 43rd St. Continue to N.E. 36th St, just beyond the I-195 flyover, turn left, and then right onto Biscayne Blvd. Residential areas between Biscayne Blvd and the bay are expensive, but the boulevard is a strip of rundown motels and abandoned buildings frequented by drug sellers and prostitutes after dark. Continue 31 blocks south on Biscayne Blvd to Bayside Marketplace, on the left.

# MIAMI–KEY WEST

The Keys are a schizophrenic marine playground, a 110-mile string of coral islets curving gracefully south and west from the tip of Florida, a riot of jungles and mangroves set in a sea of iridescent turquoise. The Keys are also a 110-mile traffic jam, a garish strip of faded billboards, shopping malls, bars, hamburger joints, motels and RV parks.

Both visions are true. Driving south along US Hwy 1, the steely blue Atlantic is on the left and the Gulf Stream sweeps rich, warm water northward along the only living coral reef in the continental US. To the right is Florida Bay and the shallow backcountry, teeming with wildlife and imperilled by agricultural runoff washing through the Everglades from the Lake Okeechobee region. Ocean and bay are sometimes as much as ten miles apart. More often, they're separated by a key barely wider than the highway and connected by a maze of channels, cuts and passes.

The 300-mile return trip from Miami to Key West can be done in one excruciatingly long day, but three to ten days allows time to enjoy the ocean and explore the land. Key Largo, Islamorada, Marathon and Key West are the best overnight stops. It's also possible to fly into Marathon or Key West and hire a car, but hire prices are considerably cheaper in Miami, Orlando and Tampa.

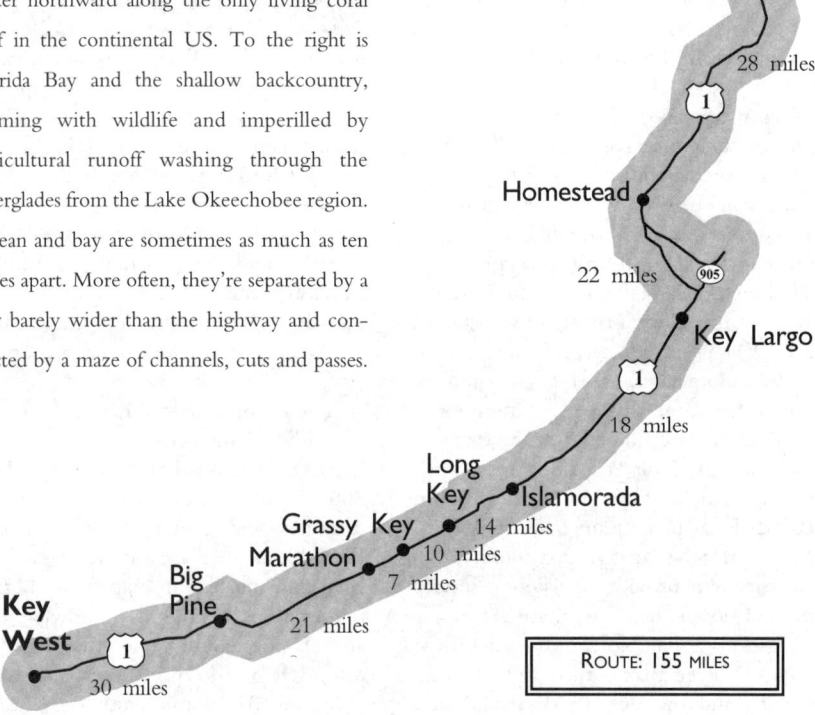

**ROUTE: 155 MILES**

# MIAMI–KEY WEST

## ROUTE

US Hwy 1 follows the route of Henry Flagler's Florida East Coast Railway (FEC), which connected Miami and Key West from 1912 until the Labor Day Hurricane in Sept 1935. Winds of more than 200 mph and storm surges topping 14 ft knocked trains from the track, washed out miles of landfill, and killed more than 400 people in the Keys. But Flagler's concrete bridges survived to become the foundation for US Hwy 1, which opened in 1938.

Route-finding in the Keys is easy: Follow the small green mile marker (MM) signs at the right side of the highway. Most addresses and directions are given in the form 'MMXXX'. MM126 is just south of Florida City, MM0 is in Key West. 'Oceanside' is the Atlantic side of US 1, 'bayside' and 'gulfside' are the Florida Bay/Gulf of Mexico side.

US 1 expands to four lanes through Key Largo, which is lined with scuba dive suppliers and outfitters, souvenir shops, petrol stations, motels, bars and restaurants. The town centre is *MM100*. The next major town is **Islamorada**, on Upper Matecumbe Key, *MM82*. **Marathon** is on Key Vaca, *MM50*. The **Seven Mile Bridge** is the longest on the Overseas Highway. **Pigeon Key**, two miles south of Key Vaca, was one of Henry Flagler's railroad construction camps. **Big Pine Key**, home of the endangered **Key Deer**, surrounds *MM30*. **Key West** is at *MM0*.

## MIAMI TO HOMESTEAD

From **Bayside Marketplace** in Miami, take Biscayne Blvd south to E. Flagler St. Turn right. Go one block to S.E. Second Ave and turn left. Follow S.E. Second Ave over the Miami River, where it becomes Brickell Ave. Continue south to SR 913, the Rickenbacker Causeway (to Key Biscayne). Veer right to **US Hwy 1**, the **South Dixie Highway**. Continue south on US 1 through **Coral Gables** and **South Miami** into Dade County, past **Miami Metrozoo** and the **Gold Coast Railroad Museum** (S.W. 151st St), **Monkey Jungle** (S.W. 216 St), the **Fruit & Spice Garden** (S.W. 248 St), and **Coral Castle** (S.W. 157 Ave).

Damage from Hurricane Andrew, which swept through the area in Aug 1992, becomes more visible toward Homestead/Florida City. Wind, rain and waves shattered trees, stripped away roofs and windows, and tore thousands of buildings from their foundations. A jet fighter on a pedestal on the east side of the highway 1.5 miles south of Coral Castle marks **Homestead City**, the town that grew up around **Homestead Air Force Base** and absorbed the worst of Hurricane Andrew.

## HOMESTEAD

**Tourist Information:** Greater Homestead/Florida City Chamber of Commerce, *43 N. Krome Ave, Homestead, FL 33030; tel: (305) 247-2332,* open Mon–Fri 0830–1700, and **Tropical Everglades Visitor Association**, *160 US Hwy 1, Florida City, FL 33034; tel: (305) 245-9180.*

Nobody stays in Homestead. Sleep in Miami or Key Largo, where there is a much wider choice of accommodation.

### SIGHTSEEING

The Chamber of Commerce publishes a walking and shopping guide with a heavy emphasis on antiques. **Florida Keys Factory Shops**, *250 E. Palm Dr, Florida City, FL 33034; tel: (305) 248-4727,* is the biggest shopping opportunity. **R.F. Orchids, Inc.**, *28100 S.W. 182 Ave,*

Homestead, FL 33030; tel: (305) 245-4570, has one of the finest commercial orchid displays in South Florida.

## HOMESTEAD TO KEY LARGO

Shopping malls line most of US Hwy 1, although fruit and vegetable fields still resist creeping development near Homestead. The **Tropical Everglades Visitor Association**, three miles south of Homestead, *160 US Hwy 1, Florida City, FL 33034; tel: (305) 245-9180*, is just south of the junction of US 1 and SR 9336. SR 9336 leads east to Everglades National Park and west to Biscayne National Park.

US Hwy 1 continues south to the Keys and narrows to two lanes just beyond Card Sound Rd (see side track below), running through swamps lush with new growth after Hurricane Andrew. Large lorries often slow traffic. Traffic also slows to a near standstill at weekends and holidays. The worst jams are southbound Fri and afternoons before holidays and northbound on Sun afternoons and the final day of holiday breaks. Try to schedule travel against the rush, i.e., southbound on Sun and northbound on Fri, or travel midweek. Watch for cars and motorcycles overtaking slower vehicles. The road follows a low dike with extremely narrow verges that drop into the water.

Monroe County begins 14 miles south of Card Sound Rd. Monroe originally included what is now Dade and Broward Counties, but was split as Miami and Fort Lauderdale grew. Today, Monroe covers the Everglades and the Keys, an area that probably has more alligators and ospreys, or sea eagles, than permanent residents. Osprey nests are untidy piles of sticks atop the tallest tree, which is more often a utility pole than a real tree.

Key Largo is connected to the mainland by a drawbridge 19 miles south of Card Sound Rd. At **Key Largo**, US Hwy 1 literally becomes **The Overseas Highway**, a mystical path that barely skims the waves to suddenly arc high above a deep water channel.

### SIDE TRACK FROM HOMESTEAD

**Card Sound Rd**, an alternative route to Key Largo, turns left a half-mile south of the Tropical Everglades Visitor Association. Card Sound Bridge ($1 toll each way) provides a splendid view of blue water and mangroves with the Turkey Point nuclear power station on the eastern horizon. Enormous flocks of ibis, herons and other shore birds stalk the mud flats at low tide and roost in the thick mangroves the rest of the time.

**Alabama Jacks**, *58000 Card Sound Rd, Florida City, FL 33034; tel: (305) 248-8741*, a local restaurant, bar, and country and western dance spot, is just north of the bridge. South of the bridge, on upper (northern) Key Largo, the highway crosses a deserted mangrove swamp that shelters poisonous snakes, the very rare American crocodile and (most dangerous of all) humans involved in the illegal drug trade. The narrow road is quite safe, the mangroves are not.

Turn right at the only stop sign to join SR 905, which runs through some of the last hardwood forest in the Keys. The road rejoins US Hwy 1 at Key Largo, adding about 30 mins to the trip.

## KEY LARGO

**Tourist Information: Key Largo Chamber of Commerce**, *MM106 bayside, 105950 Overseas Highway, Key Largo,*

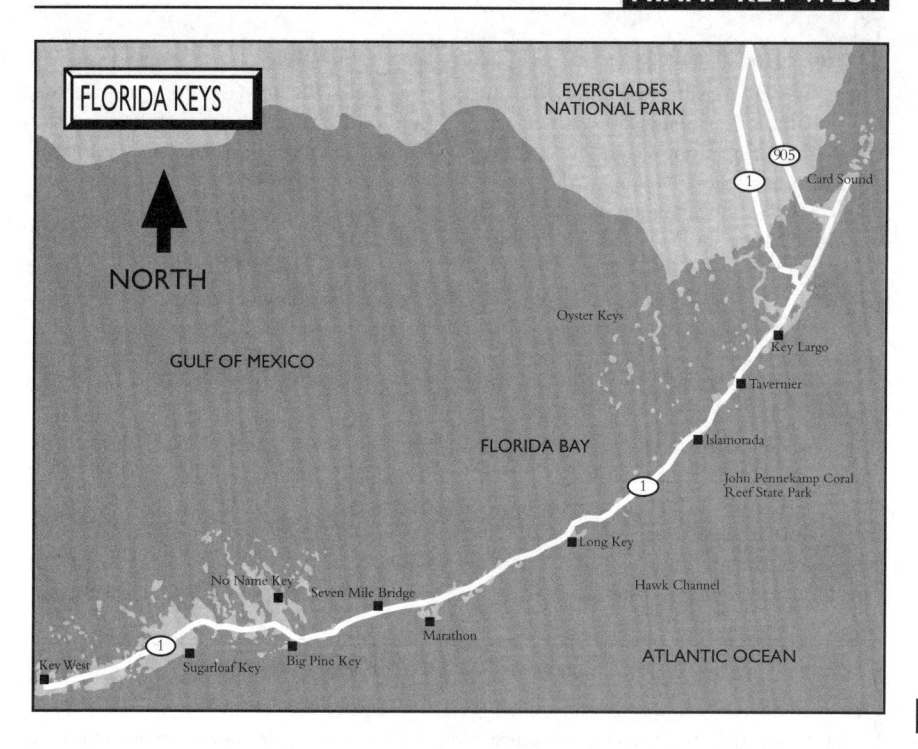

FL 33037; tel: (800) 822-1088 or (305) 451-1414, open daily 0900–1800.

### Accommodation

Key Largo is one of the most popular snorkelling and scuba diving destinations in the world and the favourite Keys getaway for Miami. The town has *BW, DI, Hd, HJ, Ma, Sh* and *TL*, but chain hotels have made little headway elsewhere in the Keys. The expensive–pricey **Sheraton Key Largo Resort**, *MM97 bayside, 97000 US Hwy 1; tel: (305) 852-5553*, is south of town with the best sunset view of any chain.

**Holiday Inn Key Largo**, *MM100 oceanside, 99701 Overseas Hwy; tel: (800) 843-5997* or *(305) 451-2121*, also expensive–pricey, has its own harbour with diving and fishing trips and the *African Queen*, the original steam boat from the 1951 Humphrey Bogart-Katharine Hepburn film. **Amoray Dive Resort**, *MM104 bayside, 104250 Overseas Hwy; tel: (800) 426-6729* or *(305) 451-3595*, moderate–expensive, has several efficiency units and excellent diving/snorkelling services.

**Jules Verne Undersea Lodge**, *MM102 oceanside, 51 Shoreland Dr; tel: (305) 451-2353*, is expensive and 30 ft underwater. The only access is by scuba diving, but the lodge teaches the basics. Anyone who can swim can get down to the hotel and back. Book 1–4 months in advance.

**Freelancer**, *103100 Overseas Hwy; tel: (305) 451-0349*, and **Keysearch Realty Corp.**, *101487 Overseas Hwy; tel: (800) 210-6246* or *(305) 451-4321*, have the largest stock of holiday flats in all price ranges.

## Eating and Drinking

There are few chain restaurants in the Keys. Cuban restaurants are particularly good value for money and dependably good. **Denny's Latin Cafe**, *MM100 bayside, 99600 Overseas Highway; tel: (305) 451-3665*, open 24 hrs, is one of the best cheap–budget choices. **Mrs. Mac's Kitchen**, budget, *MM99.4 bayside; tel: (305) 451-3722* is popular with locals for fresh fish, burgers, chili and a good beer selection. **Pilot House**, *MM99.5 oceanside, 13 Sea Gate Blvd; tel: (305) 451-3142*, moderate, is a lively waterfront fish restaurant. **Caribbean Club**, *MM104; tel: (305) 451-9970*, a popular local hangout, claims to have been the set for the Humphrey Bogart film *Key Largo*. True or not, the bar has splendid sunset views.

## Sightseeing

Anyone with an aversion to the sea shouldn't venture south of Homestead, but the Keys can be a paradise for anyone who enjoys activities in, on, above, under, or about the ocean.

Key Largo is the most popular scuba diving and snorkelling destination area in the US, possibly the world. The lure is an expansive system of coral reefs spreading from the Dry Tortugas, 75 miles west of Key West, to the outer reaches of Biscayne Bay. Many reefs near Key Largo are barely awash at low tide, and perfect for snorkelling when the tide is high. **Sharkey's**, bayside at *MM106 Plaza; tel: (305) 451-5533*, and **Sundiver**, *MM100 oceanside; tel: (800) 654-7369 or (305) 451-2220*, offer reef trips for snorkellers

## The Florida Keys

The Keys have three distinct subregions. The **Upper Keys**, Key Largo to Long Key Channel, is the centre for scuba diving and a growing dormitory community for Homestead, South Dade and Miami. Many residents are transplants from the US Northeast and Midwest, including a large number of retirees. The **Middle Key**s, Long Key Channel to Marathon and the Seven Mile Bridge, are dominated by fishing and other water-related activities. Most residents are the children and grandchildren of migrants from other Southern US states. The **Lower Keys**, Seven Mile Bridge to Key West, revolve around tourism and the military. The permanent population is a quirky mixture of salt water conchs (pronounced 'konks', anyone born in the Keys); freshwater conchs (long term residents originally from somewhere else); refugees from the sprawl of Miami, Fort Lauderdale and New York; Cubans; homosexuals; transient military personnel; students; world travellers (especially from the UK) and a sprinkling of drifters searching for nirvana at the end of the road.

One thing the Keys lack is beach. The coral reefs surrounding the Keys slowly decompose into sand, but the Gulf Stream sweeps nearly everything not anchored in place north and east toward the Bahamas. **John Pennekamp Coral Reef State Park**, *MM102.5*, has two artificial beaches. **Harry Harris Park**, *MM93*, has a small natural beach. **Islamorada County Park**, *MM81.5*, has a natural beach near the mouth of a stream, but ocean currents are strong. **Calusa Cove Beach**, *MM74*, and **Annie's Beach**, *MM73*, are shallow and protected, good spots for small children. The two are connected by a shady boardwalk. **Long Key State Recreational Area**, *MM67.5*, has a sand and coral beach that is good for snorkelling. **Sombrero Beach**, *MM50*, has good ocean swimming. **Bahia Honda State Park**, *MM37*, has the largest sand beaches in the Keys and excellent snorkelling.

only. Snorkellers who join scuba dive trips should expect to spend more time in the boat waiting for divers to return than snorkelling. The glass-bottomed **Key Largo Princess**, *MM100, Holiday Inn Harbour; tel: (305) 451-4655*, gives non-swimmers a look at the underwater world.

Most Florida reefs are 20–60 ft deep, home to hundreds of species of reef and ocean fish as well as dolphins, turtles and shipwrecks. Ships have been foundering on the reefs since the days of Columbus. One of the first books on Florida was written by Hernando de Escalante Fontaneda, from Carthegna, Columbia, who spent 17 years in the Keys after a 1549 shipwreck. The Keys hold hundreds of historic wrecks as well as modern ships that have been sunk to provide habitat for fish and interest for divers.

Most of the early wrecks were Spanish, often carrying tonnes of gold, silver and gemstones home to the royal treasury. The **Maritime Museum**, *MM102, 102670 Hwy 1; tel: (305) 451-6444*, open daily 1000–1700, has the best shipwreck maps and displays in the Keys. The narrow Florida Straits, fringed with jagged reefs, is the only dependable channel from Cuba (centre of the Spanish Empire in the Americas for three centuries) to the Atlantic Ocean and Spain. The same strait was later the best route from New Orleans and the Mississippi River to the ports of Europe and the Eastern US. The museum displays – and sells – antique jewellery and coins salvaged from local reefs.

The same reefs are part of **John Pennekamp Coral Reef State Park**, *MM102.5 oceanside, 102601 US Hwy 1; tel: (305) 451-1202*, 75 square miles of the third-largest barrier reef on the planet. The **Key Largo National Marine Sanctuary**, *PO Box 1083, Key Largo, FL 33037; tel: (305) 451-1644*, protects more reef. The entire Keys are within the **Florida Keys National Marine Sanctuary** (see p. 97).

All dive and snorkel operators hire out the necessary gear. The most reasonable place to purchase snorkelling or diving equipment locally is **Divers City USA**, *MM104, 104001 Overseas Highway; tel: (305) 451-4554*. **Stephen Frink Photographic**, *MM102.5 bayside, PO Box 2720, Key Largo, FL 33037; tel: (305) 451-3737*, has the best local selection of underwater cameras for sale or hire.

Pennekamp has adequate snorkelling from shore, a well-stocked aquarium display, picnic areas and two artificial beaches. Most shoreside hotels advertise snorkelling, but the best reefs are several miles offshore. The **Coral Reef Park Company**, *PO Box 1560, Key Largo, FL 33037; tel: (305) 451-1621*, is the official Pennekamp operator, but all dive and snorkel operators use the same reefs. **Amoray Divers**, *MM104 bayside, 104250 Overseas Hwy; tel: (800) 426-6729* or *(305) 451-3595*, runs excellent diving trips. **Ocean Divers**, *522 Caribbean Dr.; (bayside); tel: (800) 451-1113* or *(305) 541-1113*, also has a solid reputation.

**Capt. Sterling's Everglades Experience**, *MM102, PO Box 3343, Key Largo, FL 33037; tel: (800) 959-0742* or *(305) 451-4540*, offers small boat tours of Florida Bay and the Everglades. For an even closer look at the mangroves, sand bars and underwater meadows of the backcountry, **Florida Bay Outfitters**, *MM104 Overseas Hwy; tel: (305) 451-3018*, offers kayak and canoe tours from several hours to seven days. Expect to meet dolphins, manatees, turtles, herons, ibis, spoonbills, egrets and mosquitoes.

**Dolphins Plus**, *PO Box 2728, Key*

Largo, FL 33037; tel: (305) 451-1993, specialises in helping the mentally and physically handicapped by introducing them to dolphins. Therapy schedules permitting, the general public can also swim with the dolphins, but bookings must be

## Scuba Diving in Florida

The Florida Keys are famous for miles of brilliant coral reefs and limpid water, but there is diving – and snorkelling – throughout the state. North Florida is pockmarked with sinkholes, springs and caverns. The Atlantic Coast is littered with wrecks and Spanish treasure. Even the sandy Gulf Coast offers occasional wrecks.

Reef, spring, or wreck, there remains one constant: a valid diver certification card. All divers must have a C card and all dive operators must see it *before* the dive. Most operators also check divers' logbooks to verify their experience level. Without a logbook, don't expect more than a shallow dive.

Warm water, clouds of fish and easy depths make the Keys one of the most popular places in the world to learn to dive. Certification can take as little as three or four days. For non-divers, most coastal resorts offer 'resort courses' – an hour or two of basic instruction and a closely supervised dive on a shallow reef.

The best all-round guide to Florida diving and dive shops is the monthly magazine *Florida Scuba News, 1324 Placid Pl., Jacksonville, FL, 32205; tel: (904) 693-0474*. Water temperatures range from 65–70°F in northern springs to 80–85°F in the Keys in summer. Most divers wear 3 mm or heavier wet suits all year. Dive shops and dive boats hire out all the necessary gear, but at least think about buying equipment – price competition among dive shops is fierce.

There are more than 300 springs in North–Central Florida and the Panhandle. Some operators claim visibility up to 300 ft. Even when it's less, expect to see anything from fish and turtles to fossilised mastodons and live alligators – divers are supposedly too big and noisy for gators to attack. Divers are too noisy for manatees, too. To see them up close, trade the scuba gear for snorkelling. Manatees and snorkellers often meet at **Manatee Springs State Park**; *tel: (904) 493-6072*. Other popular freshwater dives include **Ginnie Springs**; *tel: (800) 874-8571*, **Blue Springs State Park**; *tel: (904) 775-3663*, and **Devil's Den**; *tel: (904) 528-3344*.

Uncounted Spanish ships went down on the rocky reefs along the Treasure Coast, Sebastian Inlet to Palm Beach. Gold and silver coins from the vanished fleets still wash ashore after violent storms but known Spanish wrecks have been picked clean. There's always the chance of stumbling across a new treasure trove, but most divers explore reefs and modern wrecks. Genuine wrecks are scattered south from Jupiter; artificial reefs are concentrated off Fort Lauderdale and Miami. There are also wreck dives off Key Largo (the *Duane*, at 100 ft and the *Benwood*, 45 ft, are popular), but more divers come for the coral and fish. Favourite reefs include Molasses off Key Largo, Sombrero and Coffin's Patch off Islamorada, and Looe Key National Marine Sanctuary near Little Torch Key. The most crowded diving site is **Christ of the Abyss**, near Key Largo. The nine-ft bronze statue looks up through 16 ft of water with open arms. It looks like he's beckoning divers and snorkellers down, but the statue is also a popular backdrop for underwater weddings.

made at least four weeks in advance. For those who would rather take their chances on the water, **Holiday Casino Cruises**, *MM100, Holiday Inn; tel: (800) 843-5397* or *(305) 451-0000*, has gambling cruises.

## ISLAMORADA

**Tourist Information: Islamorada Chamber of Commerce**, in a red railroad caboose bayside, *MM82.5, US Hwy 1, Islamorada, FL 33036; tel: (305) 664-4503*, open Mon–Fri 0900–1700.

### ACCOMMODATION

**Chesapeake Resort**, *MM83.5 oceanside; tel: (800) 338-8811 or (305) 664-4662* is moderate–expensive, but has an expansive lagoon as well as swimming pools. **Holiday Isle Resort & Marina**, *MM84 oceanside; tel: (800) 327-7070 or (305) 664-2321*, lures a younger and livelier crowd. The moderate–pricey hotel and efficiency complex has an enormous artificial beach, several pools, multiple bars, and the busiest nightlife north of Key West. **Cheeca Lodge**, *MM82 oceanside; tel: (800) 327-2888 or (305) 664-4651*, pricey, is favoured by Americans from the North East who prefer their informality to be as ostentatious as possible. Cheeca is a favourite with former US President George Bush. There are also a number of budget–moderate motels in the area.

### EATING AND DRINKING

The **Islamorada Fish Company**, *MM81.5 bayside; tel: (305) 664-9271*, has a budget lunch and dinner restaurant and fish shop. The best tables are on the dock, with the broad expanse of Florida Bay on one side and fishing boats unloading the fresh catch on the other. **Manny and Isa's Kitchen**, *MM81.5; tel: (305) 664-5019*, offers budget–moderate Cuban and Spanish dishes. **Hog Heaven**, *MM85;* *tel: (305) 664-9669*, is the hottest popular local sports bar and late night venue.

### SIGHTSEEING

The **Florida Keys Wild Bird Center**, *MM93.6 bayside, Tavernier, FL 33070; tel: (305) 852-4486*, a bayside nature reserve and wild bird rehabilitation centre south of Key Largo, is the best place in the Upper Keys for land-based birdwatching. **Windley Key Fossil Reef State Geologic Site**, *MM85.5 bayside, Windley Key*, a former quarry, shows how the Keys developed. The fine limestone was created as coral between ice ages about 125,000 years ago. As the water level dropped during the Wisconsin Ice Age 25,000 years later, what had been living reefs emerged as low islands. Mangroves began to appear along the fringes of the island, trapping plant matter that slowly decayed into soil. As the water level continued falling to current levels, birds and tides carried plant seeds north from the Caribbean. Rock-hard lignum vitae, gumbo limbo, mahogany, cinnamon, poison and other trees formed forests.

The Keys and surrounding mangroves became important rest stops for millions of migrating birds. Deer, racoons, alligators, crocodiles and other animals spread down from the Everglades. Many of the Keys even had water, shallow pools that have largely disappeared as ground water has been sucked out of South Florida and the Everglades for agriculture and people. By the time immigrants from America and the Bahamas began settling the Keys in the 1810s, the area was rich in fish, birds, land animals and hungry insects. Rangers at **Long Key State Park**, *MM67.5* have keys to quarries.

**Theater of the Sea**, *MM84.5 oceanside; tel: (305) 664-2431*, is another abandoned quarry. Regular shows feature trained dolphins and sea lions, a 'bottomless' boat that opens a window into the underwater world; swims with dolphins can be booked in advance.

Islamorada grew up as a fishing community. Fishing, commercial and sport, remains a major industry. **Bud 'n' Mary's Marina**, *MM79.8 oceanside*, is one of the busiest sport fishing marinas for ocean fish. **Papa Joe's**, across US Hwy 1, *MM79.7; tel: (800) 539-8326 or (305) 664-5005*, specialises in backcountry fishing for tarpon, bonefish, permit, redfish, and snook as well as water tours.

Two of the most popular destinations are **Indian Key State Historic Site**, *oceanside from the Triangle of History* (a state historical marker), *Indian Key Fill, MM77.5*, and **Lignumvitae Key State Botanical Site**, *bayside*, both at *PO Box 1052, Islamorada, FL 30336; tel: (305) 664-4815*. **Indian Key** was a wrecking, or marine salvage, base in the 1830s, the third largest town in Florida after St Augustine and Key West. The town was destroyed in an 1840 Indian raid during the Second Seminole War and has been partially excavated. Ranger-guided tours available Thur–Sun at 0900 and 1300.

**Lignumvitae Key** was a private holiday island until recent years. It has the original caretaker's mansion and the largest patch of virgin forest remaining in the Keys. The key is named after its lignum vitae forest. Guided ranger tours Thur–Sun at 1000 and 1400. Access to both Keys is by boat, either private or charter, from **Papa Joe's** and **Robbie's**, *MM84.5; tel: (305) 664-8498*. Departures are timed to join ranger tours.

**San Pedro Underwater Archaeological Preserve**; *tel: (305) 664-4815*, is just south of Indian Key. The preserve protects the remains of the *San Pedro*, a Spanish treasure ship that sank in 1733.

The wreck, in 27 ft of water, has been picked clean of valuables, but ballast bricks, cannon and other large artefacts remain for divers to explore.

## LONG KEY

Much of the key is part of **Long Key State Park**, *MM67.5, PO Box 776, Long Key, FL 33001; tel: (305) 664-4815*. The park has a long natural beach as well as hiking trails, a lagoon canoe trail, camping and picnicking. The small town of **Layton** is all that remains of a bustling railroad station and fishing lodge built by Henry Flagler.

The **Long Key Viaduct**, connecting Long Key with the fishing town of Conch Key, is just over two miles long. **Duck Key**, once a salt factory, was deserted from the 1830s until a causeway was built in the 1950s. **Hawk's Cay Resort and Marina**, *MM61, Duck Key, FL 33050; tel: (800) 432-2242 or (305) 743-7000*, a pricey resort and dolphin research facility, share the key with an equally pricey residential community.

## GRASSY KEY

The huge grey statue of Mitzi, *Flipper* of television and cinema fame, marks the **Dolphin Research Center (DRC)**, *MM59 bayside, PO Box 522875, Marathon Shores, FL 33052; tel: (305) 289-1121*. The DRC has one of the world's largest populations of domesticated dolphins, which move freely between artificial lagoons and Florida Bay. There are continuing language and training projects as well as daily tours and swims with the dolphins. Dolphin swims should be booked at least a month in advance, but there are occasional last minute cancellations.

The **Grassy Key Dairy Bar**, *MM58.5 oceanside, Rte 1, Box 355, Marathon, FL 33050; tel: (305) 743-3816*, is a local budget favourite for fresh fish and burgers.

## MARATHON

**Tourist Information: Greater Marathon Chamber of Commerce**, *MM53.5 gulfside, 12222 US Hwy 1, Marathon, FL 33050; tel: (800) 262-7284* or *(305) 743-5417*, open daily 0900–1700. **Marathon Airport**, *MM52, 900 Aviation Blvd; tel: (305) 743-2155*, has flight information.

### ACCOMMODATION

Marathon is the second largest town in the Keys (after Key West). There are a number of older moderate motels along US 1, but Hd and HJ are the only chains. The Chamber of Commerce and **Florida Keys Reservations**; *tel: (800) 853-7737* or *(305) 289-1104*, can make bookings.

### SIGHTSEEING

**The Museum of Natural History of the Florida Keys**, *MM50 gulfside, PO Box 536, Marathon, FL 33050; tel: (305) 743-3900*, open Mon–Sat 1000–1700 and Sun 1200–1700, explains the natural history of the Keys. Walking trails through **Crane Hammock** explore the largest undisturbed hardwood hammock in the Keys; a restored 19th-century Bahamian home shows the cultural contributions made by immigrants from the Bahamas.

The **Florida Keys National Marine Sanctuary**, *PO Box 500368, Marathon, FL 33050; tel: (305) 743-2437*, headquartered on the museum property, protects the entire Florida Keys. Local feelings about new coral and wildlife protection measures run high: commercial fishermen and treasure hunters expect their access to the reef to be curtailed; tour operators (dive and snorkel boats, fishing outfitters, etc) expect to see business grow.

**Sombrero Beach**, *MM50 oceanside, 3 miles east from US Hwy 1*, has an expansive lawn, picnic facilities and a natural beach. Beach lovers should save themselves for Bahia Honda State Park (see p. 98).

The **Pigeon Key Visitors Center**, *MM48 oceanside, PO Box 500130, Marathon, FL 33050; tel: (305) 289-0025*, is a green train carriage once used on Henry Flagler's FEC Railway. Follow signs for Knight's Key Resort, then continue to the centre. The centre is also the terminus for shuttles to **Pigeon Key**, a primary construction and maintenance facility for the railroad from 1908 to 1935. Seven historic buildings that survived hurricanes are being restored to their original condition. The four-acre island is 2.2 miles from Knights Key at the end of an original section of the **Seven Mile Bridge**. Visitors can walk or cycle to Pigeon Key, but private vehicles are banned from the old span. The two lane span, which originally carried train tracks, was featured in Arnold Schwarzenegger's 1994 film *True Lies*.

Seven Mile Bridge is the longest span in the Keys. The high rise section is also the highest point in the Keys, but unfortunately no stopping is allowed. The original bridge is visible from the new span, compete with fallen railings (the original train tracks) and trees growing in the old roadbed.

## BIG PINE

**Tourist Information: Lower Keys Chamber of Commerce**, *MM31 oceanside, Big Pine, FL 33043; tel: (305) 872-2411*, open Mon–Fri 0900–1700.

### ACCOMMODATION

**Dolphin Marina**, *MM28.5, Rt 4, Box 1038, Little Torch Key, FL 33042; tel: (800) 553-0308* or *(305) 872-2685* has moderate–expensive self-catering flats just a few steps away from the water. **Little Palm Island**, *28500 Overseas Highway, Little Torch Key, FL 30042; tel: (800) 343-8567 or (305) 872-2524*, is the most expensive and exclusive resort in the Keys, a private island three miles from Dolphin Marina. **Sugarloaf Lodge**, *MM17 gulfside, PO Box 440148, Sugarloaf Key, FL 33044; tel: (305) 745-3211*, moderate, has wonderful sunset views and daily dolphin shows.

### Eating and Drinking

Sun brunch at **Little Palm Island** is pricey, but the food may be the best in Florida. **Sugarloaf Lodge**, budget–moderate, has sunsets to rival Key West without the crowds or high prices. **Peddler's Bakery**, *MM30.5 gulfside, Big Pine Shopping Plaza; tel: (305) 872-4725*, has budget breakfasts and good take away Key Lime pie. The **Good Food Conspiracy**; *tel: (305) 872-3945* and **Mark's Place**; *tel: (305) 872-1230*, both *at MM30 oceanside, Big Pine Key, FL 33043*, have excellent sandwiches.

### Sightseeing

**Bahia Honda State Park**, *MM37.5 oceanside, Rte 1, Box 782, Big Pine Key, FL 33043; tel: (305) 872-2353*, has the best beach in the Keys, a series of sandy crescents opening onto the Atlantic Ocean. The park also has swimming areas, excellent snorkelling (the north end of the ocean beach is best), moderate–expensive oceanside cabins, a marina, kayaks for hire and a lagoon trail to use them, walking trails, a concession shop and a restaurant. The scenic peak is **Old Bahia Honda Bridge**, a railroad bridge with the roadway atop the superstructure. A short portion of the old bridge is open to foot traffic; follow the path from the toilets opposite the concession store. The new Bahia Honda Bridge is the second longest span on the Overseas Highway.

Big Pine Key is the last refuge for the endangered **Florida Key deer**, the smallest North American deer. Whitetailed deer, marooned on the Keys by rising ocean levels about 4000 years ago, evolved into a subspecies the size of dogs. Once hunted almost to extinction, there are now about 300 of the 24-inch high deer. The **National Key Deer Refuge** headquarters, *MM30.5 gulfside, Big Pine Shopping Plaza, PO Box 430510, Big Pine Key, FL 33043; tel: (305) 872-2293*, is open Mon–Sat 0830–1700. The best time to see Key deer is at dawn and sunset. The most likely places to find them are at the **Blue Hole**, *Key Deer Blvd, four miles north of Refuge headquarters*, along the **nature trail**, *¼ mile further north on Key Deer Blvd*, and **No Name Key**, *east of Big Pine Key on Watson Blvd*.

The Blue Hole, which is actually green most of the year from algae, is a former quarry that has filled with rain water. The pond holds a variety of fish, turtles and several alligators. Walking either the nature trail or No Name Key requires long sleeves and insect repellent against voracious mosquitos and flies.

**Looe Key National Marine Sanctuary**, *offshore from Little Torch Key, Rt 1, Box 782, Big Pine Key, FL 33043; tel: (305) 872-4039*, was named after HMS *Looe*, pronounced 'loo', which sank on the reef in 1744. The reef is a popular destination for snorkelling and diving boats. The best-equipped snorkel-only boat is **HMS Looe**, *MM28.5 oceanside at Dolphin Marina; tel: (800) 553-0308 or (305) 872-2685*. Ultralight aeroplane flights over the reef and Keys are also available at the marina; *tel: (305) 744-7202*. **Blue Water Tours**, *PO Box*

431386, Big Pine Key, FL 33043; tel: (800) 822-1386, and **Outback Safari**, Rte 3, Box 226, Big Pine Key, FL 33043; tel: (800) 522-2824 or (305) 872-3355, offer guided tours of the gulfside backcountry.

A pair of white blimps is usually visible on the north shore of Cudjoe Key at **Cudjoe Key Air Force Station**, MM22.5 gulfside, at the end of Blimp Blvd. The blimps, which sometimes hover 15,000 ft above the key, carry radar used for drug traffic surveillance and transmitters for TV Marti, an anti-Castro television station supported by the US government and beamed to Cuba. **Perky's Tower**, MM17 behind Sugarloaf Lodge, is an unpainted wooden tower built in the 1920s to attract bats, which a would-be developer hoped would control the mosquitoes that plagued his customers. The bats fled, and so did the customers, but modern spraying and drainage has turned the mosquito plague into a mere nuisance. Key West (see p. 100) is another 17 miles west.

## Florida Foods

The surest way to start a food fight in Florida is to disparage the state's unofficial icon, Key Lime pie. Second best is to ask what makes a 'real' Key Lime pie. The basic ingredient – Key Lime juice, condensed milk, eggs and sugar – make a custard, but even that much is subject to debate.

Key Limes, a lumpy, tart, yellowish fruit not much larger than a giant olive, once grew wild throughout the Keys. Housing developments replaced most native vegetation and the most common limes became the bland green rounds floating atop drinks. A few pie makers still import the real fruit from the Yucatan (Mexico) or Caribbean island orchards.

Then there's the question of what surrounds the limey custard. Purists insist that the *only* topping is meringue baked to a golden brown, the only proper crust is made of crushed wholemeal biscuits called Graham crackers (Digestive biscuits).

But modern tastes run more towards whipped cream on top and traditional tart pastry beneath. At least that's how many bakeries make Key Lime pie, in part because whipped cream and pie crust are cheaper to prepare than meringue and Graham cracker crusts. Weather and technology play a part, too. On a hot day, which is most of the year in Florida, a piece of frozen Key Lime pie is wonderfully rich and cool. And unlike whipped cream, meringue just doesn't freeze well.

Conch is another culinary icon as well as the State shell. The giant marine snails have been a staple food for centuries, the horned, pink-lipid shell a tourist trinket as long as there have been tourists. Conch is even the name used by residents of the Keys, after early Bahamian immigrants who made the common creature a major part of their diet. Once a term of approbation applied by 'strangers' from the mainland, conch, pronounced 'conk', has become a title of pride.

Unfortunately, the growing popularity of the sweet-fleshed conch led to overfishing in the 1980s. Too few conch and growing water pollution have brought the conch to the brink of extinction in Florida waters. It is now illegal to harvest conch anywhere in Florida. The tons of conch consumed as chowder, salad, fritters (minced with onions and spices, then fried) and other preparations are all imported from the Caribbean.

# KEY WEST

Key West is the cul de sac of the Overseas Highway, a tropical island in all but location. Island and town lie low on the glistening sea, backyards and gardens filled with the scent of frangipani, hibiscus and ginger. Sidewalks sit shadowed beneath the spreading branches of mango and kapok trees. Harbours are home to fleets of battered fishing boats, sleek new yachts, glass-bottomed sightseeing boats and refugee rafts. Heat is the norm, but the sea breezes keep summer days cool and Arctic cold fronts sometimes send thermometers plunging. Key West is a traveller's haven, replete with exclusive resorts and ramshackle buildings that haven't seen a can of paint in decades. Key West is the end of the road.

## Weather

Key West lies 70 miles north of the Tropic of Cancer, but the weather is strictly tropical. Average temperatures hover around 70–80°F, but summer days regularly peak above 90°F with humidity near 100%. And while winter frost has never been recorded in the town, cold fronts occasionally follow seasonal refugees from northern climes, keeping temperatures around 40–45°F for days at a stretch. Aug and Sept are the hottest, Jan and Feb the coolest. Rain can fall any time during the year, but storms are usually short and localised – Key West may have a downpour while Stock Island, four miles north, is dry and sunny. The height of the hurricane season is Aug–Oct, but Key West itself has not suffered significant hurricane damage since 1919. Believers credit this to a stone shrine to Our Lady of Lourdes that was built in the 1920s.

## Tourist Information

**Key West Chamber of Commerce**, *402 Wall St, Key West, FL 33040* (Mallory Square, behind the Sponge Market); *tel: (800) 527-8391* or *(305) 294-2587*, is open seven days 0830–1700. The **Key West Welcome Center**, *3840 N. Roosevelt Blvd, Key West, FL 33040; tel: (800) 296-4482* or *(305) 296-4444*, is open daily. The Chamber of Commerce has more brochures on things to do, but the Welcome Center has more complete information on accommodation and provides free bookings for lodgings and activities. Welcome Center souvenirs are somewhat less expensive than similar items along Duval St.

## Arriving and Departing

### Airport

**Key West International Airport**, *S. Roosevelt Blvd; tel: (305) 296-5439*, is on the Atlantic (south-eastern) coast of the island, three miles (10 mins) from the historic district. A taxi to city centre hotels costs $6.50.

### By Car and Bus

US Hwy 1 is the only road in, or out, of Key West. The highway becomes Roosevelt Blvd at the east end of the island. North Roosevelt, along the north shore, is US 1, leading to the historic Old

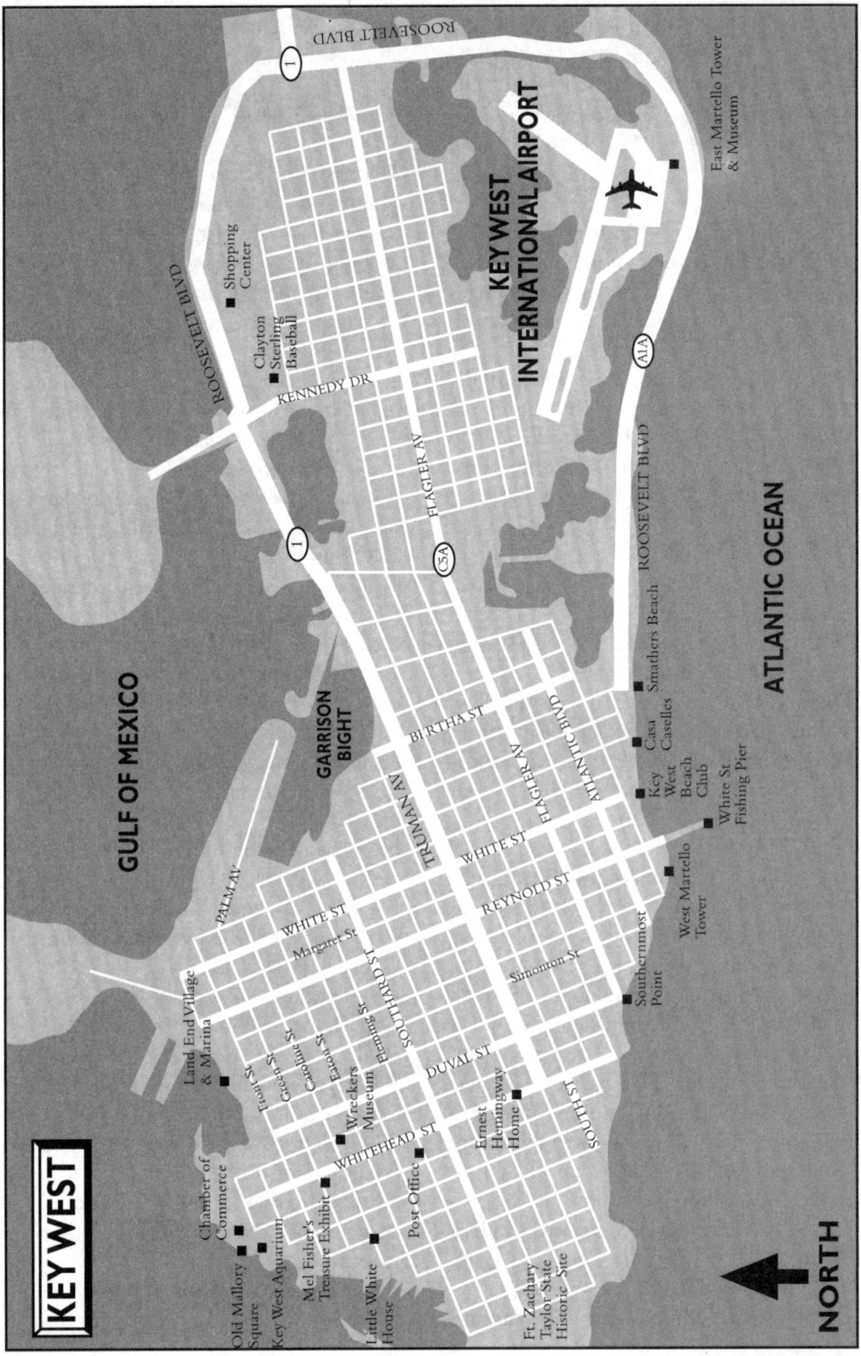
KEY WEST
GULF OF MEXICO
ATLANTIC OCEAN
KEY WEST INTERNATIONAL AIRPORT
GARRISON BIGHT
NORTH
ROOSEVELT BLVD
ROOSEVELT BLVD
ROOSEVELT BLVD
KENNEDY DR
FLAGLER AV
BERTHA ST
TRUMAN AV
FLAGLER AV
ATLANTIC BLVD
WHITE ST
WHITE ST
REYNOLD ST
PALM AV
Margaret St
SOUTHARD ST
Simonton St
Fleming St
Eaton St
Caroline St
Green St
Front St
DUVAL ST
WHITEHEAD ST
SOUTH ST
1
1
C5A
A1A
Shopping Center
Clayton Sterling Baseball
East Martello Tower & Museum
Smathers Beach
Casa Caselles
Key West Beach Club
White St Fishing Pier
West Martello Tower
Southernmost Point
Land End Village & Marina
Chamber of Commerce
Old Mallory Square
Key West Aquarium
Mel Fisher's Treasure Exhibit
Wreckers Museum
Little White House
Post Office
Ernest Hemingway Home
Ft. Zachary Taylor State Historic Site

Town district. South Roosevelt, along the south shore, is US A1A, leading past the airport and Smathers Beach. The **Greyhound Bus Lines** depot is at *615-1/2 Duval St; tel: (305) 296-9072.*

## By Boat

Cruise ships dock at **Mallory Square** or the **Truman Annex**, both off Front St south of Duval St. Other large passenger vessels use the same docks, but all vessels must leave before sunset. To protect the Key West sunset, local laws allow nothing to come between Conchs (the locals) and the setting sun. Most day boats and private vessels tie up at the **Lands End Marina**, at the foot of Margaret St.

## GETTING AROUND

The entire island of Key West is just four miles long by two miles wide. Most areas of interest are concentrated in the 13-block historic district centred around **Duval St** at the west end of the key. Traffic in the tourist area is heavy from late morning until early the next morning. Duval St can seem more like a linear car park than a major street, especially on Fri and Sat evenings.

Parking is extremely limited throughout the island. Large hotels have car parks, but most guesthouses leave visitors to find parking on the street. The easiest way to get around is on foot, although many visitors hire bicycles or motor scooters.

Cycles are the better (and cheaper) choice. Speed makes scooters more fun than cycles, as well as considerably more dangerous on the island's poorly paved roads. Most scooters are uninsured, leaving the driver responsible for any accident damage, and helmets are rare. Cycles are more manoeuvrable in heavy traffic than scooters, and cycling is easy. The summit of Key West is Solares Hill, all of 18 ft above sea level.

## STAYING IN KEY WEST

### Accommodation

Limited space, especially in and around the historic district, keeps Key West lodging prices among the highest in the state. The most desirable addresses are on or around lower Duval St, near Front St, where most shops, restaurants and bars are concentrated. Lodgings on Duval are likely to be on the noisy side, but it is often possible to ask for a room at the back. Properties on the side streets (Caroline, Whitehead, Fleming, Simonton, Petronia etc.) are equally convenient and considerably quieter.

The only special concern for safety is to watch out for drunken drivers, especially when traffic begins to thin out around midnight. Street crime is rare in the historic district; there is some reported night-time criminal activity in Little Bahama, west of Whitehead St and south of Petronia St. It is always a good idea to ensure that nothing of any value or interest is visible inside parked cars.

Key West chains include *BW, DI, Hd, HJ, Hy, Ma, Rm* and *Sh*. Booking services include the **Key West Welcome Center**, *3804 N. Roosevelt Blvd; tel: (800) 284-4482* or *(305) 296-4444*; **I Love Key West**, *1601 N. Roosevelt Blvd; tel: (800) 733-5397* or *(305) 294-4265*; and **AA Accommodation Center**, *816 Eaton St; (800) 732-2006* or *(305) 296-7707*. The **Key West Innkeeper's Association**; *tel: (800) 492-1911*, books more than two dozen guesthouses and Bed and Breakfast inns. All booking services are free.

Most Key West lodging is in guesthouses or Bed and Breakfast inns, usually

# Key West

Key West was discovered by Spanish explorers in the 16th century. Officially, nothing more happened until 1815, when Spain gave the island to Juan Pablo Salas, an artillery officer. In reality, it was the occasional haunt of Native Americans, then of pirates who preyed on rich ships sailing between Europe and colonies in the Caribbean and South America. In 1822, the United States bought Florida, including the Keys.

The growing sea trade between New Orleans and the Eastern United States was squeezed into the same narrow Florida Straits that had troubled Spanish mariners for three centuries. The channel, passing between Key West and Cuba, then turning north between the Atlantic coast of Florida and the Bahamas, was lined with treacherous reefs.

John Simonton, a New Jersey speculator, bought Key West from Salas and convinced the US government to establish a naval base at the west end of the island. As Commodore David Sydney Porter cleared out the pirates, Simonton and his partners turned the barren key into the most successful wrecking, or ship salvage, base North America had ever seen.

Key West quickly became the largest town in Florida. Mallory Square, on the harbour, was lined with cavernous warehouses. Lookouts climbed tall watchtowers before dawn each day to scan the horizon for ships that had run up on the reefs the previous night. When a ship was spotted, wrecking crews raced to the scene in shallow draft boats. The first wrecker on the scene became master of the wreck, taking charge of the beleaguered ship, its crew, passengers and cargo.

Passengers and crew were put ashore free of charge, but the wreck was pure profit. Saleable merchandise was sold at auction or parcelled out to family and friends. Wreckers towed damaged ships into Key West and resold them to the original owners, or to anyone else, for the right price.

Key West led a charmed life. As lighthouses began warning ships off the reefs and wrecking declined, a sponge fishing industry developed. Political unrest in Cuba brought an influx of refugees and Key West became the Cigar Capital of the World. During much of the 19th century, Key West had the highest per capita income in America. In 1912, Henry Flagler's Overseas Railroad, the first direct land connection to Miami, brought a steady stream of tourists. Fishing, shipping, smuggling and military bases brought more wealth.

When the Great Depression hit in 1929, Key West collapsed. Nearly all private businesses died. The US government closed military bases. In 1935, the Labor Day hurricane washed away the railroad and tourism. Local government surrendered and turned Key West over to the Federal Emergency Relief Program.

Federal officials decided that Flagler had been right about turning Key West into a tourist destination. Federal funds turned what was left of Flagler's Folly into the paved Overseas Highway, which opened in 1938, Tourists returned in droves. World War II brought the military back. After the war, soldiers and sailors kept coming back for the pleasant winter weather and the relaxed attitude that valued pleasure over profit.

Gay holidaymakers enjoyed the same easy tolerance. So did van loads of hippies who wandered down the Overseas Highway in the late 1960s and early 1970s. The long-haired strangers brought a taste for Grateful Dead music and added square grouper (marijuana) to the list of preferred intoxicants, but the town hardly noticed. Quarter of a century later, there still isn't much in Key West so important that it can't wait for just one more beer.

historic homes that have been subdivided into several guest units. Guesthouses seldom serve breakfast, Bed and Breakfast's do. Air conditioning is universal, swimming pool and spa or Jacuzzi facilities common. Guests usually have to fend for themselves to find parking on the street. Guesthouse or Bed and Breakfast prices are comparable to hotel and motel rates.

The most coveted rooms in Key West are at the **Pier House**, *One Duval St; tel: (305) 296-4600*, and the **Ocean Key House**, *Zero Duval St; tel: (305) 296-7701*. On opposite sides of the foot of Duval St, both are luxurious, pricey, and provide spectacular sunset views from most rooms – non-guests can enjoy the same view for the price of a drink at their ground floor sunset bars. Pier House has the unadorned sunset; the Ocean Key House pool deck bar overlooks the sunset hubbub at Mallory. The Ocean Key House is all suites (it was built as a time-share resort); Pier House is a traditional hotel. The **Hyatt Key West**, *601 Front St; tel: (305) 296-9900*, has similar ocean views and prices. The other flash hotel is **Marriott's Casa Marina**, on the Atlantic coast toward the airport at *1500 Reynolds St; tel: (305) 296-3535*. It was originally built as the luxury finale to Henry Flagler's Overseas Railroad.

**Atlantic Shores**, at the east (Atlantic) end of Duval, *510 South St; tel: (800) 526-3559* or *(305) 296-2491*, has the largest clothing-optional pool in Key West and moderate–expensive prices. Good inn and guesthouse choices include **Casablanca**, moderate, *900 Duval St; tel: (305) 296-0637* (with an outstanding restaurant, also moderate), **Pilot House**, *414 Simonton St; tel: (800) 648-3780* or *(305) 294-8719*, the expensive **Cuban Club**, *1108 Duval St; tel: (800) 432-4849* or *(305) 296-0465*, the pricey **Curry Mansion Inn**, *511 Caroline St; tel: (800) 253-3466* or *(305) 294-5349*, moderate **Courtney's Place**, *720 Whitmarsh Lane; tel: (800) 869-4639* or *(305) 294-3480*, moderate–expensive **Authors of Key West**, *725 White St (at Petronia); tel: (800) 898-6909* or *(305) 294-7381*. **Curry House**, expensive, *806 Fleming St; tel: (800) 633-7439* or *(305) 294-6777* is one of the leading guesthouses catering for homosexuals. The least expensive lodgings may be the budget **Key West International Youth Hostel**, somewhat removed from the action at *718 South St; tel: (305) 296-5719*.

Accommodation prices generally fall with distance from the western end of Duval St and Mallory Square. Low season (May 1–Oct 1) also brings a sharp drop in rates. Motels near the separation of US 1 and US A1A at the east end of the key are generally the least expensive as well as the least convenient to Duval St.

## Eating and Drinking

Don't take the brochures exclaiming about Key West museums, beaches, sailing, fishing, snorkelling and scuba diving too seriously. The attractions and activities are real enough, but most visitors go lightly during the day to save themselves for eating and drinking. The city's unofficial slogan is 'any excuse for a party', whether it's the Conch Republic in April, Hemingway Days in July, or Fantasy Fest in Oct, a licentious Halloween celebration that rivals Mardi Gras in New Orleans.

Whatever the season, New World and Floribbean cuisine are ubiquitous, though they too often appear as sweet tropical fruit sauces poured over perfectly ordinary pieces of fish, chicken or beef. It's always best to ask what fish is fresh. Dolphin (the fish, not the mammal) is caught locally most of the year, but grouper, swordfish, stone crab and other favourites are seasonal. The most popular starting time for dinner is the hour after sunset, whether it falls at 1730 in Dec or 2030 in June. Bookings are always advisable for dinner, especially during the busy winter season.

**Casablanca**, *914 Duval St; tel: (305) 296-0637*, moderate, has some of the tastiest seafood, best service and most tempting sweets in town. Deep verandas and ceiling fans keep the indoor-outdoor restaurant comfortable on even the hottest and wettest days. **Blue Heaven**, budget–moderate, *729 Thomas St; tel: (305) 296-8666*, has excellent Caribbean fare and outside tables, but don't sit too near the rope swing. **Applerouth Grille**, *416 Lewinski* (off Duval St between Fleming and Southard Sts); *tel: (305) 294-5662*, has budget Caribbean fare as well as the biggest burgers and hot dogs in Key West, a good selection of microbrew beer and evening entertainment. **El Siboney**, budget–moderate, *900 Catherine St; tel: (305) 296-4184*, may be the best Cuban restaurant in Key West.

**Turtle Kraals**, moderate, *1 Lands End Village; tel: (305) 294-2640*, adds a Southwest bent instead of the usual Caribbean flavours. It's also one of Key West's livelier and noisier night spots. The budget–moderate **Half Shell Raw Bar**, across the street at *231 Margaret St; tel: (305) 294-7496*, has a great selection of seafood and beers but can get noisy. **Kelly's Caribbean Bar Grill & Brewery**, *301 Whitehead St; tel: (305) 293-8484*, has the country's southernmost brewery in an elegant mansion that was the first office for Pan American World Airways, but the beer and food are eminently forgettable. **Louie's Backyard**, *700 Waddell Ave; tel: (305) 294-1061*, is the most prestigious, and by far the priciest, restaurant in Key West. A sunset drink on the oceanside deck is a more affordable alternative to dinner.

Best bets for cheap breakfast are **Croissants de France** (croissants, *café au lait* and quiche), *816 Duval St; tel: (305) 294-2624*, and **Pepe's Cafe** (Cuban and American with fabulous *café con leche*), *806 Caroline St; tel: (305) 294-7192*. Lunch and dinner are budget–moderate at both. Most bars along Duval St also serve light meals, some from counters that open onto the pavement. Fast food outlets are found on N. Roosevelt Blvd.

## Communications

The **post office** is at *400 Whitehead St, Key West, FL 33040*. Mail can also be addressed to hotels.

## ENTERTAINMENT

Key West is an adult playground, a tradition that goes back to the town's earliest days. Bar owners and patrons ran a number of 19th-century preachers out of town when the men of the cloth persisted in inveighing against the evils of alcohol and sex. The four dozen or so local churches and synagogues have learned to turn a blind eye to bars that boom until 0400 most mornings, but little else has changed. Competition keeps beer and spirit prices low, especially during the slow summer season. Drink specials and hangovers are the order of every day. Police generally ignore laws forbidding open containers of alcohol on the streets so long as revellers remain reasonably controlled.

The nightly party is centred on the bars, clubs and lounges that have settled near the first eight blocks of Duval St. Many offer live music from mid-afternoon until closing, but the intensity

# KEY WEST

increases noticeably around 1700. **Sloppy Joe's**, *201 Duval St; tel: (305) 294-5717*, is one of Key West's oldest, largest, loudest and most popular bars. Named after Sloppy Joe Russell, the bar owner who became one of Ernest Hemingway's closest friends in Key West, the bar features a string of hard-driving rock bands every night. The original Sloppy Joe's that Hemingway frequented, now called **Capt. Tony's Saloon**, *428 Greene St; tel: (305) 294-1838*, is smaller but equally raucous.

**Barefoot Bob's**, *525 Duval St; tel: (305) 296-5858*, bills itself as a 'local's hangout', but the steady diet of Grateful Dead-style music lures as many tourists as Conchs.

Parrotheads (Jimmy Buffett fans) flock to **Margaritaville**, *500 Duval St; tel: (305) 292-1435*, which is as much restaurant and Buffett paraphernalia shop as it is bar and music venue. **Hog's Breath Saloon**, *400 Front St; tel: (305) 296-4222* serves up a varied diet of rock and blues. **Turtle Kraals**, *1 Lands End Village; tel: (305) 294-2640*, prides itself on offering the best line up of Blues bands in the Keys. **Schooner Wharf**, *202 William St; tel: (305) 292-9520*, is probably the liveliest night-spot in town.

Even the sunset is lively in Key West. In the early 1970s, resident hippies began gathering at **Mallory Square**, which faces west, to watch the sun go down and share whatever beer, rum and marijuana they could afford. As musicians, magicians, jugglers, mimes and buskers began showing up to perform and pass the hat, sunset gradually evolved into Sunset.

Mallory Square is still one of the best places in Key West to watch the sun go down, but it's more a maelstrom of tourists jostling for a view than a party. Count on sharing the small square with a mime artist, a magician, an escape artist, a juggler, a singer and a thousand or so strangers packed elbow to elbow.

For a less crowded view of the sunset, stake out a table at the waterfront bars in front of the **Pier House** or **Ocean Key**

## The Conch Republic

Key West has always been a place apart. In April 1982, federal agents threw a surprise roadblock across US 1 at Florida City. Northbound traffic backed up toward Key Largo as immigration officers and drug agents searched boots, glove boxes and ashtrays while demanding proof of US citizenship from all who wanted to pass, documentation that Americans were not required to carry. Key West city officials rebelled.

When legal protests failed to budge the federal roadblocks, Mayor Dennis Wardlow read an official proclamation of secession on the steps of the Miami Federal Courthouse. The next day, Wardlow led a crowd of 500 to the Key West Chamber of Commerce, on Mallory Square, struck a federal representative on the head with a loaf of stale Cuban bread, and declared war on America in the name of the Conch Republic.

The Conch Republic (under the motto 'We succeeded where others failed') immediately surrendered and demanded $2 billion in aid. The money never arrived, but the world press did, and the Florida City roadblock quietly disappeared.

The Conch Republic is alive and well throughout the Keys, but it's cause for April celebration in Key West. The annual party is part of the island's odd place in the world, legally part of the United States but psychologically and physically closer to the Caribbean than to Miami.

**House** (see p. 102). The best seats fill up about 90 mins before sundown. Another choice spot, if somewhat isolated, is the top floor bar of the **Holiday Inn La Concha Hotel**, *430 Duval St; tel: (305) 296-2991*, the tallest building in Key West since its opening day in 1926.

There are also a variety of sunset cruises. Most leave from Lands End Marina with recorded music and open bars. Cruises last about two hours. **Seebago**; *tel: (305) 294-5687*, has two 60-ft catamarans with plenty of shade on deck. **Floridays**; *tel: (305) 744-8335*, carries passengers aboard a traditional 60-ft yacht. **Rumrunners**; *tel: (305) 294-1017*, masquerades as a floating island with reggae, palm fronds and rum punch. **Moondancer Cruises**; *tel: (305) 294-0990*, is a floating discotheque, complete with flashing neon.

There are more sedate activities, but not many. **Applerouth Grille** and **The Green Parrot**, *601 Whitehead St; tel: (305) 296-9198*, stage regular evening poetry slams – readings by local poets who may, or may not, deserve the time they get at the microphone. The **Tennessee Williams Fine Arts Center**, at the Florida Keys Community College, *5901 West College Rd; tel: (305) 296-1520*, sponsors visiting music, dance and dramatic performances as well as local stage productions. The **Spirit Theatre**, *802 White St; tel: (305) 296-0442*, stages a nightly re-creation of a Victorian seance. **Theatre Key West**, *1075 Duval St; tel: (305) 292-3725*, **Waterfront Playhouse**, *Mallory Square; tel: (305) 294-5015*, and the **Red Barn Theatre**, *319 Duval St; tel: (305) 296-9911*, offer stage productions.

## SHOPPING

Shopping is Key West's number two activity after drinking, or so shop owners would like visitors to believe. Bars from Hog's Breath to Margaritaville and Sloppy Joe's seem to sell as many souvenir T-shirts, beer coolers and hats as they do beers and rum drinks.

The packaging and selling of Key West is a time honoured tradition. The speculators who founded the place and the wreckers who settled came with the express intent of creating a shopping centre. They succeeded beyond anyone's wildest imagination. The risks were high, but so were the profits from selling salvaged cargoes to merchants from New Orleans, Havana and New York. By 1840, Key West was the largest town in Florida.

Duval remains the main shopping street, a mix of souvenirs, clothing, jewellery, artworks and T-shirts amidst the bars and restaurants. T-shirts and other merchandise that is unpriced is open to bargaining, a rarity in America. If the final price seems too high, walk away. There's bound to be another shop with identical merchandise a few doors away. **Mallory Market**, *Mallory Square; tel: (305) 294-5168*, has the largest concentration of shopping on the island.

T-shirt shops with prices that seem too good to be true probably are. The surprisingly low prices usually buy only a plain white shirt. Adding any kind of decoration can double or triple the final price. The **T-shirt Factory Outlet**, *316 Simonton St; tel: (305) 292-2060*, has some of the best genuine prices in town. For more formal clothing, **Fast Buck Freddie's**, *500 Duval St; tel: (305) 294-2007*, has a good selection at somewhat elevated prices. **Key West Aloe Factory**, *524 Front St; tel: (305) 294-5592*, open daily 0900–1700, makes and sells aloe vera sun and cosmetic products.

# KEY WEST

For serious shopping, wait for Miami or try one of the shopping centres on N. Roosevelt Blvd. The one exception is **Key West Island Bookstore**, *513 Fleming St; tel: (305) 294-2904*, open daily 1000–1800, which is the best stocked bookseller in the Keys.

## SIGHTSEEING

Key West has three sightseeing areas: the Old Town historic district surrounding Duval St, the Dry Tortugas islands (70 miles west) and the beaches.

The best bet for beach fun is to drive north to MM37 and **Bahia Honda State Park** (see p. 98). Key West beaches are almost entirely artificial: sand is barged in from the Bahamas, packed onto the rocky shore, washed back out to the Bahamas, and is barged back again a few years later. **Fort Zachary Taylor** has one of the best beaches on Key West, and one of the least used. **Smathers Beach**, along S. Roosevelt Blvd from the airport to Bertha St, is the most popular. It offers two miles of sand with volleyball nets, gazebos, shade trees, toilets, food vendors along the street and watercraft rentals offshore. **Higgs Beach**, at the end of White St, is smaller, but has similar facilities. **Marriott's Casa Marina** beach is open to hotel guests and anyone who rents a cabana for the day. **South Beach** is a tiny patch of sand opening onto the **South Beach Seafood and Raw Bar**, *1405 Duval St; tel: (305) 294-2727*. **Pier House Beach**, surrounded by the Pier House Hotel, is reserved for beach club guests.

## Tours

The **Conch Tour Train**; *tel: (305) 294-5161*, and the **Old Town Trolley**; *tel: (305) 296-6688*, offer 90-min rolling tours of Old Town. The Tour Train stops at the corner of Duval and Front Sts and the Key West Welcome Center on N. Roosevelt Blvd. The Trolley makes 14 stops along a more complete route through Old Town. Riders can leave and reboard their tour at any stop. Several companies offer cycling tours. **Island Aeroplane**, *Key West International Airport; tel: (305) 294-8687*, offers biplane tours of Key West and surrounding reefs. **Discovery Tours**, *251 Margaret St; tel: (305) 293-0099*, has daily boat tours of nearby reefs out of Lands End Marina with underwater viewing windows. A number of companies offer daily snorkelling tours.

## Walking Tours

The **Old Island Restoration Foundation**, *Old Mallory Square; tel: (305) 294-9501*, the group responsible for the preservation of many of Key West's original buildings, has created a 50-stop walking tour of Old Town. The **Pelican Path** visits most of the historic homes and buildings open to the public as it passes dozens of guesthouses and private residences. The walk takes about an hour, plus time for house and museum visits. The **Key West Historical Homes Association** has its own **Museum Walk** tour of seven historic buildings. Brochures for both self-guided walks are free at the Welcome Center and the Chamber of Commerce.

For visitors in a hurry, Caroline St is the most scenic walk in Key West. The three blocks between Simonton and Front Sts range from the gates of President Harry Truman's **Little White House**, *111 Front St; tel: (305) 294-9911*, open daily 0900–1700, to the **Curry Mansion Inn**, *511 Caroline St; tel: (305) 294-5349*, open daily 0900–1700. The street continues eastward toward the Lands End Marina.

## Museums

Many ships wrecked on the Key West reefs were too badly damaged to refloat, but their timbers and planks made solid building materials. Thanks to the times when Key West was too poor to knock down its old buildings and rebuild, the city has more entries on the National Register of Historic Places than any other municipality in the United States – more than 3000 buildings, many of them constructed from shipwreck wood.

The oldest building in Key West is the **Wrecker's Museum**, *322 Duval St; tel: (305) 294-9503*, open daily 1000–1600. The house, built about 1829, displays artefacts and furnishings of the era. A list of licensed wreckers and a list of wreckers cashiered for misconduct both reflect family names that still control the politics and fortunes of Key West. The **Shipwreck Historeum**, *1 Whitehead St; tel: (305) 292-8990*, is a museum and theatrical re-creation of the heyday of wrecking during the successful salvage of the *Isaac Allerton* in Aug 1856. The **Key West Lighthouse**, *938 Whitehead St; tel: (305) 294-0012*, follows the evolving history of the Keys lighthouses that eventually put the wreckers out of business. The museum is on the grounds of the 90-ft tall Key West Lighthouse, built in 1847. The lighthouse is no longer operational.

Key West took the Union side during the American Civil War, not because Conchs were against slavery (city merchants sold slaves as well as anything else), but because of four brick forts: East and West Martello Towers, Fort Zachary Taylor, and Fort Jefferson. **Fort Zachary Taylor State Historic Site**, *PO Box 289, Key West, FL 33041; tel: (305) 292-6713*, open daily, on the south-west corner of the key, was the island's main defence. Much of the ruined red brick fort has been excavated, uncovering the largest arsenal of Civil War cannon in the US. The fort is now a popular picnic and Atlantic Ocean swimming beach, more frequented by locals than visitors.

The towers, East and West Martello, were built to protect the approaches to Fort Taylor. Advances in armament made the towers and fort obsolete before they were completed. **East Martello Museum & Gallery**, *3501 S. Roosevelt Blvd; tel: (305) 296-3913*, is overflowing with artefacts from Key West history, from ship models to railroad memorabilia and local art. West Martello has become the **Key West Garden Club**, *north end of Higgs Memorial Beach; tel: (305) 294-3210*, open most weekends.

Fort Jefferson is the centrepiece of **Dry Tortugas National Park**, *PO Box 6208, Key West, FL 33041; tel: (305) 242-7700*, 70 miles west of Key West. Once the haunt of British, Dutch, French and Spanish pirates, the Dry Tortugas and surrounding reefs dominated North Caribbean sea lanes for centuries. Construction of the fort was started in 1846 to control sea traffic between New Orleans and the Atlantic, but was never finished.

During the Civil War, Fort Jefferson was a desolate Union prison. The most famous inmate was Dr. Samuel Mudd, convicted of treason for innocently setting the leg John Wilkes Booth broke after killing President Abraham Lincoln in 1865. Mudd was eventually pardoned in return for medical work during a yellow fever epidemic that ravaged the island. The military had largely abandoned the island by the 1880s.

Today, Fort Jefferson is the most complete Civil War-era brick fort on

America's East Coast, its only wards are the thousands of sooty terns and other migratory birds that stop in the Tortugas each year. Park and fort are open for tours, primitive camping (no water, housing, meals or supplies), snorkelling, swimming and birdwatching, but the only access is by seaplane or boat. The **Yankee Fleet**, *PO Box 5903, Key West, FL 33040; tel: (800) 942-5464 or (305) 294-7009*, runs all-day boat trips to the fort. Seaplane visits can take as little as

## Ernest Hemingway

Hemingway sailed into Key West in 1928 with his second wife, Pauline Pfeiffer, and called it 'the St Tropez of the poor'. He spent most of the next 12 years in Key West, writing between bouts of fishing, big game hunting, and reporting on the Spanish Civil War. They were some of his most productive years: *A Farewell To Arms, Death In The Afternoon, Green Hills of Africa, To Have and Have Not, For Whom The Bell Tolls* and *The Snows of Kilimanjaro* are among the most famous products of mornings spent writing and evenings spent boozing with his buddies at Sloppy Joe's bar.

Hemingway worked hard developing the persona of Papa Hemingway, the macho fisherman, hunter, brawler, drinker and gambler, but the reality was considerably less glamorous. He kept a strict working regimen in Key West, home by 2300, up at dawn, writing in his first floor studio until noon, and being a father to two growing sons. Hemingway's workaday life in Key West may not have matched his mythology, but it created the literary reputation that won him a Nobel Prize in 1954.

Novelist John Dos Pasos had originally suggested that Hemingway try Key West. After a decade of chilly winters in Paris, the 29-year old Hemingway was entranced with the warmth of Key West. When the local bank refused to cash a royalty cheque because they had never heard of him, Hemingway tried the nearest bar as the second most likely source of cash. Bar owner Joe Russell had never heard of Ernest Hemingway either, but liked his look and cashed the cheque. The two remained fast friends until Sloppy Joe died in 1941.

The abandoned house at 907 Whitehead St that Hemingway bought had been built in 1851 by shipping magnate Asa Tift. The coral block home had one of the few cellars in Key West, the quarry the building materials had been taken from, and the island's first swimming pool. Pauline imported most of the tropical plants that still grace the garden, including many of the spreading shade trees. When an early guidebook listed the house as a tourist attraction, Hemingway built the brick wall around the property to keep the crowds at bay.

Hemingway also collected cats, their only common feature having six toes instead of the usual five. Descendants of his cats still loll about the house and grounds, consuming five tonnes of cat food yearly.

In 1936, writer Martha Gelhorn travelled to Key West to interview Hemingway for a magazine article. They met again in Spain the next year while both were covering the Spanish Civil War. She eventually became his third wife.

Hemingway divorced Pauline in 1940. He moved his personal papers and possessions into a storeroom at Sloppy Joe's and left Key West for Cuba and Martha. Pauline and the two boys remained in the Whitehead St house until Hemingway's suicide in 1961.

The **Hemingway House Museum**, *907 Whitehead St, Key West, FL 33040*, is open daily 0900–1700, admission: $6.

two hours, but cost two to four times more than the boat journey.

## Duval St

Those who boast about Key West like to call Duval the longest street in the world, stretching from the Atlantic to the Caribbean in 14 blocks. It *is* the tourist artery of Key West and, like many arteries, has become clogged with the advancing decades. But despite the crowds, Duval St reflects more of the changes that have built Key West than any other part of town.

**Havana Dock**, the outdoor waterside bar at the Pier House, *One Duval St*, was once the dock for steamers bound for Havana, Cuba. Just up Duval at the corner of Front St, the ornate **First Union Bank**, *422 Front St; tel: (305) 292-6603*, reflects the wealthy years seen by Key West early this century, from the marble-lined lobby to the ornate gilt ironwork protecting the teller cages.

In the 1890s, Key West produced more than 100 million cigars a year until Cuban cigar makers were lured north to Tampa. Today, two of the few cigar makers left in Key West work in the lobby of the **Southern Cross Hotel**, *326 Duval St; tel: (305) 294-3200*, rolling, moulding and cutting cigars by hand for the tourist trade. **Rodriguez Cigar Factory**, *113 Kino Plaza; tel: (305) 296-0167*, and **Key West Cigar Factory**, *3 Pirates Alley (off Front St); tel: (305) 294-3470*, are the only other cigar makers in town. But despite historic connections, cigar smoke is not welcome in most restaurants, bars, or other enclosed spaces in Key West.

**Ripley's Believe It or Not! Odditorium**, *527 Duval St; tel: (305) 293-9694*, features oddities from around the world, including a selection of antique diving equipment that could have been used in Key West. One of the oddities that Ripley's omitted is the **Southernmost Point**, a buoy-shaped monument *at the corner of Whitehead and South Sts*, that may be the most photographed spot in Key West. The marker sits at the most southerly point in the continental United States (most of the state of Hawaii is further south). A sign points the way to Cuba, just 90 miles due south but off limits to US citizens and residents.

**Mallory Market** and **Clinton Square Market**, *Front and Whitehead Sts*, are probably the second most photographed areas. What was once the centre of the old waterfront is now a busy tourist complex of shops and attractions. **Key West Aquarium**, *1 Whitehead St; tel: (305) 296-2051*, has an excellent collection of local marine life, from colourful reef fish to fully-grown sharks and several species of endangered turtles. The **Mel Fisher Maritime Heritage Society Museum**, *200 Greene St; tel: (305) 294-2633*, is usually just called the Treasure Museum. Modern-day wrecker Mel Fisher (he prefers 'salver') has built a successful career finding and salvaging ancient shipwrecks, including colonial Spanish ships loaded with tons of treasure. The museum details Fisher's methods and discoveries with artefacts from ships including the *Nuestra Señora de Atocha* and *Santa Margarita*, Spanish treasure ships that went down in a hurricane on 5 Sept 1622.

Displays run the gamut from corroded cannon, sparkling pieces of eight and million-dollar gemstones to iron manacles from an English slave ship. The gift shop sells treasure pieces, including silver coins and bars and genuine (or less expensive reproductions) 18th-century gold jewellery salvaged from ancient wrecks. The museum building was originally a naval storehouse.

# EVERGLADES NATIONAL PARK

Everglades National Park, 1.5 million acres and only one-seventh of the actual Everglades region, occupies the southern tip of the Florida peninsula, stopping just short of the Keys.

Away from the burgeoning cities and ever-encroaching suburban building spree, the Everglades are a land-based island, a relic of the swamps, estuaries and rich wildlife habitat that once covered much of southern Florida. Sharp-bladed, slender shafts of green sawgrass shelter birds wintering over in the subtropical warmth of one of the lushest flyways on earth. Basking alligators laze unchallenged by the bounty hunters lurking just outside the national park borders. Airboats, plentiful on the park's perimeter, may not cross the boundary. Hardy souls canoe or kayak around the numerous small islands in Whitewater and Florida Bays. A ranger leads a 'slough slog' through quicksand-like muck to find delicate spongy lifeforms and multi-coloured apple snails bobbing in the water.

The Everglades hide more than overhanging trees, gators and greenish waters and the wide expanses visible from a vehicle. Four areas define the Everglades: the protected sea of Florida Bay, jungle, mangrove swamps and the prairies swaying with sawgrass and cypress hammocks. The American crocodile, peregrine falcon, Florida panther, West Indian manatee, wood stork and four varieties of turtle are among the fifteen endangered species sheltered within Everglades National Park. Take at least three days to get out into or onto the park's watery element; walk the boardwalks near bald cypresses; spot a myriad of birds, from raptors to woodpeckers, herons to roseate spoonbills. Bicycle, canoe, kayak, fish, or hike the paths into raw nature.

From Apr to Sept mosquitos thicken the air and the Everglades is only for those well-swathed with insect repellent, long sleeved shirts, trousers and hats. Hurricanes may lash in Aug. From Dec–Feb, Everglades skies, trees and ponds are thick with thousands of birds. Deer, rabbits and the ubiquitous gators wander paths threatened by few predators.

## TOURIST INFORMATION

The **Main Visitor Center** is ten miles south-west of Homestead at the park's east side; *tel: (305) 242-7700,* open 0800–1700 daily. **Shark Valley Visitor Center**; *tel: (305) 221-8776,* is open 0830–1700 daily, and **Gulf Coast Visitor Center;** *tel: (941) 695-3311,* opens 0730–1700. Must-haves are the Everglades Park brochure, the *Everglades & Biscayne National Parks Guide* and the *Visitor Guide to National Parks and Preserves of South Florida,* free at park entrances and visitor centres.

Contact **Everglades National Park Headquarters**, *40001 State Rd 9936,*

# EVERGLADES NATIONAL PARK

**EVERGLADES MAP**

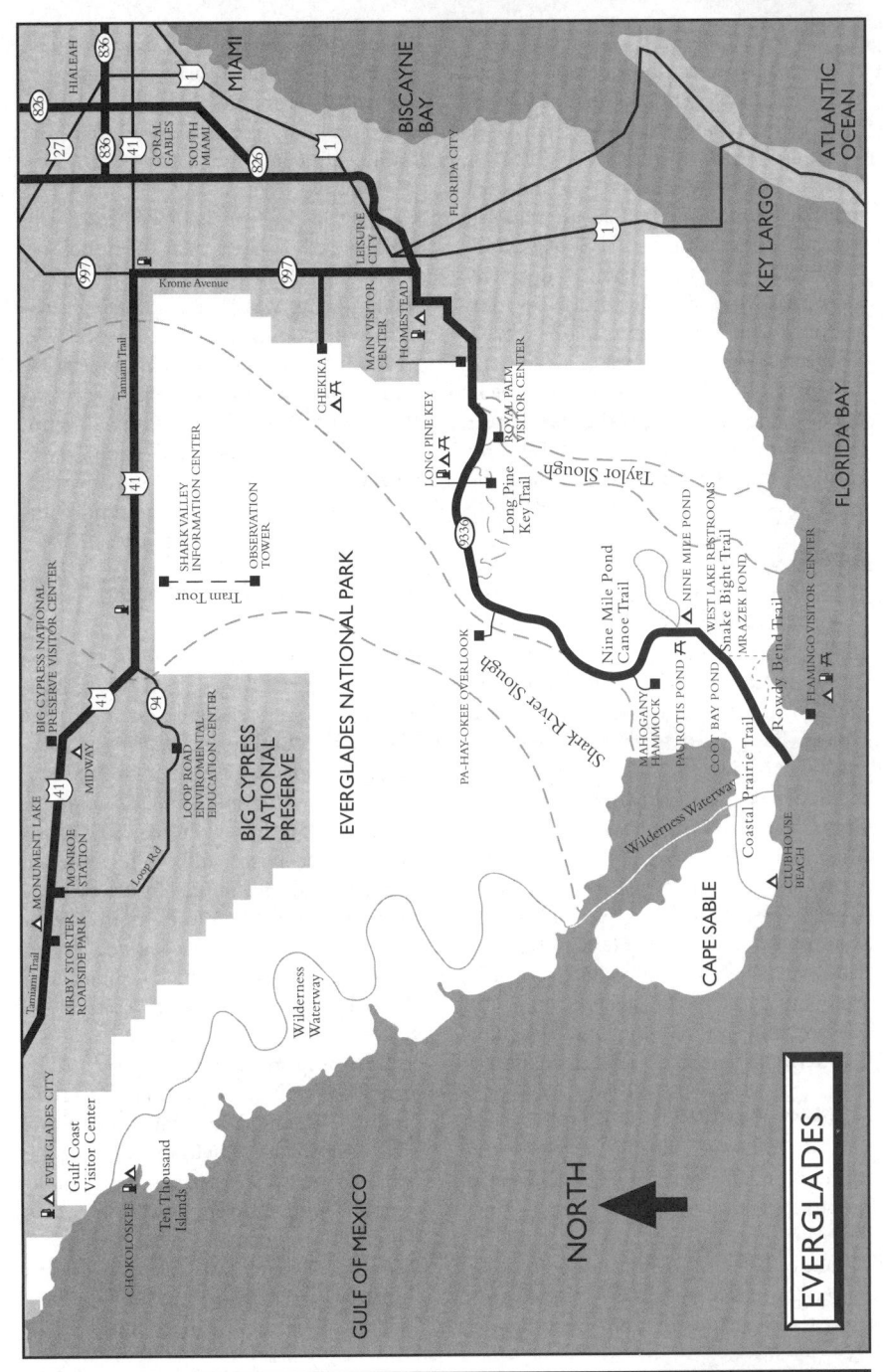

# EVERGLADES NATIONAL PARK

Homestead, FL 33034; tel: (305) 242-7700, for advance information and to request schedules of seasonal activities. **TW Recreational Services, Inc.**; tel: (800) 600-3813 or (305) 253-2241 or (941) 695-3101, books lodging and boat and tram tours. To anticipate regional weather near Miami, tel: (305) 661-5065.

Not all areas of the park are disabled-accessible. Muddy trails and observation platforms and towers can make wheelchair access impossible. Seasonal rains can turn normally dry areas into wet muck. Accessible trails include **Pineland** near the Main Visitor Center, **Mahogany Hammock**, **West Lake Trail** and the paved **Shark Valley Loop Road**.

## Arriving

There are three entrances to the Everglades, all offering differing scenery and appeal. From the Main Visitor Center south-west of Homestead, it is 38 miles to the Flamingo Visitor Center on Florida Bay. Thirty-five miles west of Miami along Hwy 41 (Tamiami Trail), is the **Shark Valley Entrance**. Just west is **Big Cypress National Preserve** (See Miami–Fort Myers route, p. 118). Eighty miles west of Miami, just south of Hwy 41 in Everglades City, is the Gulf Coast Visitor Center, the Ten Thousand Islands Gateway. The roads into the Everglades are not connected. Decide what to explore and go to that area's Visitor Centre for orientation and information.

## Getting Around

Car, motorcycle and RV are the main means of seeing the Everglades. There are no bus tours in Everglades National Park. To access the park, you must arrive by vehicle or bicycle. **Greyhound**; tel: (800) 231-2222, offers the closest bus connection, from Miami to Homestead, about 10 miles from the park. Covered, open-air tram tours and bicycle rentals are offered at Flamingo and Shark Valley; boat tours and canoe and boat hire can be found at Flamingo and Gulf Coast (Everglades City).

The 38-mile main road has well-marked parking areas near overlooks and ponds. Arrange for drop-off at hiking trailheads, as verges are sometimes too narrow to accommodate a vehicle. Mosquitoes and other nipping insects can make unprotected walking a torture. Wear long trousers, long-sleeved shirts, closed walking shoes and apply insect repellent before venturing onto any path. Clouds of mosquitoes can descend without warning, a stinging agony.

## Staying in the Everglades

### Accommodation

Except for tent camping and RV pitches, in-park accommodation is limited to the **Flamingo Lodge**, *1 Flamingo Lodge Hwy, Flamingo, FL 33034-6798*; tel: (800) 600-3813 or (305) 253-2241 or (941) 695-3101, which has 102 motel rooms, 20 cottages with fully-equipped kitchens, and one suite. Florida Bay is a lawn away from the motel rooms. Prices vary by about $20 between the lowest season, May–Oct, and high season, mid-Dec–Mar, but are always moderate. Book well in advance for high season.

**Camping information** is provided by Everglades National Park Headquarters; tel: (305) 242-7700, for **Flamingo, Lone Pine Key** and **Chekika**, though no bookings are made. **Flamingo** is the only campsite with showers – all cold water. For Chekika's open season dates, tel: (305) 251-0371. Pitches are filled on a first come, first served basis.

Unique to the Everglades are backcountry pitches, used by hikers and canoeists. Covered wooden *chickees*, lean-tos with chemical toilets, stand above the water and mosquito-ridden mangroves. Designated beach sites have pitches on massive piles of shells, or sandy beaches where loggerhead sea turtles nest in season. Ground sites are clearings once used by Native Americans or early residents. Backcountry permits must be obtained in advance, in person, from a ranger at the Flamingo or Gulf Coast Visitor Centers. The permit must be carried while camping. All supplies must be carried in and all trash must be carried back out.

### Eating and Drinking

TW Recreational Services controls food and drink facilities as well as park lodging. **Flamingo Lodge Restaurant** affords excellent views of Florida Bay sunrises and is open 0700–2100, Nov–Apr for budget–moderate meals. Beneath the restaurant, from Dec–Apr, the **Buttonwood Lounge and Cafe** serves budget salads, pizza and the like. Both restaurants are open for lunch and dinner from 1130–2000, May–Oct. A store has snacks and beverages, suitable for light breakfasts or picnic provisions. Everglades City, the park's north-west gateway, has several restaurants.

### Sightseeing

Southern Florida's traditional landscape and wildlife survive in the Everglades. While a vehicle is necessary for access to the national park areas, canoeing, bicycling or walking brings the experience closer. From Dec to Mar, park rangers lead a 'slough slog', 'swamp tromp' or 'slog and trog' walk through the sawgrass prairies or swamps. Watching for snakes makes wading thigh- or waist-deep in water a thrill, and hones observation.

### Flamingo

Along the 38-mile road from the Main Visitor Centre to Flamingo, it's possible to have the illusion that the world ends just across the green-gold sawgrass prairie or among the twisting vines curling around trees. Birds are hushed, masking their numbers. The road slopes gradually downhill as it moves to the south-west. Each stop along the road and every trail is different, requiring at least a half-day to drive to Flamingo.

If time is limited, get a succinct glimpse of the Everglades by hiking the trails at **Royal Palm Hammock**, two miles from the Main Visitors Center. The **Anhinga Trail's** half-mile boardwalk zigzags over sawgrass prairies and the profuse bird life of **Taylor Slough**. The **Gumbo Limbo Trail's** exotic name comes from the common tree with paper-thin peeling red bark. The trail wanders through a tropical hardwood hammock, an area about a metre above water level, where tree roots thrust from the water. Hardwoods and royal palms form a jungle, towering over air plants, orchids, ferns and mosses. Four miles down the road, picnic under the slash pines at **Long Pine Key**.

En route to Flamingo the landscape changes from pine woods to prairies broken by elevated islands, or hammocks, of bald cypresses. So-called dwarf cypresses, perhaps a century old, grow angular but no taller than 15 ft. At 10.7 miles along the road the elevation is three ft, just high enough above water to support trees, not marshes. At 12.5 miles, a boardwalk on the **Pa-hay-okee** (Seminole language for 'Grassy Waters') **Overlook Trail** leads to a covered two-storey observation platform with a panoramic view of the hammocks, sawgrass prairies and resident local hawks.

Stroll on a cool and shady boardwalk around the **Mahogany Hammock** at 19.5 miles. One magnificent, sprawling mahogany tree is the largest in the US. Orchids and tree ferns cling to live oaks, mahoganies and other hardwood species, as meandering vines and tree snails confirm the feeling of a dense green jungle.

Tiny **Paurotis Pond**, named after the rare paurotis palms at mile 24, has picnic tables and a small boat ramp. Angling is permitted, but don't eat the pond fish which are contaminated with mercury. A few miles down the road is the trailhead for **Nine Mile Pond Canoe Trail**, a 5.2-mile loop trail navigated by non-motorised watercraft.

Toilets, a 7.7-mile one-way canoe trail and a nature trail make **West Lake**, at 30.3 miles, a welcome stop. The four species of mangrove; red, white, black, and buttonwood, line the half-mile-long boardwalk to the lake, clearly showing the mixture of fresh, brackish and salt water flowing around the area. Ducks and coots glide over the lake's surface; mullet, snook and redfish break the surface as they feed; racoons patrol the shoreline mangroves for oysters and crabs.

At 32.7 miles, narrated tram tours along the **Snake Bight Trail** describe flora, fauna and waterfowl in screened comfort from Dec–Apr. A 1.8 mile walking trail is favoured by mosquitoes, chiggers, alligators, snakes and treefrogs. It terminates in a boardwalk view of Florida Bay, with excellent birdwatching year round at low tide. A 2.6-mile alternative return to the main road is via **Rowdy Bend Trail**, with an incongruous variety of flora: buttonwood (mangrove) mixed with cactus and yucca.

**Mrazek Pond** at 33.6 miles is a birdwatcher's paradise from Dec–Mar when wading birds arrive to feed on abundant fish in shallow water. The water shimmers with natural activity; no boating, canoeing or fishing is permitted. Just beyond are picnic tables and a canoe launch at **Coot Bay Pond** (channel).

**Flamingo** has lodging; a campsite; restaurants; a lounge; general store; excursion bookings; bicycle, boat and canoe hire; petrol; and a National Park Visitor Center which dispenses information and issues camping and backcountry permits. An amphitheatre treats evening visitors to ranger talks on wildlife, ecosystems and astronomy under a panoply of real stars.

Flamingos, the symbol of Florida, are very rare in Flamingo. The former fishing village, known for its mosquitoes and frequent hurricanes in the late 19th century, became infamous as the centre of plume hunting. Egrets, herons and spoonbills were slaughtered for feathers, used to adorn women's hats. An outcry in 1905 led to the criminalisation of plume sales in 1910 and to the decline of the village on stilts. The establishment of the national park in 1947 resurrected the town.

On the main park road's west side is **Eco Pond**, a mecca for visitors day or night. This artificial evaporation pond receives treated effluent from Flamingo. A 0.2-mile trail follows the pond shore from a wooden observation platform. From Dec–Apr, wildlife experts loan out binoculars and lead early morning, hour-long walks around the pond. Roseate spoonbills fly off, white ibis flutter in mangrove limbs, coots swim between the grasses, red-tailed hawks swoop through the sky, and painted buntings flutter by. Gators bask on the banks, and anhingas spread their wings to the sun. Rabbits frisk in the underbrush, while frogs croak nearby. At dusk, clouds of birds fly to safety in the trees growing in the pond's

# EVERGLADES NATIONAL PARK

centre, and squawking ensues as the birds settle for the night. A winter full moon illuminates white birds roosting around Eco Pond.

## Shark Valley

Access **Shark Valley** on the park's northern side from Hwy 41 (the Tamiami Trail), across the road from the Miccosukee Cultural Center. (See Miami–Fort Myers route, p. 117) There are numerous alligators along the 15-mile **Lookout Tower Road** which loops through **Shark Slough**, the park's largest slough. Park at the **Shark Valley Visitor Center**, then take the two-hr covered tram tour. Seven miles south of the Visitors Center is a circular staircase up the 65-ft high **Observation Tower**. Yellow-crowned night herons roost close by; take the quarter-mile-long **Tower Trail** for butterfly spotting. Except for a stop at the tower, tram tourists stay seated in the vehicle. A hired bicycle requires more energy, but is more flexible, and allows for walking en route. Lack of shade demands judicious walking. Dec–Mar, take a ranger-led slough slog to experience nature's wet grandeur. Depart from the Visitor Center for all activities equipped with water, snacks and cover-ups.

## Everglades City – Gulf Coast

Just west of Big Cypress National Preserve and south-east of Naples is **Everglades City**, launching point for kayaks, canoes and boats through the mangroves, sandy shoals and small dots of land that make up the **Ten Thousand Islands**. Dolphins are seen year-round, and manatees inhabit the area.

Park at the **Gulf Coast Visitor Center** car park lot to catch guided boat tours with **Everglades National Park**

**Boat Tours;** *PO Box 119, Everglades, FL 33929; tel: (941) 695-2591 or (800) 445-7724, only in Florida.*

The ultimate canoe or kayak trip involves navigating for 7–10 days along the 99-mile **Wilderness Waterway Canoe Trail** from the Gulf Coast Visitor Center to Flamingo. Backcountry camping permits must be obtained from either visitor centre. Canoeists are instructed as to routes and necessary provisions. Water is unavailable en route and transport from the trail's terminus should be arranged in advance. Even day trip canoeists or kayakers should be aware that the isolated wilderness has a price – water is often choppy, winds and tides are high, lightning often races over the water, and there is no shade away from chickee campsites.

Fifteenth-century Calusa Indians left mounds of shells for burials, houses and refuse piles on many of the small mangrove islands, like Sandfly Island. **Chokoloskee** town is on a 20-ft-high, 150-acre shell mound. Chokoloskee **Outdoor Resorts;** *tel: (941) 695-2881,* offers a launch site for fishing boats. Find fishing guides through the **Everglades City Chamber of Commerce;** *tel: (941) 696-3941,* to lead anglers to mangrove snapper and other gamefish. Purchase saltwater fishing licenses at Flamingo Marina. Freshwater licenses for fishing from Nine Mile Pond north must be obtained outside the national park.

Everglades sunsets are beautiful. Prime spots for watching romantic sunsets are the boardwalk by the **Gulf Coast Visitor Center** and **Clubhouse Beach** overlooking Florida Bay at the west end of the **Coastal Prairie Trail** near Flamingo. Flamingo's sunrises are opalescent pastel, quiet except for the island-based birds feeding noisily on Florida Bay.

**SIGHTSEEING**

# MIAMI–FORT MYERS

Before the Atlantic and Gulf Coasts were filled with strip malls, housing developments and fashionable barrier island resorts, the swamps and estuaries of South Florida were little disturbed. Occasional hunters and fishermen forayed into the glades, meeting the small bands of Native Americans who lived in stockaded villages. Alligators and tawny panthers hunted. Birds of prey found snakes and small rodents among the grasses and low-lying palms. Bald cypress trees clumped in mounds on hammocks, and millions of birds wintered in the lush feeding grounds.

Railroads, the automobile, and a land boom changed the glades forever. By the late 19th century, Henry Flagler's Florida East Coast Railway and Henry Plant's rail operation in the south-west demanded a land connection. Unstable swampland was available, but it cost a great deal to create and stabilise a roadbed above water.

The Tamiami Trail, now part of Hwy 41, was created by dredging a canal and parallel road out of the wilderness between Miami and Naples from 1915–28. The 'Tampa to Miami Trail' proved a boon when completed, bringing tourists and settlers lured by a land boom that went bust with the Great Depression.

Hwy 41 is arguably both Florida's most interesting and mind-numbing route. The law requires drivers to turn on headlights, both to warn oncoming traffic and to prevent lurching off the road into the endless sea of grass between Sweetwater and Ochopee. Stops at some of the parks and nature preserves can extend the 150-mile route between Miami and Fort Myers from a three-hour drive to a multi-day excursion.

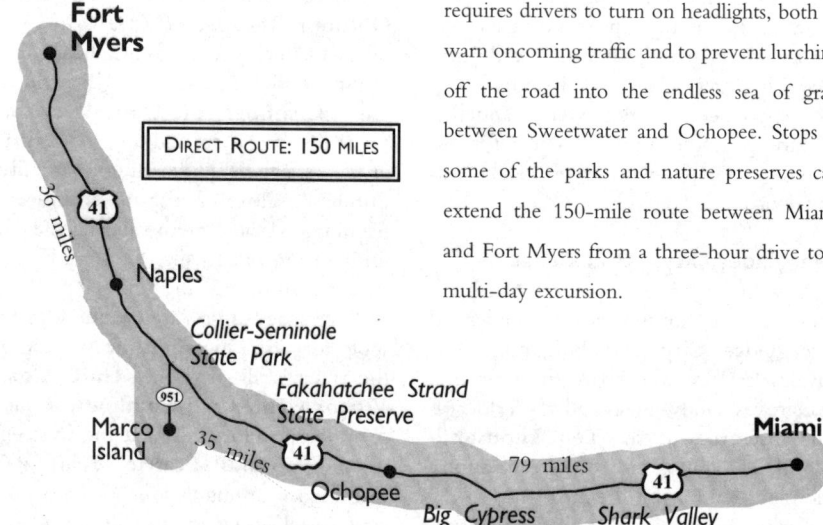

DIRECT ROUTE: 150 MILES

# MIAMI-FORT MYERS

## ROUTE

From Bayside Marketplace in downtown Miami, take Biscayne Blvd south and turn right onto E. Flagler St. The road jogs right, goes under I-95 and continues as W. Flagler. Turn left on Le Jeune Rd (S. W. 42nd Ave), then turn right onto the **Tamiami Trail** (S.W. 8th St), west of Little Havana. Follow Hwy 41, the Tamiami Trail, west from Sweetwater to **Everglades National Park** and its **Shark Valley** and **Miccosukee Tribal Headquarters**. Hwy 41 turns north-west to **Big Cypress National Preserve**, and **Ochopee**, passing a turn-off to Everglades National Park's Gulf Coast Visitors Center in **Everglades City**. Further west are **Fakahatchee Strand State Preserve** and **Collier-Seminole State Park**. Take a side track south on CR 951 to **Marco Island** and **Briggs Nature Center**. Return to Hwy 41 and drive north to **Naples** and **Fort Myers**. There are few verges on Hwy 41, as the raised road is just wide enough for one lane in each direction. Fill the petrol tank before the Tamiami Trail.

## SHARK VALLEY

Everglades National Park **Shark Valley Visitors Center;** *tel: (305) 221-8776,* open 0830–1700, is 35 miles from central Miami. (See Everglades chapter, p. 112). There is no accommodation. The nearest camping is at Big Cypress National Preserve; for hotels and motels try Everglades City. A two-hour **tram tour;** *tel: (305) 221-8455,* or a hired bicycle are the ways to explore Shark Valley (see p. 117).

### Miccosukee Indian Village

West of Shark Valley is one of three **Miccosukee Tribe of Indians of Florida** reservation areas; *PO Box 440021, Tamiami Station, Miami, FL 33144; tel: (305) 223-8380.* Before 1700, these Native Americans belonged to the Creek Confederacy in Georgia, Alabama and North Florida. Gradual migrations south landed the band in central Florida; the Seminole Wars forced them into hiding in the Everglades. The building of the Tamiami Trail drained hunting lands; the establishment of the national park took much of the remaining traditional land.

**Miccosukee Indian Village**, open 0900–1700, offers guided tours (price $5) of traditional *chickees* (open-sided huts on stilts), men carving wood, women sewing bright patchwork clothes, a museum displaying tribal clothing of several eras and **alligator wrestling**. Tribal members run **airboat tours** through the river of grass. The budget **Miccosukee Restaurant;** *tel: (305) 223-8388,* on the north side of Hwy 41, specialises in fry bread, fried catfish and frogs legs.

## BIG CYPRESS NATIONAL PRESERVE

**Big Cypress National Preserve,** *Superintendent, HCR 61, Box 11, Ochopee, FL 33943; tel: (941) 695-2000* or *Oasis Visitor Center; tel: (941) 695-4111,* open 0830–1630, has information on hiking and camping. Hunting, oil and gas exploration and cattle grazing continue in this 2400-square-mile area partially covered with water flowing from the Okeechobee Waterway south to Everglades National Park. One-third of the swamp, hammock, marshes, prairies and mangrove estuaries are covered with dwarf bald cypress. Birds like the red cockaded woodpecker and wild turkey and animals such as mink and the rare Florida panther range through the preserve. Avoid deer and wild–hog hunting season mid-Nov–Dec.

A 24-mile **Loop Road**, Rte 94,

leaves Hwy 41 at the Tamiami Ranger Station at Forty Mile Bend, then rejoins it at Monroe Station, west of the Oasis Visitor Center. The first nine miles are paved; the remaining 13 miles have deep potholes. Near Pinecrest is the **Tree Snail Hammock Nature Trail**. The preserve also has the southernmost 35 miles of the **Florida Scenic Trail**. Rangers lead swamp walks in winter. Drinking water and food must be carried in.

## OCHOPEE

Don't blink, but Ochopee boasts the **smallest post office** in the US. Tourists over-run the place, snapping photographs and getting letters stamped. **Turner River Road**, Rte 839, runs north from Hwy 41 in Big Cypress for 18 miles. On Hwy 41, you can't miss the noise on both sides of the road as **Wooten's**, *Hwy 41, Ochopee, FL 33943; tel: (800) 282-2781,* the best-advertised airboat operator in the state, revs its airboat (rides $13) and swamp buggy (lorry) engines. Airboats are obliged by the US Park Service to skirt the edge of the national park.

Other airboat and water concessionaires operate out of Everglades City, three miles south of Hwy 41 on Hwy 29.

## EVERGLADES CITY

**Tourist Information: Everglades Area Chamber of Commerce,** *32016 E. Tamiami Trail, PO Box 130, Everglades City, FL 33929; tel: (941) 695-3941,* and the **Everglades City Chamber of Commerce Welcome Station,** *junction of Hwys 41 and 29; tel: (941) 695-3941,* have information on lodging and dining in town, airboat rides and the **Ten Thousand Islands** area served by the **Everglades National Park Gulf Coast Visitor Center,** *tel: (941) 695-3311,* open 0730–1700 (see Everglades, p. 112).

The town was created in the 1920s when Barron Collier completed the last few miles of the Tamiami Trail. Dredged soil formed the company-run town. The 1940s saw sponge fishing; the 1950s, shrimping. Since the 1960s the area has been known as the stone crab capital of Florida.

## FAKAHATCHEE STRAND STATE PRESERVE

If you stop nowhere else en route, stop at the astoundingly beautiful Big Cypress Bend entrance to the **Fakahatchee Strand State Preserve,** *PO Box 548, Copeland, FL 33926; tel: (941) 695-4593.* Park on the wide verge by the stockaded Miccosukee Village, then wander the 2000-ft boardwalk through the undeveloped slough which drains Big Cypress Swamp. Signs describe the old growth cypresses which survived earlier logging.

bald cypress and native royal palms mix with the largest concentration of orchids in the US. The variety and magnificence of the ecozones, animals and birdlife is not over-run by visitors who can easily miss the preserve sign on Hwy 41. **Janes Scenic Drive**, a few miles north of Hwy 41 on Rte 29, is unpaved, but is good for bicycling, wildlife spotting, and walking the 'trams', old logging roads. Just north of the 74,000-acre preserve is the inaccessible **Florida Panther National Wildlife Refuge**.

## COLLIER-SEMINOLE STATE PARK

**Collier-Seminole State Park,** *20200 E. Tamiami Trail, Naples, FL 33961; tel: (941) 394-3397,* offers RV and camping pitches, fishing, canoeing and boat tours. A 6½-mile hiking trail winds through a cypress swamp and slash pines. The park has many rare Florida royal palms. Near the entrance is the huge restored **Bay City Walking Dredge**, used in the 1920s to move ancient limestone beneath swamp muck to become the foundation of the Tamiami Trail.

### SIDE TRACK TO MARCO ISLAND

En route to Marco Island detour to visit **Briggs Nature Center**, *401 Shell Island Rd, Naples, FL 33942; tel: (941) 775-8569.* Go left 2.5 miles on CR ¹51 south, then drive right one mile ⁾n Shell Island Rd. The Centre, open Mon–Sat 0900–1630, Sun 1300–1700 (Jan–Mar), is favoured by its remote location in Rookery Bay National Estuarine Research Reserve. A half-mile boardwalk wanders through oak scrub, bay, brackish ponds, mangrove and pines, with a pond overlook, a birdfeeder trail and butterfly garden. The estuary, sheltering wading birds and their shrimp, crab and snail food supply, is open Dec–May to individual or guided canoe trips and pontoon boat tours.

### MARCO ISLAND

**Tourist Information: Marco Island & The Everglades**, *1102 N. Collier Blvd, Marco Island, FL 33937; tel: (800) 788-6272;* UK: *0800-89-1411;* Germany: *0130-81-0110,* provides information on accommodation, restaurants and Tamiami Trail and Everglades attractions.

#### ACCOMMODATION AND FOOD

*Hn, Ma* and *Rd* are expensive resorts along the strip offering substantial discounts upon request, and, like the suites at the **Radisson Suite Beach Resort, Marco Island**, *600 S. Collier Blvd, Marco Island, FL 33937; tel: (941)* *394-4100,* have kitchens and can accommodate 4–8 persons.

### SIGHTSEEING

Four-mile-long Marco Island sits at the north-west tip of the Everglades, the only inhabited island of the Gulf Coast's Ten Thousand Islands. The island's past includes pirates, pineapple plantations, a clam cannery and the 1883 **Olde Marco Inn**, now a pricey German and French cuisine restaurant, *100 Palm St; tel: (941) 394-3131.* Today, Marco Island is a beach resort with high-rise hotels along the Gulf, golf courses, tennis courts, commercial and sport fishing and birds nesting in inland marshy areas. **Marco Island Trolley Tours**, *601 Elkcam Circle, Suite A-7; tel: (941) 394-1600,* offers narrated tours of the isle for $9, stopping at a Calusa Indian mound and spotting bald eagles and manatees. **Tigertail Beach Park**, north of the hotel strip, is undisturbed dunes. **Coral Isle Factory Stores**, *on CR 951; tel: (941) 775-8083,* has outlet shopping Mon–Sat 0900–2000, Sun 1000–1800.

Return to the Tamiami Trail and go north-west to **Naples**.

### NAPLES

**Tourist Information: Naples Area Tourism Bureau**, *853 Vanderbilt Beach Rd, Suite 351, Naples, FL 33963; tel: (941) 598-3202;* UK: *0800-96-2122;* Germany: *0130-81-1954.*

#### ACCOMMODATION

From Apr–mid-Dec, lodging prices drop by half. Among the hotels that can claim to be on the beach, the **Edgewater Beach Hotel**, *1901 Gulf Shore Blvd N., Naples, FL 33940; tel: (800) 821-0196* or *(941) 262-6511,* is expensive–pricey. The moderate **Tides Motor Inn**, *1801 Gulf Shore Blvd N.; tel: (800) 438-8763 or (941) 262-6196*, includes breakfast.

Convenient Tamiami Trail accommodation includes the moderate–expensive **Howard Johnson Resort Lodge**, *221 9th St S. (Hwy 41), Naples, FL 33940; tel: (800) 206-2888 or (941) 262-6181*, the budget–moderate **Sea Shell Motel**, *82 Tamiami Trail S.; tel: (941) 262-5129*, and the moderate–expensive **Stoney's Courtyard Inn**, *2630 N. Tamiami Trail; tel: (800) 432-3870 or (941) 261-3870*, to enjoy a poolside breakfast, with citrus juice from the owner's own groves.

The **Ritz-Carlton Naples**, *280 Vanderbilt Beach Rd, Naples, FL 33963; tel: (800) 241-3333 or (941) 598-3300*, is posh with great service. The **Naples Registry Resort**, *475 Seagate Dr.; tel: (800) 962-7537 or (941) 597-3232*, is equally pricey. A cheerful breakfast is served in the lobby of the moderate **Inn at Pelican Bay**, *800 Vanderbilt Beach Rd; tel: (800) 597-8770 or (941) 597-8777*.

### EATING AND DRINKING

Some estimates hold that Naples has more than one restaurant per resident. The *Naples Daily News* Fri 'Applause' section has extensive restaurant listings. Budget **Kenny Rogers Roasters**, *975 Pine Ridge Rd; tel: (941) 597-2560*, one of a chain owned by the singer, serves excellent mesquite-grilled chicken, salads and corn bread. Find a cheap–budget breakfast along Hwy 41 at **The Bagel Place**, *2132 Tamiami Trail N.; tel: (941) 649-0055*. When exploring the Tin City/Dockside area, have a strong, rich *café latte* at **Caffe Becca Expresso**, *Dockside Boardwalk; tel: (941) 434-7478*.

### SIGHTSEEING

The 'Palm Beach of the West Coast' prefers flamingo-pink architecture and unostentatious wealth, but locals claim more old money millionaires per capita than anywhere in the US. In the last decade, the average age of residents has shifted from 60-something to the late 30s. Housing estates appear between Hwy 41 and I-75 seemingly overnight. Banking and computer professionals have moved in, a few hours from the Everglades, Miami, resort Gulf Coast barrier islands or Sarasota culture. Neapolitans are relaxed, golf courses are everywhere, and there's no glitzy night-life.

When Louisville, Kentucky *Courier Journal* publisher Walter N. Haldeman's consortium purchased local land in 1887, South-west Florida's climate and landscape were compared to Italy. Naples was born. Until railroad services reached the area in 1927 and the Tamiami Trail was completed in 1928, Naples remained the holiday venue for those who could afford to sail to it. **Naples Trolley Tours**, *179 Commerce St, Naples, FL 33963: tel: (941) 262-7300*, has narrated, two-hour tours of town and beach attractions.

Fine mansions line three short driving routes running parallel to the beaches: **Gordon Dr.** west of the 5th Ave S. shopping area; west off Hwy 41 on Harbour Dr. then north on **N. Gulf Shore Blvd** to the Venetian-canal look of Park Shore Dr.; and west off Hwy 41 on Vanderbilt Beach Blvd, past the Ritz-Carlton Hotel, then north on **N. Gulf Shore Dr.** to the **Delnor-Wiggins Pass State Recreation Area**, *11100 Gulf Shore Dr. N., Naples, FL 33963; tel: (941) 597-6196*. Swimming is not permitted in the pass, the treacherous mouth of the Cocohatchee River, but fishing is. Endangered loggerhead sea turtle nesting sites are protected. Shelling is popular but avoid collecting live starfish and sand dollars. Climb the wooden observation tower before having a leisurely picnic.

Stroll along **Naples Pier**, *12th Ave S., south of downtown Naples.* Two blocks away, **Palm Cottage**, *137 12th Ave S.; tel: (941) 261-8164*, once Haldeman's winter home, now houses the Collier County Historical Society which conducts tours mid-Nov–mid-Apr. **Olde Naples** is just east, from Gordon Dr./2nd St S. to 4th St S., and from 14th Ave S. for three blocks north to Broad Ave S. Shops, restaurants, fashion boutiques and art galleries have taken over the original town centre. There is more shopping and dining on **5th Ave S.** between 3rd and 9th St (at the Tamiami Trail) and at **Tin City**, two blocks east, *Hwy 41 E. at Goodlette Rd; tel: (941) 262-4200*, originally a 1920s clam and oyster processing plant. Bay cruises and sport fishing boats leave from the Tin City dock. One block west at *1100 6th Ave S.* are **Dockside Boardwalk's** clothing stores, chandlery and fast food shops.

The **Teddy Bear Museum**, *2511 Pine Ridge Rd, Naples, FL 33942; tel: (941) 598-2711*, admission $5 (children aged four–12 $2), open Wed–Sat 1000–1700, Sun 1300–1700 and Mon Nov–mid-Apr, displays 3000 teddy bears in settings like a Beard (*sic*) of Directors Room and by era. The charming stuffed critters are costumed and labelled with city and country of origin; a **Little Bear Shop** sells bear paraphernalia.

**Jungle Larry's Caribbean Gardens**, *1590 Goodlette Rd; tel: (941) 262-5409*, is an example of how Florida's nature parks used to be run. Tiger, elephant and gator shows go on most days; exotic African animals are penned within beautiful landscaped gardens. Admission $11. Next door is the real thing, the **Conservancy's Naples Nature Center**, *14th Ave N., tel: (941) 262-0304*. Sign up immediately with the volunteer guide for free electric, non-polluting, boat rides up the Gordon River. On one side is the protected natural area; on the other bank of the river, developers have removed the mangroves and greenery, levelled the land and left concrete piers. Hire a canoe, walk mangrove, hammock and arboretum nature trails, see the birds in the wildlife rehabilitation centre and visit the Center's museum for an overview of the area's ecology. **Butterflies in Flight**, *6151 Everett St, Naples, FL 33962; tel: (941) 793-2359*, has a walk-in aviary and butterfly breeding tour.

Continue north on Hwy 41 to **Bonita Springs**. Lodging information from **Bonita Springs Area Chamber of Commerce**, *8801 W. Terry St, Bonita Springs, FL 33959; tel: (941) 992-5011*. The **Naples-Fort Myers Greyhound Track**; *tel: (941) 992-2411*, runs year-round, entrance fee $1. **Everglades Wonder Gardens**; *tel: (941) 992-2591*, is a relic of gatormania when the only good gators were performers, and animals and birds were only for display.

Dr. Cyrus Teed and Chicago-area followers set up a utopian community in 1893 at **Koreshan State Historic Site**, *Hwy 41 and Corkscrew Rd, PO Box 7, Estero, FL 33928; tel: (941) 992-0311*, on the south bank of the Estero River. Teed believed himself immortal and set out to build a communal New Jerusalem. The Koreshan community's tropical plantings and some buildings remain. Fishing, boating and hired canoes are enjoyed by onsite campers, who can access nearby **Mound Key State Archaeological Site**, believed to have been the main town of an ancient Calusa tribal leader by the mid-16th century. **Fort Myers** is fifteen miles north on the Tamiami Trail.

# Miami–Fort Lauderdale

The 30-mile journey from Miami north to Ft Lauderdale joins two burgeoning cities that have engulfed several small towns. But despite the lack of distinct physical boundaries, many coastal communities along SR A1A have maintained their own identities.

DIRECT ROUTE: 30 MILES

Direct Route

Fort Lauderdale • 3 miles
• Dania
5 miles
• Hollywood
3 miles
• Hallandale
2 miles
• Aventura
2 miles
• Sunny Isles
4½ miles
• Bal Harbour
½ mile
• Surfside

30 miles

15 miles

Miami

Scenic Route

## ROUTES

### Direct Route

➡ The only advantage of taking I-95 north is speed. Freeway builders stayed inland, cutting through light industry, residential tracts, and shopping malls to avoid miles of Atlantic beaches.

From Miami's **Bayside Marketplace**, take Biscayne Blvd south to N.E. 1st St. Turn right and follow the signs to I-95 northbound. Remain on I-95 through **North Miami**, **Aventura**, **Hallandale**, **Hollywood** and **Dania**, past **Fort Lauderdale-Hollywood International Airport**, and into **Fort Lauderdale**. The journey should take no more than 60 mins in the worst of traffic.

### Scenic Route

➡ From **Bayside Marketplace**, take Biscayne Blvd north to the MacArthur Causeway, turn right and follow the causeway to Miami Beach. Take 5th St to Collins Ave (SR A1A) and turn left. Collins Ave runs from the rejuvenated Art Deco Historic District through increasingly modern developments toward the north. The narrow strip of sand spits and islands have become some of the most sought-after real estate in America, sandwiched between the Atlantic Ocean on the right and the Intracoastal Waterway on the left. Sandy beaches are the norm from South Pointe Park in Miami Beach all the way to Fort Lauderdale and beyond.

The **Sans Souci Resort and Spa** near 31st St, the **Fontainebleau Hilton** near 44th St and the **Eden Roc** near 45th St, are the epitome of Miami

# MIAMI–FORT LAUDERDALE

Beach's post World War II boom. What looks to be a rectangular entrance into the Fontainebleau is a *trompe l'oeil* mural modelled on the authentic interior. Collins Ave takes a sharp left turn at 44th St around the hotel. To the left is **Indian Creek**, a long, narrow inlet from Biscayne Bay, and a line of expensive creekside homes with backyard docks. Collins dives into a canyon of high rise condominiums around the 5000 block that runs to 87th St and the town of **Surfside**. **Bal Harbour**, which begins at 96th St, is a mixture of high rise housing and low rise shopping, both equally expensive.

Parks separate Bal Harbour from **Sunny Isles** and **Golden Beach**, the last two communities in North Dade County. Both are older, established resort areas mired in a building boom that is replacing budget–moderate motels and restaurants with more expensive facilities. **Aventura**, a new resort community, is west across the Intracoastal Waterway.

County Line Rd marks the boundary between Dade and Broward Counties. **Hallandale** lies just inside Broward County, followed by **Hollywood**, for decades the unofficial winter capital of French-speaking Canada and the centre of Native American culture in South Florida. SR A1A turns inland at the city of **Dania**, leaving **John U. Lloyd State Recreation Area**, a quiet refuge from the busy marine traffic in and out of **Port Everglades** and Ft Lauderdale. SR A1A joins Hwy 1 in Dania to skirt the east side of **Ft Lauderdale-Hollywood International Airport** and enter the city of **Fort Lauderdale**. Allow 1–2 hours for the drive. Traffic is slowest at weekends.

## SURFSIDE

Tourist Information: Town of Surfside Tourist Board, *9301 Collins Ave, Surfside, FL 33154; tel: (800) 327-4557 or (305) 864-0722, open Mon–Fri 0900–1700.*

**Surfside** is precisely what the name promises, a small town on the surf that exists for the tourist trade.

## BAL HARBOUR

Tourist Information: Greater Miami Convention and Visitors Bureau, *701 Brickell Ave, Suite 2700, Miami, FL 33131; tel: (800) 283-2707 or (305) 539-3063,* covers Bal Harbour.

**Bal Harbour** is a modern version of what Miami Beach used to be, an exclusive resort area catering to the need to consume as conspicuously as possible.

### ACCOMMODATION

Choices include **The Sea View Hotel**, *9909 Collins Ave, Bal Harbour, FL 33154; tel: (800) 447-1010 or (305) 866-1898,* and **Sheraton Bal Harbour Beach Resort**, *9701 Collins Ave, Bal Harbour, FL 33154; tel: (800) 325-3535 or (305) 865-7511,* pricey and on the beach.

### SHOPPING

**Bal Harbour Shops**, *9700 Collins Ave, Bal Harbour, FL 33154; tel: (305) 866-0311,* has the largest concentration of name boutiques south of Palm Beach: Bulgari, Chanel, Tiffany, Louis Vuitton, Gucci, Cartier, Hermès, Fendi and Bottega Veneta, plus Florida's largest Saks Fifth Avenue and Nieman Marcus stores..

## SUNNY ISLES

Tourist Information: Sunny Isles Beach Resort Association Visitor Information Center, *17100 Collins Ave, Suite 217, Sunny Isles, FL 33160; tel: (800) 327-6366 or (305) 947-5826,* open Mon–Fri 0900–1700.

# MIAMI–FORT LAUDERDALE

## ACCOMMODATION

More than 40 hotels and resorts are clustered along three miles of beach, a moderate–expensive alternative to pricey Miami Beach.

Chains include *BW* and *Sh*; most properties use Miami Beach addresses to suggest locations several miles farther south.

## AVENTURA

**Tourist Information: Aventura Marketing Council**, *20901 Biscayne Blvd, Suite 445, Aventura, FL 33180; tel: (305) 932-5334*, open Mon–Fri 0830–1730.

Aventura is a recent residential resort community on the inland side of the Intracoastal Waterway.

### ACCOMMODATION

**Turnberry Isle Resort & Club**, *19999 W. Country Club Dr., Aventura, FL 33180; tel: (800) 327-7028* or *(305) 932-6200*, is one of the most private – and most expensive – resorts in South Florida. The pricey restaurants are outstanding.

## HALLANDALE

**Tourist Information: Fort Lauderdale Convention and Visitors Bureau**, *200 E. Las Olas Blvd, Suite 1500, Fort Lauderdale, FL 33301; tel: (800) 356-1662* has information on the town.

Hallandale, once a block of tomato fields settled by Swedish farmers, has become a retirement and racetrack community with high-rise condominiums along A1A and an appealing beach park with limited parking.

**Gulfstream Park**, *901 S. Federal Hwy (US 1) at S. E. 7th St; tel: (305) 454-7000*, is open for horse racing Jan–Mar. The $500,000 Florida Derby is the leading preview to the Triple Crown races.

**Hollywood Greyhound Dog Track**, *831 N. Federal Hwy (US 1) at Pembroke Rd; tel: (305) 545-9400*, is open for dog racing late Dec–late Apr.

## HOLLYWOOD

**Tourist Information: Greater Hollywood Chamber of Commerce**, *4000 Hollywood Blvd, Suite 265, Hollywood, FL 33021; tel: (305) 985-4000.*

### ACCOMMODATION

Chains include *BW, CI, DI, HJ* and *Hd*, but Hollywood is filled with budget–moderate motels that make no pretence at offering more than a clean, safe and affordable place to sleep. Best areas to look are along US 1, S. 18th Ave, south of Hollywood Blvd and Young Circle or N. 18th Ave north of the roundabout, and along A1A, Ocean Dr. The **Hollywood Beach Resort**, at the foot of Hollywood Blvd, *101 N. Ocean Dr., Hollywood, FL 33019; tel: (800) 331-6103* or *(305) 921-0990*, moderate–expensive, was Hollywood's first beach resort in 1926.

### SIGHTSEEING

Hollywood was founded as a tourist town in the 1920s. It's still the most popular spot in Florida for Canadians, but the ageing downtown is being renovated into a chic business and arts centre. Backers hope to combine the panache of Miami with the less frenetic atmosphere of Ft Lauderdale.

Hollywood has worked hard to maintain its family image. The 2.5 miles of beach between Hollywood Blvd and Sheridan St are backed by a **boardwalk**, actually a paved pedestrian walkway, lined with cheap–budget restaurants, fast food stands, convenience stores and souvenir shops. Police on bicycles strictly enforce local laws against roller bladers, speeding cyclists, loud music and any sort of rowdy behaviour.

The boardwalk begins at **Ocean Walk**, *101 N. Ocean Dr., Hollywood, FL 33019; tel: (305) 922-3438*, an electric pink hotel/condominium/entertainment complex at the foot of Hollywood Blvd that incorporates the Hollywood Beach Resort. For fewer people and easier parking, hold out until you reach **Hollywood South Beach Park** and **Hollywood North Beach Park**, Broward County parks extending north from the boardwalk. North Beach Park also has a real boardwalk along the Intracoastal Waterway just across Ocean Dr. from the beach.

The **Art and Culture Center of Hollywood**, *1650 Harrison St, Hollywood, FL 33019; tel: (305) 921-3275*, stages sculpture, photography, jewellery and antique exhibits as well as cultural and educational programmes. Look for classical and jazz concerts on Sun.

Hollywood is also the centre of Native American life in South Florida. The few remaining signs of what was once the dominant culture are place names and a handful of tourist attractions, including the **Native Village**, *3551 N. SR 7, Hollywood, FL 33021; tel: (305) 961-4519*, and **Seminole Indian Poker Casino**, *4150 N. SR 7, Hollywood, FL 33021; tel: (800) 323-5452* or *(305) 961-3220*.

## DANIA

**Tourist Information: Dania Chamber of Commerce**, *102 W. Dania Beach Blvd, Dania, FL 33004; tel: (305) 927-3377*.

### ACCOMMODATION

Chains include *Hd* and *Sh*, both near the Ft Lauderdale-Hollywood International Airport. (See Ft Lauderdale, p. 126.)

### SIGHTSEEING

Dania began life as tomato farms settled by Danish immigrants, hence the name. The farms have long since disappeared, leaving Dania as a busy beach resort town with a growing sideline in antique shops.

**Dania Beach**, *Ocean Dr. and Dania Beach Blvd*, just beyond A1A's left turn into Dania, has showers, fishing, lifeguards and relatively few people. Just north is **John U. Lloyd State Recreation Area**, *6503 N. Ocean Dr., Hollywood, FL 33019; tel: (305) 932-2833*, one of South Florida's most scenic beaches. Two miles of golden sand are lined with spreading Australian pines. The west side of the park overlooks Port Everglades and Ft Lauderdale.

**Dania Jai-alai Frontón**, *301 E. Dania Beach Blvd, Dania, FL 33004; tel: (305) 927-2841*, is Florida's second largest *frontón* (the court in which the game is played) after Miami. Children at least 39 inches tall are allowed in with a parent, but they must have a reserved seat.

Jai-alai is based on a traditional Basque game: players, or *pelotaris*, use wicker baskets to hurl a ball, or *pelota*, at 185 mph. The idea is to bounce the ball off walls and floor so your opponent can't catch and return it.

**Graves Museum of Archaeology and Natural History**, *481 S. Federal Hwy, Dania, F, 33004; tel: (305) 925-7770*, has the best local coverage of the Tequesta Indians, Broward County's original settlers. Look for the skull sign on the east side of US 1 at S.E. 4th St. **Antique Row** just north, has 150 antique shops along S. Federal Hwy between Dania Beach Blvd and Griffin Rd.

# FORT LAUDERDALE

Fort Lauderdale hasn't always been famous for Spring Break. Spanish explorers named it Rio Nuevo in the early 17th century, but they weren't interested in the mosquito-ridden swamp that surrounded the waterway. Neither was Major William Lauderdale, whose troops built a fort along the New River in 1838 during the Second Seminole War, then went home to Tennessee as quickly as possible. Insects and isolation defeated two later Fort Lauderdales before Henry Flagler's Florida East Coast Railway finally opened South Florida to settlement.

In the 1920s, real estate speculators dredged much of Fort Lauderdale's marshy bayside into muddy building sites separated by canals, then called their creation the 'Venice of America'. The same kind of single-minded boosterism is still at work. Once known as a raucous resort for students on spring holiday, sailors on shore leave, and hard drinking beach bums in all seasons, Fort Lauderdale is spending serious money on new museums, new hotels and new attractions for families. The city name is frequently abbreviated to Ft Lauderdale.

## TOURIST INFORMATION

**Greater Fort Lauderdale Convention & Visitors Bureau**, *200 E. Las Olas Blvd, Suite 1500, Ft Lauderdale, FL 33301; tel: (800) 356-1662* or *(305) 765-4466,* provides information for Fort Lauderdale, Pompano Beach, Lauderdale-by-the-Sea and Deerfield Beach. The **Greater Fort Lauderdale Chamber of Commerce**, *512 N.E. 3rd Ave, Ft Lauderdale, FL 33301; tel: (305) 462-6000,* is open Mon–Fri 0800–1700.

The Visitors Bureau **Arts & Entertainment Hotline**; *tel: (305) 357-5700,* has pre-recorded information on events throughout Broward County; the **Fort Lauderdale Parks and Recreation Hotline**; *tel: (305) 761-5363,* provides information on most outdoor events.

## ARRIVING AND DEPARTING

### By Air

**Ft Lauderdale-Hollywood International Airport,** *between I-95, I-395 and US 1 between Ft Lauderdale and Dania; tel: (305) 357-6100,* is 20 mins from beachfront hotels and 45–60 mins from northern and western Broward County.

Taxi and shuttle service is approximately $15 to major hotels, but most visitors pick up hire cars at the airport. Private transport is absolutely essential as most public transport is slow, impractical and unreliable.

### By Car

The major approaches from the north and south are SR A1A, US 1, I-95 and Florida's Turnpike. I-75, Alligator Alley, is the main western approach. Streets are generally well-marked, but US 1 is variously signed as Federal Hwy and N.E. or S.E. 6th Ave.

# FORT LAUDERDALE

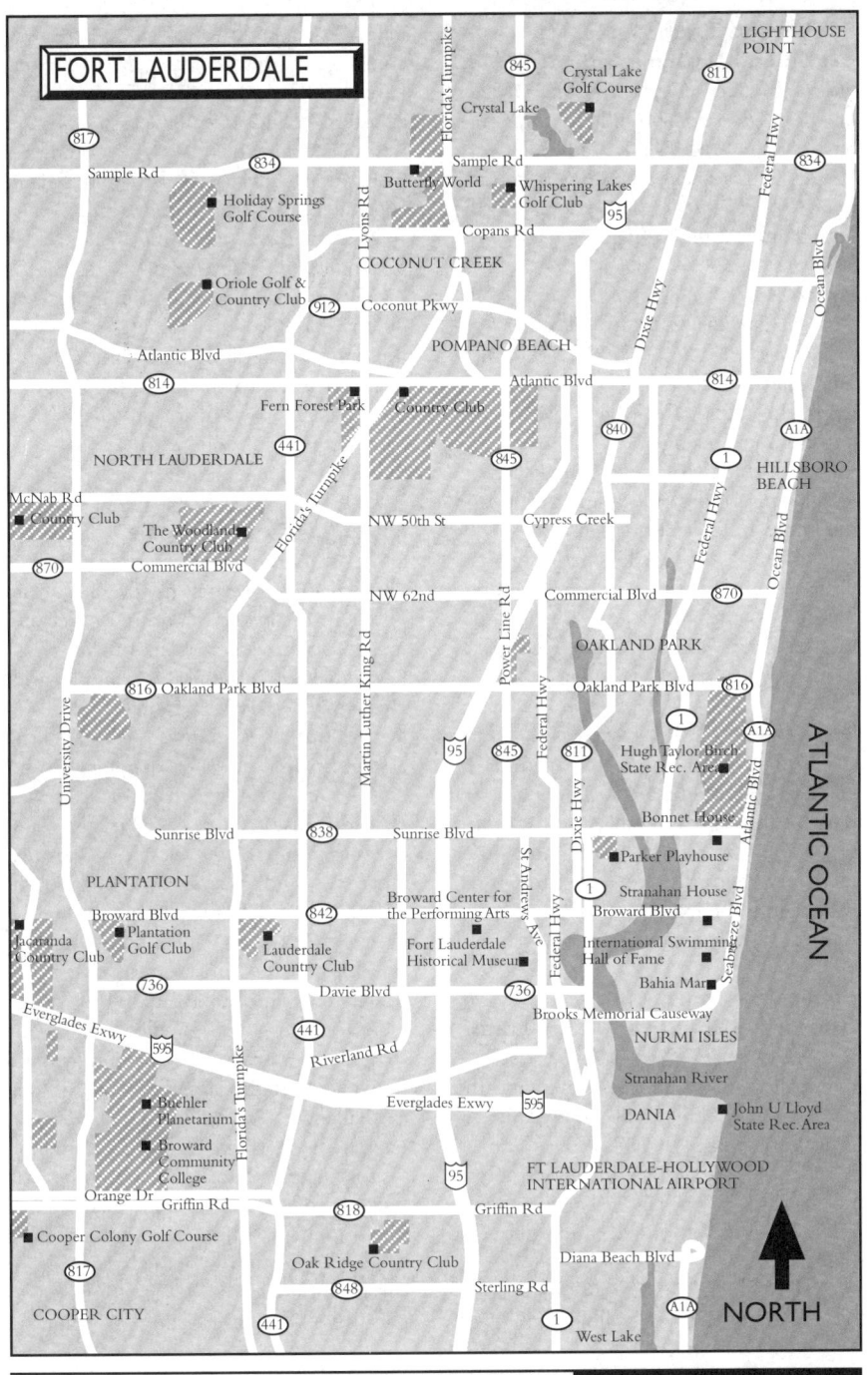

# FORT LAUDERDALE

## By Bus and Train
Greyhound Bus Lines, Inc., *513 N.E. 3rd St, Ft Lauderdale; tel: (800) 231-2222* or *(305) 764-6551* provide long distance bus services. **AMTRAK**, *200 S.W. 21st Terrace, Ft Lauderdale; tel: (800) 872-7245* or *(305) 587-6692*, has services northbound and south to Miami.

## By Boat
Port Everglades, *180 Eller Dr., Ft Lauderdale, FL 33316; tel: (305) 523-3404*, is the second busiest cruise terminal in the world after Miami. More than two million passengers a year board ships for everything from gambling cruises, which sail around in circles just beyond the three-mile territorial limit, to 100-day 'round the world' extravaganzas. Cruise ship companies generally arrange transfers to the airport; car hire companies have free shuttles to their car parks near the airport.

## GETTING AROUND
It's difficult to navigate around Ft Lauderdale without a car. There are taxi ranks at most larger hotels, but cabs must be ordered by telephone for most other locations. Because taxis are little used, they tend to be expensive for any but the shortest of excursions.

## Public Transport
Broward County Mass Transit (BCMT); *tel: (305) 357-8400*, operates free trolleys between downtown and the beach, daily 0730–1730 approximately every 30 mins. BCMT's three dozen other routes are designed for commuters, not tourists. Service is daily 0500–2230, with intervals of 15–90 mins between buses.

**Tri-Rail**; *tel: (305) 728-8445*, commuter trains run 67 miles from West Palm Beach south to Miami, where they connect to Metrorail and Metromover. Fares are $3 single or $5 daily, with free transfers to Metrorail. Most Tri-Rail trains are scheduled for the commuter rush, but a public transport trip to Miami is possible, if slower than driving.

Water Taxi, *651 Seabreeze Blvd, Ft Lauderdale, FL 33316; tel: (305) 467-6677*, picks up passengers at more than 80 marinas, hotels, beaches, restaurants, museums, shopping malls and cinemas near the water. The bright yellow boats cost $6 single or $14 for an all-day pass. Water tours and pub crawls are available by special arrangement.

## Driving in Ft Lauderdale
The best source of maps is the **American Automobile Association**. Check the phone directory for the nearest office and make enquiries in person. In theory, Ft Lauderdale streets follow a simple grid. **Broward Blvd** divides addresses north–south; **Andrews Ave** is the east–west division. The quadrant, N.E., S.W., etc., is a vital part of addresses. **Boulevards**, **Courts**, **Drives** and **Streets** run east–west. **Avenues**, **Terraces** and **Ways** run north–south. Many residential areas, however, follow their own pattern, which bears no relationship to the city pattern. Map out routes in advance to avoid getting lost.

Looping flyovers, endless road construction, drawbridge openings and unexpected traffic jams can make driving a challenge. So can other drivers. Ft Lauderdale gets well over four million visitors every year, about four times the number of residents. The chances are quite good that the driver just ahead has only a vague notion about where he or she is going and no idea at all of how to get there. Watch for drivers making a

'New York turn' – suddenly turning left from the far right lane, or stopping dead in traffic to consult a map, usually followed by frantic attempts to reverse direction.

## STAYING IN FORT LAUDERDALE

### Accommodation

Ft Lauderdale is largely a residential city, but there are 30,000 hotel rooms in the area. Hotels are concentrated near the beach close to SR A1A, on the harbour and near the airport. All of the major chains are represented, usually with several properties each. Prices are generally lower in the towns to the south (Dania, Hollywood, Hallandale; see Miami–Ft Lauderdale route, pp. 124–127) and the north (Lauderdale-by-the-Sea, Pompano Beach, Hillsboro Beach, Deerfield Beach; see Ft Lauderdale–West Palm Beach route, p. 139–143) of Ft Lauderdale. Flats can be hired for longer stays. Self-catering rates start at $30 per night during the summer, and $45 in winter. The **Greater Fort Lauderdale Convention & Visitors Bureau**; *tel: (800) 227-8669, ext 747 or (305) 765-4466*, can make limited bookings.

The **Bonaventure Resort & Spa**, *250 Racquet Club Rd, Ft Lauderdale, FL 33326; tel: (305) 389-3300*, expensive–pricey, is one of the most pleasant landscaped spa resorts in the area, though it is on the west side of the city and not convenient for the beach. **Doubletree Suites**, *440 Seabreeze Blvd, Ft Lauderdale, FL 33316; tel: (800) 222-8733 or (305) 524-8733*, is directly across the street from the busiest section of the Ft Lauderdale beach near Las Olas Blvd; moderate–expensive. **Hyatt Regency Pier Sixty-Six Resort & Marina**, expensive–pricey, *2301 E. 17th St, Ft Lauderdale, FL 33316; tel: (800) 327-3796 or (305) 525-6666*, sits between the 17th St Causeway and what may be the world's largest concentration of marinas. **Marriott's Harbor Beach**, *3030 Holiday Dr., Ft Lauderdale, FL 33316; tel: (800) 228-9290 or (305) 525-4000*, pricey, has one of the longest hotel beaches in the area. **Radisson Bahia Mar**, *801 Seabreeze Blvd, Ft Lauderdale, FL 33316; tel: (800) 333-3333 or (305) 764-2233*, expensive, has splendid water views.

### Eating and Drinking

Ft Lauderdale claims more than 2500 restaurants, from the Polynesian kitsch of **Mai Kai**, *3599 N. Federal Hwy, Ft Lauderdale, FL 33394; tel: (305) 563-3272*, to old fashioned formality at **Raindancer**, *3031 E. Commercial Blvd, Lauderdale, FL 33316; tel: (305) 772-0337*, both pricey. **15th Street Fisheries**, *1900 S.E. 15th St, Ft Lauderdale, FL 33316; tel: (305) 763-2777*, moderate, overlooking the harbour, is a local favourite for fish and alligator. **Aruba Beach Cafe**, *Commercial Blvd and Ocean Ave, Lauderdale-by-the-Sea; tel: (305) 776-0111*, budget–moderate, is a casual local spot for seafood and pasta. **Dicey Riley's**, *217 S.W. 2nd St, Ft Lauderdale, FL 33316; tel: (305) 522-2202*, budget–moderate, is a lively jazz bar with simple meals.

### Communications

There are dozens of post offices in the Ft Lauderdale area. Mail can also be sent to hotels.

### Money

**Thomas Cook Foreign Exchange**, *3526 N. Ocean Blvd, Ft Lauderdale, FL 33308; tel: (305) 566-2666*.

## FORT LAUDERDALE

### Entertainment

With several million tourists pouring through town every year, Ft Lauderdale has an active night-time scene. Most major hotels offer dancing, entertainment, or both. The club scene is centred in downtown and the beachfront, **Oakland Park** and **Commercial Blvds**. For a listing of current clubs and evening entertainment venues, check the local newspaper, the *Fort Lauderdale Sun-Sentinel*, and the *Guide to the Gold Coast Sun Spots*, available at most news-stands and lodging.

### Music and Theatre

**Broward Center for the Performing Arts**, *624 S.W. 2nd St, Ft Lauderdale, FL 33312; tel: (305) 462-0222*, hosts special events and performances including ballet, opera, touring shows, children's theatre and concerts. **Coral Ridge Concert Series**, *555 N. Federal Hwy, Ft Lauderdale, FL 33308; tel: (305) 491-1103*, offers a season of varied concerts in the Coral Ridge Presbyterian Church, which has one of the largest pipe organs in the world.

**Fort Lauderdale Children's Theatre**, *640 N. Andrews Ave, Ft Lauderdale, FL 33304; tel: (305) 763-8813*, is the area's leading professional theatre for children. **Gold Coast Opera**, *1000 Coconut Creek Blvd, Pompano Beach, FL 33066; tel: (305) 973-2323*, stages opera in Ft Lauderdale, Pompano Beach, Coral Springs and Boca Raton. **Parker Playhouse**, *707 N.E. 8th St, Ft Lauderdale, FL 33304; tel: (305) 764-1411*, hosts national touring theatre companies.

The **Philharmonic Orchestra of Florida**; *tel: (305) 561-2997*, performs at the Broward Center for the Performing Arts as well as venues in Boca Raton, Miami and West Palm Beach.

### Sports

The **New York Yankees** baseball team have their spring training camp and exhibition games at *5201 N.W. 12th Ave, Ft Lauderdale, FL 33309; tel: (305) 776-1921*, through the end of 1995.

Ocean **fishing** off Ft Lauderdale is among the best north of the Keys, thanks to the Gulf Stream that runs as close as one mile offshore. Inland waters are also popular, although fishing is generally better in less populated areas to the north. Deep sea fishing charters and inland boats can be arranged at Bahia Mar, Marina del Americana, and Pier 66. Ask your hotel for current recommendations. Nearly all of the piers up and down the coast are also open for fishing. Bait and tackle is usually available on the pier or from shops nearby.

**Golf** and **tennis** are two of Florida's most popular sports. Most local golf courses are semi-private with very restricted public hours, but many hotels make special arrangements with one or more courses. The larger hotels have their own tennis courts; there are also a number of public courts. Check with your hotel for the nearest tennis centre.

**Scuba diving** is excellent off the three reef lines that guard Ft Lauderdale beaches. There are also a number of artificial reefs, most of them ships sunk deliberately in the middle of empty, sandy stretches of the sea bed to provide habitat for fish and visual interest for divers. One of the most famous is the 197-ft freighter *Mercedes*, washed onto a beachside terrace during a fierce storm several years ago. The ship was eventually towed one mile off shore and sunk in 60–100 ft of water. Most divers wear lightweight wet suits all year. Gulf Stream currents can be unexpectedly strong. For safety, dive with someone who knows the local conditions.

# FORT LAUDERDALE

## SHOPPING

Las Olas Blvd was once the area where settlers traded with Native Americans. It's still an important shopping venue, a low-rise street of dreams developed in the 1940s to compete with Palm Beach's Worth Ave. Las Olas never quite attained the hoped-for stature, but the six blocks between S.E. 6th and 11th Aves draws a lively crowd to tiny boutiques, art galleries, outdoor cafés and bridal shops. Parking is usually available on side streets. Many shops are closed on Sundays. Las Olas means 'The Waves' in Spanish. The street led to what was once Ft Lauderdale's first bridge to the Atlantic beaches.

**Festival Flea Market**, *Sample Rd and Florida's Turnpike, Pompano Beach, FL; tel: (305) 979-4555*, gathers more than 600 vendors under a single roof. **Sawgrass Mills**, *near I-75 west of Ft Lauderdale, 12801 W. Sunrise Blvd, Sunrise, FL 33323; tel: (800) 356-4557 or (305) 846-2350*, claims to be the world's largest outlet mall with over 200 shops. **Swap Shop of Ft Lauderdale**, *3501 W. Sunrise Blvd (between I-95 and Florida's Turnpike); tel: (305) 791-7927*, claims more than 2000 merchants plus an 11-screen drive-in cinema.

## SIGHTSEEING

### The Strip

The public beach stretches six miles from the **Ocean Lane** area, directly north of the Port Everglades channel entrance, to well beyond Sunrise Blvd. Most visitors go to Ft Lauderdale for the beach, a tradition that goes back at least to 1935, when the town sponsored its first Collegiate Aquatic Forum. The Christmas swimming competition drew university students from across the Eastern US and Canada, anxious for an excuse to escape the throes of winter. Thirty years later, Connie Francis enshrined **Spring Break** with an almost-forgotten 1960 film, *Where the Boys Are*. The swimming competition had been moved to the Easter school holiday to boost attendance. In Hollywood's vision of the Easter holiday, the boys, the girls and their cars all gathered at The Strip, the Atlantic beach at the foot of Los Olas Blvd.

The film lured 50,000 students to Ft Lauderdale in 1961. By 1985, the peak year, Spring Break had grown to 350,000 hormone-laden revellers guzzling oceans of beer, diving into swimming pools from the nearest balcony (and occasionally missing), packing every available motel room with dozens of bodies, blocking streets and generally having a rowdy good time. Too good a time, Ft Lauderdale decided, and cancelled the festivities.

City authorities decided that the $140 million students spent each year wasn't worth the additional policing and clean-up costs from too much beer and lost business. Everyone else avoided Ft Lauder-dale like the plague so long as the students were in town. Police crackdowns and 'the wall', a concrete barricade that kept cars out of the beach area, convinced most of the revellers to decamp to Daytona Beach, Panama City and other more welcoming places.

Today, The Strip has sprouted $25 million worth of new palm trees, sidewalk cafés and broad pavements that have become almost as popular with roller bladers as with pedestrians. The centre of beach activity stretches from the junction of Seabreeze Blvd and SR A1A/Atlantic Blvd north beyond the foot of Los Olas Blvd. Spring Break remains, too, but the crowds are smaller and far more restrained.

SHOPPING • SIGHTSEEING

## FORT LAUDERDALE

Just two short blocks west of The Strip is the **International Swimming Hall of Fame**, *One Hall of Fame Dr., Ft Lauderdale, FL 33316; tel: (305) 462-6536,* open daily 0900–1900, admission $5. The world's leading swimming museum displays mementoes of great swimmers of the last 100 years. The hall's swimming pools are open to the public.

**Cruises and Boat Tours**

One block south of the Swimming Hall of Fame is **Bahia Mar Resort & Yachting Club**, *601 Seabreeze Blvd, Ft Lauderdale, FL 33316; tel: (305) 764-2233,* with 350 slips and almost as many hotel rooms. Bahia Mar once billed itself as the largest marina in the world. It remains a bewildering maze of charter fishing boats, houseboats, plush yachts, sightseeing vessels and ordinary sailboats. Bahia Mar's most famous occupant is *The Busted Flush,* a houseboat owned by private detective Travis McGee. McGee, a self-described knight in slightly tarnished armour, is the wildly successful creation of local novelist John D. MacDonald. The bulk of MacDonald's 20-plus Travis McGee mystery novels are set in Ft Lauderdale and South Florida, offering a very perceptive window into the harsher realities behind the surf and sunshine of tourist brochures.

**Jungle Queen Cruises**, *2455 E. Sunrise Blvd, Ft Lauderdale, FL 33316; tel: (305) 462-5596,* docks near McGee's literary mooring. Two *Queens* cruise the inland waterways of Ft Lauderdale daily, complete with vaudeville entertainment and sing-along songs that predate many of today's grandparents. The act has been sailing the Intracoastal Waterway for nearly 40 years with no signs of fatigue. The nightly four-hour dinner cruise includes an all-you-can-eat barbecue on a private island. Price: $8–22.95

Other Ft Lauderdale sightseeing cruises include the **Carrie B**, *1402 E. Las Olas Blvd; tel (305) 768-9920,* a replica 19th-century riverboat, and **Paddlewheel Queen Cruises**, *2950 N.E. 32nd Ave; tel: (305) 564-7659,* a sternwheel paddleboat. **Lolly the Trolley**, *419 S. Atlantic Blvd; tel: (305) 768-0700,* and **South Florida Trolley**; *tel: (305) 429-3100,* offer similar land tours and both cost $10.

**Coral Princess**, *425 Seabreeze Blvd, Ft Lauderdale, FL 33316; tel: (305) 832-9078,* and **Pro Diver II**, *Bahia Mar Yacht Basin; tel: (305) 467-6030,* tour the reefs off Ft Lauderdale in glass-bottomed boats. Snorkellers are also welcome.

For those who prefer ships, **Discovery Cruises**, *1850 Eller Dr., Suite 402, Ft Lauderdale, FL 33316; tel: (800) 999-3646* or *(305) 467-5777,* and **SeaEscape**, *PO Box 13002, Ft Lauderdale, FL 33316; tel: (305) 476-9999,* offer one-day ocean cruises to the Bahamas or to nowhere, priced from $39. Cruises include dancing, entertainment and casino gambling.

**The Riverwalk**

The easiest way to get an overview of downtown Ft Lauderdale is to stroll the **Riverwalk**, *along the New River; tel: (305) 468-1533,* a narrow parkway running one mile along the north bank and a half mile along the south bank of the New River. Riverwalk begins at **Cooley's Landing Park**, *S.W. 7th Ave,* on Sailboat Bend, a hairpin turn in the river that was once the site of a Tequesta Indian village, and runs through the **Arts and Science District,** an entertainment and educational complex at *S.W. 2nd St and S.W. 7th Ave.*

**Museums**

**Museum of Discovery and Science and Blockbuster IMAX Theater,** *401*

## FORT LAUDERDALE

S.W. 2nd St, Ft Lauderdale, FL 33312; tel: (305) 467-6637, has the only interactive IMAX cinema in the region as well as seven interactive exhibit areas focusing on science, ecology and health, plus travelling exhibitions. Admission: museum $6, IMAX cinema $5. The easiest parking is across S.E. 2nd Ave at the public parking garage. The same car park is convenient for the **Fort Lauderdale Historical Museum**, 219 S.W. 2nd Ave, Ft Lauderdale, FL 33312; tel: (305) 463-4431, which houses artefacts from the Seminole Wars period (1830s) to the 1930s, including an extensive collection of local photography. Admission $2. Museum staff also lead historical walking, river and coach tours. The Broward Center for the Performing Arts is directly east of the museum.

**Stranahan House**, 1 Stranahan Place, (335 S.E. 6th Ave), Ft Lauderdale, FL 33312; tel: (305) 524-4736, built on the river in 1901, is Broward County's oldest surviving structure. It was also the home of Ivy Cromartie Stranahan, the first teacher in the county. The roots of modern Ft Lauderdale sprang from a nearby landing where Frank Stranahan opened a ferry service across the New River in 1893. Admission: $3. **Bonnet House**, 900 N. Birch Rd, Ft Lauderdale, FL 33316; tel: (305) 563-5393, open May–Nov, an eclectic beach estate from the 1920s, is still occupied during the winter season. Admission $7.

**Ah-Tha-Thi-Ki Museum**, 5845 S. SR 7, Ft Lauderdale, FL 33314; tel: (305) 792-0745, explores the Native American side of Broward County. It's a history which is more often ignored after a perfunctory mention of the Seminole Wars which led to the elimination of Native Americans from most of South Florida. The only obvious signs of Native culture today are place names and a few tourist attractions, including the **Native Village**, 3551 N. SR 7, Hollywood, FL 33021; tel: (305) 961-4519 and **Seminole Indian Poker Casino**, 4150 N. SR 7, Hollywood, FL 33021; tel: (800) 323-5452 or (305) 961-3220.

**Buehler Planetarium**, 3501 S.W. Davie Rd, on the central campus of Broward Community College, Davie, FL; tel: (305) 475-6680, creates imaginary voyages through space and time. Admission $4. **Butterfly World**, 3600 W. Sample Rd, Coconut Creek, FL 33073; tel: (305) 977-4400, admission $8.95, has two-storey tropical aviaries stocked with butterflies from around the world. The facility includes an extensive research laboratory and insectarium.

### Parks and Gardens

**Flamingo Gardens**, 3750 Flamingo Rd, Davie, FL 33073; tel: (305) 473-2955, is a former citrus grove and private arboretum that has grown into a major botanical garden and tourist attraction. Admission $8. The gardens, with splendid tropical and subtropical specimens from around the world, include a wetlands area, complete with alligators, a hammock, parrots and the namesake flamingo flock. The only access to much of the garden is aboard a 1.5-mile narrated tram tour. **Everglades Holiday Park**, 21940 Griffin Rd, Ft Lauderdale, FL 33332; tel: (800) 226-2244 or (305) 434-8111, south-west of downtown, offers airboat tours of the Everglades outside the National Park boundaries that career through immense tracts of reeds at 60 mph and float almost silently past cautious alligators. Airboats also stop at a hammock for alligator wrestling and trinket sales. There is also fishing, with or without a guide, picnicking and an RV park.

# FORT LAUDERDALE–FORT MYERS

Suspend imagination on one of Florida's most efficient but featureless routes. Interstate 75 replaced State Route 84 as an east-west corridor more fondly remembered as Alligator Alley. The fast, partial toll road on the 135-mile route between Ft Lauderdale and Ft Myers is still called Alligator Alley by all Floridians, a tribute to the critters that were once a menace on the road in this northern patch of the Everglades.

A detour off I-75 to an Audubon Society sanctuary spices up the two-hour drive through an area still largely inhabited by Seminole and Miccosukee bands.

ROUTE: 135 MILES

## ROUTE

Pick up the beginning of **I-595** at US 1 by **Ft Lauderdale Hollywood International Airport** and go west 13 miles to the junction with **I-75**. Continue on I-75 west 84 miles to **Naples**, then follow the interstate 38 miles north to **Ft Myers**. For a Side Track to **Corkscrew Swamp Sanctuary**, take Exit 17, CR 846, 16 miles east and north. There will be only one opportunity to fill the petrol tank and drive between Ft Lauderdale and Naples, at the Indian Reservation station.

Take I-595 west from Ft Lauderdale. Ignore the temptation to

## FORT LAUDERDALE-FORT MYERS

take Florida's Turnpike or the Sawgrass Expressway. Instead, continue straight as dense city business areas yields to apartment complexes built on lagoons. After 13 miles, pick up I-75 as it turns left, west, rather than continuing north on the Sawgrass Expressway. A toll plaza is 5.5 miles west on I-75 ($0.75).

Emergency call boxes are spaced at every mile between the two toll booths along this route. The posted speed limit is 65 mph; most motorists go 75–85 mph.

Though designed to get travellers quickly across Southern Florida, I-75 is actually a good glimpse of what the everglades would look like if left undisturbed. The median between the two lanes in each direction is wide enough to give sanctuary to herons, anhingas, osprey, wood storks and other birds. Alligator Alley follows a canal.

Both sides of the interstate have 6–7 ft-high fences topped with barbed wire, but the vista is clear as the I-75 roadbed was constructed to rise every mile or so to allow swampy water to flow freely below. Cypress clumped in hammocks are more numerous onto the north side of the road.

Two marked Recreation Areas are on the left side, eight miles apart. Both are favourites of fishermen who enjoy the fishing and ample parking. Neither area has restrooms. The first recreation area has a boat-launching ramp on to the north side canal, to the right.

Midway across the peninsula is the **Indian Reservation**, *Snake Rd*, at the Broward-Collier County line a combination petrol station, lorry stop, food market, restaurant and souvenir shop, run by the Miccosukee Native Americans. The **Seminole Tribe of Florida**; *tel: (800) 949-6101*, operates **Billie Swamp Safari** tours; *tel: (305) 257-2134*, with jeep and hiking tours, overnight camping in *chickees*, wildlife viewing and wildlife and cultural shows.

Beyond the Indian Reservation, I-75 traverses **Big Cypress Swamp/ National Preserve** (see Miami–Fort Myers p. 118). Fourteen miles west of the reservation is the point where the last 35 miles of the **Florida National Scenic Trail** head south.

Seventeen miles west at Exit 14A, SR 29 goes south to Everglades City (see Everglades chapter p. 112 and Miami – Fort Myers p. 118) or north to Immokalee (pronounced im-mack-o-lee). To the north is the protected, inaccessible **Florida Panther National Wildlife Refuge**. The second I-75 toll booth is 19 miles west of the SR 29 junction.

At Exit 15, you can turn left on CR 951 to head to Marco Island, or go straight on SR 84 to downtown Naples (see Miami–Fort Myers chapter p. 118 for details of Naples and Marco Island). To complete this route continue on I-75 the 39 miles to downtown Fort Myers.

---

### The Big Banyan

You see something to marvel at even before you enter the Thomas Edison Museum at Fort Myers - one tree that makes a small forest. It's a banyan tree, claimed to be world's largest.

Banyans put down suckers which take root, forming new trunks, and this one has spread to a circumference of more than 400 ft.

# FORT LAUDERDALE–FORT MYERS

### ▶ SIDE TRACK TO CORKSCREW SWAMP SANCTUARY.

Take Exit 17, Immokalee Rd, east 10 miles past the Pelican Nursery and the Naples Quarry gravel pit to the National Audubon Society **Corkscrew Swamp Sanctuary**, *Sanctuary Rd, Route 6, Box 1875-A, Naples, FL, 33964; tel: (941) 657-3771,* open Dec–Apr 0700–1700, May–Nov 0800–1700. Admission $6.50. Early settlers named an unusually winding river Corkscrew, and the name stuck. A boardwalk over the swamp passes red maple hammocks, the world's largest remaining swamp for its buoyancy. Birds and volunteer naturalists are everywhere. In 1912, the Audubon Society stationed a warden in the area to enforce recent laws against plume poaching which had decimated the bird population in the southern half of the state.

By 1937, the birds had returned, part of a natural system that protects delicate green frogs and the much-appreciated mosquito fish which eat mosquito larvae and reduce the nipping that plagues visitors to most natural areas in the South. ◂

## *Alligators*

**S**panish explorers called it *el lagarto*, the lizard. That very large lizard, a throwback to 250 million years ago, was the alligator. Ugly? Perhaps, but size, thick body armour and powerful jaws make it an efficient survivor. On land, a seemingly lethargic beast can suddenly start running on very short legs at 35 mph. Its long, flexible tail turns a gator into an even more efficient predator in watery areas.

Yellow and black patterns on youngsters are camouflage against turtles and birds. For the first five years gators grow a foot a year as the armour hardens and darkens. Adult 'gators have black skin with a greenish sheen and a wide snout. The American crocodile, seldom seen, is grey with a narrow snout and a tooth protruding from the lower jaw.

Gators make holes in the mud, usually near a protected shore or bank of a river or pond, and can remain submerged for 20 mins. They are silent hunters, and a speedy 700-pound adult gator will protect its young fiercely.

A Native American tradition, now a tourist attraction, is gator wrestling. A tribesman grabs the jaw, strokes the throat, forces the mouth open, then flips the animal over to scratch the seemingly hypnotized creature's belly. The American alligator is no longer on the US Endangered Species list, and some restaurants serve alligator meat, especially 'gator tail. Hunting is left to professionals, licensed bounty hunters, many of whom have the scars to prove the effectiveness of the gator's survival techniques.

# FORT LAUDERDALE–WEST PALM BEACH

The 45-mile drive from Ft. Lauderdale to Palm Beach covers most of the Sun Coast, the nearly uninterrupted beach that lines Broward and Palm Beach Counties. Much of the beach, especially in Palm Beach County, is not open to the public. Beaches themselves are public throughout Florida, but access to the beach can be blocked by private land owners and beach parking may be prohibited by local laws.

SR A1A follows the barrier islands north, islands barely 1.5 miles wide in many places. There is seldom as much as three miles of semi-dry land between the surf and the calm Intracoastal Waterway. North Broward County merges imperceptibly into South Palm Beach County, the Atlantic Ocean surf slowly gaining strength to the north. Waves aren't the only thing getting higher on the way north. Prices for food, lodging and almost everything else rise with proximity to Palm Beach.

### Direct Route

DIRECT ROUTE: 45 MILES

**West Palm Beach**
A1A
15 miles
95 | Delray Beach
8 miles
45 miles | Boca Raton
2 miles
Deerfield Beach
8 miles
95 | Pompano Beach
10 miles
A1A | **Scenic Route**
Fort Lauderdale

### ROUTES

#### DIRECT ROUTE

➡ From downtown Ft Lauderdale, take I-95 north. The interstate passes through a patchwork of towns, including **Oakland Park, Pompano Beach, Deerfield Beach, Boca Raton**,

# FORT LAUDERDALE–WEST PALM BEACH

Delray Beach, Boynton Beach and Lake Worth on the way into West Palm Beach. Take Exit 54 eastbound onto SR 704 and cross Lake Worth (the Intracoastal Waterway) into the city of Palm Beach.

## Scenic Route

From central Ft Lauderdale, take S.E. 17th St (SR A1A) eastward over the **17th St Causeway**, which opens for ship traffic on the half hour. 17th St becomes Seabreeze Blvd, which turns into Atlantic Blvd near **Bahia Mar**, on the left. Continue northbound on The Strand, past Las Olas Blvd and Sunrise Blvd, to **Hugh Taylor Birch State Recreation Area**, *3109 E. Sunrise Blvd, Ft Lauderdale, FL 33304; tel: (305) 564-4521*. Birch, a Chicago attorney, settled in the village of Ft Lauderdale in 1893 and bought 3.5 miles of beachfront property. Appalled by post-World War II real estate development, he donated the property to the state as a public park. Birch's home is the visitor centre; the grounds shelter the last significant section of maritime hammock in Broward County and numerous endangered animal and plant species. A self-guiding nature walk explores the forest; a canoe trail explores a system of freshwater lagoons running the length of the park. There are also extensive picnic areas and beach access.

Ft Lauderdale continues north of the park, merging into the tiny community of **Lauderdale-by-the-Sea**, a cluster of low rise family-orientated motels clustered around **Anglin's Fishing Pier**. The town also offers some of the only walk-in off-the-beach scuba diving in South Florida. Dive shops have equipment for hire. The easiest beach access in **Pompano Beach** is between Atlantic Blvd and N.E. 5th St around the fishing pier. The **Goodyear Blimp**, based at the city airport, is a common sight. SR A1A swings inland to meet a drawbridge over **Hillsboro Inlet** to **Hillsboro Beach** and the **Hillsboro Mile**, some of Florida's finer homes. Skilful landscaping and imposing gates keep most of the estates extremely private. There's a better view of similarly posh homes west across the Intracoastal Waterway.

**Deerfield Beach** has some of the least-used beaches in the area because the strand is located well east of A1A. The road makes a sharp right turn back to the ocean and the Deerfield Beach **fishing pier**, just south of the boundary with Palm Beach County.

**Boca Raton**, the first community in Palm Beach County, charges theme park prices to enjoy its impressive string of city parks. **South Inlet Park**, on the south side of **Boca Raton Inlet**, is the first easy beach access north of Deerfield Beach. **South Beach Park**, **Red Reef Park**, and **Gumbo Limbo Nature Reserve** create an expansive strip of public lands opening onto the ocean and inland waters. **Spanish River Park** is Boca Raton's largest park.

The highway continues north along the barrier islands into **Highland Beach**, **Delray Beach**, **Boynton Beach**, and **Manalapan**, increasingly affluent suburbs of Palm Beach, with **Lake Worth** to the west. Most traffic turns west at Southern Blvd, US 98, into **West Palm Beach**. SR A1A continues north into **Palm Beach**.

### POMPANO BEACH

*Tourist Information*: Greater Pompano Beach Chamber of Commerce, *2000 E. Atlantic Blvd, Pompano Beach, FL 33062; tel: (305) 941-2940.*

# FORT LAUDERDALE–WEST PALM BEACH

## ACCOMMODATION

Chains include *BW, DI, Hd, HJ, QI* and *Rd*, but SR A1A from Ft Lauderdale north is lined with an ever-changing mix of moderate–pricey motels and hotels.

The Ft Lauderdale Convention and Visitors Bureau (see Ft Lauderdale p. 128) can make limited bookings for smaller motels throughout Broward County.

**Palm-Aire Resort and Spa**, *2501 N. Palm-Aire Dr. (at Powerline Rd), Pompano Beach, FL 33069; tel: (800) 272-5624 or (305) 972-3300*, very pricey, is Pompano's ultimate luxury spa and golf/tennis/swimming resort.

## EATING AND DRINKING

**Cap's Place**, *Cap's Dock, 2765 N.E. 28th Ct, Lighthouse Point, FL 33064; tel: (305) 941-0418*, is pricey but claims not to have changed a board since it was frequented by Winston Churchill and F. D. Roosevelt half a century ago. It is best known for broiled seafood, hearts of palm salad, and the free boat ride from the dock to the island restaurant.

**Fisherman's Wharf**, *on the pier, 222 Pompano Beach Blvd, Pompano Beach, FL 33304; tel: (305) 941-5522*, cheap–budget, is the most convenient stop for a quick meal on the pier.

**Pelican Pub**, *2635 N. Riverside Dr., Pompano Beach, FL 33304; tel: (305) 785-8550*, moderate, has docking space for diners and daily fish deliveries by boat.

## SIGHTSEEING

Pompano Beach is named after the popular white-fleshed fish that are caught off shore much of the year. The city's biggest draws are family-oriented beaches and fishing.

The 1080-ft **Municipal Pier** is the longest fishing pier on the Atlantic Coast of Florida and a popular spot for anglers. The city is also home to a large fleet of sport fishing boats, many of them specialising in swordfish.

The **Pompano Beach Fishing Rodeo**, held each May, is one of the largest sport fishing events in the US.

**Hillsboro Lighthouse**, *on Hillsboro Inlet at the north end of Pompano Beach*, is not open to the public, but the 1907 iron tower still warns mariners of reefs just 200 ft offshore. The reefs are as shallow as 15 ft, giving Pompano Beach and Lauderdale-by-the-Sea, just south, some of the easiest scuba diving on the Florida coast. There are another two dozen artificial reefs not far from shore, most of them derelict ships that were cleaned and sunk intentionally.

Pompano's unique attraction is the **Goodyear Blimp Base**, at *Pompano Air Park, 1001 N.E. 10th St (at Powerline Rd), Pompano Beach, FL 33311*. Visitors are welcome to watch the lighter-than-air ships take off and land every half hour during the day, but blimp rides are by invitation only – the tiny cabins hold no more than six passengers.

Pompano also has one of Florida's few surviving harness racing tracks, **Pompano Park Harness Track**, *1800 S.W. Third St (at Powerline Rd), Pompano Beach, FL 33311; tel: (305) 972-2000*.

**Gold Coast Opera**, *1000 Coconut Creek Blvd, Pompano Beach, FL 33066; tel: (305) 973-2323*, the area's oldest opera company, performs in Ft Lauderdale, Pompano Beach, Coral Springs and Boca Raton.

## DEERFIELD BEACH

**Tourist Information: Deerfield Beach Chamber of Commerce**, *1601 E. Hillsboro Blvd, Deerfield Beach, FL 33441; tel: (305) 462-0409*.

# FORT LAUDERDALE–WEST PALM BEACH

## Sightseeing

The city came by its name honestly. Until recent decades, deer grazed the banks of the Hillsboro River, which forms the boundary with Palm Beach County and becomes part of the Intracoastal Waterway.

The mile-long stretch of Atlantic Ocean beach that forms the town's eastern boundary has a pedestrian promenade lined with palm trees, a beach pavilion and a fishing pier. **Deerfield Island Park**, was once (mistakenly) thought to be the winter residence of Chicago gangster Al Capone, *from the dock at Hillsboro Blvd and the Intracoastal Waterway; tel: (305) 360-1320*, open daily 0800–sunset, has lush gardens, nature trails, wildlife, picnic areas and volleyball courts.

## BOCA RATON

**Tourist Information: Boca Raton Chamber of Commerce**, *1800 N. Dixie Hwy, Boca Raton, FL 33432; tel: (407) 395-4433*; the **Boca Raton Historical Society**, *71 N. Federal Hwy, Boca Raton, FL 33432; tel: (407) 395-6766*; and the **Palm Beach County Convention & Visitors Bureau**, *15555 Palm Beach Lakes Blvd, Suite 204, West Palm Beach, FL 33401; tel: (800) 554-4256 or (407) 471-3995*, provide information. Their brochures generally provide telephone numbers, but inexplicably omit addresses.

## Accommodation

Chains include *BW, ES, Hd, HJ, Ma, Rd, Rm, RI* and *Sh*. The **Boca Raton Resort and Club**, *501 E. Camino Real; tel: (407) 395-3000*, pricey, was Boca's original resort and remains the height of local luxury. Historical tours are offered Tues at 1300; *tel: (407) 392-3003*.

## Eating and Drinking

Boca Raton, a working city rather than a resort town, has many of the region's finest restaurants.

**The Cuban Cafe**, *3350 N.W. Boca Raton Blvd; tel: (407) 750-8860*, budget–moderate, is the best Cuban restaurant in town.

**Bagels With**, *Knightsbridge Shopping Center, 2 blocks north of Yamato Rd on N. Federal Hwy; tel: (407) 997-7108*, has excellent budget meals. **Maxluna**, *5050 Town Center Circle; tel: (407) 391-7177*, pricey, is *the* trendsetting restaurant north of Miami.

## Sightseeing

Boca Raton, usually called 'Boca', was built as a middle class version of Palm Beach by Addison Mizner, the same architect who created a corner of the Mediterranean in South Florida for Henry Flager. But where Mizner built mansions in Palm Beach, he designed hotels and homes for Boca. A burgeoning high tech community, started when IBM created its now-famous PC in Boca, has helped keep the economy vibrant and the population relatively young.

Boca also has the county's greatest concentration of parks, including **Gumbo Limbo Nature Center**, *1801 N. Ocean Blvd; tel: (407) 338-1473*, easily the best environmental education complex in south-east Florida. The centre offers a clear explanation of plant and animal communities from the beach to the dunes, hammocks and mangroves that once stretched the entire length of Florida. **Red Reef Park** surrounds the centre.

**Spanish River Park**, *just north on A1A*, has nature trails, extensive picnic and beach facilities, an observation tower, and, at the north end, an information

# FORT LAUDERDALE–WEST PALM BEACH

centre for the city park system. Fees for city parks, almost the only public access to the beaches, where you have to pay to get into the park and use the facilities, can run up to $10 per day.

**Arthur R. Marshall Loxahatchee National Wildlife Refuge**, *Rte 1 Box 278, Boynton Beach, FL 33437; tel: (407) 732-3684*, protects the marshy northern tip of the Everglades.

A five-mile canoe trail starts at headquarters on Lee Rd, south of SR 7. **Loxahatchee Ever-glades Tours**, *15490 West Lox Rd; tel: (407) 482-6107*, offers Everglades airboat tours. Polo season runs Dec–Apr at **Royal Palm Polo**, *6300 Old Clint Moore Rd; tel: (407) 994-1876*.

The **Royal Palm Dinner Theatre Center**, *303 S.E. Mizner Blvd; tel: (407) 392-3755*, offers a respectable Broadway season with good food. **Little Palm Theatre**, *same stage; tel: (407) 392-3755*, stages plays for children.

**Caldwell Theatre Company**, *7873 N. Federal Hwy; tel: (407) 241-7432*, is known for presenting challenging new scripts during the Oct–May season. **Children's Museum**, *498 Crawford Blvd; tel: (407) 368-6875*, has hands-on science exhibits, including a static-electricity generator that literally puts your hair on end.

**Boca Raton Museum of Art**, *801 Palmetto Park Rd; tel: (407) 392-2500*, has a solid collection of 20th-century paintings to support a full schedule of touring exhibitions. The **International Museum of Cartoon Art** is scheduled to open in early 1996 with the earliest known sketches of Mickey Mouse and other famous cartoon works.

**Boca Raton Historical Society**, *71 N. Federal Hwy; tel: (407) 395-6766*, has mementoes dating back to the 1920s and founder Addison Mizner. **Old Floresta**, *Oleander and Alamanda Sts between Palmetto Park Rd and 7th St*, is a fine example of his original 1920s neighbourhood design.

## DELRAY BEACH

**Tourist Information: Greater Delray Beach Chamber of Commerce**, *64 S.E. 5th Ave, Delray Beach, FL 33483; tel: (407) 278-0424.*

### SIGHTSEEING

Delray is a genuine small town, complete with a real main street, **Atlantic Ave**, lined with a succession of small stores, affordable restaurants, and local bars.

Nearby is **Old School Square**, *51 N. Swinton Ave; (407) 243-7922*, with three early 20th-century school buildings, including the **Crest Theatre**; *tel: (407) 243-3183*, and the **Cornell Museum of Art and History**. **Cason Cottage Museum**, *5 N.E. 1st St; tel: (407) 243-0223*, depicts typical life from the early 1900s.

The **Morikami Museum and Japanese Gardens**, *4000 Morikami Park Rd (off Carter Rd, near Florida's Turnpike); tel: (407) 495-0233*, is a tribute to the Yamato Colony, a nearby early 20th century Japanese farming community. Admission is $4.75. The restaurant has excellent budget Japanese meals.

**Blood's Hammock Groves**, *Linton Blvd, 2 miles west of I-95; tel: (800) 255-5188 or (407) 498-3400*, open Nov–Apr, has accessible citrus groves as well as seasonal citrus to taste and to buy. The public beach at the foot of Atlantic Blvd is one of the finest in Palm Beach County, with ample parking and sidewalk restaurants just across SR A1A – and it's free.

# THE PALM BEACHES

Palm Beach and West Palm Beach are Siamese twins who remain inextricably intertwined. Palm Beach began as a mosquito infested island on the ocean side of Lake Worth, the shallow bay between mainland and barrier islands. The world saw worthless scrub, but Henry Flagler saw a playground. Flagler's railway brought his rich and famous friends south for the winter, his hotels put them up, his real estate company sold them land for ornate mansions and Florida provided weather that looked little short of heavenly compared to New York City in January.

Flagler's elite enclave couldn't run itself, of course, so he built the town of West Palm Beach on the mainland to house the construction workers, household servants, shopkeepers and fawning sycophants that let America's upper crust create its own private and exclusive world. Palm Beach remains a tiny, glittery enclave replete with unspoken rules and *No Parking* signs.

Madame wouldn't dream of taking the family dog for a morning walk without first checking both of their respective coiffures and donning pearls to match her designer jogging-suit. But the people and the services that keep her community functioning, from maids to stock brokers and airports, remain in West Palm Beach.

## TOURIST INFORMATION

**Palm Beach County Convention & Visitors Bureau**, *1555 Palm Beach Lakes Blvd, Suite 204, West Palm Beach, FL 33401; tel: (800) 833-5733 or (407) 471-3995;* **The Chamber of Commerce of the Palm Beaches**, *401 N. Flagler Dr., West Palm Beach, FL 33401; tel: (407) 833-3711;* **Palm Beach Chamber of Commerce**, *45 Cocoanut Row, Palm Beach, FL 33480; tel: (407) 655-3282;* and the **Chamber of Commerce of Greater Lake Worth**, *1702 Lake Worth Rd, Lake Worth, FL 33463; tel: (407) 582-4401,* all provide information.

## ARRIVING AND DEPARTING

### Airport
**Palm Beach International Airport**, *1000 Turnage Blvd, West Palm Beach, FL 33406; tel: (407) 471-7420,* is three miles west of West Palm Beach. Unless you plan to spend the entire holiday in one place, hire a car. Taxis are few and expensive; public transport is impractical.

### By Car
**I-95**, **Florida's Turnpike** and **SR A1A** are the primary north–south roads into the Palm Beach Area. **Hwy 98** is the main highway from the west.

### By Boat
**The Port of Palm Beach**, *PO Box 9935, Riviera Beach, FL 33419; tel: (407) 842-4201,* is a busy passenger port. Cruise ship lines provide transport between airport and ship or ship and hotels, or hire cars can be picked up at the port.

# THE PALM BEACHES

## Getting Around

Public transport is one of the few things that money can't buy in Palm Beach. **CoTran**, Palm Beach County Transit, *Bldg S-1440, Palm Beach International Airport, West Palm Beach, FL 33406; tel: (407) 233-1111*, has a limited service that bypasses most tourist areas. **Tri-Rail**, *305 S. Andrews Ave, Suite 200, Ft Lauderdale, FL 33301; tel: (800) 874-7245*, has a daily service south to Ft Lauderdale and Miami.

## Staying in the Palm Beaches

### Accommodation

All of the major chains are represented in the Palm Beach area, primarily on the mainland. Palm Beach is quite seasonal. Much of the town closes down for the summer, May–Oct. Hotels are pricey in winter, moderate–pricey in summer. **The Breakers**, *One S. County Rd, Palm Beach, FL 33480; tel: (407) 655-6611*, is the ultimate Palm Beach experience. This Historic Landmark hotel has been a grand social centre since it opened at the height of the flapper era in 1926, but is now as much tourist attraction as hotel. **Brazilian Court Hotel**, *301 Australian Ave, Palm Beach, FL 33480; tel: (407) 655-7740*, was built to house the mistresses who discreetly followed their moneyed benefactors south for the winter. The hotel, built around fountains and courtyards, is far less forbidding than The Breakers. **The Ritz-Carlton Palm Beach**, *100 S. Ocean Blvd, Manalapan, FL 33462; tel: (407) 533-6000*, ten miles south of Palm Beach, has Palm Beach's elegance with friendlier staff and better food.

On the mainland, **MacArthurs' Holiday Inn**, *4431 PGA Blvd, Palm Beach Gardens, FL 33410; tel: (407) 622-2260*, is convenient to I-95. The **PGA National Resort & Spa**, *400 Ave of the Champions, Palm Beach Gardens, FL 33418; tel: (407) 627-2000*, is headquarters for both the Professional Golfers of America and the United States Croquet Association. Chain hotels offer moderate–expensive lodging. West Palm Beach has budget motels along US Hwy 1, but recent economic problems have left much of the highway area unsavoury at night. Singer Island, just north of Palm Beach, is a better budget choice.

### Eating and Drinking

It's hard to eat in Palm Beach without slipping into the upper end of the pricey range. It's even harder to eat well when image overpowers taste. The fanciest restaurants are fine, but hardly unusual (the clientele excepted), while the most famous rely more on reputation than excellence. The *Palm Beach Daily News* and *Palm Beach Life* document the comings, goings and dining preferences of local toffs in exquisite detail.

For food that actually tastes good, drive ten miles south to **The Ritz-Carlton Palm Beach**; *tel: (407) 588-4555*. The pricey hotel gets top marks for its Floridian cuisine. In Palm Beach itself, **Hamburger Heaven**, *314 S. County Rd, Palm Beach, FL 33480; tel: (407) 655-5277*, budget, has thick, drippy and delicious burgers. Look for the cow wearing a halo. **Green's Pharmacy and Luncheonette**, *151 N. County Rd, Palm Beach, FL 33480; tel: (407) 832-9171*, budget, has hearty American fare; the thick milk shakes and ice cream sodas are worth a trip in themselves. **Cape Cod Cafe**, *410 S. County Rd, Palm Beach, FL 33480; tel: (407) 659-4349*, budget–moderate, has reliable salads and sandwiches, more than 300 flavours of ice cream (32 on tap daily) and prime people-watching at the head of Worth Ave. **Au Bar**, *Royal Poinciana Plaza, 336 Royal Poinciana Way, Palm Beach, FL 33480; tel: (407) 832-4800*, pricey, is a long-time Kennedy family haunt. Since 1991, it's best known as the place William Kennedy Smith met a woman who accused him the next morning of rape.

### SIGHTSEEING

West Palm Beach welcomes visitors, Palm Beach grudgingly puts up with them. Society is closed, the streets are narrow, parking is rare and the beaches private.

But the ingrown, expensive, snobbish, and formal atmosphere that has kept Palm Beach so exclusive is also its biggest attraction. Most of the world treats decorating, design, landscaping and entertaining as useful trades, possibly even minor arts. In Palm Beach, they define existence. Nowhere else is the life of upper crust America in the 20th century on such public display. There are mansions from every decade, many of them associated with names like Kennedy, Vanderbilt, Pulitzer, Trump and Windsor.

The island is 14 miles long and four blocks wide. Larger homes and estates lie toward the south. The best way to see Palm Beach is slowly, the pace at which traffic generally moves. Cycling is even better: the views are closer and there is almost no parking outside the commercial heart of town. A bicycle trail follows the Lake Worth shoreline, much of N. County Rd and parts of S. County Rd (SR A1A). One of the most scenic rides is north on N. County Rd to the end of the island. Hotels can direct you to a bicycle hire stand.

Many homes are hidden behind tall walls and lush landscaping, but it *is* possible to see a few interiors. One way is to wait for Sun, when homes for sale go on public display. The other is to visit **Whitehall**, *One Whitehall Way* (off Cocoanut Row), *Palm Beach, FL 33480; tel: (407) 655-2833*. Once the palatial home of Henry Flagler, the white colonnaded mansion has become the **Henry Morrison Flagler Museum**, admission $5, filled with original and period furnishings. Flagler's private railroad carriage 'The Rambler' is on the south lawn.

Flagler set the tone for Palm Beach homage to wealth and power. **The Breakers** (see p. 145) is the third hotel on the site, the first being one of Flagler's original Palm Beach hostelries. **Worth Ave**, *Cocoanut Row east to S. Ocean Blvd*, was designed by Addison Mizner, whose Spanish and Mediterranean style formed Palm Beach. He created a fantasyland for shoppers with spotless sidewalks, a warren of flower-filled *vias*, or side streets, and a galaxy of famous-name designer boutiques. Most shops offer valet parking or validations (with a purchase) for car parks. Worth Ave is among the most exclusive shopping streets in the world, but there's less than meets the eye. Selections are thin compared to Miami or Boca Raton. **Via Mizner**, *west end of Worth Ave*, is the most spectacular arcade, with winding curves, Spanish-tiled vaults and bougainvillea creeping up every wall.

**The Church of Bethesda-by-the-Sea**, *141 S. County Rd, Palm Beach, FL 33380; tel: (407) 655-4554*, is a gothic wonder in coral stone, complete with stained glass windows and a 4000-pipe organ. Don't miss **Cluett Memorial Gardens**, *through the east arcade*, a grand moss-covered re-creation of an ancient formal Italian garden filled with tropical plants. **The Society of the Four Arts**, *Four Arts Plaza (near the east end of Royal Park Bridge), Palm Beach, FL 33480; tel:*

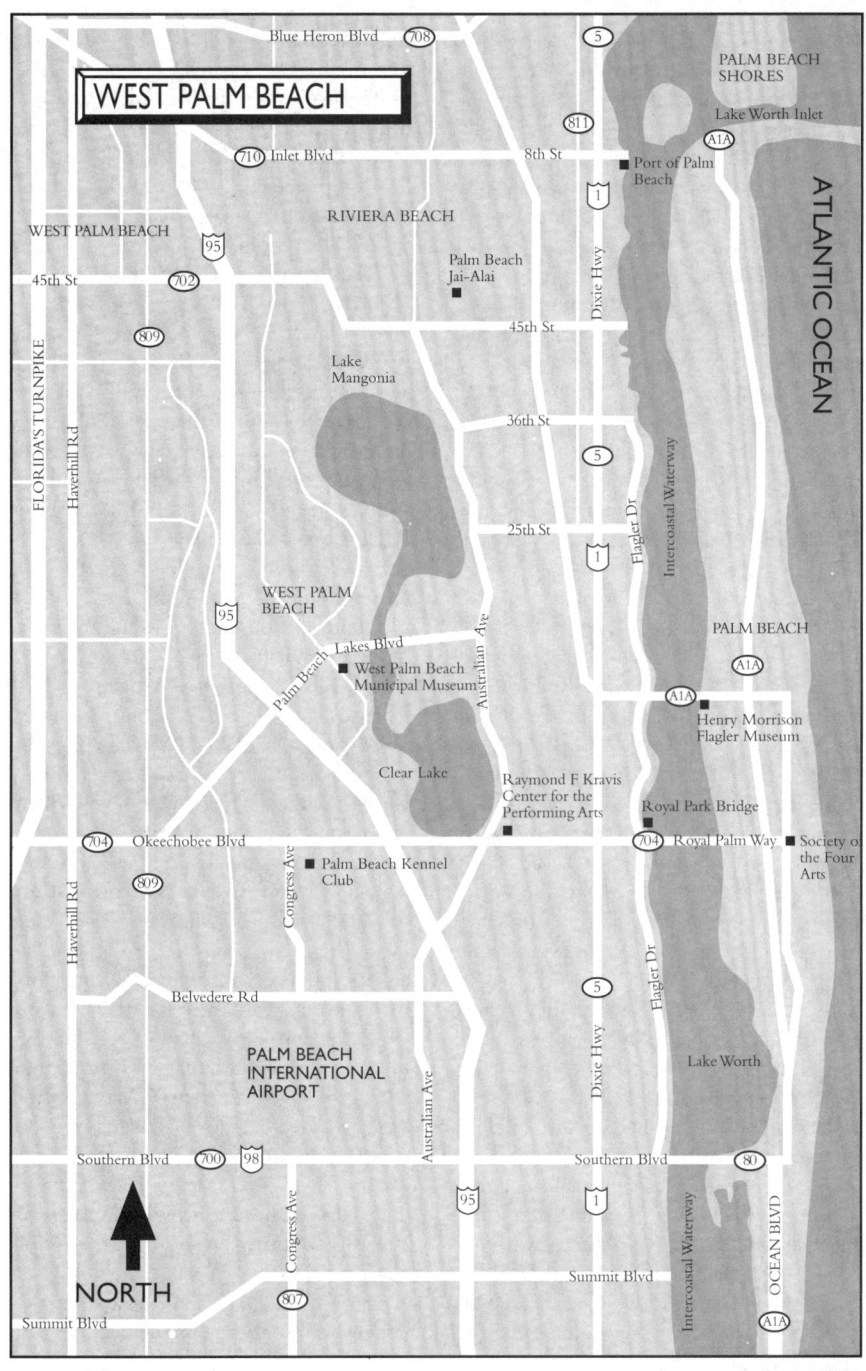

# THE PALM BEACHES

## WEST PALM BEACH

Blue Heron Blvd — 708
PALM BEACH SHORES
Lake Worth Inlet
811
A1A
710 Inlet Blvd
8th St
Port of Palm Beach
1
WEST PALM BEACH
RIVIERA BEACH
ATLANTIC OCEAN
95
Palm Beach Jai-Alai
45th St
702
Dixie Hwy
45th St
809
Lake Mangonia
36th St
FLORIDA'S TURNPIKE
Haverhill Rd
5
25th St
1
Flagler Dr
Intercoastal Waterway
95
WEST PALM BEACH
Palm Beach Lakes Blvd
West Palm Beach Municipal Museum
Australian Ave
PALM BEACH
A1A
A1A
Henry Morrison Flagler Museum
Clear Lake
Raymond F Kravis Center for the Performing Arts
Royal Park Bridge
704 Okeechobee Blvd
704 Royal Palm Way
Society of the Four Arts
809
Palm Beach Kennel Club
Congress Ave
Haverhill Rd
Belvedere Rd
5
Flagler Dr
PALM BEACH INTERNATIONAL AIRPORT
Australian Ave
Dixie Hwy
Lake Worth
Southern Blvd
700 98
Southern Blvd
80
OCEAN BLVD
95
1
Congress Ave
Summit Blvd
Intercoastal Waterway
A1A
↑ NORTH
807
Summit Blvd

**PALM BEACHES MAP**

*(407) 655-7226*, is a building devoted to art, music, drama and literature with an all-year programme at bargain prices.

Palm Beach was named after the palms that grew wild on the island when Flagler arrived. They are a rarity in South Florida. The palms sprouted after a ship carrying coconuts was wrecked on the island. Most of the island beaches are private and many Ocean Blvd homes have tunnels beneath the road leading to the surf. The only public beach in town worth noting is at *Gulfstream Rd and S. Ocean Blvd*, with very limited parking on side streets. The best public beaches on the island are **Phipps Ocean Park**, nine miles south of Palm Beach, and **Lake Worth Bathing Beach**, *Lake Ave and SR A1A*, another mile south.

On the mainland side of Lake Worth, **Flagler Drive** runs five miles *from Belvedere Rd north to 36th St* with a broad paved walkway on the water and sweeping views across to Palm Beach. **Currie Park**, *2400 N. Flagler Dr., West Palm Beach, FL 33480; tel: (407) 659-8071*, offers expansive lawns as well as playground and picnic facilities. **Star of Palm Beach**, *900 E. Blue Heron Blvd, Singer Island, FL 33404; tel: (407) 848-7827*, offers sightseeing and party cruises on Lake Worth. **Viking Princess**, *Port of Palm Beach; tel: (800) 841-7447*, has day-long cruises to the Bahamas. **Palm Beach Air Service**; *tel: (407) 585-5200*, offers low altitude sightseeing flights over Palm Beach in a biplane.

Palm Beach is famous for its polo club, which counts England's Prince Charles among its regular players, but **The Palm Beach Polo Club** is actually on the mainland at *13420 South Shore Blvd, Wellington, FL 33414; tel: (407) 793-1440*. Most other sports attractions are also in West Palm Beach: spring training for the **Atlanta Braves**; *tel: (407) 683-6100*, and the **Montreal Expos**; *tel: (407) 684-6801*, at **West Palm Beach Municipal Stadium**, *715 Hank Aaron Dr.*, dog races at the **Palm Beach Kennel Club**, *111 N. Congress Ave; tel: (407) 683-2222*, and **Palm Beach Jai-alai**, *1415 W. 45th St; tel: (407) 844-2444*.

**Lion Country Safari**, *Southern Blvd West* (off Hwy 98), *West Palm Beach; tel: (407) 793-1084*, entrance $11.95, is the country's oldest and largest drive-thru zoo. Lions, rhinos, elephants, giraffes and antelopes wander freely while humans drive through in cars. The lions are somewhat stand-offish, but ostriches and other animals regularly block traffic. **Dreher Park Zoo**, *1301 Summit Blvd, West Palm Beach, FL 33405; tel: (407) 533-0887*, is a more traditional zoo. Admission $5.

Children sometimes seem an afterthought in Palm Beach, but not at the **South Florida Science Museum**, *4801 Dreher Trail North, West Palm Beach, FL 33405; tel: (407) 832-1988*. The museum includes a native plant garden, an observatory with a 15.75-inch Newtonian reflector telescope, a planetarium, an aquarium and a hands-on light and sound hall. Admission $5. The **Norton Gallery of Art**, *1451 S. Olive Ave, West Palm Beach, FL 33401; tel: (407) 832-5194*, has an outstanding collection of impressionists and 20th-century artists, from Gauguin and Picasso to O'Keeffe. Admission free, but a donation is requested. The Art Deco **Armory Art Center**, *1703 S. Lake Ave, West Palm Beach, FL 33401; tel: (407) 832-1776*, hosts rotating exhibits by contemporary Florida artists. The **Raymond F. Kravis Center for the Performing Arts**, *701 Okeechobee Blvd, West Palm Beach, FL 33401; tel: (407) 659-2000*, stages theatre, dance, concerts and other performances.

# PALM BEACH–TITUSVILLE

It's possible to drive the 150 miles along the Atlantic Ocean from Palm Beach to Titusville in a single day, but only by ignoring some of the most historic and scenic stretches of Florida coastline. The coastal route runs from the semi-rural reaches of North Palm Beach to the Treasure Coast, where gold and silver coins from ancient Spanish wrecks still wash ashore, to the Space Coast, where all eyes are focused on the Kennedy Space Center when they aren't otherwise occupied with miles of beaches. Allow at least three days for the journey, stopping near Jensen Beach, Vero Beach and Cocoa Beach. To save time, drive a few miles west and take I-95.

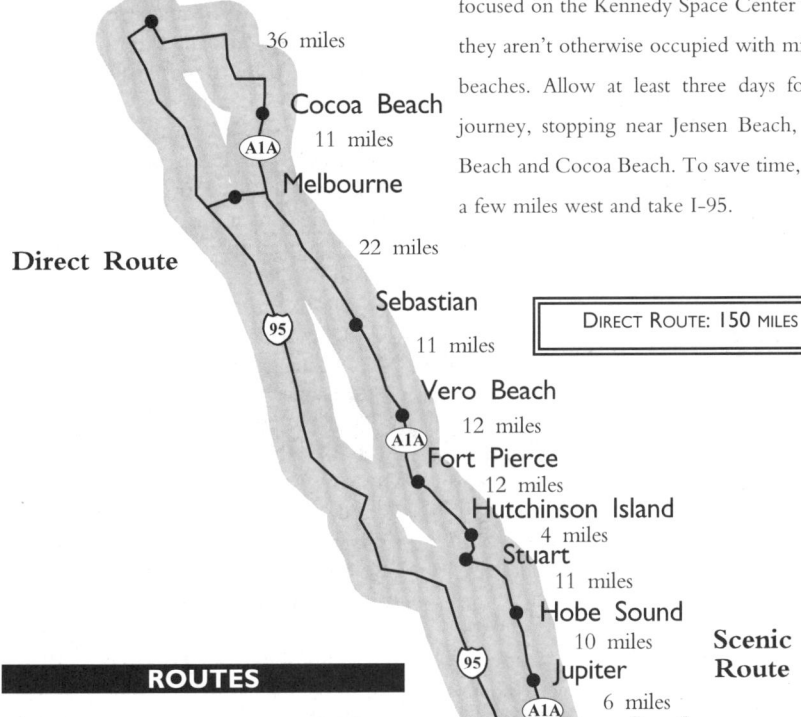

**Titusville**
36 miles
**Cocoa Beach** (A1A)
11 miles
**Melbourne**
22 miles
**Sebastian**
11 miles
**Vero Beach** (A1A)
12 miles
**Fort Pierce**
12 miles
**Hutchinson Island**
4 miles
**Stuart**
11 miles
**Hobe Sound**
10 miles
**Jupiter**
6 miles (A1A)
**Juno Beach**
6 miles
**Singer Island**
5 miles
**West Palm Beach**

**Direct Route**

DIRECT ROUTE: 150 MILES

Scenic Route

## ROUTES

### DIRECT ROUTE

From Palm Beach, cross any bridge west to the mainland and US 1, then take Okeechobee Blvd or Palm Lakes Blvd west to I-95 and turn north. I-95 traverses suburban housing estates, orange groves and light industrial areas. Much of the freeway is posted for 65 mph, though actual speeds are 10–15 mph faster despite heavy traffic. The roadway bypasses most towns until **Melbourne**, 121 miles north of West Palm Beach, but exits for petrol and food are clearly marked.

To reach **Orlando**, continue north on I-95 and go west at *Exit 75, SR 520; Exit 77, SR 528 (Beeline Expressway, toll)*; or *Exit 79, SR 50*. To reach **Titusville**, *take Exit 80 eastbound*.

## Scenic Route

From Palm Beach, take SR A1A across the Flagler Memorial Bridge to West Palm Beach and turn right onto Olive Ave, US 1/SR A1A. At the end of Olive Ave. turn left one block, then right onto S. ixie Hwy. Follow the road through a sharp left onto Northwood Rd, then a sharp right onto Broadway. **Northwood**, a 1920s neighbourhood, extends north to 59th St. The **Port of Palm Beach** is to the right on 8th St, Martin Luther King St, just north of a large power station on the Intracoastal Waterway.

Continue north to Blue Heron Blvd and turn right, crossing the **Blue Heron Blvd Bridge** onto **Singer Island**. The broad lawns and playgrounds of **Phil Foster Park**, *north-east foot of Blue Heron Blvd Bridge; tel: (407) 964-4420*, open onto the Intracoastal Waterway. Concessionaires sell Lake Worth sightseeing cruises and hire small boats and jet skis. Follow SR A1A toward the Atlantic Ocean and N. Ocean Blvd. **Singer Island Beach**, to the right, is often called the best beach in Palm Beach County for fine white sand that feels like silk. To the north along SR A1A is **John D. MacArthur Beach State Park**, *10900 SR 703 (A1A), North Palm Beach, FL 33408; tel: (407) 624-6950*. The park offers 1.5 miles of ocean beach, a 1600-ft boardwalk spanning Lake Worth Cove and walking paths through a hardwood hammock and mangroves. Rangers lead midnight turtle-spotting walks during the summer.

N. Ocean Blvd becomes PGA Blvd near **Lost Tree Village**, a private community. Turn right onto Ocean Dr. at **Oakbrook Square**, an expensive shopping plaza. Stay to the right, on SR A1A, at the **Seminole Golf Course**. Continue to the town of **Juno Beach**, **Loggerhead Park** and the **Marine Life Center of Juno Beach**. SR A1A continues through relatively undeveloped countryside toward the town of **Jupiter**, passing **Carlin Park**, **Jupiter Beach Park** and **Dubois Park** on the way to a drawbridge over **Jupiter Inlet**. The bright red **Jupiter Lighthouse** is just across the inlet.

Cross the bridge and turn right toward the lighthouse. SR A1A becomes SR 707, passing **Roaring Rocks Nature Preserve** and **Hobe Sound National Wildlife Refuge** before rejoining US 1. At **Palm City**, SR A1A turns right to cross **St. Lucie Inlet** onto **Hutchinson Island**. At the end of the island, SR A1A turns left into **Fort Pierce**, then right over **Fort Pierce Inlet** to **Fort Pierce Inlet State Recreation Area**. SR A1A follows the string of barrier islands all the way to Cape Canaveral. **Vero Beach** and **Sebastian Inlet** are the heart of the Treasure Coast. The reefs offshore claimed numerous ships laden with treasure during the Spanish colonial era. The Space Coast begins near **Melbourne**, south of the missile test centre at **Patrick Air Force Base**. **Cocoa Beach**, just north of Patrick, is a beach and dormitory community for the **John F. Kennedy Space Center**, which lies directly north. SR A1A turns eastward at the town of

Cape Canaveral and the cruise ship centre of Port Canaveral. Turn right (north) onto SR 3 and Merritt Island to enter the Kennedy Space Center. The road is closed during rocket launches. Continue northbound on SR 3 to SR 406 and turn left to pass the Kennedy Space Center Visitors Center. Follow SR 406 to US 1, turn right, and continue eight miles into Titusville.

## SINGER ISLAND

Tourist Information: The Chamber of Commerce of Northern Palm Beach, *1983 PGA Blvd, Suite 104, Palm Beach Gardens, FL 33408; tel: (407) 694-2300.*

### ACCOMMODATION

In the 1920s, the island was owned by Paris Singer, of the sewing machine family, who planned to turn it into a second Palm Beach. Singer lost the island in a divorce settlement. Chains include *DI, Hd, QI* and *Sh*. Both chains and local motels are moderate–expensive alternatives to pricey Palm Beach.

## JUNO BEACH

Tourist Information: Jupiter-Tequesta-Juno Beach Chamber of Commerce (see under 'Jupiter', right) covers Juno Beach.

### SIGHTSEEING

The area's first railroad, the Jupiter and Lake Worth Railroad, started from Juno in 1888. Called the 'Celestial Railroad' for its main stops of Jupiter, Mars, Venus and Juno, the line continued south to Lake Worth and eventually became part of Henry Flagler's Florida East Coast Railway. The Mars and Venus stations have disappeared.

The Marine Life Center of Juno Beach, in Loggerhead County Park, *1200 Hwy 1, Juno Beach, FL 33408; tel: (407) 627-8280*, has late-night summer beach walks to spot sea turtles. Don't look for sparkling lights to illuminate Atlantic Ocean beaches at night. Laws prohibit artificial lights from shining on the sand most of the year to avoid confusing endangered sea turtles.

The turtles use the beacon of the moon to help find their way to beaches to lay eggs during the summer months. What look like tread marks between the surf line and the dunes in the morning light are the tracks of female turtles which have come ashore during the night to lay their eggs in the sand. The hatchlings, which emerge six to eight weeks afterwards, also use the moon to find their way over the open beach, where they are an easy meal for any passing predator, into the relative protection of the water. Bright lights from shore can cause both adult and baby turtles to crawl in the wrong direction. Most beachside hotels request that light-proof curtains be drawn between sunset and sunrise.

## JUPITER

Tourist Information: Jupiter-Tequesta-Juno Beach Chamber of Commerce, *800 N. US 1, Jupiter, FL 33477; tel: (407) 746-7111.*

### ACCOMMODATION

The Jupiter Beach Resort, *5 N. A1A, Jupiter, FL 33477; tel: (407) 745-7154*, pricey, is the only beach resort in town. Area chains include *Hd* and *HJ*.

### EATING AND DRINKING

Harpoon Louie's Restaurant, *1065 SR A1A, Jupiter, FL 33468; tel: (407) 744-1300*, budget–moderate, has ordinary seafood and a spectacular dusk view of the bright red lighthouse across Jupiter Inlet. **Charlie's Crab**, *1000 N. Hwy, Jupiter, FL 33468; tel: (407) 744-4710*, budget–moderate, has better food but lesser views.

### SIGHTSEEING

Jupiter was founded as an army post in 1838 during the Seminole Indian Wars. The **Jupiter Lighthouse**, *US 1 and Alt SR A1A just north of the Jupiter–Tequesta Bridge; tel: (407) 747-8380*, was completed in 1860 but extinguished during the Civil War. The light was relit in 1866 and can still be seen 27 miles out to sea. The tower is open Sun–Wed. Children must be at least 48 inches tall to climb the spiral staircase. The lighthouse is part of the **Florida History Center & Museum**, *805 N. Hwy 1, Jupiter, FL 33477; tel: (407) 747-6639*, admission $3, in **Burt Reynolds Park** on the south side of the inlet. The centre's excellent **Loxahatchee Museum** concentrates on regional seafaring history. The **Dubois House** is one of the oldest surviving structures in the area. The 1898 house was built atop a Native American shell mound, or midden, believed to be the site of the village where Jonathan Dickinson (see under Hobe Sound) and other shipwreck survivors lived before trekking north.

The easiest way to see the Jupiter Inlet area is by boat. **Louie's Lady**; *tel: (407) 744-5550*, sightseeing and dining cruises leave from the dock at Harpoon Louie's. The **Manatee Queen**; *tel: (407) 744-2191*, leaves from the dock near Charlie's Crab. Both cruises pass **Jupiter Inlet Colony**, a tiny private community at the end of Jupiter Island, on the north side of the inlet. The Colony is the winter home for many of the captains of America's richest industrial enterprises. **Canoe Outfitters of Florida**, *16346 N. 106th Terrace, Jupiter, FL 33478; tel: (407) 746-7053*, hires canoes to explore the **Loxahatchee River**, the only surviving cypress freshwater river system in South Florida. An eight mile canoe trail heads north to Jonathan Dickinson State Park.

Local son and cinema star Burt Reynolds founded the **Jupiter Theater**, *1001 E. Indiantown Rd, Jupiter, FL 33477; tel: (407) 746-5566*. A full season of musicals and dramas draws crowds from as far away as Ft Lauderdale. **Burt Reynolds Ranch**, *16133 Jupiter Farms Rd, Jupiter, FL 33478; tel: (407) 746-0393*, part horse ranch, part cinema/television studio, has daily tours and a petting zoo.

On the north side of Jupiter Inlet, **Blowing Rocks Preserve**, *PO Box 3795, Tequesta, FL 33469; tel: (407) 575-2297*, preserves one of the longest stretches of virgin beach between Cape Canaveral and Key West, less than one mile in length. An ancient coral reef along the shore funnels incoming waves into huge spouts of blowing spray. No swimming is allowed, but the Nature Conservancy, which owns the preserve, has well-marked trails through beach, dune, hammock and mangrove.

## HOBE SOUND

**Tourist Information: Hobe Sound Chamber of Commerce**, *PO Box 1507, Hobe Sound, FL 33475; tel: (407) 546-4724*, covers the southern end of Martin County.

### SIGHTSEEING

**Jonathan Dickinson State Park**, off *US 1, 16450 S.E. Federal Hwy, Hobe Sound, FL 33455; tel: (407) 546-2771*, is named after the merchant who led a band of shipwrecked Quakers from Jupiter Inlet north to St. Augustine in 1696. Dickinson's journal was an important source of information about coastal

Florida as well as the first best-seller written in North America. The park preserves several important habitats, including upland pine forests, much of the Loxahatchee River, and rare coastal pines. Entrance $3.25. **Loxahatchee River Adventures**, *16450 S.E. Federal Hwy, Hobe Sound, FL 33455; tel: (800) 746-1466*, offers narrated Loxahatchee River tours and hires canoes for do-it-yourself exploration. There are also extensive walking trails and campsites in the park.

**Hobe Sound National Wildlife Refuge**, *PO Box 214, Hobe Sound, FL 33475; tel: (407) 546-2067*, protects a large section of upland forest and coastal marsh from development. A self-guided walking trail explores the diverse plant and animal communities. A privately-operated Nature Center oversees several research projects and the visitor centre.

## STUART

**Tourist Information**: Stuart/Martin County Chamber of Commerce, *1650 S. Kanner Hwy, Stuart, FL 34944; tel: (800) 524-9704 or (407) 287-1088*.

### ACCOMMODATION

Hd is the only chain, but there are a number of motels and Bed and Breakfasts throughout the area. Other chain hotels are located just north, in and around Jensen Beach, on Hutchinson Island. **Harbor Front Inn**, *310 Atlanta Ave, Stuart, FL 34994; tel: (407) 288-7289*, moderate, is a relaxed Bed and Breakfast overlooking the St. Lucie River.

### SIGHTSEEING

Stuart is the eastern terminus of the Okeechobee Waterway, which crosses Florida to the Gulf of Mexico via Lake Okeechobee. There is excellent fishing in the Indian River (the Intracoastal Waterway) and deep sea fishing in the Gulf Stream, about 10 miles offshore. A Chamber of Commerce brochure details a self-guided walking tour of the city.

**Island Water Taxi**; *tel: (407) 285-6292*, provides transport and easy sightseeing along the waterfront from Stuart to Jensen Beach and Hutchinson Island.

## HUTCHINSON ISLAND

**Tourist Information**: The Greater St Lucie County Chamber of Commerce, *1626 S.E. Port St Lucie Blvd, Port St Lucie, FL 34592; tel: (407) 595-9999*, concentrates on Southern St Lucie County. **Jensen Beach Chamber of Commerce**, *1910 N.E. Jensen Beach Blvd, Jensen Beach, FL 34957; tel: (407) 334-3444*, covers Hutchinson Island and can book late-night turtle watching tours.

### ACCOMMODATION

**Indian River Plantation Beach Resort**, *555 N.E. Ocean Blvd, Stuart, FL 34996; tel: (407) 225-0003*, pricey, is the only flashy resort in the area. More typical is the **Holiday Inn Oceanside**, *3793 N.E. Ocean Blvd, Jensen Beach, FL 34957; tel: (407) 225-3000*, quiet and extremely convenient to I-95. Other chains include BW, CI, DI, HJ and Ma. SR A1A, N.E. Ocean Blvd, is lined with small moderate motels. Motels along US 1, on the mainland side of the S. Lucie River, tend toward the budget range. The **Hutchinson Inn**, *9750 S. Ocean Dr, Jensen Beach, FL 34957; tel: (407) 339-2000*, moderate–expensive, may be the only Bed and Breakfast on the island.

### SIGHTSEEING

South Hutchinson Island runs from the north side of St Lucie Inlet 16 miles north to Fort Pierce Inlet. Most of the Atlantic Ocean side of the island is open beach.

## PALM BEACH–TITUSVILLE

**Bathtub Reef Park**, just north of St Lucie Inlet, is named after a shallow reef near shore. The reef is exposed at low tide, creating a broad, shallow wading area for young children. **Stuart Beach Park** is popular with teenagers and young adults. **Jensen Beach Park**, just north, is filled with families.

**Gilbert's Bar House of Refuge Museum**, *301 McArthur Blvd, Hutchinson Island, FL 34597; tel: (407) 225-1875*, is Florida's last surviving coastal life-saving station. The 1875 house and observation tower are now a museum; admission $2. **Elliot Museum**, *825 N.E. Ocean Blvd, Hutchinson Island, FL 34597; tel: (407) 225-1961*, admission $4, is filled with everyday technology from the 19th and early 20th centuries. The **Florida Power & Light Energy Encounter**, *Gate B, FP&L St Lucie Nuclear Power Station, 6501 S. SR A1A, Hutchinson Island; tel: (407) 468-4111*, explores the ways modern society uses and produces energy. The **FP&L Turtle Beach Nature Trail**, *just north of the power station on the east side of SR A1A*, is a well marked path through coastal mangrove, hammock and dunes. **Island Princess Cruises**, *555 N.E. Ocean Blvd, Stuart, FL 34996; tel: (407) 225-2100*, offers sightseeing cruises along the St Lucie and Indian Rivers.

### FORT PIERCE

**Tourist Information: The Greater Saint Lucie County Chamber of Commerce**, *2200 Virginia Ave, Fort Pierce, FL 34982; tel: (407) 595-9999*, covers northern St Lucie County.

### ACCOMMODATION

Hotels and motels are concentrated along SR A1A on North and South Hutchinson Islands and US 1 on the mainland. Chains include *BW, CI, DI, Hd, HJ* and *Ma*.

### SIGHTSEEING

Fort Pierce was once a military base during the Seminole Wars. Most of North Hutchinson Island, like its twin to the south, is lined with open beaches.

The easiest way to see the town is with a self-guided **historic walking tour** brochure from *Fort Pierce Main Street, 131 N. 2nd St, Fort Pierce, FL 34950; tel: (407) 466-3880*. The **St Lucie County Historical Museum**, *414 Seaway Dr, Fort Pierce, FL 34949; tel: (407) 462-1795*, begins its fine displays with the pre-Columbian Ais Indians, admission $2. **Heathcote Botanical Gardens**, *210 Savannah Rd, Fort Pierce, FL 34982; tel: (407) 464-4672*, surround a 1922 home. **The Savannas Recreation Area**, *1400 E. Midway Rd, Fort Pierce, FL; tel: (407) 464-7855*, is 550 acres of freshwater wilderness with fishing, boating, camping and walking. The **Spirit of St Joseph**, *414 Seaway Dr., Fort Pierce, FL 34949; tel: (407) 467-2628*, offers Intracoastal Waterway cruises Nov–Apr.

**Fort Pierce Jai-Alai**, *Kings Hwy; tel: (407) 464-7500*, is open Nov–Apr. The **New York Mets** spring baseball training camp is at **St Lucie Stadium**, *525 N.W. Peacock Blvd, Port St Lucie, FL 34986; tel: (407) 871-2100*. **Manufacturer's Outlet Center**, *I-95 and SR-70 (Okeechobee Rd)*, is the area's major shopping centre.

**Fort Pierce Inlet State Recreation Area**, *905 Shorewinds Dr, Fort Pierce, FL 34949; tel: (407) 468-3985*, has two sections. The smaller, on the north shore of Fort Pierce Inlet, provides camping, picnicking, fishing and a hammock nature trail. The larger, **Jack Island Preserve**, *1.5 miles north on SR A1A*, is a mangrove peninsula with several miles of walking trails and hordes of mosquitoes.

The **UDT–SEAL Museum**, usually called **The Frogmen Museum**, *3300 N.*

SR A1A, Fort Pierce, FL 34954; tel: (407) 595-1570, admission $2, graphically shows the history of the US Navy's underwater demolition teams (UDT) and sea, air, land (SEAL) commando units. UDT training began on the museum site in the 1940s. The **Urca de Lima Underwater Archaeological Preserve**, *0.6 miles north of the museum and 200 yards offshore in 10–15 ft of water*, harbours the wreck of the *Urca de Lima*, a Spanish treasure and supply ship that sank in a July, 1715 hurricane. Displays from an 11-ship fleet that foundered off the Treasure Coast can be seen at the **St Lucie County Historical Museum**, Fort Pierce, the **McLarty Treasure Museum**, Sebastian (see next page) and the **Museum of Florida History**, Tallahassee (p. 303). **Harbor Branch Oceanographic Institution**, *5600 US 1 N., Fort Pierce, FL 34946; tel: (407) 465-2400*, offers a detailed tour of one of the world's top marine research institutions.

## VERO BEACH

**Tourist Information: Vero Beach–Indian River County Chamber of Commerce**, *1216 21st St, Vero Beach, FL 32961; tel: (800) 338-2768 or (407) 567-3491*.

### ACCOMMODATION

Chains include CI, DI, Hd and HJ. **Days Hotel–Vero Beach Resort**, *3244 Ocean Dr., Vero Beach, FL 32963; tel: (407) 231-2800*, moderate, is among the most reasonable beachfront choices.

### SIGHTSEEING

Vero Beach has long been a quietly prosperous beach and residential community, but business is likely to increase in late 1995 when Disney opens its **Vero Beach Resort** at *SR 510 and SR A1A*. The **Indian River Citrus Museum**, *2140 14th Ave, Vero Beach, FL 32960; tel: (407) 770-2263*, celebrates Vero Beach's continuing success with citrus growing. The museum has antique citrus labels and packing equipment, historic tools, photographs, and can arrange tours of citrus packing plants. **Hale Groves** has citrus shops on *S. US 1 north of 4th St; Beachland Blvd, one block west of SR A1A; and I-95 at SR 60*. The **Indian River County Historical Society** has turned the town's 1903 railroad station into a local museum, *2336 14th Ave, Vero Beach, FL 32961; tel: (407) 778-3435*.

**The Center for the Arts**, *3001 Riverside Park Dr., Vero Beach, FL 32963; tel: (407) 231-0707*, hosts art exhibitions, lectures, films, concerts and theatrical performances. The surrounding **Riverside Park** has quiet, expansive lawns and picnic areas opening onto the Intracoastal Waterway and an active tennis centre.

**Horizon Outlet Center**, *SR 60 at I-95, Vero Beach, FL 32963; tel: (800) 866-5900*, has about 60 outlet shops. The major sporting attraction is **Dodgertown**, *Holman Stadium, 3901 Dodger Rd, Vero Beach, FL 32961; tel: (407) 569-6858*, the **Los Angeles Dodgers** spring baseball training camp. **Windsor Polo Club**, *10155 Hwy A1A, Vero Beach, FL 32963; tel: (407) 589-9800*, holds matches most Suns Nov–May.

**McKee Botanical Gardens**, *4871 N. A1A, Vero Beach, FL 32963; tel: (407) 234-1949*, was opened in 1932, then gradually sold off to developers. Eighteen acres of the original landscaped 'jungle' have survived and been reopened. The **Environmental Learning Center**, *on CR 510, Wabasso Island; tel: (407) 589-5050*, has extensive displays and education programs on the 160-mile long Indian River lagoon that stretches south from Cape Canaveral. The paddlewheel

River Queen, *1606 Indian River Dr., Sebastian; tel: (407) 589-6161,* is an easy way to see the river.

## SEBASTIAN

**Tourist Information: Sebastian River Area Chamber of Commerce**, *1302 US 1, Sebastian, FL 32958; tel: (407) 589-5969,* covers Northern Indian River County.

### SIGHTSEEING

In July 1715, the 1500 treasure fleet survivors made camp just south of Sebastian Inlet and began to salvage what they could, soon aided by divers from Havana and St Augustine. The **McLarty Treasure Museum**, *9700 S. A1A, Melbourne Beach, FL 32951; tel: (407) 589-2147,* built on the site of the original salvage camp, covers the fleet and successive efforts to recover the tons of gold, silver and jewels that never made it to Spain's royal treasury. Admission $1. **Mel Fisher's Treasure Museum**, *1322 US 1, Sebastian, FL 32958; tel: (407) 589-9875,* admission $5, explores the same fleet, plus Fisher's successful efforts to find and salvage other Spanish treasure ships. The museum extols Fisher's ventures to the virtual exclusion of other salvagers, but has the area's best exhibits of genuine Spanish colonial gold, silver and other artefacts.

Sebastian Inlet is surrounded by **Sebastian Inlet State Recreation Area**, *9700 S. A1A, Melbourne Beach, FL 32951; tel: (407) 984-4852,* with fishing, picnicking and beach facilities on both the Indian River and the Atlantic Ocean. The inlet is artificial, like most of the passes through the Florida East Coast barrier islands. The inlets provide access to the sea, but they are also responsible for the disappearance of beaches up and down the coast.

Florida's beaches began as sand washed down from the Appalachian Mountains, then carried south along the Carolinas and Georgia to Florida. Storms wash Florida's beaches out to sea; southbound currents from the north replenish them. Sebastian and other artificial inlets disrupt the natural flow of sand south along the coast, creating dramatic erosion. Atlantic waves now lap at the foundations of buildings that were well over 100 yards from the water within living memory.

## MELBOURNE

**Tourist Information: Melbourne Palm Bay Area Convention and Visitors Bureau**, *1005 E. Strawbridge Ave, Melbourne, FL 32901; tel: (800) 771-9922* or *(407) 724-5400,* covers the Southern Space Coast. **Florida's Space Coast Office of Tourism**, *2725 St Johns St, Melbourne, FL 32940; tel: (800) 872-1969* or *(407) 633-2110,* also has information booths at Kennedy Space Center and Melbourne International Airport.

### ARRIVING AND DEPARTING

**Melbourne International Airport**, *One Airterminal Pkwy, Suite 220, Melbourne, FL 32901; tel: (407) 723-6227,* is one mile north of Melbourne. **Cocoa Beach Shuttle**; *tel: (800) 633-0427* or *(407) 784-3831,* provides transport between Space Coast cities and Orlando International Airport.

### ACCOMMODATION

SR A1A is lined with hotels and motels. Chains include *CI, Hd, Hn, Ma, QI, Ra* and *Rm;* density and prices increase toward Cocoa Beach and the Kennedy Space Center. US 1 motels are usually older and cost somewhat less than their barrier-island counterparts.

**Days Inn Palm Bay**, *4700 Dixie Hwy, Palm Bay, FL 32905; tel: (407) 951-0350*, moderate, has unusually spacious rooms. The **Melbourne Beach Hilton Ocean-front**, *3003 N. A1A, Indiatlantic, FL 32903; tel: (407) 777-5000*, is particularly convenient to I-95. Advance bookings are a must during the winter season and anytime a rocket launch is scheduled. Most hotels in this area offer **NASA Select** television coverage of launches.

### SIGHTSEEING

Melbourne and the rest of the Space Coast are satellites of the space industry and Kennedy Space Center (see also Space Coast, p. 158). Mainland towns are also involved in agriculture and light industry; island towns rely on tourism.

Natural areas are increasingly hard to find in heavily populated Brevard County. **Turkey Creek Sanctuary**, *Port Malabar Blvd N.E., Palm Bay, FL 32906; tel: (407) 952-3433*, has a nature centre and boardwalks through freshwater hammock and sand pine ecozones.

The **Florida Institute of Technology Botanical Gardens**, *150 W. University Blvd, Melbourne, FL 32940; tel: (407) 768-8000*, has an outstanding palm collection.

The **Maxwell King Center for the Performing Arts**, *3865 N. Wickham Rd, Melbourne, FL 32935; tel: (407) 242-2219*, is the county's leading venue for top touring performers.

The **Florida Marlins** hold spring baseball training at **Space Coast Stadium**, *5600 Stadium Parkway, Melbourne, FL 32940; tel: (407) 633-9200*. **Melbourne Greyhound Park**, *1100 N. Wickham Rd, Melbourne, FL 32935; tel: (407) 259-9800*, has dog racing and betting.

## COCOA BEACH

**Tourist Information: Cocoa Beach Area Chamber of Commerce**, *400 Fortenberry Rd, Merritt Island, FL 32952; tel: (407) 459-2200*.

### ACCOMMODATION

Chain hotels in Cocoa Beach include BW, DI, CI, Hd, HJ and Rd.

### SIGHTSEEING

Cocoa Beach was a local favourite long before America's space program brought astronauts and fame to the area. **Cocoa Beach Pier**, *401 Meade Ave, Cocoa Beach, FL 32931; tel: (407) 783-8549*, 800 ft long, offers fishing, surfing, dining and dancing. **Port Canaveral**, *just north on SR A1A; tel: (407) 783-7831*, is one of the busiest cruise ports in Florida. **Ron Jon Surf Shop**, *4151 N. Atlantic Ave, Cocoa Beach, FL 32931; tel: (407) 799-8888*, an Art Deco-style palace open 24 hrs, has the best selection of surf and beach gear in the area *and* some of the highest prices.

**Cocoa Village**, *Brevard and Delannoy Aves just south of SR 520* in the mainland town of Cocoa, is the turn-of-the-century heart of the area. The **Historic Cocoa Village Association**, *274 Brevard Ave, Cocoa, FL 32922; tel: (407) 631-9075*, publishes a self-guided walking tour brochure. **The Brevard Museum**, *2201 Michigan Ave, Cocoa, FL 32926; tel: (407) 632-1830*, has a solid local history collection, including fine exhibits on the Windover People, Native Americans who lived in the area about 7000 years ago. **Valiant Air Command War Bird Air Museum**, *6600 Tico Rd, Titusville, FL 32765; tel: (407) 268-1941*, has an extensive display of World War II and Vietnam-era military aircraft, many in flying condition. Admission $6.

## THE SPACE COAST

# THE SPACE COAST

Florida's Space Coast has landscapes unchanged since before the first Europeans arrived in the 16th century side by side with the highest technical achievements of the 20th century. This is a compact stretch of marshland, savannah, beaches and islands with Titusville at its centre. Here, where those early explorers sailed, modern mankind is reaching out to the boundless horizons beyond the solar system.

### TOURIST INFORMATION

**Florida's Space Coast Office of Tourism**, *2725 St John's St, Melbourne, FL 32940; tel (800) 872-2110*, has information about lodgings and attractions. It also has an information booth at Kennedy Space Centre.

### ARRIVING AND DEPARTING

US Hwy 1, the north–south coastal route that runs parallel with I-95 for much of the way between Miami and the Georgia State line, goes through Titusville. From the west, the city is reached by Hwy 560 or the Beeline Expressway (Hwy 528) and Hwy 407. Four miles south of downtown Titusville Hwy 405 crosses the Intracoastal Waterway via the NASA Causeway to reach Spaceport USA.

### TITUSVILLE

**Tourist Information: Titusville Area Chamber of Commerce**, *2000 S. Washington Ave; tel: (407) 267-3036*. Regional maps, an accommodation directory and a guide to restaurants are available.

### ACCOMMODATION

There is a reasonable selection of hotels and motels mostly within easy reach of downtown Titusville. Hotel chains include: *BW, CI, Hd, HJ, QI, Rd*. Accommodation will obviously be under pressure at the time of a Space Center launch. See Palm Beach–Titusville chapter, pp. 149–157 for accommodation to the south. The nearest *KOA* campsite is the **Cape Kennedy KOA**, *4513 W. Main St (Rte 46), Mims* (seven miles north of Titusville); *tel: (407) 269-7361 or 1-800-848-4562*. Other campsites are **Holiday Village Travel Park**, *3550 N. Hwy 1, Mims; tel: (407) 269-6542*; **Manatee Hammock Park**, *7275 S. Hwy 1, Titusville; tel: (407) 264-5083*.

### SIGHTSEEING

Fronting the Indian River, **Titusville** is a workaday community of about 40,000 residents. Not surprisingly, the city's major industries are related to space technology, and with NASA's pads barely ten miles away, it's a great place to view a launch.

The city has some splendid riverfront homes and its *Main St* is a designated National Historic District with a number of fine buildings from the late 18th and early 19th centuries. The **Valiant Air Command Warbird Museum**, *6600 Tico Rd* (part of the Space Coast Executive Airport); *tel: (407) 268-1941*, houses a collection of more than 350 vintage World War II and post-war military aircraft. There are static aircraft displays and memorabilia, and visitors can watch aircraft restorers at work. Each Mar, some

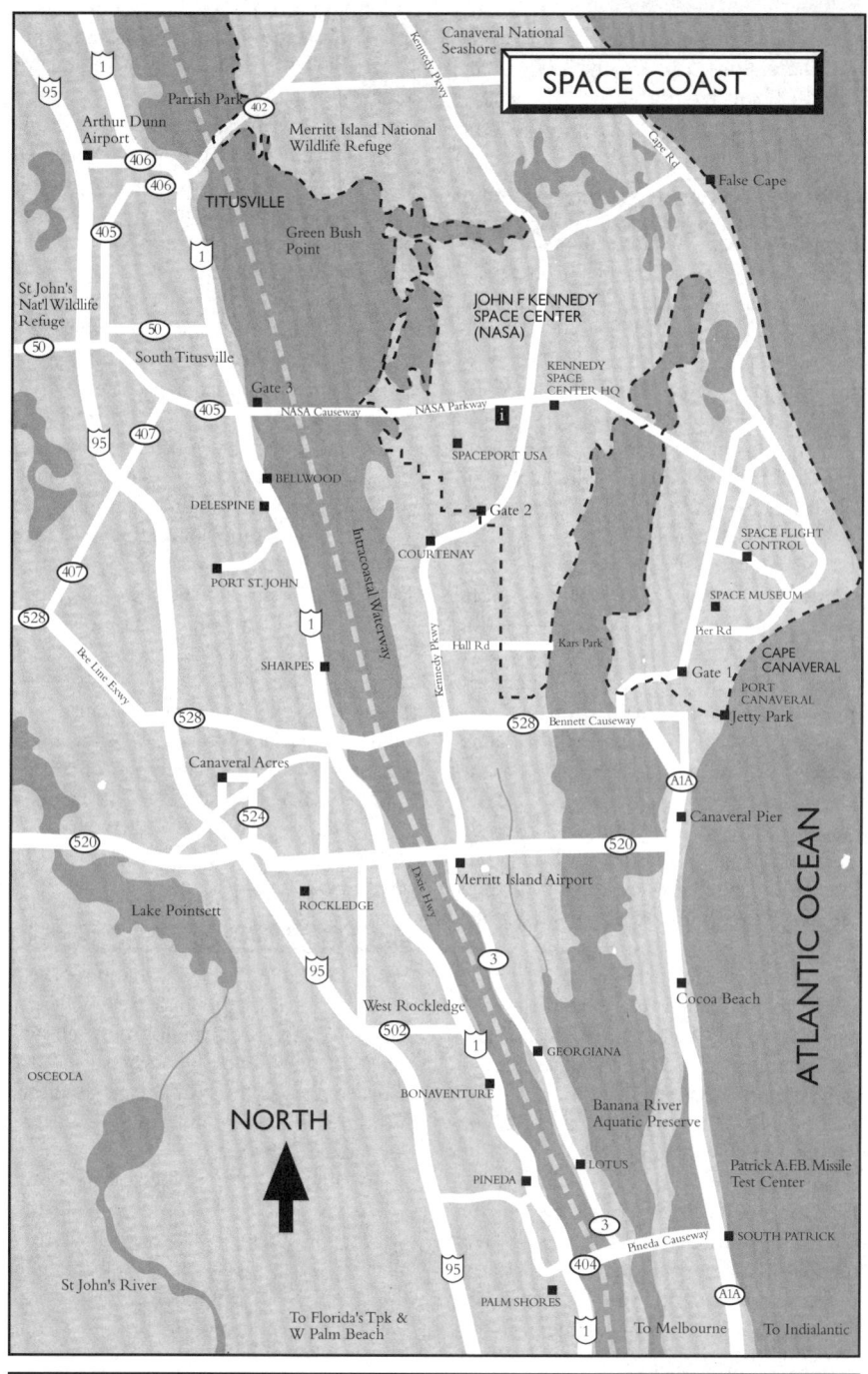

# THE SPACE COAST

# SPACE COAST MAP

of the 'warbirds' take wing in the VAC annual air show. Open daily 1000–1800; closed Thanksgiving Day, Christmas Day, New Year's Day. Admission: $6; seniors $5; children five–12 years: $4.

## US ASTRONAUT HALL OF FAME

Located on *NASA Parkway (Rte 405); tel: (407) 269-6100*, the US Astronaut Hall of Fame traces the history of the American space programme and honours the men and women who have contributed to the pioneer work.

A 'time tunnel' takes visitors back to the start of the space race – the launch of the Soviet *Sputnik* in 1957 and America's response with *Explorer 1*.

The Hall of Fame is administered jointly by the US Space Camp Foundation and the Mercury Seven Foundation. A major section pays tribute to the seven pioneers, with a special feature on each individual astronaut. The Mercury Seven Foundation was founded by the six surviving members of the Mercury Seven mission and Betty Grissom, widow of Gus Grissom who died in a launch pad fire in 1967. The foundation raises money for scholarships for students seeking an aerospace career. Like the US Space Camp Foundation, it is a non-profit organisation.

Audio-visual presentations in the Hall of Fame show Alan B. Shepard Jr on his historic moon walk, Gus Grissom desperately swimming as his spacecraft sinks on returning to Earth and John H. Glenn making the first Earth orbit. Malcolm Scott Carpenter, Walter M. Schirra Jr and L. Gordon Cooper are seen during increasingly longer orbital flights, and there is footage of Donald K. Slayton's meeting in space with Soviet cosmonauts.

In addition to such memorabilia as space suits, equipment, medals and rare photographs, there is a roll of honour of all astronauts who have flown. Future space programmes, including possible return trips to the moon and manned voyages to Mars, are also featured. Visitors can conclude their tour of the hall with a simulated trip aboard a full-scale orbiter mock-up.

A special viewing area enables visitors to watch activities in the adjoining **US Space Camp Florida**, where youngsters can experience the excitement of a space training programme.

During a five-day course, trainees gain hands-on experience in astronaut simulators from the Mercury, Gemini and Apollo programmes, build and launch model rockets and a space station and take part in a simulated shuttle mission.

US Space Camp Florida, *6225 Vectorspace Blvd, Titusville, FL 32780; tel: (407) 267-3184*, is open daily 0900–1700. Youngsters from other countries, as well as American schoolchildren in Grades four–seven, may apply for places.

The US Astronaut Hall of Fame is open daily 0900–1700 (0900–1800, June–Sept). Admission: $7.95; children aged three–12 $4.95.

## SPACEPORT USA

From Titusville, Rte 405 becomes NASA Parkway, crosses the Indian River on a causeway and enters the John F. Kennedy Space Center, which shares its 84,000 acres with the Merritt Island National Wildlife Refuge and the Canaveral National Seashore.

In this unlikely location, **Spaceport USA**, the Space Center's visitor centre, is one of Florida's top ten attractions. It is also almost certainly the best bargain in the state – if not the entire nation. Parking is free and entrance is free. You

# THE SPACE COAST

can even leave your pet dog or cat in a kennel without charge – remember, it is illegal to leave an untended animal in a car in Florida.

You will be required to pay for a bus tour of the Space Center and there is a charge for admission to the IMAX Theatre presentations (see p. 163), but these amount to a small price when you consider just how much you can experience for nothing.

Special assistance is available for the hearing-impaired – *tel: (407) 454-4198* in advance – and disabled visitors. Free wheelchairs are provided and all exhibits and tours are accessible.

A special playground, housed in a large geodesic dome, enables children aged three–12 to experience some of the excitement of being an astronaut in space. It features a one-fifth scale Space Shuttle and Space Station gym.

The Kennedy Space Center is probably the closest ordinary mortals can get to the infinity of the Universe, and the 70-acre Spaceport USA is certainly the closest most tourists will ever come to the excitement of space exploration. It's an excitement that begins even before you park your car – for there, in front of the whole complex, is the **Rocket Garden**.

Here, many of the rockets used for both manned and unmanned space flight are displayed, including a full-scale model of the lunar module in which astronauts landed on the moon. A fully-suited 'spaceman' is on hand to add authenticity to your photographs.

But the first thing you should do after parking the car is to head for the **Ticket Pavilion** and book your places for the scheduled bus tours and IMAX shows. These are popular activities and if you leave it too late you may miss out. The next place to visit is the information area at **Spaceport Central**, where you can pick up a guide map and the latest news on activities, presentations and imminent launches. This is a good place for orientation, too, and it pays to spend a little time working out a priority list of things to see.

A new exhibit in Spaceport Central allows visitors to use touch-screen technology to learn about the men and women who have flown in space. The exhibit is in three sections.

**Meet Your Astronauts** gives biographical data on all 232 past and present members of the Astronaut Corps, including places and dates of birth, educational backgrounds and flight experience.

**Current/Next Mission** provides information on current or imminent flights, listing the Orbiter's name, mission designation, mission duration, time and date of launch and live input from NASA Select Television. Immediacy is added to the display by a clock showing elapsed mission time in days, hours, minutes and seconds.

**Mission History** provides synopses of all manned missions, from Freedom 7 in 1961 to the present.

Spaceport Central also houses a Space Coast area information booth where you can obtain information on other local attractions, as well as accommodation and restaurants.

A typical visit to the Space Centre lasts from four to six hours. The bus tour alone takes up two hours. As elsewhere in Florida, especially in the heat of summer, don't try to rush things. Spaceport USA is a large complex and there is a lot to see. A good place to start your visit is the **Gallery of Space Flight**, located next to the Ticket Pavilion. It has displays of real space hardware and models that highlight developments in space exploration.

## THE GREAT SPACE RACE

The Kennedy Space Center owes its existence to the development of military rockets in the years immediately following World War II. It wasn't long before the range in the desert region of western USA became inadequate for the new generation of long-range guided missiles, so the War Department chose Cape Canaveral as a more suitable testing ground.

Formal approval was given in June 1949 when the Joint Long Range Proving Ground was designated by President Truman as a missile test launching site. Cape Canaveral Air Force Station is still Station One of a test range that covers 10,000 miles – to as far away as the Indian Ocean.

NASA – the National Aeronautics and Space Administration – was established in 1958, a year after the Soviet Union put the first man into space. NASA's brief was to carry out the peaceful exploration and use of space.

In the early days NASA's operations were confined to Cape Canaveral, where existing rockets and launch pads were modified to launch the early satellites and astronauts of the Mercury and Gemini programmes. The Cape is still used for the launching of communications and science satellites as well as robot spacecraft on exploratory missions of the solar system.

In the thick of the Cold War, President John F. Kennedy pledged in May 1961 that the US would land a man on the Moon and return him safely to Earth within the decade.

Boosted by apparently limitless supplies of money and brainpower, NASA captured the headlines from the Soviets in a series of spectacular space achievements, and in July 1969 America's Apollo 11 astronauts landed on the Moon.

Since the 1970s, American accomplishments in space have been no less dramatic in scientific terms, although they have been something of an anti-climax for the layman. Cost has been the greatest inhibition to headline-grabbing deeds.

Nevertheless, the success of the Space Shuttle – the first re-usable space ship – has captured hearts and minds right round the world, while unmanned probes like Magellan and Galileo and projects like the Hubble Telescope have greatly expanded human knowledge.

Now, NASA is deeply involved in a project to construct Space Station Freedom, an orbiting outpost that will act as a springboard for manned journeys to the moon and Mars. About 20 Space Shuttle flights will be needed to transport sections which will be assembled in orbit by astronauts.

With living and working quarters for up to eight people, Space Station Freedom is expected to be fully assembled by the end of this century. Orbiting 250 miles above the Earth, the station will allow astronomers to study the stars and planets in a pollution-free environment. The weightless conditions will allow the processing of medicines, metals and other products that cannot be produced in Earth's gravity. Astronauts assemble, service and repair satellites and send them out to explore space.

NASA wants to use the station as a launching point to send astronauts back to the moon and hopes to mount a manned expedition to Mars early in the 21st century.

Space Station Freedom is to be an international effort involving the USA, Canada, Japan and the European Space Agency.

A self-guided path leads visitors through the history of manned and unmanned flights. Exhibits include authentic Mercury, Gemini and Apollo capsules, models of a Lunar Rover and the Viking Mars Lander and a piece of moon rock.

**Satellites and You**, close to Spaceport Central, is a walk-through exhibit offering a 45-min journey through a simulated space station of the future.

One of the newest and most popular exhibits at Spaceport USA is the orbiter **Explorer**, which opened in July 1994. Equipped with actual flight hardware, Explorer is a full-scale model of a Space Shuttle, accurate in every detail from its flight deck control panels to its 60-ft long cargo bay.

Adjacent to Explorer, overlooking a quiet lagoon on a six-acre site is the **Astronauts Memorial**, also known as the Space Mirror. The 42.5 ft by 50 ft monument honours the 16 US astronauts who have given their lives in the line of duty. Constructed of black, mirror-finished granite, the $6.2 million memorial is on a computer-controlled framework which enables it to track the sun throughout the day. Specially placed reflectors direct sunlight out through the names, which appear to be written in the sky. At night, or when the sunlight is feeble, powerful supplementary lighting illuminates the names.

The **Galaxy Center** is a huge futuristic complex that houses the IMAX and Spaceport theatres, a gallery of space art and space exhibits, including a 61-ft long model of a module from the proposed International Space Station and a four-section audio/visual presentation which examines the spin-off benefits of space technology.

Spaceport USA is said to be the only attraction in the world to offer a back-to-back twin **IMAX theatre** complex. Three spectacular large format films are shown on huge screens five and a half storeys tall.

*The Dream is Alive*, an established favourite, is an awesome space adventure in which the huge screen and thunderous sound system make you feel as if you are standing on the launch pad during a Space Shuttle launch.

*Blue Planet* is described as a space film about Earth. Like *The Dream is Alive*, it was produced by the Smithsonian Institution's National Air and Space Museum and the Lockheed Corporation in co-operation with NASA. Made by the crews of five Space Shuttle missions, who had been trained to operate the IMAX cameras, the film presents views of Earth shot from as high as 330 miles in space. The film demonstrates the effects of the constantly interacting natural forces at work in the world and contrasts these with the damage caused by river pollution, deforestation and rapid population growth.

The third and newest IMAX production, *Destiny in Space*, takes viewers on a 40-min voyage to the far reaches of the universe. Narrated by Leonard Nimoy – Mr Spock in the TV series *Star Trek* – the film features exterior views of the Space Shuttle in flight around Earth, the mission in which the Hubble space telescope was retrieved and redeployed and flights over the rugged contours of Venus and Mars.

Each film lasts about 40 mins and is shown several times daily. Admission $4; children aged three–11, $2.

Live shows featuring a variety of space-related topics are presented in the **Spaceport Theater**, and the **NASA Art Gallery** exhibits 250 works in a complete range of artistic styles.

Facilities at Spaceport USA include the **Gift Gantry**, a souvenir store with a stock of more than 1200 space-related items, ranging from clothing and collectables to photographs and videos, and a number of eating and refreshment places. The **Orbit Cafeteria** opens at 1130 and specialises in sandwiches and salads. The **Lunch Pad** opens at 0900 and offers breakfast and lunch entrées.

Spaceport USA is open daily (except Christmas Day) 0900–1900.

**Bus Tours**

Two different bus tours are available from Spaceport USA, both in luxury, double-decker vehicles. The **Red Tour** – the most popular – covers the actual working areas of the Kennedy Space Center. The **Blue Tour** – which is more likely to appeal to space history buffs – visits Cape Canaveral Air Force Station, developed as a testing centre for guided missiles and later used for pioneer space launchings.

Because of security restrictions, the Red Tour is the only way you can visit the Space Center, but the tour is surprisingly unfettered by the kind of conditions you might expect. You do get the opportunity to leave the bus at a number of locations and you can take pictures. That said, certain restrictions may apply at times and there are no tours when a launch is imminent.

The tour takes visitors by the centre's administrative and communications buildings, including the **Communications Distribution and Switching Center** where a huge dish-shaped radio antenna maintains links between the Kennedy Space Center, Mission Control in Houston, Texas, NASA headquarters in Washington, D.C. and other NASA centres.

The largest structure in the centre's industrial area is the **Operations and Checkout Building** where spacecraft used for the Moon landing missions, as well as Skylab and the joint mission with the Soviet Union in 1975 were prepared for launch. This is where Spacelab, the European Space Agency's contribution to the Space Shuttle programme, is checked out before being fitted into the Shuttle Orbiter's cargo bay.

Astronaut crews who have been assigned to a mission occupy living quarters on the third floor of the Operations and Checkout Building.

Visitors experience a simulated Apollo 11 moon launch countdown in the **Flight Crew Training Building**. Here, complex simulators enabled Apollo astronauts to rehearse every detail of their Moon voyage. Today, visitors can examine the Apollo Command Module and see a real Apollo Lunar Module, complete with Lunar Rover, on a mocked-up Moon landing site.

The largest structure on the entire Space Center – and one of the largest in volume in the world – is the **Vehicle Assembly Building**. Reaching a height of 52 storeys, this is the building you can see for miles around, distinguished by its huge Stars and Stripes and massive louvred doors. The building is so large that a special air-conditioning system had to be installed to prevent clouds from forming *inside* it.

Enclosing more than 129 million cubic feet, the VAB – as everyone calls it – is where Space Shuttles are assembled and made ready for flight in space before being taken to the launch pad.

Outside the VAB, visitors can take a close-up look at a **Saturn V** rocket, separated at its staging points to allow a good view of the engines for each stage. The Saturn V is 363 ft long, weighs 2812 metric tons and is the world's most powerful launch vehicle. It carried the Apollo missions to the Moon.

Space vehicles – these days that means the Space Shuttle and all the hardware needed to get it off the ground – are transported to the launch pad on a massive **Crawler Transporter**, about half the size of a football field, that covers the 3.5 mile journey in about seven hours. Unloaded, its top speed is two mph. It takes a crew of 26 to operate the transporter. The Red Tour bus follows the crawlerway, a stretch of superhighway specially constructed to take the enormous payloads.

Dwarfed by the neighbouring VAB, the four-storey **Launch Control Center** is where pre-launch testing of the Space Shuttle is controlled and monitored and where the launch command is issued.

Visitors also get the chance to examine the **launch pads** and there may be an opportunity to see and photograph the Shuttle as it waits to be launched. The pad itself is constructed of 52,000 cubic metres of reinforced concrete. During a launch water spouts located in the flame trench and on the mobile launch platform will slosh 300,000 gallons of water on to the pad area in 20 seconds to provide sound suppression and cooling.

Blue Tour passengers can see the sites at **Cape Canaveral Air Force Station** where the first astronauts were launched in the Mercury and Gemini programmes. They can also examine the current launch pads used for various scientific, commercial and military missions. The **Air Force Space Museum** has a unique collection of early military rockets and space memorabilia and visitors can see the old **Mission Control** building.

Bus tours operate daily from Spaceport USA. There are departures every 15 minutes from 0945 until two hours before dusk. Admission: $7; children aged three–11, $4.

**Viewing a Launch**

Launch dates are posted at entrances to the Space Center and updated information is available from NASA; tel: (407) 867-4636 or Spaceport USA; tel: (800) KSC-INFO (Florida only).

Complimentary launch viewing car passes are available from NASA. Each pass allows one private vehicle inside the Space Center to a viewing site six miles from the launch area. You must apply in writing three months in advance to: **NASA Visitor Services**, Mail Code: PA-PASS, Kennedy Space Center, FL 32899.

Spaceport USA sells some 1500 tickets to board the buses that transport visitors to the viewing site six miles from the pad on launch day. A ticket costs $7; children aged three–11 $4. Reservations begin about a week before launch date and applicants must telephone (407) 452-2121 ext 260/261. Tickets must be collected in person before launch day.

You can also view a launch from outside the Space Center – in fact, you can scarcely miss it anywhere within 40 miles. Prime sites are along Hwy 1 in Titusville and on Hwy A1A in the cities of Cape Canaveral and Cocoa Beach.

## MERRITT ISLAND

NASA shares its island home with more endangered and threatened wildlife species than are found anywhere else in continental USA. The **Merritt Island Wildlife Refuge** was founded soon after the establishment of the Kennedy Space Center in the 1960s, when NASA realised it would not need the whole island for its rocketry.

The refuge **visitor centre** is on Hwy 406 north-east of Titusville and can also be reached by Rte 3 north of Spaceport USA.

Administered by the US Fish and Wildlife Service, the refuge first served as a winter sanctuary for wildlife drawn to its sub-tropical environment. In fact, the island is a year-round home to a very wide range of wildlife, thanks to the habitat provided by the many temperate and sub-tropical plants which thrive here side by side.

The island harbours 25 species of mammal, including alligators, armadillos, bobcats and racoons. There are more than 300 species of birds, including bald eagles and ospreys, 117 fish species and 65 types of amphibians and reptiles. Among the endangered species which have found refuge in the surrounding waters is the manatee, the docile sea cow whose population has been reduced to an estimated 1200 in the US.

Twenty-two species on the island are among those listed by Federal and State authorities as endangered or threatened.

There are three way-marked walking trails and one which visitors can follow by car. Maps of the trails and lots of other information is available from the refuge visitor centre.

The area's wildlife viewing and recreational facilities were extended in 1975 when the **Canaveral National Seashore** was created and the US National Parks Service took on the role of protecting the 25 miles of beach that acts as a barrier between the island's **Mosquito Lagoon** and the Atlantic Ocean.

The National Seashore can be reached by Hwy 406 from Titusville or Rte 3 from Spaceport USA. There is also access from New Smyrna Beach via Rte A1A.

Two beaches adjoin the refuge and are open to visitors, but care is needed when swimming: there are strong currents, surf conditions can be rough and you need to keep an eye open for stinging jellyfish. There are no lifeguards.

The beaches – Apollo and Playalinda – both have parking areas and boardwalks which provide access while protecting fragile vegetation. Picnics are permitted and Apollo Beach has picnic tables. The only drinking water is at the Apollo Beach information centre.

Limited simple camping is allowed within the refuge, but you will need a permit from The Manager, **Merritt Island National Wildlife Refuge**, *PO Box 6504, Titusville, FL 32782*. Within the Canaveral National Seashore area, camping is permitted – and free – on the North Beach and on the islands in the north end of Mosquito Lagoon. The campsites are closed May–Oct.

Make sure you have insect repellent with you – Mosquito Lagoon is well named.

Humans have been involved with Merritt Island for centuries. Ancient burial mounds and aboriginal shell mounds are to be found around Mosquito Lagoon. Spanish explorers certainly passed this way, as did British colonists and American pioneers, but there was no permanent settlement until the 1840s. Major movement into the area came after the Civil War.

Before the Space Center arrived, the island's economy was largely based on citrus fruit, sugar cane, pineapples and cattle. Outside the wilderness area there is a permanent population of around 40,000 people.

The Wildlife Refuge is open daily 0800–two hours before dusk. Canaveral National Seashore is open daily 0600–1800. Admission to both is free.

# West Palm Beach– Sebring

The lure of Florida's highlands pulls travellers past the fish camp communities around Lake Okeechobee straight to Sebring and the lakes of Central Florida. North-west of the lake, pasture land rises towards Florida's geographic spine, making Sebring in the highlands cooler than the coasts. With a single lane in each direction, plan on several hours for this 107-mile route.

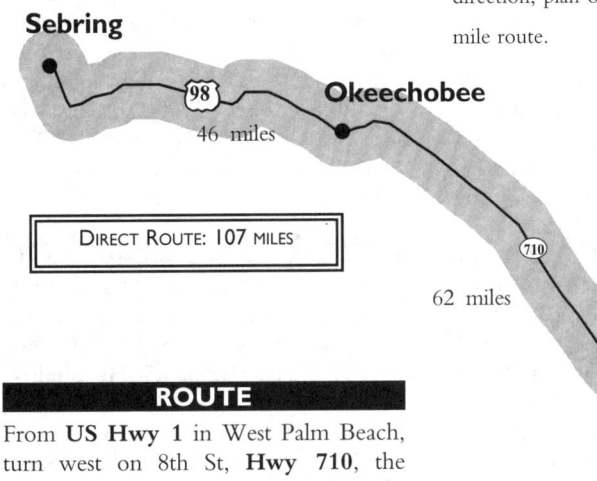

**Sebring** — 98 — 46 miles — **Okeechobee** — 710 — 62 miles — **West Palm Beach**

DIRECT ROUTE: 107 MILES

## ROUTE

From **US Hwy 1** in West Palm Beach, turn west on 8th St, **Hwy 710**, the **Coast-to-Coast Hwy** or **Martin Luther King Jr Blvd,** for 58 miles. Go left on **Hwy 70** for four miles through Okeechobee, then take **US 98** 42 miles north-west. Continue north on **US 98/ US 27** four miles to **Sebring**.

Leaving West Palm Beach behind, go west on Hwy 710 through marshland and sawgrass. Hwy 710 narrows as it turns north-west to parallel the AMTRAK railroad track. If following a lorry or tractor, prepare for a slow drive. In winter, large lorries haul citrus from the groves on the north-east side of Hwy 710 to processing plants. Slash pine trees and palms are on the left.

Cross the St. Lucie Canal on the Intracoastal Waterway's east side, built by the US Army Corps of Engineers during World War I. Widened and deepened in 1923, it accommodates a boat 250 ft long and 50 ft wide with an 8-ft draft. During World War II, coastal freighters and oil barges entered Lake Okeechobee via the canal to hide from submarines patrolling the Florida coast.

Across the canal is **Indiantown.** After Seminole warriors were defeated at nearby Okeechobee battlefield, the US Army established a fort at Indiantown to protect inter-fort telegraph communications. The moderate 1928 **Seminole Country Inn**, *15885 S.W. Warfield Blvd, PO Box 1818, Indiantown, FL 34956; tel: (407) 597-3777*, was built by S. Davies Warfield, a Baltimore banker who wanted a lodge for his Seaboard Airline Railroad passengers. Wallis Warfield (later Simpson and Duchess of Windsor), his niece, worked in the dining room and later was a guest. The lobby has a roaring fireplace and 25 individually-decorated rooms including the Duchess' Room. The **Foxgrape Café** has lunch and dinner Tues–Sat and a Sun brunch buffet. Picnic by the Indiantown Marina on the north bank of the canal.

Fertiliser and citrus processing plants are north-west on Hwy 710. Florida Power & Light's Martin Power Plant on the left includes the 450-acre **Barley Barber Swamp**; *tel: (800) 257-9267*, two miles east of Lake Okeechobee. Call for tours of the rookery and an Indian mound where artefacts have been dated to 1000 AD. Wood storks, buzzards, hawks, eagles and owls and live and hunt in the preserve.

Hwy 710 descends for 14 miles to **Okeechobee**, through slash pines, palm trees and cow pasture. Turn left on Hwy 70 for four miles, through Okeechobee.

From Hwy 70, take US 98 north-west. The odour of local cattle can be overpowering. Cross the Kissimmee River to Highlands County. **Basinger** is dairy country. Cross the Istokpoga Canal and drive through **Lorida**. Locals say Lorida is Florida without the 'F'. Watch for the 'cowboy crossing' sign. Drive through Spring Lake and turn right on US 98/Hwy 27. **Sebring International Raceway** is to the right. Drive four miles north on US 98/Hwy 27 towards Lake Jackson and **Sebring**.

## OKEECHOBEE

**Okeechobee County Chamber of Commerce**, *55 S. Parrott Ave, Okeechobee, FL 34972; tel: (941) 763-6464*, has information on lodging, dining and activities around the lake. (See also Lake Okeechobee chapter, p. 170.)

### ACCOMMODATION AND FOOD

There is a range of budget–moderate lodging near Lake Okeechobee. **Budget Inn**, *210 S. Parrott Ave, Okeechobee, FL 34974; tel: (941) 763-3185*, and **Days Inn Okeechobee**, *2200 S.E. Hwy 441, Okeechobee, FL 34974; tel: (941) 763-8003*, are moderate chains. Try the usual fast food chains for budget eating.

## SEBRING

**Tourist Information**: The **Greater Sebring Chamber of Commerce**, *309 S. Circle, Sebring, FL 33870; tel: (941) 385-8448*, and **Highlands Hospitality, Inc. Convention & Visitors Bureau**, *PO Box 2001, Sebring, FL 33871-2001; tel: (800) 255-1711*, have information on lodging, dining, car racing and golf. **Sebring Community Redevelopment Agency**; *tel: (941) 471-5104*, provides information on the downtown **Circle**.

In 1912, pious Ohio-born teetotaller George Sebring founded the town for retired clergy and college professors. Planners avoided the popular street grid design with Sebring Circle Park. In 1952, auto racing began next to Sebring Airport, and the Grand Prix of Endurance took off. Orange and grapefruit groves, caladium bulb nurseries and dairy and beef cattle ranching dominate the surrounding highlands around lakes and rolling countryside. Golf is the area's other passion.

## WEST PALM BEACH–SEBRING

### ACCOMMODATION

During the four days of the 12 Hours of Sebring, lodging is at premium prices. To attend racing events in Mar, book months in advance. Highlands Hospitality, Inc. has an accommodation guide. *DI, Hd* and *HJ* are on US 27. **Kenilworth Lodge**, *836 S.E. Lakeview Dr, Sebring, FL 33870; tel: (800) 423-5939* or *(941) 385-0111*, is a moderate Spanish-style inn built by Sebring in 1916. In cooler winter weather, ask for the old-fashioned third-floor rooms without air conditioning. The **Inn on the Lakes**, *3100 Golfview Rd and US 27 S., Sebring, FL 33870; tel: (800) 531-5253* or *(941) 471-9400*, is modern, moderate and has golf packages.

### EATING AND DRINKING

**Takis Family Restaurant**, *2710 Kenilworth Blvd; tel: (941) 385-7323*, cheerfully serves budget Greek and American food, with early-bird specials 1100–1800. **Tony's Italian Restaurant**, *130 N. Ridgewood Dr.; tel: (941) 471-2227*, near the Circle, has cheap early-bird specials. The **Cathouse Restaurant**, *213 S. Circle Ave, Sebring, FL 33870; tel: (941) 385-6653*, Mon–Sat 0630–1500, Sun 0700–1400, boasts more than 4000 feline-related articles and the slogan, 'the only legal cathouse in Florida'. Taste local citrus juice at **Sebring Packing Co., Inc.**, *3954 US 27 S.; tel: (941) 385-1348*.

### SIGHTSEEING

March is race month. The **12 Hours of Sebring International Grand Prix of Endurance Race**; *tel: (800) 626-7223*, mid-Mar, is the oldest endurance road race in the US. Ticket prices start at $35. The 3.7-mile circuit, draws thousands of racing fans to **Sebring International Raceway, Inc.**, *113 Midway Dr., Sebring, FL 33870; tel: (941) 655-1442*. There are viewing hills and 400 acres of camping for spectators. Tickets for the paddock cost a few dollars more. Book months in advance for low prices.

The downtown **Circle**, on the east side of Lake Jackson, is a historic 1920s district. A tree-shaded park is at the centre of the circle, complete with classical-to-pop loudspeaker music. Merchants around the circle sell antiques, clothing and crafts. **Kubies Kris Kringle House**, *200 N. Circle Dr.; tel: (941) 382-1220*, sells Christmas gifts all year. Near the **City Pier** on Lake Jackson is Sebring's civic and cultural centre. The **Highlands Museum of Fine Arts**, *351 W. Center Ave; tel: (941) 385-5312*, displays work of local artists and archaeological finds. Next door is a performing arts theatre, library and museum. The **Sebring Tourist Club**, *N. Lime and Pomegranate Aves*, has outdoor shuffleboard courts.

Take CR 634 to **Highlands Hammock State Park**, *5931 Hammock Rd, Sebring, FL 33872; tel: (941) 386-6094*. Camp, picnic or hire bicycles. Rangers lead narrated tram tours. Expect armadillos along the **Young Hammock Trail**; a narrow catwalk across **Cypress Swamp Trail** through a virgin cypress forest; a twisted, millennium-old oak on **Big Oak Trail**, a lush **Garden Trail** and wild pigs, racoons, alligators, scrub jays and otters. At the end of the **Lieber Memorial Trail** boardwalk is a green sheen on the surface of a swamp so brooding and primeval it could be the glades before man's arrival. There is a **Civilian Conservation Corps Museum**, notable for photographs of workers building the park during the Great Depression. **Bailey's Camp Store**; *tel: (941) 471-6400*, in the park, has wild-orange milkshakes and pies made from citrus growing outside the log cabin store.

# Lake Okeechobee

Lake Okeechobee, 'big water' to the Seminoles, is the second-largest freshwater lake in the US after Lake Michigan. Much of the lake's 730 square miles are hidden from view by a dyke, levee or trees which screen the shore. Water flows in from the Kissimmee River in the north and drains south into the Everglades. In the 1920s and 1930s, the US Army Corps of Engineers constructed the Okeechobee Waterway, to connect the Intracoastal Waterway lock and dam canal system linking Stuart on the Atlantic Coast with Fort Myers on the Gulf Coast.

Most of the recreation and views along the lake's 150-mile circumference are on the east side, north of Belle Glade between Pahokee and Taylor Creek. Much of the rest of Lake Okeechobee's shoreline wanders through farmland. Sugar cane burning, pesticide and chemical use mean that polluted water is flushed from Lake Okeechobee into the fragile Everglades ecosystem.

For visitors, game fishing is the prime lure. Largemouth bass and pike are prized. Clewiston and Okeechobee, known as the crappie or speck (speckled perch) capital of the world, are the main towns. When wading into the shallow lake, watch for alligators and poisonous cottonmouth water moccasin snakes. In a car, but never in an RV, drive carefully up narrow steep slopes to the tops of levees to look at the lake. The invisible opposite shore is more than 30 miles away. Lake Okeechobee's western side is overrun with Australian melaleuca trees, impervious to floods and droughts; fire explodes and scatters seed pods which propagate in the sheltered waters, blocking the western access to the Intracoastal Waterway. Four sections of the Florida Scenic Trail circle the tops of Lake Okeechobee's dike, though greenery obscures many views of the water. Allow a full day to drive around the lake, where traffic and the pace of life slows dramatically.

## ROUTE

From **Belle Glade** at the south end of Lake Okeechobee, go west two miles, then turn right to begin circumnavigating Lake Okeechobee's east side. On SR 715, drive 11 miles to **Pahokee**. Continue north on Hwys 441 and 98 to the town of **Okeechobee** (see p. 170). From the lake's north end, follow SR 78 southwest, then south to Hwy 27. Turn left on Hwy 27 and go through **Moore Haven** 18 miles to **Clewiston**. From Clewiston, drive east on Hwy 27/SR 80 through South Bay to return to Belle Glade.

## TOURIST INFORMATION

**Okeechobee County Chamber of Commerce**, *55 S. Parrot Ave, Okeechobee, FL 34972; tel: (941) 763-6464*, and the **Lake Okeechobee & Okeechobee**

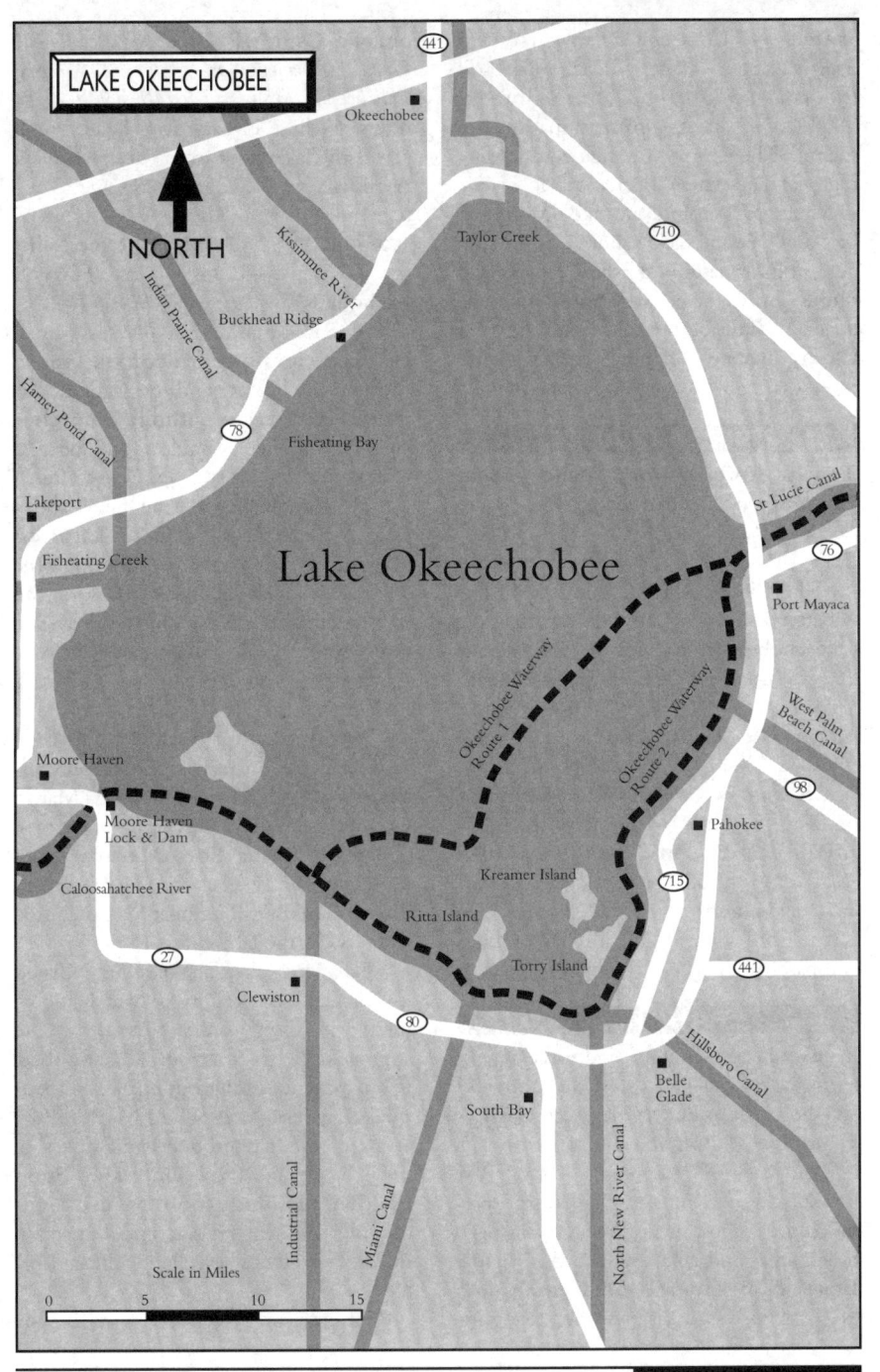

# LAKE OKEECHOBEE

# LAKE OKEECHOBEE

Waterway, US Corps of Engineers, 525 Ridgelawn Rd, Clewiston, FL 33440-5399; tel: (941) 983-8101, open Mon–Fri 0800–1630, have information on the region. The Corps of Engineers have a regional map which lists recreational facilities and parks around the lake. Local boat hire and bait and tackle shops can provide current information on fishing conditions, dining and accommodations in their locality. Outside of Okeechobee and Clewiston most lodging is modest, little more than a place to sleep for the night.

## BELLE GLADE

**Tourist Information: Belle Glade Chamber of Commerce,** *540 S. Main St, Belle Glade, FL 33430; tel: (407) 996-2745.*

Belle Glade is the site of a prison, but is better known as the gateway to Lake Okeechobee's fishing resorts. **Days Inn,** *1075 S. Main St, Belle Glade, FL 33430; tel: (407) 992-8600,* and the **Belle Glade Marina & Campground**; *tel: (407) 996-6322,* are budget lodgings.

Go west two miles, then head north on SR 715. Drive to the top of the levee at **Paul Rardin Park**, *4600 Bacom Point Rd*, before having a picnic on shaded tables. **Padgett Park**, *3701 SR 715*, across from a small airport, has parking and baseball fields.

## PAHOKEE

Pahokee, 'grassy waters', is a town spread between Hwy 441, SR 715 and the lakeshore. **Pahokee Marina & Campground,** *171 N. Lake Ave, Pahokee, FL 33476; tel: (407) 924-7832,* has 82 RV hookups, boat ramps, a small store, tennis, shuffleboard, fishing piers, two small beach areas and lake excursions. **Florida Boat Club Houseboat Rentals;** *tel: (407) 996-5154,* is another lodging option. **Capt. JP Boat Cruises**, *200 Upper Lakeview Dr., Pahokee Marina, Pahokee, FL 33476; tel: (407) 924-2100,* offers six-hr 350-passenger boat cruises across the lake to or from Moore Haven. A bus is available to take passengers back to Moore Haven. The cruises are priced at around $50. Sail with **Pahokee Sails;** *tel: (407) 924-3556,* or try **Harry's Airboat Rides;** *tel: (407) 996-5154.*

SR 715 joins Hwy 441 north of Pahokee. Houses are built off the ground to catch the breezes and to escape floodwaters. **St. Mary's Catholic Church** is an old-fashioned shingled buiding. At **Canal Point**, cross the **West Palm Beach Canal.** Sugar cane fields and a refinery are to the right. To the left across the railroad tracks, drive to the top of the levee for a lovely lake view. Back on SR 715, modest homes with verandas and insect screens house sugar cane workers. Cows graze near the levee, and there is fresh catfish for sale.

**Cypress Plantation** is a white 1913 private mansion to the right as you cross from Palm Beach County to Martin County at **Port Mayaca**. Fishermen congregate at the **Port Mayaca Lock and Dam** on Okeechobee Waterway **St Lucie Canal**. Fishing boats are anchored to buoys in the lake.

Walk across the dam at **Henry Creek** in Okeechobee County to watch fishermen and birds fishing. As the route approaches the town of Okeechobee, RV parks and fishing camps fill the roadside. **Cypress Hut Flea Market**, the area's oldest, has produce and boxes of small rummage, Sat–Sun. The **Food Peddler's Dining Room** has live country entertainment Fri–Sat, and a breakfast on Wed–Fri that is excellent value at only $0.99.

Continue on Hwy 441/98 to **Taylor**

## LAKE OKEECHOBEE

Creek south of **Okeechobee**. On Christmas Day, 1837, Colonel (later US President) Zachary Taylor's troops defeated a band of 400 Seminoles at Okeechobee in the final major battle of the Second Seminole War.) Campers have budget lodgings near the lake: **Zachary Taylor Camping Resort**, *2995 US 441 S. E., Okeechobee, FL 34974-6899; tel: (941) 763-3377*, and **Lake Okeechobee Resort and KOA Kampground**, *4276 Hwy 441 S., Okeechobee, FL 34974-7214; tel: 800-845-6846*, which has 713 RV and tent pitches, 10 cabins and a golf course.

Follow Hwy 78 around the north end of the lake. The **National Audubon Society** runs 44-passenger pontoon boat cruises through the organisation's 28,500 acre wildlife sanctuary: **Swampland Tours**, *10300 Hwy 78 W. at Kissimmee River Bridge, Okeechobee, FL 34974; tel: (941) 467-4411*. The fare is $17.50. **Okee-Tantee Recreation Area**, *10430 Hwy 78 W.; tel: (941) 763-2622*, is a 224-pitch RV park with a restaurant; boat hire is available.

Cross the Kissimmee River into Glades County. To the right (west) of **Buckhead Ridge** are pastures, grassland and grazing cows. **Elderberry Cottage Restaurant & Gift Shop**, run by Seminoles, serves budget meatloaf and sells small gator skulls and non-native bisque dolls in the store. To the west is **Brighton Seminole Indian Reservation**, with bingo, cheap cigarettes, hunting and cows grazing through arid scrub.

**Lakeport**, a few blocks long, has several modest hotels and RV parks. The fishing resort is on the north shore of **Fisheating Creek**, one of the few places Lake Okeechobee is visible from its west shore. Hwy 78 slopes down as it goes south towards Moore Haven.

Take Hwy 27 left (east) to **Moore Haven**. Tourist Information: **Glades County Chamber of Commerce**, *PO Box 490, Moore Haven; FL 33471; tel: (941) 946-0440*.

Cross the **Caloosahatchee River**, western outlet for the Intracoastal Waterway, to watch the water falling over the spillway at the **Moore Haven Lock & Dam**.

Take Hwy 27 south past vast sugar cane fields into Hendry County, then follow the highway east to **Clewiston** (see West Palm Beach–Fort Myers, p. 174), which is the centre of Florida's sugar and rice production.

East of Clewiston, as Hwy 27/SR 80 crosses into Palm Beach County, the route again approaches the levee. To the right are farms and cattle. Stop at **Herbert Hoover Dam Access** where steps lead to the top of the levee and a view of birds on the lake.

**John Stretch County Park**, *47225 Hwy 27*, open 0800–sunset, has RV camping, a boat launch and covered picnic tables. At **Lake Harbor**, palm tree plantations alternate with winter vegetable greenhouses. Approaching **South Bay, Okeechobee Access Point Boat Ramp** is on the left.

## SOUTH BAY

South Bay, the 'Crossroads of South Florida' is known for sugar cane and winter vegetable production. The moderate 115-room **Okeechobee Inn**, *265 N. US Hwy 27, South Bay, FL 33493; tel: (407) 996-6517*, easily spotted next door to Fat Boy's Bar-B-Que, is conveniently en route to Belle Glade. Cross **North View River Canal** and complete the circuit at **Belle Glade**.

# WEST PALM BEACH– FORT MYERS

Leave the posh existence of West Palm Beach for the sweet heartland and the dams and locks along the Caloosahatchee River which flows to Fort Myers. Sugar cane plantations and citrus groves are a reminder of the rural past of South-central Florida; today the farms are huge agri-business operations. The 120-mile highway route can be driven in three hours, with a stop to see the Intracoastal Waterway locks.

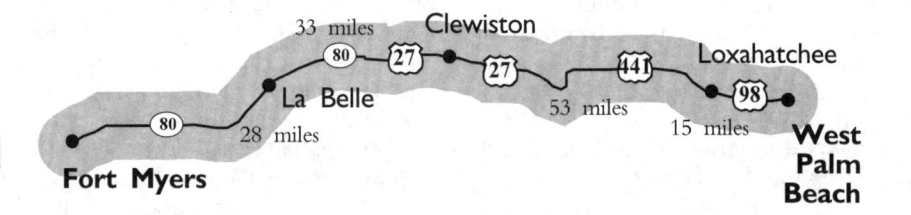

> DIRECT ROUTE: 120 MILES

## ROUTE

Take **Southern Blvd** in West Palm Beach west from US 1, the Dixie Hwy, and cross over I-95. Southern Blvd, or **Hwy 98/SR 80/SR 700** continues west, beneath Florida's Turnpike to the junction of Hwy 441. **Hwy 441** turns west and joins Hwy 98 and SR 80 as the westerly route designations.

The **West Palm Beach Canal** parallels Southern Blvd from Glen Rd in West Palm Beach to **Loxahatchee**. From Loxahatchee, **Hwy 441/SR 80** continues west to **Belle Glade**, then heads left to **South Bay**. Follow the southern fringes of **Lake Okeechobee** along **Hwy 27/SR 80** through **Clewiston**, and continue through **La Belle** and **Alva** to I-75 and **Fort Myers**.

Tourist information for the region is provided by **Lake Okeechobee & Okeechobee Waterway**, *US Corps of Engineers, 525 Ridgelawn Rd, Clewiston, FL 33440-5399; tel: (941) 983-8101,* open Mon–Fri 0800–1630. The Corps of Engineers has a regional map which lists recreational facilities and parks around the lake.

## LOXAHATCHEE

**Tourist Information: Palms West Chamber of Commerce**, *PO Box 1062, Loxahatchee, FL 33470; tel: (407) 790-6200*, has information on the one post office, several-building town.

**Loxahatchee Groves County Park**, open 0800–sundown, is 12 miles west of US 1. A winding, unpaved one-mile road through chalky sand leads past cabbage palms and slash pines to unshaded picnic tables and a baseball field.

Drive through roaming wild animals (keep car windows closed) at **Lion Country Safari**, *Southern Blvd W., West Palm Beach, FL 33416; tel: (407) 793-1084*. An attached **KOA Kampground**; *tel: (407) 793-9797*, offers RV and tent camping. A hard-to-find boat ramp near Hwy 441 is one access to the **Arthur R. Marshall Loxahatchee National Wildlife Refuge**, *Rte 1, Box 278, Boynton Beach, FL 33437; tel: (407) 732-3684*, a small bit of the Everglades.

Sugar cane fields appear ahead on Hwy 441/SR 80, often under a thick brown pall of smoke from a controlled cane burn. A processing plant is on the left. (See Lake Okeechobee, p.170, for **Belle Glade – Clewiston** area.)

## CLEWISTON

**Tourist Information: Clewiston Chamber of Commerce**, *544 W. Sugarland Hwy, PO Box 275, Clewiston, FL 33440; tel: (941) 983-7979*, has lodging, dining and sugar history information.

### ACCOMMODATION

**The Clewiston Inn**, *US 27 & 108 Royal Palm Ave, PO Box 1297, Clewiston, FL 33440; tel: (800) 673-9528 or (941) 983-8151*, a moderate Bed and Breakfast inn, built in 1938, resembles a white-painted Southern plantation. Cypress panelling and wood-burning fireplaces add atmosphere. The **Cane Court Motel**, *335 W. Sugarland Hwy; tel: (941) 983-3141*, **Motel 27**, *412 W. Sugarland Hwy; tel: (941) 983-4115*, and **Porterhouse Motel East & West**, *433 W. Sugarland Hwy; tel: (941) 983-9161*, are budget choices.

Near **Lake Okeechobee Access Point** are **Roland Martin's Lakeside Marina**, *910 E. Del Monte Ave; tel: (800) 473-6566 or (941) 983-3151*, and **Angler's Marina**, *910 Okeechobee Blvd; tel: (800) 741-3141 or (941) 983-2128*, both of which have a moderate motel and condominiums, and a budget RV park.

### EATING AND DRINKING

**The Clewiston Inn**, *US 27 & 108 Royal Palm Ave, PO Box 1297, Clewiston, FL 33440; tel: (800) 673-9528 or (941) 983-8151*, has a popular daily budget buffet lunch and moderate dinners with Southern fried chicken and Okeechobee catfish. The Inn's **Everglades Lounge** has a colourful and detailed mural of Everglades wildlife on the walls.

**Old South Bar-B-Q**, *602 E. Sugarland Hwy; tel: (941) 983-7756*, budget–moderate, is well-advertised with signs on the approach to town. Eat catfish and barbecue food surrounded by Florida memorabilia. **Cafeteria Cubano**, *San Pedro St and W. Sugarland Hwy*, is a cheap Spanish-only sample of real Cuban cooking and huge cups of sweet *café cubano* in a former petrol station. A Madonna shrine in front has replaced petrol pumps. Fast food outlets are on the west side of Clewiston.

### SIGHTSEEING

Clewiston calls itself 'America's Sweetest Town', after the sugar cane cultivation and processing that has been the town's mainstay since the late 1920s. The 'Sweet Taste of Sugar Festival' celebrates the sugarcane harvest in late Apr. United States Sugar Corporation, the USA's largest raw sugar producer, is Clewiston's *raison d'être*, though the agricultural area also supports citrus, rice and winter vegetable production and cattle ranching.

Recreational fishing on Lake Okeechobee draws visitors who prefer to use the town as a base for exploration of the lake. Clewiston is a bird sanctuary for a colony of smooth-billed ani – large black birds found in South-Central Florida and the Everglades. British RAF pilots trained at Flying Training School Number Five at Riddle Field during World War II.

**Clewiston Museum**, *112 S. Commercio St, Clewiston, FL 33440-3706; tel: (941) 983-2870*, open Tues–Sat 1300–1700, in the former city hall, has local artefacts, old photographs of sugar production and a good selection of books on Seminole customs and history. A bag of Clewiston rice makes a delicious souvenir. At **Clewiston Park**, **Okeechobee Waterway Routes 1** and **2** meet at the south end of the lake, a pleasant picnic spot.

Continue west on Hwy 27/SR 80 about 17 miles to **Ortona Lock & Dam**; *tel: (941) 675-8400*, reached by driving past an alpaca farm and through the **Ortona Lock Campground (RV) Park**. There is a walkway across the powerful pulsing water spilling over the dam, open 0600–2130. Anglers can fish from the pier below the spillway, and there is a walking trail along the riverbank.

On the north side of the Callosahatchee River is the tree-shaded **Ortona Cemetery** and **Ortona Indian Mound Park**. SR 340 continues west.

The Model A car on top of the Country Store is easy to spot. Golf courses line the route, but may be an unsightly brown in winter due to a lack of water.

## LA BELLE

**Tourist Information: Greater La Belle Chamber of Commerce**, *PO Box 456, La Belle, FL 33935; tel: (941) 675-0125*, has local information on La Belle's Swamp Cabbage Festival, held the last weekend in Feb. The sleepy-looking town is 10 blocks long with many churches. La Belle's red brick, Georgian-style City Hall has white columns. Across the highway is the (bright red) Log Cabin Bar-B-Que.

**Alva** is west. **Murphy Grove**, *7800 Hwy 80 W., Alva, FL 33920; tel: (800) 223-5204* or *(941) 728-2424*, has an excellent assortment of fresh citrus juice. **Eden Vineyards**, *19709 Little Lane, Alvra, FL 33920; tel: (941) 728-9463*, open daily 1100-1600, is the southernmost vineyard and winery in the US. The owners make seven varieties of wine, from Bordeaux-style Lake Emerald to Alva Rouge spaghetti wine and the odd Carambola, from tropical starfruit. There is a charge to taste the wines, but a thoughtful explanation of winemaking and local conditions enhances the tasting and compensates for the fee.

Take **Old Olga Rd** right from SR 80 to **W. P. Franklin Lock & Dam**; *tel: (941) 694-2582*, a good place to watch a lock in action on the Caloosahatchee River. The recreation area, open only during the day, has a beautiful but unshaded white-sand beach. Citrus groves and cane fields are ahead on SR 80. Continue towards the red-and-white-banded smokestacks of Florida Power & Light. Enter Fort Myers, ending the route at I-75's Exit 25.

# FORT MYERS AND CAPE CORAL

Fort Myers' most famous citizen, inventor Thomas Alva Edison, chose the Caloosahatchee River shore for a winter home in the 1880s. Edison's search for a pleasant, healthy climate blended with his search for a plant that would yield a cheap supply of rubber. Admirers like car mogul Henry Ford and tyre tycoon Harvey Firestone joined Edison when it was chilly in the Northern US.

The Caloosahatchee River is the western outlet of Florida's Intracoastal Waterway. The islands at the mouth of the river, Sanibel and Captiva in particular, are famed for white sand and beautiful shells. Each island enclave has a distinct personality: posh, relaxed, exclusive or quaint.

Fort Myers is a business and convention centre, home to financiers. To the east, agri-business raises cattle, vegetables and citrus. Fort Myers Beach to the south-west is home to a shrimping fleet and a beach resort strip. North Fort Myers and Cape Coral, north of the river, are residential. Pine Island raises tonnes of tropical fruit. Sanibel and Captiva Islands are environmental gems.

Plan on four days to explore this region; longer if planning an extended stay on Sanibel or Captiva.

## TOURIST INFORMATION

**Lee County Visitor & Convention Bureau**, *2180 W. 1st St, Suite 100, PO Box 2445, Fort Myers, FL 33902-2445; tel: (800) 533-4753 or (941) 338-3500,* provides information and can make lodging reservations. **Greater Fort Myers Chamber of Commerce**, *PO Box 9289, Fort Myers, FL 33902; tel: (941) 332-3624,* provides area information.

There is a **Visitor Welcome Booth** at each concourse of **Southwest Florida International Airport**. Visitors can contact barrier island Chambers of Commerce direct. For Lee County **cultural and arts events;** *tel: (941) 939-2787.*

## ARRIVING AND DEPARTING

**Southwest Florida International Airport (RSW)**, *Chamberlin Pkwy, Fort Myers, FL 33913; tel: (941) 768-1000,* is 10 miles south-east of Fort Myers on SR 876. Take Exit 21 from I-75/SR 93. Check with your hotel to see if it has a courtesy van service.

## GETTING AROUND

**I-75** and **US Hwy 41 (Tamiami Trail)** run parallel, south–north. Choose I-75 for speed. US Hwy 41 is closer to beach areas, but slows near downtown Fort Myers. Near the Caloosahatchee River, **Business 41** separates from US 41, then rejoins it on the north side of the river in North Fort Myers. Take **CR 869, Summerlin Rd**, to Sanibel Island; **CR 865, San Carlos Blvd**, from Fort Myers, through San Carlos Island to Fort Myers

## FORT MYERS AND CAPE CORAL

Beach (Estero Island); **SR 78, Pine Island Rd**, through North Fort Myers and Cape Coral, west to Little Pine Island and Pine Island; or, take **SR 867** south from downtown Fort Myers, then west to Cape Coral. Hire cars are available at Southwest Florida International Airport.

**Public Transport**
**LeeTran;** *tel: (941) 275-8726*, operates bus services in Fort Myers, Fort Myers Beach, North Fort Myers and Cape Coral, as well as winter trolley service to many of the historic sites in downtown Fort Myers and a tram service in Fort Myers Beach.

### ACCOMMODATION
**Lee County VCB** can help with booking area lodging; area Chambers of Commerce have information but do not make bookings. Chains include *BW, CI, DI, Hd, Rd, Rm* and *Sh*. Long-term rates are much cheaper than overnight rates.

### EATING, DRINKING AND ENTERTAINMENT
The Fri 'Gulf Coasting' section of the *Fort Myers News-Press* has extensive listings of activities and where to eat in the Fort Myers area.

## FORT MYERS

**Tourist Information: City of Fort Myers Marketing & Tourism Dept**, *2310 Edwards Dr., Fort Myers, FL 33901; tel: (941) 332-6679.*

**Money**
**Thomas Cook Foreign Exchange** office at *Southwest Florida International Airport, 1600 Chamberlin Parkway, Suite 8638, Fort Myers, FL 33913; tel: (941) 768-6575*, handles travellers' cheques refunds.

### ACCOMMODATION
**Sheraton Harbor Place**, *2500 Edwards Dr., Fort Myers, FL 33901; tel: (800) 833-1620* or *(941) 337-0300*, moderate–expensive, is downtown with good views of the Edison Bridge (carrying Business 41), and the Caloosahatchee Bridge (carrying US 41), over the Caloosahatchee River. *DI, Hd* and *Rm* have moderate–expensive airport area hotels.

### SIGHTSEEING
Fort Myers' premiere attractions are the **Edison-Ford Winter Estates**, *2350 McGregor Blvd, Fort Myers, FL 33901; tel: (941) 334-7419*, Mon–Sat 0900–1600, Sun 1200–1600. Rapid group tours see Edison's magnificent experimental tropical botanical gardens, research laboratory, and, through screens, the furnishings of the Edison and Ford houses.

After the tour, visitors may wander the Edison Museum at leisure. Edison's inventions, amongst them the light bulb, phonograph, telephone and stock-market ticker-tape machine, and his tests of goldenrod as a reliable rubber substitute are on display. Separate tours are offered of only the Edison House or the botanical gardens. Admission to both houses is $10; to the Edison House only is $8; and to the botanical gardens $16.

From the 1890s–1920s, Fort Myers was a fashionable winter refuge for wealthy Americans from the Northern US. **The Burroughs Home**, *2505 1st St, Fort Myers, FL 33902; tel: (941) 332-1229*, Tues–Fri 1000–1600, is an elegant 1901 Georgian Revival riverside home. Living-history guides greet visitors in the parlour, then wander through the house showing off the furnishings, clothing and pictures. Admission $3.18.

**Fort Myers Historical Museum**, *2300 Peck St, Fort Myers, FL 33901; tel:*

# FORT MYERS AND CAPE CORAL

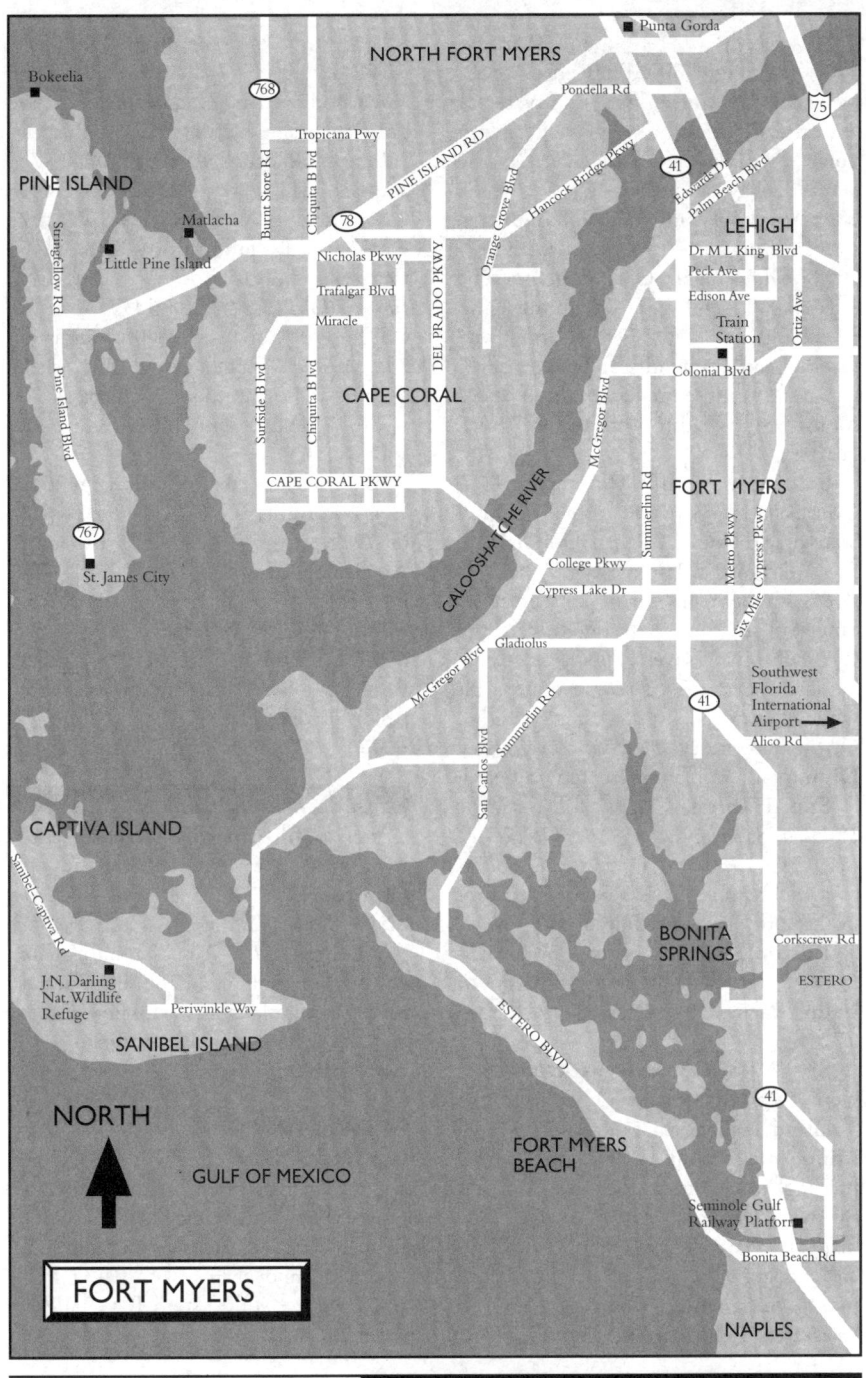

## FORT MYERS AND CAPE CORAL AREA MAP

*(941) 332-5955*, is open Mon–Fri 0900–1630, Sun 1300–1700, entrance $2. The museum covers local history better than most, using a few well-chosen objects to illustrate early events: the Seminole Wars, early settlers, the Koreshan Unity utopian community, a 1920s fishing dock, a Cooper Glass collection and a replica Cracker house. The *Esperanza*, weighing 101 tonnes and stretching for 84 ft, was the largest and last Pullman Railroad Car built, according to the museum, with three staterooms, four bathrooms and servants' quarters.

**Seminole Gulf Railway**, *4110 Centerpointe Dr.* (Metro Mall Railway Station at Colonial Blvd), *Fort Myers, FL 33916; tel: (800) 736-4853* or *(941) 275-8487*, runs two-hr lunch tours north to dine sitting on a bridge over the Caloosahatchee River. There's no panoramic scenery; the cars sway quite a bit while passing backyards. Price: $12.50. On weekends, **Murder Mystery Dinners** for $55, are presented on board.

**Sun Harvest Citrus**, *14810 Metro Parkway S., Fort Myers, FL 33912; tel: (800) 743-1480* or *(941) 768-2686*, offers free juice samples with a self-guided tour of the sorting and packing plant.

**Boston Red Sox** baseball brings fans to see their spring training at **City of Palms Park**, *2201 Edison; tel: (941) 334-4700.*

**Six Mile Cypress Parkway** is a scenic transit between Hwy 41, the Tamiami Trail, north-east to I-75. Watch **Minnesota Twins** baseball team spring training workouts at the **Lee County Sports Complex**; *tel: (800) 338-9467* or *(941) 768-4200.*

A boardwalk and observation deck make **Six Mile Cypress Slough Preserve**, *7751 Penzance Crossing at Six Mile Cypress Pkwy, Fort Myers, FL 33918; tel: (941) 432-2004*, a cypress and mixed hardwood wetland, a quiet place to see birds including herons, egrets, ibis and anhingas. Guided walks start at 0930 Wed and Sat. The parking fee is $3. Three miles north is the **Calusa Nature Center and Planetarium, Inc.**, *3450 Ortiz Ave, (near I-75, Exit 22) Fort Myers, FL 33906; tel: (941) 275-3435*, Mon–Sat 0900–1700, Sun 1100–1700, admission $3. Museum guides demonstrate snake behaviour; an outdoor trail passes an aviary, a replica Seminole Village, pines and cypress.

Biplane rides take off from Page Field: **Classic Flight, Inc.**; *tel: (800) 824-9464* or *(941) 939-7411*, and **Barnstormer Air Incorporated**; *tel: (941) 542-1768.* For longer-range flightseeing, fly **Sound Flight of Fort Myers**; *tel: (941) 277-5777*, in an amphibian Dehavilland Beaver or a **SeaCoast Airlines** small propellor driven aeroplane; *tel: (800) 742-6278* or *(941) 531-8520.*

## FORT MYERS BEACH

**Tourist Information: Greater Fort Myers Beach Area Chamber of Commerce**, *17200 San Carlos Blvd, Fort Myers Beach, FL 33931; tel: (800) 782-9283* or *(941) 454-7500*, has information on lodging, dining and golf, but does not make accommodation bookings for the area, also known as **Estero Island** and **Estero Beach.**

### ACCOMMODATION

Fort Myers Beach has white sand and lower lodging prices than downtown Fort Myers or Sanibel and Captiva Islands. Cottages, motels, condominiums, RV parks and chains like *BW, DI, Hd* and *Rm*, are along Estero Rd, the main street on the narrow island. At the island's north end is the pricey **Best Western Pink Shell Beach & Bay Resort**, *275 Estero Blvd; tel: (800) 237-5786 or (941) 463-6181*, with suites, cottages, apartments and water sports.

## Sightseeing

Separating San Carlos Island from the mainland is Hurricane Bay, part of the **Estero Bay Aquatic Preserve,** sheltering manatees, dolphins and birds. **Island Water Tours;** *tel: (941) 765-4354*, cruises the bay in a pontoon boat. **Matanzas Pass Wilderness Preserve,** *School Rd; tel: (941) 338-3300*, on Estero Bay, is for strolling and birdwatching amidst live oaks and mangroves.

**Island Rover Cruises,** *Snug Harbor Restaurant Marina, 645 San Carlos Blvd; tel: (941) 765-7447*, operates two-hr sailing cruises on a 72-ft long tall ship. **Europa SeaKruz,** *Palm Grove Marina, 1500 Main St; tel: (800) 688-7529 or (941) 463-5000*, offers six-hr cruises with dining, entertainment and gambling. Inquire at the dock for deep sea fishing. Estero Island water activities include parasailing, Wave Runners, Jet Skis, paddle boat hire and shell collecting.

South on CR 865 via the **Bonita Beach Causeway** is **Lovers Key State Recreation Area and Carl E. Johnson County Park**, *c/o Delnor-Wiggins Pass State Recreation Area, 11100 Gulf Shore Dr. N., Naples, FL 33963; tel: (941) 597-6196*, a pleasant shelling, hiking and picnic area on three islands: **Black Island**, **Inner Key** and **Lovers Key**. A footbridge provides access from a parking area on Black Island. Swimming is treacherous, but boating, canoeing and fishing are popular. Osprey, red egrets and roseate spoonbills are easily spotted. Manatees and bottle-nosed dolphins swim offshore.

**Days Inn at Lovers Key,** *8701 Estero Blvd; tel: (800) 329-7466 or (941) 765-4422*, expensive–pricey with breakfast, is just north of Lovers Key.

## SANIBEL AND CAPTIVA ISLANDS

Tourist Information: **Sanibel-Captiva Chamber of Commerce**, *Causeway Blvd, PO Box 166, Sanibel, FL 33957; tel: (941) 472-1080*, has racks of brochures and sells island maps and its own brochures, but does not make bookings for accommodation.

### Arriving and Departing

CR 869, Summerlin Rd, the only road access to Sanibel, becomes the **Sanibel Causeway**. A $3 toll is levied.

### Getting Around

Once on Sanibel, the Sanibel Causeway gives onto **Periwinkle Way.** To the left (east) is **Lighthouse Point**. Three miles to the right, turn right onto **Tarpon Bay Rd**. Go left on **Sanibel-Captiva Rd**, past J. N. 'Ding' Darling Wildlife Refuge, and continue across **Blind Pass** to Captiva Island. Most homes have names: 'Overlook South', 'No-See-Ums', 'Captiva Cottage'. With one lane in each direction, traffic slows dramatically at rush hour, 0700–0900 and 1600–1800.

On Sanibel's south side, **Gulf Drive** is divided into three sections, with increasing street numbers: East Gulf Dr., 0–1000; Middle Gulf Dr., 1200–1400; and West Gulf Dr., 2100–4400.

Roadside parking is prohibited on Sanibel. Parking in marked, patrolled areas is $0.75 per hour. Secure annual beach access parking permits from the **Sanibel Police Dept**, *Sanibel City Hall, 800 Dunlop Rd*, for a fee during business hours. There are twenty miles of well marked bike paths.

Sanibel Island Taxi; *tel: (941) 472-4160*, Sanibel Island Limosine; *tel: (941) 472-8888*, and Sanibel-Captiva Airport Shuttle, Inc.; *tel: (800) 566-0007*, provide return transport from Southwest Florida International Airport. The Sanibel-Captiva Trolley Tour; *tel: (941) 472-6374*, circles the islands in two hrs and costs $10.

## STAYING IN SANIBEL AND CAPTIVA

### Accommodation

Sanibel and Captiva are chock-a-block with lodging, from cottages to condominiums and resort hotels. Lee County Visitors and Conventions Bureau can make bookings or give recommendations.

South Seas Plantation Resort, *PO Box 194, Captiva Island, FL 33924; tel: (800) 237-3102* or *(941) 472-5111*, at the north end of Captiva Island, has 600 expensive–pricey rooms, suites, homes and cottages in a setting large and exclusive enough to occupy days with tennis, golf, yachting, swimming, fitness training and dining in a South Pacific atmosphere. Sundial Beach & Tennis Resort, *1451 Middle Gulf Dr., Sanibel, FL 33957; tel: (800) 237-4184* or *(941) 472-4151*, pricey, has huge condominiums with water views. A marine life touch tank, salt water tank, hermit crab petting tank and other ecology exhibits are in Sundial's Environmental Coastal Observatory Center.

The Island Inn, *3111 W. Gulf Dr., PO Box 659, Sanibel, FL 33957; tel: (800) 851-5088* or *(941) 472-1561*, pricey, was the first inn on the island, complete with a butterfly garden, croquet courts, a pool, beach proximity, and tables outside each room for shell displays. Near Sanibel Lighthouse are two sets of cottages:

Seahorse Cottages, *1223 Buttonwood Lane; tel: (941) 472-4262*, moderate–pricey, with lace curtains, antique oak furniture and paddle fans; and moderate Buttonwood Cottages, *1234 N. Buttonwood Lane; tel: (941) 472-2609*.

### Eating and Drinking

Fast food to seafood, Sanibel has it. Choose the seafood, preparation, and sauce at moderate–pricey Bud's Any Fish You Wish, *1473 Periwinkle Way; tel: (941) 472-5700*, which also has fresh pasta, a bakery and ice cream. Sea-motif murals adorn the walls. The Jacaranda, *1223 Periwinkle Way; tel: (941) 472-1771*, offers jazz, reggae and blues music with moderate–pricey dinners.

On Captiva, the Mucky Duck, *Andy Rosse Lane; tel: (941) 472-3434*, budget–moderate, approximates a British pub – with barbecued, bacon-wrapped shrimp the speciality. Girl Scout staff uniforms and 1940s decor is served with the food at Captiva's pricey Bubble Room, *15001 Captiva Rd; tel: (941) 472-5558*.

### SHOPPING

Shells are widely sold, but Sanibel's best shopping is found in its numerous art galleries. Aboriginals, Art of the First Person, *2340 Periwinkle Way; tel: (941) 395-2200*, has fine tribal art from the US, Africa and Australasia. A Touch of Sanibel Pottery, *1544 Periwinkle Way; tel: (941) 472-4330*, is a working ceramics studio.

### SIGHTSEEING

White sand beaches, shells and beautiful sunrises make the two islands a mecca for visitors. J. N. 'Ding' Darling Wildlife Refuge teems with wildlife and birds, easily visible from a five-mile loop road. The beaches beckon, but the multiple wildlife santuaries along the Sanibel-Captiva Rd are more alluring, with the extraordinary natural range that has disappeared from most of Florida forever.

**J. N. 'Ding' Darling Wildlife Refuge**, *1 Wildlife Dr., Sanibel, FL 33957; tel: (941) 472-1100*, open Sat–Thur sunrise–sunset, entrance fee $5, was named after a Pulitzer-prize-winning political cartoonist who headed the US Biological Survey and helped establish America's National Wildlife Refuge system. Ding – a shortened form of his name – was used as his signature on his work. To decrease stress on animals and birds, the refuge is closed on Fri.

The five-mile, one-way **Wildlife Drive**, can be driven, bicycled, or hiked. Hire canoes to paddle along two canoe trails wending through red mangroves. Narrated tram tours leave from **Tarpon Bay Recreational Area**, *900 Tarpon Bay Rd; tel: (941) 472-8900*. Trams are fine for visitors without a vehicle, though stops are few and camera vantage points poor, especially from the right side. The Wildlife Road was originally built for salt water marsh mosquito control, but the campaign was only partially successful. Parking is permitted on verges within the refuge, if it does not cause a traffic hazard.

Naturalists recommend low tide conditions for optimum wildlife sighting. Anhingas, roseate spoonbills, snowy egrets, white ibis, small grey herons, great blue herons and great egrets are easy to see. Birds feed in the shallows, swooping to pluck small prey. Wading birds peck for crabs and shrimp hiding in the bottom muck, as mullet, bottom-feeding fish, churn the mud for food. Racoons patrol the mudflats for crabs and oysters. Alligators are quite visible. An elevated platform provides year-round protection for ospreys.

It is possible to park and walk the **Cross Dike Trail** to its junction with the **Indigo Trail**. Anhingas, wings outstretched, absorb the sun's warmth. An alligator, harassed by a small grey heron, takes off from a pond at top speed. A lone crocodile holds court for 750,000 annual 'Ding' Darling visitors.

Across from 'Ding' Darling is **C.R.O.W. (Care and Rehabilitation of Wildlife)**, *Sanibel-Captiva Rd; tel: (941) 472-3644*, which has guided tours, Mon–Fri 1100, Sun 1300, for $13, of birds and animals recuperating in habitats. **Sanibel-Captiva Nature Conservation Center**, *3333 Sanibel-Captiva Rd; tel: (941) 472-2329*, admission $2, provides an extensive trail system through wetlands, with guided trail walks, beach walks, a natural history boat cruise, marine touch tank, native plant nursery and Fri science lectures.

As on most of the South-west Gulf Coast, female loggerhead turtles arrive on the islands between May–Sept to lay a hundred or so eggs in the sand, where the young hatch six–eight weeks later. Females and hatchlings are distracted by artificial lights, which act as beacons. By law, hoteliers and homeowners must extinguish all beach lights during those months. A moonlit stroll on the beach should be a watchful one. **Caretta Research, Inc.**; *tel: (941) 472-3177*, conducts informational beach walks.

The **Sanibel Lighthouse**, at the east end of the island, built in 1884, resembles a petroleum rig on stilts topped with a tower. A white lightkeeper's cottage is nearby.

The **Sanibel Historical Museum**, *800 Dunlop Rd; tel: (941) 472-6848*, is a restored Cracker home at the centre of a reconstructed village with a general store, post office and tea room. The 1896 **Old**

**Schoolhouse Theatre**, *1905 Periwinkle Way; tel: (941) 472-6862*, stages musicals and local theatre productions. A 70-year-old Captiva plantation worker's cottage is a museum, the **Captiva History House**, *South Seas Plantation entrance; tel: (941) 472-5111*. The **Bailey-Matthews Shell Museum Preview Center**, *2431 Periwinkle Way; tel: (941) 395-2233*, open 1000-1600, has extensive displays of shells from the islands, Everglades and fossil pits. Not a shell shop, the approach is colourful but educational.

Captiva's **Offshore Sailing School**, *c/o 16731 McGregor Blvd, Fort Myers, FL 33908; tel: (800) 221-4326*, claims to turn landlubbers into experienced sailors in four, six or eight days, complete with a length of rope for pre-arrival knot-tying practice.

## CAPE CORAL

**Tourist Information: Chamber of Commerce of Cape Coral**, *1625 Cape Coral Parkway E., PO Box 747, Cape Coral, FL 33910-0747; tel: (800) 226-9609* or *(941) 549-6900*, or **Chamber of Southwest Florida Welcome Center**, *2051 Cape Coral Parkway, Cape Coral, FL 33904; tel: (941) 542-3721*.

### ARRIVING

Cross the **Cape Coral Bridge, SR 867**, from south Fort Myers to Cape Coral.

### SIGHTSEEING

Cape Coral is residential, partly a dormitory community for Fort Myers. For variation from beach watersports, complete with waterslides, there's **Sun Splash Family Waterpark**, *400 Santa Barbara Blvd; tel: (941) 574-0557*, open mid-Mar–Oct; admission $8.50.

Find inexpensive dining and fast food along **Pine Island Rd, SR 78**, on the way west to **West Island, Little Pine Island,** and **Pine Island**.

## PINE ISLAND

**Tourist Information: Greater Pine Island Chamber of Commerce**, *PO Box 525, Matlacha, FL 33909; tel: (941) 283-0888*.

### SIGHTSEEING

The road to Pine Island leaves Cape Coral's suburbia for fresh fish sold by fishmongers on the narrow Matlacha strip between West Island and Little Pine Island. **The Griffin**, *4303 Pine Island Rd, Matlacha; tel: (941) 283-0680*, open Wed–Sun 1200-2100, also called **The Mad Hatter's Teas of Matlacha**, has moderately priced fresh seafood and other entrées served dockside. A *papier mâché* flower in front marks the small entrance, which is also entry to the **American Center for Haitian Art** gallery; *tel: (941) 283-3486*. Kayak the **Matlacha Pass Aquatic Preserve** at sunset or under a full moon for birdwatching with **Gulf Coast Kayak**, *4882 N.W. Pine Island Rd, Matlacha, FL 33909; tel: (941) 283-1125*.

On **Pine Island,** turn north onto Stringfellow Rd. The small **Museum of the Islands**, *572 Sesame Dr.; tel: (941) 283-1525*, open 1000–1630, has a Calusa Indian canoe and other artefacts. Toward **Pineland**, exotic tropical fruit nurseries appear, cultivating fruits like sapodilla, calmondin, pomelo (grapefruit), sour orange, sugar apple, mamey sapote and avocado. Some growers sell to passers by: **Tropicaya Fruit & Gift Mart**, *3220 S.W. Pine Island Rd; tel: (941) 283-0656*; and **Blind Hog Groves, Ltd**, *6935 Pineland Rd; tel: (941) 283-4092*. **Sunburst Tropical Fruit Co.**, *7113 Howard Rd; tel: (941) 283-1200*, conducts tours

through mango groves and offers visitors samples of chutney, preserves and fruit.
**Gulf Island Groves**, *12101 N.W. Harry St, Bokeelia; tel: (941) 283-0240,* is at the north end of Pine Island. A small, cheap restaurant and gift shop are at the end of Main St on **Ebb Tide Way**. There is a fee to use the pier. Drive along **Main St** to view large wooden seaside 'cottages'. From Bokeelia's **Four Winds Marina, Tropic Star Cruises;** *tel: (941) 283-0015,* take day-long cruises to **Cayo Costa** and **Cabbage Key**. Water taxis run from Captiva to Upper Captiva, Cayo Costa and Cabbage Key from **Jensen's Twin Palm Marina**, *15107 Captiva Dr.; tel: (941) 472-5800.* **Captiva Cruises**, *South Seas Plantation; tel: (941) 472-5300,* cruise to Useppa Island, Cabbage Key and Cayo Costa.

**Cayo Costa State Island Preserve;** *c/o PO Box 1150, Boca Grande, FL 33921; tel: (941) 964-0375* or *(941) 966-3694,* is south of Boca Grande. The seven-mile-long preserve is covered with dunes and forest. Twelve budget cabins with a view of the Gulf are for hire; other activities are primitive camping, fishing, boating, bicycling, five miles of trails and excellent winter shelling.

**Cabbage Key**, *Box 200, Pineland, FL 33945; tel: (941) 283-2278,* sits on a Calusa shell mound. In 1938, playwright and novelist Mary Roberts Rhinehart built the moderate–expensive **Cabbage Inn** with six rooms, six cottages, a marina and paths. A wooden water tower has a view of Pine Island Sound and coconut palms on the beach. The inn's dining room walls have thousands of autographed $1 bills.

**Useppa Island**, *c/o PO Box 640, Bokeelia, FL 33922; tel: (941) 283-0290,* is a private island with a 25-room inn, and the posh Barron Collier Inn Restaurant. The **Useppa Museum**; *tel: (941) 283-9600,* open Tues–Sun 1300-1500, has artefacts recovered from local archaeological digs.

## NORTH FORT MYERS

**Tourist Information: North Fort Myers Chamber of Commerce**, *3444 Marinatown Lane, North Fort Myers, FL 33903; tel: (941) 656-2002.*

### SIGHTSEEING

Much of North Fort Myers along Hwy 41 is taken up with fast food restaurants and petrol stations. **The Shell Factory**, *North Tamiami Trail (US 41), North Fort Myers, FL 33903-2787; tel: (941) 995-2141,* open 0900–1800, is the exception. A huge collection of shells are in display cases around the store entrance. Inside are collectable shells, shell jewellery, magnets, trinkets, lamps and even shell toilet seats. There are also souvenirs, tables, clothing, moccasins, live fish in aquariums, baby sharks in bottles, marbles and gemstones. A **Christmas Shop** has a fine assortment of delicate ornaments.

**Babcock Wilderness Adventures,** *8000 SR 31, Punta Gorda, FL 33982; tel: (941) 338-6367* or *(941) 489-3911,* north-east of Fort Myers, is a 90,000-acre cattle ranch with an egg-incubation alligator farm, lumber, sand and gravel sales, fruit, vegetables, corn seed and turf cultivation. Admission is $16. Narrated tours wind through Telegraph Swamp in a 32-passenger truck, or 'swamp buggy', to see American bison, egrets, sandhill cranes, white-tailed deer, wild pigs, snakes, baby and adult alligators and specially-bred relatives of the Florida panther kept in a shady enclosure. Animal spotting varies seasonally. A small Cracker-style house holds a few exhibits; it was built for the Sean Connery film, 'Just Cause'.

# FORT MYERS–
# ST PETERSBURG

Forty years after Thomas Alva Edison, the great inventor, chose Fort Myers' tropical garden atmosphere for his winter residence, the Ringling Brothers chose a town about seventy miles north as pleasant winter quarters for their circus. Sarasota, close to several brilliant white sand keys, was to become the Gulf Coast's cultural centre, a playland for rich patrons of the arts from Chicago to Miami.

Sarasota's economy now boasts financiers, banks, stock brokers and a booming medical specialities establishment. The city centre thrives on art galleries, theatres and clubs.

Powdery white sand, long beaches and few shells are features of Sarasota's barrier islands. Longboat Key is up-market. Siesta Key is Caribbean in atmosphere. Anna Maria is casual, in attitude and dress.

The 95 miles from Fort Myers to St Petersburg leaves the Everglades and South-west Florida behind. Driving direct from the Caloosahatchee River in Fort Myers to downtown St. Petersburg takes two hours. Allow several days for a visit to the keys, Myakka River State Park and the splendid Ringling Museum complex in Sarasota.

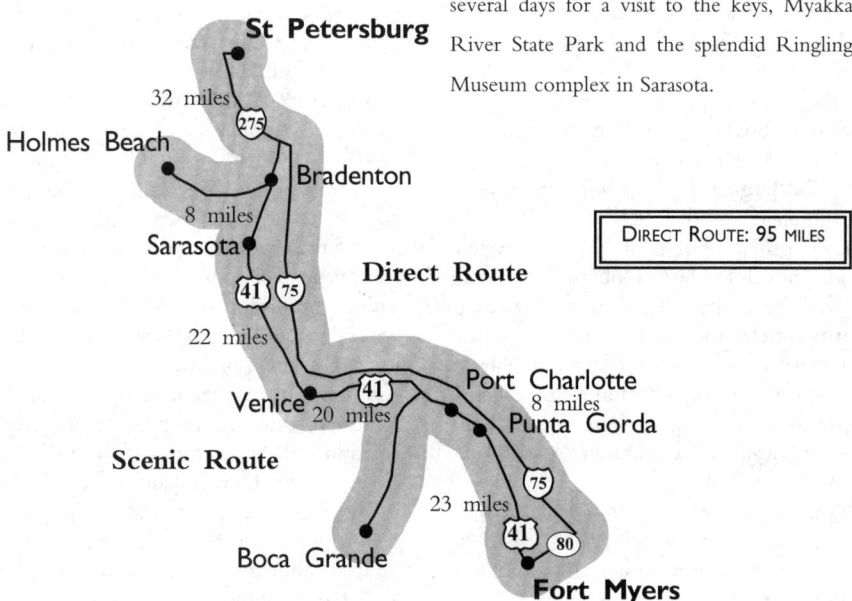

**DIRECT ROUTE: 95 MILES**

St Petersburg
32 miles (275)
Holmes Beach
Bradenton
8 miles
Sarasota
(41) (75)
22 miles
Direct Route
Venice (41)
20 miles
Port Charlotte
8 miles
Punta Gorda
Scenic Route
23 miles (75)
(41) (80)
Boca Grande
Fort Myers

## FORT MYERS–ST PETERSBURG

### ROUTES

#### DIRECT ROUTE

From downtown Fort Myers, take **Palm Beach Blvd**, **SR 80**, northeast. At (I-75) **Exit 25** turn onto **I-75** going north. I-75 parallels Hwy 41. Take **Exit 44**, **I-275** west and north-west over the **Sunshine Skyway** to **St Petersburg**. Take **Exit 9** off I-275 east on **I-175** towards downtown. Take **Exit 2** onto **5th Ave S.** towards **Bayfront Center**.

#### SCENIC ROUTE

Follow **Hwy 41**, the **Tamiami Trail**, north from downtown **Fort Myers** through **Punta Gorda, Port Charlotte, North Point, Venice, Nokomis, Osprey, Sarasota** and **Bradenton**. North of **Memphis**, take **US 19** north, then turn left onto **I-275** at **Terra Ceia** and cross the **Sunshine Skyway** to **St. Petersburg**. Take **Exit 3**, **Pinellas**, for one long block, then turn left onto **31st St S.** Go right on **35th Terrace**, which becomes **Fairway Ave S.** then **Country Club Way S.** as it winds south of **Lake Maggiore**. Continue north on **9th St S.**, head right on **Harbordale**, left on **4th St S.**, right on **22nd Ave S.E.**, north on **Beach Dr.** Turn west on **14th Ave S.E.**, then north on **Bay St**, left on **13th Ave S.E.**, north on **3rd St S.**, east on **5th St S.** then continue on **Bayshore Dr.** to **The Pier** in downtown **St Petersburg**.

### PUNTA GORDA

**Tourist Information:** Charlotte County Chamber of Commerce, *326 W. Marion Ave, Suite 112, Punta Gorda, FL 33950; tel: (941) 639-2222.*

#### ACCOMMODATION

Chain hotels include *DI, Hd* and *HJ*. The three-room **Gilchrist Bed & Breakfast Inn**, *115 Gilchrist St; tel: (941) 575-4129*, is a moderate choice.

Twenty-three miles from Fort Myers, turn left on **Airport Rd** for one short block, right on **Shreve St** and left on **W. Retta Esplanade** to shop for souvenirs and local crafts at **Fisherman's Village**, *1200 W. Retta Esplanade, Punta Gorda, FL 33950; tel: (941) 639-8721.* Go one block south to **W. Marion Ave**, then west to **Ponce de Leon Historical Park** at **Marion Creek**. A stone memorial surmounted with a cross marks the spot where the Spanish explorer may have landed and been wounded by Native Americans in 1513. To return to Hwy 41, retrace the route on **W. Marion Ave**, but veer right going north-east on **W. Olympia Ave**, then turn right onto the **Collier Bridge** over the **Peace River** to continue north to **Port Charlotte**.

### PORT CHARLOTTE

**Tourist Information:** Charlotte County Chamber of Commerce, *2702 Tamiami Trail, Port Charlotte, FL 33952; tel: (941) 627-2222.*

#### ACCOMMODATION

*DI* and *QI* are amongst the chains. Inquire at the Chamber of Commerce or continue to Boca Grande.

**SIDE TRACK TO BOCA GRANDE**

At **Murdock**, take **SR 776** south through **El Jobean**. Baseball fans watch the **Texas Rangers** spring training at **Charlotte County Stadium**, *SR 776, El Jobean Rd; tel: (941) 625-9500.* Cross the **Myakka River**, then continue south on **CR 771** to **Placida**.

**Placida** is a small fishing pier, a

187

restaurant and a few buildings. Three art galleries on Fishery Rd sell crafts, from windchimes to fine silk-screen clothing: **Margaret Albritton Gallery**; *tel: (941) 698-0603*; **The Sassy Seagull**; *tel: (941) 698-1919*; and **Placida Cove Gifts and Crafts**; *tel: (941) 697-2451*. The moderate **Fishery Restaurant**; *tel: (941) 697-2451*, has a wide range of seafood with waterfront views. **Grande Tours**, *11 Fishery Rd, PO Box 281, Placida, FL 33946-0281; tel: (941) 697-8825*, leads boat and kayak tours. A private ferry service goes to **Don Pedro Island State Recreation Area**, *c/o Cayo Costa State Park; tel: (941) 964-0375*, a mile-long white sand beach barrier island a few miles north. Follow a causeway and a toll bridge ($3.20) to **Boca Grande** on **Gasparilla Island**.

## BOCA GRANDE

**Tourist Information: Boca Grande Chamber of Commerce**, *PO Box 704, Boca Grande, FL 33921; tel: (941) 964-0568*, on Gasparilla Island, has local information. The local paper, the *Boca Beacon, PO Box 313, 431 Park Ave, Boca Grande, FL 33921; tel: (941) 964-2995*, publishes a visitors' guide.

### ACCOMMODATION

**Gasparilla Inn & Cottages**, *5th St at Palm Ave, PO Box 1088, Boca Grande, FL 33921; tel: (813) 964-2201*, expensive–pricey, prides itself on never advertising and has catered to New England's Social Register from the hotel's inception in 1913. The lemon-yellow clapboard building has elegant porticoes. Golf, tennis, croquet, wicker furniture and afternoon tea preserve the old-time ambience.

### SIGHTSEEING

Gasparilla Island is named after José Gaspar, a legendary pirate who may have frequented the waters from Fort Myers to Tampa. Boca Grande tidal inlet is one of Florida's deepest, used from 1885–1979 as a deep water port for phosphate shipment. Following a century's tradition, the very rich return to their enclave year after year during the winter season. Boca Grande Pass is the 'Tarpon Fishing Capital of the World', and the Gasparilla Inn and other lodging is full for **Tarpon Season**, mid-Apr–July.

At the southern tip of the island is **Gasparilla Island State Recreation Area**, *c/o Cayo Costa State Park, PO Box 1150, Boca Grande, FL 33921; tel: (941) 964-0375*. The beach, on the Gulf of Mexico, is a mile long, flanked at the northern end by impressive houses, and, at the island's southern tip, by the 1890 **Boca Grande Lighthouse**, girded by a wooden balcony. Picnic tables are at either end of the recreation area. Bicycles are popular transport on the converted railbed that runs the island's length.

Continue west on Hwy 41 to North Port. One mile north is the **Resort and Spa at Warm Mineral Springs**, *12200 San Servando Blvd, Warm Mineral Springs, FL 34287; tel: (941) 426-1692*. Accommodation is moderate; the 87ºF waters are the focus, with tubs, whirlpool sauna, hotpack and massage.

Cross the Myakka River and go west to **South Venice** and **Venice**. Hwy 41 splits on the outskirts of Venice; take Business 41, the Tamiami Trail, to the left to go through town or the **Venice Bypass**, east of the Intracoastal Waterway, to pass it by.

## VENICE

**Tourist Information: Venice Area Chamber of Commerce**, *257 N. Tamiami Trail, Venice, FL 34285-1534; tel: (941) 488-2236*, has information and packets of fossilised shark teeth.

### ACCOMMODATION

Chain hotels include BW and DI. **Banyan House Bed & Breakfast Inn**, *519 Harbor Dr. S., Venice, FL 34285; tel: (941) 484-1385*, expensive, matches the Mediterranean style of Venice's 1920s design. Lodging a block or two from the beach is cheaper than a beachfront room.

### GETTING AROUND

**Sarasota County Area Transit (SCAT)**; *tel: (941) 951-5851*, provides bus services. **Venice Trolley**; *tel: (941) 488-2779*, has narrated sightseeing tours from 20 downtown stops.

### SIGHTSEEING

Venice lacks the barrier islands which proliferate along the Gulf of Mexico. Visit **Casperson Beach, Venice Beach** or **Golden Beach** to search for flat shiny black **shark teeth**. The obsidian-coloured triangles wash ashore, the product of centuries of shark shedding up to 2000 teeth per year.

The Homestead Act brought the first European settlers to the area in the 1860s. The hamlet of Horse and Chaise became Venice in 1888 when a resident concluded the town was laid out on canals like its Italian namesake. A few fingers of land are surrounded by water, but the resemblance is more striking in the Mediterranean architecture of the historic district around **W. Venice Ave**. From 1960–91, Venice was the winter headquarters of Ringling Bros. and Barnum & Bailey Circus.

At **Nokomis**, take **Albee Rd** left from Hwy 41, across a bridge to **Nokomis Beach** on **Casey Key**. Follow **Jetty Rd** south to **North Jetty Park**, open 0600–midnight, for a fine view of pleasure boats on Venice Inlet. Pelicans and fishermen line up for the show.

Early homesteaders settled the coast around **Osprey**. **Oscar Scherer State Park**, *1843 S. Tamiami Trail, Osprey, FL 34229; tel: (941) 483-5956*, has trails, camp pitches and Florida scrub jays, a threatened species. Canoeing and fishing are popular; beware of alligators basking in the shadows of the creek bank and shuffle your feet in shallow water to discourage sting rays. **Historic Spanish Point**, *500 N. Tamiami Trail, Osprey, FL 34229; tel: (941) 966-5214*, Mon–Sat 0900-1700, Sun 1200–1700 (Dec–Apr), admission $4, has outstanding native plant gardens, Native American shell middens, historic buildings and 0.8 miles of pathways along Little Sarasota Bay. On Sun, costumed guides narrate the history of the building. The **Webb Citrus Packing House** at Historic Spanish point is Florida's best demonstration of early processing techniques and the history of the state's most important product.

Follow Hwy 41 eight miles north to **Sarasota**.

## SARASOTA

**Tourist Information: Sarasota Convention & Visitors Bureau**, *655 N. Tamiami Trail, Sarasota, FL 34236; tel: (800) 522-9799* or *(941) 957-1877*, has information on Sarasota County, but does not make accommodation bookings.

### ARRIVING AND DEPARTING

**Sarasota-Bradenton International Airport (SRQ)**; *tel: (941) 359-2770*, is at the north end of town.

## GETTING AROUND

At **Wood St**, Hwy 41 turns west, then continues north. From downtown Sarasota, take **John Ringling Causeway**, SR 789, to **St Armands Key, Lido Key** and north-west to **Longboat Key**. Take **Siesta Dr.**, Hwy 758, or **Stickney Point**, SR 72, to **Siesta Key**.

## Public Transport

**Sarasota County Area Transit (SCAT)**, *5303 Pinkney Ave, Sarasota, FL 34233; tel: (941) 951-5851*, operates area-wide buses. The open-air **Sarasota Trolley** runs downtown around Main St every half hour, 0945–1645.

## ACCOMMODATION

Sarasota has a wide variety of lodging in town and on the barrier islands. *BW, CI, DI, Hd, Hy* and *Rm* are chain hotels in Sarasota. The moderate–expensive **Sleep Inn**, *900 University Parkway, Sarasota, FL 34234; tel: (800) 627-5337* or *(941) 359-8558*, across from Sarasota-Bradenton Airport and convenient for Hwy 41, nestles in a small forest with resident ducks.

## EATING AND DRINKING

The **Granary**, *8421 N. Tamiami Trail; tel: (941) 651-4671*, open Mon–Sat 0830–2100, Sun 1000–1800, is a well-stocked budget natural foods store with delicious home-made breads. Next door, **Captain Brian's Seafood Market & Restaurant** has stone crabs, Maine lobster and Nova Scotia whitefish.

## ENTERTAINMENT

Sarasota's 24-hr **Artsline;** *tel: (941) 365-2787*, details cultural events. The *Sarasota Herald Tribune* Fri 'Ticket'; *tel: (941) 957-5210*, lists entertainment, supplemented by the monthly club list in the *Eclispe* paper; *tel: (941) 365-6776*.

The **Asolo Theater Company,** *5555 N. Tamiami Trail, Sarasota, FL 34243; (941) 351-8000* or *351-9010*, performs plays from Oct–Jun. From Oct–Apr the **Van Wezel Performing Arts Hall**, *777 N. Tamiami Trail; tel: (941) 953-3366*, hosts internationally-renowned musicians, concerts and films. The Sarasota Opera performs four operas annually at the 1926 **Opera House**, *61 N. Pineapple Ave; tel: (941) 953-7030*.

Sarasota's many art galleries are on Main St or Palm and Pineapple Aves. **In Extremis**, *at Sarasota Quay, Hwy 41 and Fruitville Rd; tel: (941) 954-2008*, is a laser and video night-club in a major shopping, dining and entertainment complex. **The Gator Club**, *1490 Main St; tel: (941) 366-5969*, has live jazz. Piano clubs centre around Palm Ave and Main St. The **Paradise Café**, *1311 1st St; tel: (941) 955-8500*, has cabaret. **Café Saint Louie**, *1258 N. Palm Ave; tel: (941) 955-8550*, is a romantic piano bar in the Theater District.

The **Chicago White Sox** train during spring at **Ed Smith Stadium;** *2700 12th St; tel: (941) 954-7699*. Greyhounds race mid-Jan–mid-Apr at **Sarasota Kennel Club**, *5400 Bradenton Rd, Sarasota, FL 34234; tel: (941) 355-7744*.

## SHOPPING

**Main Book Shop**, *1962 Main St, Sarasota, FL 34236; tel: (941) 955-1978*, has long hours, free coffee and a eclectic collection of new and used books. Shop for *objets d'art*, postcards and glassware at the **Ringling Museum of Art**, the **Circus Museum** and **Ca'd'Zan gift shops**.

## SIGHTSEEING

Cattle ranching, citrus and fishing may have been Sarasota's 19th century mainstays, but the **John & Mable Ringling**

**Museum of Art,** *5401 Bay Shore Rd; tel: (941) 359-5700,* open 1000–1730; free Sat except Medieval Fair weekends, is the area's finest attraction today. The museum complex, admission $8.50, includes the **Art Galleries**, **Circus Museum**, the circus impresario's fanciful residence, **Ca'd'Zan** (House of John), the **Asolo Theater**, and a **Rose Garden** gazebo.

The **Art Galleries** are in a villa built around an Italian Renaissance-style courtyard. Inside, the walls of the 21 galleries are painted to match the paintings or objects on exhibit; if the art is Gothic, so are the ceilings and portals. The fascinating collections range from late Medieval–Renaissance Northern Europe to 19th-century American. Many paintings are huge, including a collection of wall-sized Peter Paul Rubens. John Ringling collected what he liked, and the oil paintings frequently show large fleshy people or odd, bold expressions. The Astor Room Southeast Salon has a unique collection of delicate fans.

**Circus Museum** artefacts were collected after Ringling's death by the State of Florida. Circus posters from the 1890s–1940s and early engravings of English circuses fill the walls. Elaborately-carved menagerie, ticket taker and calliope wagons seem to wait for occupants. Circus costumes, props, a mechanised circus and Tom Thumb's personal effects fill other rooms with colour and oddity.

**Ca'd'Zan**, finished in 1926, shows wear. The golden Venetian-style house has a patterned marble terrace overlooking Sarasota Bay, tinted Venetian glass windows and more than 20 rooms, some outfitted with the Ringlings' furnishings.

**Marie Selby Botanical Gardens,** *811 S. Palm Ave, Sarasota, FL 34236: tel: (941) 366-5731,* open 1000–1700, entrance $6, has more than 6000 orchids amongst its 15 tropical gardens. The **Tropical Display House** showcases torch ginger, carnivorous plants, bromeliads, heliconias and the most concentrated **epiphyte** (non-parasitic air plants) collection in the US.

**Bellm's Cars & Music of Yesterday,** *5500 N. US 41; tel: (941) 355-6228,* open 0930–1730, price $7.50, has 120 classic restored cars, music machines from organs to music boxes and antique mechanised games.

Sarasota's cultural attractions are complemented by the quality of its outdoors. **Myakka River State Park,** *13207 SR 72, Sarasota, FL 34241-9542; tel: (941) 361-6511,* nine miles east of town, has the usual alligators, shorebirds, ponds, lakes, hammocks, prairies and pine flatwoods of South-west Florida. An airboat tour of Upper Myakka Lake's basking gators, sunning anhingas and egrets, combined with a tram safari tour through Cracker pioneer homestead land is a splendid, informative and economical introduction to Florida's wilderness. Abundant alligators prevent swimming, but (hired) canoes and fishing are popular. Hike or bicycle along trails, walk a boardwalk to the Bird Walk Observation Area, camp or stay in a log cabin.

## SIESTA KEY

**Tourist Information: Siesta Key Chamber of Commerce,** *5263 Ocean Blvd, Siesta Key, FL 34242; tel: (941) 349-3800.*

### GETTING AROUND

The **Siesta Key Trolley**; *tel: (941) 346-3115,* caters to visitors Nov–May.

Museums around Florida display samples of Siesta Key sand, which is 99% quartz and possibly the whitest powder sand in the world. Artists live and work at the key's north end. Further south are condominiums and beautiful homes overlooking wide, white beaches. **Midnight Pass Rd, SR 758,** traverses six-mile-long Siesta Key, though **Ocean Blvd/Beach Dr.** skirt **Sandy Cove** and **Sarasota Point** on the west side. Venetian-style canals snake between the two routes. **Siesta Key Beach**, at the junction of Midnight Pass Rd and Beach Dr., has plenty of free parking, picnic tables and weekend arts fairs. At the extreme southern end of the island, the two fingers of **Turtle Beach Park** attract sun worshippers and sunset watchers to the dunes. The moderate **Crescent House Bed & Breakfast**, *459 Beach Rd, Siesta Key, FL 34242; tel: (941) 346-0857,* is a 1920s-era home near the white sand beaches.

Across the John Ringling Causeway from downtown Sarasota is **St Armands Key**. The circus man's dream was to build deluxe residences around a posh shopping area. St Armands Circle, the small island's centre, today has 160 upmarket shops, boutiques, restaurants, jewellers, estate agents (realtors) and art galleries. Plaques on the **Circus Ring of Fame** honour 39 performers and groups.

Take **John Ringling Parkway** north from St Armands Circle and turn right on **Ken Thompson Parkway** onto **City Island**. **Mote Marine Aquarium**, *1600 Ken Thompson Parkway, Sarasota, FL 34236; tel: (800) 691-6683 or (941) 388-4441,* open 1000–1700, admission $6, is a part of a major marine research facility. Skates, used for cancer research, are shown in embryonic development. Sharks, also used in research, are visible in a large tank. Aquarium guides passionate and knowledgeable about the sealife, which includes Gulf and river fish, game fish like grouper, snook and bass, spiny lobsters and loggerhead turtles. Across the parkway is **Mote Marine Mammal Rehabilitation Center**, which shows films of its animal care programme. **Pelican Man's Bird Sanctuary**, *1708 Ken Thompson Pkwy; tel: (941) 388-4444,* open 1000–1700, is a rehabilitation facility for injured birds. Permanently disabled birds are on display while their saviour, Dale Shields, rolls between their enclosures in a wheelchair.

To see **Lido Key**, take **John Ringling Blvd** west to **Benjamin Franklin Dr.** Drive south past **Lido Beach**, condominiums, and moderate–expensive lodging like the **Half Moon Beach Club**, *2050 Benjamin Franklin Dr.; tel: (800) 358-3245 or (941) 388-3694,* to **South Lido Park**. Trees shade picnic tables as boats cruise through **Big Pass**. The beach curves 180º around the island's south side, drawing spectators to watch deep-pink sunsets.

North of Lido Key is **Longboat Key**, accessible from St Armands Key via John Ringling Parkway, SR 789. The **Longboat Key Chamber of Commerce**, *The Centre, 5360 Gulf of Mexico Dr., Suite 107, Longboat Key, FL 34228; tel: (941) 383-2466,* has information on lodging. Residents are proud of the 'Rolls Royce of Islands' reputation, typified by manicured lawns, gated residences and pricey resorts. Fishing, tennis, golf and jogging, bicycling or rollerblading along the 10.5-mile-long Gulf of Mexico Dr. bikepath is excellent.

### BRADENTON

**Tourist Information: Bradenton Area Convention & Visitors Bureau**, *PO Box 1000, Bradenton, FL 34206; tel: (800) 462-6283 or (941) 729-9177,* has lists of accommodation and 15 **manatee spotting areas** in Manatee County. The **Manatee Chamber of Commerce**,

# FORT MYERS–ST PETERSBURG

*222 10th St W., Bradenton, FL 34205; tel: (941) 748-3411*, also has information.

## ACCOMMODATION

Bradenton area lodging is generally less expensive than Sarasota and the barrier islands. Bradenton chain hotels include *DI, Hd, HJ* and *M6*. **Holmes** and **Bradenton Beaches** on **Anna Maria Island** also have accommodation.

## SIGHTSEEING

Bradenton's most famous resident is **Snooty the Manatee**, housed in his huge **Parker Aquarium** pool at the **South Florida Museum & Bishop Planetarium**, *201 10th St W., Bradenton, FL 34205; tel: (941) 746-4131*, open Mon–Sat 1000–1700, Sun 1200–1700. Bi-level viewing of the winsome 40-something Snooty's feeding time is a unique perspective of the animal and its gentle, responsive ways that make it so vulnerable in open waters.

The museum's Spanish-style building has 1880s–1950s sportsfishing equipment, displays of comparative sand whiteness, arrowheads, shells and 19th-century artefacts.

One mile east is **Manatee Village Historical Park;** *SR 64 and 15th St E.; tel: (941) 749-7165*, the county's restored courthouse, school, store and a house, with picnic facilities.

Go five miles west of the museum/planetarium/aquarium, then north on 75th St N.W. to the **De Soto National Memorial,** *PO Box 15390, Bradenton, FL 34280-5390; tel: (941) 792-0458*, open 0900-1700. A nature trail follows the Manatee River shoreline. Call in advance for the schedule of crossbow and arquebus demonstrations by costumed rangers. The visitors centre has 16th-century armour and a short film of Hernando de Soto's explorations of the Gulf Coast and Mississippi River.

### SIDE TRACK TO ANNA MARIA ISLAND

## ANNA MARIA ISLAND/HOLMES BEACH

**Tourist Information: Anna Maria Island Chamber of Commerce,** *3214 E. Bay Dr., PO Box 1892, Holmes Beach, FL 34218; tel: (941) 778-1541*.

Anna Maria Island thrusts into Tampa Bay and is connected by bridge with Longboat Key on the southern end and by **Cortez Bridge (SR 684)** and **Anna Maria Island Bridge (SR 64)**, to Bradenton. **Anna Maria** town is north; **Holmes Beach** and **Bradenton Beach** are further south.

Condominiums are prohibited, so buildings are low; the lifestyle is relaxed and oriented towards deep sea fishing for snook, redfish, tarpon and sea trout.

North of Bradenton, on US 301 between Hwy 41 and I-75, is **Gamble Plantation State Historic Site;** *3708 Patten Ave, Ellenton, FL 34222; tel: (941) 723-4536*, open Thurs–Mon 0900–1700, the only extant plantation house in Southern Florida. It was built by slave labour in 1844 as the centre of a 3500-acre sugar plantation. The plantation house is also called the **Judah P. Benjamin Confederate Memorial** after the Secretary of State who took refuge there after the Civil War, before fleeing to England and becoming a member of the English Bar.

Return to Hwy 41 and continue north on US 19 to the junction with I-275. Take I-275, the Sunshine Skyway, to St. Petersburg.

# ST PETERSBURG

St Petersburg has a relaxed charm, resting between the ambience of the Gulf of Mexico (from Clearwater Beach to St Pete Beach) and the business centre to the east, Tampa. Arts and culture define downtown St Petersburg, or St Pete, as locals call it. The Salvador Dali Museum gives St Petersburg a world-class draw, but its jewel-like setting on Tampa Bay and the south-east side of the Pinellas Peninsula demands a closer look.

## TOURIST INFORMATION

The **St Petersburg/Clearwater Area Convention & Visitors Bureau (SPCACVB);** *St Petersburg ThunderDome, One Stadium Dr, Suite A, St Petersburg, FL 33705-1706; tel: (813) 582-7892,* has information on the Pinellas Peninsula. A **Visitor Center;** *tel: (813) 821-6164,* is located on the main level of **The Pier** (see p. 200) **St Petersburg Area Chamber of Commerce**, *100 2nd Ave N., Suite 150, St Petersburg, FL 33701; tel: (813) 821-4069,* has information about the city.

### Weather

Lots of sunshine is the claim, backed up by history. From 1910–86, the *St Petersburg Evening Independent* gave a free newspaper away any day the sun didn't shine. During the 76 years before the paper folded, the publisher had to make good the offer only 295 times. June–Sept brings thunderstorms and high humidity. Winter nights can be chilly enough to need a cover-up. For weather forecasts; *tel: (813) 645-2506.*

## ARRIVING AND DEPARTING

### Airports

While a few planes, especially charters, use **St Petersburg-Clearwater International Airport,** *Administration Bldg, Suite 221, Clearwater, FL 34622; tel: (813) 535-7600,* most passengers arrive at **Tampa International Airport (TIA);** *tel: (813) 870-8700* or *(800) 767-8882* (see Tampa, p. 216). The **Limo,** *tel: (813) 572-1111,* and **Red Line Limo**, *tel: (813) 535-3391,* cost about $12 from TIA to St Petersburg; taxis are a little less.

### By car

Interstate highways flow conveniently near downtown St Pete. From I-275, take Exit 10 east on I-375. Take Exit 1 from I-375, then turn right on M. L. King St (9th St N.). Turn left onto 1st Ave and drive east through downtown to Tampa Bay. Or, take Exit 9 off I-275, onto I-175. Then take Exit 1 onto 5th Ave and go east through downtown. To find the Dali Museum, take Exit 2 off I-175 onto 5th Ave, then turn right onto 4th St. Go right at 11th Ave for one block, then go left. The Dali Museum is on the right on the Bayboro Harbor side.

### By bus

**Greyhound Lines, Inc.,** *180 9th St N.; tel: (800) 231-2222,* connects with other major cities in Florida.

## GETTING AROUND

One-way streets direct traffic flow around downtown St Petersburg. All avenues run east–west and streets run

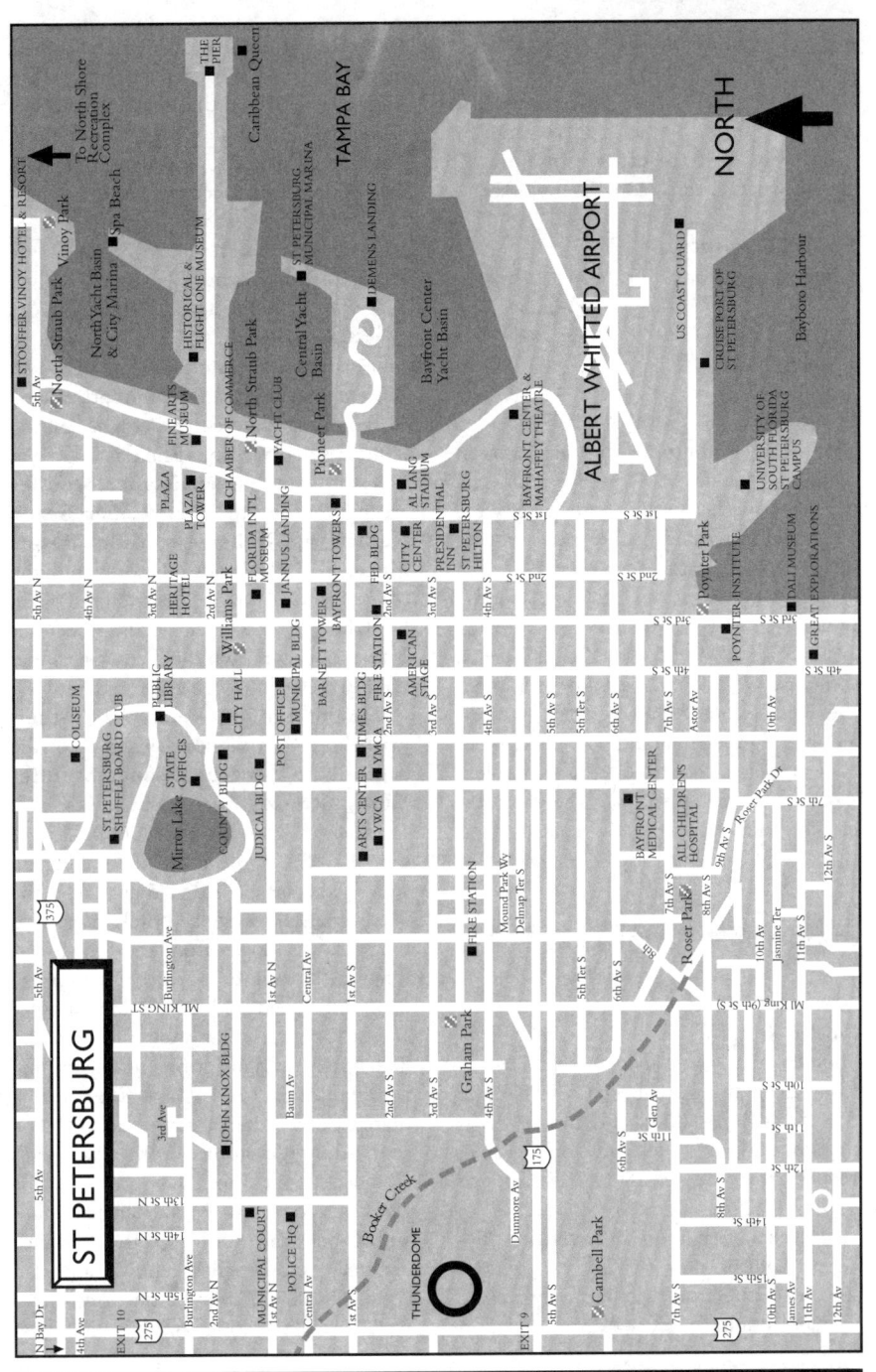

# ST PETERSBURG

# ST PETERSBURG MAP

195

north–south. **Central Ave** is the north–south divide for all streets and avenues. Paralled to Central Ave are **1st Ave N.** (one way west), and **1st Ave S.** (one way east towards downtown). **Bayshore Dr.** runs along Tampa Bay.

**Public Transport**
**Pinellas Suncoast Transit Authority (PSTA)**; *tel: (813) 530-9911*, has bus services for St Petersburg and Pinellas County.

**Driving**
Avoid St Petersburg's rush hour between 0700–0900 and 1630–1800. Traffic signals are slow. Downtown streets are wide and well marked. One-way routes include 1st Aves N. (west) and S. (east), 5th Aves N. (west) and S. (east), southbound M.L. King and 4th Sts, and northbound 8th, 3rd, and 1st Sts. There is some parking along Bayshore Dr. near the Renaissance Stouffer Vinoy Resort, along 2nd Ave N. along The Pier, or in paid car parks close to The Pier complex. A trolley shuttle runs from the car parks to The Pier. There is free parking near the Dali Museum and Great Explorations.

**STAYING IN ST PETERSBURG**

**Accommodation**
Pinellas County's 23,000 rooms offer a wide range of prices and styles of lodging, from chain hotels to beach resorts. The **SPCACVB** has hotel and motel information, and books lodging for the area; **reservation line**; *tel: (800) 345-6710*, or *0130-518976* in Germany.

Seasonal variations, unadvertised discounts and long-term (weekly, monthly, seasonal) rates can dramatically lower average lodging prices. Accommodation with even a rudimentary kitchen can be a bargain if some meals are eaten in. (See Tampa, p. 217 and the Pinellas Peninsula Circular Tour, pp. 202–212 for more Tampa Bay lodging.) St Petersburg and Pinellas Peninsula accommodation is centred in three areas: downtown St Petersburg; Hwy 19, 34th St, from the Sunshine Skyway north to Gandy Blvd; and the Gulf Beach Cities from Clearwater Beach to St Pete Beach. Major chains, including *BW, CI, DI, Hd, HJ, Hn, Rd, RI* and *Rm* are represented.

Room rates are 10–20% higher during high season, Jan–Apr. Priciest lodging is at historic hotels (**Renaissance Stouffer Vinoy Resort**; the **Don CeSar Beach Resort**; and **Belleview Mido Resort Hotel**); TradeWinds Resort and the resort hotels along Clearwater Beach. Find budget–moderate accommodations between downtown St Petersburg and the beaches, along Hwys 19 and 92.

**Downtown St Petersburg**'s landmark hotel is a salmon pink palace, the expensive–pricey **Renaissance Stouffer Vinoy Resort**, *501 5th Ave N.E., St Petersburg, FL 33701; tel: (800) 468-3571* or *(813) 894-1000*. From its opening in 1925 until World War II, the Mediterranean-Revival hotel catered to the social set down from the North-east US for the winter 'season'. Authors F. Scott Fitzgerald and Ernest Hemingway and actor Jimmy Stewart were guests. The hotel was transformed into a training centre during World War II, then deteriorated during the post-war period. The restored hotel, home of the Women's Tennis Association, overlooks Tampa Bay and The Pier. Wicker chairs, palms and paddle fans wait on the entrance veranda. Two beaches, tennis courts and a golf course are prime attractions, but a walk down the long, brightly-lit lobby,

## ST PETERSBURG

with stencilled pecky cypress beams, a glazed quarry tile floor and chandeliers evokes the 1925 atmosphere.

Also in downtown are the moderate–expensive restored 1920s-era **Heritage Hotel, Holiday Inn**, *234 3rd Ave N.; tel: (813) 822-4814*, and the **Hilton St Petersburg**, *333 1st St S.; tel: (813) 894-5000*.

St Petersburg boasts three moderate Bed and Breakfast hotels. The six room, Welsh-style **Mansion House**, *105 5th Ave N.E.; tel: (813) 821-9391*, is near the Vinoy. **Bay Gables**, *136 4th Ave N.E.; tel: (813) 822-8855*, has nine rooms in a Key West-style building, a garden with gazebo and a lunch restaurant and tearoom in a Victorian-era mansion. **Bayboro House**, *1719 Beach Dr. S.E., St Petersburg, FL 33701; tel: (813) 823-4955*, has four rooms, an apartment, and a veranda with wicker chairs, a rocking chair and a swing.

Lodging on **Hwy 19**, also known as **34th St**, lacks ambience but makes up for it in convenient midway access to either downtown St Petersburg or the beaches. Most lodging is moderate, though some rates fall within budget range during low season. Always ask for discounts – there's lots of competition down the street. There are many chain hotels. Among them are the **Best Western Mirage**, *5005 34th St N., St Petersburg, FL 33714; tel: (800) 843-4669* or *(813) 525-1181*; **La Quinta Inn**, *4999 34th St N., St Petersburg, FL 33714; tel: (813) 527-8421* and the **Days Inn St Pete Central**, *650 34th St N., St Petersburg, FL 33713; tel: (813) 321-2985*. The moderate **Suncoast Executive Inn**, *3000 34th St S., St Petersburg, FL 33711; tel: (813) 867-1111*, has nine tennis courts.

The **Gulf Beach Cities** are close to sun and sand. Causeways provide access to the Pinellas Peninsula, including downtown St Petersburg. No accommodation is more than a few blocks from a beach. The **SPCACVB** makes bookings. (See Pinellas Peninsula Circular Tour, pp. 202–212, for beach cities' lodging).

### Eating and Drinking

Many dining establishments in the region are near water and specialise in seafood. Local residents don't hesitate to drive to Clearwater Beach, St Pete Beach (see Pinellas Peninsula Circular Tour, pp. 202–212) or to Tampa (see p. 218) for a fine dining experience.

St Petersburg has **The Heritage Grille**, *256 2nd St N.; tel: (813) 823-6382*, where steak is supplemented by grilled swordfish stuffed with arugula, prosciutto, olives and sarteno cheese. The 'casual American cuisine' is a moderate choice for lunch, pricey for dinner.

**The Pier**, *800 2nd Ave N.E.*, has good fast food, including *gyros* sandwiches and mouth-watering ice cream. **Nick's on the Water**; *tel: (813) 898-5800*, is The Pier's pricey mall level Italian restaurant, serving veal, steak, chicken, fish, pasta, lasagne and Italian Egg Rolls. **Columbia at the Pier**, *tel: (813) 822-8000*, on the fourth level with a view, is another in the moderate Tampa chain of excellent Cuban/Spanish cuisine restaurants. On the fifth level is one of the area's budget–moderate **Cha Cha Coconuts** restaurants; *tel: (813) 822-6655*, with tasty grilled or lime-garlic marinated grouper, and the unusual Cha Cha Krunchy Fish, deep fried whitefish rolled in corn flakes, smothered with cheese, french fries and coleslaw. Be prepared for raucous music inside and strong breezes if dining outside.

**The Garden**, *217 Central Ave; tel: (813) 896-3800*, serves moderate French-Mediterranean cuisine, especially tapas

197

STAYING IN ST PETERSBURG

## ST PETERSBURG

and lamb couscous, in a chic atmosphere. **Saffron's,** *537 Central Ave; tel: (813) 898-9200,* serves Caribbean/Jamaican budget fare with imaginative names like '96 Degrees In The Shade' (baked potato) and 'Trenchtown Rock' (goat curry). **Bay Gables Tea Room,** *136 4th Ave N. E.; tel: (813) 822-0044,* serves afternoon tea and lunch. **Mrs. B's Doe-al Restaurant,** *226 4th Ave N.; tel: (813) 898-4416,* opens for lunch and dinner. Telephone for opening hours.

Budget dining is easy to find. During the week, the **Firehouse,** *260 1st Ave S.; tel: (813) 895-4716,* serves generous portions of ribs, grilled chicken, burgers, grouper sandwiches and a huge salad. **Fourth Street Shrimp Store,** *1006 4th St N.; tel: (813) 822-0325,* has fried shrimp, flounder, popcorn shrimp, clams, scallops and oysters, sandwiches and several all-you-can-eat days. Try the cheap hot dogs and chili dogs at the **Coney Island Sandwich Shop,** *250 9th St N.; tel: (813) 822-4493.* For budget dining on 34th St try **Piccadilly Cafeteria,** *1900 34th St N.; tel: (813) 328-1501.* **Adriano's Restaurant & Pizzeria,** *3090 34th St N.; tel: (813) 527-0009,* has a bargain seafood buffet on Fri night.

### ENTERTAINMENT

Find up-to-date regional night-club and night-life listings in the Fri *St Petersburg Times* 'Weekend' and *Tampa Tribune* 'Extra' sections, or call the **St Petersburg Hotline;** *tel: (813) 825-3333.* In May, St Petersburg hosts the **Artworks** festival: several weeks of free or inexpensive theatre, music and dance productions, including outdoor Shakespeare; *tel: (813) 821-4069.* New Year's Eve sees more arts presentations celebrating **First Night;** *tel: (813) 893-7627.*

**Coconuts Comedy Club,** at *Bleacher's Sports Bar and Restaurant, 10478 Roosevelt Blvd, St Petersburg; tel: (813) 578-0232,* is part of a chain of clubs that goes for laughs – and a cover charge. **Cha Cha Coconuts** at The Pier; *tel: (813) 822-6655,* has live popular music nightly. At **Pockets Billiards,** *6220 4th St N.; tel: (813) 522-6214,* you will find a rock/pop singer or a blues jam. For ballroom and Big Band orchestra dancing, there's the 1924 **Coliseum Ballroom,** *535 4th Ave N.; tel: (813) 892-5202,* whose 13,000 square foot maple floor was used in the film *Cocoon.*

Performing Arts are found downtown at the **Bayfront Center,** *400 1st St S., St Petersburg, FL 33701; tel: (813) 893-7211.* But sports are an important part of St Pete's time off. For general information, call the **Sports Activity Line;** *tel: (813) 444-4444, ext. 8.* Watch the greyhounds race Jan–June at **Derby Lane,** *10490 Gandy Blvd, St Petersburg, FL 33702; tel: (813) 576-1361,* where there's also parimutuel betting. Two baseball teams, the **Baltimore Orioles** and the **St Louis Cardinals,** hold spring training every Mar at **St Petersburg's Al Lang Stadium;** *tel: (813) 892-5491.* The National Hockey League team **Tampa Bay Lightning** (Aug–Apr) and the Arena Football League team **Tampa Bay Storm** (summer season) teams play at the **St Petersburg ThunderDome,** *One Stadium Dr.; tel: (813) 825-3334* or *(813) 898-2100* for tickets.

Pinellas County claims about 20 percent of Florida's golf courses. **Tee-Times USA** provides general **golf** information for courses and tee times and makes advance bookings; *tel: (800) 374-8633* or *(813) 733-0900. Golf Coast/Golfer's Guide* is a free magazine offering brief descriptions of golf courses and resorts in the Tampa Bay Area, *PO Box 20578, St*

# ST PETERSBURG

*Petersburg, FL 33742; tel: (800) 864-6101.*

## Shopping

Most St Petersburg area shopping is confined to malls anchored by major department stores. Watch local newspaper advertisements for sales. **Tyrone Square**, *66th St and 22nd Ave N.; tel: (813) 345-0126*, houses 150 stores, shops and fast food outlets. The **Golfer's Attic**, *2420 9th St N.; tel: (813) 822-9588*, carries unusual and antique golf clubs and accessories. **Florida Craftsmen Gallery**, *237 2nd Ave S.; tel: (813) 821-7391*, displays and sells locally made blown glass, ceramics, stoneware, jewellery, painted silk and textiles. The **Salvador Dali Museum**, *1000 3rd St S.; tel: (813) 823-3767*, sells everything from Dali keyrings to beautifully rendered Dali prints. **Haslam's Book Store**, *2025 Central Ave, St Petersburg, FL 33713; tel: (813) 822-8616*, has more than 300,000 books, in a store large enough to attract school tours. Greater Tampa Bay has many **antique** shops. Request a copy of the *Florida Central West Coast Antique Shopping Guide* from Sue Tiffin; *tel: (813) 586-3006* or *(813) 581-5626*. (See Tampa, p. 220 for more area shopping.)

## Sightseeing

The **Salvador Dali Museum**, *1000 3rd St S., St Petersburg, FL 33701; tel: (813) 823-3767*, is open Tues–Sat 0930–1730, Sun–Mon 1200–1730 except some holidays. This world class gallery with the eccentric artist's work put St Petersburg on the international art map. The paintings, water-colours and sketches, each individually spotlit, are arranged on spacious gallery walls in chronological order, from 1914, when Dali was 10 years old, to 1980. The collection periodically rotates the 94 oil paintings, 100 water-colours and 1300 other pieces. Among the most famous are 'The Disintegration of the Persistence of Memory', the 'Hallucinogenic Toreador' and 'The Discovery of America by Christopher Columbus'. An hour-long tour provides an easy introduction to the work of an artist who said, 'The only difference between myself and a madman is that I am not mad'.

One block away is **Great Explorations**, *1120 4th St S.; tel: (813) 821-8885*, open Mon–Sat 1000–1700, Sun 1200–1700. A visit to the 'Hands On Museum' requires bodily participation and loose, comfortable clothing. *The Touch Tunnel* is pitch black with twists and turns, and challenges fears of darkness, getting lost, falling, and losing direction. *Phenomenal Arts* uses touch, audio (a 'boing' sound), or motion to create unique colour spectrum patterns or outlines. Fingers inserted in a tube causes the pulse to flip sand. *The Body Shop* explores in detail 'what's in your lunch?' Proposed exhibits, raw wires, crude boxes and all, can also be played with.

The **Florida International Museum**, *100 2nd St N.; tel: (813) 822-3693*, has periodic international-scale exhibitions. The **Museum of Fine Arts**, *255 Beach Dr. N. E.; tel: (813) 896-2667*, is best known for French impressionist paintings and prints by American photographers, while also housing European, pre-Columbian, Far Eastern and North American art.

Along the way to The Pier's dining places, gift shops and aquarium is the **St Petersburg Historical & Flight One Museum**, *335 Second Ave N. E.; tel: (813) 894-1052*, open Mon–Sat 1000–1700, Sun 1300–1700. Suspended in the museum entrance is a replica of the 1914 Benoist airboat in which Tony Jannus flew the first commercial passengers. Museum exhibits flow along a historical timeline, from the Weedon Island (Native) Culture excavations (from six miles north of the city) and 'Before the Train', to vertical pull-out drawers of mounted clothing to try on for size in mirrors. Computers show then-and-now of views historic hotels and buildings. A slightly risqué mermaid sign shows off the happy beach culture of St Pete's winter season playground.

Outside is the reconstructed pier, the seventh on the site since the 1800s. **The Pier**, *800 2nd Ave N.E.; tel: (813) 821-6164*, is a teal blue and tan five-storey inverted pyramid at the end of an actual pier. There is an observation deck on the top level for excellent views of the North Yacht Basin (where dolphins occasionally jump) in front of the Renaissance Stouffer Vinoy Resort. The Columbia Restaurant, Cha Cha Coconuts, and Nick's at the Pier all have fine views with drinks and dining. The **Pier Aquarium,** open Mon–Sat 1000–2000, Sun 1200–1800, starts on the main (entry) level with three two-storey cylindrical tanks. The aquarium's main area is on the first level (second floor). Tank specimens are beautifully displayed and there are good explanations of sharks' DNA, coral degradation, and the drilling of underwater core samples. On the main level, the US Geological Survey has an excellent photographic exhibit on the effects of hurricane destruction. Hire waverunners, jet boats, boats, bicycles, or in-line skates at The Pier; *tel: (813) 363-0000*.

The *Caribbean Queen*; *tel: (813) 895-2628*, has four daily one-hour sightseeing excursions. The *Yankee Clipper*; *tel: (813) 896-0188*, makes sunset cruises. Both depart from The Pier.

The **Sunken Gardens**, *1825 4th St N.; tel: (813) 896-3187*, combines botanical gardens, caged birds, an aviary, performing bird shows, alligator wrestling and a Christ-themed Biblical waxworks. For a free nature experience convenient to Hwy 19 (34th St N.), there's **Sawgrass Lake Park**, *7400 25th St N., St Petersburg, FL 33702; tel: (813) 527-3814*. A mile-long elevated boardwalk through a hardwood maple swamp leads to an observation tower with its view of Sawgrass Lake.

St Petersburg has a **downtown scenic drive**. Take Bayshore Dr. north along the waterfront to 5th Ave N.E. Turn left onto North Shore Dr. in the **Old Northeast North Shore** area. A continuous shoreline park is marked by signs showing a pink ocean on a tropical blue field and a white boat. On the right, bayside, are a ball park, public swimming pool, tennis courts and the disabled-accessible **Gisella Kopsick Palm Arboretum**, *at the east end of 10th Ave N.E.; tel: (813) 893-7335*, with 200 palms and cycades planted outdoors amidst a gazebo and wooden benches. **North Shore Park** has more benches and a children's playground. A cycle path winds along the water in **Flora Wylie Park**. Turn left on **Coffee Pot Blvd,** and follow it past palatial mansions. Take a white bridge over **Coffee Pot Bayou**, past a small hammock with roosting water birds to **Snell Isle Blvd**, where the private **Vinoy Resort Golf Club** is a fanciful Moorish-style brown building with green trim and minaret tower.

South-west of downtown St Petersburg is **Lake Maggiore**, a large urban green area with the splendid 245-acre **Boyd Hill Nature Park**, *1101 Country Club Way S., St Petersburg, FL 33705; tel: (813) 893-7326*. Gather bird, plant, and animal checklists from park information and nature centres, then walk the three miles of trails and boardwalks through six ecosystems: an oak and pine hammock, swamp woodlands, willow marsh, scrub oak, pine flatwoods, and the lake itself. Enjoy a lakeside picnic lunch, but remember, even in the city, the alligators can be dangerous.

## St Petersburg

The Pinellas Peninsula has been inhabited for 3500 years. Until the 16th century, when Spanish explorers like Hernando de Soto arrived, native bands had been living near the water, using shell and bone tools, trading shell beads, and burying their dead above water level in middens or mounds. By 1700, native mound cultures had dwindled. The Great Gale of 1848 pushed Gulf waters to Tampa Bay and rearranged islands and keys dramatically. Most middens, and therefore most traces of native culture, had disappeared by the early 20th century; midden shells had been appropriated for road foundations.

General John C. Williams purchased 1600 acres of peninsula land for $1600 in 1875. In 1879, he spent a month travelling in a covered wagon from Gainesville to the St Petersburg site with his family. Scattered settlers grew citrus fruit and pineapples and made sugar syrup and turpentine; Williams, not as productive, decided to promote his land as a railroad terminus when his Michigan (Northern US) farming methods failed.

Peter Demens, an immigrant Russian aristocrat, wanted to extend his narrow-gauge Orange Belt Railroad from Lake Apopka to Gulfport, just west of the present city. Williams sold Demens acreage, and despite inadequate financing, heavy rains and yellow fever, the Demens railroad reached downtown St Petersburg (named after Demens' birthplace in Russia) in 1888.

Both men began land investment companies, selling land cheaply with the requirement that houses be on brick or stone piers and be painted. The town became a summer resort for residents of other parts of Florida who arrived by train because they considered St Petersburg 'cooler', especially after an 1885 American Medical Society paper which asserted that Point Pinellas 'offers the best climate in Florida'. St Petersburg citrus survived a bad freeze in 1894–95, so some growers from further north relocated to the peninsula. Henry Plant bought the Orange Belt Railway in 1895, and built the Tampa Bay Hotel.

In 1914, pilot Tony Jannus flew a Benoist airboat from St Petersburg to Tampa, the first regularly scheduled US passenger aeroplane flight, beginning ccommercial aviation. The same year, several major league baseball teams held spring training in St Pete. After World War I, land speculation became a suckers market. For a while, a $10,000 purchase with only $500 down for 'sight unseen' land brought $50,000 profit after 30 days. The boom went bust in 1926, and a few local business men, fishermen, railroad workers and draymen started building a downtown where speculation had left only bare lots.

In the 1930s, St Pete became the set for South American and African scenes in films. The town offered an exotic-seeming locale with the bright Florida light then unreproduceable in a studio. Celebrities followed, lured by the promise of a month's free rent. In 1954, the Sunshine Skyway bridge replaced a ferry system to connect Pinellas Point to Bradenton and points south. Race relations between African-Americans and Whites generated desegregation battles until 1968. Today, St Petersburg boasts banks and mutual fund companies, medical centres and marine science researchers, and its famous Salvador Dali Museum.

# PINELLAS PENINSULA CIRCULAR TOUR

The Pinellas Peninsula, halfway down Florida's Gulf Coast, gathers beaches, culture, history, constant vehicular traffic and bicycling into a getaway frame of mind. The pace is less frantic than the state's Atlantic Coast, less dedicated to tourism than Orlando and less devoted to the pursuit of business than Tampa, its Hillsborough County neighbour. The Peninsula shares the Tampa Bay Region's mania for sports; many Pinellas County residents who work in Tampa prefer the housing prices, social services and gentler ambience of St. Petersburg's suburbs and beaches.

The Pinellas Peninsula is girded by Dunedin and Clearwater in the north-west, Safety Harbor on Old Tampa Bay in the north-east, and St. Petersburg on its eastern side. Gulf barrier islands run south from Honeymoon and Caladesi Islands State Parks to St Petersburg Beach, Fort de Soto Park and Egmont Key. The Gulf Beach cities, most a few blocks wide, cater to visitors with many of the region's hostelries and restaurants. There are whiter, finer sand beaches on the barrier islands near Sarasota and Fort Myers, but Pinellas Peninsula beaches are long, easy to access and a few hours' drive from Orlando theme parks.

Major east–west arterial roads are SR 60, the Courtney-Campbell Causeway from Tampa's West Shore which becomes Gulf-to-Bay Blvd before entering Clearwater and Clearwater Beach; Ulmerton Rd, SR 688, from Old Tampa Bay to Indian Rocks Beach; Central Ave, St Petersburg to Treasure Island; and the Pinellas Bayway, SR 682, from north of the Sunshine Skyway to the Don CeSar in St Pete Beach. Many causeways to the Gulf Island are toll roads.

The 75-mile circuit begins at the Pier in St Petersburg, but can begin just as easily in Clearwater or north of where the Sunshine Skyway bridge (I-275) causeway joins the peninsula. Exploring Weedon and Honeymoon Islands, Fort de Soto State Park and an 8.5-mile Belleair side track adds about 20 miles to the route.

Allow two days to complete the peninsula circuit, more if visiting the attractions in St Petersburg.

## ROUTE

Begin the circuit driving north from **The Pier** in St Petersburg towards **Weedon Island**. Continue north to **Philippe Park** at **Safety Harbor**, head north on County Road 611, go west on Curlew Rd, SR 586, to Causeway Blvd. Side

# PINELLAS PENINSULA CIRCULAR TOUR

track west to **Honeymoon Island**, or turn south on US 19 through **Dunedin** to **Clearwater**. Take Hwy 60 west to **Clearwater Beach**, then head south on **Gulf Blvd** along the **Gulf Beaches**. At the Don CeSar Resort, 21 miles south in **St Petersburg Beach**, turn east on SR 682, Pinellas Bayway. Pass 34th St S. (Sunshine Skyway is to the right) and turn left on 31st St S. Go right on 35th Terrace, which becomes Fairway Ave S., then Country Club Way S. as it winds south of Lake Maggiore. Continue north on 9th St S., right on Harbordale, left on 4th St S., right on 22nd Ave S.E., north on Beach Dr., west on 14th Ave S.E., north on Bay St, left on 13th Ave S.E., north on 3rd St S., east on 5th St S. then continue on Bayshore Dr. to **The Pier**.

## TOURIST INFORMATION

The **St Petersburg/Clearwater Area Convention & Visitors Bureau (SPCACVB)**; *St Petersburg Thunderdome, One Stadium Dr., Suite A, St Petersburg, FL 33705-1706; tel: (813) 582-7892*, has information on accommodation throughout the Pinellas Peninsula. The **Greater Clearwater Chamber of Commerce**, *128 N. Osceola Ave, Clearwater, FL 34615; tel: (813) 461-0011*, and **St Petersburg Beach Area Chamber of Commerce**, *6990 Gulf Blvd, St Petersburg Beach, FL 33706; tel: (813) 360-6957*, have a list of accommodation.

## ACCOMMODATION

Find lodging in St Petersburg (see p. 196), motels along 34th St N. and S. in the centre of the Peninsula or along the Gulf Beaches. Gulf Beach lodging is dense in Clearwater Beach/Sand Key and St Pete Beach. In between are modest motels and cottages, many priced for long-term stays.

## THE PIER TO DUNEDIN

Near **The Pier**, the **St Petersburg Historical and Flight One Museum** *335 Second Ave N.E., St Petersburg, FL 33701; tel: (813) 894-1052*, admission $4.50, is a good introduction to the history and geography of the Pinellas Peninsula. The circuit begins where The Pier meets the mainland at 2nd Ave N. and Bayshore Dr. The yacht basin, bordered by Straub Park's pleasant walking strip, is east of Bayshore Dr.

Straight ahead is the stately pink **Renaissance Stouffer Vinoy Resort**, *501 5th Ave N.E., St Petersburg, FL 33701; tel: (813) 894-1000*, a Mediterranean-revival hotel with wicker chairs on a wide veranda. Inside the lobby, marble and chandeliers evoke the fashionable stroll of 1925 guests. Turn right in front of the hotel onto 5th Ave N.E. On the right is **Vinoy Park**, a small waterfront area. Turn left and follow the road for three blocks, then turn north onto North Shore Dr. in the **Old Northeast North Shore area**. On the right, a continuous series of parks runs 0.5 miles north along Tampa Bay, with a playing field, public swimming pool, tennis courts, the 200-palm **Gisella Kopsick Palm Arboretum**, **North Shore Park** children's playground and **Flora Wylie Park** lawn and bicycle path.

Mansions are on the left as North Shore Dr. turns left into Coffee Pot Blvd for 0.2 miles. Turn right onto **Snell Isle Blvd** and cross a white bridge to Snell Isle Estates, a residential area with fabulous mansions well-screened by lush foliage and guarded by marble and stone animals and birds. Snell Isle Blvd jogs right at the private **Vinoy Resort Golf Club**, its ostentatious Moorish-style clubhouse resplendent with a minaret. Follow the curve of Snell Isle Blvd

ROUTE • THE PIER TO DUNEDIN

# PINELLAS PENINSULA CIRCULAR TOUR

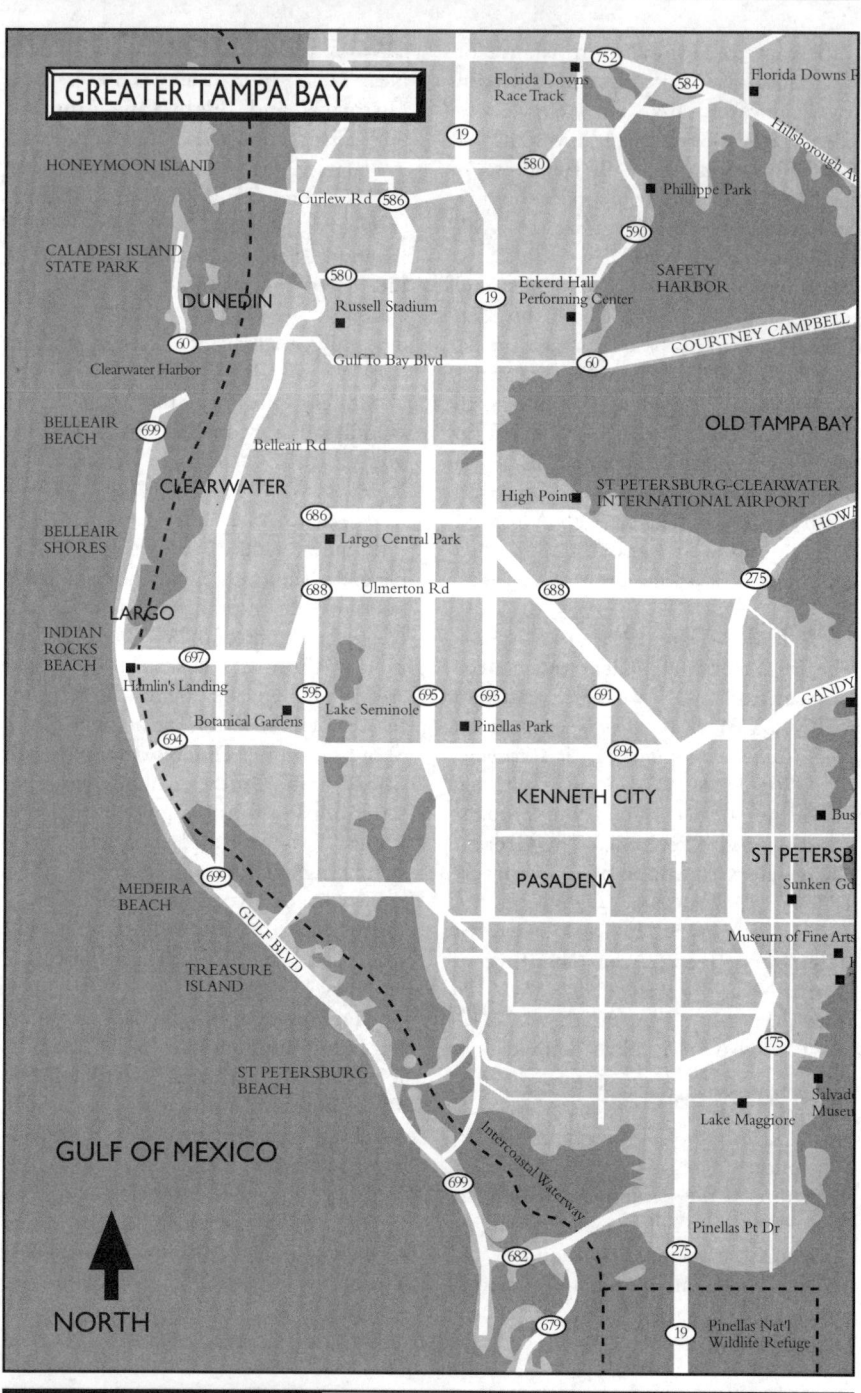

## GREATER TAMPA BAY MAP

# PINELLAS PENINSULA CIRCULAR TOUR

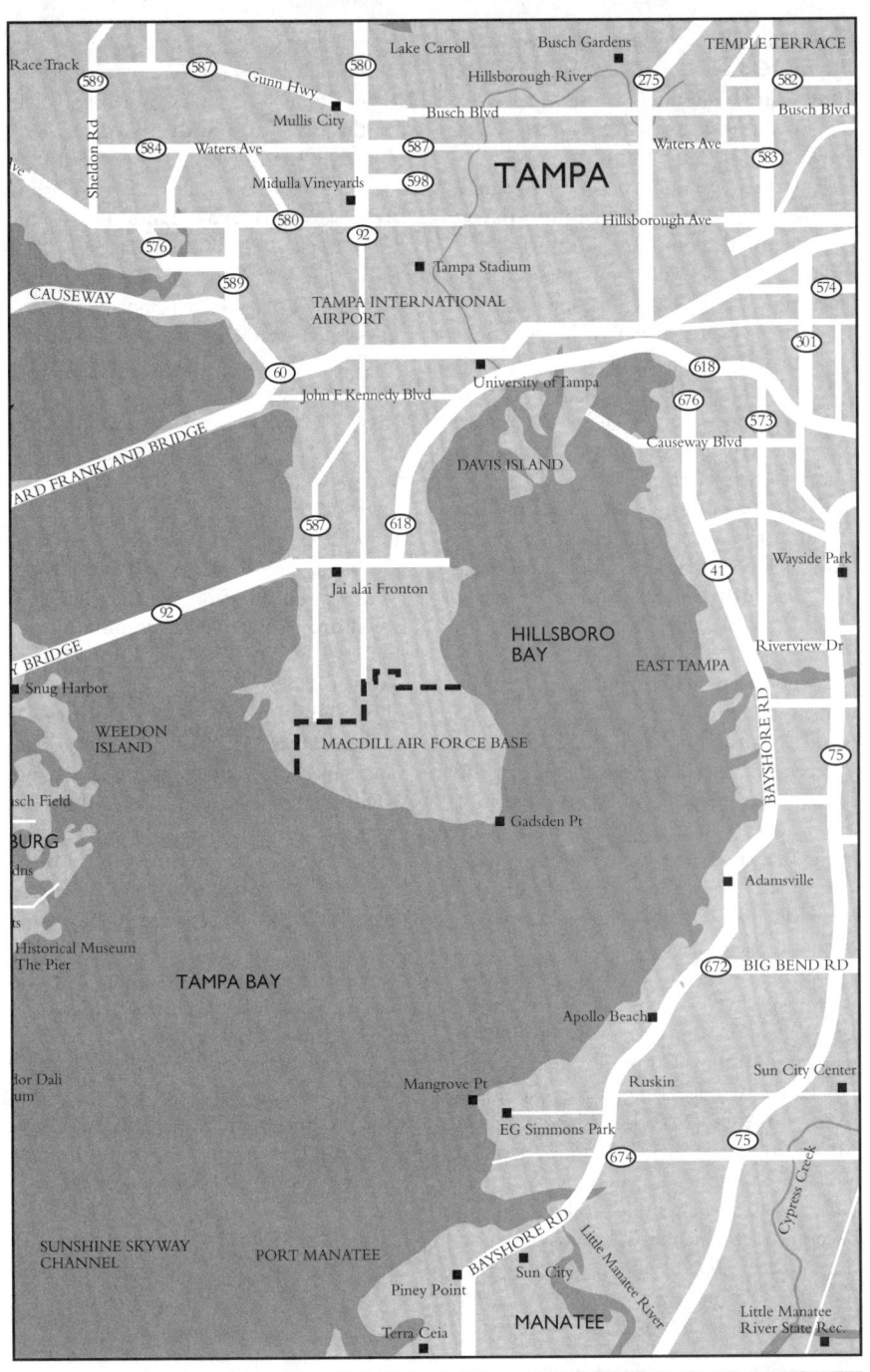

**GREATER TAMPA BAY MAP**

## PINELLAS PENINSULA CIRCULAR TOUR

Overlook Dr., crossing over **Smacks Bayou**. Go left on Shore Acres, where houses are built on bayous, canal-style, on short fingers of land. **Shore Acres Park** is on the left at 40th Ave N.E.

Turn left at Venetian Blvd, crossing a channel over **Bayou Grande**. Bayou Grande Blvd continues north for 0.6 miles. Go left 1.5 miles at 62nd Ave N.E. Turn right on 1st St N. for one mile, left on 78th Ave N.E. for two blocks, right on 4th St N. then right again on 83rd Ave N. (County Rd 823). The avenue veers left and becomes Patica Rd before crossing Riviera Bay where it changes names to San Martin Blvd.

To see **Weedon Island**, turn right at Weedon Dr. and skirt the north and east sides of Riviera Bay to a boat ramp and pier. **Weedon Island State Preserve,** *1500 Weedon Island Dr., St Petersburg, FL 33702; tel: (813) 570-5146,* is a 1250-acre environmentally fragile area used by humans and birds. Hike and picnic on the island, or fish for sea trout, snook and sheepshead. Arrange canoe hire at the Preserve Visitor Centre and paddle four miles down Old Tampa Bay from Mud Hole Island, between Benjamin, Snake, Christmas, Ross, and Googe Islands and Weedon Island, into Papys Bayou on Weedon Island's west side.

Weedon Island Culture Native Americans lived on the isle from 10,000 BC–1200 AD, burying their dead with painted and stencilled pottery in mounds. Dr. Leslie Weedon bought the island as a retreat in 1898. Weedon Island Culture excavations began in 1923, when Weedon's homestead became a dance club. In 1925, the rebuilt San Remo Club became St Petersburg's hot dance spot; during the 1930s it was a production studio for eminently forgettable films. Largely abandoned, the island reverted to the mangrove habitat favoured by roosting birds and offshore oyster beds.

Continue 0.7 miles north on San Martin Blvd to **Gandy Blvd**, US 92. (**Gandy Bridge**, right, goes east to Tampa.) Go one mile left on Gandy Blvd, passing **Derby Lane** greyhound racing track, *10490 Gandy Blvd; tel: (813) 576-1361,* to a five-way junction. Take Roosevelt Blvd, SR 686, north-west 2.7 miles, then turn left and go west one mile on Ulmerton Rd, SR 688, before rejoining Roosevelt Blvd with a right turn. After 1.3 miles, take County Rd 611 (49th St N.) right, north on the Bayside Bridge over Old Tampa Bay to Gulf-To-Bay Blvd, Hwy 60. Go right in the direction of the Courtney-Campbell Pkwy for one block (the **Welcome Center** is 0.5 miles east on the parkway) then left onto **Bayshore**. Attractive condominiums line the road by Sunfish Bay; **Old Tampa Bay** is east.

Bayshore Blvd becomes **Bayshore Dr** at the **Safety Harbor** city limit. The Safety Harbor Native American Culture which flourished from 1000–1700 AD also built burial middens. Safety Harbor, nestling towards the northern end of the bay, is widely considered to be Hernando de Soto's main 1539 landing site in the Tampa Bay Area, the base for his explorations of mangrove-lined shoreline and islands. The **Safety Harbor Museum of Regional History,** *329 S. Bayshore Blvd, Safety Harbor, FL 34695; tel: (813) 726-1668,* Tues–Fri 1000–1600, Sat–Sun 1300–1600, exhibits Native American artefacts. The pricey 183-room **Safety Harbor Spa and Fitness Center**, *105 N. Bayshore Dr., Safety Harbor, FL 34695; tel: (813) 726-1161,* one of Florida's largest spas, is housed in a two-storey tan stucco building with red terracotta roof tiles.

Continue north-east on Bayshore Dr. N. for 1.5 miles past huge houses with bay overlooks. The road appears to end at **Philippe Point**, a spot with graceful old trees dripping with Spanish moss. Drive around the circle at the end and turn right at the first corner.

Take Bayshore Dr. N. to the formal entrance to **Philippe Park**, *2355 N. Bayshore Dr.; tel: (813) 726-2700*. The park, filled with tree-shaded picnic tables, is named after Napoleon's surgeon, Count Odet Philippe, who settled the point and is buried there. Tocobago Indian Burial Mounds are protected within the park, which also shelters large numbers of shorebirds.

Take Bayshore Dr. north-west from the park entrance to Philippe Pkwy, SR 590. One mile north, turn left onto SR 580. Rejoin County Rd 611, McMullen-Booth Rd, and drive two miles north. Turn left on SR 586, Curlew Rd, and go west for four miles to the Alt US 19 junction in **Dunedin**. Take a side track to visit **Honeymoon** and **Caladesi Islands** or take a detour through **Belleair**, or turn right onto Hwy 60, Memorial Causeway, towards downtown **Clearwater Beach**.

### SIDE TRACK TO HONEYMOON AND CALADESI ISLANDS

Continue west 2.3 miles to **Honeymoon Island State Recreation Area**, *#1 Causeway Blvd, Dunedin, FL 34698; tel: (813) 469-5942*, open daily 0800–sunset. Once in the park, a flat road winds between low palms and brush towards beach dunes.

Shell collectors along the beach find a wide variety of species including the crown conch, alphabet cone, angle wing, common American auger, Pennsylvania lucine, apple and lace murex, baby's ear, slipper shell, whelk, turkey wings, prickly cockle, banded tulip shell, skate egg, brittle star, bleeding tooth, clam, coquina, ivory bush coral, saw tooth pen shell, star shell, calico scallop, purple sea plume, Florida stromb, operculum, nautilus, Florida cone, jewelbox, keyhole urchin, top shell, jingle shell, fighting stromb (conch), shark eye, cat's paw, oyster drill, seahorse, horse conch, sunray venus, harp cockle, common bubble, and ponderous ark. Collecting shells with sea animals inside is prohibited, but surf fishing is popular.

A few feet inland from the shelling activity are sand hummocks sheltering birds like (wintering) piping plovers, pelicans, egrets, peregrine falcons, (summering) roseate spoonbills and the rare year-round resident, Wilson's plover. Nesting areas are well-marked. Ospreys nest in a virgin slash pine strand along the northern loop trail.

Near beach life-saving stations, **Café Honeymoon** sells burgers, snacks and jewellery. There are plenty of picnic tables. Near the park entrance is the **Caladesi Island Ferry Dock**; *tel: (813) 734-5263*. The other ferry access is near the Memorial Causeway, Hwy 60, in Clearwater. Inter-island ferry services begin daily at 1000, but frequency varies.

**Caladesi Island State Park**, *#1 Causeway Blvd, Dunedin, FL 34698; tel: (813) 469-5918*, actually five small islands surrounding a large one, is accessible only by ferry or private boat. Ferries from Honeymoon Island cross Hurricane Pass, formed in 1921 after a storm created Caladesi Island from the Honeymoon (then Hog) Island land mass. Boaters can anchor offshore or register for an overnight stay in the 99-slip dock.

## PINELLAS PENINSULA CIRCULAR TOUR

Picnic, swim or hike a short nature trail on the quiet, undeveloped island. Birds and turtles nest unmolested amidst coastal sand dunes, along with the burrowing gopher tortoise and the dangerous eastern diamondback rattlesnake. Mangroves cluster on the east shore while slash pines hold the high ground.

From SR 586, Curlew Rd, in Dunedin, turn south onto Alt US 19. The detailed *Guidebook to the Pinellas Trail*, **Pinellas Trails, Inc.**, *1100 Cleveland St, Suite 900B, Clearwater, FL 34615-4805; tel: (813) 441-1466,* describes the 47-mile abandoned railroad route that closely parallels Alt US 19 from Tarpon Springs to Seminole, some 30 miles south. Pedestrians, bicyclists and skaters use the trail, a shady green ribbon through highly-developed suburbs. Trees and modest inns line the route. Five miles south on Alt US 19 in N. Clearwater, turn right onto N. Fort Harrison Ave.

### SIDE TRACK TO BELLEAIR

Continue south on Alt US 19, S. Fort Harrison Ave. Turn right on Belleview Blvd and continue to the **Belleview Mido Resort Hotel;** *tel: (813) 442-6171,* another Henry Plant creation built in 1897 to receive the wealthiest of industrialists arriving in private railway cars on Plant's railroad. The Duke of Windsor was among visiting dignitaries. The white wooden building with gables, stained glass windows and a green roof sprawls amidst huge pine and oak trees. A small museum has old photographs; historical tours are conducted daily at 1100.

Five miles south on Indian Rocks Rd is the **Sturgeon Memorial Rose Garden** at **Serenity Gardens Memorial Park,** *13401 Indian Rocks Rd, Largo, FL 34644; tel: (813) 595-2914,* 850 rosebushes from 125 All American Rose varieties.

Continue south to Walsingham Rd, SR 688. One mile left (east) is the **Pinellas County Heritage Park & Museum,** *11909 125th St N., Largo, FL 34644; tel: (813) 588-8123,* Tues–Sat 1000–1600, Sun 1300–1600. A walking path threads around restored buildings. The McMullen-Coachman 1852 log house, the oldest structure in the area, is a typical Cracker settler's residence. A barn, train depot, church, mercantile store and grand houses are on view; costumed guides lead tours of two mansions.

Go west on Walsingham Rd, cross Indian Rocks Rd, and turn right at 146th St to the parking lot at **Largo Narrows Nature Park and Nature Center,** *11901 146th St N., Largo, FL 34644; tel: (813) 587-6775,* open daily 0700. A few hundred feet from the busy thoroughfare, there's serene tropical vegetation. A mile of trails wanders through slash pine flatwoods thickly overgrown with saw palmetto. Boardwalks appear to go right into the water as they traverse a hardwood hammock and black and red mangrove estuaries.

Go west on Walsingham Rd. **Hamlin's Landing** and the **Starlite Princess** are visible to the left while crossing **Indian Rocks Bridge** to 5th Ave. 5th Ave ends at Gulf Blvd, SR 699, in Indian Rocks Beach.

### CLEARWATER AND CLEARWATER BEACH

**Tourist Information:** The **Greater Clearwater Chamber of Commerce**, *128 N. Osceola Ave, Clearwater, FL 34615; tel: (813) 461-0011.* **Clearwater**

## PINELLAS PENINSULA CIRCULAR TOUR

Beach Welcome Center, *40 Causeway Blvd*, is open daily 0900–1700.

### GETTING AROUND

The **Jolley Trolley**, daily from 1000, $25, runs along Clearwater Beach and Sand Key, then crosses Memorial Causeway to downtown Clearwater. **Clearwater Ferry Service**; *tel: (813) 442-7433*, operates water taxis Tues–Sat between Clearwater Beach and City Beach Marina, $2 one-way.

### ACCOMMODATION

Both Clearwater and Clearwater Beach have a wide range of accommodations. Lodging is generally more expensive in Clearwater Beach because of the resort atmosphere.

The **St Petersburg/Clearwater Area Convention & Visitors Bureau**; *tel: (813) 582-7892*, and the **Greater Clearwater Chamber of Commerce**; *tel: (813) 461-0011*, have lodging lists. Most chains in **Clearwater**, including BW, CI, Hd, HJ, RI and TL, are on US Hwy 19. Clearwater's *grande dame* is the pricey 292-room **Belleview Mido Resort Hotel**, *25 Belleview Blvd, Clearwater, FL 34617; tel: (800) 237-8947* or *(813) 442-6171*. The resort's golf course is a mile away.

**Clearwater Beach** chains include BW, DI, Hd, HJ, QI, Rd, Rm and Sh. Moderate motels are a few blocks from the water. The **Best Western Sea Stone Resort**, *445 Hamden Dr., Clearwater Beach, FL 34630; tel: (800) 444-1919* or *(813) 441-1722*, sits on a marina and has huge moderate rooms with kitchens. On the island resort strip is the pricey **Radisson Suite Resort on Sand Key**, *1201 Gulf Blvd; tel: (800) 333-3333* or *(813) 596-1100*, with water views and a shopping mall adjacent to the hotel.

### EATING AND DRINKING

In season, Jan–mid-April, restaurants are packed and Clearwater Beach streets are lively. In other months, restaurant hours are curtailed. The **Show Queen**, *25 Causeway Blvd; tel: (813) 461-3113*, offers pricey dinner cruises around Clearwater Bay. The **Admiral Dinner Boat**, *Clearwater Beach Marina; tel: (813) 462-2628*, has moderate–pricey dinner/dance cruises. **Empress Cruise Lines**, *Clearwater Bay Marina; tel: (813) 895-3325*, adds a full casino to dinner and dancing.

Local people talk glowingly about budget **Frenchy's Café**, *41 Baymont St, Clearwater, FL 34630; tel: (813) 446-3607*. It's worth a pilgrimage to sample any version of the ultra-fresh grouper, tuna, clams or mussels, served plain or in burgers and sandwiches. The atmosphere is beach dive bar, but the French Canadian owner assures that the seafood gumbo and grouper rueben sandwich are mouth-watering for the businessmen in suits, beach bums and tourists who wander in. Look for a bright parrot mural on the tiny building's exterior. The Frenchy's Clearwater Beach empire includes the more up-market **Frenchy's Rockaway Grill**, *7 Rockaway St; tel: (813) 446-4844*, **Frenchy's Salt Water Café**, *419 Pointsettia; tel: (813) 461-6295*, and **Frenchy's Mandalay Seafood Company**, *435 Mandalay Ave; tel: (813) 443-2100*. **Bobby's Bistro & Wine Bar**, *447 Mandalay Ave; tel: (813) 446-9463*, is known for an extensive wine list. Check local give-away papers like *Bee Publications* for coupon specials and moderate all-you-can-eat buffets.

### ENTERTAINMENT

Much of the Clearwater area's nightlife centres around the season Jan–mid-Apr.

## PINELLAS PENINSULA CIRCULAR TOUR

The *St Petersburg Times* 'Weekend' section has complete listings of current nightclub offerings, including **Coconut's Comedy Club**, *430 S. Gulfview Blvd (Adam's Mark Caribbean Gulf Resort); tel: (813) 443-5714.*

For dinner theatre listings; *tel: (813) 582-7892.* **Showboat Dinner Theater**, *3405 Ulmerton Rd; tel: (813) 573-3777*, has Broadway shows; **Musicana Dinner Theater**, *560 McMullen-Booth Rd; tel: (813) 791-3204*, and **Bill Irle Early Bird Dinner Theater**, *1310 N. Fort Harrison Ave; tel: (813) 446-5898*, have musicals and dramas. **Mystery Dinner Theater**, *691 Gulfview Blvd; tel: (813) 584-3490*, and at the *Belleview Mido Resort Hotel*, requires audience participation to solve the crime. **Ruth Eckerd Hall**, *1111 McMullen-Booth Rd; tel: (813) 791-7400*, presents live music and dance performances. **Philadelphia Phillies** baseball team trains during Mar at **Jack Russell Stadium**, *800 Phillies Dr.; tel: (813) 441-9941.* Drag racing and stock car racing are featured spring–Nov at **Sunshine Speedway**, *4500 Ulmerton Rd; tel: (813) 573-4598.*

### SIGHTSEEING

Clearwater Beach's main street is **Mandalay**, lined with restaurants, bars and T-shirt shops. **Clearwater Ferry Service**, *Drew St Dock, Clearwater; tel: (813) 442-7433*, offers sightseeing dolphin encounters and excursions to Caladesi Island State Park, Tarpon Springs and Sarasota. **Pier 60**, Clearwater Beach, charges $0.50 to walk its 1007-ft length, but is most famed for excellent fishing – day or night. At **Clearwater Marina, Captain Memo's Pirate Cruise**; *tel: (813) 446-2587*, offers excursions on the *Sea Hogge* for $25. **Tradewinds**; *tel: (813) 581-4662*, is a 60-ft three-masted windjammer. **Little Toot**; *tel: (813) 446-5503*, is a tugboat ride. Hop on a 73-ft speedboat or para-sail with **Sea Screamer**, *Slip # 10; tel: (813) 447-7200.*

The **Clearwater Marine Science Center Aquarium Museum**, *249 Windward Passage, Clearwater, FL 34630-2250; tel: (813) 441-1790*, open Mon–Fri 0900–1700, Sat 0900–1600, Sun 1100–1600, is a marine life rehabilitation centre and aquarium. **Sand Key Park**, *1060 Gulf Blvd*, on the Gulf, has the sculptured look of a golf course, plots of oleander and very small palm trees, grassy areas and picnic tables. The park is free but parking is metered. The pond between the Sheraton Sand Key Resort and the park is favoured by birds.

From Sand Key south to St Pete Beach, Gulf Blvd, SR 699, is modest lodging and low-rise strip malls. Drive through **Belleair Beach** and **Belleair Shore** to **Indian Rocks Beach**, where birds sit on pier posts. **Hamlin's Landing**, *401 2nd St E.; tel: (813) 595-9484*, near Indian Rocks Bridge, is a modern version of a Victorian waterfront, with dining, shops and paddlewheel riverboat cruises on the **Starlite Princess**; *tel: (800) 722-6645* or *(813) 595-1212.* Small beach cottages line Gulf Blvd in **Indian Shores**.

Ralph T. Heath Jr. founded the **Suncoast Seabird Sanctuary, Inc.**, *18328 Gulf Blvd, Indian Shores, FL 34635; tel: (813) 391-6211*, in 1971 to care for injured seabirds, brown pelicans and birds of prey. Birds are rehabilitated and released when possible. Heath also breeds and releases offspring of permanently crippled birds at the largest wild bird hospital in the US. The Sanctuary, the prime attraction between Clearwater Beach and St Pete Beach, is free, open

## PINELLAS PENINSULA CIRCULAR TOUR

daily 0900–dark. Surfboards are the tables at **Mahuffer's Sloppy John's**, *19201 Gulf Blvd, Indian Shores; tel: (813) 596-0226*, which features blues music on weekends.

Further south at the north end of **Boca Ciega Bay** is **Redington Shores** and the 1021-foot **Redington Long Pier**. **North Redington Beach** has boardwalk beach access and free parking. Warnings are posted against stingrays or disturbing May–Oct turtle nesting. Egrets, pelicans, cormorants and gulls use the beach to fish or rest. The sand is fine, white and powdery; shells are small but colourful. Just south of Redington Beach is **Madeira Beach**.

### MADEIRA BEACH

Tourist Information: Madeira Beach Chamber of Commerce/Gulf Beaches on Sand Key Chamber of Commerce, *501 150th Ave, Madeira Beach, FL 33708; tel: (813) 391-7373, (813) 595-4575 or (800) 944-1847*, have maps, lodging and restaurant listings.

**John's Pass Village & Boardwalk**, *12901 Gulf Blvd E.* (north of the John's Pass Bridge), is marked by a lighthouse. The three-block-long pier accommodates three seafood restaurants, including the **Friendly Fisherman**; *tel: (813) 391-6025*, a snack bar with fruit shakes, shell and T-shirt shops, East End cappuccino house's pink plastic flamingo, and **Europa FunKruz**; *tel: (800) 688-7529*, offering six-hr gambling cruises. The **Holocaust Memorial Museum**, *5001 Duhme Rd; tel: (813) 392-4678*, Mon–Fri 1000–1600, Sun 1200–1600, has exhibits on sombre aspects of World War II.

### TREASURE ISLAND

Tourist Information: Treasure Island, Treasure Island Chamber of Commerce, *152 108th Ave, Treasure Island, FL 33706; tel: (813) 367-4529*, claims the widest public beaches on the Central Gulf Coast, including pavilion-shaded **Municipal Beach** and **Treasure Island Beach Access Park**, *104th Ave and Gulf Blvd*. Kingfish fishing tournaments are held in Apr and Oct.

SR 699 curves left and crosses east over Blind Pass into **St Pete Beach**, then veers to the right as Blind Pass Rd. Go left at 75th Ave for one block, then pick up Gulf Blvd, SR 699, going south. Along the way is a Baskin Robbins Twisty Treat shop shaped like a huge ice cream cone.

### ST PETE BEACH

Tourist Information: St Petersburg Beach Area Chamber of Commerce, *6990 Gulf Blvd, St Petersburg Beach, FL 33706; tel: (813) 360-6957*. The town is affectionately and legally called **St Pete Beach**, drawing local people to its gulf waterfront for dining and sunbathing. The *St Petersburg Times* 'Weekend' section lists dining and nightlife in Southern Pinellas County.

#### ACCOMMODATION

St Pete Beach has many smaller motels and efficiencies. Chains include *BW, DI, Hd, Hn* and *Rd*.

The **Radisson Sandpiper Beach Resort**, *6000 Gulf Blvd; tel: (800) 333-3333 or (813) 360-5551*, is an expensive–pricey suite hotel with an unusually friendly staff. **Tradewinds**, *5500 Gulf Blvd; tel: (800) 237-0707 or (813) 367-6461*, the largest beachfront resort in the Tampa Bay Area, is landscaped with tropical foliage and Victorian gazebos. Expensive–pricey.

The shimmering pink pricey landmark of the Gulf Beaches is the **Don CeSar**,

## PINELLAS PENINSULA CIRCULAR TOUR

*3400 Gulf Blvd; tel: (800) 282-1116 or (813) 360-1881*, built by an Irish real estate tycoon in 1928 to resemble the pink Royal Hawaiian Hotel in Waikiki. Even the hibiscus growing profusely in front matches the flamingo pink façade with its Moorish bell towers. F. Scott Fitzgerald put his wife Zelda through detoxification at 'The Don', which later served as a Yankees baseball spring training centre and army hospital and convalescent centre. A beach club and spa are recent additions. Guides dressed à la Gatsby conduct historical and ecological tours of the resort hotel.

The **Lady Anderson Dining Yacht,** *3400 Pasadena Ave S.; tel: (800) 533-2288 or (813) 367-7804*, Sept–May, offers sightseeing and dining cruises, with gospel music cruises on Tues and Thurs evenings. Dolphin watching and other excursions leave from **Dolphin Landings Charter Boat Center**, *4737 Gulf Blvd (Dolphin Village Shopping Center); tel: (813) 367-4488*. Shoppers have a wide choice at **Silas Bayside Market** (across from Tradewinds) *5505 Gulf Blvd; tel: (813) 360-6961*. Look for the elaborate cement statue of Neptune and a sea monster.

At the southern end of Gulf Blvd is the small, mostly residential village and beach dunes of **Pass-A-Grille**, named by 19th-century Cuban fishermen who smoked fish there. **Island's End Cottages**, *1 Passe-A-Grille Way; St Pete Beach, FL 33706; tel: (813) 360-5023*, are moderate–expensive. **Hurricane Seafood Restaurant**, *9th Ave and Gulf Way; tel: (813) 360-9558*, moderate, is good for sunset watching. The **Gulf Beaches Historical Museum**, *115 10th Ave; tel: (813) 360-2491*, open weekends, delves into the history and development of the barrier islands.

## ST PETE BEACH TO THE PIER

Drive east on Pinellas Bayway, SR 682. The toll to Isla del Sol is $0.50. Turn right, going south on Pinellas Bayway, SR 679. Pay another toll before arriving at **Tierra Verde**, where pelicans and fishermen vie with windsurfers around a key with a large Native American burial mound. Five miles ahead, beyond another toll booth at Bunce's Pass, is **Fort de Soto County Park**; *tel: (813) 866-2484*, actually 900 acres spread over five keys. Most of the park is on Mullet Key, with 233 camp pitches plus swimming beaches, bicycle path, picnic tables, boat launches, snack bar and bait shop, and the 1898 fort's forgettable battery and barracks.

Walk the self-guiding **Arrowhead Nature Trail**, cushioned by soft, springy pine needles. Deer flies, salt marsh mosquitoes and poison ivy are hazards, but the 1.5 mile trail is a good introduction to the flora and wildlife of the Gulf Coast. Bunce's Pass Overlook is one of South Florida's finest views of mangroves emerging from water.

Return to Isla del Sol and turn right onto SR 682. Pinellas Bayway becomes 54th Ave S., going east. Cross US 19 and drive under I-275, then turn left (north) onto 31st St S. Turn right at 35th Terr, and curve right on Fairway Ave. S. Lakewood Golf & Country Club is on the left. Jog left, then immediately right onto Country Club Way S. **Boyd Hill Nature Park** is on the left (See St Petersburg, pp. 194–201). Follow 9th St S. around the east side of **Lake Maggiore**. Turn right on Harbordale, left on 4th St S, right on 22nd Ave S.E., north on Beach Dr., west on 14th Ave S. E., north on Bay St, left on 13th Ave S. E., north on 3rd St S. past the **Dali Museum**, east on 5th St S., and continue on **Bayshore Dr.** to **The Pier**.

# ST PETERSBURG–TAMPA

If Tampa Bay's culture is in St Petersburg and its business is in Tampa, its less developed past remains on the east side of Tampa and Hillsborough Bays. The 45-mile direct route leaves downtown St Petersburg, crosses the Sunshine Skyway and goes north through rural areas and Apollo Beach on the Tamiami Trail, Hwy 41, before ending in downtown Tampa. Allow three hours to make a leisurely loop, or make Bahia or Apollo Beach an inexpensive base for exploration of the region's attractions.

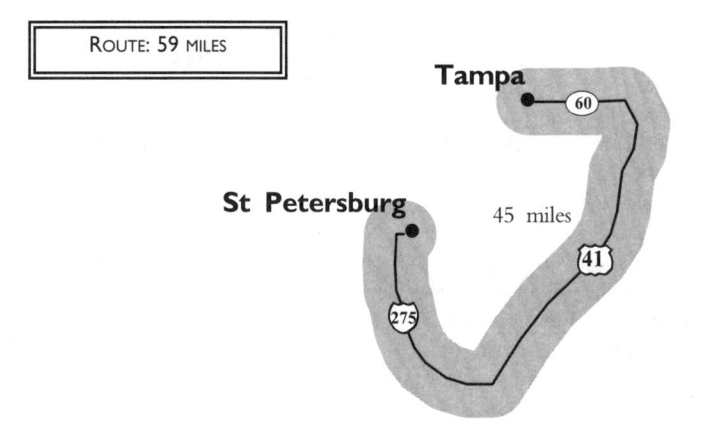

ROUTE: 59 MILES

Tampa
St Petersburg    45 miles

## ROUTE

Take Bayshore Dr. north from The Pier in St. Petersburg and turn left onto 5th Ave N.E. Follow signs for the I-375 transition to I-275 south, and continue south five miles to the Sunshine Skyway. For a more scenic route on surface streets, drive the last eight miles of the Pinellas Circular Tour, p. 202, in reverse. Take the Sunshine Skyway bridge, I-275, 15 miles south-east over Tampa Bay to North Manatee County. Go left on Hwy 41, the Tamiami Trail. Twenty-three miles north, turn left on Hwy 60 and proceed to downtown Tampa.

The **Sunshine Skyway** toll road is St Petersburg's icon, pictured in advertisements for banks, scientific research, and beach delights. First built in 1954, then rebuilt after a freighter smashed through a span in 1980, the skyway is a 15-mile long bridge and causeway system linking Pinellas County in the north with Manatee County. Designed after the Brotonne Bridge over the Seine River, the 4.1-mile 'skyway' rises 175 ft above Lower Tampa Bay. The long and steep crossing is enhanced with delicate-looking yellow cables in the shape of upside-down fans attached to pylons. At dusk, the skyway's illuminated cables glitter on the surface of the bay. On the St Petersburg side, there is an area for swimming and picnics, and a fishing pier.

The Sunshine Skyway ends at **Terra Ceia** in **Palmetto** in Manatee County. To the left is **Terra Ceia** (federal) **Aquatic Preserve.** Turn right on Hwy 41. A cluster of RV parks lines the Tamiami Trail near the highway junction, including **Winterset Travel Trailer RV Park**, *8515 US 41 N., Palmetto, FL 34221-9634; tel: (941) 722-4884*, and the adult-only **Fiesta Grove RV Resort**, *8615 Bayshore Rd, Palmetto, FL 34221-9615; tel: (941) 722-7661*. **Gillette** is the next hamlet. The **Midway Flea Market**, Sat–Sun 0800-1600, is two miles north of the I-275–Hwy 41 junction.

A huge water tower is emblazoned with the words **Port Manatee. Regal Cruises'** terminal, *S. Dock St,* with Oct–Apr *M/V Regal Empress* cruises, shares the port with two cement factories and a petroleum refinery. Book tours of Port Manatee; *tel: (941) 722-6221*, Florida's fourth-largest deepwater port, which ships 1.3 million pounds of produce daily, in addition to phosphate, petroleum, asphalt, cement, lumber, citrus concentrate and bananas.

Piles of phosphates are on the left as the route enters Hillsborough County. Foliage is green on both sides of Hwy 41 near **Sun City. Sundance Growers** greenhouses are on the right. To the left is **Cockroach Bay**, enjoyed by canoeists, but under threat from powerboats which destroy the seagrass habitat. Too many anglers fish for the snook, redfish and sea trout which shelter in shallow water. Aggressive commercial night-time gill netting has endangered the beautiful bay's natural balance. Cockroach Bay is part of the Cockroach Bay Aquatic Preserve.

Hwy 41 passes **Gulf City** and enters **Ruskin,** a small resort patronised mainly by Floridians. The **Ruskin Chamber of Commerce,** *315 S. Tamiami Trail, Ruskin, FL 33570; tel: (813) 645-3808,* has information on local accommodation and recreation. On the south bank of the **Little Manatee River** is the **Hide-A-Way RV Resort**, *2206 Chaney Dr, Ruskin, FL 33570-5908; tel (813) 645-6037.* **Days Inn at Bahia Beach,** *611 Destiny Dr., Ruskin, FL 33570; tel: (800) 282-8116* or *(813) 645-3291*, moderate-expensive, has a peaceful beach, hot and cold pools, two restaurants, tennis, volleyball and shuffleboard.

Find home-style dining at the corner of Hwy 41 and Shell Point Rd. The **Ruskin Café** is open 0600–2000 to accommodate fisherfolk. Across the road is **The Coffee Cup,** *105 US 41, Ruskin, FL 33570*. The 1910-era building decor is basic and not shiny-clean, but a budget lunch includes meat, a vegetable, salad, bread and butter. Sugar-cured ham, fried chicken and black-eyed peas join the usual burgers, but pie and coffee are the magnet. A dozen varieties of mouth-watering home-made pies, including coconut cream, banana and chocolate, are served in huge wedges. A bonus is the attached General Store which sells plaid shirts, straw hats, cigars, syrups, local honey and blackstrap (sulphured) molasses along with regular groceries.

## ST PETERSBURG–TAMPA

Hire pleasure boats at **Shell Point Marina**, *end of Shell Point Rd*, half day $30; full day $50. The neighbourhood has small, custom-built houses with dozens of citrus trees in lush gardens. **E. G. Simmons County Park**, *19th Ave N.W. (at Hunter Pass); tel: (813) 671-7655*, has saltwater swimming off a narrow beach, fishing, protected birding areas and is popular with canoeists. **Wilderness Canoe Adventures**, *18001 US 301 S., Wimauma, FL 33598; tel: (800) 229-1371 or (813) 634-2228*, conducts Nov–Mar tours of Cockroach Bay and two–five-hour canoe trips down the shallow Little Manatee River. Ruskin holds an annual **Seafood Festival** at Bahia Beach in mid-Nov, featuring craftspeople displaying their wares.

Next to a McDonald's at the corner of 19th Ave and Hwy 41 is a deserted spot labelled the **Last Family Drive-in In the USA**. As the Tamiami Trail approaches **Apollo Beach**, tomato processing plants and pick-your-own farms proliferate. **Apollo Beach Chamber of Commerce**, *5914 Fortune Place, Apollo Beach, FL 33572; tel: (813) 645-1366*, has local information. **Ramada Bayside Inn & Resort**, *6414 Surfside, Apollo Beach, FL 33572; tel: (800) 672-3224 or (813) 645-32731*, offers 102 moderate rooms on the beach. Just north, at the west end of **Big Bend Rd,** is a huge power plant. At night the lights sparkle, but the chemical fumes are overpowering.

North of **Adamsville**, water landmarks have quaint names: **Whiskey Stump Key**, **Hog and Hominy Cove** and the **Kitchen**. Tiny **Bullfrog Creek** has one-room cottages, a small flea market, and bait shops selling perch, chub and worms. **Gibsonton**, at the mouth of the **Alafia River**, is well-known for mural-bedecked **Showtown USA**, *Hwy 41; tel (813) 677-5443*, with dancing to live country music bands and circus performances. About 25 mobile home parks house Gibsonton residents, many of whom are retired circus people.

Cross the Alafia River on the **Doyle E. Carlton Bridge**. A boat-launching ramp and fishing piers are on the north side. Cargill Fertilizer, Inc. has a huge plant on the left. The Tamiami Trail crosses a railway track and the speed limit increases from 50–55 mph. A sign points to a trout restocking area near the bay. Pass another power plant to the left on Port Sutton Rd.

One mile north, Hwy 41 continues north while Bus Hwy 41 turns northwest. Both meet Hwy 60 1.5 miles beyond the split.

Take Hwy 41 (S. 50th St) straight north, drive past a brake shop, mobile homes, statuary, used lorries and the Old Car Co.'s Model T Ford display. A pontoon boat centre is to the right as Hwy 41 crosses over the Palm River. There is an excellent view of downtown Tampa to the left.

Ironically, the more **scenic alternative** is the Hwy 41 Business route. Turn left on Causeway Blvd, which curves right, with **McKay Bay** on the right. To the left across **East Bay** are the **Port of Tampa** and the Holland America Cruise Ship Terminal. On land again, the Causeway becomes S. 22nd St, with Ybor City ahead. Before joining Hwy 60, Bus Hwy 41 traverses an African-American neighbourhood with graceful old houses.

From either Hwy 41 route, turn left (west) on Hwy 60, E. Adamo Dr. Turn left on 13th St to visit the **Florida Aquarium,** then continue south on 13th St until it becomes Platt St and goes west into downtown Tampa.

# TAMPA

Tampa is a no-nonsense business centre. Glass and rock skyscrapers point heavenward, and the Port of Tampa, Florida's most active port, churns with activity a mile away. Locally mined phosphates, petroleum refineries, cruise ship passengers and the Florida Aquarium add to the port's bustle. Tampa is also home to Busch Gardens and the Gulf Coast's version of Cuban culture.

When Hernando de Soto sailed into the Tampa Bay in 1539, he encountered natives in a bayside village named Tanpa, 'sticks of fire'. Mapmakers drew 'Tampa', which became the name of the Fort Brooke trading settlement in 1855. Exiled Cuban cigar makers led that industry's boom in Ybor City, north-east of Tampa's present downtown, in the late 19th century. At the same time, Henry B. Plant placed his railroad system terminus in Tampa, with a steamship service from Tampa to Havana, Cuba, via Key West. The railroad brought visitors to Plant's Tampa Bay Hotel, a Moorish style building with silver onion–dome turrets. Settlers arrived to work in the cigar industry, mining, agriculture, and at the port.

Today, Florida's third most populous city is adding museums and arts venues to erase a reputation as a cultural wasteland.

## TOURIST INFORMATION

The **Tampa Hillsborough Convention and Visitors Association, Inc. (THCVA)**, *PO Box 519, Tampa, FL 33601-0519, 111 Madison St, Suite 1010, Tampa, FL 33602-4706; tel: (800) 448-2672, or (813) 223-2752*, open Mon–Sat 0900–1700, provides 24-hr recorded information on attractions lists of hotels in both moderate and deluxe categories. It also has a with connection to a direct booking line for each hotel, car hire information, and Busch Gardens hours and admission.

The **Greater Tampa Chamber of Commerce**, *PO Box 420, Tampa, FL 33601-0420; tel: (813) 228-7777*, has area information. The **North Tampa Chamber of Commerce**, *4819 E. Busch Blvd, Suite 206, Tampa, FL 33617; tel (813) 980-6966*, covers activities around Busch Gardens, Adventure Island and the Museum of Science & Industry (MOSI). The **Tampa Bay Visitor Information Center**, *3601 E. Busch Blvd; tel: (813) 985-3601*, is open daily 1000–1800, across from Busch Gardens.

The **Ybor City Chamber of Commerce**, *1800 E. 9th Ave, Tampa, FL 33605; tel: (813) 248-3712*, has both general Tampa area tips and information about the historic Cuban cigar-making district.

### Weather

Tampa's climate is temperate, but semi-tropical conditions and June–Sept thunderstorms raise summertime humidity levels. Oct–Jan are the driest months, when temperatures plummet to lows of

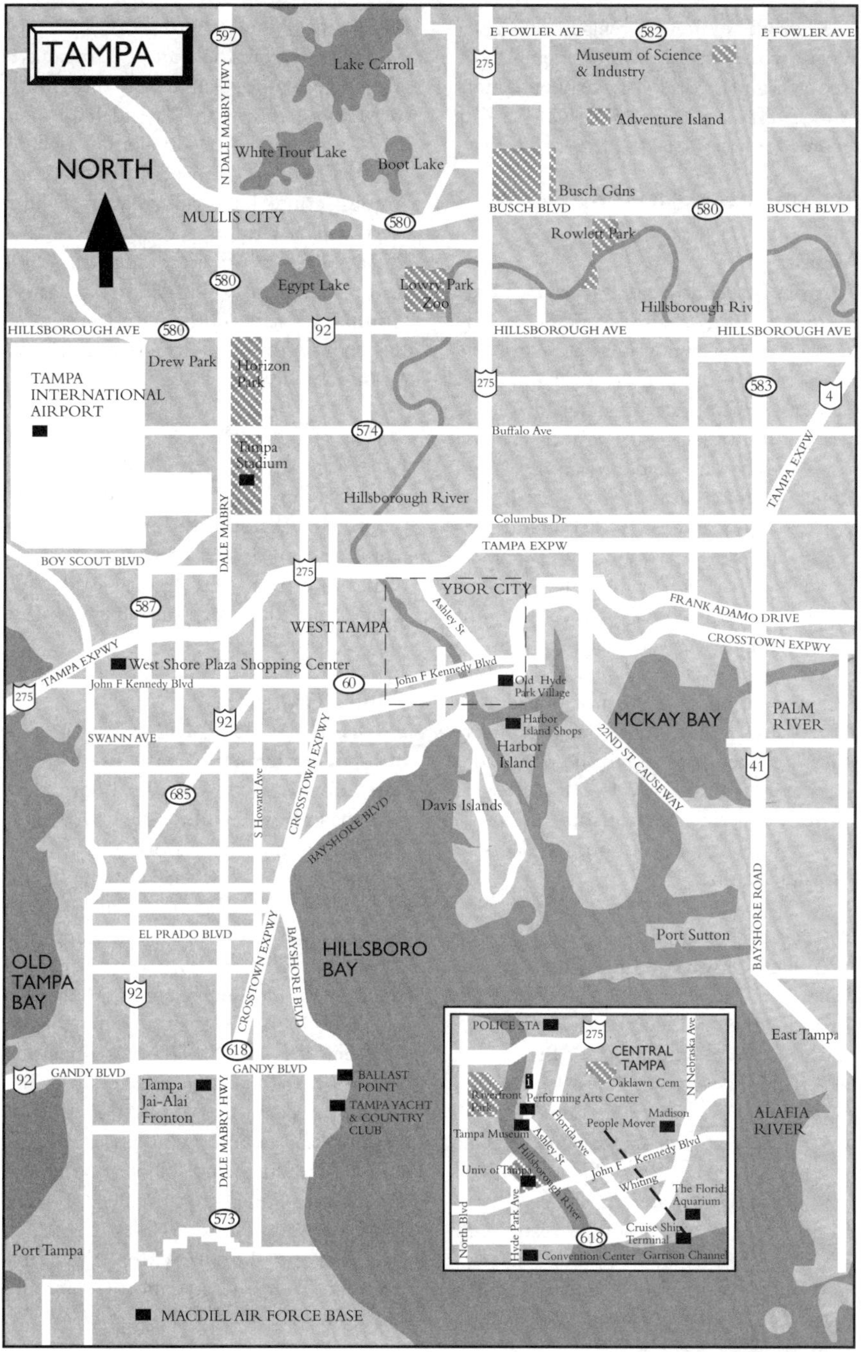
TAMPA
NORTH
E FOWLER AVE
Lake Carroll
Museum of Science
& Industry
Adventure Island
White Trout Lake
Boot Lake
N DALE MABRY HWY
Busch Gdns
BUSCH BLVD
MULLIS CITY
Rowlett Park
Egypt Lake
Lowry Park
Zoo
Hillsborough Riv
HILLSBOROUGH AVE
Drew Park
Horizon
Park
TAMPA
INTERNATIONAL
AIRPORT
Buffalo Ave
Tampa
Stadium
TAMPA EXPW
Hillsborough River
Columbus Dr
TAMPA EXPW
BOY SCOUT BLVD
DALE MABRY
YBOR CITY
FRANK ADAMO DRIVE
WEST TAMPA
Ashley St
CROSSTOWN EXPWY
TAMPA EXPWY
West Shore Plaza Shopping Center
John F Kennedy Blvd
John F Kennedy Blvd
Old Hyde
Park Village
Harbor
Island Shops
MCKAY BAY
PALM
RIVER
SWANN AVE
CROSSTOWN EXPWY
Harbor
Island
22ND ST CAUSEWAY
Davis Islands
BAYSHORE BLVD
S Howard Ave
EL PRADO BLVD
CROSSTOWN EXPWY
BAYSHORE BLVD
HILLSBORO
BAY
Port Sutton
BAYSHORE ROAD
OLD
TAMPA
BAY
GANDY BLVD
GANDY BLVD
BALLAST
POINT
TAMPA YACHT
& COUNTRY
CLUB
Tampa
Jai-Alai
Fronton
DALE MABRY HWY
POLICE STA
CENTRAL
TAMPA
N Nebraska Ave
Oaklawn Cem
Riverfront
Park
Performing Arts Center
Florida Ave
Madison
People Mover
Tampa Museum
Ashley St
John F. Kennedy Blvd
Univ of Tampa
Hillsborough River
Whiting
The Florida
Aquarium
North Blvd
Hyde Park Ave
Cruise Ship
Terminal
Convention Center
Garrison Channel
East Tampa
ALAFIA
RIVER
Port Tampa
MACDILL AIR FORCE BASE
597
582
275
580
580
580
580
92
275
583
4
574
275
587
60
275
92
41
685
92
618
92
573
275
618

# TAMPA

10°C from summer averages of 27°C. Wear a cover-up for winter evenings, or breezy nights. For local weather conditions; *tel: (813) 645-2506*. (24-hr recorded forecast), or *(813) 645-2323*.

### Arriving and Departing

**Airport**
**Tampa International Airport (TIA)**; *tel: (813) 870-8700*, is seven miles northwest of downtown via Exit 20 from I-275 to SR60, or 12 miles west of Busch Gardens. Visitors arriving at airside terminals take shuttlecars to airport Galleria shops, restaurants and an onsite hotel. Huge metal sculptures of sea birds 'fly' over elevators and the Galleria, and lifesize metal pelicans around a copper mangrove tree mark TIA's meeting place.

TIA is a US model for ease of transit between plane and transport. A monorail provides access to car parks. Car hire agency parking stalls are just outside the hire desks. Many hotels have courtesy shuttles to downtown and the Westshore Plaza area. Taxi to downtown, $12–$15. **Central Florida Limousine**; *tel: (813) 396-3730*, covers Hillsborough County (Greater Tampa).

**By Car**
Interstate highways are the swiftest way to drive into Tampa. Take I-4 west from Orlando, then follow the signs to I-275 north of downtown. From St Petersburg, take I-275 east across Howard Frankland Bridge, then veer right onto SR 60 towards downtown skyscrapers, or take Exit 25, Ashley Dr. From TIA, take SR60 south, then east towards Tampa. To bypass Tampa, take the Crosstown Expressway (Hwy 618, a toll road beginning at Hwy 92, Gandy Blvd in west Tampa) 14 miles east to I-75, east of Tampa.

**By Boat**
Cruise ships from the Port of Tampa take advantage of the Gulf Coast's proximity to Mexican resorts in Playa del Carmen and Cozumel. A few itineraries include Grand Cayman Island in the Caribbean. Among cruise lines sailing from Tampa are Carnival Cruise Line; *tel: (800) 327-9501*, Holland America Line; *tel: (800) 426-0327*, the OdessAmerica Cruise Company; *tel: (800) 375-4661*, and Regency Cruises (Port Manatee); *tel: (800) 388-5500*.

### Getting Around

One way streets direct traffic flow in Tampa's surprisingly compact downtown. SR60, Kennedy (or JFK) Blvd, a main artery, divides downtown street names into north and south; Florida Ave divides the downtown into east and west on the grid plan.

**Public Transport**
**Hart Line**; *tel: (813) 254-4278*, Tampa's bus system; runs a free **HartLine Shuttle Bus** around a downtown Loop. The **Tampa-Ybor Trolley**; *tel: (813) 254-4278*, running daily from 0730–1730, makes 17 stops between Harbour Island, the Garrison Seaport Cruise Ship Terminal, the Florida Aquarium, and Ybor City. The trolley stops are marked with green and orange signs. Adult fares are $0.50. An elevated rail **People Mover**; *tel: (813) 223-4141*, operating Mon–Sat 0700–2400, Sun 0800–1200, runs from level three of Old Fort Brooke Parking Garage in downtown to the east end of Harbour Island's Shops on the second level. Rides from 1100–1400 are free; other times, adult fares are $0.25. The **Tampa Town Water Taxi** runs between Tampa Convention Center and Harbour Island across the Garrison

**Tourist Information • Getting Around**

Channel, Mon–Fri, every six mins, 1100–1400, $0.50. **Tampa Town Ferry, Inc.**; *tel: (813) 253-3076*, includes stops at the convention centre, Harbour Island, the Performing Arts Center, University of Tampa (Plant Museum), the Museum of Art and the Florida Aquarium.

### Driving

Avoid Tampa's rush hour between 0700–0900 and 1630–1800. One-way streets, long traffic signals, and lack of on-street parking necessitate route pre-planning. Meters in city-owned lots are $0.75 per hour, up to $5 per day. **Old Fort Brooke Parking Garage**, *Whiting and Florida Sts*, is convenient for downtown and Harbour Island (via People Mover). Harbour Island's car park has 3 hrs of free parking. Other public car parks are: **Poe Parking Garage**, *Ashley and Polk Sts*; **NationsBank Garage**, *Franklin and Whiting Sts*; and the Convention Center, *via S. Tampa St*.

For driving in Greater Tampa, use interstates (I-275, I-4, I-75) when possible to reach a specific area like Busch Gardens. Surface travel is frequently clogged with slow drivers and lorries blocking all lanes.

## STAYING IN TAMPA

### Accommodation

Seasonal variations, unadvertised discounts and long-term (weekly, monthly) rates can dramatically lower average lodging prices. Accommodation with even a rudimentary kitchen can be a bargain if some meals are eaten in. Other Tampa Bay lodging is covered in the St Petersburg chapter (see p. 194). Tampa's lodging is centred in four areas: downtown; Westshore Plaza/Airport; Rocky Point Island/Bayfront Beaches; and near Busch Gardens in North Tampa. The **THCVA**; *tel: (800)-448-2672*, lists hotels in each area by price category, and connects callers with the booking desk of their chosen hotel. Major chains are represented, including *DI, Hd, HJ, Hy, Ma, Rd, Rm, Sh* and *Tl*.

Room rates are 10% higher during high season, Jan–Mar. Fri–Sat prices are lower at most hotels and motels. Priciest accommodation is downtown and Westshore Plaza/Airport; there is a good choice of budget–moderate accommodations near Busch Gardens.

**Downtown** hotels are convenient for Harbour Island, Ybor City or cruise ship stopovers. At Harbour Island is the pricey **Wyndham Harbour Island Hotel**, *725 S. Harbour Island Blvd, Tampa, FL 33602; tel: (813) 229-5000* or *(800) WYNDHAM*, posh lodgings with views of downtown skyscrapers. The **Hyatt Regency Tampa**, *Two Tampa City Center, Tampa, FL 33602; tel: (813) 225-1234* or *(800) 233-1234*, has moderate–pricey rooms in the business district. Many rooms at the moderate–expensive **Quality Hotel Riverside**, *200 N. Ashley Dr., Tampa, FL 33602; tel: (813) 223-2222*, have balconies overlooking the Hillsborough riverfront.

The **Holiday Inn Ashley Plaza Convention Center**, *111 W. Fortune St, Tampa, FL 33602; tel: (813) 223-1351*, is a moderate–expensive hotel that is close to I-275's Exit 25 to downtown and is adjacent to Tampa's Performing Arts Center.

**Airport** or **Westshore** locations offer easy access to the Tampa Bay Area; take I-275 south-west to St Petersburg, SR60 west to Clearwater, or I-275 south and SR60 east to downtown Tampa. The **Tampa Airport Marriott**, *Tampa International Airport, FL 33607; tel: (813)*

979-5151, located in the main terminal, is expensive, but convenient for arrival–night rest. Four miles east of TIA is the **Budget Host Tampa Motel**, *3110 W. Hillsborough Ave, Tampa, FL 33614; tel: (813) 876-8673 or (800) 283-4678*, including a few cottages among 33 motel rooms.

The **Holiday Inn Express Tampa Stadium/Airport**, *4732 N. Dale Mabry Hwy, Tampa, FL 33614; tel: (813) 877-6061 or (800) 868-4484*, east of the airport, has moderate rooms and excellent weekly rates. Two other moderate hotels just south of TIA are **Hampton Inn Tampa International Airport**, *4817 W. Laurel St, Tampa, FL 33607; tel: (813) 287-0778 or (800) 426-7866*, and **AmeriSuites Westshore**, *4811 W. Main St, Tampa, FL 33607; tel: (813) 282-1037 or (800) 833-1516*.

**Rocky Point Island** along the Courtney Campbell Pkwy adjoins the Westshore area. At the **Hyatt Regency Westshore**, *6200 Courtney Campbell Causeway, Tampa, FL 33607; tel: (813) 874-1234, or (800) 233-1234*, rooms overlook a protected salt marsh. **Radisson Bay Harbor Inn**, *7700 Courtney Campbell Causeway, Tampa, FL 33607; tel: (813) 281-8900 or (800) 333-3333*, has a beach and balcony views of the city or Old Tampa Bay. Both are expensive. **Days Inn Rocky Point Island**, *7627 Courtney Campbell Causeway, Tampa, FL 33607; tel: (813) 281-0000 or (800) 237-2555*, moderate, has rooms just down the block. The moderate **Sailport Resort**, *2506 Rocky Point Dr., Tampa, FL 33607; tel: (813) 281-9599 or (800) 255-9599*, has bunkbeds in some rooms and a beach for sunning.

**North Tampa** accommodation serves Busch Gardens visitors. Moderate priced lodging close to the theme park entrance are **Days Inn Busch Gardens Maingate**, *2901 E. Busch Blvd, Tampa, FL 33612; tel: (813) 933-6741 or (800) 325-2525*, and **Howard Johnson's Busch Gardens Main Gate**, *4139 E. Busch Blvd; tel: (813) 988-9191 or (800) 874-1768*. **Econo Lodge Busch Gardens**, *1701 E. Busch Blvd; tel: (813) 933-7681 or (800) 783-7681*, has close to budget prices.

### Eating and Drinking

Luckily, only one Tampa restaurant has stretched the appetiser menu to include a salmon and peach tart. The usual fast food burgers and submarine sandwiches are dependable cheap–budget fare.

**Bern's Steak House**, *1208 S. Howard Ave, Tampa, FL 33606; tel: (813) 251-2421*, is one of Florida's best-known eateries. Sixty-three varieties of wood-grilled steak, a separate dessert room with accordion music and dancing, produce grown locally without pesticides, and claim to the largest wine selection in the world makes dinner pricey and advance booking a must. Bern's adds a 12% gratuity to the bill. For a touch of Americana, there's steak at **Don Shula's**, *Sheraton Grand Hotel, 4860 W. Kennedy Blvd, Tampa, FL 33609; tel: (813) 286-4400*, where the pricey menu is printed on an American-style football in honour of the restauranteur, a football team manager. **CK'S Restaurant**; *tel: (813) 878-6500*, is the pricey revolving rooftop restaurant atop the *Tampa Airport Marriott*.

For authentic budget American food near Busch Gardens, sample **Mel's Hot Dogs**, *4136 E. Busch Blvd; tel: (813) 985-8000*. The Jewish Jitsu Big Kosher sandwich combines corned beef, pastrami and Swiss cheese for lunch fare at **Zudar's**, *4315 Bay-to-Bay Blvd; tel: (813) 839-3354*, open for breakfast Sat–Sun, lunch, and late Fri–Sat night coffee with homemade coconut cream and apple pies. The original **Columbia Restaurant**, *2117 E. 7th Ave; tel: (813) 248-4961*, began in Ybor City in 1905, and still serves Cuban specialities like chicken with yellow rice and the enormous 1905 salad, with lettuce, ham, Swiss cheese, tomatoes, olives, Romano cheese and garlic dressing. There's a typical hot Cuban sandwich with ham, pork, salami, Swiss cheese, gherkin and mustard, as well as entrees with grouper, Gulf shrimp, and roast pork. The original location has a flamenco revue. Another **Columbia Restaurant** location at Harbour Island, *tel: (813) 229-2992*, has outdoor dining with an excellent view of downtown. Both are moderate.

### ENTERTAINMENT

Inventing a colourful past where one was lacking, city fathers encourage the **Gasparilla Pirate Fest Street Festival** the first Sat in Feb. Following legendary exploits of a highly fictitious pirate named Gaspar, a fully-rigged wooden ship filled with costumed buccaneers sets sail across Hillsborough Bay from Ballast Point to the Tampa Convention Center. The pirates rampage through downtown, initiating a street festival with live music and fireworks.

The *Tampa Tribune* 'Extra' and the *St Petersburg Times* 'Weekend', both published Fri, have listings for night-clubs and comedy clubs throughout the Tampa Bay region. Flamenco, jazz, blues, reggae, soul, rock – look for most of Greater Tampa's music and night-life scene in Ybor City, a mecca for the youth and homosexual communities. Find Ybor City jazz at **The Jazz Cellar**, *1916 N. 14th St; tel: (813) 248-1862*, open Thurs–Sat, and **Blues Ship**, *1910 E. 7th Ave; tel: (813) 248-6097*. For rock 'n' roll, there's **Killian's**, *1509 E. 8th Ave; tel: (813) 247-6606*.

The **Comedy Works**, *3447 W. Kennedy Blvd*. (Westshore); *tel: (813) 875-9129*, has live stand-up comedy Tues–Sun. The **Harry Waugh Room** at **Bern's Steak House**, *1208 S. Howard Ave; tel: 251-2421*, serves more than 80 desserts from a stainless steel menu, accompanied by the accordion and dancing. Find legitimate theatre and free Wed and Sat backstage tours at the **Tampa Bay Performing Arts Center**, *1010 N. MacInnes Pl., Tampa, FL 33601; tel: (813) 229-7827 or (800) 955-1045*. Concerts and films are presented at the 1926 Moorish decor **Tampa Theatre** movie palace, *711 Franklin St, Tampa, FL 33602; tel: (813) 274-8981*. **ArtsLine**; *tel: (813) 229-2787*, has Hillsborough County arts events listings. The **Seminole Gaming Palace**, *5223 N. Orient Rd, Tampa, FL 33610; tel: (813) 621-1302*, has bingo, poker and video gambling.

The Tampa Bay area is sports crazy. The **Tampa Bay Buccaneers**, *One Buccaneer Pl. Tampa, FL 33607; tel: (813) 879-BUCS or (800) 282-0683*, play American football from Aug–Jan in Tampa Stadium. Tickets are $20–40. The **New York Yankees** baseball team; *tel: (813) 875-7753*, will begin spring training at an adjacent facility at *Dale Mabry Hwy and Dr Martin Luther King, Jr Blvd* in 1996. Year-round, there's pari-mutuel betting at **Tampa Jai Alai Fronton**, *5125 S. Dale Mabry at Gandy Blvd; tel: (813) 831-1441*, entrance $1, **Tampa Greyhound Track**, *I-275, Exit 32 to Bird St; tel: (813) 932-4313*, July–Dec, entrance $1, and **Tampa Bay Downs Thoroughbred Racing**, *one mile north of Hwy 580; tel: (813) 855-4401*, Jan–May, entrance $1.50.

# TAMPA

## Shopping

**West Shore Plaza**, *West Shore and Kennedy Blvds near I-275; tel: (813) 286-0790*, has convenient department store shopping. **The Shops on Harbour Island**, *610 S. Harbour Island Blvd; tel: (813) 229-5093*, are an eclectic mix of up-market clothing boutiques, Chinese porcelain shops, antique dealers and an 'under $1' shop, with ever-changing costume jewellery bargains. **Old Hyde Park Village**, *712 S. Oregon Ave; tel: (813) 251-3500*, is known for up-market speciality shops like The Sharper Image (gadgets) and Williams-Sonoma (kitchenware). **Ybor Square**, *1901 N. 13th St; tel: (813) 247-4497*, is a transformed red-brick cigar factory with hand-rolled cigars at the **Tampa Rico Cigar Co. Inc.**; *tel: (813) 247-6738*, and other shops selling old postcards and cigar-box labels (**Red Horse Book Stall**), woven goods and afghans, Cuban snack food and coffee. **Henry B. Plant Museum** gift shop has excellently priced crafts and *objets d'art*, many Victorian reproductions.

## Sightseeing

Tampa's attractions are found in three areas: Downtown, Ybor City and North Tampa.

### Downtown

**Bayshore Blvd**, said to be the longest continuous paved walkway in the world, is also a driving road lined with small mansions and oaks dripping with Spanish moss. From **MacDill Air Force Base** gate at N. Boundary Rd, 6.5 miles north to the Platt St Bridge into downtown, the road hugs Hillsborough Bay. One mile north of the base, take Interbay Blvd right to **Ballast Point**, for a city pier view of fishing waterbirds, stables and a glimpse of the elegant Georgian-style **Tampa Yacht & Country Club**. Soon, more palatial mansions in Georgian and New England clapboard styles mix with pastel-coloured apartment complexes. Off to the west is posh **Hyde Park**, O.H. Platt's 1886 subdivision, built in 'bungalow' and 'Princess Anne' (Victorian) styles.

To accommodate winter season rail passengers voyaging on his Tampa–Key West–Cuba steamships, railroad baron Henry B. Plant built a fanciful lodging, the Tampa Bay Hotel, in 1891. A long, red–brick, vaguely Moorish-style building curves to follow the line of the Hillsborough River. Silver onion domes surmounted by golden crescent moons are the building's turrets. Arabesque-arched windows vie with the turrets and white carved wooden trim on doorways and windows. Teddy Roosevelt trained troops in sweltering heat at the Tampa Bay Hotel for duty in Cuba during the Spanish American War, 1898–1899. Today, the building is divided between the University of Tampa and the **Henry B. Plant Museum**, *401 W. Kennedy Blvd, Tampa, FL 33606; tel: (813) 254-1891*. Rooms at the former hotel, admission $5, are filled with heavy period furniture, rugs, and monogrammed china. The first three weeks of Dec, local designers transform each room into a celebrity guest's purported Christmas-time lodging and costumed actors playing historic figures like Roosevelt, Nellie Melba, and US orator-politician William Jennings Bryan talk about their arrival at the amazing fantasy hotel. Holiday music plays and hot mulled cider complete the image for the festive **Victorian Christmas Stroll**. Tickets are $5.

**The Tampa Bay History Center**, *601 S. Harbour Island Blvd, #224–226 (Upper Level); tel: (813) 228-0097*, has a few well-explained displays of 500 years

# TAMPA

of Tampa area Native culture, settlement, immigrant groups, industrial and agricultural development near convenient dining and shopping. Exhibitions change frequently at five of the seven galleries at the **Tampa Museum of Art**, *600 N. Ashley Dr., Tampa, FL 33602; tel: (813) 274-8130.* Admission $3.50 adults.

Rich canvases and powerful sculpture stock two floors of galleries at the **Museum of African American Art**, *1308 Marion St; tel: (813) 272-2466.* Black American culture, from African roots and plantation life to back-alley jazz, bloody urban ghettos, racism, family ties, and neighbourhoods are vividly portrayed. Drive by the beautiful brick and white flagstone **St Paul AME Church** at *N. Marion* and *Harrison Sts*, and, just behind, the **Oaklawn Cemetery's** old gravestones and moss-covered trees.

The **Florida Aquarium**, *300 S. 13th St; tel: (813) 273-4020,* admission $14, is Tampa's newest waterfront attraction, halfway between Harbour Island and Ybor City at the Garrison Seaport Center. About 4300 creatures from 485 Florida native species populate habitats, most in natural sunlight. Allow several hours for wandering and watching the wildlife and sealife.

## Ybor City

**Ybor City Chamber of Commerce**, *1800 E. 9th Ave, Tampa, FL 33605; tel: (813) 248-3712,* has information on activities in Ybor City. There is no lodging in the 50–block historic district. The **Tampa-Ybor Trolley**; *tel: (813) 254-4278,* runs daily 0730–1730, or use convenient free parking at 8th and 9th Aves at 13th St. There is an anti-cruising law (prohibiting more than two drives a night down 7th Ave between 12th and 22nd Sts), Fri and Sat 2000–0400.

An enclave of Cuban culture is unexpected amidst the building boom of south Florida. Ybor City is pre-revolutionary 1880s Cuba. Don Vicente Martinez Ybor fled Cuba, first to Key West, then to Tampa where there were no threats of political or labour unrest. In 1886, he opened the first cigar factory, a haven for Cuban refugee worker. Rolling and cutting cigars was a skilled hand art, still seen today in Ybor City.

Prosperity brought families and a café scene to Ybor City in the late 19th century. Bakeries flourished, Spanish and Cuban music and literature made the rounds, and merchants set up shop in solid red and gold brick buildings along 'La Septima', E. 7th Ave. Two old-time social clubs remain, **Centro Asturiano** and **Circulo Cubano**, where older men drink Cuban coffee, gossip and play dominoes and checkers.

Seventh Ave, with its iron grillwork balconies, and gas-lamp era street lighting still pulses with art galleries, poetry readings, jazz and honky-tonk music till the early morning, and is a favourite with the homosexual crowd. Unusual shops include **Adams City Hatters**, 12,000 hats at *1621 E 7th Ave; tel: (813) 229-2850,* and **The Spitting Gargoyle**, *1605 E. 7th Ave; tel: (813) 247-7877,* a haven for an eclectic mix of statues and body parts in plaster.

Most days, the Ybor City State Museum Society leads free, 90-min **Historic (Area) Walking Tours**; *tel: (813) 247-6323,* leaving from the lower level of **Ybor Square**, *1901 N. 13th; tel: (813) 247-4497.* The **Ybor City State Museum**, *1818 E. 9th Ave, Tampa, FL 33605; tel: (813) 247-6323,* open Tues–Sat 0900–1200, 1300–1700 admission $1, is housed in the gold brick La Ferlita Bakery building. The history of

223

SIGHTSEEING

# TAMPA

Ybor City's founding, Cuban politics and society of the turn of the century, immigrant workers, Teddy Roosevelt's Rough Riders training for the Spanish-American War, the decline during the Depression, and mechanised cigar rolling and cigarettes' new popularity are explained. A **Cigar Worker's Home**, **La Casita**, *1804 E. 9th Ave*, open Tues–Sat 1000–1500, is a separate part of the museum. Across the street in **Centennial Park** is a statue of Cuban immigrants.

**Ybor Square**, *1901 N. 13th St; tel: (813) 247-4497*, open Mon–Sat 1000–1800, Sun 1200–1730, once the largest cigar factory in town, has restaurants, boutiques, antique shops and cigar rolling and cutting demonstrations at **Tampa Rico Cigar Co. Inc.**; *tel: (813) 247-6738*. Take a guided tour through **Ybor City Brewing Company**, *2205 N. 20th St, Tampa, FL 33605; tel: (813) 242-9222*, Tues–Sun 1100–1500 for $2. The red-brick cigar factory-turned-brewery offers samples of **Ybor Gold** lager.

## North Tampa

**Busch Gardens**, *3000 E. Busch Blvd, Tampa, FL 33612; tel: (813) 987-5082*, is Tampa's 335-acre theme park, complete with wild roller coasters, African animals, a Tangiers shopping bazaar, and a giant Anheuser-Busch brewery. North from Tampa, take Exit 33 off I-275, and follow Busch Blvd 2 miles east, or take Exit 54 off I-75 and drive 2 miles west. Free shuttle trams run from pay parking lots to the entrance. The park is open longer hours in summer. Adult admission is about $35; children three–nine years $28. Not all rides are wheelchair-accessible. Drinks, ice cream and snacks are available; sandwiches, grilled chicken and ribs, and pizza are harder to locate.

The African theme carries through eight park areas. A snake charmer totes a python near the requisite American alligator pen. Chimpanzees and gorillas run and leap about **Nairobi's Myombe Reserve**. Stroll on the other side of the glass along a jungle-without-the-bugs walkway lined with ferns, bamboo, banana trees, and other tropical plants. Take the festive steam train from **Nairobi Train Station** around camels, kudus and Cape buffalo lounging among other animals on the **Serengeti Plain**.

Disembark at the **Congo Train Station** for wild roller coasters. **Kumba** plungers into a loop from 110 ft, spirals into weightlessness for a few seconds, then loops up 108 ft. The yellow **Python**, almost as exciting, is a double spiral corkscrew. Below Kumba is the **Congo River Rapids**, a soaking experience in a 12-person round raft. Games and arcades, kiddie rides and the **Scorpion** roller coaster are in the adjacent **Timbuktu** area. **Claw Island**, which separates the Congo from Stanleyville, has two white tigers and a mixed–gene Bengal tiger.

**Stanleyville**'s roller coaster streaks above **Stanley Falls**, but Stanleyville's excitement is the **Tanganyika Tidal Wave**, which drops boats off a 55 ft edge, dousing pedestrians caught on an observation bridge. Nearby, **Orchid Canyon** has real orchids and bromeliads cascading over fake limestone. **Bird Gardens** have sad-looking parrots and winged creatures in the Birds of the Pacific and aviary walk-through; the signature Busch Gardens pink flamingos; a koala display; **Land of the Dragons**, a youngster area with a three-storey house and wandering dragon named Dumphrey; and the **Anheuser-Busch Brewery** and **Hospitality House**. Self-guided brewery tours are unenlightening; find free beer samples at the Hospitality House. Ice skating,

German song and dance, American big band and country music add to the amusement park atmosphere.
**Adventure Island**, *4500 Bougainvillea Ave; tel: (813) 987-5660*, admission $19, open late Mar–Sept, is a pool and plunge splash park half a mile from the Busch Gardens entrance. Visitors push rapidly through the **Aruba Tuba**, a connected set of enclosed, water-filled tubes.
The **Museum of Science & Industry (MOSI)**, *4801 E. Fowler Ave, Tampa, FL 33617-2099; tel: (800) 998-MOSI or (813) 987-6300*, one mile north of Busch Gardens, is interactive. Entrance is $8 faor adults, children under 12 $5. Book in advance for the simulated space shuttle flight. Experience the force of a 74-mph Gulf Coast hurricane, complete with debris, or a 3.5 million volt Tesla coil in action. Coral geode 'diamonds' from Ballast Point shimmer with luminescence. Beneath a manatee skeleton in the LifeLab, five tanks form simulated wetlands to create clean water. There's a Butterfly Encounter garden, 3.5 miles of nature trails, a planetarium and an IMAX® dome theatre.
**Lowry Park Zoo**, *7350 North Blvd, Tampa, FL 33604; tel: (813) 935-8552*, admission $6.50, five miles north of downtown Tampa, has Asian animals, Florida wildlife including alligators, snakes, panthers, red wolves, and river otters and a manatee research and rehabilitation centre. The **Seminole Cultural Center**, next to the **Seminole Gaming Palace**, *5223 N. Orient Rd, Tampa, FL 33610; tel: (813) 621-1302*, has Seminole alligator wrestling and tours.

## *SPORT*

Florida is sport crazy. Twenty of North America's 28 professional baseball teams train in Florida, pumping $300 million into local economies every year. Spring training is big business, but it's also the closest that most fans ever get to America's most famous folk heroes.

Tampa called on legendary pirate history to name its professional football team the Buccaneers; Miami named its footballers after the dolphins that once teemed throughout the bay. Orlando evokes a Disneyesque tone by calling its basketball team Magic. Miami sardonically calls its basketballers The Heat. There hasn't been a sheet of natural ice in Florida since the last Ice Age, but that doesn't stop ice hockey fans from packing the arenas to watch the Ft Lauderdale Panthers and the Tampa Lightning.

Professional golf and tennis both have their headquarters in Florida. Even soccer, which the rest of the world knows as football, attracts respectable crowds thanks to the state's large immigrant population.

Professional sport is only the beginning. Every university and college has its own stable of athletes who raise local fans to a fever pitch. And even those who don't actively root for the home team are likely to sport team colours in hats, T-shirts and other official regalia.

Horse and dog races take on an almost religious significance during the autumn–spring seasons, with the added attraction of legal betting. Florida has even turned Jai-alai, a ball game that almost no one has heard of and even fewer have seen, into a big-time wagering sport – and never mind that the game moves so quickly the ball is all but invisible.

# TAMPA–ST AUGUSTINE

This route takes you diagonally from central west to north-east Florida from Tampa Bay on the Gulf of Mexico to the historic city of St Augustine on the Atlantic coast. The terrain varies from the citrus groves of the west and the lush grasslands of the horse-breeding country surrounding Ocala to the camping and hiking paradise of Ocala National Forest, the subtropical reaches of the St John's River and the white beaches of the east coast, fringed with sea oats.

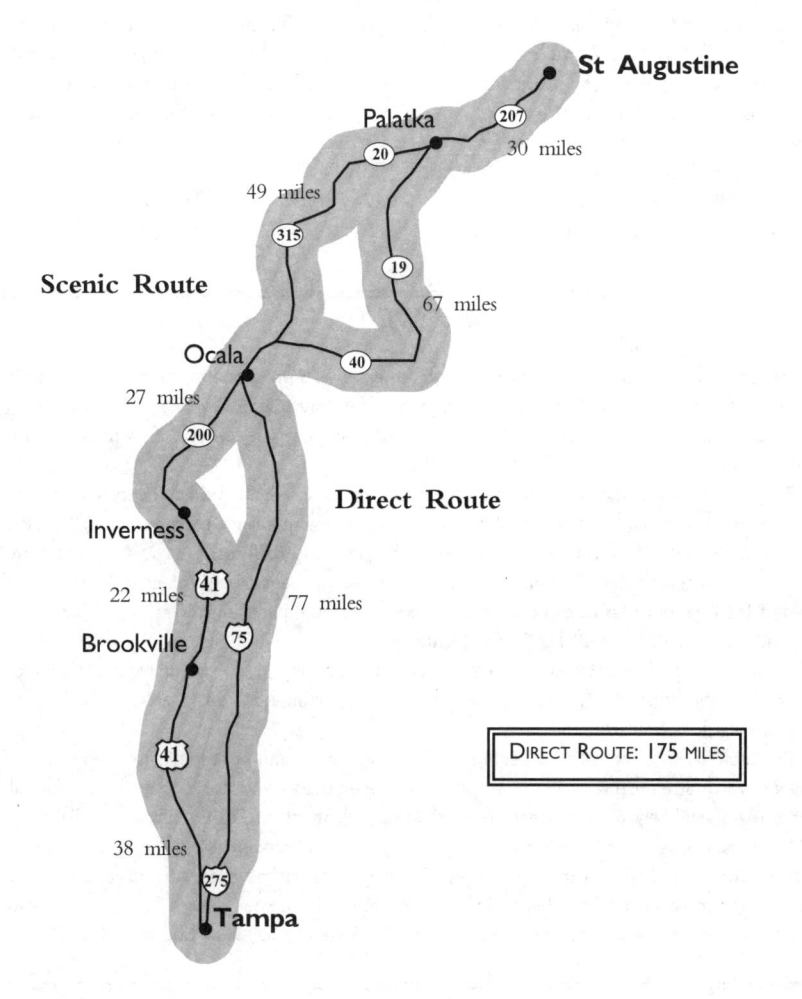

**St Augustine**

Palatka (207)
(20) 30 miles

49 miles
(315)
(19)

**Scenic Route**
67 miles

Ocala (40)
27 miles
(200)

**Direct Route**

Inverness
22 miles (41)
77 miles
Brookville (75)

(41)

DIRECT ROUTE: 175 MILES

38 miles
(275)
Tampa

## ROUTES

### DIRECT ROUTE

From downtown Tampa take I-275 north for eight miles then turn off to I-75 north. After 72 miles, leave I-75 and head east on Hwy 200, reaching **Ocala** after five miles. Bear right on to Hwy 40 and in nine miles – just after **Silver Springs** – turn left on Hwy 315 and drive north for 32 miles until the intersection with Hwy 20, where you turn right and head east for another 17 miles to reach **Palatka**.

Cross the St John's River to **East Palatka**, then turn left on Hwy 207 which reaches **St Augustine** (see p 272) in 30 miles after passing under I-95 and crossing Hwy 1.

This direct route should take just a little under three hrs.

### SCENIC ROUTE

From downtown Tampa take Florida Ave north, turning right on to Cass St and left into Nebraska Ave. From Busch Blvd, the avenue becomes Hwy 41 and continues through increasingly rural countryside, reaching **Brooksville** after 38 miles, where it bears to the east, passing between Withlacoochee State Forest and Apopka Lake before reaching Inverness after another 22 miles. The countryside now is a mixture of woodland, rolling pastures and lakes.

At **Hernando** turn right on to Hwy 200, which reaches Ocala after 27 miles. At Ocala bear right on Hwy 40. Remain on Hwy 40 as it passes through Ocala National Forest, where there are plenty of campgrounds and picnic locations. After 32 miles from Ocala, turn left on to Hwy 19.

The route now heads due north, with Hwy 19 running parallel with the course of the St John's River and continuing through the national forest. After 35 miles, Hwy 19 reaches Palatka, where you cross the river to East Palatka and continue to St Augustine as shown in the Direct Route.

### BROOKSVILLE

Tourist Information: Hernando County Tourist Information Center, *16110 Aviation Loop Dr., Brooksville, FL 34609; tel: (904) 796-4580.* **Hernando Chamber of Commerce**, *101 E. Fort Dade Ave; tel: (904) 796-2420.*

Brooksville is often called Hernando County's Southern Belle. The little town of about 7500 people has plantation homes, brick streets, antique shops and an imposing columned courthouse.

**Hernando Heritage Museum**, is at the intersection of *May Ave and Jefferson St; tel: (904) 799-0129.*

All kinds of Christmas items; trees, baubles, ornaments, nativity scenes, coloured lights, gifts, wrappings and fantastic centrepieces for the festive table can be found at **Roger's Christmas House and Village**, *103 Saxon Ave; tel: (904) 796-2415.* Open daily 0930–1700, except, wait for it, Christmas. Admission: free. If you can endure Christmas all year-round and plenty of people shop here months in advance this is where you can avoid a last-minute rush. There are ten rooms in which to browse and buy.

At **Boyett's Citrus Grove**, *4355 Spring Lake Hwy; tel: (904) 796-2289,* you can buy refreshing oranges and see some Florida marine species in the zoo and aquarium at the site.

**Hernando County Fairground**, *Brooksville; tel: (904) 796-4552,* hosts a number of horse-riding events during the year. Horse shows and show-jumping take place in summer, and at the end of

October there's a **Cattlemen's Rodeo**; *tel: (904) 796-2290*.

The three-day **Octoberfest**; *tel: (904) 796-4552*, with country and blues music, takes place at the same venue towards the end of October.

North of Brooksville, *off I75 and Hwy 48 west of Hwy 301*, is **Dade Battlefield State Historic Site**, *PO Box 938, Bushnell, FL 33513; tel: (904) 793-4781*.

This was the scene of ghastly carnage on a Dec day in 1835. The battle marked the start of the Second Seminole Indian War. In the Visitor Centre the story unfolds of how 108 exhausted soldiers entered the battle arena just as they thought they were going to enjoy a belated celebration of Christmas. Of the 108, only three survived. A re-enactment takes place every Dec. The site is open daily 0800–sunset, Visitor Centre open daily 0900–1700.

## INVERNESS

British visitors will feel at home in Inverness. A double-decker London bus stands outside the moderately priced **Crown Hotel**, *109 N. Seminole Ave; tel: (904) 344-5555*. A replica display of the Crown Jewels can be seen inside the premises. You can dine in the Churchill Restaurant and drink in the Fox and Hounds bar.

Inverness is a small town (pop 6,000) but busy. People stock up here before setting out on a canoe trip on the Withlacoochee River. Canoes can be launched from the Hooty Point car parking area in Potts Preserve, just west of Inverness on Hwy 581, just off Hwy 41.

There are miles of trails for hikers, cyclists and horseriders, accessible from Eden Drive off Hwy 41 in Inverness. Trails information from **SWFWMD Land Resources Dept**, *2379 Broad St,*

*Brooksville, FL 34609; tel: (904) 796-7211*.

East and north of Inverness is a chain of lakes. **Apopka Lake** is the largest and most southerly.

## OCALA

**Tourist Information: Ocala/Marion County Chamber of Commerce**, *110 E. Silver Springs Blvd, PO Box 1210, Ocala, FL 34478; tel: (904) 629-8051*.

Ocala (pop 42,000) is the county seat of Marion County. Its most attractive quality is its setting gently undulating, white rail-fenced meadows sustaining the top-quality thoroughbreds reared and trained in the area and the **Ocala National Forest**, *Box 701, Silver Springs, FL 32688; tel: (904) 625-2520*, with its springs and watercourses.

Members of the public can arrange to visit a working thoroughbred farm on weekdays by appointment; *tel: (904) 629-2160*. It's worth making a dawn start to see the racehorses pounding round the track on their early morning gallops.

Another kind of horse power is on show at the **Don Garlits Museum of Drag Racing and International Drag Racing Hall of Fame**, south of the city near Exit 67 off I-75, *13700 S.W. 16th Avenue, Ocala, FL 34473; tel: (904) 245-8661*.

Don Garlits, holder of a record number of drag-racing awards, founded the museum with his wife, Pat. It traces the sport's development from the 1940s and it has on display more than 75 cars and many items of memorabilia. There is also a collection of antique and classic cars. The museum is open daily 0900–1730, admission is $7.50.

Ocala's **Appleton Museum of Art**, *4333 E. Silver Springs Blvd, Ocala, FL 34470; tel: (904) 236-5050*, contains collections of fine arts from West Africa and South and Central America. Paintings, sculptures and decorative arts from Europe and other parts of the world are exhibited. Open daily except Mon and some public holidays, Tues–Sat 1000–1630, Sun 1300–1700. Admission $3.

Ocala National Forest has hiking trails amid the pines, palms, scrub, rivers and swamp and plenty of campgrounds, some with showers, laundromats and playgrounds, others deep in the wilderness where you can commune with nature. Most of them are near good fishing waters information from the Chamber of Commerce.

The springs in the sub-tropical forest gush amazingly clear water. Canoes can be hired year-round at **Alexander Springs, Juniper Springs** and **Salt Springs**. The water is a steady 72°F. Alexander Springs sends out nearly 80 million gallons of water a day. Swimming, snorkelling and scuba diving are permitted in the 'boil' of the springs.

Fees are charged for camping and day use in Alexander Springs Recreation Area. A blue-waymarked spur trail connects the Recreation Area with the orange-marked **Florida National Scenic Trail** (see p. 68) which runs the 66-mile north south length of the Ocala National Forest.

Within the Recreation Area there is also the **Timucuan Nature Trail**, which forms a loop just over a mile long. Vegetation used by early Indians and wildlife can be seen along the trail.

Privately-owned canoes can be launched and canoe rentals are available for a two-hour or half-day trip, or for a seven-mile one-way trip. This takes about four hours, allowing for a short picnic stop and the negotiation of shallows and obstacles like fallen or overhanging trees. A mini-bus fetches canoeists back to base, and the canoes are towed back. Sightings of white-tailed deer, turtles, alligators and bald eagles can almost be guaranteed. The forest contains many bird and mammal species, including bobcats and the threatened southern black bear and Florida panther.

Don't miss a chance to visit **Silver Springs**, off I-75 about a mile east of Ocala on Hwy 40, *5656 E. Silver Springs Blvd, PO Box 370, Silver Springs, FL 34489; tel: (904) 236-1732.*

The world's largest artesian spring can be cruised by glass-bottom boat. The water is gin-clear, enabling you to see a wide range of aquatic life and objects scores of feet below the surface.

The long-established 350-acre multi-theme park provides a jungle cruise this is Tarzan country where some of the Johnny Weissmuller films were shot a jeep safari among imported African creatures, a petting zoo and close encounters with snakes and spiders. Open daily year-round 0900–1730, extended hours in summer and public holidays. Admission: $21.50.

## PALATKA

**Tourist Information: Putnam County Chamber of Commerce**, *PO Box 550, Palatka, FL 32178; tel: (904) 328-1503.*

Pleasure boats moor near the bridge that crosses the St Johns River in Palatka.

**Ravine State Gardens**, *PO Box 1096, Palatka, FL 32178; tel: (904) 329-3721, are off Twigg St.* The steep ravine was created by the flow of water from beneath sandy ridges along the river's western shore. The gardens were first planted in 1933. Peak flowering time is during Mar and Apr. An annual Azalea Festival is held in spring.

# ORLANDO

Orlando stops short of calling itself the *Fantasy Capital of the World*, although it justifiably could. Instead, it settles for the slogan, *Go for the Magic!* There's certainly plenty of that around, whether it's the high-tech magic of flight simulator rides, the magic of skilfully trained animals or the magic of good old-fashioned entertainment. The hype could be awful, but somehow it all works, a tribute perhaps to the dedication and professionalism of the people who bridge the gap between dream and reality.

Fantasy, however, is a profitable business. With a resident population of just over one million, metropolitan Orlando attracts 13.5 million tourists a year, bringing in close to $4 billion. More than 120,000 people are employed in tourism-related industries.

## TOURIST INFORMATION

**Orlando/Orange County Official Visitor Information Center**, *Mercado Mediterranean Village, 8445 International Dr. (prominently located left of the main entrance to the village); tel: (407) 363-5871.* Open daily (except Christmas Day) 0800–2000. Although the centre gets very busy at peak times, the staff manage to remain relaxed, helpful and informative. Free literature and maps in abundance – make sure you get a copy of the *Official Visitors Guide*. Admission tickets to the area's attractions and theme parks are available at discount prices. Two other free publications – *Best Read Guide to Orlando* and *See Orlando*, both packed with information and discount coupons, are widely available.

A **Florida State Tourism** information booth (not always manned, but with serve-yourself literature) is located in the Mercado food court.

### Weather

Central Florida is rarely short of sunshine. Summer arrives in Orlando in late May and lasts to the end of Sept. High temperatures range from 85–95°F, dropping to 65–75°F at night. High summer sees a considerable increase in humidity with frequent afternoon thunder showers. From Oct–May daytime temperatures range from 75–85°F with night-time lows of 50–65°F. The temperature occasionally drops close to freezing between Dec and Feb.

Sunburn can be a hazard at any time of year. Restraint and a good sunscreen are advised.

## ARRIVING AND DEPARTING

### Airports

**Orlando International Airport**; *tel: (407) 825-2001*, is nine miles south of downtown, just off the Beeline Expressway (Hwy 528), which provides access to the major routes into and around the city. The airport is all very art deco, with pastel shades, subdued lighting and palm trees, and its two terminal buildings – 'A' Side and 'B' Side – are spacious and carpeted. Smoking is allowed only in

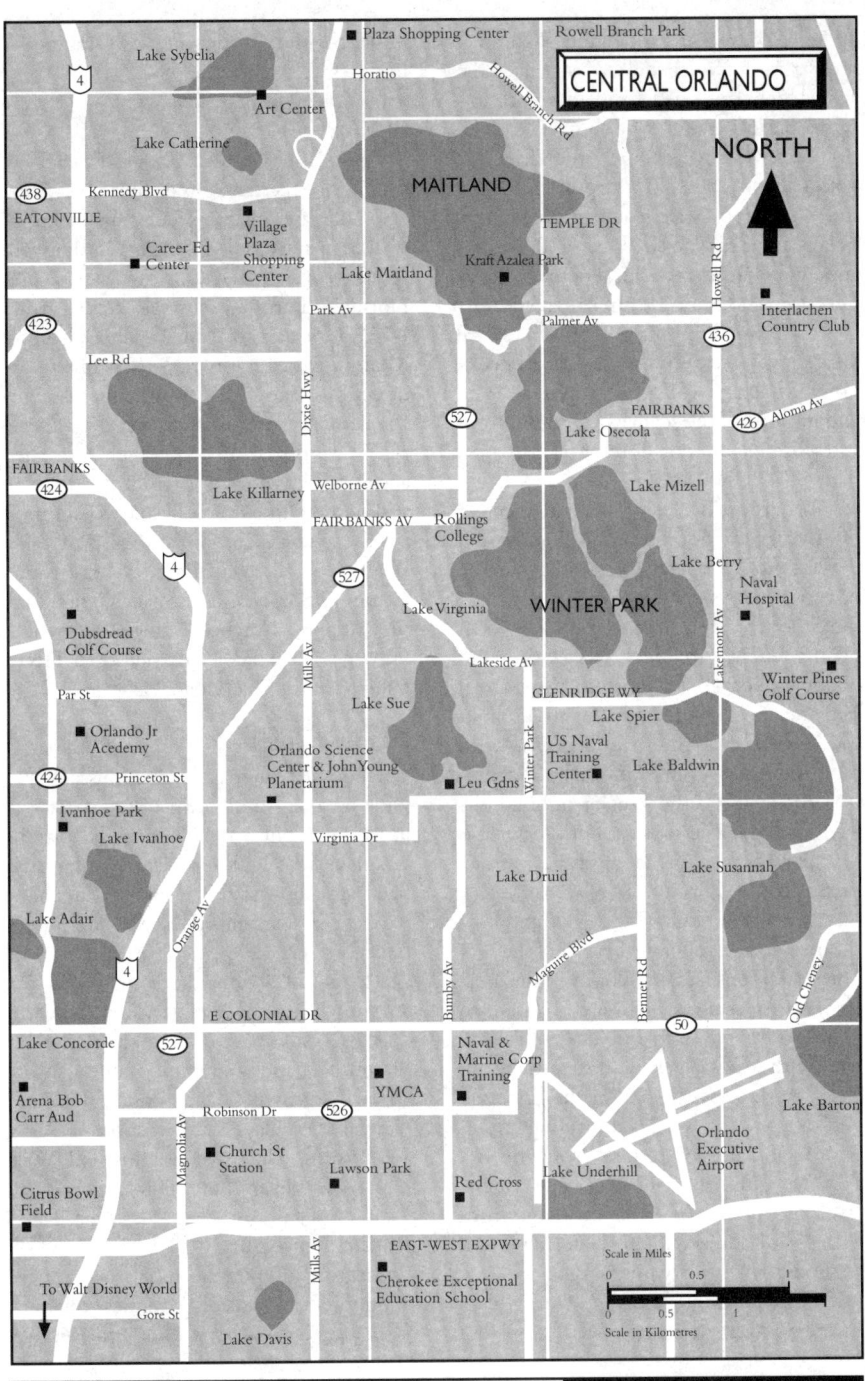

# ORLANDO

# CENTRAL ORLANDO

**NORTH**

- Plaza Shopping Center
- Rowell Branch Park
- Lake Sybelia
- Horatio
- Howell Branch Rd
- Art Center
- Lake Catherine
- MAITLAND
- Kennedy Blvd
- EATONVILLE
- TEMPLE DR
- Career Ed Center
- Village Plaza Shopping Center
- Kraft Azalea Park
- Lake Maitland
- Howell Rd
- Park Av
- Palmer Av
- Interlachen Country Club
- Lee Rd
- Dixie Hwy
- FAIRBANKS
- Lake Osceola
- Aloma Av
- FAIRBANKS
- Lake Killarney
- Welborne Av
- Lake Mizell
- FAIRBANKS AV
- Rollings College
- Lake Berry
- Naval Hospital
- Dubsdread Golf Course
- Lake Virginia
- WINTER PARK
- Lakemont Av
- Winter Pines Golf Course
- Par St
- Lake Sue
- Lakeside Av
- GLENRIDGE WY
- Lake Spier
- Orlando Jr Acedemy
- Mills Av
- Orlando Science Center & John Young Planetarium
- Winter Park
- US Naval Training Center
- Lake Baldwin
- Princeton St
- Leu Gdns
- Ivanhoe Park
- Lake Ivanhoe
- Virginia Dr
- Lake Druid
- Lake Susannah
- Lake Adair
- Orange Av
- Bumby Av
- Maguire Blvd
- Bennet Rd
- Old Cherry
- E COLONIAL DR
- Lake Concorde
- Naval & Marine Corp Training
- Arena Bob Carr Aud
- Robinson Dr
- YMCA
- Lake Barton
- Orlando Executive Airport
- Church St Station
- Lawson Park
- Red Cross
- Lake Underhill
- Citrus Bowl Field
- Magnolia Av
- Mills Av
- EAST-WEST EXPWY
- To Walt Disney World
- Gore St
- Cherokee Exceptional Education School
- Lake Davis

Scale in Miles
Scale in Kilometres

**CENTRAL ORLANDO MAP**

designated areas in restaurants. Monorail trains run between the terminals and the arrival/departure gates and there are lots of people-movers.

The airport is extremely user-friendly, with banks, shops, a 24-hr post office and souvenir shops where you can also buy tickets for Sea World, Universal Studios and Walt Disney World. There are three duty-free shops airside. Information centres offering multilingual services are located in front of the security checkpoint for gates 1–59 in the Great Hall, and in front of the security checkpoint for gates 60–99 in the Hotel Atrium; open daily 0700–2300.

The airport is served by buses operated by **Lynx**, the local transport authority. Service no.11 operates to and from the downtown bus station, with buses running hourly from the airport between 0640 and 2340 (reduced service Sun and public holidays). Buses from downtown operate 0552–2245. Service no.42 links the airport and International Dr., with buses running hourly in each direction from 0525–1950 (no Sun or public holiday services). The stop for both services is on the airport's 'A' Side and the journey time is about 50 mins. The fare is $0.75.

A number of taxi, shuttle bus and limousine services operate between the airport and hotels and attractions in the area. Passengers using a taxi are advised to choose a metered cab and/or confirm the fare with the driver before setting off. Taxi rates average $2.50 for the first mile and $1.50 for each additional mile. Shuttle and limousine fares from the airport to International Dr., Lake Buena Vista or downtown Orlando range from $10–25 for adults and $5–15 for children.

Those in a hurry might like to consider the helicopter service that whisks travellers from the roof of the main terminal building to downtown Orlando in minutes. The cost: $50–$75.

### By Car

In Florida, it seems, all roads lead to Orlando – certainly the city lies at the heart of a net of intersecting major highways. I-4 sweeps from Tampa in the west to Daytona Beach on the east coast. Florida's Turnpike funnels traffic from I-75 south-east to Palm Beach and on to Miami. Other highways reach out in all directions. From the airport, the Beeline Expressway intersects to the west with the turnpike and I-4, which provides access to downtown Orlando to the east and Walt Disney World and Kissimmee to the west. East of the airport, the Beeline, a toll road, provides a fast route to the John F. Kennedy Space Center and the Atlantic beaches. Hwy 192 is also known as Irlo Bronson Memorial Hwy, Vine St and Space Coast Parkway.

## GETTING AROUND

Orlando and its many attractions cover a wide area, so some form of transport is a must for sightseers. There was a time when visitors without a car would have been at a distinct disadvantage, but there have been big improvements in public transport. However, no matter how you get to an attraction, there will be a fair amount of foot-slogging. Wear footwear that gives support to the ankles and soles of your feet and dress comfortably – shorts and a T-shirt will be fine most of the time. The quietest days for attractions such as Sea World, Universal Studios and Walt Disney World are Sun, Thur and Fri.

### Public Transport

**Lynx**, the transport authority for Orange, Seminole and Osceola counties, operates from the **Downtown Bus Station**, *78*

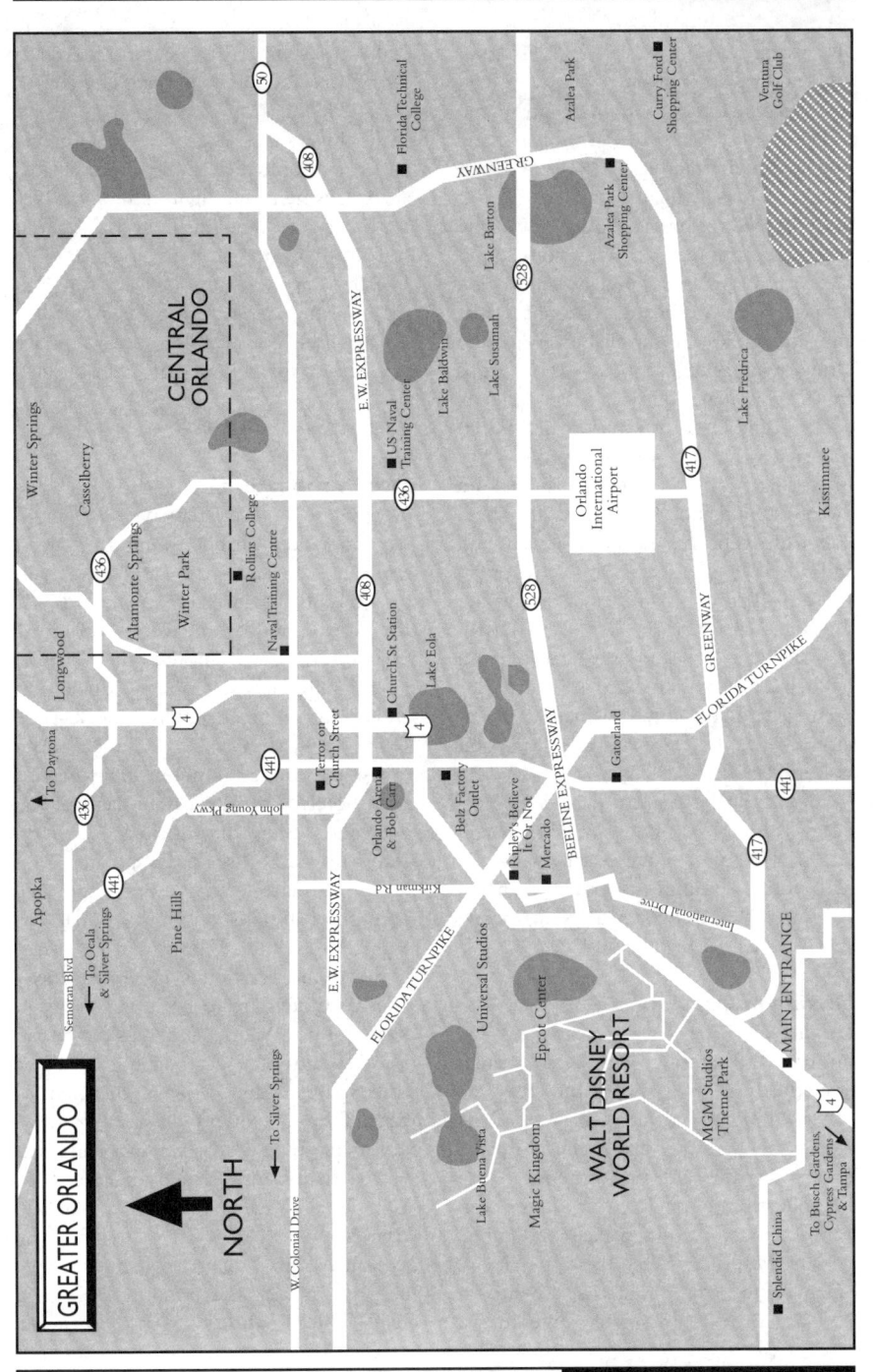

# ORLANDO

**GREATER ORLANDO MAP**

W. Central Blvd; tel: (407) 841-8240. Lynx claims that a bus will take you almost any place you want to go in the Orlando area. The cash fare for a single ride is $0.75; transfers, which save you having to pay a second full fare if you need to change buses, cost $0.10. The exact fare must be tendered if you pay on the bus. Otherwise purchase multi-ride tickets before you board. Discount tickets and timetables are available from the Downtown Bus Station. Lynx bus stops carry a paw mark logo.

A recent Lynx innovation is **I-Ride**, otherwise known as the International Dr. Resort Area Shuttle, a fleet of buses in a livery of blue, hot pink and teal. These colourful vehicles transport visitors up and down International Dr.'s tourist strip every 5–10 mins, from Sea World at the south end to American Way at the north. In summer the buses run from 0700–0200 daily. The fare is $0.75 (children free). Lynx hopes to make the service free to hotel guests and attraction visitors.

**Taxis** can be found in ranks at most hotels. Orlando's longest-established and largest fleet, with metered rates and the city's only computer-operated despatch system, is the **Yellow Cab Company**, *234 W. Gore St; tel: (407) 422-4561.*

## Driving in Orlando

Driving in Orlando is a fairly relaxed business and although the most popular attractions are well spread out they are easy to find and reach. There is an abundance of parking space. Downtown, there's a park and ride scheme – the FreeBee shuttle service – so drivers can park in central parking garages and public parking lots, then take a free bus on a circular route over about 12 downtown blocks. Buses run every five mins, 0640–1900 Mon–Fri. For information on the service and public parking charges *tel: (407) 246-2154.*

Highways are wide and well maintained and traffic, by European standards at least, is generally light, although Hwy 50 can be busy in the industrial section just east of downtown Orlando. The *Florida Official Transportation Map* and maps in the *Official Visitors Guide* and *See Orlando* (see Tourist Information, p. 230) are suitable for sightseeing.

## STAYING IN ORLANDO

### Accommodation

You name it and Orlando is certain to have it – and probably several times over. Almost every international hotel chain has at least one property in the area. At the last count there were well over 80,000 rooms, with more in the pipeline.

Orlando/Orange County Convention and Visitors Bureau publishes a 60-page *Official Accommodations Guide* listing everything from campsites to up-market suite hotels. The guide is available at the Mercado Visitor Information Center on International Dr. (see p. 230).

The smartest and most expensive accommodation is on International Dr. and in Lake Buena Vista and Walt Disney World. Cheaper hotels and many inexpensive motels are to be found between Walt Disney World and Kissimmee on Hwy 192. Another reasonably priced area is in South Orlando close to the international airport. Downtown Orlando has a dozen or so hotels of varying standards. Hotel chains in Orlando include *BW, Ch, DI, GT, Hd, HJ, Hn, Hy, Ma, Rd, Rm, Sh, TL.*

Some of Orlando's hotels have become tourist attractions in their own right. **The Peabody**, *9801 International*

## ORLANDO

*Dr., Orlando, FL 32819; tel: (407) 352-4000* or *800-PEABODY* (toll-free in US), is a 27-storey luxury hotel with an eccentric tradition. Daily at 1100 a squad of mallards – four ducks and a drake, who live in a Royal Duck Palace within the hotel – take a lift to the lobby where they march along a red carpet to the tune of Sousa's *The King Cotton March* before spending the day in a marble fountain.

**Disney's Contemporary Resort**, *PO Box 10,000, Lake Buena Vista, FL 32830-1000; tel: (407) 934-7639*, is one of nine up-market properties within Walt Disney World (WDW). This ultra-modern hotel has a monorail station inside its lobby. Guests can take a free ride to Magic Kingdom and EPCOT Center.

Not surprisingly perhaps, Disney hotels tend be heavily themed, a fashion underscored in three of the newest WDW properties.

The moderately-priced **Disney's All-Star Music Resort** is a 1920-room hotel with giant musical instruments, top hats, musical notes, DJ equipment and an over-sized neon-lit juke box. One swimming pool is in the shape of a guitar, the other a grand piano.

Huge football helmets, megaphones, surfboards and basketballs decorate **Disney's All-Star Sports Resort**, also containing 1920 rooms and moderately priced. **Disney's Wilderness Lodge**, a pricey 728-room property, is all logs and stone, reflecting the Wild West of a century ago. There are tepees, totem poles, Indian artefacts, sketches, maps and watercolours.

Bed and Breakfast facilities are thin on the ground in Orlando. **Buckets Bermuda Bay Hideaway**, *1825 N. Mills Ave, Orlando, FL 32803; tel: (407) 896-4111* or *800-929 2428* (toll-free in US), has an award-winning restaurant and a wine cellar with 35,000 bottles. Another moderately priced establishment is **Perrihouse Bed & Breakfast Inn**, *10417 State Rd 535, Orlando, FL 32836; tel: (407) 876-4830* or *800-780-4830*.

Campers and RV travellers have a good choice. Disney's **Fort Wilderness Resort and Campground**, within Walt Disney World, (contact Disney's Contemporary Resort, above) has 1200 pitches and facilities for watersports, cycling, jogging and horse-riding on 740 acres.

**Kampgrounds of America** (KOA) has two locations. **Kissimmee/Orlando KOA**, *4771 W. Bronson Hwy, Kissimmee, FL 34746; tel: (407) 396-2400*, has a tent village and cabins. It is on Hwy 192, close to Walt Disney World and has a shuttle service to the attractions. **Orlando SE KOA**, *12343 Narcoossee Rd, Orlando, FL 32827; tel: (407) 277-5075*, is on County Rte 15, five miles south off the Beeline, and has cabins and an attractions shuttle. Both KOA grounds have a range of on-site recreational facilities.

**Yogi Bear's Jellystone Camp Resort**, *9200 Turkey Lake Rd, Orlando, FL 32819; tel: (407) 351-4394*, is handy for Walt Disney World and Sea World. More campsites are strung along US-192 near Kissimmee.

**HI: Orlando International Youth Hostel**, *227 N. Eola Dr., Orlando, FL 32801; tel: (407) 843-8888*. This Spanish-style hostel is downtown, overlooking Lake Eola. Female members of AYH can stay at the **Young Women's Community Club**, *107 E. Hillcrest St; tel: (407) 425-2502*.

### Eating and Drinking

The *Official Visitors Guide* devotes 20 pages to a list of eating places, ranging from haute cuisine restaurants in five-star hotels to fast food cafés, but there are many other places that are not listed. There can hardly be a taste or budget that isn't accommodated.

International Dr. has the widest choice, but the Church St area downtown and Hwy 192 out towards Kissimmee are also well served. The cost of eating out can be reduced by discount coupons from tourist publications.

Each of the area's major attractions has a host of restaurants, cafés and food stalls. One of the cheapest places to eat – especially for breakfast – is the food court in the Mercado Village on International Dr.

Supermarkets with extensive delicatessens can be found at shopping centres like **Colonial Plaza Mall** on *E. Colonial Dr.*, **Crossroads of Lake Buena Vista** and the **Florida Mall** on *S. Orange Blossom Trail* near the Sand Lake Rd intersection.

Among a wide range of establishments offering frankly American fare is **Austin's**, *8633 International Dr.; tel: (407) 363-9575*, a moderately-priced restaurant where hickory-grilled dishes of the south-west are served by gaslight. **Clarkie's Restaurant**, *3110 S. Orange Ave; tel: (407) 859-1690*, has been serving budget-priced Florida dishes since 1959. Guitar-shaped **Hard Rock Cafe** at *5800 Kirkman Rd; tel: (407) 351-7425*, adjoins Universal Studios and offers a moderate to pricey menu for those who care more about rock 'n' roll than they do about food. **The B-Line Diner** at the Peabody Hotel (see Accommodation, p. 234) serves classic burgers, steaks, seafood, milkshakes and home-made ice cream in the chrome and pastel decor of the 1950s, with prices ranging from budget to moderate.

**Ming Court**, *9188 International Dr.,* *tel: (407) 351-9988*, is a favourite with Orlando business folk. It's pricey, but the Chinese dishes are legendary.

### Communications

Branches of the US Post Office are to be found in most Orlando neighbourhoods. The main office, open 24 hrs, is at *10401 Tradeport Dr.; tel: (407) 850-6288*. The Downtown office is at *46 E. Robinson St; tel: (407) 843-5673*.

Other branches handy for visitors are: *12541 State Rd 535; tel: (407) 828-2606, 440 Orange Blossom Trail; tel: (407) 843-6400, 501 S. Kirkman Rd; tel: (407) 293-6410, 7707 S Orange Ave; tel: (407) 855-3010, 10450 Turkey Lake Rd; tel: (407) 361-9037*. Business hours: 0900–1700 Mon–Fri, 0900–1200 Sat.

The area tel code for Orlando is *(407)*.

### Money

There is a **Thomas Cook Foreign Exchange** office at *55 West Church St, Suite 120, Orlando, FL 32801; tel: (407) 839-1700*.

## ENTERTAINMENT

Orlando is devoted to entertainment, day and night. Theme parks apart (see p. 241), there are lots of things to see and do for visitors of all ages. The daily newspaper, *Orlando Sentinel,* lists concerts, operas, recitals, ballets, plays and other entertainment and cultural activities in its *Calendar* section published on Fri. Listings also appear in the tourist publications mentioned above.

### Theatres

For theatre-lovers, **Orlando Broadway Series** presents a late-Oct–May season of national and touring productions of Broadway plays and musicals at the 2500-seat **Bob Carr Performing Arts**

Centre, *201 S. Orange Ave; tel: (407) 423-9999*. The professional **Orlando Opera Company** performs at *1111 N. Orange Ave; tel: (407) 426-1717*.

**Hilarities Comedy Theatre**, *5251 International Dr.; tel: (407) 352-7161*, features live stand-up comedy by well-known television entertainers. Teams of comedy actors compete in improvised acts at **Sak Theatre Comedy Labs**, a 150-seat theatre at *45 E. Church St; tel: (407) 648-0001*.

## Entertainment Complexes

The city's premier night-time entertainment centre is undoubtedly **Church Street Station**, at *124 W. Church St; tel: (407) 422-2434*. This complex of restaurants, shopping arcades, bars and discos is an eccentric collection of restored warehouses, hotels and shops associated with the old downtown railroad station. Dixieland is the sound at Rosie O'Grady's Good Time Emporium, with blue grass and folk at Apple Annie's Courtyard. The Cheyenne Saloon and Opera House features country and western and Phineas Phogg's Balloon Works is the place for disco dancing to the current hits. Live music from the 1950s onwards can be heard in the Victorian-style Orchid Garden Ballroom. Church Street Station is open daily 1100–0200. Admission: $15.95.

Nearby is **Terror on Church Street**, at the *corner of Church St and Orange Ave; tel: (407) 649-FEAR (3327)*. Featuring a Dracula-themed set, this showplace combines theatre, state of the art sound and lighting and the element of surprise to satisfy those who like to be scared. Open Tues–Thur and Sun 1900–midnight, Fri–Sat 1900–0100. Admission: $12.

New Year's Eve is celebrated every night of the year at **Pleasure Island**, part of the Walt Disney World complex; *tel: (407) 934-7781*. Lots of music here: rhythm and blues to modern jazz at the Pleasure Island Jazz Club; rock 'n' roll on skates at the XZFR ('zephyr') Rockin' Roller Drome; country and western in the Neon Armadillo Bar and the authentic New Orleans sound aboard the *Empress Lily* riverboat. The nightly New Year is announced with cannonfire, bells, fireworks and dancing in the streets. Open daily 1900–0200. Admission: $14.95.

## Dinner Shows

Dinner shows form a major part of Orlando's night-time entertainment programme.

**Arabian Nights Dinner Attraction**, *6225 W. Irlo Bronson Memorial Dr.; tel: (407) 239-9221 or 1-800-553-6116 (toll-free)*, combines virtuoso horsemanship with a four-course prime ribs dinner. Admission: $34.95; children $19.95; discount for senior citizens.

Italian fare accompanies speakeasy entertainment, with gangsters, dames and cops, at **Capone's Dinner and Show**, *4740 W. Hwy 192; tel: (407) 397-2378*. Admission: $29.50; children half price.

At **King Henry's Feast**, *8984 International Dr.; tel: (407) 351-5151 or 1-800-883-8181 (toll-free)*, guests are entertained by minstrels and magicians as costumed wenches serve a 'banquet' of roast chicken and ribs. Admission: $31.95; children $19.95. A similar meal is served by similar wenches at **Medieval Times**, *4510 W. Irlo Bronson Memorial Hwy, tel: (407) 239-0214 or 1-800-229-8300 (toll-free)*, but here the entertainment is provided by knights indulging in jousting, swordplay and other tournament games. Admission: $31.95; children $21.95.

## ORLANDO

**Sleuth's Mystery Dinner Show**, *Republic Sq, Republic Dr.; tel: (407) 363-1985*, is murder-while-you-eat, with the mystery unfolding as the meal progresses. Admission: $31.95; children $21.95.
**Wild Bill's Wild West Dinner Extravaganza**, at *Fort Liberty, 5260 W. Hwy 192; tel: (407) 363-3550 or 1-800-883-8181*, is a dinnertime romp with the US Cavalry, cowboys, Indians, ropers, knife throwers, chorus girls and clog dancers. Admission: $31.95; children $19.95.

### Nightclubs

Most nightclubs are located in the major hotels, but there are a number of independent establishments with very elastic opening times. Prices are moderate.

**Baja Beach Club**, *8510 W. Palm Parkway, tel: (407) 239-99629*, boasts outrageous DJs, claims to be Orlando's only party bar and offers 'high energy' dancing. Open Mon–Fri 1700–0300, Sat–Sun 1900–0300.

**Club Juana**, *6150 S. Hwy 17-92, Fern Park; tel: (407) 831-1855*, features female entertainers and 'adult' entertainment. Open Mon–Sat 1200–0200, Sun 1800–0200.

**Cricketers' Arms**, *8445 International Dr.; tel: (407) 354-0686*. Budget eating and drinking with an English pub atmosphere and nightly entertainment. Open daily 1100–0200.

**Fat Tuesday**, *8445 International Dr.; tel: (407) 351-5311*, specialises in frozen drinks and offers free entertainment. Crawfish and shrimp boil nights are a special feature. Open Mon–Fri 1600–0200, Sat–Sun 1100–0200. There's another Fat Tuesday at *41 W. Church St; tel: (407) 843-6104*. Open Mon–Sat 1100–0200, Sun 1200–0200.

Karaoke addicts will doubtless head for the **Star Search Lounge** at *Howard Johnson Universal Tower, 5905 International Dr.; tel: (407) 351-2100*. Karaoke and other entertainment is staged seven nights a week and there's a happy hour from 1700–1900.

**Howl at the Moon Saloon**, *55 W. Church St, Suite 244; tel: (407) 841-9118*, has duelling pianists pounding out classic

---

### How It All Began

Orlando was first known as Jernigan, named after Aaron Jernigan, a settler who arrived from Georgia in 1842. According to local lore the city's name was changed in 1857 to honour a soldier, Orlando Reeves, who was killed by an arrow after warning sleeping colleagues of an Indian attack.

As more people moved into the area after the turn of the century, Orlando started to develop as a railhead and distribution point for the surrounding citrus groves – and that, very largely, is what it still was when Walt Disney woke up to the area's dream potential.

Today, Orlando is the seat of Orange County, although its metropolitan area spills over also into neighbouring Osceola and Seminole Counties.

About 122,000 people are employed in tourism and tourism-related industries – about 35,000 in hotels, an estimated 41,000 in attractions and 46,000 in restaurants.

The importance of tourism to the area is underlined by the fact that visitors spend an average of $73 a day, a collective spend of $5.1 billion. Tourists save local taxpayers $95 million a year, or $203 per household.

## ORLANDO

rock 'n' roll and leading the crowd in a noisy singsong. Open daily 1800–0200.

Las Vegas-style revues with 65 showgirls are produced on three stages at **Pure Platinum**, *5581 S. Orange Blossom Trail; tel: (407) 859-4146*. Open Mon–Fri 1300–0200, Sat–Sun 1900–0200.

### Sport and Activities

Like the rest of Florida, Orlando is golf and tennis crazy and lots of facilities are available to visitors.

The **Arnold Palmer Golf Academy**, *9000 Bay Hill Blvd; tel: (407) 876-2429*, offers top-class tuition daily 0800–1800.

**Cypress Creek Golf and Country Club**, *5353 Vineland Rd; tel: (407) 351-3151*, has an 18-hole championship course, driving range, restaurant, lounge and tennis academy. Open daily 0630–2100.

**Grand Cypress Academy of Golf**, *1 Grand Cypress Blvd; tel: (407) 239-1975*, has full teaching facilities with computer/video analyses for individuals or groups. At the same location are the **Grand Cypress Racquet Club**, *tel: (407) 239-1234*; and the **Grand Cypress Equestrian Center**; *tel: (407) 239-4608*.

The **International Golf Club**, *6351 International Golf Club Rd; tel: (407) 239-6909*, has an 18-hole championship course, driving range, snack bar/lounge and club and shoe rentals. Open daily 0630–2200.

Adventurous souls may like to take to the air. Orlando has a number of companies offering hot air balloon flights, among them **Airborne Balloons**, *5465 Lake Margaret Dr.; tel: (407) 380-7146*, **Balloon Flights of Florida**, *3529 Edgewater Dr.; tel: (407) 841-8787*; **Rise and Float Balloon Tours**, *5767 Major Blvd; tel: (407) 363-4418* and **Orange Blossom Balloons**, *Lake Buena Vista; tel: (407) 239-7677*. If you fancy your chances as a dogfight ace try **Fighter Pilots USA**, *3033 W. Patrick St, Kissimmee; tel: (407) 931-4333*. You fly a plane in combat conditions with an expert fighter pilot.

For spectator sports **Florida Citrus Sports**, *1 Citrus Bowl Pl; tel: (407) 423-2476*, promotes and stages high school, collegiate and professional world class events.

There are four major splash parks in the Orlando area. **River Country**, *Lake Buena Vista; tel: (407) 824-4321*, has twisting water slides, swings, white water rapid ride, sandy beach and a nature trail. At **Walt Disney World Typhoon Lagoon**, *Lake Buena Vista; tel: (407) 843-4321*, you can snorkel, plummet down flumes and ride in the world's biggest wave lagoon.

New in 1995, **Blizzard Beach** is another Disney water park – the largest yet. The bizarre theme is winter sports, so the various slides and rides are based on ski jumps and toboggan runs. It also has what Disney claims is the world's longest family white water raft ride. The whole thing is built around a snow-capped mountain.

**Wet 'N Wild**, *6200 International Dr.; tel: (407) 351-1800*, has 25 acres of rides, slides and flumes – including one that is seven storeys high. There are safe, diminutive versions of most things for toddlers.

### SHOPPING

Shopping opportunities in the Orlando area include large retail malls, speciality centres, discount or factory outlets and open-air bargain 'flea' markets. Most malls and shopping centres are open Mon–Sat 1000–2100, Sun 1200–1800.

# ORLANDO

Speciality shops are usually open Mon–Sat 1000–1800.

The area's largest factory outlet – claimed to be the largest anywhere – is **Belz Factory Outlet World**, *5401 W. Oakridge Rd*, (at the north end of International Dr.); *tel: (407) 352-9600*. More than 160 outlets are housed in two massive enclosed malls and four shopping centres, all within walking distance of each other. Almost every type of commodity you can think of is available at savings of up to 75 per cent.

Other factory outlets include **International Diamond Centre**, *5536 International Dr.; tel: (407) 352-6620*, and **Quality Outlet Centres**, *5527 International Dr.; tel: (407) 423-5885*. The **Central Florida Resale Association**, *6309 Grand National Dr.; tel: (407) 352-2446*, represents 30 resale and consignment stores in the area. It publishes a free map and organises group shopping tours by bus.

The Orange Blossom Trail, known locally as OBT, is lined with superstores and shopping malls, with the greatest concentration between Sand Lake Rd and the Central Florida Parkway.

Major shopping malls in Greater Orlando include **Church Street Station Exchange**, *129 W. Church St; tel: (407) 422-2434*, **Colonial Plaza Mall**, two miles east of downtown Orlando on *Colonial Dr. (Hwy 50), tel: (407) 894-3603*, **Fashion Sq Mall**, *3201 Colonial Dr.; tel: (407) 896-1131*, **Florida Mall**, *8001 S. Orange Blossom Trail; tel: (407) 851-6255*, **Marketplace at Dr Phillips**, *Dr Phillips Blvd and Sand Lake Rd; tel: (407) 345-8668*, **Mercado Mediterranean Village**, *8445 International Dr.; tel: (407) 345-9337*.

Speciality shops range from the **American Tourister Factory Outlet**, *5431 International Dr.; tel: (407) 352-7207*, which specialises in quality luggage, business cases, sports bags and backpacks, to **Yes Brasil**, *5571 International Dr.; tel: (407) 351-3684*, where you can buy cameras, videos, hifi and other goods.

If Florida's sunshine becomes a strain, a trip to the **U.S. Sunglass Exchange** might be advisable. Located at *5544 International Dr.; tel: (407) 345-8504*, the Exchange claims to have the nation's largest selection of sunglasses and accessories. And if you get hooked on the state's oranges and grapefruit, **Orange Blossom Indian River Citrus**, *5151 S. Orange Blossom Trail; tel: (407) 855-2837 or 1-800-624-8835 (toll-free)*, will pack and deliver fruit to any American destination. The store is open daily 0800–1800.

International travellers visiting Orlando may purchase tax-free goods to take home. Thousands of tax-free items are available at **Orlando Duty Free** *8480 Palm Parkway; tel: (407) 239-8165*, which runs a free shuttle bus service to and from hotels. Open daily 1000–2200.

Outside Orlando, but worth visiting, are two big flea markets. **192 Flea Market**, *4301 W. Vine St, Kissimmee; tel: (407) 396-4555*, has over 400 booths selling everything from Disney souvenirs to clothing, jewellery and electronics. Open daily 0900–1800. **Flea World**, *4311 North Hwy (Hwy 17-92), Sanford; tel: (407) 628-2233*, is said to be America's largest, with 1600 stalls spread over 104 acres. Lots of food stalls and entertainment. Open Fri–Sun 0800–1700.

Collectors may want to head for **Antique Row**, *N. Orange Ave*, where the road is lined by about 30 antique stores and malls. From I-4 take Exit 43 (Princeton Ave) and go east to traffic lights; turn right on to N. Orange Ave.

## Sightseeing

Orlando's attractions are big and spread over a wide area, so transport is a must. The major theme parks can be reached by shuttle buses and public transport.

### Walt Disney World

To reach Walt Disney World, from the Mercado, turn right onto International Dr., then left on to Sand Lake Rd. Head west on I-4. From Exits 27, 26 or 25, follow signs to Walt Disney World.

**Disney-MGM Studios**, *Walt Disney World Resort, Lake Buena Vista; tel: (407) 824-4321*, is Disney's answer to Universal Studios Florida. The entertainment is non-stop, spectacular and sometimes spontaneous. 'Film stars' wander along Hollywood Boulevard, gossip writers and talent scouts chat up the customers. The newest experience is *The Twilight Zone Tower of Terror*. Visitors enjoy a number of 'supernatural' encounters in a deserted, ramshackle hotel and plunge 13 storeys in a failed lift. Open daily 0900–2300 (Feb–Aug), daily 0900–2100 (Sept–Jan). Admission: $36; children aged three–nine $29.

Dominated by the huge golf ball shape of Spaceship Earth, its communications pavilion, **Epcot Center** is a 260-acre examination of the world from technological and social viewpoints. *Future World* deals with land and sea, communications and transportation, health, energy and imagination – with lots of whizzbang effects. The latest exhibit is *Innoventions*, where visitors see and use the products of tomorrow. *World Showcase* presents the culture, cuisine, crafts and entertainment of various countries in 11 pavilions built around a lagoon. Open daily 0900–2300

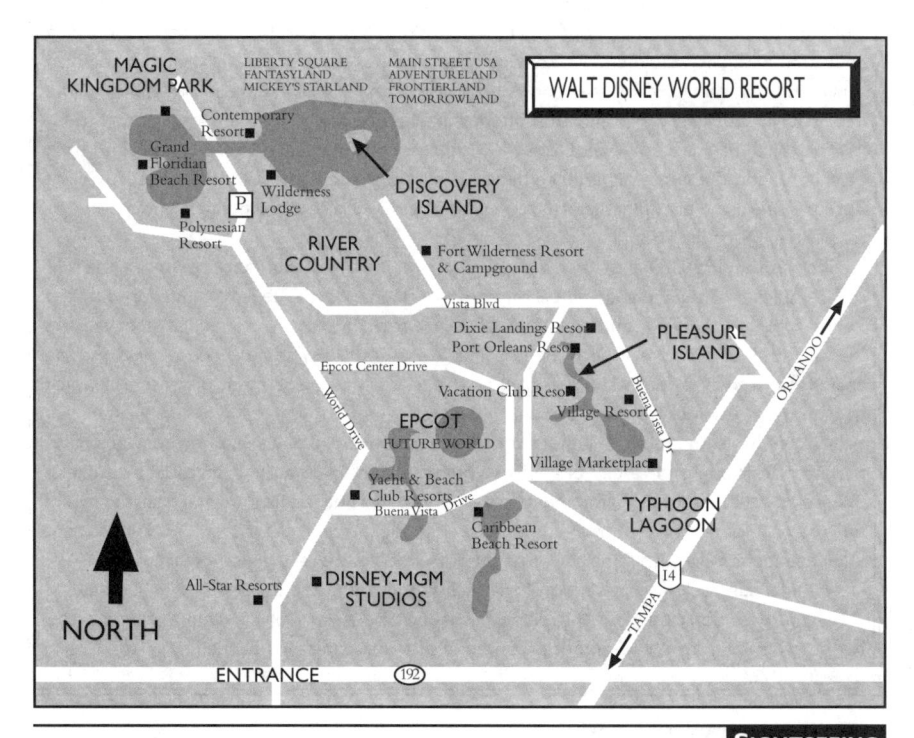

## A World Of Its Own

Every day Florida's Walt Disney World Resort welcomes about 100,000 visitors. Servicing their needs or entertaining them are up to 35,000 employees. All these people are there because of the way a black-eared, white-gloved mouse and his entourage of cartoon characters have been marketed worldwide.

Mickey Mouse qualified for his retirement pension several years ago, but he still packs them in to the Magic Kingdom day after day, with ever more fanciful exploits. The latest is Mickey Mania, a zany parade held every afternoon, with Mickey as grand marshal.

Floats, stilt-walkers, dancers, roller bladers, bikers, skateboarders, Minnie Mouse, Donald Duck, Pluto, Goofy and a couple of dozen of their mates roll along Main Street, USA, amid a medley of music and monster-size Mickey toys – Mickey Mouse clocks, cameras, BMS bikes, trikes, punchbags and puppets.

Mickey's famous bright yellow shoes, four ft high, and his gloves blown up to giant size, dance along the street. Pinocchio, Peter Pan, Snow White, Chip and Dale, Winnie the Pooh – all jumping up and down, tireless in the heat, put on an incredible whizz-bang show.

A cast of 'Disney Humanimals' perform in a live version of *The Lion King* film. Larger-than-life characters identical to their animated counterparts perform in the Fantasyland Theatre.

As well as Main Street, USA and Fantasyland, the 100-acre Magic Kingdom, which opened in 1971, presents dozens of shows and adventures in Frontierland, Adventureland, Liberty Square, Tomorrowland and Mickey's Starland.

Behind the fantasy lies reality, and the Epcot Centre – the Experimental Prototype Community of Tomorrow – opened in 1982, has a more cerebral approach combining education with entertainment. The newest innovation is 'Innovention', in which visitors can touch and test things which may soon enter their lives – wrist radios and telephones, the information superhighway, television phones, filmless cameras.

The third main area of Walt Disney World resort, Disney MGM Studios, takes us back to fantasy, and the latest experience here to chill the spine is the Twilight Zone Tower of Terror. There are also Pleasure Island, which offers a choice of nightclubs, and a zoological park at Discovery Island.

Back in the 1960s Disney cast a canny eye over nearly 30,000 acres – more than 40 square miles – of swampland and pasture at Lake Buena Vista. The land is bordered by the Reedy Creek waterway, and the Walt Disney World Resort is still officially called the Reedy Creek Improvement District. Within a few years the swamp was developed and the crowds poured in. There's still plenty of water, and a wide assortment of vessels in which to explore it, from submarines to sternwheelers.

Visitors have a memorable time, but not a cheap one. You pay separately for each park, though a four-day or five-day pass gives you access to them all and saves a few dollars. Where some of Florida's major theme parks are concerned, adulthood starts at the age of ten years. A four-day pass for an adult costs $124 (at the time of writing) plus six per cent sales tax. Your daily admission ticket to the park you've selected gives you access to every show, ride, spectacle and attraction for which you can find the energy.

By the way, don't take a picnic. Walt Disney World Resort offers many eating options, but bringing your own food and drink isn't one of them. In fact it's banned.

# ORLANDO

(Feb–Aug), daily 0900–2100 (Sept–Jan). Admission $36; children $29.

**The Magic Kingdom** was the first of the Walt Disney World theme parks. Opened in 1971, it features nearly 50 major shows and adventures on a 100-acre site which is divided into seven fantasy lands. Mickey Mouse reigns over them all and is the star of a noisy, colourful parade that rolls down Main Street USA every afternoon. One of the newest stage shows at the Magic Kingdom is *Legend of the Lion King* featuring the music of Elton John and Tim Rice. Open daily 0900–2300 (Feb–Aug), daily 0900–2100 (Sept–Jan). Admission: $36; children $29.

**Sea World of Florida**
Sea World, *7007 Sea World Dr.; tel: (407) 351-3600*, is at the intersection of I-4 and the Beeline Expressway, ten mins south of downtown Orlando and 15 mins from Orlando International Airport. More than 20 major shows and displays are featured at this long-established marine life park, which has entertainment, educational, research and conservation elements. You need a full day to see everything.

Opened in 1974, the Anheuser-Busch theme park has expanded considerably in the past few years, adding a number of major new attractions and shows. One of these, *Manatees: the Last Generation?*

## Manatees Please

Although manatees are a highly endangered species, getting to meet one - or several – is made easy in Florida. These amiable, slow-moving and docile creatures are vulnerable to injury by boat propellers and fishing lines.

There are places like Homosassa Springs State Wildlife Park in the central west of the state, and Sea World of Florida in Orlando, where injured and orphaned manatees are treated and cared for, where the public can see them in a relaxed natural environment.

Sea World has introduced a *Manatees: The Last Generation?* feature, an education programme geared towards saving the manatee from extinction.

At Homosassa Springs (see St Petersburg–Tallahassee route, p. 292) you can view manatees and thousands of fish of various species from an underwater observatory. There are regular presentations in which the manatees meet the public.

The West Indian manatee – the type native to Florida – is typically about 9 ft long and 1000 lbs in weight, though it can grow up to 13 ft and 3000 lbs. It cannot be described as beautiful, being simply built, rather like an inflated oval-shape with a spatula-like tail, two forelimbs and nostrils which close when the animal is submerged – it can stay under water for up to 15 minutes when resting.

The manatee has a benevolent expression and is indeed quite harmless, with no means of defending itself. Although known in some countries as the sea cow, the herbivorous manatee is believed to share a common ancestry with the elephant.

Manatees are protected by federal and state laws. 'Manatee Area' notices are displayed in waters where manatees are known to be present. In these areas and others where the presence of manatees is likely motor boats must be operated at idle/no wake speed.

Estimates put the US manatee population at fewer than 1800.

enables visitors to enter the underwater world of the manatee and other creatures in its habitat – fish, birds and the native Florida turtle.

*Shamu Close Up* presents a killer whale habitat, showing playtimes and training sessions and outlining Sea World's successful killer whale breeding programme. Another presentation, *Shamu, New Visions,* introduces Shamu and two baby killer whales born in 1993. Through live action and video imagery, *Shamu: World Focus* shows killer whales in remote locations and stages an underwater 'ballet'.

A laser and fireworks show with a 60-ft screen of water which produces wonderful effects is the new after-dark extravaganza *Mermaids, Myths and Monsters.*

The park's most ambitious project, *Wild Arctic,* opened in 1995 to provide polar excitement for visitors . The attraction simulates a hazardous helicopter trip in the frozen north and explores the hull of an ancient ship. From above and below water visitors see polar bears, seals, walruses, beluga whales and fish.

As well as the performances by whales, dolphins and other marine mammals for which Sea World is famous, there are many shows and exhibits, like *Penguin Encounter, Terrors of the Deep (*a display of barracuda, poisonous fish, sharks and other dangerous sea creatures), *Tropical Reef* and *Caribbean Tide Pool.*

Open daily 0900–1900 (hours vary during summer and holidays). Admission: $34.90; children $29.95, under three free. Parking costs $5 per car and $7 per RV or camper. Strollers and wheelchairs can be rented.

## Gatorland

**Gatorland**, *14501 S. Orange Blossom Trail; tel: (407) 855-5496.* More than 5000 alligators and crocodiles inhabit the park's extensive pools. *Crocodiles of the World* is an exhibit showing the differences between indigenous alligators and their cousins. There is alligator wrestling, a marsh with an observation tower, a natural cypress swamp and lots of other animals, birds and reptiles. When hunger strikes, you can try alligator cooked Southern style. Open daily 0800–dusk. Admission $11.95.

## Splendid China

**Splendid China**, *3000 Splendid China Blvd, Kissimmee, Fl 34747; tel: (407) 397-8800.* The attraction opened in Dec 1993 and is 12 miles south-west of Orlando on Hwy 192. It is three miles west of I4 (Exit 25B), one mile west of the Walt Disney World entrance. From Hwy 27 exit at Hwy 192 and drive east. Admission is $23.55 for those aged 13 and over, $13 for children aged five to 12. There is no charge for children aged four and under. The attraction is open daily.

Splendid China has replicas of 60 Chinese historical and cultural landmarks and sites, most of them – like the Great Wall of China and the Terra Cotta Warriors – miniaturised. It took exactly a year and a day to construct, at a cost of $100 million, and is conceived as a 10,000-mile journey through 3000 years of history. Live entertainment, shops and restaurants are on the 76-acre site.

The entrance is through a lifesize replica of Suzhou Gardens, an urban area in eastern China. It gives visitors a view of a typical Chinese main street in about AD 1300.

The 4200-mile Great Wall of China has been reproduced as a half-mile version. Even so, more than six million bricks reduced from the original three-ft blocks to bricks one and two inches long, were meticulously laid by hand by Chinese artisans.

The re-creation of Beijing's Forbidden City provides a majestic focal point. The original Imperial Palace was built in 1420 and was the residence and official headquarters for a succession of emperors, their families and staff. Even in miniature, the Potala Palace is impressive. The original, in Lhasa, Tibet, is the most sacred place on earth for millions of Buddhists.

The Mausoleum of Genghis Khan, who died in 1227 and whose empire stretched from mid-Asia to Europe, is carefully reproduced.

The carved Terra Cotta Warriors and their horses, copies of some of the army of more than 6000 discovered by archeologists in 1974, are an impressive sight.

The Leshan Grand Buddha, carved out of the side of a mountain and the height of a 23-storey building, has been scaled down to 35 ft. The original, begun in 719 AD, took 90 years to complete. More 'giants' which are still a spectacle even when miniaturised, are the limestone peaks of the Stone Forest, carved by nature over eons of time into curious forms, some grotesque, others graceful.

The Temple of Confucius, the White Pagoda, the Marco Polo Bridge, the Longman Grottoes, these and many more wonders can be seen at Splendid China, not only in Florida but also in Shenzhen, China, where a similar display opened in 1989. The Florida version operates with a staff of up to 500, mostly Central Floridians but including 160 Chinese employed in specialist entertainment and craft roles.

Among the live entertainments are dancing displays, Mongolian wrestling, martial arts, acrobatics and juggling demonstrations. Shops sell Chinese merchandise. The choice of cuisine covers Cantonese, Tibetan, Mongolian, Mandarin, Hunan, Peking, Szechwan, dim sum and Chiu Chow.

**Universal Studios**
Universal Studios Florida, *1000 Universal Studios Plaza, Orlando, Fl 32819; tel: (407) 363-8000.* The Universal Studios complex is near the intersection of I-4 and the Florida Turnpike. Take I-4 to Exit 30B and the main entrance on Kirkman Rd (Hwy 435) about ½ mile north of I-4. Another entrance on Turkey Lake Rd is reached by leaving I-4 at Sand Lake Rd (Exit 29).

Opening times vary according to the season. Admission: one-day ticket $36; children aged three–nine $29. A two-day ticket is $55 (children $44). Prices do not include tax. Children aged two and under go free. There is parking for more than 7000 vehicles at $5 a day for cars and $7 for RVs and trailers.

Universal Studios Florida is a $650 million project open 365 days a year. It is a working film and television production studio with movie-themed attractions and daredevil stunt shows.

'Ride the Movies' features take you right inside blockbuster films like *Earthquake* (feel the heat of the flames), *King Kong* (smell his banana breath), *Back to the Future* (hurtle through fog made of liquid nitrogen), *Jaws* (hang on tight as he tries to capsize your boat) and *ET* (travel through space amid hundreds of planets and thousands of stars). Coming soon under the guidance of producer/director Steven Spielberg: *Jurassic Park* and *Casper*.

At other attractions on-site you can see *Ghostbusters* at work, get a backstage view of the *Flintstones* and find out how Alfred Hitchcock presented the shower scene in *Psycho*.

The magic of *Back to the Future – The Ride* is achieved with two domed theatres and seven-storey Omnimax screens which envelop the peripheral vision, giving the feeling that you are being transported into the image. The apparent speed is terrifying. King Kong in *Kongfrontation* weighs six tons, has 7,000 lbs of fur and a 54-ft arm span – he lifts your tram into the air with ease. The mega-tremor in *Earthquake* releases and recycles 65,000 gallons of water every six mins.

One of the most popular entertainments is the Animal Actors Show, in which a varied cast of famous animal and bird movie stars demonstrate their talent in an outdoor theatre.

Within the present Universal Studios site you can walk in sets of New York, San Francisco, New England and Hollywood street scenes. Here and in the restaurants you are likely to meet Marilyn Monroe, Mae West, the Marx Brothers, Laurel and Hardy, Lucille Ball, Charlie Chaplin and other celebrity look-alikes. You can see how horror make-up is applied, watch a Wild West stunt show and daring high-speed boating stunts involving pyrotechnics.

Plans for a major multi-billion dollar expansion called **Universal City Florida** are underway. The development, to the south of the existing attraction, will include a night-time entertainment complex, shops, five themed hotels with a total of 4300 guest-rooms, extensive conference facilities, an 18-hole PGA golf course and a championship tennis centre, all inter-connected by waterways and lakes. The entire complex, including Universal Studios, is expected eventually to employ 18,000 people, which will make it Orlando's biggest single employer. The first two hotels are scheduled for completion in 1997 and the others by 2000.

## Other Attractions
**Church Street Station Historical Tours**. To celebrate its 20th anniversary, Church Street Station has introduced walking tours of its block-long complex in downtown Orlando. Visitors learn the history of the city's original railroad depot and its development into a tourist attraction. They also get the chance to examine at leisure the many antiques and other artefacts on display in the buildings. It all ends up in a sing-song with the banjo player in Rosie O'Grady's Good Time Emporium. Tours daily 1100–1500. Admission: $8; tour/lunch packages from $13.28.

**Leu Gardens and House**, *1730 N. Forest Ave; tel: (407) 246-2620*. The house is a fine example of a turn-of-the-century Florida farmhouse and has been restored to reflect the lifestyle of successful farmers and their families during the period 1910–30. The magnificent gardens feature camellias, azaleas, roses, dogwood and orchids and there is a floral clock. Open Tues–Sat 1000–1600, Sun–Mon 1300–1600. Admission: $3; children aged six–16 enter for $1.

**Medieval Life**, *Vine St and Hwy 192, Kissimmee; tel: (407) 396-1518*. An 11th-century village brought to life, with artisans at work with the tools of their day, a bird of prey demonstration and a dungeon and torture chamber for sensation-seekers. Open daily 1600–2100. Admission: $8; children $6.

**Mystery Fun House**, *5767 Major Blvd; tel: (407) 351-3335*. Trails of the unexpected, with magic floors, laughing doors and lots of electronic wizardry. It also encompasses **Starbase Omega**, a laser game featuring adventures in the past and future. Open daily 1000–2300. Admission: Fun House $7.95; Starbase Omega $5.95.

**Turkey Lake Park**, *3401 Hiawassee Rd; tel: (407) 299-5594.* A 300-acre recreational haven with picnic tables, a three-mile cycle trail, hiking trails, two beaches, a swimming pool, a 200-ft fishing pier, canoe rentals, petting zoo and a children's playground designed to accommodate the physically disabled. There is also a campsite with 32 pitches. Open daily 0930–dusk or 1900. Admission: adults $2; children $1.

**U.S. Navy Training Center**, *General Rees Rd; tel: (407) 646-4474.* Commissioned in 1968 and one of the largest military training facilities in the country, the centre is staffed by 16,000 military and civilian personnel. Each Fri at 0945 *sharp* some 600 recruits – men and women – parade with the Navy Band Orlando, the Blue Jacket Chorus, a 50-state flag team and a precision drill team. The ceremonies last about one hour. Admission: free.

**Winter Park Scenic Boat Tour**, *tel: (407) 644-4056.* A gentle cruise through 12 miles of lakes and canals. Daily 1000–1600. Admission charge.

## Art Galleries

**Cornell Museum of Fine Art**, *Rollins College Campus, Fairbanks Ave, Winter Park; tel: (407) 646-2526.* This small gallery contains collections of works by European Old Masters, 19th-century American painters, prints, modern graphics, French bronzes, American decorative art, Indian artefacts and more than 1200 watch keys. Special exhibits are mounted throughout the year. Open Tues–Fri 1000–1700, Sat–Sun 1300–1700. Admission: free.

**Maitland Art Center**, *231 W. Packwood Ave, Maitland; tel: (407) 539-2181.* The center was founded by André Smith in 1937 as a retreat for avant-garde artists and has recently been added to the National Register of Historic Places. It consists of a number of buildings in a walled compound with garden courtyards. Its simple architecture is embellished by 200 Aztec and Mayan carvings. Carvings on the wall of a garden chapel depict the life of Christ. The main building houses a permanent art collection and temporary exhibitions are also staged. Open Mon–Fri 1000–1630, Sat–Sun 1200–1630. Admission: free.

**Charles Hosmer Morse Museum of American Art**, *133 Welbourne Ave, Winter Park; tel: (407) 644-3686.* Founded in 1942, the museum contains an impressive collection of art nouveau by Louis Comfort Tiffany. Its displays of priceless paintings, stained glass windows, jewellery, lamps and other items are drawn from a collection of more than 4,000 pieces, many salvaged from the burnt-out ruins of Tiffany's art nouveau mansion on Long Island. Works by artists such as Emile Galle, John LaFarge, Frank Lloyd Wright, Maxfield Parrish, George Innes and Rene Lalique are frequently shown. Open Tues–Sat 0930–1600, Sun 1300–1600. Admission: $2.50; students and children $1.

**Orlando Museum of Art**, *2416 N. Mills Ave; tel: (407) 896-4231.* The museum's permanent pre-Columbian Gallery houses more than 250 pieces from Mexico, Guatemala, Colombia, Costa Rica, Panama and Peru dating from 1200 BC to AD 1500. Among its permanent collections is a rotating exhibition of 20th-century American and African art. Changing exhibits include collections on loan from international museums and private collectors. Open Tues–Sat 0900–

1700, Sun 1200–1700. Admission: $4; children aged four–ten $2.
**Polasek Foundation**, *633 Osceola Ave, Winter Park; tel: (407) 647-6294.* The home of the sculptor and painter Albin Polasek for the last 16 years of his life is now maintained as a museum-studio. The house and grounds are filled with the artist's most prized pieces and replicas of works which earned him international acclaim. Open Wed–Sat 1000–1600, Sun 1300–1600 (Oct–June). Admission: free.

## Museums
**Central Florida Railroad Museum**, *101 S. Boyd St, Winter Garden: tel: (407) 656-8749 or (904) 748-4377.* Built in 1913, the museum is the former Tavares and Gulf Railroad depot. Faithfully restored, it contains more than 3,000 items – antique whistles, switchlights and other memorabilia. Open Sun 1400–1700 (other visiting times by arrangement). Admission: free.

**Classic Chevy International**, *8235 N. Orange Blossom Trail; tel: (407) 299-1957.* An exhibition of classic Chevrolet cars of 1955–57 – chrome, fins and all. Open Mon–Fri 0800–1700; Sat 0900–1500. Admission: free.

**Fire Station No.3**, *812 E. Rollins St, Loch Haven Park; tel: (407) 897-6350.* Built in 1926 and now a division of Orange County Historical Museum, this two-storey red brick building is the oldest standing firehouse in Orlando. One of only two such museums in Florida, it houses a fascinating collection of firefighting memorabilia, including an 1885 hose cart, a 1908 horse-drawn steamer and a 1915 American La France, the city's first motorised fire truck. A gallery has photographs and murals of Orlando's most devastating fires. Open Mon–Sat 1700, Sun 1200–1700. Admission: $2; senior citizens $1.50; children aged six to 12 $1, under six free.

**Orange County Historical Museum**, *812 E. Rollins St, Loch Haven Park; tel: (407) 897-6350.* The museum traces the history of the county from the days when it was known as Mosquito County, through the Seminole wars, the citrus bonanza, the big freeze of 1894, the 1920s land boom and on to the present. Open Mon–Sat 0900–1700, Sun 1200–1700. Admission $2.

**Orlando Science Center**, *810 E. Rollins St, Loch Haven Park; tel: (407) 896-7151.* A museum and planetarium, the centre features exhibits on astronomy, Florida's natural history, health and physical science, many designed to encourage hands-on participation. Presentations on astronomy are shown in the planetarium on a 40-ft domed screen. At weekends visitors can attend a 'cosmic concert' with music and lasers. Open Mon–Thur 0900–1700, Fri 0900–2100, Sat 0900–1700, Sun 1200–1700. Admission: $6.50; children and seniors $5.50.

**Ripley's Believe It Or Not!** *8201 International Dr.; tel: (407) 345-0501.* Hundreds of unbelievable exhibits in an eccentric showplace. Open daily 1000–2300. Admission charge.

## Wildlife
**Alligatorland Safari Zoo**, *4580 W. Hwy 192; tel: (407) 396-1012.* Alligators, crocodiles and a petting zoo of more approachable animals. Open daily 0830–dusk. Admission $5.95; children $4.50.

**Audubon House**, *1101 Audubon Way, Maitland; tel: (407) 260-8300.* Headquarters of the Florida Audubon Society, which was founded in 1900 and is one of the state's oldest and largest conservation organisation, Audubon House

## ORLANDO

has an exquisite art gallery, a gift shop and an aviary of Florida's native raptors. Open Tues–Sat 1000–1600. Admission: free.
**Discovery Island Zoological Park**, *Walt Disney World Resort, Lake Buena Vista; tel: (407) 824-3784*. Many species of mammals, birds and reptiles may be seen on this island site, and there's a bamboo jungle to explore. Open daily 0900–1900. Admission: $9.50.
**Reptile World Serpentarium**, *5705 E. Bronson Memorial Hwy, St Cloud; tel: (407) 892-6905*. Visitors can watch as snake venom is 'milked' for use in biomedical research. Venom extractions are performed at 1100, 1400 and 1700. The serpentarium houses 60 species of reptiles – including cobras and rattlesnakes – from Florida and the rest of the world. Open Tues–Sat 0900–1730 (closed Sept). Admission: $4.25; children aged six–16 $3.25, aged three–five $2.25.

## The Real Orlando

Behind all the razzmatazz and fantasy there lies a real place called Orlando. It has a few skyscrapers and is enmeshed by long-distance highways, but it still has the soul of a Southern city and is a place where some people, at least, do comparatively normal things for a living.

On the surface, downtown Orlando is not too far removed from the sleepy community that once depended on citrus fruit as the mainstay of its economy. Its streets are pleasantly tree-shaded and it skirts Lake Eola, where you can take a ride on the waterfront in a horse-drawn carriage. In fact, it's a dynamic metropolis rated by *Fortune* magazine as one of the top business cities in the US.

Tourism is only one aspect of the city's economy. Other industries are manufacturing, financial and professional services, agriculture and high technology – there are so many computer-based industries that the area has been called 'Silicon Swamp'.

Among internationally known corporations who have made their home in Orlando are the American Automobile Association, the communications group AT&T, Siemens Stromberg-Carlson and Westinghouse Electric Corporation.

The region boasts a respected technology-orientated university and one of the country's leading research parks, with internationally recognised centres for the study of simulation and training in electro-optics and lasers.

Transportation is a major factor in the city's success. Located more or less in the centre of the state, it has a modern, efficient airport that is said to be the fastest-growing in the US and one of the world's top 25 gateways. Air services, which carry a high volume of business and tourist traffic, include many flights reaching all parts of the world.

The network of major highways that converges on Orlando also gives it easier access to markets and lower costs to distributors and shippers based there.

Relatively low land values and housing prices below the national average enable businesses to keep costs relatively low. Labour costs are competitive and taxes are among the most equitable in the country.

Metropolitan Orlando's workforce is young and well educated. Nearly 700,000 people with an average age of 32 are employed in the area and thousands more move in each year. The number of new jobs rises by more than five per cent a year.

**SIGHTSEEING**

# ORLANDO–TAMPA

Here is a chance to see central Florida's citrus-growing heartland, some of its cattle country and to drive along a highway that actually goes up and down hills. Beyond Kissimmee, the rural countryside is punctuated by small but attractive communities, usually with a lake somewhere in view.

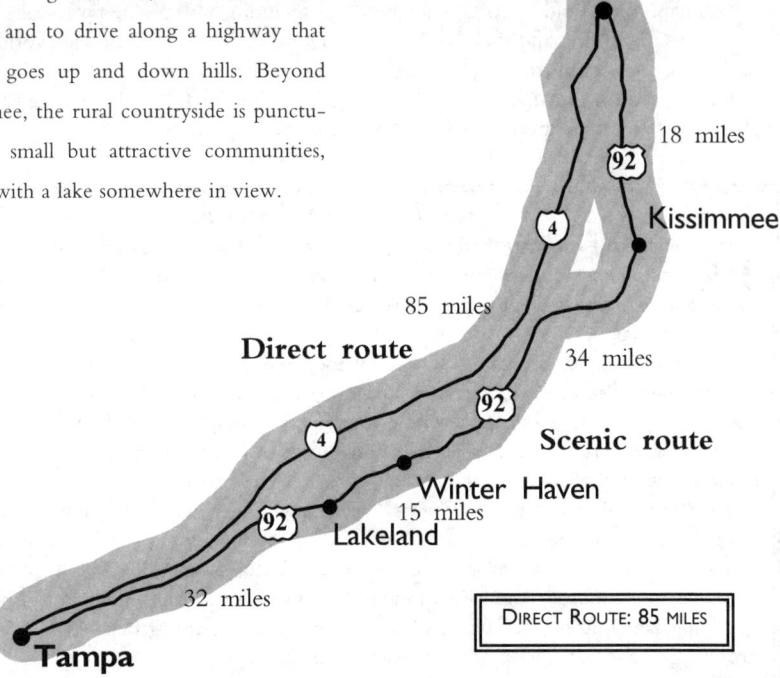

*Orlando to Kissimmee: 18 miles*
*Kissimmee to Winter Haven: 34 miles*
*Winter Haven to Lakeland: 15 miles*
*Lakeland to Tampa: 32 miles*
*Direct route: 85 miles*

DIRECT ROUTE: 85 MILES

## ROUTES

### DIRECT ROUTE

From the Mercado Village on International Dr. turn right, then left on to Sand Lake Rd. Take I-4 west and Tampa is reached in 78 miles. Continue on I-275 south exits 27, 26 and 25 lead downtown.

### SCENIC ROUTE

After leaving the Mercado Village, turn right on to Sand Lake Rd and after 4½ miles turn right again on to the Orange Blossom Trail (OBT), which confusingly carries three highway numbers: 17, 92 and 441. For this journey, it's best to keep 17/92 in mind.

The first three or four miles of the OBT are taken up by shopping malls, discount stores and specialist outlets – computers, books, office equipment and the like. Six and a half miles from the Sand Lake Rd intersection, almost on the boundary of Orange and Osceola counties – and of Orlando and

Kissimmee – is **Gatorland**, billed as 'The Alligator Capital of the World'. The park is on the left and easily recognised by the gaping 'gator jaws through which all visitors must enter.

After running the usual gauntlet of used car lots, the OBT sweeps into Kissimmee and becomes *N. Main St.* After crossing Hwy 192 in the heart of downtown Kissimmee, where it parts company with Hwy 441, the combined Hwy 17/92 takes a sharp right turn and peels off to the south west.

Before long the highway is rising and falling among the orange groves of Polk County. **Haines City**, a small commercial centre with a number of distribution depots, is reached 36 miles after leaving the Mercado Village. At Haines City, the road crosses Hwy 27 and continues a winding and generally westerly course as it skirts the lakes in the area of **Winter Haven**. Here Hwy 17 leaves us and continues south, and Hwy 92 steers us on a solo course west towards the aptly-named city of **Lakeland**.

From Lakeland the highway runs more or less parallel with I-4, passing through the pleasant suburbs of **Winston** and **Plant City**. After passing under I-75, Hwy 92 continues as *Hillsborough Ave*. To reach the heart of downtown Tampa, turn left on to *Florida Ave* (Business Rte 41 south) after passing under I-275.

## KISSIMMEE

**Tourist Information:** Kissimmee-St Cloud Convention and Visitors Bureau (CVB), *PO Box 422007, Kissimmee, FL, 3472-2007; tel: (407) 847-4000 or 1-800-831-1844*. The bureau's well-stocked **Visitor Information Center** is on *Hwy 192*, near the intersection with *Bill Beck Blvd*, one mile west of Exit 244 from the *Florida Turnpike*. Open daily 0800–1800. The centre offers a wealth of free maps, brochures booklets and leaflets with information on attractions, accommodation and dining throughout central Florida as well as the immediate area. The CVB's own *Vacation Guide*, a useful 80-page glossy production, contains 16 pages of accommodation and dining discount vouchers.

### ACCOMMODATION

Kissimmee is the major accommodation centre for Greater Orlando, handily located for Walt Disney World along Hwy 192. The Kissimmee St Cloud CVB runs an accommodation reservations service; *tel: 1-800-333-KISS*, available daily 0700–0200. In addition to the accommodation details listed in the *Vacation Guide*, the bureau also publishes a *Campground and Fish Camp Guide*.

Hotel chains in Kissimmee include *BW, Ch, CI, DI, Ev, Hd, HJ, Hn, Hy, QI, Rm, Rd, RI, Sh, TL*.

For self-catering aficionados, the area has a wide range of condominiums, villas, cabins and cottages available for holiday rentals. Many of these are let through agencies. Two of these which participate in the CVB's telephone reservations scheme are **Condolodge**, *4145 W. Vine St, Kissimmee, FL, 34741; tel: (407) 931-2683*, (75 condominiums available); and **Fantasyworld Club Villas**, *2960 Vineland Rd, Kissimmee, FL, 34746; tel: (407) 396-1808*, (230 villas available). A smaller agency is **Feel Like Home**, *714 N. Bermuda Ave, Kissimmee, FL, 34741; tel: (407) 438-1613*. It has 15 two- to three-bedroom villas and homes with swimming pools.

For campers and RV travellers, the area has about 20 well-equipped sites,

## CITRUS

Nothing conveys the golden promise of Florida quite like fresh citrus. During the Oct–Jul harvest season, migrant farm workers swarm over the groves. Each picker spills up to 7000 pounds of oranges, tangelos, temples and grapefruit into waiting lorries every day, worth nearly two thousand million dollars every year.

Columbus brought the first citrus to the New Word in 1493, but Ponce de Leon usually gets credit for planting Florida's first orange trees in St. Augustine. Spanish missions planted their own groves and passed seeds to Native Americans. It was the scent of wild oranges that drew Capt. Douglas Dummitt to the north end of what is now Merritt Island in 1807. Dummitt planted seeds from wild trees around his homestead to create the first orange grove in what became the Indian River Citrus District. The grapefruit that eventually made the Indian River label famous came later. Count Odet Philippe, once Napoleon's surgeon, planted the state's first grapefruit grove near Tampa in 1823.

Roadside fruit stands generally have the freshest and widest selection of fruit and juice, although nearby supermarkets are often less expensive. Most stands offer free samples. Navel, valencia and hamlin are the most common orange varieties, but temple oranges, which ripen mid-Jan–mid-Mar, are the richest and the sweetest. Tangelos are a hybrid between tangerines and grapefruit; the Minneola, or Honeybell Tangelo is the sweetest. Most varieties of grapefruit ripen Oct–Jul. Tangerines are picked Oct–mid-Apr. The Murcott, or Honey Tangerine, is king of the crop.

some along Hwy 192, others in remoter locations. Some have cabins, mobile homes or cottages available for short-term rentals. **Kissimmee KOA**, *4771 W. Irlo Bronson Memorial Hwy; tel: (407) 396-2400 or 800-331-1433;* 39 tent pitches, 227 hook-up RV sites and some cottages. Free shuttle service to major attractions.

A quieter, more remote location is **Richardson's Fish Camp**, *1550 Scotty's Rd; tel: (407) 846-6540.* With ten cabins and 16 RV sites, the camp is located on the north-east shore of Lake Tohopekaliga, accessible from *Neptune Rd* at the southern end of the Orange Blossom Trail.

### Eating and Drinking

There's no need to go hungry or thirsty in Kissimmee, especially along Hwy 192 and in the downtown area near the Orange Blossom Trail intersection. You can try dishes from many nations at a wide range of prices. Here's a small selection.

**Atlantic Bay Seafood**, *2901 Parkway Blvd; tel: (407) 7736*, seafood, steaks and barbecue – moderate to pricey. **Black-Eyed Pea**, *5305 W. Irlo Bronson Hwy; tel: (407) 397-1500*, Southern-style home-cooking – budget. **Bruno's Restaurant**, *8556 W. Irlo Bronson Hwy; tel: (407) 397-7577* authentic Italian and pizzas – cheap to budget. **Hollywood Diner**, *4559 W. Irlo Bronson Hwy; tel: (407) 396-1212;* classic American fast food – cheap to moderate. **Kobe**, *2901 Parkway Blvd; tel: (407) 396-8088*, Japanese cuisine, sushi bar – budget to moderate. **New Punjab**, *3404 W. Irlo Bronson Hwy; tel: (407) 931-2449*, Indian cuisine – cheap to moderate.

## ENTERTAINMENT

When it comes to entertainment, Kissimmee and Orlando merge to such an extent along Hwy 192 that it's hard to know where one area ends and the other begins. This is especially true of the themed dinner shows, many of which are in Kissimmee but which we have listed for the sake of convenience in Orlando's entertainments sections (see p. 237).

**Airship International**, *301 Dyer Blvd; tel: (407) 351-0011*. Dirigible flights over Central Florida depart from Kissimmee Municipal Airport, *301 N. Dyer Blvd*. Open daily 0900–1700. Admission: $99.

**Fortune Feast Game Show and Dinner**, *5515 W. Irlo Bronson Hwy; tel: (407) 397-9797*, gives visitors the chance to take part in the excitement of a network TV game show as they eat dinner. Admission: $35.95; children $22.95.

**Great American Racing Place**, *5285 W. Irlo Bronson Hwy; tel: (407) 396-1996*, has five go-kart tracks, two 18-hole miniature golf courses, a games arcade and bumper boats. Open daily 1000–midnight. Admission: $5; children $2.50.

**Horse World Poinciana Riding Stables**, *3705 S. Poinciana Blvd; tel: (407) 847-4343*, offers horseback riding on 750 acres of woodland trails. Open daily from 0900. Charges: from $24.95.

**A.J. Hackett Bungy**, *5782 W. Irlo Bronson Hwy; tel: (407) 397-7866*. Take the plunge from a 80 ft tower. Open daily 1700–midnight. Admission: $29.

**Haunted House at Old Town**, *5770 W. Irlo Bronson Hwy; tel: (407) 397-2231*. More than 4,000 sq. ft of fearful fun on two floors, with 20 rooms full of live (?) characters and special effects. Open Mon–Thur 1000–2200. Admission: $5; children $3.

**High Expectations Balloon Tours**, *312 Chiquita Court; tel: (407) 846-1110*. Champagne flights over the Greater Orlando area. Open daily 0900–2000. Admission: $120.

**Kissimmee Rodeo**, *958 S. Hoagland Blvd; tel: (407) 933-0020*. Cowboys and cowgirls compete in calf roping, bareback riding, steer wrestling, team roping and bull riding at the Kissimmee Sports Arena. Open Fri 2000-2200. Admission: $8; children $3.

**Osceola County Center for the Arts**, *2411 E. Irlo Bronson Hwy; tel: (407) 846-6257*. Home of the Osceola Players Theater group and art gallery. Open various times. Admission: theatre prices vary; gallery free.

**Osceola County Stadium and Sports Complex**, *1000 Bill Beck Blvd; tel: (407) 933-5400*. Spring training home of the Houston Astros baseball team and the Florida State League's Osceola Astros. Open various times. Admission: $6–8 for spring training events.

## SHOPPING

Kissimmee has its fair share of shopping malls and discount outlets, and you can also save money by using the discount coupons in tourist publications such as *See Orlando and Kissimmee*, *Best Read Guide* and *Orientation*.

**Kissimmee Manufacturers Outlet Mall**, *4673 W. Irlo Bronson Hwy; tel: (407) 396-2204*, has an information centre where you can obtain a book with even more savings coupons. The mall has stores selling internationally known brand name goods at very low prices. Closer to downtown Kissimmee, the **Osceola Square Mall** is at *3831*

W. Vine St; tel: (407) 847-6941 and is the only enclosed shopping mall in Osceola County. Among the 35 stores and restaurants are Wal-Mart, Eckerd Drugs and the Osceola Terrace Food Court.

Almost an attraction in its own right, **Old Town** is at *5770 W. Irlo Bronson Hwy; tel: (407) 396-4888*, a mile east of I-4. Built in the style of a 19th-century pioneer town, with brick-lined streets, raised sidewalks and timber buildings, it contains more than 70 speciality shops and restaurants as well as entertainment features and a train museum.

Stores in Old Town include **Electronic Town Outlet**, *Suite 209*, selling merchandise by Sony, Minolta, Canon, Sharp, Panasonic, etc, and **Gold Factory Outlet**, *Suite 205*, which offers savings on gold, diamonds, gemstones, pearls and fine jewellery.

For sports goods, clothing and footwear **Sports Dominator**, *7550 W.Irlo Bronson Hwy; tel: (407) 397-4700*, has a very wide range of international brand names. And if you have to buy an extra suitcase to take all your purchases home, **American Tourister**, the luggage specialist, has a factory outlet with discounts of 40–70 per cent off retail prices at *2547 Old Vineland Rd; tel: (407) 396-8853*, part of the Kissimmee Manufacturers Mall.

### Sightseeing

'Location is our biggest attraction,' proclaims the Kissimmee St Cloud CVB and it is certainly true that if you are staying in Kissimmee you won't have far to travel to visit most of Greater Orlando's major attractions – many of which are geographically in Kissimmee, anyway. However, Kissimmee does have a number of attractions which are inarguably its very own.

**Brave Warrior Wax Museum**, *5260 W. Irlo Bronson Hwy; tel: (407) 363-3610*. Tableaux featuring six Indian nations, General George Custer and scenes from American history. Open daily 1000–2100. Admission: $4; children $2.

**Cypress Island**, *Lake Tohopekaliga; tel: (407) 935-9202*. The area's newest attraction features exotic animals on a 200-acre historic island in Florida's second largest lake. In addition to emus, peacocks and llamas, the island houses bald eagles, osprey, blue heron, white egret and alligators. There are two miles of nature trails, airboat and seaplane rides, watersports and horseback riding.

During the mid-19th century, Cypress Island served as a sanctuary for a powerful Seminole Indian chief. It is reached by a tour boat which leaves the mainland every 30 mins, or visitors may travel there by airboat. Open daily 0900–dusk. Admission: $18; child $14 ($19.75/16.50 with airboat transfer).

**Flying Tigers Warbird Air Museum**, *231 N. Hoagland Blvd; tel: (407) 933-1942*. A working museum where visitors can see World War II aircraft on display, being restored and flying. Open daily 0900–1730. Admission: $6; children $5.

**Green Meadows Farm**, *1368 S. Poinciana Blvd; tel: (407) 846-0770*. Here's a chance to observe the gentler side of animal life during a two-hour guided tour of more than 200 farm animals. Children can learn to milk a cow and ride a pony. There are tractor-drawn hayrides and a picnic area. Open daily 0930–1730. Admission: $12.

**Spence-Lanier Pioneer Center**, *750 N. Bass Rd; tel: (407) 396-8644*. The centre encompasses an 1899 Cracker house in typical Floridian pioneer style, a

1900 general store, a museum of pioneer artefacts, a nature preserve and shaded picnic areas. Open daily 1000–1600. Admission: $2; children under six free.
**Water Mania**, *6073 W. Irlo Bronson Hwy; tel: (407) 396-2626*, is a 36-acre water park where there are rides and slides with such awesome names as Wipe Out, The Abyss and Riptide.

There's a giant Pirate Ship for children to play on and paddling pools for toddlers. Open daily, times vary according to season. Admission: $21.35; children $19.20.

**World of Orchids**, *2501 N. Old Lake Wilson Rd; tel: (407) 396-1887*. A permanent indoor display of flowering orchids from around the globe set in a climate-controlled tropical rain forest. Open daily 1000–1800. Admission: $8.95; children $6.95.

## WINTER HAVEN

**Tourist Information: Winter Haven Area Chamber of Commerce**, *401 Ave B, N.W., PO Drawer 1420, Winter Haven, FL, 33882; tel: (803) 293-2138*.

Winter Haven owes its tourism popularity to **Cypress Gardens**, *2641 South Lake Summit Dr; tel: (813) 324-2111 or (800) 282-2123*. Covering more than 220 acres, the attraction opened in 1936 and is claimed as Florida's oldest theme park. Edged by lakes and ancient cypress swamps, it features more than 8,000 varieties of plants and flowers from 75 countries. Southern Belles wearing elegant ball gowns stroll along the lawns and pathways.

Other things to see include exciting water-ski performances, stage shows, an old-fashioned circus, performing birds and a colourful butterfly conservatory. There are lots of shops and restaurants.

Cypress Gardens is one of ten theme parks belonging to the Anheuser-Busch brewery chain. Adults can sample the company's products in the hospitality centre located in an antebellum-style mansion. Open daily 0930–1730. Admission: $26.45; children $17.40.

## LAKELAND

**Tourist Information: Lakeland Area Chamber of Commerce**, *35 Lake Morton Dr., PO Box 3607, Lakeland, FL, 33802-3607; tel: (813) 688-8551*. Literature dispensed in the office includes a free walking tour map. Open Mon–Fri 0900–1630.

Accommodation options include **Holiday Inn North**, *4645 Socrum Loop Rd; tel: (813) 858-1411*. Moderate.

The **Sanlan Ranch Campground**, *3929 Hwy 985; tel: (813) 665-1726*, has an 18-hole 72-par golf course, canoe and hiking trails, swimming pools and pitches for RVs and tents.

**Valencia Estates and RV Park**, *3325 Bartow Hwy; tel: (813) 665-1611*, has a mobile home section as well as RV pitches.

This attractive city is surrounded by lakes and a pleasant, tree-shaded square lies at the heart of the downtown **Munn Park Historic District**. Here you will find the Art Deco-style **Polk Theater**, *124 S. Florida Ave*.

The **Polk Museum of Art**, *800 E. Palmetto St; tel: (813) 688-7743*, one of the largest in Central Florida, features a permanent exhibition of pre-Columbian artefacts and stages shows of work by artists based in the state.

Lakeland's major claim to fame is probably the **Florida Southern College**, on the city's southwestern outskirts. Here is the largest collection of buildings by the innovative American architect, Frank Lloyd Wright.

# ORLANDO–COCOA

This is the shortest – and probably least interesting – trip in the book. But it happens to be the only practicable way of travelling by road from Orlando to the Space Coast.

DIRECT ROUTE: 40 MILES

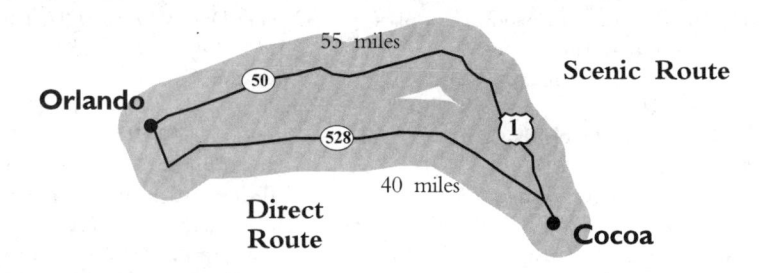

## ROUTES

### DIRECT ROUTE

The quickest route – less than an hour – is Hwy 528, the **Beeline Expressway** (toll road). This intersects with I-4 at Exit 28 and heads due east for 40 miles. To reach the Beeline from the Mercado Village, turn right on International Dr. then right again on to Sand Lake Rd. Cross the Orange Blossom Trail into McCoy Rd (Hwy 482) which leads into the Beeline, and the toll booths, just before Orlando International Airport.

After reaching its eastern toll plaza, the Beeline curves to the south-east, crossing I-95 and intersecting with Hwy 1. Cocoa is three miles to the south.

### SCENIC ROUTE

For the first 4.5 miles, follow the route as above from the Mercado to the Orange Blossom Trail, then turn left (Hwy 17/92 north). This is a busy stretch, lined with topless bars, used car lots and tyre and car repair workshops. After seven miles you'll be glad to reach Hwy 50, where you head east. Factories and warehouses gradually thin out and open countryside is soon reached.

Beyond **Bithlo**, Hwy 50 reaches the tiny community of **Christmas**, where crowds flock to the post office each Dec to get their cards and gift parcels appropriately franked.

Christmas is also the gateway to the **Tosohatchee State Reserve**, *3365 Taylor Creek Rd; tel: (407) 568-5893*, a 28,000-acre mosaic of marshes, swamps, pine flatwoods and hammocks with 19 miles of frontage on the St Johns River. Open daily 0800–dusk. Admission: $3.25 per vehicle.

Twelve miles east of Christmas head south on Hwy 1. You will reach Cocoa in 15 miles.

# ORLANDO–DAYTONA BEACH

This route links Florida's fantasy capital with the rather more down-to-earth dreamland of one of the state's longest-established seaside resorts. Leaving Orlando's blue collar districts and chic northern suburbs behind, the route soon encounters the rural landscapes of Seminole and Volusia Counties, with farmland, lakes and the meandering St John's River flowing sedately northwards on its way to Jacksonville. It's a leisurely and interesting drive – 59 miles if you take the Interstate route, 75 miles if you decide to dawdle.

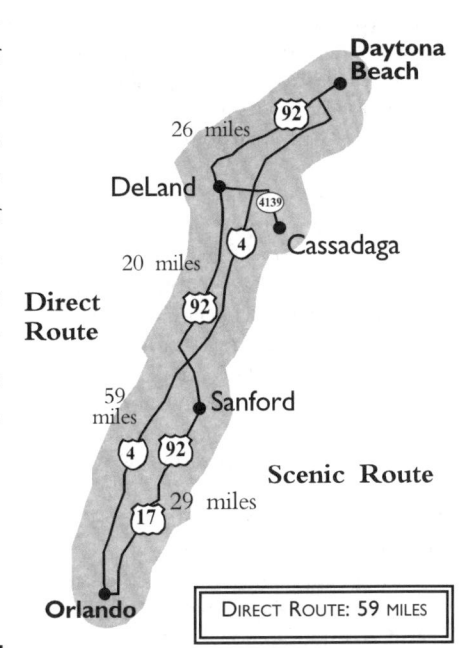

DIRECT ROUTE: 59 MILES

## ROUTES

### DIRECT ROUTE

→ From the Mercado Village on International Dr., turn right, then left on to Sand Lake Rd. Head east on I-4 for 52 miles then turn off on to I-95 north for three miles. Hwy 92 then takes you east and leads directly into downtown Daytona Beach (see p. 267) after four miles.

### SCENIC ROUTE

→ After leaving the Mercado Village, you can turn right on to Sand Lake Road and after 4½ miles turn left on the Orange Blossom Trail. This is Hwy 17-92 and leads directly to **Sanford**. It also takes you through some of Orlando's drearier commercial and industrial parts, before reaching the more rarefied ambience of such suburban places as Winter Park, Maitland and Winter Springs, so an alternative is to take I-4 east for 20 miles, then exit onto Hwy 46 east. This leads into Sanford after four miles.

From Sanford, take Hwy 17-92 north through increasingly rural countryside to the genteel university city of **DeLand**. A mile or so north of downtown DeLand Hwys 17 and 92 part company. Follow Hwy 92 east for 25 miles into Daytona Beach. The massive stadium of the famous international speedway track, unmissable on the right, indicates that your journey is coming to an end.

## SANFORD

**Tourist Information: Greater Sanford Chamber of Commerce**, *400 E. First St; tel: (407) 322-2212*. A useful map is available which allows visitors to take a self-guided tour of the nearby old downtown district, which contains more than 20 buildings dating from the city's boom in the early years of this century.

### SIGHTSEEING

Formerly an inland port and agricultural centre, Sanford today has gained from tourism, thanks to **Lake Monro** and the **St John's River**. The city's history is traced in the **Shelton Sanford Memorial Museum**, *520 E. First St.* Open Tues–Fri 1100–1600. Admission: free. For a broader view of the surrounding area, visit the **Seminole County Historical Museum**, *300 Bush Blvd.* Open Mon–Fri 0900–1300, Sat–Sun 1300–1600. Admission: free.

Cruises with dining and live entertainment can be taken aboard **Rivership Grand Romance**, *433 N. Palmetto Ave; tel: (407) 321-5091 or (800) 423-7401*. Departures daily at various times; reservations required, prices: from $20. Two-hour trips with the opportunity to view wildlife are also offered by **St John's River Cruises**, *4359 Peninsula Point; tel: (407) 330-1612*. Open Tues–Sun 1100–1300, 1330–1530; price: $10–15.

Those who prefer to cruise at their own pace should head for **Katie's Wekiva River Landing**, *190 Katie's Cove* (one mile off Hwy 46, on Wekiva Park Dr.); *tel: (407) 628-1482*. Katie Moncrieff and her husband Russ offer canoe rentals with a programme of downstream 'runs' along the **Wekiva River** system, a tributary of the St John's River. Runs range from a six-mile trip taking two–three hours to a 19-mile odyssey with an overnight camping stop. Open daily 0800–1800. Rentals from $15. The Moncrieffs also have cabins to rent.

The Wekiva River, protected as an Outstanding Florida Waterway, runs through the **Lower Wekiva River State Preserve**, a 4636-acre wilderness bordering two miles of the St John's River and four miles of the Wekiva River and Blackwater Creek. The preserve's system of backwater streams and wetlands provides superb habitat for black bears, otters, alligators and waterfowl. Recreational facilities include canoeing, hiking, primitive camping and nature study. The park's entrance is nine miles west of Sanford on Hwy 46. Information: Lower Wekiva River State Preserve, *c/o Wekiwa Springs State Park, 1800 Wekiwa Springs State Park, 1800 Wekiwa Circle, Apopka, FL 32712; tel: (407) 884-2009*.

**Central Florida Zoological Park**, *3755 N. Hwy 17-92, Lake Monroe*, (four miles north-west of Sanford); *tel: (407) 323-4450*, includes alligators, crocodiles, elephants, reptiles and birds. Open daily 0900–1700. Admission: $5.

## DELAND

**Tourist Information: DeLand Area Chamber of Commerce Welcome Center**, *336 N. Woodland Blvd; tel: (904) 734-4331 or (800) 749-4350*. Located at the back of the Chamber of Commerce offices (limited car parking), the centre has a wealth of information in its well-stocked racks. There is an excellent free map of Volusia County, of which DeLand is the county seat, and the chamber produces self-guided driving tour leaflets, with maps of the area. A self-guided tour leaflet of the city, with a list of major points of interest and a clearly drawn map, is suitable for walkers or visitors who would rather drive.

## Getting Around

**Votran**, the West Volusia County Transit Authority; *tel: (904) 943-7033*, runs buses between DeLand and the city of Deltona, a few miles to the south east. These buses provide a restricted service to a number of points between north and south DeLand. Your own car is the best bet for local travel.

## Shopping

DeLand is old-fashioned enough to have a main street, **Woodland Blvd,** which is still lined with shops, boutiques and restaurants. **Brandywine Shopping Center**, with department stores and other amenities, is at the south end of the city, just beyond the intersection of Hwy 17-92 and Orange Camp Rd.

## Entertainment

The Chamber of Commerce Welcome Center is the best place for information on the current entertainment scene. Listings are also given in the local newspaper, *The News-Journal*.

The recently-opened **DeLand Cultural Arts Center**, *600 N. Woodland Blvd; tel: (904) 736-7232*, is the city's entertainment and cultural heart. Performances by the **Rivertown Players**, a community theatrical company, *tel: (904) 736-7456*, are staged in the centre. **DeLand Little Symphony**, *tel: (904) 736-7372*, holds rehearsals in the centre, but its performances of classical, jazz and bluegrass music take place at various locations. Concerts are also staged regularly at **Stetson University**, *N. Woodland Blvd; tel: (904) 822-7000*, which has a respected School of Music.

## Sightseeing

DeLand was founded in 1876 by Henry Addison DeLand, a manufacturer from Fairport, New York, who saw his new city as the 'Athens of Florida'. In 1883 he opened the DeLand Academy, later renamed the **John B. Stetson University** in honour of his friend, the renowned hat-maker.

The **Henry A. DeLand House**, *137 W. Michigan Ave; tel: (904) 734-7029*, restored home of the city's founder, displays furnishings and artefacts relating to the development of DeLand. Open Mon–Sat 0900–1200 1300–1600. Admission: donation.

**DeLand Museum of Art**, *DeLand Cultural Arts Center, 600 N. Woodland Blvd; tel: (904) 734-4371*. The permanent collection includes Native American basketware. Visiting exhibitions include internationally known works as well the works of Florida artists. Open Tues–Sat 1000–1600, Sun 1300–1600.

**Downtown DeLand**, the area encompassed by *Woodland Blvd, Alabama Ave, New Ave* and *Indiana Ave*, is listed as a National Historic District. Revitalised after restoration, it is the venue for frequent street fairs and festivals. Stetson University and a residential area in northwest DeLand are also designated National Historic Districts.

**Duncan Gallery of Art**, *Sampson Hall, Stetson University Campus; tel: (904) 822-7386*. Changing exhibitions are featured periodically. Open Mon–Fri 1000–1600, Sat–Sun 1300–1600. Closed during vacations. Admission: free.

Some 25,000 rocks, minerals and fossils are displayed in the **Gillespie Museum of Minerals**, part of the Stetson University Campus, *234 E., Michigan Ave; tel: (904) 822-7330*. Open Mon–Fri 0900–1200, 1300–1600. Admission: free.

**Stone Street Memorial Museum**, *230 N. Stone St; tel: (904) 734-5333*, was DeLand's first hospital. Listed on the

National Register of Historic Buildings, it has been restored to display the original operating theatre and pharmacy. There are displays of early medical equipment and international medical artefacts.

## State and National Parks
**Blue Spring State Park**, *seven miles south-west of DeLand on Hwy 17-92; tel: (904) 775-3663*, is a great place for viewing endangered manatees, which swim into the spring's constant 72°F water from the colder St John's River. Recreational activities include camping, picnicking, swimming and canoeing, with fishing and boating also available on the St John's River. Open daily 0800–dusk. Admission: $3.25 per vehicle; $1 per person on foot.

**De Leon Springs State Recreation Area**, *at the corner of Ponce De Leon Rd and Burt Parks Rd, De Leon Spring; tel: (904) 985-1212*, is five miles north of DeLand on Hwy 17. The spring which gives the park its name delivers 19 million gallons of water a day. Facilities include swimming, picnicking, nature study and canoeing (rentals available). Open daily, 0800–dusk. Admission: $3.25 per vehicle; $1 per person on foot.

**Hontoon Island State Park**, *2309 River Ridge Rd, De Land, six miles west of downtown, off Hwy 44; tel: (904) 736-5309*, covers 1650 acres. Its first inhabitants were Timucuan Indians whose mounds can still be seen on the park's nature trail. Later, it served as a boatyard, cattle ranch and pioneer homestead before becoming a state park in 1967. The island, bordered by the St John's River and the Hontoon Dead River, is accessible only by private boat or free passenger ferry. Open daily 0800–dusk.

**Lake Woodruff National Wildlife Refuge**, *County Rd 4053, off Hwy 17,* five miles north of DeLand; *tel: (904) 985-4673*. The refuge offers fishing, camping, hiking and picnics, as well as the chance to see bald eagles, limpkins, ospreys, wood storks, alligators, manatees and – if you are lucky – round-tailed muskrat. Open daily 0800–dusk. Admission: free.

### SIDE TRACK FROM DELAND
This is a round trip to visit one of Florida's oddest communities: the spiritualist village of **Cassadaga**, five miles east of downtown DeLand. From the Chamber of Commerce Welcome Center drive south along Woodland Blvd and turn left on to New York Ave (Hwy 44), which skirts the southern end of Lake Winnemissett after two miles. Turn right on to County Rd 4139 which leads through the small town of **Lake Helen** and on to Cassadaga, a sleepy hamlet with post office and a couple of shops.

Cassadaga's dominant features are the **Cassadaga Hotel**, the gateway to the **Cassadaga Spiritualist Camp** where there is also a bookshop and information centre, and a profusion of signs offering 'psychic readings' and clairvoyancy services. A 30-min session costs around $30. Cassadaga was founded by George Colby, a medium from New York, who claimed he was led to the site by an Indian spirit guide in 1875. Information: **Southern Cassadaga Spiritualist Camp Meeting Association**, *PO Box 319, Cassadaga, FL 32706; tel: (904) 228-3171*.

CR 4139 continues through Cassadaga and crosses I-4 to intersect with Hwy 472. Turn right here and continue along Hwy 472 until it joins Hwy 17-92 north which leads back into downtown DeLand.

# ORLANDO–LAKE CITY

This route takes you through the heart of central and north–central Florida – from the lakes and citrus orchards to the northwest of Orlando, on through the racehorse breeding and training area around Ocala and into the university city of Gainesville.

DIRECT ROUTE: 159 MILES

## ROUTES

### DIRECT ROUTE

From the Mercado Village, turn right into International Dr., then left left into Sand Lake Rd. Take I-4 east, and within three miles (Exit 31) head north on the Florida Turnpike (toll). After 52 miles the road I-75. Head north on the interstate, passing **Gainesville** and **Alachua**. After 101 miles take Hwy 90 east which reaches Lake City in three miles.

### SCENIC ROUTE

Avoid Orlando's messier northern outskirts by taking the Florida Turnpike (see above) and after 14 miles exit on to Hwy 50 west to **Clermont**. Take Hwy 27 north for 24 miles to **Leesburg**. Beyond Leesburg, Hwy 27 merges with Hwy 441 and continues for 34 miles to Ocala,. where the highways split. Stay on Hwy 441 for another 64 miles to Gainesville, Alachua and **High Springs**. Here Hwy 27 appears again and continues to **Fort White**, where Hwy 47 heads north to merge with Hwy 441 after 18 miles. Lake City is reached after a further three miles.

### WINTER GARDEN

**Tourist Information: West Orange Chamber of Commerce**, *PO Box 770522, Winter Garden, FL 34777; tel: (407) 656-1304*. It has city and regional maps, a restaurant guide and an accommodation directory.

The Central Florida Railroad Museum, *101 S. Boyd St, Winter Garden; tel: (407) 656-8749*, has lanterns, locomotive bells and historical photographs displayed in the former Tavares and Gulf Railroad Depot. Open Sun 1400–1700 or by appointment. Admission: free.

## CLERMONT

**Tourist Information: Lake County Official Welcome Center**, *20763 US Hwy 27, Groveland, FL 34736; tel: (904) 429-3673*. **Clermont Area Chamber of Commerce**, *PO Box 120417, 691 W. Montrose St, Clermont, FL 34712; tel: (904) 304-4191*.

On a clear day you can see 2000 sq miles from the top of the 226 ft **Citrus Tower**, *US Hwy 27, Clermont; tel: (904) 394-8585*. There are also two glass-enclosed observation decks at slightly lower levels. Lakes and woodland, hills, urban areas and millions of citrus trees can be seen. Visitors get a guided tour by tram through the citrus grove. They can visit the Candy Kitchen and Marmalade House – and sample the goods. A gift shop, basket shop and restaurant are on the site. Open daily 0800–1800. Admission: $5.

Next to the Citrus Tower is **The House of Presidents Wax Museum**, *123 N. Hwy 27, Clermont; tel: (904) 394-2836*. It is a 60 by 20 ft replica of The White House, complete with Oval Office. Life-sized wax figures of all US presidents from are shown in appropriate settings. Open daily 0900–1700. .

For people from cooler climates, visiting the **U-Pick Citrus Farm**, *5010 Hwy 27, Clermont; tel: (904) 394-4377*, is a novelty. Phone to check dates for picking oranges, grapefruit, limes, kumquats, peaches and other fruit. Purchases can be shipped home. Open Oct–June.

Free wine tours and tastings are available at **Lakeridge Winery and Vineyards**, *19239 US 27 N, Clermont; tel: (904) 394-8627*.

The annual **Great Florida Triathlon** attracts 500 contestants in Oct. Activities in the area include fishing and canoeing in the **Clermont Chain of Lakes**, water skiing and golf. Glider flights are offered by **Seminole-Lake Gliderport**, *PO Box 120458, Clermont; tel: (904) 394-5450*. Motels and inns include the **Ramada Inn**, *20349 Hwy 27, Clermont; tel: (904) 429-2163*.

## LEESBURG

**Tourist Information: Leesburg Chamber of Commerce**, *PO Box 490309, Leesburg, FL 34749; tel: (904) 787-2131*.

This township of 15,000 people has more than a dozen motels and inns and several fishing camps. Bass fishing is a major pursuit at **Lake Griffin State Recreation Area**, *2miles north of Leesburg, 103 Hwy 441/27, Fruitland Park; tel: (904) 787-7402*. Camping, canoeing and boating are other activities. Open daily 0800–dusk. Admission: $3.25 per vehicle.

## GAINESVILLE

**Tourist Information: Gainesville Area Chamber of Commerce**, *PO Box 1187, Gainesville, FL 32602; tel: (904) 336-7100*. **Alachua County Visitors and Convention Bureau**, *30 E. University Ave, Dept FVG, Gainesville, FL 32601; tel: (904) 374-5231*.

Gainesville has been the home of the **University of Florida** since the academic institution was founded more than 140 years ago, and with about 40,000 students it is quite a lively city. A number of the university buildings are on the National Register of Historic Places, and a carillon in the Century Tower plays at 15-min intervals. **Florida Museum of Natural History**, *Museum Road, University of Florida, Gainesville; tel: (904) 392-1721*, is considered one of the top 10 in the US. Exhibits range from a limestone cave and Florida fossil specimens to computer games. Hundreds of natural science specimens can be seen in the Object Gallery. Open Tues–Sat 1000–1700, Sun and holidays 1300–1700. Admission: free.

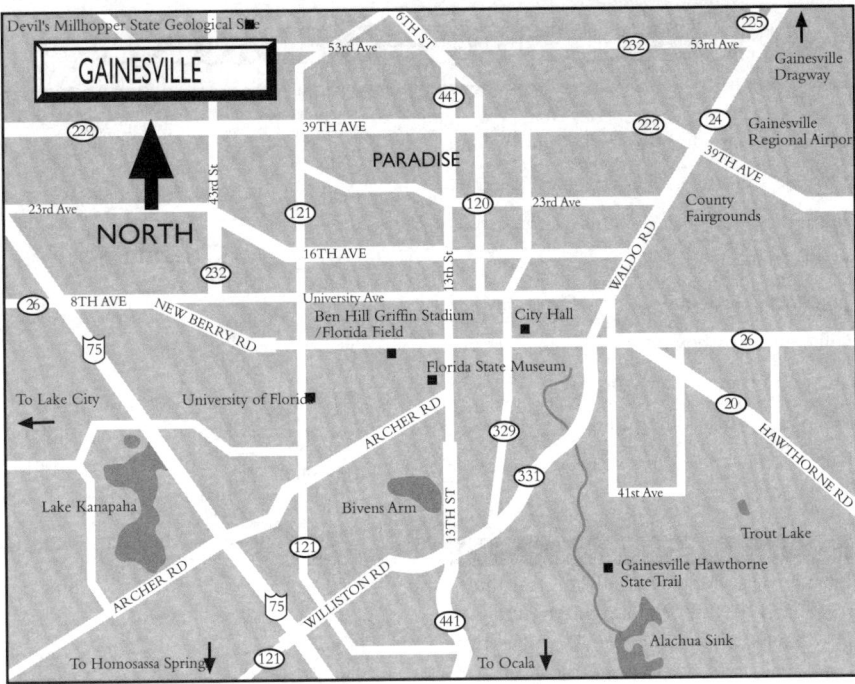

Contemporary plays are staged at the **Hippodrome State Theatre**, *25 S.E. 2nd Place, Gainesville; tel: (904) 375-4477*, which also houses a cinema and a gallery displaying the work of local artists. Pop, jazz, country and classical music; Broadway plays; opera and dance are presented at the 1800-seat **Centre for the Performing Arts**, *315 Hull Road, University of Florida, Gainesville; tel: (904) 392-2787*. Next door is the new **Samuel P. Harn Museum of Art**, *Hull Rd and S.W. 34th St, University of Florida, Gainesville; tel: (904) 392-9826*. Collections from pre-Columbian to contemporary are on show. Open Tues–Fri 1100–1700, Sat 1000–1700, Sun 1300–1700. Free admission.

A 120 ft deep sinkhole which you can enter down 232 steps, amid waterfalls and rare plants, is in **Devil's Millhopper State Geological Site**, *4732 Millhopper Road, Gainesville; tel: (904) 336-2008*. Its geological history is outlined in the visitor centre. Open 0900–sunset in summer, 0900–1700 Oct–Mar. Admission charge.

Once vital to Gainesville's economy, the railway constructed in the 1850s has become a 17-mile trail for hikers, cyclists and horseriders. **Gainesville-Hawthorne State Trail**, *Region 2 Administration, 4801 S.E. 17th St, Gainesville; tel: (904) 336-2135*, leads through lake and forest country. It is located off S.E. 15th St.

# ORLANDO–SEBRING

Here's proof that there is life beyond Orlando's dream world and a pleasant, rural life at that, with real lakes, hills, citrus groves and people who work well outside the entertainment industry. You'll probably see some real cowboys, too, wearing Stetsons and jeans, though they'll be driving a pickup truck rather than riding a horse.

## ROUTE

From the Mercado Village on International Dr. turn right, then right again into Sand Lake Rd. After 4½ miles turn right again into the Orange Blossom Trail (Hwy 441, 17/92). Continue on the OBT for 11 miles to Kissimmee, cross Hwy 192 and continue south on Hwy 17/92 (Hwy 441 continues to the east in company with 192).

A few miles south of Kissimmee the highway enters Polk County and gentle hills begin. Orange groves line the road, and during harvest-time (Dec–Jan) tractors pull massive wagons laden with fruit. Roadside stalls sell sacks of oranges and grapefruit at ridiculously low prices.

**Haines City**, a small commercial and distribution centre, is 23 miles beyond Kissimmee. Maps, restaurant guides and accommodation directories are available at **Haines City Chamber of Commerce**, *908 Hwy 27, PO Box 986, Haines City, FL, 33844; tel: (813) 422–3751.*

At Haines City we abandon Hwy 17/92 in favour of Alt Hwy 27 south. Hwy 27 proper also passes through the

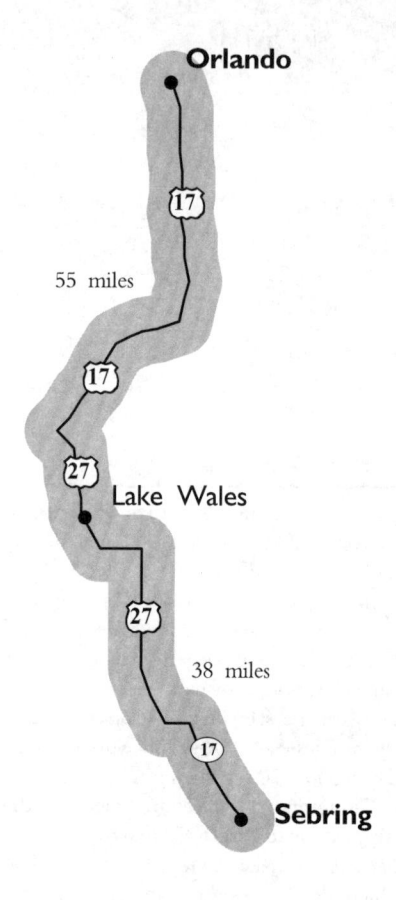

ROUTE: 93 MILES

city and heads in the same direction. It doesn't matter which road you take, but Alt 27 follows a quieter, prettier course.

Passing through the small communities of **Lake Hamilton, Dundee** and **Waverly**, Alt 27 winds its way for another 17 miles to **Lake Wales**. The entrance to the **Bok Tower Gardens** is three miles north of the town and the **Black Hills Passion Play** theatre is about the same distance to the south.

The highway curves round the northern tip of Caloosa Lake and continues south for a dozen miles through **Babson Park** and **Hillcrest Heights** to the confidently named little town of **Frostproof**. There was a time when central Florida's citrus farmers believed they lived in a frostproof environment, but there have been occasions when the climate has proved them wrong and their industry has suffered.

Six miles south of Frostproof, Alt 27 ends and we continue south on Hwy 27 for another seven miles to reach **Avon Park**. From there, Hwy 17 runs south for another 11 miles to Sebring.

## LAKE WALES

**Tourist Information:** Lake Wales Chamber of Commerce, *340 W. Central Ave, PO Box 191, Lake Wales, FL, 33859; tel: (813) 676-3445.*

This quaint little town has some well preserved shops and office buildings from the early 1920s and a new mural featuring some of its structures. The low-level town is dominated by the 10-storey **Grand Hotel**, painted in two tones of green (currently closed and awaiting a purchaser).

But it is the **Bok Tower Gardens**; *tel: (813) 676-1408*, three miles north of the downtown area, that attracts the multitudes. The attraction owes its origins to a Dutch immigrant, Edward Bok, who presented it to the American people in 1929. This is one of the higher points in Florida at 298 ft above sea level and is known as Iron Mountain. Bok's highly ornate pink and grey tower, built of coquina stone from St Augustine and marble from Georgia, is set in 128 acres of flowering plants, shrubberies, palms, oaks and pines. Part of it is left natural, and wild creatures can be viewed from a wooden hide. From Dec–May azaleas, magnolias and camellias bloom.

Carillon music is played half-hourly from 1000, and a 'live' recital of the 57-bell carillon is given daily at 1500. The bronze bells in the tower range in weight from 17 lb to nearly 12 tons. A visitor centre, cafe and gift shop are on site. Open daily 0800–1800 (latest entry 1700). Admission: $3.

Founded on a shoestring in the early 1930s Depression, **Chalet Suzanne**, *3800 Chalet Suzanne Dr.; tel: (813) 676-6011*, is not only one of Florida's most prestigious restaurants and inns, it also has a certain curiosity value. People can take a free peek even if they are not staying or eating there, to goggle at the luridly painted, bizarre building and sniff appreciatively at the incorporated soup-canning plant. A ceramic workshop, gift shop and antique store complete the set-up. Open daily 0900–1600.

From early Feb–mid-Apr, the annual **Black Hills Passion Play** is presented at the *Amphitheatre, Passion Play Rd, Lake Wales; tel: (813) 676-1495.*

Fifteen miles east of Lake Wales, off Hwy 60, in the heart of what was Florida's pioneer cattle country, a 'living history' demonstration of an 1870s cow camp is run at **Lake Kissimmee State Park**, *14248 Camp Mack Rd, Lake Wales; tel: (813) 696-1112.* Open daily 0800–dusk. Admission: $3.25 per vehicle.

# TITUSVILLE–JACKSONVILLE

DIRECT ROUTE: 140 MILES

**Jacksonville**

10

39 miles

A1A

**Direct Route**

95

**St Augustine**

A1A **Scenic Route**

140 miles

53 miles

**Daytona Beach**

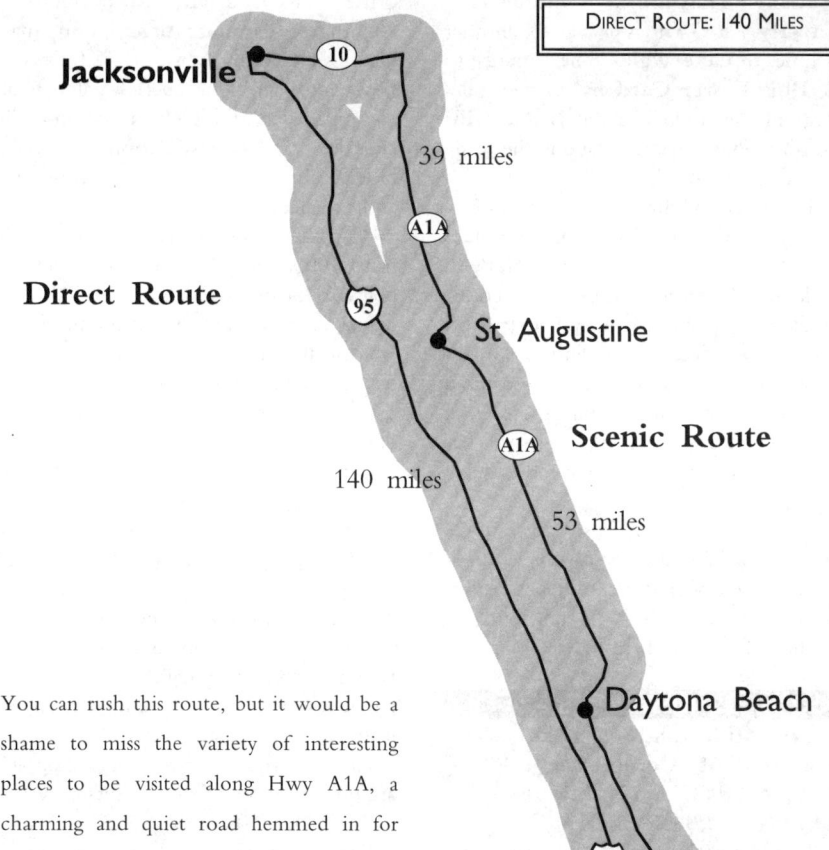

95 | 1

46 miles

**Titusville**

You can rush this route, but it would be a shame to miss the variety of interesting places to be visited along Hwy A1A, a charming and quiet road hemmed in for much of its length between the Atlantic Ocean and the Intracoastal Waterway.

State historic sites and state parks punctuate the spaces between a string of resorts, most of them tiny communities of seaside cottages and seafood shacks. The sea and waterway are frequently hidden from view by dunes covered with a thick growth of palmettoes and Spanish bayonet plants.

## ROUTES

### DIRECT ROUTE

From downtown Titusville head north on Hwy 1 to **Mims**, eight miles away, then take Hwy 46 west and two miles later take I-95 north. The interstate runs parallel with Hwys 1 and A1A for much of the remaining 130 miles, varying from about two to 10 miles inland. After 128 miles take Hwy 13 north for another two miles then head west on Hwy 90, which leads into downtown Jacksonville.

### SCENIC ROUTE

From Titusville proceed to Mims as on the Direct Route, then continue north on Hwy 1 for 46 miles, travelling to **Daytona Beach** through **New Smyrna Beach** and **South Daytona**.

The stretch of highway between Mims and South Daytona is full of variety, passing the **Canaveral National Seashore** (see the Space Coast, p 158) and running through a number of small communities with a definite holiday coast ambience.

When the high-rise hotels and condominium blocks of Daytona Beach appear, turn right on to I-92 east, here known as E. *International Speedway Blvd*, and cross the bridge over the Intracoastal Waterway. Turn left into *Atlantic Ave*, also Hwy A1A, our route for much of the rest of the journey.

Atlantic Ave is a wide seaside boulevard, though the sea is out of view because of high-rise blocks standing shoulder to shoulder for the next five miles or so to **Ormond Beach**.

North of Ormond Beach, Hwy A1A soon loses its boulevard character and becomes what it will remain for the next 40 miles: a quiet country road. Twenty-five miles north of Ormond Beach, is **Marineland of Florida**, *9507 Ocean Shore Blvd, Marineland; tel: (904) 471-1111*, where dolphins entertain six times a day and marine life can be observed. Opened in 1938, the park also features land wildlife and tropical plants. Open daily 0900–1730. Admission: $12.

At **St Augustine** Hwy A1A makes a spectacular crossing of Matanzas Bay, part of the Intracoastal Waterway, over the elegant **Bridge of Lions**.

From historic St Augustine, Hwy A1A hugs the coast and in the next 27 miles passes only three communities – **Vilano Beach, South Ponte Vedra Beach** and **Ponte Vedra Beach** – before hitting the fleshpots of the fast-living Jacksonville Beaches. From **Atlantic Beach**, turn left on to Hwy 10 east (*Atlantic Blvd*) which reaches downtown Jacksonville in 10 miles.

## DAYTONA BEACH

Tourist Information: **Daytona Beach Area Convention and Visitors Bureau**, *126 E. Orange Ave; tel: (904) 255-5478.* **Daytona Beach/ Halifax Area Chamber of Commerce**, *PO Box 2475, Daytona Beach, FL 32115; tel: (904) 255-0981.* Both authorities have accommodation directories and restaurant guides.

More than 20 miles of sandy beaches line the Daytona Beach area, which includes the seaside communities of Ponce Inlet and Daytona Beach Shores to the south and Ormond Beach and Ormond-By-the-Sea to the north.

The sand is so hard-packed here that you can drive your car along the 18 miles of beach, except at night in autumn when baby turtles are hatching out in the sand. The speed limit, 10 mph, is strictly enforced. From Feb to Labor Day (first Mon in Sept) there's a $5 charge for driving and parking on the beach. At other times it's free. Disabled people may drive and park on the beach without charge if their vehicles have appropriate stickers. Specially adapted beach wheelchairs with fat tyres are available at a number of lifeguard stations – information from **Volusia County Beach Management Dept**; tel: (904) 239-7873.

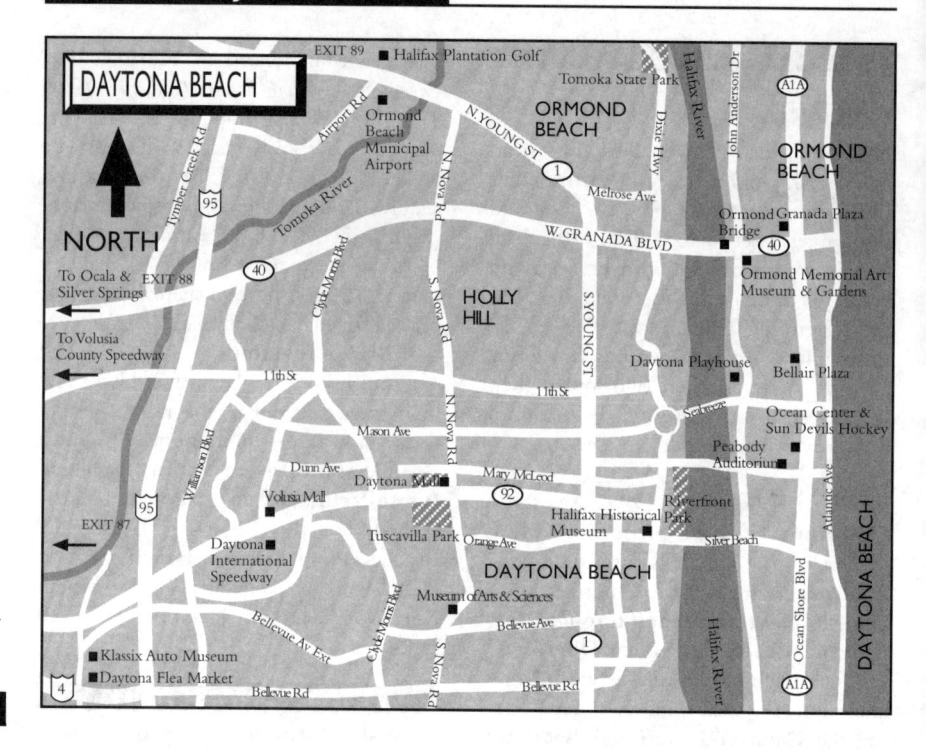

Some parts of the beach are up to 500 ft wide at low tide and provided a testing ground and race track for early car makers from 1902. The Winter Speed Carnival was an annual beach event until the 1950s.

### GETTING AROUND

Buses and trolleys operated by **VOTRAN** (Volusia County Transit System) serve the area. The strip of land between the Atlantic Ocean and the Halifax River (part of the Intracoastal Waterway) is known as **Beachside**. It is connected to the mainland by a number of bridges.

Turn-of-the-century-style trolleys run every 45 mins on Hwy A1A (Atlantic Ave) and are popular with holidaymakers as they stop near the beaches between Daytona Beach Shores and Ormond Beach. The trolleys run from Jan–early Sept. Fare: 75 cents.

Buses go to the Ocean Centre, Volusia Mall, Daytona International Speedway, Daytona Beach Airport and other points. Several bus companies have services to many of Central Florida's theme parks and attractions.

### ACCOMMODATION

More than 16,000 guest rooms are available, from budget to luxury, from family-owned motels and inns to all-suite hotels, and from youth hostels and campgrounds to beachside resorts.

This is not one of Florida's most expensive areas, and although you can choose a luxuriously appointed suite in a hotel with many amenities and off-load a walletful of dollars, there are plenty of easy-on-the-pocket lodgings where one modestly-priced room sleeps a family of four.

Hotel chains in the area include *BW, DI, EL, Hd, Hn, HJ, Ma, QI, Ra, Tl*.

**Perry's Ocean-Edge Resort**, *2209 S. Atlantic Ave, Daytona Beach; tel: (904) 255-0581*, has 700 ft of beachfront, one indoor and two outdoor pools, 204 rooms, tropical gardens, complimentary coffee and doughnuts, spacious rooms with kitchenettes and discounted golf at local courses. Prices are moderate.

Also overlooking the ocean is the modestly-priced **Ivanhoe Beach Resort**, *205 S. Atlantic Ave, Ormond Beach; tel: (904) 672-6711*. It has a choice of rooms, suites and efficiencies.

### EATING AND DRINKING

More than 400 restaurants provide options from fast food to fine dining, with freshly-caught seafood to the fore. Many restaurants are open all day, serving breakfast, lunch and dinner. Some do not serve alcohol, so if you want a beer with your meal, check before you're committed.

A sign saying 'Early Bird Specials' means people can tuck into a main meal at about 1630 at extraordinarily low prices, before the evening rush starts. This can be about 1800 – people tend to eat early here and some restaurants close at 1930, like the long-established **Middle East Foods**, *909 W. International Speedway Blvd, Daytona Beach; tel: (904) 257-7753*. Budget-priced kebabs, hummous-tab-barlen and other Middle East dishes are served here.

As well as Middle East food, ethnic options include Greek, Italian, Caribbean, Southern, Spanish, Chinese and Japanese.

Most restaurants close at 2200, though late-night eating is provided at nightspots and some sports bars.

Most establishments are in the budget or moderate price range. Even in the more upscale restaurants in riverside or ocean-side locations, most main courses are below $14.

**St Regis Bar and Restaurant** (moderate), *509 Seabreeze Blvd, Daytona Beach; tel: (904) 252-8743*, has a 'happy hour' daily 1630–1800, offering free *hors d'oeuvres*. Pre-prandial cocktails are available and on Fri and Sat there's live music 2100–midnight.

### ENTERTAINMENT

Varied stage productions are held at **Daytona Playhouse**, *100 Jessamine Blvd, Daytona Beach; tel: (904) 255-2431*, Sept–late-June. Community and children's-theatre workshops, concerts and touring productions take place at **Ormond Performing Arts Center**, *399 N. Hwy 1, Ormond Beach; tel: (904) 676-3375*.

Jazz, musicals, dinner theatre, pop, classical concerts and the Seaside Music Theatre's professional repertory productions are held at **Daytona Beach Community College**, *1200 International Speedway Blvd, Daytona Beach; tel: (904) 254-3042*.

The biggest arena for the performing arts is the **Peabody Auditorium**, *600 Auditorium Blvd, Daytona Beach; tel: (904) 254-1314*. It seats 2,500 people.

Six cinemas showing current movies – you can stay all day for $1 – are within **Daytona Mall**, a shopping and entertainment centre at the corner of *W. International Blvd* and *Nora Rd; tel: (904) 255-4503.*

Leisure activities around Daytona Beach include boat trips past riverside estates and wildlife, themed miniature golf courses, more than a dozen full–size golf courses, greyhound racing, game fishing and diving charters.

Scuba diving is popular among wrecks in the area, including a ship and two aircraft which came to grief in World War II. Sailboards, sailing boats and jet skis can be rented.

Ice hockey is played at the **Ocean Center**, Daytona Beach; *tel: (904) 254-4545*, where the Sun Devils play home games Nov–Apr. The rink is available for public use at certain times throughout the year.

### Events

Twice a year Daytona Beach Area Convention and Visitors Bureau publishes a full list of events. Some of the major ones are listed here – it's wise to check the exact dates.

**Daytona 500** at Daytona International Speedway; *tel: (904) 253-7223*; late Jan–mid-Feb.

**Bike Week**, Daytona International Speedway and throughout the area; *tel: (904) 255-0981*; Mar.

**Daytona Beach International Kite Festival**, on beach between Bandshell and Oceanfront Park; *tel: (904) 239-6414*; May.

**Jazz Matazz**, The Casements and Rockefeller Gardens; *tel: (904) 677-3454*; Fourth of July weekend.

**Biketoberfest/Fall Cycle Scene Championship Cup** (motorcycle races), Daytona International Speedway, Main St and throughout the area; *tel: (904) 253-7223*.

### Shopping

Six major department stores and more than 100 shops and restaurants are in the **Volusia Mall**, *International Speedway Blvd*. The area has several shopping malls. **Bellair Plaza** is the largest Beachside shopping centre. **Fountain Square**, *Granada Blvd*, is a picturesque courtyard of shops in Ormond Beach.

Specialist motorbike shops with all the gear and airbrushed tee shirts as well are grouped in *Main St*. Clothing and other goods sell at factory prices at **Daytona Beach Outlet Mall**. Self-caterers will find fresh produce and seafood at the **Farmers' Market** in downtown Daytona Beach at City Island. Open Sat 0700–early afternoon.

A 40-acre **flea market** with more than 1,000 booths is open Fri–Sun 0800–1700 one mile west of Daytona International Speedway at the corner of Hwy 92 and I-95.

### Sightseeing

**Birthplace of Speed Museum**, *160 E. Granada Blvd, Ormond Beach; tel: (904) 672-5657*. The area's role in the development of the car industry and racing. Exhibits include a replica of the Stanley Steamer which set a 27 mph record on the beach in 1902. Open Tues–Sat 1300–1700. Admission: $1.

**Bulow Plantation Ruins State Historic Site**,; *three miles west of Flagler Beach, north of Ormond Beach (Hwy 100, then south on county road 2001; tel: (904) 439-2219*. Scattered ruins, including several wells, can be seen – all that remains from a plantation producing sugar, cotton, rice and indigo which was destroyed in the Second Seminole Indian war. Canoe rentals, fishing and picnic tables available. Open daily 0900–1700. Admission: free.

The **Casements**, *25 Riverside Dr., Ormond Beach; tel: (904) 676-3216*, was multi-millionaire John D. Rockefeller's winter home from 1918 until his death in 1937, aged 97. Now it is Ormond Beach's cultural centre and museum. Open Mon–Thur 0900–2100, Fri 0900–1700, Sat 0900–noon. Tours Mon–Fri 1000–1430, Sat 1000–1130. Admission: donation.

**Daytona International Speedway**, *1801 International Speedway Blvd, Daytona Beach; tel: (904) 254-2700*. The annual Daytona 500 stock car racing event (in Feb) the Rolex 24 sports car race and major motorcycle races are held at this world centre of racing. Visitor Center open daily 0900–1700 with free admission to the **Gallery of Legends**. On non-racing days, a guided minibus tour is available for $3.

**Halifax Historical Museum**, *252 S. Beach St, Daytona Beach; tel: (904) 255-6976*, has a 600-year-old Timucuan dugout canoe, a 1909 time capsule, prehistoric Indian relics and modern motor racing artefacts among its exhibits. Open Tues–Sat 1000–1600. Admission $2 (free Sat).

A collection of Corvette cars from every year since 1953 can be seen at the new **Klassix Auto Museum**, *2909 W. International Speedway Blvd, Daytona Beach; tel: (904) 252-3800*. Motor bikes from the early 1900s are also displayed. Open daily 0900–2100. Admission charged.

A 13ft tall skeleton of a giant ground sloth, found nearby in 1974 and calculated to be 130,000 years old, is displayed in the Prehistory of Florida wing at the **Museum of Arts and Sciences**, *1040 Museum Blvd, Daytona Beach; tel: (904) 255-0285*. A new 'Window in the Forest' interpretive centre introduces the local environment. The 60-acre site includes a planetarium, sculpture garden, a Cuban arts museum, an Africa wing

## Speed City

The sand is so hard-packed at Daytona Beach that you can drive along it for miles. The speed limit is 10 mph, and there's a regular police patrol to enforce it.

At one time there was no speed limit. The beach was used as a racetrack from 1902, when an Oldsmobile clocked up 57 mph. In 1935 Sir Malcolm Campbell set a record of 276 mph in Bluebird. Stock car racing took place in the 1950s.

In 1959 motor racing moved 2½ miles inland to the **Daytona International Speedway**. The first meeting was a stock car event. Some of the world's most important sports car and motor cycle events are held at the speedway, known as the **World Centre of Racing**. The Visitors' Centre, at *1801 West International Speedway Boulevard*, opens daily from 0900–1700, with free admission to the Gallery of Legends.

A generous section of downtown Daytona Beach is devoted to bikers. In and around Main street you'll find D & I House of Leather, Choppers World, Crazy Bob's and T-shirt empires like Shirt World and T-Shirt Paradise offering shirts decorated with the skull motifs beloved by bikers. The Froggy Saloon has a motor cycle park and displays in its window a skeletal motor bike made up entirely of bones.

Bikers from far and wide converge on Daytona Beach in Oct for the main motor cycling event of the year at the Speedway. Motor cycle shows and a group touring ride in Volusia County take place.

and the Arts in America wing covering the period 1640–1910. Open Tues–Fri 0900–1600, Sat–Sun noon–1700. Reservations needed for guided tours. Admission: $3.

Tropical gardens with fishponds, fountains, waterfalls, winding paths, nature trails and a gazebo provide a pleasurable stroll at **Ormond Memorial Art Museum and Gardens**, *78 E. Granada Blvd, Ormond Beach; tel: (904) 677-1857*. To add to the romantic atmosphere, there may well be a wedding taking place during your visit.

The museum and gardens were established in 1946 in memory of local wartime servicemen and women. Exhibits of Florida artists' works, historical displays and items of children's interests are changed monthly. Open Tues–Fri 1100–1600, Sat–Sun noon–1600. Admission: free.

Anyone with the energy and determination to climb the 203 steps spiralling to the top of the 175 ft **Ponce de Leon Inlet Lighthouse**, *4931 S. Peninsula Dr., Ponce Inlet; tel: (904) 761-1821*, will be rewarded with a panoramic view of the Daytona Beach resort area. The lighthouse was operational from 1887 to 1978 and was re-activated as a working lighthouse by the US Coast Guard in 1982. It is a historic monument and museum and has a gift shop. Open daily 1000–2100 in summer, 1000–1700 in winter. Admission: $3.

Part of **Tomoka State Park**, three miles north of downtown Ormond Beach at *2099 N. Beach St; tel: (904) 676-4050*, is on the site of a former Timucuan Indian village. By the 18th century, part of the area was used for the cultivation of indigo, grown for its blue dye, sugar and rice.

Live oaks 400 years old can be seen at the park, which is at the confluence of the Tomoko and Halifax rivers. Swimming is not permitted but canoeists can explore marshlands and tidal creeks.

In a wooded riverside location is a 40ft sculpture of an Indian group, *The Legend of Tomokie* by Fred Dana Marsh. More of his work can be seen in the Visitor Center which has gifts for sale.

The park offers camping, canoe rentals, fishing, boating and a nature trail. Open daily 0800–dusk. Admission: $3.25 per vehicle.

## ST AUGUSTINE

**Tourist Information: St Augustine/ St John's County Chamber of Commerce**, *1 Riberia St, St Augustine, FL, 32084; tel: (904) 829-5681*. **Visitor Information Centre**, *10 Castillo Dr., St Augustine, FL, 32084; tel: (904) 825-1000*. Open daily 0800–1730. The spacious visitor centre, rich in natural wood, has maps of the area and information on accommodation, restaurants and attractions.

### GETTING AROUND

St Augustine is a compact, stroll-around city, but to spare your feet let the train take you sightseeing or take a carriage drawn by a fit, glossy horse. Either way, you'll get an entertaining narration.

**Sightseeing Trains**, *170 San Marco Ave, St Augustine; tel: (904) 829-6545*, has six boarding points, mostly near free parking areas. Bright Toytown-style trains leave every 15 or 20 minutes. You get off at any stop and re-board to get to another place of interest. Inquire about discounted tours. Tours take approximately two hours (from $12.50) or six to eight hours (from $38). Tickets may be used over three consecutive days. They run from 0830 to 1700.

Colee's Sightseeing Carriage Tours, *115 LaQuinta Place, St Augustine; tel: (904) 829-2818*. The one-hour tours ($9 per person) leave from Bayfront near the entrance to Fort Castillo de San Marcos, daily 0830–1700. Evening tours are also available.

The St Augustine skyline can be admired during a 75-minute narrated cruise in Matanzas Bay in the daytime, at sunset or by moonlight, aboard *Victory III* with **Scenic Cruise**, *4125 Coastal Hwy, St Augustine; tel: (904) 826-0897*. There are six daily sailings (between 1100 and 2030) in summer, five (1100–1815) in spring and fall, and four (1100–1630) from mid-Oct–Mar. Cruises leave from Municipal Marina.

Also leaving from the Municipal Marina are **Sea-Light Cruises** several times daily mid-Feb–mid-Dec. A limited schedule runs in the remaining few weeks. The cruises take you under the multi-arched **Bridge of Lions**, built in the Mediterranean style in 1927 across Matanzas Bay (Intracoastal Waterway).

### ACCOMMODATION

With more than 7000 guest rooms, St Augustine offers plenty of choice. For gracious living you can't beat bed and breakfast. There are two dozen interesting upmarket properties in the historic district and around Matanzas Bay.

If you fancy communing with a friendly ghost, try Room 3A at the 200-year-old **St Francis Inn**, *279 St George St; tel: (904) 824-6068*.

Or how about a superb breakfast on the patio opposite Matanzas Bay at the **Casablanca Inn**? Its suites and rooms are furnished with carefully-chosen antiques. It's at 24 Avenida Menendez; tel: (904) 829-0928.

A golf course and six tennis courts appeal to sporty clients at the 193-room **Ponce de Leon Golf & Conference Resort**, *4000 Hwy 1 N, St Augustine; tel: (904) 824-2821*.

Most motels in the city and Anastasia Island are modestly priced. Condominiums can be rented. The island has a dozen campgrounds, including KOA's, which also has cabins. Among hotel and motel chains are: HJ, Ra.

### EATING AND DRINKING

At least 150 restaurants, cafes and shrimp shacks compete for your custom. Among the top-notchers is **Compton's Seafood Restaurant**, beside the water on A1A on the North Beach; *tel: (904) 824-8051*. Compton's, open on weekdays at 1600 and for Saturday lunch from 1130–1600, is famous for Sunday Brunch, from 1030–1430. Tables groan under all-you-can-eat breakfast and lunch offerings at under $16.

**Scarlett O'Hara's**, *70 Hypolita St, St Augustine; tel: (904) 824-6535*, is a rocking-chairs-on-the-porch establishment with an outdoor oyster bar. **Raintree**, a Victorian property at *102 San Marco Ave; tel: (904) 824-7211*, offers fine dining and free transport within the city to and from the restaurant.

### ENTERTAINMENT

Florida's official state play depicting some of its history, *Cross and Sword*, is performed nightly except Mon and Tues from Jul 1 to late Aug at the 2000-seat **St Augustine Amphitheatre**, *Hwy A1A S, PO Box 1965, St Augustine; tel: (904) 471-1965*. Admission under $10.

The latest movies are shown at **Pot Belly's**, *36 Granada St, St Augustine; tel: (904) 829-3101*. Admission $2.

# TITUSVILLE–JACKSONVILLE

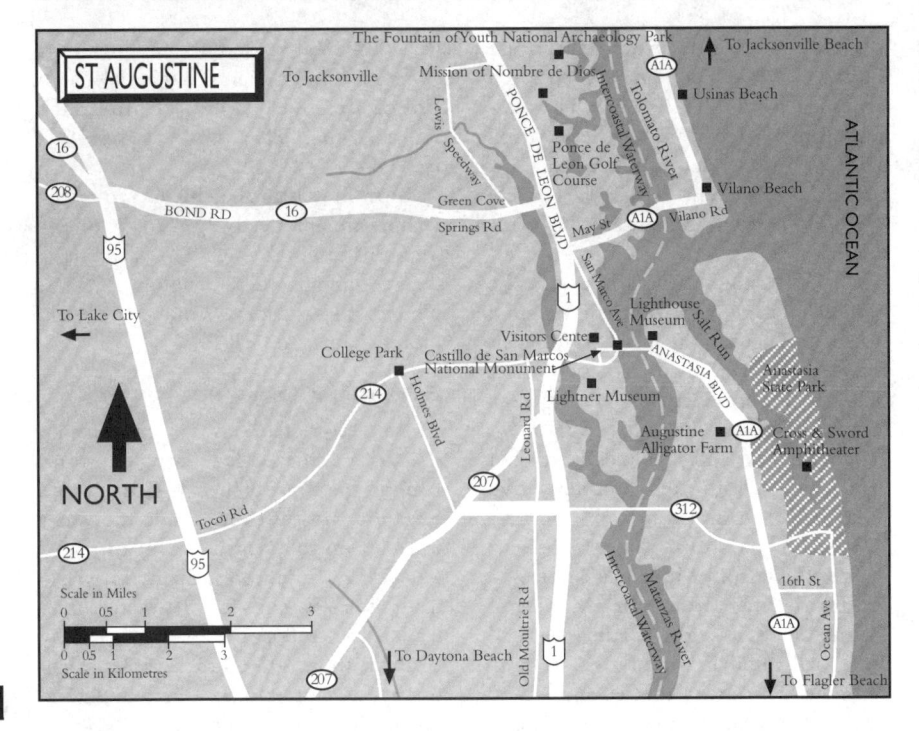

### Events
Festivals are held throughout the year about 45 in all with much music and pageantry, from the Palm Sunday Blessing of the Fleet, with decorated boats, to a torchlight procession through the Spanish Quarter re-enacting 18th-century British colonial customs.

### Shopping
The pedestrianised St George Street area is the place for unusual purchases in good quality specialist shops in the historic district. The Dat'l Do-It Hot Shop at Pueblo Español Mall, *George St,* sells hot chilli sauces. San Agustin Imports has genuine Panama hats, ponchos and embroidered clothing. Hand-made Indian arts, pottery, rugs and basketry can be found at The American Indian in Cuna Street. The Out of This World Dream Street Bookstore is in Hypolita Street, and you can watch wire jewellery being made in the traditional way at Gem & Wire Artists in Aviles Street.

For feet-on-the-ground shopping try the huge St Augustine Outlet Center on *Hwy 16* (turn right off I-95 at Exit 95). There are nearly 100 brand-name discount stores.

### Sightseeing
Opened in 1893, Florida's original **Alligator Farm**, *999 Anastasia Blvd, Anastasia Island; tel: (904) 824-3337,* also features crocodiles 22 living species of them, including a 17½ footer from New Guinea. Monkeys, birds and giant tortoises are viewed from an elevated trail. Open daily 0900–1700. Admission: $8.95.

**Anastasia State Recreation Area**, *Hwy A1A, St, Augustine Beach; tel: (904)*

*461-2033*, offers five miles of beach, coastal camping, fishing, canoeing, birdwatching, surfing and sailboarding. Sailboard tuition and rentals are available.

The moated **Castillo de San Marcos**, a National Monument, *1 Castillo Dr. E., St Augustine; tel: (904) 829-6506*, was built by the Spanish as a defence against the British. Its walls of coquina, a local shell stone, are 16 ft thick in places it took 23 years to build and was finished in 1695. It was never conquered and is largely intact. On summer weekends and some other occasions, cannons are fired from the ramparts by interpreters in 1740 Spanish military uniforms. Open daily 0845–1645. Admission $1.

**Flagler College**, *74 King St, St Augustine; tel: (904) 829-6481*, was the Ponce de Leon Hotel for more than 50 years, built in 1887 by railway magnate Henry Flagler in the extravagant Spanish renaissance style. Under its towers and turrets, it is rich in mosaic floors and Tiffany glass. The building is a liberal arts college. Guided tours are available in summer, daily 1000–1600.

While the Castillo de San Marcos defended the mouth of Matanzas Bay, its outpost, **Fort Matanzas**, a small Spanish tower built in 1742, protected Matanzas Inlet, from pirates as well as British attack. The fort, on Rattlesnake Island, about 8 miles south of St Augustine on *Hwy A1A; tel: (904) 471-0116*, is reached by a short free ferry service with a narration. It departs daily every 15 minutes from 0900–1630, year round, weather permitting. The Visitor Center is open from 0900–1700. A self-guided walk with labelled trees and plants is in the grounds.

**The Fountain of Youth National Archeology Park**, *155 Magnolia Ave, St Augustine; tel: (904) 829 3168*, is the Spring of Eternal Hope at which Ponce de Leon is believed to have ended his search for eternal youth in 1513. Visitors laughingly hope a sip of the water will send their wrinkles packing. The site of the first Christian Indian burials can be seen, and giant live oaks draped with Spanish moss provide welcome shade. Open daily 0900–1700.

Climb 219 steps to the lantern room at the **Lighthouse Museum**, *Old Beach Road, Anastasia Island; tel: (904) 829-0745*, for a great view of St Augustine. A film, nautical artefacts and paintings by local artists can be seen. Open daily 1000–1700. Admission $3.50.

Another of Flagler's former hotels is now the **Lightner Museum**, *City Hall Complex, King St, St Augustine; tel: (904) 824-2874*. It contains antique cut glass, Oriental art, antique dolls and musical instruments. Open 0900–1700.

A 208 ft high steel cross was erected at the **Mission of Nombre de Dios** in 1865 to mark the 400th anniversary of St Augustine's founding and of the first Catholic mass celebrated in St Augustine in 1565. The Mission is at *San Marco Ave and Ocean Ave; tel: (904) 824-2809*.

**Memorial Presbyterian Church** (1889), *36 Sevilla St, St Augustine; tel: (904) 829-6451*, was built in the Venetian renaissance style by Henry Flagler as a memorial to his daughter and grandchild. Open Mon–Fri, 0830–1630.

**Museum of St Augustine's History**, within *Government House, 48 King St, St Augustine; tel: (903) 825-5033*, traces local history from the days of its early native population to European colonisation and modern times. Exhibits include the hold of a 16th century ship and old coins from 18th century shipwrecks. Open 1000–1600. Admission: $2.

# TITUSVILLE–JACKSONVILLE

## Florida's Railroad Barons

Henry Morrison Flagler and Henry Bradley Plant deserve much of the credit for turning Florida from a frontier outpost into one of the busiest tourist destinations in the world. The two men worked largely independently, but both followed the same strategy: build a railroad and people will come. They gambled that freight would come, too, oranges from Florida's expanding citrus groves, timber, cattle and other agricultural products

There were other similarities as well. Each was born poor and had become rich through hard work, luck, and the right friends. Each had wives in ill health who craved warm weather. Each came as far south as practicable, to Jacksonville, Florida, liked what he found, and determined to move farther south. And each staked what were already considerable fortunes on railroads.

Flagler, born in upstate New York, first brought his wife to Jacksonville in 1878, where they were surprised at the lack of appropriately ostentatious accommodations. His wife died in 1881 and Flagler remarried two years later. He brought his new wife back to Jacksonville for their honeymoon, then continued on to St. Augustine, which had even poorer lodgings. Flagler's solution was to build the Ponce de Leon, the most luxurious hotel Florida had ever seen.

It was an instant success, prompting Flagler to build the slightly less grand Alcazar Hotel across the street. It, too, was a money spinner from opening day. Flagler had found the means to turn the swamps of Florida into wealth.

He bought a narrow gauge railroad to Ormond Beach, then invested heavily in the Ormond Beach Hotel. Julia Tuttle, the business pioneer who launched the city of Miami, used her considerable skills of persuasion to lure Flagler southward. His Florida East Coast Railway reached New Smyrna in 1892, Fort Pierce in early 1894, and Palm Beach by April of the same year.

Flagler stopped in Palm Beach long enough to break ground for several, including The Breakers, and Whitehall, his personal mansion which outshone the Ponce de Leon. He might

---

The city's **Oldest House**, the Gonzales-Elvarez House, said to date from 1706, is at *14 St Francis St; tel: (904) 824–2872*. It houses a history museum and the **Museum of Florida's Army**. Open daily with guided tours 0900–1700. Admission: $5.

It's back to the classroom at the red cedar and cypress **Oldest Wooden Schoolhouse**, built before 1763 at *45 St George St; tel: (904) 824-0192*. Visitors attend a history lesson in the company of animated wax figures and get their diplomas. Open daily 0900–1700, extended hours in summer. Admission $1.50. **The**

**Old Jail**, built in 1891, still served as St John's County penitentiary until 1953. See the sheriff with horse thieves and train robbers at *167 San Marco Ave, St Augustine; tel: (904) 829-3800*. Admission: $4.25.

Thousands of goods from yesteryear are displayed in the **Oldest Store Museum**, *4 Artillery Lane; tel: (904) 829-9729*. Admission: $2.50.

Nearly 200 historical figures in wax, a workshop where they are made and a multi-image presentation attract crowds to **Potter's Wax Museum**, *17 King St, St Augustine; tel: (904) 829-9056*. Open win-

## TITUSVILLE-JACKSONVILLE

have been content with Palm Beach, but Tuttle and fellow developer William Brickell proffered so much free land in Miami that he couldn't afford not to continue south. The FEC chugged into Miami in 1896.

Plant, a Connecticut native, had been equally busy on the Gulf Coast. He and his wife first saw Jacksonville in 1853 after an arduous eight day steamship journey from New York. They eventually settled in Augusta, Georgia, and Plant began building a rail empire with the outbreak of the US Civil War in 1861. By 1885, he had linked Jacksonville and Tampa with a combination of rail lines and steamship routes.

When Flagler's Ponce de Leon opened as an instant success, Plant began building his own grand hotel in Tampa. The Tampa Bay Hotel, complete with Moorish styling and glittering onion domes, opened in early 1891. Plant had 4,300 guests in the first two months alone, enough to convince him to concentrate his efforts in Tampa. Plant poured money and energy into the Port of Tampa. What had been a sleepy coastal facility became the busiest waterfront in Florida, with links to New Orleans, Key West, Havana and beyond.

Flagler charted a different course. In 1905, he broke ground on the first land link to Key West and steamers bound for Havana, then a major agricultural producer for America. More than 400,000 men worked on his Overseas Railroad, more often called Flagler's Folly. Seven years, hundreds of deaths, and $20 million later, Flagler triumphantly rode the first train into Key West – and promptly set about building the Casa Marina hotel for his wealthy passengers.

A hurricane destroyed much of the Overseas Railroad in 1935, but every one of Flagler's bridges survived. By 1938, the Overseas Highway, now US Hwy 1, extended from Miami to Key West, built atop Flagler's railroad bridges and the abandoned rail bed. The Casa Marina (now a Marriott) and La Concha (a Holiday Inn), built for train passengers, are still catering to upmarket visitors.

The Ponce de Leon now houses Flagler College in St. Augustine; the Alcazar has become the Lightner Museum. Henry Plant didn't do badly, either. His Tampa Bay Hotel is now the University of Tampa and the port he built remains the busiest in the state.

ter 0900–1700, summer 0900–2100. Admission charged. Nothing concentrates the mind on the eccentricities of human endeavour more than a visit to **Ripley's Believe It or Not!** Who could sculpt a manatee out of old soft–drink cans or build a 24- ft replica of the Eiffel Tower from toothpicks? See it all at *19 San Marco Ave; tel: (904) 824-1606.* Open daily 0900–2100. Admission: $7.50.

**St George Street** is the core of the city's 11-block pedestrianised historic district; *tel: (904) 829-5681.* Street musicians stroll among the restored 18th century cottages and courtyards.

The restored **Spanish Quarter** is a living history museum at the northern end of the St George Street Historic District; *tel: (904) 825-6830.* Costumed settlers and soldiers in a mid-1700s timewarp chat to sightseers about their everyday lives and demonstrate their crafts. Open daily 0900–1700.

A mummy's foot, a rug 2,300 years old and the harem quarters are among the exhibits at **Zorayda Castle**, *83 King St, St Augustine; tel: (904) 824-3007*, a scaled-down version of awing of the Alhambra, the Moorish castle in Granada, Spain. Open daily 1900–1700. Admission: $5.

# JACKSONVILLE

Jacksonville, a busy commercial and industrial port and city 12 miles inland from the Atlantic coast, straddles the north-flowing St John's River. It was named after General Andrew Jackson in 1822. Before that it was a small community called Cowford. Seven major bridges carry traffic over the wide river, and there is also the Mayport car ferry.

Claimed to be the largest city in the US by volume – it covers 840 square miles – it is a connurbation of more than 700,000 people, but its boundaries stretch out into much of the rural and oceanside regions of north-east Florida. The tourism organisation is called Jacksonville and the Beaches Convention and Visitors Bureau. Atlantic Beach, Neptune Beach and Jacksonville Beach are sand and surf playgrounds.

With its long-established military links Jacksonville was the busiest military port in the US during the Gulf War in 1991, with movements of troops and supplies. Nearly a dozen historical sites and museums reflect the African-American heritage of the area.

Jacksonville Landing, a development of shops, restaurants and entertainment, on the river's north bank, is opposite the Southbank Riverwalk. In 1901 the city lost more than 2000 Victorian buildings in a fire. Skyscrapers dominate today.

### TOURIST INFORMATION

**Jacksonville and the Beaches Convention and Visitors Bureau (CVB)**, *3 Independent Dr.; Jacksonville FL 32218; tel: (904) 798-9148*. Open Mon–Fri 0800–1700. City and regional maps, accommodation directories and restaurant guides are available here.

### Weather

Far enough north to have recognizable seasons, Jacksonville has mild winters (daytime high temperatures averaging 66°F) and hot summers, with average highs of 90°F, which is 10–12°F higher than average spring and autumn temperatures.

### ARRIVING AND DEPARTING

**Jacksonville International Airport**, *2400 Yankee Clipper Rd; tel: (904) 741-4902*. The airport is ten miles north of the city on I-95 and I-295 and is served by 13 international and regional airlines. The **Greyhound** bus station is at *10 Pearl St; tel: (904) 356-9976*. **Jacksonville Tranportation Authority (JTA)**; *tel: (904) 630-3100*, provides local daily bus services covering 50 routes. JTA also operates the **Automated Skyway Express (ASE)**, a monorail service which serves the downtown area and is likely to be extended. **Amtrak** provides train services. The railway station is at *3570 Clifford Lane; tel: (904) 766-5110*, six miles north-west of downtown.

**Water taxis** provide a ferry service between the north and south banks of the St John's River, but the service is withdrawn when the weather is wet and

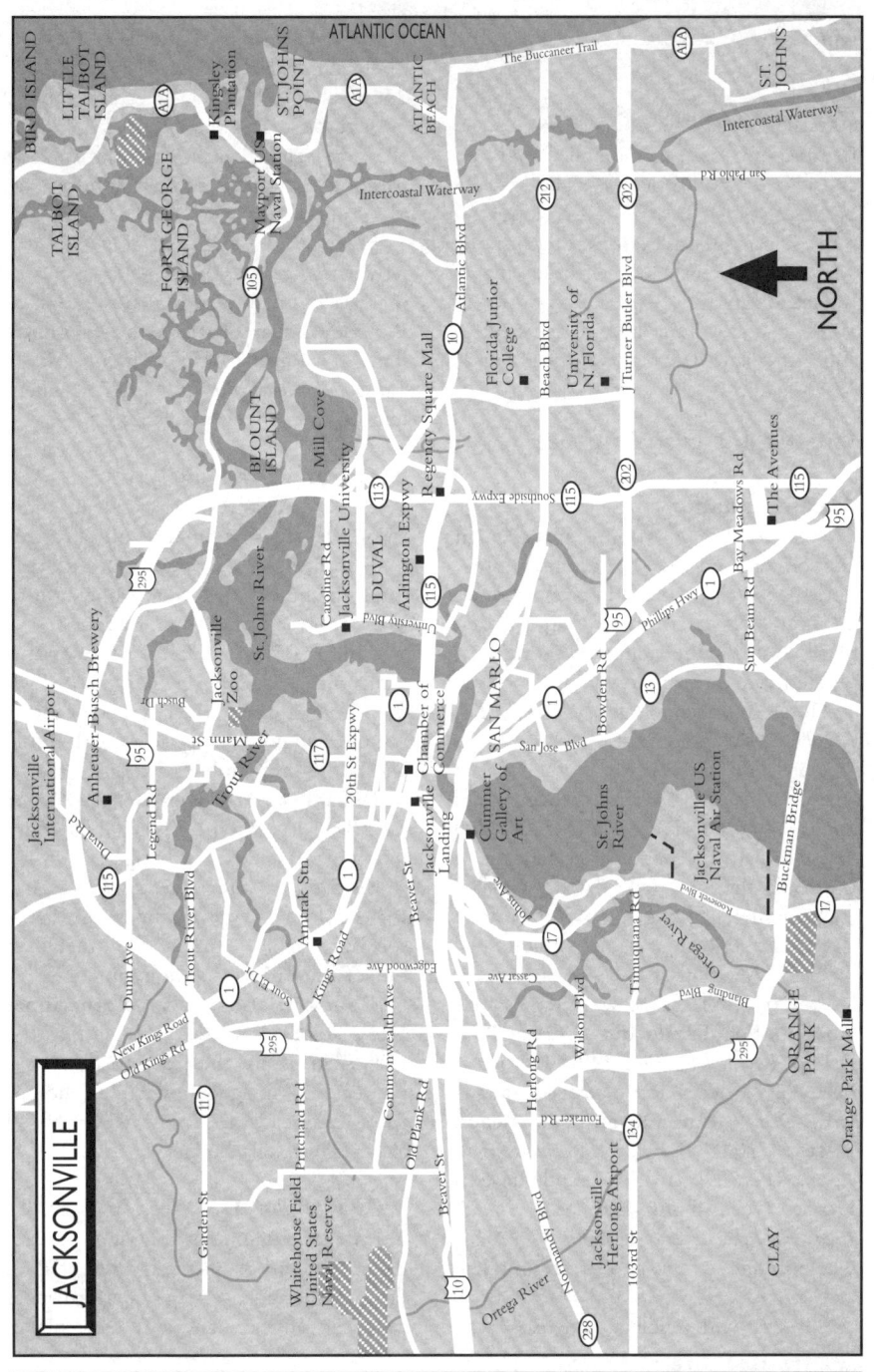

# JACKSONVILLE

**.DOWNTOWN JACKSONVILLE MAP.**

# JACKSONVILLE

windy. The fare is $2 one way, $3 for the round trip.

## GETTING AROUND

Because of its size, Jacksonville cannot be considered a walkabout city. The 12-mile bus ride to the Beaches takes about 50 mins. A car is the ideal form of transport. The city is served by three major Interstate highways – I-95, I-295 and I-10 (I-75 is a 30-min drive to the west) – and four major US highways – Hwys 1, 17, 90 and 301.

## STAYING IN JACKSONVILLE

### Accommodation

There are 12,000 rooms available in Jacksonville and the Beaches, in motels, hotels, resorts, bed and breakfast homes and inns. There are more than a dozen places to stay in the vicinity of the airport, where room rates are lower.

Hotels chains include *BW, CI, DI, ES, Hd, Ma, QI, Rd, TL.*

The only Jacksonville hotel on the riverfront is the **Marina Hotel** at *St John's Place, 1515 Prudential Dr.; tel: (904) 396-5100*. In the upper price bracket, it overlooks the Riverwalk, with a view of Jacksonville Landing across the wide river. The 184 guest-rooms are reached by glass-walled lifts.

Among the seaview choices are **Adeeb's Sea Turtle Inn**, *1 Ocean Blvd, Atlantic Beach; tel: (904) 249-7402*, it has nearly 200 rooms and a seafood restaurant, **Day's Inn Oceanfront Beach Resort**, *1031 S. First St, Jacksonville Beach; tel: (800) 321-2037*, and the **Sea Horse Oceanfront Inn**, *120 Atlantic Blvd, Neptune Beach; tel: (800) 881-2330*. These beachside properties are moderately priced.

Visitors with trailers and RVs can camp at **Flamingo Lake RV Resort**, *3640 Newcomb Rd, Jacksonville, Fl 32218-1510; tel: (904) 766-0672*. This is a new, 50-acre park near the airport has a large lake and sandy beach. Facilities include bathhouses, games room, laundry and playground.

**Fleetwood Park**, *5001 Phillips Hwy, Jacksonville; tel: (904) 737-4333*, is nearer the Beaches and the Gator Bowl. East of Regency Square Mall is the **Regency Trailer Park**, *10557 Atlantic Blvd, Jacksonville; tel: (904) 641-2273*, where tent campers are also welcome.

### Eating and Drinking

With varied cultures in its resident population, the city's restaurants and cafés present a diversity of options, from fresh catch-of-the-day to Cajun, from sushi to steak, from fast food to fine dining.

The **River City Brewing Company**, *835 Museum Circle; tel: (904) 398-2299*, is one of the city's latest eateries, offering good varied food with music and home-brew; moderate.

**Bella Pizza by Renna's**, *9426 San José Blvd; tel: (904) 733-1976*, provides filling pizzas and pastas; budget.

**Sterling's Café**, *3551 St John's Ave; tel: (904) 387-0700*, is among the 1920s speciality shops. An enticing menu of out-of-the-ordinary dishes; moderate.

**Coney Island Joe's International Deli**, *420D Wharfside Way; tel: (904) 399-5736*, is just the place to pick up a burger or a sausage sandwich and homemade lemonade to enjoy as you stroll along Riverwalk; budget.

## ENTERTAINMENT

Formal entertainment on the theatre, dance and music scene is presented in Jacksonville and a variety of performances by street musicians and entertainers takes

## JACKSONVILLE

place, particularly at **Jacksonville Landing**. Free concerts and festivals are held in **Metropolitan Park**.

The city is justifiably proud of its **Jacksonville Symphony Orchestra** and **St John's River City Band**. **Theatre Jacksonville**; *tel: (904) 396-4425*, has been operating continuously since it opened in 1919.

A variety of plays by local and national actors is performed at the **Alhambra Dinner Theatre**, *12000 Beach Blvd, Southside; tel: (904) 641-1212*. Dinner and show, Tues–Sat 1800; matinees, Sat 1100, Sun 1200. Admission: $24.50–29.50. Show only, Tues–Sat 2015; matinees, Sat 1315, Sun 1400. Admission: $15.

---

*Fairway Florida*

Golf is an obsession in Florida. There are at least 1,100 golf course – around 200 more than in any other state.

It has been reckoned that a minimum 55 million rounds of golf are played each year in the Sunshine State and 20 major professional tournaments are hosted annually by Florida.

Many courses are open to the public, some offering discounted green fees. The state has a number of high-ranking golf resorts. Overseas guests are pleasantly surprised at the modest cost of golf packages, which may include accommodation in a fairway villa, unlimited use of the driving range, guaranteed tee times and other services.

For a copy of the official Florida golf guide, *Fairways in the Sunshine*, contact Florida Sports Foundation, *107 W. Gaines St, Suite 466, Tallahassee, FL 32399; tel: (904) 488-8347*.

---

Live jazz can be heard nightly at **Partners**, *3585 St John's Ave, Avondale; tel: (904) 387-3585*, and *1222 S. Third St, Jacksonville Beach; tel: (904) 249-9550*. Live jazz or blues bands play at the **Ragtime Tap Room and Brewery**, *207 Atlantic Blvd, Atlantic Beach; tel: (904) 241-7877*, Thur–Sun. Jazz piano sessions are held Fri and Sat nights at **River City Brewing Company**, *835 Museum Centre, Southbank Riverwalk, Jacksonville; tel: (904) 399-5684*. River City also has live local jazz or blues bands Wed–Sun. Local guitar soloists and rock or reggae bands play at the **Sun Dog Diner**, *207 Atlantic Blvd; tel: (904) 241-8221*, Tues–Sun.

### Events

Jacksonville's football team, the **Jaguars**, plays at the newly renovated 73,000-seat **Gator Bowl**. The annual football match between Florida and Georgia in Oct has been a fixture since 1933.

Professional baseball is played at **Jacksonville Suns Baseball and Wolfson Park Complex**, a multi-purpose stadium which hosts motorcycle races, equestrian shows and other events.

As well as the Jacksonville Marathon, the **River Run 15K**, held in March, sees good local and national runners competing on the cross-river course.

### SHOPPING

As you might expect of a city as large as Jacksonville, the shopping opportunities are enormous.

Downtown, **Jacksonville Landing**, *2 Independent Dr.; tel: (904) 353-1188*, is an attraction in its own right. Located on the St John's River, this busy marketplace contains 65 retail and speciality shops and 17 restaurants. Open Mon–Sat 1000–2100, Sun 1200–1730.

# JACKSONVILLE

Other large shopping malls are located in the major districts. The **Avenues**, *10300 Southside Blvd, Southside; tel: (904) 363-3060*, has 125 stores, including Dillard's, Sears, Gayfers and JC Penney. Open Mon–Sat 1000–2100, Sun 1200–1800.

The **Gateway Marketplace**, *5320 Norwood Ave, Northside; tel: (904) 764-7745*, is a complex of 50 clothing, footwear and speciality shops. Open Mon–Sat 1000–2100, Sun 1230–1730.

An ice skating rink is a feature at **Market Square Mall**, *3637 Phillips Hwy, Southside; tel: (904) 396-5000*, a cluster of discount stores. Open Mon–Sat 1000–2000, Sun noon–1700.

More big names appear among the 134 stores at **Orange Park Mall**, *1910 Wells Rd, Orange Park; tel: (904) 269-2422*. Open Mon–Sat 1000–2100, Sun noon–1730.

**Regency Square Mall**, *9501 Arlington Expressway, Arlington; tel: (904) 725-1220*, is handy for both Downtown and the Beaches, being about halfway between the two. It has 165 stores, services and restaurants. Open Mon–Sat 1000–2100, Sun 1230–1730.

**Roosevelt Mall**, *4529 Roosevelt Blvd, Westside; tel: (904) 387-6255*, has more than 30 retail and service stores. Open Mon–Sat 1000–2100, Sun 1230–1730.

There are a number of shopping areas where opening hours vary from store to store.

**North Beach Area Shopping**, *at Atlantic Blvd and Hwy A1A (Third St)*, is a revitalised neighbourhood of small speciality shops, restaurants and bars close to the sea front on the edges of Atlantic Beach and Neptune Beach.

**San Marco Square** is a collection of speciality stores, restaurants and services in 1920s Mediterranean revival buildings on *San Marco Blvd, San Marco*.

The **Sandcastle Shopping Center**, *at J. Turner Blvd and Hwy A1A, Jacksonville Beach*, has more than 40 retail stores, speciality shops and restaurants.

**Shops of Historic Avondale**, *St John's Ave, Avondale*, is two blocks of some 60 stores, boutiques, food shops, art galleries, services and restaurants.

Collectors and bargain-hunters will have a great time rummaging through Jacksonville's wealth of antique stores.

**Avondale Antique Mart**, *3960 Oak St, Avondale; tel: (904) 384-9810*, is an emporium of art, books, collectables, furniture and toys. Open Mon–Sat 1000–1700.

A vast collection of antiques from local and regional interior designers and dealers is on show at **Interiors Market**, *5133 San Jose Blvd, San Jose; tel: (904) 733-2223*, which also has a café. Open Mon–Sat 1000–1700.

**Old Towne Antiques**, *2020 Carnes St, Orange Park; tel: (904) 269-3613* is a mall featuring antiques, collectibles and furniture. Open Mon–Sat 1100–1700.

Dozens of dealers trade at **Southside Antiques Mall**, *11000 Beach Blvd, Southside; tel: (904) 645-0806*. Open Mon–Sat 1000–1800, Sun noon–1800.

An exhibition of articles from the Jacksonville home of writer Harriet Beecher Stowe is featured at **Worth Antiques**, *1254 Beach Blvd, Jacksonville Beach; tel: (904) 247-2211*. Antiques, collectables and furniture are for sale. Open Mon–Sat 1000–1900, Sun 1000–1800.

## SIGHTSEEING

Jacksonville's attractions are scattered over a wide area, but you can see the city at its best by taking a stroll along the **Southbank Riverwalk**, a 1.2 mile boardwalk that runs from just east of

Acosta Bridge to about half a mile east of Main St Bridge.
Another relaxing option is to take a cruise on the river. The *Annabelle Lee*, moored at *1011 Riviera St, San Marco; tel: (904) 396-2333*, is an 1890s-style sternwheeler with room for 150 passengers. Admission: $5–20. The *Viking Sun* at *917 Dante Place, San Marco; tel: (904) 398-0797*, is a 130-ft ship offering lunch and buffet party cruises and also available for private charters. Admission: $18–31.

### General attractions

**Anheuser-Busch Brewery Tour**, *111 Busch Dr.; Northside; tel: (904) 751-8117*. Take an hourly guided or self-guided tour to find out how beer is brewed and bottled. If you are over 21 you may also taste the beer. Open Mon–Sat 0900–1600. Admission: free.

**The Beaches**; *tel: (904) 249-3868*, are a string of coastal resorts 12 miles east of Jacksonville and accessible via *Atlantic Blvd (Hwy 10), Beach Blvd (Hwy 90), J. Turner Blvd* and *Hwy A1A South*. They are **Atlantic Beach, Jacksonville Beach, Neptune Beach, Ponte Vedra Beach** and to the south **South Ponte Vedra Beach, North Beach** and **Vilano Beach**. In addition to miles of sandy white beaches, there are shopping areas and restaurants.

By following the **Black Heritage Trail** you can trace Northeast Florida's black history through a number of local sites, including Bethel Baptist Institutional Church, Edward Waters College, Olustee Battlefield and Edwin M. Stanton School. Free trail guide from Jacksonville CVB, *3 Independent Dr.; tel: (904) 798-9148*.

**Jacksonville Zoo**, *8605 Zoo Rd, Northside; tel: (904) 757-4462*, has an 11-acre recreation of the African savannah, with ostriches, gazelles, kudus and antelope. Other features are the Okavango Village, a lion exhibit, Chimpanorama, Elephant Encounters, the Florida Wetlands and an outdoor aviary. There is also a petting zoo and a railroad. Open daily 0900–1700. Admission: $4; children $2.50.

**Jacksonville Beach Fishing Pier**, *3 Sixth Ave; tel: (904) 246-6001*, is popular with anglers and sightseers. Open daily 0600–2200. Admission: fishing, $3.50; seniors and children under 8 years, $1.75; sightseers $0.75 cents.

**Kingsley Plantation**, *11676 Palmetto Ave, Fort George Island; tel: (904) 251-3537*, is Florida's oldest standing plantation, dating from the 1800s when Zephaniah Kingsley used slaves to produce sugar cane and Sea Island cotton. A nonconformist scholar and agricultural pioneer, Kingsley married a black woman, Anna Madgigine Jai. Open daily 0900–1700, admission: free.

**Mayport and the Mayport Ferry**; *tel: (904) 246-2822*. Mayport is one of the oldest fishing villages in the US and home to a large commercial shrimp boat fleet. The ferry; *tel: (904) 246-2922*, transports cars across the St John's River between Mayport, Fort George Island and Amelia Island. Open daily 0615–2215. Admission: $2.50 per car, $0.50 per bicycle.

**Mayport Naval Station**; *tel: (904) 250-5226*, is one of the largest naval ports on the East Coast. Visitors can tour the base and visit aircraft carriers and other warships. Open Sat 1000–1630, Sun 1300–1630. Admission: free.

### Museums

**Alexander Brest Museum**, *Jacksonville University, 2800 University Blvd N., Arlington; tel: (904) 744-3950 ext. 3371*.

# JACKSONVILLE

## St John's River

In many ways, the St John's River reflects the course of Florida's history. It has played an important part in the state's development, the survival of its people, exploration, industry, commerce and tourism.

The state's mightiest river, the St John's rises in marshlands 25 miles north of Lake Okeechobee and becomes one of the world's rarer north-flowing waterways as it meanders from lake to lake among the lowlands of the east coast.

Throughout its course the river provides a habitat for a wide range of wildlife: egrets, herons, ospreys and other birds, as well as many kinds of fish, alligators and the much-loved but endangered manatee, the gentle, slow-moving sea cow which may have given rise to the mermaid myth.

Humans who have found themselves relying upon the river at various stages in history have given it different names. The region's original inhabitants, the Timucua Indians, called it Welaka. To the Spanish explorers who found it in the early 16th century it was *Rio de Corrientes* – 'river of currents'.

In 1562 French Huguenots who settled along its banks named the river *Riviére de Mai* to celebrate the fact that they landed on 1 May. With help from the Timucuan people, they established a Protestant colony and built a fort on the south bank near the river's mouth, and named it *La Caroline* in honour of King Charles IX. A replica of the fort now stands near the original site, just upstream from Mayport.

Led by Pedro Menendez de Aviles, the Spanish recaptured the river in 1565, massacred the Huguenots and renamed the river the *San Mateo*. By the early 17th century, however, the river was known as the *San Juan* after a Spanish mission established on the estuary.

When the British took over Florida in 1763 they kept the name San Juan but anglicised it – and it has been known as the St John's River ever since.

Like many other rivers, the St John's was an important route for exploration and was later used to transport raw materials, goods and supplies. Commerce and industry led to the development of inland ports such as Sanford and Palatka. It also brought Florida's first tourists. Towards the end of the 19th century, wilderness trips from Jacksonville aboard steam-driven sternwheelers became popular with adventurous northerners.

The river continues to provide for tourists today. In addition to fishing, swimming, tubing, canoeing and taking excursions aboard luxury vessels of near-liner proportions, visitors can rent houseboats – floating apartments with showers, microwave ovens, television, air-conditioning and ship-to-shore radio – to explore the river in style and comfort.

---

Steuben glassware, ivory and pre-Columbian art are included in the permanent collection. Open Mon–Fri 0900–1630, Sat 1200–1700. Admission: free. **Cummer Museum of Art**, *829 Riverside Ave, Riverside; tel: (904) 356-6857.* Twelve galleries contain a collection of western art from 2000 BC onwards. A formal garden runs down to the St John's River. Open Tues–Fri 1000–1600, Sat 1200–1700, Sun 1400–1700. Admission: $3. **Jacksonville Art Museum**, *4160 Boulevard Center Dr., Southside; tel: (904) 398-8336.* Works by Picasso and Louise Nevelson are in the permanent collec-

SIGHTSEEING

tion, which also includes pre-Columbian art. There is a contemporary sculpture garden. Open Tues, Wed and Fri 1000–1600, Thur 1000–2200, Sat–Sun 1300–1700. Admission: free.
**Jacksonville Historical Center**, *Southbank Riverwalk; tel: (904) 398-4301.* The history of Jacksonville is traced from the time of the Timucua Indians to its development as a major port. Open Mon–Sat 1100–1700, Sun noon–1700. Admission: free.
**Jacksonville Maritime Museum**, *Jacksonville Landing; tel: (904) 355-9011, and Southbank Riverwalk; tel: (904) 398-9011*, has lots of model ships, paintings, photographs and maritime artefacts. Open: Landing, Mon–Sat 1100–1900, Sun 1200–1700; Riverwalk, Tues–Sun 1100–1600. Admission: free.
**Karpeles Manuscript Library**, *101 W. First St, Springfield; tel: (904) 356-2992*, houses a private collection of historical documents. Open daily 1200–1600, admission free.
**Museum of Science and History**, *1025 Museum Circle, Southbank; tel: (904) 396-7062*. Permanent hands-on exhibits and presentations include studies of bats, the history of the St John's River and medical science. Laser 3-D shows are presented in the **Alexander Brest Planetarium**. Open Mon–Fri 1000–1700, Sat 1000–1800, Sun 1300–1800. Admission: $5.

## Parks
**Big Talbot Island**, *12157 Heckscher Dr.; tel: (904) 251-2320* – an undeveloped beach area popular with bathers and watersports enthusiasts. You can park your car on the sand. Open daily 0800–dusk. Admission: $2 'honour' donation per vehicle.
**Fort Caroline National Memorial**, *12713 Fort Caroline Rd, Arlington; tel: (904) 641-7155*, was where French Huguenots landed in 1564, establishing North America's first Protestant colony. Its 680 acres contain a replica of the Huguenots' fort, a museum of French and Native American artefacts and a nature trail. Open daily 0900–1700. Admission: free.
**Huguenot Memorial Park**, *10980 Geckscher Dr.; tel: (904) 251-3335*. Another popular beach area offering surfing, windsurfing, fishing and swimming. Tent and RV camping (no hook-ups) available. Open daily 0600–dusk. Admission: $0.50.
**Little Talbot State Park**, *12157 Heckscher Dr., Jacksonville; tel: (904) 251-2320*, is a beach park with campsites, nature trails, fishing and picnic areas. Open daily 0800–dusk, admission: $3.25 per vehicle.
**Pablo Historical Park**, *425 Beach Blvd, Jacksonville Beach; tel: (904) 246-0093*. Jacksonville Beach was known as San Pablo until 1925. There are guided tours of historic buildings and remains of the Florida East Coast Railway. The museum features artefacts and photographs. Open Mon–Sat 1000–1600, Sun 1300–1600. Admission: free.

## Wildlife
**BEAKS**, *12084 Houston Ave, Big Talbot Island; tel: (904) 251-2473*. The name is an acronym for Bird Emergency Aid and Kare Sanctuary. BEAKS rescues and cares for thousands of injured wild birds. Among the patients are eagles, ospreys, owls and pelicans. Open Fri–Sat 1200–700. Admission: donation.
**Tree Hill**, *7152 Lone Star Rd, Arlington; tel: (904) 724-4646*. A hardwood forest, nature trails and environmental exhibits are contained within this 42-acre nature centre.

# JACKSONVILLE–LIVE OAK

This route takes us away from big city Jacksonville and into the drowsy Deep South ambience of Northern Florida. It even gives us a peep into a fascinating corner of Georgia. Apart from the 12-mile stretch between Jacksonville and Atlantic Beach and a similar distance of modern highway west of Fernandina Beach, much of the journey is along rural state and county highways.

ROUTE: 175 MILES

## ROUTE

From downtown Jacksonville follow Atlantic Blvd (Hwy 10) east for 12 miles. At **Atlantic Beach** head north on Hwy A1A. At Mayport cross the St John's River on the Mayport Ferry (fare: $2.50 per car). It takes five minutes to reach Fort George Island. From here the route is known as the **Buccaneer Trail**.

After another eight miles, a bridge on Hwy A1A crosses the Nassau River to **Amelia Island**, one of the most attractive places on Florida's Atlantic coast.

At **Fernandina Beach** stay on A1A by turning left at the crossroads at the start of the downtown area (traffic lights at the intersection of *Atlantic Ave, Centre St* and *8th St*) and continue west for 12 miles to **Yulee**. Bear right on to Hwy 17, which passes under I-95 after seven miles then crosses the state line into Georgia.

At **Kingsland** turn left on to Hwy 40 and drive west for 21 miles to **Folkston**. Cross the Amtrak railway and follow Hwy 23/121 south, passing the entrance to **Okefenokee National Wildlife Refuge** and continuing for 23 miles to Toledo and Saint George. Turn right and head east on Hwy 94 towards **Fargo**, 20 miles away, where there is another entrance to Okefenokee National Wildlife Refuge.

On the outskirts of Fargo peel south on Hwy 89, which becomes Hwy 441 as it crosses the Florida state line. Turn right on to Hwy 6 after 17 miles. After another three miles turn left on to Hwy 135 which passes through **Big Shoals State Forest** and reaches **White Springs**, home of the **Stephen C. Foster State Folk Culture Center**. From White Springs, Hwy 135 continues for 14 miles to Live Oak.

## AMELIA ISLAND

Tourist Information: Amelia Island Tourist Development Council, *PO Box 472, Fernandina Beach, FL, 32035-0472; tel: (904) 277-0717 or 1-800-2-AMELIA.*

The **Chamber of Commerce visitor centre** is located in the depot of Florida's first cross-state railway, at *102 Centre St; tel: (904) 261-3248*. An old locomotive serves as a memorial and landmark. The centre is well stocked with brochures on attractions, accommodation, restaurants and shopping, and the friendly staff are ready with a wealth of local knowledge. Pick up a copy of the locally published – and free – *Amelia Now*. Open Mon–Fri 0900–1700. **TelEvent** is a 24-hour telephone information guide with weather reports and information on seasonal events, restaurants, accommodation, shopping and recreation opportunities; *tel: (904) 277-1599*.

### ACCOMMODATION

The island has more than 2,000 rooms, mostly in and around Fernandina Beach, ranging from charming bed and breakfast inns and family lodges to luxurious resorts and seaside condominiums.

About half of the available rooms in the area are to be found at the **Amelia Island Plantation**, *PO Box 3000, Amelia Island, FL, 32035-1307; tel: (904) 261-6161 or (800) 874-6878*. The resort is on the island's south east shore and is signposted off *Hwy A1A*. Covering 1,250 acres, it offers 17 varying types of accommodation – all in the expensive to pricey category – ranging from deluxe hotel rooms and penthouses to three-bedroom beach townhouses and villas. Guests can choose from oceanfront, marsh or fairway views. Amenities include five restaurants and two lounges, 45 holes of golf, 21 tennis courts, 17 pools, a fitness centre, fishing and sailing.

The **Ritz-Carlton Amelia Island**, *4750 Amelia Island Parkway, Amelia Island, FL 32034; tel: (904) 277-110 or (800) 241-3333*, also signposted off *Hwy A1A*, is another expensive to pricey resort, this time with a total of 449 rooms and suites, each with a beach view and private balcony. It has 1½ miles of beach, three restaurants, two lounges, 11 tennis courts, two swimming pools and a fitness centre. Nearby is the Golf Club of Amelia Island.

The island's third upscale property is **Summer Beach Resort**, *5000 Amelia Island Parkway, Amelia Island, FL, 32034; tel: (904) 277-0905 or (800) 772-3359*, which also encompasses the Golf Club of Amelia Island. It has 52 two- and three-bedroom villas on oceanfront and poolside locations. Amenities include an 18-hole championship golf course, three pools, whirlpool and deck, shelling and fishing. Guests may use the Ritz-Carlton tennis facilities.

Fernandina Beach has half a dozen motels and small hotels, mostly in the budget to moderate price range. The town also has a dozen bed and breakfast inns, including Florida's oldest tourist hotel. This is the **Florida House Inn**, *22 S. Third St; tel: (904) 261-3300 or (800) 258-3301*, which has 11 moderate to expensive rooms. The **Hoyt House**, *804 Atlantic Ave (the intersection of Hwy A1A and Centre St); tel: (904) 277-4300 or (800) 432-2085*, is a delightful Queen Anne-style residence built by a wealthy banker in 1905 and now catering for travellers in nine superbly appointed rooms with private baths. The Hoyt House is one of the few inns in the area to serve a full as opposed to continental breakfast.

There are two campgrounds, both in **Fort Clinch State Park**, *2601 Atlantic Ave; tel: (904) 277-7274*. One campground is on the oceanside, the other is in a riverside, woodland setting and there are 62 pitches. Prices range from $12–17 a day.

### EATING AND DRINKING

Amelia has about 40 restaurants, ranging from candlelight and kitsch to 'shuck 'em yourself' shrimp and oyster eateries. There are some surprising bedfellows. The Amelia Island Plantation, for example, has both the expensive **Amelia Inn** and **The Coop**, open daily 0800–1500, with breakfast and luncheon dishes in the cheap rather than budget scale.

**Brett's Waterway Cafe**, overlooking Fernandina Harbour Marina at the foot of *Centre St; tel: (904) 261-2660*, is the most prominent of the town's eating places and certainly one of the most popular in the moderate to pricey range.

The **Crab Trap**, *31 N. Second St; tel: (904) 261-4749*, serves moderately priced dinner daily from 1700, specialising in seafood – blackened, broiled or fried – chicken steaks and oysters year round. Casual dress; pub bar upstairs.

**Down Under Restaurant**, so called because it's down under the *Hwy A1A* bridge that connects the island with mainland Florida, about four miles west of Fernandina Beach, offers moderately-priced value-for-money dinner daily from 1700.

The **Florida House Inn**, *22 S. Third St; tel: (904) 261-3300 or (800) 258-3301*, serves traditional Southern cooking complete with collard greens, blackeye peas, mashed potatoes and gravy, home-made biscuits and cornbread at budget prices – all served in chummy boarding–house style.

For something completely different, the **Great Khan**, *1521 Sadler Rd; tel: (904) 261-5887*, serves a 'do-it-yourself' Mongolian barbecue for dinner. You choose the ingredients, the chef cooks them before your very eyes.

Florida's oldest bar is said to be the **Palace Saloon**, *117 Centre St; tel: (904) 261-6320*. In the past it has served the likes of the Carnegies and Rockefellers and its speciality is a 22oz Pirate's Punch with rum *and* gin adding a kick to a mix of lemon, lime, orange and pineapple juices. The saloon's batwing doors open daily 1030–0200.

For those who like to eat with the fleet or booze as they cruise, the **Emerald Princess** sails from Fernandina Beach Marina; *tel: (800) 842-0115*, nine times a week, serving brunch or dinner and a buffet on the way back. On the way back from where? Good question, because the ship simply sails over the horizon into international waters where casino gambling is legal. There are 70 slot machines on board as well as a squadron of dealers only too pleased to introduce passengers to the pleasures of craps, blackjack, roulette and Caribbean poker. For non-gamblers there's live music and dancing. Admission: $20-45.

## Sightseeing

Daily **walking tours** of Fernandina Beach's 50-block **historic district** start from outside the visitor centre at the foot of *Centre St*. Admission: $5.

The town's major attraction is itself: a splendid a piece of vintage Americana as ever graced a Norman Rockwell painting. *Centre St* has cobblestone walks, wrought iron benches and replica gas lanterns to complement the town's ornate Victorian and Edwardian homes, many of which are listed in the National Register of Historic Places.

**Amelia Island Museum of History** is located in the old town jail at 233 S. Third St; tel: (904) 261-7378. The island's 4,000-year history and the story of the Victorian seaport are told through artefacts, maps and photographs. Open Mon–Sat 1100–1500; guided tours 1100 and 1400. Admission: donation.

**Fort Clinch State Park**, *2601 Atlantic Ave; tel: (904) 277-7274*. Covering more than 1,100 acres, the park encompasses a Civil War era fort in a remarkable state of preservation. Park rangers wearing Union uniforms bring history to life as they carry out the daily chores of the garrison soldier of 1864. Special full-garrison re-enactments are staged twice a year, reflecting the Union view in May and the Confederate in October. The park has a nature trail along which alligators, wading birds and many small animals may be seen. There are picnic sites, fishing facilities and a gift shop. Open daily 0800-dusk. Admission: $3.25 per vehicle.

## KINGSLAND

**Tourist Information: Kingsland Convention and Visitors Bureau**, *PO Box 1928, Kingsland, GA, 31548; tel: (912) 729-5999*. **Kingsland Welcome Center**, *107 S. Lee St; tel: (912) 729-5613*.

Kingsland's several antique shops attract collectors. The town is in Georgia's Coastal Corner, home of the annual Labor Day Catfish Festival (first Mon in Sept). Local rivers and creeks provide fishing, canoeing and boating.

Self-catering accommodation is available, moderately-priced, at **Mariners Suites**, *2343 Village Dr.; tel: (902) 882-3004*. South of Kingsland, on the west side of *I-95* at Exit 1 (*St Mary's Rd*) a **KOA** campground, open all year, provides shady camping with a games room, playground, swimming pool and volleyball area. For information write to **KOA**, *PO Box 18244, Jacksonville, FL, 32229;(912) 729-3232*.

### Side Track from Kingsland

## ST MARY'S

**Tourist Information: St Mary's Tourism Council**, *414 Osborne St, PO Box 1291, St Mary's, GA 31558; tel: (912) 882-6200*. **Orange Hall Welcome Center**; *tel: (912) 882-4000*, with a museum and gift shop, is housed in a Greek Revival antebellum mansion which is on the National Register of Historic Places. Tourist information is available. Open Mon–Sat 0900–1700, Sun 1300–1700.

St Mary's **historic district** dates from the late 18th century. Nearly 40 sites are on the Braille Trail, with raised letters and Braille for visitors who are sight-impaired. Local sightseeing includes the **Toonerville Trolley**, which was used on the St Mary's Railroad until 1938.

Wild horses, loggerhead turtles and

other wildlife are seen at **Cumberland Island National Seashore**. It is a popular place for saltwater fishing, swimming, shell collecting, backpacking and primitive camping.

Reservations; *tel: (912) 882-4335*, are required for the passenger ferry, *Cumberland Island Queen*, that plies between downtown St Mary's waterfront and the island. Braille plaques are provided on the island. Sun afternoon tours of **Plum Orchard, Carnegie Home** are available; *tel: (912) 882-4335*.

St Mary's also has one of the best-preserved tabby structures on the coast. **The McIntosh Sugar Mill Tabby Ruins** are on *Spur 40; tel: (912) 882-6200*, near the main gates of Kings Bay Naval Submarine Base. Tabby, a building material made of oyster shells, sand and water, is unique to the southern coast. Rooms were used to grind and boil cane for sugar products.

The public can play an 18-hole course overlooking salt marshes, lakes and woodland at a new attraction, **Osprey Cove**; *tel: (912) 882-5575*.

Air tours of coastal Georgia, including whale-watching, are available from **Air Tours**, *400 N Dandy St; tel: (912) 882-4359*.

Six miles north of St Mary's is **Crooked River State Park**; *tel: (912) 882-5256*. It has overnight camping facilities.

Bed and breakfast accommodation is available at **Goodbread House** (moderately–priced), a Victorian inn, *209 Osborne St; tel: (912) 882-7490*; **Riverview Hotel** (moderately-priced), on the waterfront at *105 Osborne St; tel: (912) 882-3242*; and the historic 14-room **Spencer House Inn** (moderate to expensive), *101 E. Bryant St; tel: (912) 882-1872*. All are close to the Cumberland Island ferry.

## FOLKSTON

**Tourist Information: Folkston/Charlton County Chamber of Commerce**, *Main St, Folkston; tel: (912) 496-2536*. The office is in the restored 1903 Old Train Depot, where there is a museum of early railway artefacts.

Camping for tents and trailers is available at **Trailers Hill Recreation Park**, 3½ miles south of Folkston on the St Mary's River. Facilities include a cooking shed for groups, showers and a boat ramp.

**Sardis Church**, dating from the early 19th century, in *Post Rd*, is the county's oldest. A hole in the pulpit is from a musket ball fired by a soldier defending the church from Indians.

## OKEFENOKEE SWAMP

**Okefenokee Swamp National Wildlife Refuge**, lies off *Hwy 23/121; tel: (912) 496-3331*. This 700-square mile unique eco-system has its east entrance eight miles southwest of Folkston, giving convenient access to the **Visitor Center**, guided boat tours, boat and canoe rentals, hiking trails, a 4½-mile wildlife drive, a 4,000-ft boardwalk over the swamp, two observation towers and a restored 1920s homestead.

The **Suwannee Canal** can be navigated by canoe and small motorboat into the heart of the Okefenokee. Those travelling wilderness canoe trails through the refuge need permission for trips lasting two to five days.

Alligators, turtles and many other reptiles, nearly 50 mammal species and more than 200 bird species, including the sandhill crane, live in the refuge.

The Visitor Center has displays showing some of the wildlife, including scenes of underwater and surface life. The refuge is open daily except Christmas Day. Admission charged.

## WHITE SPRINGS

Tourist Information: Suwannee County Tourist Development Council, *PO Drawer C, Live Oak, FL, 32060; tel: (904) 362-3071.*

The Suwannee River flows through White Springs, so this was an appropriate place to provide a memorial to the man who put the river on the world map – Stephen Foster, composer of *The Old Folks At Home*, Florida's state song. Foster's home was Pittsburgh, Pennsylvania – he was born in 1826. He probably never set foot in Florida. Well signposted from all directions, the **Stephen C. Foster State Folk Culture Center**; *tel: (904) 397-2733*, opened in 1950, displays a letter showing that Foster chose the Suwannee River for his nostalgic song because it sounded better than his original choice, the Pedee River.

Dioramas illustrating some of his songs – *Jeanie With the Light Brown Hair, Oh! Susanna, My Old Kentucky Home* - reflect a curiously romantic view of slavery. Pianos and desks at which Foster worked can be seen.

Guided tours of the centre's museum and carillon tower, which plays some of Foster's tunes, take place daily. Craftspeople demonstrate their skills in the **Craft Square**; *tel: (904) 397-1920* for a schedule of demonstrations. There is a well-stocked gift shop.

Special events take place throughout the year at the centre and in the extensive grounds, a major one being the annual **Florida Folk Festival**, held for three days in late-May. Regional and ethnic food is served, arts and crafts and music – including the official Florida State Fiddle Contest – contribute to the entertainment. Open daily 0800–sunset. Admission: $3.25 per vehicle.

White Springs, known then as White Sulphur Springs, was promoted as a health resort from the turn of the century and still had some adherents into the 1950s. Earlier, Indians had recognised the sulphur spring's curative powers. In 1906 the spring was walled to keep out the river. Shops, changing rooms and clinical examination rooms were built.

## LIVE OAK

Tourist Information: Suwanee County Tourist Development Council, *PO Drawer C, Live Oak, FL 32060; tel: (904) 362-4758.*

Unless you need fuel or fast food, Live Oak is not really worth a stop. However, 13 miles west of Live Oak, off *Hwy 90*, is the **Suwannee River State Park**; *tel: (904) 362-2746*, where fishing, camping, picnicking and canoeing can be enjoyed and there are hiking trails to follow.

An overlook, gives a panoramic view of the confluence of the Suwannee River with the Withlacoochee River, amid wooded hillsides.

In the park are earthworks built by Confederate soldiers during the Civil War and a cemetery. The landing place used by steamboats which once cruised the rivers can still be seen.

# St Petersburg–Tallahassee

Following the Gulf of Mexico from Tampa Bay north to Apalachee Bay, then inland to the state capital, this route traverses Florida's least populated coastal region with the exception of the extreme south west. It crosses a number of waterways, including the **Suwanee River** and provides opportunities to see some of the 'real Florida'.

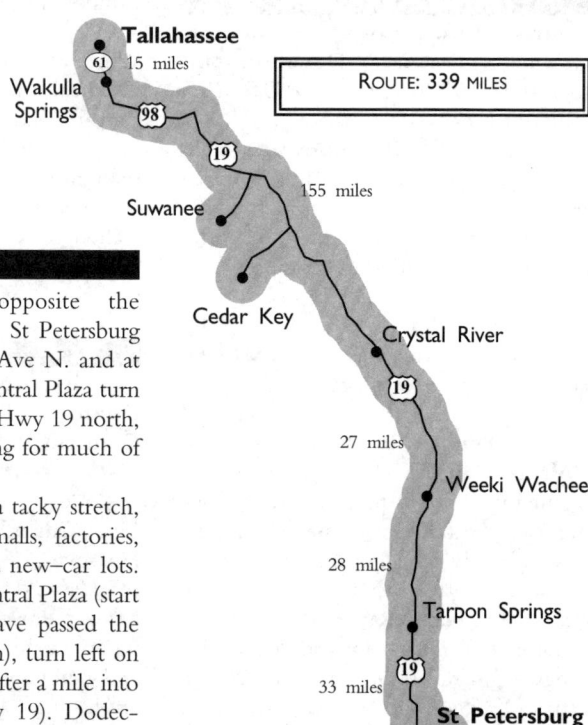

ROUTE: 339 MILES

## ROUTE

From Bayshore Dr, opposite the Municipal Marina, next to St Petersburg Pier, drive west along 1st Ave N. and at the main Post Office in Central Plaza turn right on to 34th St. This is Hwy 19 north, which you will be following for much of the journey.

The first few miles are a tacky stretch, lined with big shopping malls, factories, office blocks and used–and new–car lots. Some 25 miles north of Central Plaza (start looking as soon as you have passed the Klosterman Rd intersection), turn left on to Tarpon Ave, then right after a mile into N. Pinellas Ave (Alt Hwy 19). Dodecanese Blvd, which goes to the left just before the highway crosses the Anclote River, leads to downtown **Tarpon Springs**, a community almost as Greek as some places in the Aegean Sea.

Alt 19 swings to the north east and brings us back on to Hwy 19 after three miles. **Weeki Wachee** is reached after a further 25 miles. Another 22 miles brings us to **Homosassa Springs**, where the state park of the same name is on the left as we travel north. **Crystal River** is another 7 miles to the north.

**Otter Creek**, 35 miles north of Crystal River, is the start of a sidetrack to the quaint resort village of **Cedar Key,** and after another 25 miles Hwy 19 crosses the Suwannee River to reach **Old Town,**

## ST PETERSBURG–TALLAHASSEE

where another side track leads us to the tiny community of **Suwannee**.

Just south of **Perry**, 54 miles north of Old Town, we leave Hwy 19 and follow Hwy 98 west across the Aucilla Wildlife Management Area, an unpopulated coastal flatland, reaching the village of **Newport** in 41 miles.

Three miles south of Newport, at the southern end of Hwy 363, is tiny **St Marks** and **San Marcos de Apalache State Historic Site**; *tel: (904) 922-6007*. The ruined fort, overlooking the confluence of the St Mark's and Wakulla rivers, was built in 1679 on the site of the landing in 1528 of the explorer Panfilo de Narvaez. A museum displays pottery and tools unearthed near the original fort. Open 0800–dusk. Admission: free (small charge for admission to museum).

St Marks lies at the southern end of the **Tallahassee–St Marks Historic Railroad State Trail**. The railroad was the oldest in Florida, built in 1837 to transport cotton and other products to the port of St Marks. The tracks have been removed, but the 16-mile trail is now used by cyclists, skaters, hikers, joggers and horseback riders. Bicycles maybe rented at the northern end of the trail. For information; *tel: (904) 922-6007*.

Also in St Marks, conveniently placed at the end of the railroad trail, is **Posey's Oyster Bar** (no tel), an easy-going and moderately-priced seafood restaurant specialising in home-smoked fish and, of course, oysters.

From St Marks, Hwy 363 runs due north passing **Wakulla Springs State Park** to intersect with Hwy 61, which soon becomes Monroe St and runs into the heart of downtown Tallahassee.

### TARPON SPRINGS

**Tourist Information: Tarpon Springs**

**Chamber of Commerce**, *210 S. Pinellas Ave; tel: (813) 937-6109*. The office supplies local maps, accommodation information and a restaurant guide.

Tarpon Springs wears its Greekness like a flamboyant moustache. Greek music pours from open windows, Greek conversation is shouted across the street, the smell of Greek cooking drifts in the air. The Greek flag flutters beside the Stars and Stripes above the old **Sponge Exchange** on *Dodecanese Blvd,* and sponges of all shapes and sizes are displayed along the sidewalks. The main attractions in Tarpon Springs are the shops and tavernas located in the former sponge warehouses, chandleries and fisherfolk cottages located on Dodecanese Blvd alongside the Anclote River.

The only way to see what the place has to offer is on foot. As in Greece, driving can be a bit hazardous, with pedestrians suddenly stepping off the sidewalk and other vehicles making sudden appearances from sidestreets. Parking is plentiful (for a fee) so it's best to get rid of the car for a while.

Most accommodation is found on the approaches to the city, with a number of motels located along both Hwy 19 and *Tarpon Ave*. The most upmarket accommodation in the area is to be found at **Innisbrook Hilton Resort**, *PO Box 1088, Tarpon Springs, FL 34688-1088; tel: (813) 942-2000*. Located off Hwy 19, just south of Klosterman Rd, Innisbrook is a luxury conference, sports and leisure resort on 1,000 acres, featuring three renowned championship golf courses, 15 tennis courts, six swimming pools, a wildlife preserve and 1,000 condominium suites in 28 lodges.

The nearest **KOA** campground is at *37061 Hwy 19 N., Palm Harbor; tel: (813) 937-8412*, 2 miles south of Tarpon

## Mopping Up Souvenirs

Tarpon Springs calls itself the Sponge Capital of America and it's not difficult to see why as you walk down Dodecanese Blvd, the main street that runs alongside the Anclote River. Sponges of all shapes and sizes – some as large as coffee tables, others as small and shapely as a lady's fingers – are displayed on trestle tables and the sidewalk outside souvenir shops. There are sponges for cleaning the car, sponges for growing plants in, sponges for decoration. Few people except the British, it seems, use them in the bath.

The sponge beds in the Gulf of Mexico, off Tarpon Springs, were discovered at the end of the 19th century by John Corcoris, a buyer for a New York sponge company. He invited his two brothers and other men from the Aegean island of Kalymnos to join him in harvesting the beds – and Tarpon Springs began its rapid metamorphosis from sleepy Southern village into a lively Greek community. Tarpon Springs prospered, and by the 1940s it could justifiably regard itself as the world's leading sponge-trading centre, with sales worth more than $3 million a year. Then came the 'Red Tide', marine bacteria that destroyed the sponge beds and put divers out of work. Eventually, the epidemic ended and the beds recovered, but by then plastic sponges were being widely used and the traditional industry never got back on its feet. Thanks to a long rest and comparatively low-level harvesting, the Tarpon Springs beds are once again producing some of the best-ever sponges.

Springs. Another option is **Bay Aire RV Park**, *2242 Alt Hwy 19 N., Palm Harbor; tel: (813) 784-4082.*

If they're not selling sponges, it seems the people of Tarpon Springs are selling food. There are cafes and restaurants large and small, cheap and pricey – even a small souvlakia and kebab stall calling itself 'The Greek answer to McDonalds'.

The biggest event of the year is in Jan when Epiphany is celebrated in traditional Greek style by young men who dive for a cross thrown into the sea. **Sponge-diving** boat trips, staged strictly for tourists, depart regularly from the sponge dock on *Dodecanese Blvd.* Ashore, you can learn more about sponges at the **Spongerama Exhibition** in the Sponge Factory, *510 Dodecanese Blvd; tel: (813) 942-3771.* Open daily 1000–1730. Admission: free.

**St Nicholas Greek Orthodox Cathedral**, *36 N. Pinellas Ave; tel: (813) 937-3540,* is a replica of St Sophia in Istanbul, with richly sculptured marble, elaborate icons and stained glass. Open daily 0900–1700. Admission: donation.

### WEEKI WACHEE

**Tourist Information:** Hernando County Chamber of Commerce, *101 E. Fort Dade Ave, Brooksville, FL, 34601; tel: (904) 796-2420.* The office is 12 miles west of Weeki Wachi on Hwy 50, and it provides maps and a restaurant guide.

**Weeki Wachee Spring**, *6131 Commercial Way, Spring Hill, FL, 34606; tel: (904) 596-2062,* is the site of Florida's only spring-fed water theme park, **Buccaneer Bay**, where people can swim and enjoy a natural sandy beach, a supervised children's area and three waterslides. Buccaneer Bay is open late-Mar–Sept.

Weeki Wachee Spring, open daily 0930–1730, is not to be missed. Take the wilderness river trip. You will almost certainly see otters, raccoons, turtles and a variety of birds. Free-flying raptors are on display, directed by a demonstrator on horseback.

The park's *pièce de résistance* is over the

top and under the water. A screen provides a view of beautiful mermaids, their long hair flowing in the current as they perform in The Little Mermaids and in liquid dance routines. Open daily 0900–1800. Admission: $15.

## CRYSTAL RIVER

**Tourist Information:** Crystal River Chamber of Commerce, *28 N.W. Hwy 19, Crystal River, FL, 34428-3900; tel: (904) 795-3149*. **Homosassa Springs Chamber of Commerce,** *PO Box 709, Homosassa Springs, FL, 34447-0709; tel: (904) 628-2666*. Open Mon–Fri 0830–1700. Both offices provide maps and information on accommodation and restaurants.

Crystal River, with a number of small hotels and motels clustered around a picturesque tangle of canals, creeks and bays, is a good stopover point, especially for those keen on diving.

**Port Paradise Resort,** *1610 SE Paradise Circle, Crystal River, FL, 34428; tel: (904) 795-3111*, has a diving school and a marina where boats may be rented for birdwatching and manatee-viewing. Accommodation is in self-catering apartments and there is a dockside restaurant. *Paradise Point Rd* runs west from Hwy 19 and ends at the resort after about a mile.

There are two campgrounds in the area. **Citrus County Chassahowitzka River Campground,** *8600 W. Miss Maggie Dr., Homosassa, FL, 34446-5307; tel: (904) 382-2200*, is on the edge of the Chassahowitzka National Wildlife Refuge and has boat and canoe rentals. **Crystal Isles RV Resort,** *11419 W. Fort Island Trail, Crystal River, FL, 34429; tel: (904) 795-3774* is located on a canal leading to the Crystal River. Both campgrounds have tent pitches and full RV hook-ups.

**Crystal River State Archaeological Site,** *3400 N. Museum Point, Crystal River; tel: (904) 795-3817*, is a 14-acre temple and burial site used by Native Americans for some 1,600 years. The visitor centre has displays of ceremonial and domestic artefacts recovered from 450 graves. Open daily 0800–dusk (visitor centre 0900–1700). Admission: $3.25 per vehicle.

**Homosassa Springs State Wildlife Park,** *9225 W. Fish Bowl Dr., Homosassa; tel: (904) 628-2311*, gives visitors a chance to view manatees close up. Other wildlife displays include a Florida black bear, bobcats, alligators, birds and snakes. The most interesting feature, however, is an underwater observatory where you can watch manatees and thousands of colourful fish swimming by. Open daily 0900–1730 (ticket office closes 1600). Admission: $6.95; children, $3.95.

### SIDE TRACKS FROM CRYSTAL RIVER

For Cedar Key go to Otter Creek, 34 miles north of Crystal River, then take Hwy 24 west for 21 miles. For Suwanee go to Old Town, 31 miles north of Otter Creek, then travel 23 miles west on Hwy 349.

## CEDAR KEY

**Tourist Information:** Cedar Key Area Chamber of Commerce, *PO Box 610, Cedar Key, FL, 32625; tel: (904) 543-5600*. Maps and information on accommodation and dining. Open Mon–Tues, Thur–Fri 0900–noon, 1300–1500. The office is in the old City Hall on Second St.

Picturesque Cedar Key, with its higgledy-piggledy buildings, is a delightful small town that started out as a thriving port when the railroad came through from Fernandina Beach in the 1860s.

After a period of decline, it is now making a come-back as a 'Real Florida' destination for discerning holidaymakers. The town has a good selection of private hotels, bed and breakfast inns and holiday homes. There are pitches for tents and RVs at **Cedar Key RV Park**, a short walk from downtown at *G St; tel: (904) 543-5150*. Restaurants are plentiful, too, most of them a few minutes' walk of the pier on *Dock St*.

**Cedar Key Historical Society Museum**, *Second St at Hwy 24*. Oyster-fishing equipment and other artefacts are displayed with newspaper cuttings and photographs to tell the town's story. Open Mon–Sat 1100–1600, Sun 1300–1600. Admission: donation.

**Cedar Key State Museum**, *1710 Museum Dr.; tel: (904) 543-5350*, traces the town's history before, during and after the Civil War. Open Thur–Mon 0900–1700. Admission: 50 cents.

## SUWANEE

You may want to make this trip for no other reason than to say you have been to the very mouth of Stephen Foster's Suwannee River. It's worth making the 23-mile drive from Old Town to see a rare piece of working Floridiana.

Suwanee (pop under 1,000) is mainly a shellfishing port that attracts boating enthusiasts and campers. The **Salt Creek Shellfish Co** on the dock; *tel: (904) 542-7072*, has a roomy restaurant where you can watch the latest catch being brought in as you eat. The budget–moderate menu, featuring clams, crabs, oysters, shrimps and frogs' legs, is printed on the back of a tide table.

You can camp or rent a cabin at **Miller's**, *PO Box 280, Suwannee, FL, 32692; tel: (904) 542-7349*. You can also rent a self-skippered houseboat and set off to navigate the river. There are two other camping options in the area. **Suwannee River KOA**, a mile and a half north of Old Town on Hwy 349; *tel: (904) 542-7636*, has riverside sites for tents and RVs, cabins and a grocery store. **Yellow Jacket Landing**, nine miles south of Old Town on Hwy 349; *tel: (904) 542-8365*, also has RV and tent facilities and cabins plus four fishing lakes.

## WAKULLA SPRINGS

**Tourist Information:** Wakulla County Chamber of Commerce, *PO Box 598, Crawfordville, FL, 32326-0598; tel: (904) 926-1848*.

**Wakulla Springs State Park**, *1 Spring Dr.; tel: (904) 922-3633*. This has to be a contender for the top slot among Florida's many state parks and springs. Here is a wonderful park with one of the world's biggest, deepest natural springs, the source of the St Mark's River that winds its primeval way through cypress swamps inhabited by alligators, snakes, deer and all kinds of wild birds.

Visitors may swim within feet of the spring that pumps out 400,000 gallons of clear water a day and is so clear you can peer into its 180 ft depths from a glass-bottomed boat. Also available is a 45-minute boat tour of the wild swamp areas, including locations that appeared in several early Tarzan films and in *The Creature from the Black Lagoon*. Open daily 0900–1730. Admission: $3.25 per vehicle. Boat trips: $4.50.

You can stay in the park at the moderately priced **Wakulla Lodge**; *tel: (904) 224-5950*, a small, colonial-style hotel with an excellent dining room and conference facilities.

# JACKSONVILLE–TALLAHASSEE

Although Jacksonville and Tallahassee are both places full of interest, the routes connecting them are not among the world's most rewarding journeys. There are only two alternatives: I-10 and Hwy 90 and since one is in sight of the other for much of the way there isn't much to choose between. I-10 covers the journey in 168 miles – about three hours driving. Hwy 90 adds about 11 miles to the trip and passes through the few communities between the two major cities.

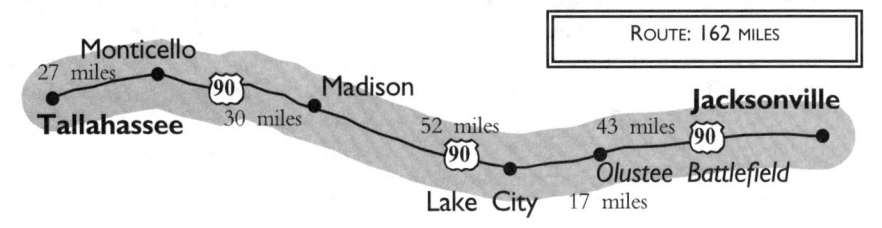

ROUTE: 162 MILES

Monticello 27 miles — 90 — 30 miles — Madison — 52 miles — 90 — 43 miles — 90 — Jacksonville
Tallahassee                                                        Olustee Battlefield
                                   Lake City    17 miles

## ROUTE

From downtown Jacksonville, head north on *Main St* and turn left (west) on to *Beaver St*, which is also *Hwy 90 west*. All you have to do now is keep going! It takes a long time to get through Jacksonville's suburbs, and the flat, open countryside is scarcely inspiring.

A change of scenery comes about at the small township of Sanderson, where Hwy 90 switches to the south side of I-10, passing **Olustee Battlefield State Historic Site** and continuing along the southern edge of **Osceola National Forest** before reaching **Lake City**.

Between Lake City and Live Oak (see **Jacksonville–Live Oak** route, p 286), the countryside becomes more pastoral. West of Live Oak the highway crosses back to the north side of the interstate, where it remains until it reaches the outskirts of Tallahassee after passing through **Madison** and **Monticello**. This last section of the journey, from Madison to the west, is most attractive, with live oaks and magnolias becoming more abundant and Spanish moss giving the area that unmistakably Southern ambience.

On the outskirts of Tallahassee, Hwy 90 becomes *Mahan Dr.*, passes under I-10 and continues for another four miles to its intersection with *Capital Circle (Hwy 261)*, where it changes to *Tennessee St*. After four miles, Hwy 90 intersects with *Monroe St N (Hwy 27)*, where a left turn takes you to the Old State Capitol and downtown Tallahassee.

## OLUSTEE BATTLEFIELD

**Olustee Battlefield State Historic Site**, on *Hwy 90, two miles east of*

*Olustee; tel: (904) 752-3866*, saw a bloody battle in 1864 during the Civil War. This was the only major Civil War battle to take place in Florida and a monument stands on the site. More than 1,800 Union troops and 946 Confederate soldiers were casualties at this quiet, tree-clad site. The battle is re-enacted at Olustee every Feb.

A trail leads through the site. Open daily 0900—1700 (interpretive centre closed Tues and Wed). Admission: free.

## LAKE CITY

**Tourist Information: Lake City/Columbia County Tourist Development Council**, PO Box 1847, Lake City, FL, 32056; tel: (904) 758-1312.

Hotels and motels to be found on Hwy 90 on the outskirts of the city include **Econo Lodge**, 5500 W. Hwy 90; tel: (904) 752-7891,budget; **Holiday Inn**, Hwy 90 and I-75; tel: (904) 752-3901, moderate; and **Piney Woods Lodge**, Hwy 13 and Hwy 90; tel: (904) 752-8334, budget. **KOA Lake City North** is 1 mile north of I-10 intersection on Hwy 441; tel: (904) 752-9131.

Lake City is on the south–west edge of the vast **Osceola National Forest**; tel: (904) 752-2577, where people cool off by tubing in the Ichetucknee River. Canoeing and diving are popular at nearby **High Springs**. The forest has some good fishing and a number of cypress swamps.

**Florida Sports Hall of Fame**, 601 Hall of Fame Dr. (at the intersection of I-75 and Hwy 90); tel: (904) 758-1310. Over 100 acclaimed sportsmen and women from the state are honoured here, with exhibits, pictures and documents. The wide range of sport in Florida is also highlighted. Open daily 0800–1800.

## MADISON

**Tourist Information: Madison County Chamber of Commerce**, 105 N. Range St, Madison, FL, 32340; tel: (904) 973-2788.

The **Friendly Inn**, Hwy 63; tel: (904) 973-2504, has 32 rooms (budget/moderate) and 120 sites for RVs and tents.

Madison is a pleasant place to pause. In the city, **Confederate Memorial Park** is on the site of a blockhouse built to defend the town in the Seminole Indian Wars.

## MONTICELLO

**Tourist Information: Monticello/Jefferson County Chamber of Commerce**, 420 W. Washington St, Monticello, FL, 32344; tel: (904) 997-5552.

Varied architectural styles and old Southern homes make this an attractive town to walk around. Its **historic district** stretches for nearly 30 blocks. Self-guided tours, on foot or by car, are available all year.

**Monticello Opera House**; tel: (904) 997-4242, is an impressive structure built in 1890. Plays and operatic productions and classical and popular music concerts are performed there.

**Jefferson Historical Society and Museum**, Pearl St; tel: (904) 997-2565, is housed in the **Wirick-Simmons House**, built in 1833.

Several antique shops and places selling collectibles keep downtown Monticello busy with visitors.

With the decline in cotton production, water melons became the town's largest crop and the **Jefferson County Water Melon Festival** has become a popular annual June event during the past half century. A Water Melon Queen leads a parade and hundreds dance in the streets and take part in sporting and fun contests – including spitting water melon seeds.

# TALLAHASSEE

Set in the first foothills of the Appalachian Mountains, Tallahassee is more like a country town of the Old South than the capital of Florida. It has been the capital since 1823, when three log cabins formed the government buildings. Today the city has two adjacent capitols – the Old Capitol, built in the classical style in 1845 and now restored to its 1902 appearance, and the New Capitol, 22 storeys high. From its top floor on a clear day, you can see the Gulf of Mexico, 20 miles south. In the foreground are the city's rolling hills, tall pines, flowering shrubs and fine architecture.

The lush greenery, nourished by the region's generous rainfall, and the famous canopy roads – tunnel-like avenues lined by great live oaks draped with Spanish moss – give Tallahassee its intimate village atmosphere. Yet this city, home to Florida State University (founded in 1860) and Florida Agricultural and mechanical University (founded in 1887) has more than 192,000 residents. It welcomes nearly 1.5 million visitors a year, many of them conference delegates.

Apalachicola National Forest (see p. 307) is on the city's doorstep. Another natural attraction, Wakulla Springs (p. 296) – one of the world's deepest freshwater springs – is 12 miles from Tallahassee. A mastodon skeleton was found here in the 1930s.

The city has 124 sites on the National Register of Historic Places, which covers buildings and areas of historic significance. They include antebellum homes, Natural Bridge Battlefield (defended by Confederate troops in the Civil War), and De Soto State Archaeological Site – the 1539 encampment of Spanish explorer de Soto and the first place Christmas was celebrated in North America.

## TOURIST INFORMATION

**Tallahassee Area Visitor Information Centre**, *New Capitol Building, PO Box 1369, Tallahassee; tel: (904) 681-9200.* Open Mon–Fri 0800–1700, weekends and public holidays 0830–1630.

## Weather

There are four distinct seasons. The climate is generally mild and moist, with an average annual temperature of 67°F. The average summer temperature is 83°F and it can get stiflingly hot. The average winter temperature is 50°F.

## ARRIVING AND DEPARTING

**Tallahassee Regional Airport**; *tel: (904) 891-7800,* is five miles south-west of downtown. **Annett Bus Lines** provides a shuttle service between the airport and city hotels and other locations by appointment; *tel: (904) 878-3216.* **Tropic Transit**; *tel: (904) 222-3375* offers an airport shuttle service. Four major highways serve the city. East and west access is by I-10 and Hwy 90, north and south access is by Hwy 27 and Hwy 319.

# TALLAHASSEE

## Getting Around

Monroe St runs north and south through the city, Tennessee/Mahon Sts go east and west, forming four sectors which make for straightforward driving. A ring road, Capital Circle, surrounds the city.

Buses serve the whole of Tallahassee. Two coach companies provide in-town and out-of-town charters. They are **Annett Bus Lines**; *tel: (904) 877-2163*, (see also Arriving and Departing p. 297) and **Capital Town Guide Service**; *tel: (904) 942-8687*. **Tropic Transit**; *tel: (904) 222-3375*, provides chauffeured transport by car, van or bus in Tallahassee and surrounding communities. Hire cars are available from five companies.

For a narrated tour of the downtown areas, including the restored Adams St Commons, you can't get a better deal than the **Old Town Trolley**. This replica streetcar has wooden slatted seats, brass handrails and gives free tours. Operating times are Mon–Fri 0700–1800. Trolley route maps are available at the Visitor Information Centre.

## Staying in Tallahassee

### Accommodation

Five thousand hotel and motel guest rooms exist in and around Tallahassee, most in the budget or moderate range, from corporate hotels – the 198-room **Ramada Inn** on *N. Monroe St* is the biggest – to family-owned budget-priced lodges. There are small, Southern-style Bed and Breakfast inns in small towns near the capital, like Quincy and Havana. In addition, the area has 15 campsites.

In the expensive bracket is the 39-room **Killearn Country Club and Inn**, at *100 Tyron Circle; tel: (904) 893-2186*. It has an Olympic-size pool, 27 holes of championship golf and eight tennis courts. In self-catering, the up-market **Lafayette Guest Club**, *384 S. Franklin Blvd; tel: (904) 222-5627*, has fully-equipped suite-style apartments with gardens. Daily rates start at $70.

Hotel and motel chains include *EL*, *Hd* and *Rd*. The moderately-priced **Ramada Inn Capitol View**, *1355 Apalachee Parkway; tel: (904) 877-3171*, is centrally situated. Budget chain **Days Inn** has four properties in the area, including one in downtown with a 24-hr restaurant.

At the upper end of the price range, with a cocktail hour for guests, is the 40-room **Governor's Inn**, in *209 S. Adams St; tel (904) 681-6855*.

One of Kampgrounds of America's (KOA) campsites is the **Tallahassee East KOA**, *tel: (904) 997-3890*, with tent camping, sites for recreational vehicles with full hook-ups and two furnished air-conditioned cabins. It is 20 miles east of Tallahassee. Take I-10, Exit 33, then south on Hwy 19 for quarter of a mile, west on CR 1588 for two miles and a half-mile north on CR 259.

### Eating and Drinking

Variety is on hand in Tallahassee. It has fast food, fine dining, family eating and all the specialist catering you would expect in a university city.

**Whataburger** has four 24-hr outlets around town, serving burgers and chicken to order at budget prices. There are five **Pizza Huts**. **International House of Pancakes**, in *Holiday Inn Parkway*, is another establishment offering low-cost food day and night. **Longhorn Steaks**, on *N. Monroe St*, prices its 'cowboy cuisine' lunches and dinners moderately. Gourmet pizzas are a speciality of the moderately priced **Mozzarella's Café** in *Governor's Sq Mall*.

Children's menus are a feature of

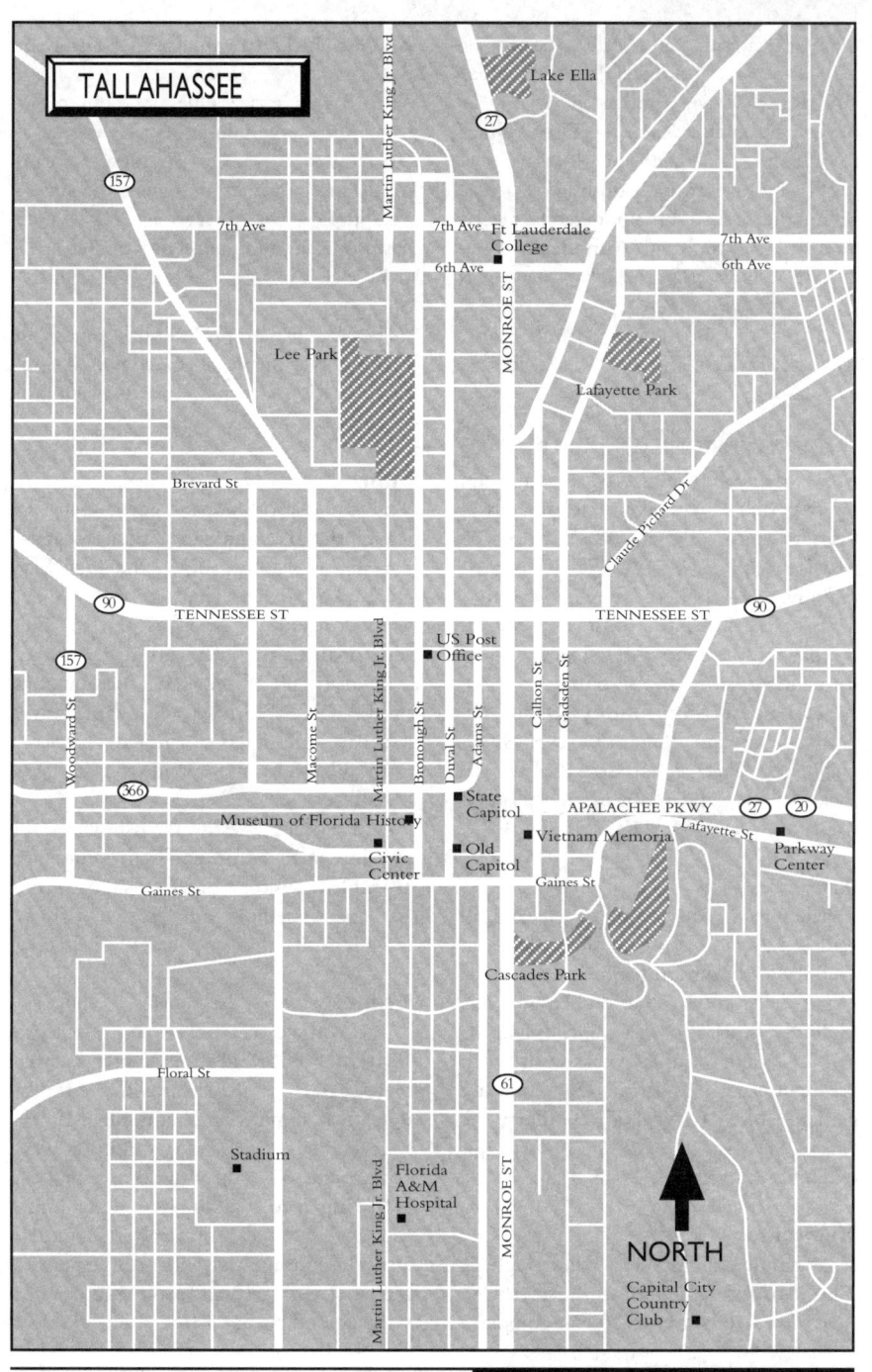

# TALLAHASSEE

**DOWNTOWN TALLAHASSEE MAP**

many restaurants and cafés. Eat-in or take-away are options at **Sonny's Real Pit Bar-BQ**, with outlets in *N. Monroe St* and *Apalachee Parkway*. **The Wharf** (moderate) on *Apalachee Parkway* is a highly-rated, award-winning seafood restaurant. Classic but moderately priced American cuisine at **Annella's**, *1400 Village Square Blvd, Village Commons Center; tel: (904) 668-1961*.

You can also choose from Swiss, Japanese, French, Chinese, Greek, Italian, Mexican and Creole cuisine.

### ENTERTAINMENT

More than 400 concerts, recitals and opera performances take place annually at Florida State University's **School of Music**; *tel: (904) 644-4774* for programme and tickets. The university's **School of Theatre**, considered one of the nation's best, has three stages for performances; *tel: (904) 644-6500*.

**Tallahassee Symphony Orchestra** performs at the *Ruby Diamond Auditorium; tel: (904) 224-0461*. Professional theatre shows and musicals take place at the *Civic Center; tel: (904) 222-0400*.

### Art

Tallahassee has four major art galleries, all with free admission. **The Artport Gallery** at the airport features local artists. Open daily 0600–1200. **LeMoyne Art Gallery,** in a restored antebellum home in *N. Gadsden St,* hosts works by artists in the region and has an outdoor sculpture garden. **The City Hall Gallery**, *S. Adams St,* has local works and two major exhibitions a year.

### Nightclubs

Fri is country night, Sat is dance night at **The Moon** nightclub, *E. Lafayette St*. Live music from country to contemporary is offered at **Diamond Jim's Lounge** at the *Silver Slipper Restaurant, Scotty's Lane,* Tues–Sat. Live jazz, blues and contemporary music entertains guests Tues–Sat at **Andrew's**, *S. Adams St*. New Orleans music and live entertainment is the attraction at **Po' Boys Creole Café**, which has properties in the downtown area at *E. College St* and near FSU at *W. Tennessee St.*

For laughs, see professional comics on Fri and Sat nights at **Comedy Zone**, *Dooley's Downunder* in the Ramada Inn Tallahassee, *N. Monroe St.*

### Sport

The only professional sports team in town, the **Tallahassee Tiger Sharks**, has an eager following in the Oct–Mar ice hockey season. The two state universities provide spectator sports. The **Seminoles** of FSU (Florida State University) play football and the **Rattlers** of FAMU (Florida Agricultural and Mechanical University) are baseball players. FSU also has men's and women's basketball teams.

Horseriding, freshwater fishing, boating, bowling, tennis, golf and cycling are available to visitors. Bicycles can be hired. An abandoned 16-mile scenic railway track to St Mark's is popular with cyclists.

### Events

The **Native American Heritage Festival**, with cultural displays, arts, crafts, dance, games and traditional foods, is celebrated mid-Sept. Seminole, Miccosukee, Creek and Choctaw peoples welcome visitors. A three-week celebration – **Springtime Tallahassee** – highlights the city's natural, historical and cultural attributes during Mar with six live performance stages, crafts and food stalls. It ends with a grand parade. Most events are free.

## TALLAHASSEE

### SHOPPING

The city has some fashionable malls and shopping centres with a mix of deparment stores and speciality shops. **Governor's Square**, a mile east of the Capitol in *Apalachee Parkway*, has 150 speciality shops. The **Tallahassee Mall** provides enclosed shopping and has a new food court. It is in *N. Monroe St*, less than a mile from I-10 exit 29. Both these shopping areas open Mon–Sat 1000–2100 and Sun 1230–1730.

Hours are variable at the **Parkway Center**, corner of *Apalachee Parkway* and *Magnolia Dr*, and in the downtown area's fashion and gift shops.

### SIGHTSEEING

**Tallahassee Museum of History and Natural Science**, *3945 Museum Dr.; tel: (904) 576-1636*. This must-see attraction is nothing like a museum – 52 acres of woodland trails, viewing Florida panthers, red wolves, alligators, owls, bald eagles and other native species in extensive natural habitats. An authentic 1880s farm has some rare breeds, old machinery (including a sugar cane crusher), a garden growing cotton and other native produce and a small farmhouse. A discovery centre, with local snakes among its exhibits, fascinates children and adults alike. Visitors can walk through an historic caboose. Open Mon–Sat 0900–1700, Sun 1230–1700. Admission: $5; seniors, $4; children aged four–15, $3.

**Museum of Florida History**, *500 S. Bronough St; tel: (904) 488-1484*. The museum's mascot is Herman, the 9 ft skeleton of a mastodon which weighed about 5 tons when it lived in prehistoric times. Exhibits include treasures from old Spanish galleons, war relics and a reconstructed steamboat. The museum is open Mon–Fri 0900–1630, Sat 1000–1630,

Sun and public holidays 1200–1630. Admission: free.

**Black Archives Research Center and Museum**, *Martin Luther King Blvd and Gamble St; tel: (904) 599-3020*, in the Carnegie Library and Florida A and M University campus, the university founded in 1887 primarily for black students. The museum has a 500-piece collection of Ethiopian crosses and memorabilia of black American heroes among its numerous exhibits.

**Old Capitol**, *corner of S. Monroe St and Apalachee Parkway; tel: (904) 407-1902*, was opened in 1845 and restored to its 1902 appearance. Open Mon–Fri 0900–1630, Sat 1000–1630, Sun and public holidays 1200–1630. Admission: free.

**New Capitol**, adjacent to Old Capitol but entered from *West Level Plaza off N. Duval St; tel: (904) 681-9200*. Free guided tours begin on the hour Mon–Fri 0900–1500, omitting 1200. There is much House and Senate activity in the Mar–May legislative session. The 22nd floor observatory gives views over rolling hills to the Gulf of Mexico. Open Mon–Fri 1800–1700, weekends and public holidays 0830–1630. Admission: free.

**Bradley's Country Store**, *Centreville Rd*, (12 miles north of the city); *tel: (904) 893-1647*. The store sells over 65,000 lbs of home-made sausages annually. Open Mon–Fri 0900–1800, Sat 0900–1700. Admission: free; guided tours cost $1.50.

**Knott House Museum**, *301 E. Park Ave; tel: (904) 922-2459*. This antebellum mansion has been restored to its 1928 appearance when state politician William Knott and his wife, Louella, moved in. It is known as 'the house that rhymes' because Louella's little poems are attached to the furnishings. Open Wed–Fri 1300–1600, Sat 1000–1600. Admission: $3; children $1.50.

# Tallahassee–Panama City

You can wander through a maze of state and county highways for hours to travel from Tallahassee to Panama City. Alternatively, you can skirt the Gulf Coast for much of the way or, if you're in a hurry, take I-10 and US Hwy 231. Whichever route you choose, you'll see a mixture of farmland, forest and coastal scenery, and for the first few miles you'll be driving along some of the state capital's famed canopy roads – lanes turned into shady green tunnels by the overhanging branches of magnificent magnolias or live oak trees.

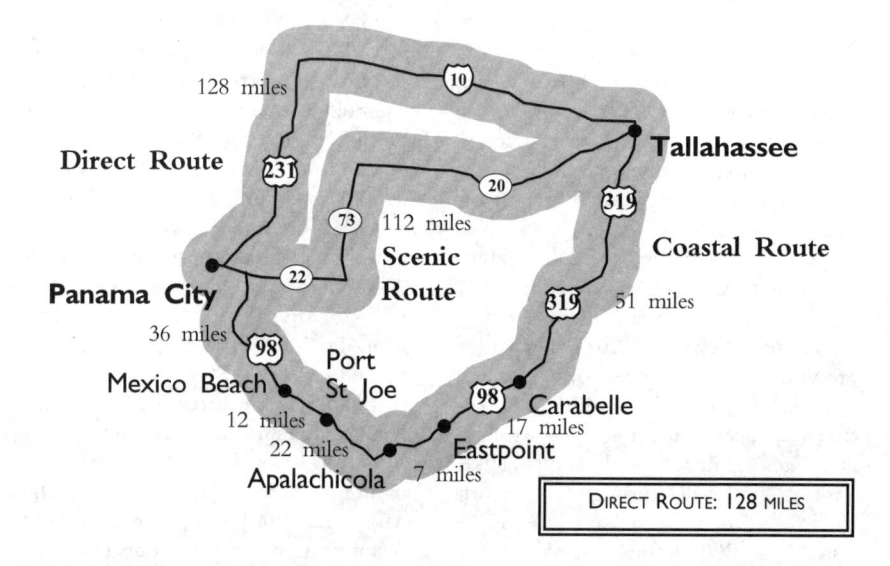

*Direct Route: 128 miles*

## ROUTES

### DIRECT ROUTE

From the front of the Old State Capitol in downtown Tallahassee take Hwy 27 (Monroe St N) north for 3½ miles then take I-10 west. After 68 miles (exit 19) take Hwy 231 south, reaching Panama City after a further 50 miles. The most noteworthy part of this journey is that soon after crossing the Apalachicola River, I-10 passes into the Central Time Zone. Remember to put your watch back one hour at the first opportunity. Without stops – and unless you stray north into **Marianna** (p.327) there really isn't anywhere worth a stop – the 128-mile journey should take around 2¼ hours.

# TALLAHASSEE–PANAMA CITY

## Scenic Route

In total, the scenic route is about 16 miles shorter than the direct route, but without a stop will probably take about the same time to cover. However, you may well be tempted to halt for a picnic in **Apalachicola National Forest**, or in a state park or recreation area. Some of the communities shown on the official state map are very small and you may pass them without knowing it.

From the Old State Capitol drive half a mile north on Hwy 27, then turn left on to Hwy 90/20 west (Tennessee St W.). After four miles turn left again on to Hwy 20 (Blountstown Highway).

Traversing the northern limit of Apalachicola National Forest, the highway reaches **Bloxham** after 16 miles. Just east of the town is **Lake Talquin State Recreation Area** on *Vause Rd; tel: (904) 922-6007*, open daily from 0800 to sunset. Admission: $3.25 per vehicle. Facilities include picnic sites, fishing, boating, nature walks among rolling hills, deep ravines and thick forests of pine and hardwoods. Wild turkey, deer, osprey and bald eagles are found in the area.

Hwy 20 continues west through **Hosford** and **Bristol**, crosses the Apalachicola River to reach **Blountstown** and 34 miles west of Bloxham reaches **Clarksville**. Turn left here on to Hwy 73 south, which joins Hwy 71 after 16 miles. Continue another 9 miles south on Hwy 71 to **Wewahitchka**, where you can enjoy fishing, boating, camping or a picnic at **Dead Lakes State Recreation Area**; *tel: (904) 639-2702*. Open daily from 0800 to sunset. Admission: $3.25 per vehicle. From Wewahitchka, Hwy 22 heads west for 23 miles, intersecting with Hwy 98 just north of **Callaway**. From here Hwy 98 runs 9 miles west into downtown **Panama City**.

## Coastal Route

This is easily the most attractive of the options open to travellers, offering a variety of forest and coastal scenery. On some stretches there are extensive pine woodlands on one side of the highway and wonderful views of the Gulf of Mexico shoreline on the other. You can do the 148-mile route in little more than four hours, but you are certain to dawdle and you may even be tempted to make an overnight stop.

Starting from the Old State Capitol in Tallahassee, take Hwy 61 south (Monroe St S), picking up Hwy 319 when both highways merge for a short time after 4¼ miles. Stay with 319 through **Crawfordville, Medart** and **Sopchoppy**.

Four miles south of Sopchoppy is **Ochlockonee River State Park**; *tel: (904) 962-2771*, where deer, bobcats, grey foxes and a wide range of birdlife live in grass ponds, pine woodlands and oak thickets and people can camp at riverside sites. Fishing, picnicking and boating facilities are available. Open daily 0800–sunset. Admission: $3.25 per vehicle.

Eleven miles south of Sopchoppy, Hwy 319 merges with Hwy 98 and from here on the route hugs the coast all the way to Panama City, passing through **Carabelle, Eastpoint, Apalachicola, Port St. Joe** and **Mexico Beach**. Between Apalachicola and Port St. Joe you can take a diversion on county Hwy 30 to visit **Cape San Blas** and **St. Joseph Peninsula State Park**; *tel: (904) 227-1327*, open daily 0800–sunset. Admission $3.25 per vehicle.

For much of the way, the highway is a joy, offering stunning views of snow white, pine-fringed beaches, offshore islands and sandspits. Roadside palmettoes and houses built on stilts emphasise the area's tropical ambience. Only as the

305

ROUTES

highway approaches Panama City – after passing through Tyndall Air Force Base for 14 miles – do things start to deteriorate into a suburban mess of filling stations, tyre fitters and industrial units. Avoid Hwy 98 Business Route into the city – it takes you well within splutter range of an eyesore chemical plant belching out noisome fumes.

## CARABELLE

**Tourist Information: Carabelle Area Chamber of Commerce**, *PO Drawer DD, Carabelle, FL, 32322; tel: (904) 697-2585*. The office is at the intersection of *Hwy 98* and *Tallahassee St*, opposite the World's Smallest Police Station (see below). Open Mon–Sat 1000–1400 (hours may vary according to availability of volunteer staff).

Carabelle's greatest claim to fame is its police station, said to be the world's smallest. It's a telephone booth located in the centre of town, just off Hwy 98. Featured in magazines, newspapers and television shows throughout the US, the station has been vandalised – and stolen – a number of times. Carabelle (pop. 2,000) is a an attractive fishing port, rather than a tourism centre, so accommodation is limited. **Ell's Court On the Gulf**, *Hwy 98; tel: (904) 697-2050*, offers moderately priced rooms with kitchenettes and cable tv and also has RV facilities. Also on *Hwy 98* is **Gulf Water Motel and Campground**; *tel: (904) 697-2840*.

With a busy fishing fleet in its harbour, it's not surprising that Carabelle is noted for seafood, and there are a number of good restaurants in town. The best-known is **Julia Mae's Seafood Restaurant**, at the foot of *Carabelle Bridge on Hwy 98 West; tel: (904) 697-3791*. The restaurant serves steaks as well as seafood and is open daily 1100–2130.

## EASTPOINT

Eleven miles west of Carabelle, Eastpoint is another small fishing community in an attractive setting. It's strung out on either side of Hwy 98, so you won't get lost. There is no tourism office – the Chamber of Commerce office in Apalachicola covers the village – but as with many of Florida's smaller communities, if you want to know anything ask anyone.

The **Sportsman's Lodge Motel and Marina**, *tel: (904) 670-8423*, has budget accommodation and RV facilities, and there are tent and RV pitches at the **Apalachicola Bay Campground**; *tel: (904) 670-8307*.

As ever, seafood is the staple diet. Eastpoint's fleet specialises in oysters and shrimps. **Sharon's Place**, just off *Hwy 98; tel: (904) 670-8646*, serves some of the freshest seafood you'll find anywhere.

Eastpoint is the gateway to two contrasting attractions.

Just west of the village, Hwy 300 heads south and crosses the bay to **St. George Island**, the largest in a chain of barrier islands just off the coastline. The island has a number of restaurants and a couple of bed and breakfast inns. It also has the 2,000-acre **St George Island State Park**, *tel: (904) 927-2111*, which has facilities for camping, hiking, fishing, swimming and nature study. There are a number of boardwalks and observation platforms where visitors can watch out for snowy plovers, least terns, black skimmers and other shore birds.

East of the village, Hwy 65 leads north for 24 miles to Sumatra, a small town located in Apalachicola National Forest. Here is **Fort Gadsden State Historic Site**; *tel: (904) 670-8988*, used by the British as a base for recruiting Indian and African American troops during the War of 1812. The fort was blown up during a raid by American gunboats in 1816. A visitor centre traces the fort's history and there are picnic sites and a nature trail alongside the Apalachicola River.

## APALACHICOLA

**Tourist Information: Apalachicola Bay Chamber of Commerce Visitor Center**, *57 Market St, Apalachicola, FL, 32320-1776; tel: (904) 653-9419.* Open Mon–Fri 0900–1700. The office has information on accommodation and attractions in the area. A free town map helps visitors to make the most of a stroll.

The town has a handful of inns. The best, a picturesque landmark in its own right, is the Victorian **Gibson Inn**, *51 Avenue C; tel: (904) 653-2191.* With verandahs surrounding its ground and first floors, the Gibson has 31 moderately priced rooms and a moderate-to-pricey restaurant. There are a number of other eating places, each serving the oysters for which Apalachicola is famous.

The major event in Apalachicola's calendar is the **Florida Seafood Festival**, staged during the first weekend in November when the normally sleepy port springs into an orgy of over-eating. A highlight of the festival is an oyster-eating contest. Apalachicola is said to produce nine out of every ten oysters eaten in Florida.

The town has a sprawling historic district with buildings as old as 150 years. There are a number of antebellum homes from Apalachicola's heyday as a cotton port. The **John Gorrie State Museum** on *Sixth St; tel: (904) 653-9347*, pays tribute to Dr John Gorrie, inventor of an ice-making machine which paved the way for modern air-conditioning. Dr Gorrie's machine was used in the treatment of malaria, a scourge in Florida in the mid-1800s. Open Thurs–Mon 0900–noon, 1300–1700. Admission: $1.

## Apalachicola National Forest

Covering some 600,000 acres, the Apalachicola National Forest offers wilderness experiences within easy reach of Tallahassee and Panama City. Its northeastern corner is less than four miles from the State Capitol, all but surrounding Tallahassee Municipal Airport.

Criss-crossed by a number of highways and minor roads, the forest's terrain of swampland and savannah dotted with springs and lakes is home to black bear, deer, wild pigs and other wildlife.

There are a dozen campsites with basic facilities – the only accommodation option available within the forest limits. Camping is free, except at Silver Lake, nine miles east of Tallahassee, where the charge is $4 a night.

Recreation areas offer picnic facilities and there are opportunities for hiking, swimming and fishing.

Fringing the forest's southern edge, between Hwy 65 and the Ochlockonee River, is the area known as Tate's Hell Swamp. This true wilderness – named, legend has it, after an early settler who disappeared after chasing a panther into the swamp – is infested with deadly water moccasin snakes.

## PORT ST JOE

**Tourist information: Gulf County Chamber of Commerce**, *PO Box 964, Port St. Joe, FL, 32456; tel: (904) 227-1223.*

Port St. Joe has restaurants and motels. **Cape San Blas Camping Resort**, *10 miles south of the town off Hwy 30; tel: (904) 229-6800*, has cottages for rent as well as tent and RV pitches in a secluded rustic setting. Another campground is **Ski Breeze Park**, *8 miles south on Hwy 30; tel: (904) 226-2136.*

Yet another fishing community – this time the specialty is scallops – Port St. Joe stands on the site of St. Joseph, once the sixth largest city in Florida and in 1838 the setting for the state's first constitutional convention. In those days it was known as the most wicked city in the Southeast, but the boom was halted by a devastating hurricane followed by a severe yellow fever epidemic.

The story is told in the **Constitution Convention State Museum**, *200 Allen Memorial Way, off Hwy 98; tel: (904) 229-8029.* Open Mon–Sat 0900–noon, 1300–1700. Admission: $1.

## MEXICO BEACH

**Tourist information: Mexico Beach Chamber of Commerce**, *PO Box 13382, Mexico Beach, FL 32410; tel: (904) 648-8196.*

Safe bathing from a beach of fine white sand has made Mexico Beach a popular place for families. And if you've already taken several hours over the journey from Tallahassee, you might consider an overnight stop here before tackling the final 40 miles or so to the fleshpots of Panama City.

Mexico Beach has waterfront self-catering houses and apartments for rent – local real estate agencies on Hwy 98 have lists – as well as the **Surfside Inn**, *Hwy 98 and 12th St; tel: (904) 648-5771*, and the **El Governor Motel and Campground**, *Hwy 98; tel: (904) 648-5432.*

## PANAMA CITY

**Tourist information: Panama City Beach Convention and Visitors Bureau**, *12015 Front Beach Rd (Alt Hwy 98 west), Panama City Beach, FL, 32417;* *tel: (904) 233-6503.* Open Mon–Fri 0800–1700. The free *See Panama City and Beaches* booklet contains useful information, street maps and discount coupons which can be used at some of the area's restaurants, shops and attractions.

### WEATHER

Panama City has an average year-round temperature of 77° F and an average water temperature of 72°. Winter 'cold snaps' occur occasionally but rarely last more than two days. Panama City Beach is virtually an all-year leisure destination, though Floridians and other Southerners prefer to visit between early Feb and Oct – the hotter months. By autumn, the sea is warm and the beaches less crowded.

### ACCOMMODATION

Even though there are more than 16,000 hotel, motel and condominium rooms available, as well as campgrounds and RV parks, it is wise to make reservations well in advance. This is an extremely popular region.

Much of the accommodation is on the beachfront, including condominiums and campgrounds, and even the most luxurious places may be the subject of generous deals outside the high season – remember, this is an acknowledged good value destination.

You can also find accommodation in tennis and golf resorts, self-catering cottages and bed and breakfast homes, and there are at least a dozen church retreats which attract many other holidaymakers from neighbouring states, where tiny communities support opulent-looking churches.

Reservations may be made through the **Panama City Chamber of Commerce Referral Service**; *tel: (904) 234-3193*. A company called **Condo**

World; *tel: (904) 234-5564*, represents several properties, including the prestigious **Edgewater Beach Resort**, where condominiums with up to three bedrooms may be rented by the day, week or month.

Hotel chains in the area include *BW, DI, HI, HJ, Ma, Rd*. Five of the area's 15 campgrounds and RV parks are in beachside locations. The **KOA** campground is near the eastern beaches at *8800 Thomas Dr.; tel: (904) 234-5731*.

### EATING AND DRINKING

There are about 100 restaurants to choose from, all but 30 of which are open year-round. Add to that some 35 lounges (bars), most of which serve food. Oyster bars, specialists in seafood, steaks and ribs, waffles, pizzas and pancakes, burger and fried chicken restaurants, coffee shops, sandwich bars, grills and diners all compete for your custom. Most of them are cheap, cheerful and fast. The same applies to the majority of ethnic restaurants – Mexican, Cajun, Chinese, Thai, English, Italian, Japanese...

For fine dining at the waterfront, indoors or out, try **Hamilton's Restaurant and Lounge**, *5711 North Lagoon Dr., tel: (904) 234-1255*. The wine list is extensive and the cooking and presentation are both good. Hamilton's opens for lunch and dinner May–Sept. At **Capt. Anderson's Restaurant**, also on *Grand Lagoon Dr.* (no reservations taken), early dockside diners can watch the fishing fleet unload. The restaurant opens at 1600.

Local specialities on many menus include seafood platters, stuffed blue crab, snapper in pesto, oysters Rockefeller, amberjack grilled over mesquite wood and charcoal, Cajun crawfish, seafood gumbo and blackened grouper.

All fish is fresh from the Gulf. Steaks are claimed to be so tender you can cut them with a butter knife. Portions in most restaurants can be dauntingly enormous, so ask for a small serving unless you are ravenous. Some fast food establishments tend to smother nearly everything in batter and deep-fry it, making delicate flavours unrecognisable.

Don't assume that a restaurant serves alcohol. The glasses of amber liquid enjoyed by other diners are probably iced tea. If you fancy a beer with your meal look for neon signs in windows advertising Budweiser, Michelob or Miller.

### ENTERTAINMENT

Hardly have you driven off Hwy 98 towards the shoreline than you are confronted by amusement centres, eateries galore, music, bars and flashing lights, and whichever entertainment, meal or service you choose is remarkably easy on the pocket. But if you are looking for peace and quiet – forget it. There are pockets of tranquility and culture, but generally the accent is on fun, fun and more fun.

Beach clubs which arrange Hobie Cat sailing, parasailing and jetskiing for visitors in the daytime turn at night into places to relax by a patio bar and listen to country, rock or a singing duo.

Weekend line dancing and live entertainment, smoochy dancing in a piano bar, guitar music, Beatles' songs and karaoke are offered at various restaurants and hotel bars.

Dinner-dance cruises and gospel music dinner cruises operate from **Capt. Anderson's Marina**, *5550 North Lagoon Dr., tel: (904) 234-3435*. Sunset and moonlight cruises are run by **Bombay Sailing Charters**, *Hathaway Marina, tel: (904) 234-7794*. MV *Stardancer* is a casino cruise ship, *tel: (904) 233-SHIP*.

**Miracle Strip** has a concentration of restaurants and entertainments. The **Ocean Opry** music and country stage show is open year round at *8400 Front Beach Rd, tel: (904) 234-5464.*

As well as being popular with families, the Panama City Beach area appeals to specialist sportspeople. Golf, tennis, sport fishing, boating, parasailing, jetskiing, diving, snorkelling, windsurfing – if you have the energy, Panama City Beach provides the opportunity. In the Spring Break students from far and wide make a beeline for the beaches.

One of the city's three fishing piers, the **Dan Russell Municipal Pier**, juts more than 1,100 ft over the Gulf. It is reckoned that a quarter of a million visitors a year go to Panama City Beach just for the fishing. Deep-sea fishing in the Gulf is available at several marinas. Party boats taking four to six dozen people anchor where red snapper, amberjack and grouper are known to feed.

Overnight fishing trips can also be arranged. A licence is required for freshwater and sea fishing. Information is available at marinas and piers.

### Events

The **Bay Art Show**, *Visual Arts Center of Northwest Florida*, and the **Panama City Beach Fishing Classic** both occur throughout Sept. The **Indian Summer Seafood Festival** is held over three days in mid-Oct.

### Shopping

Beachwear, sportswear, fun clothes, airbrush tee shirts, swimsuits, beach toys, gifts and souvenirs are widely available at shops and boutiques around the beaches. The biggest of these is **Alvin's Island Tropical Department Store** – one of several at Panama City Beach and along the Gulf Coast – at *Hwy 98 west*, across the street from Miracle Strip Amusement Park. Here you can see tropical birds and alligator and shark feedings.

In town, just east of the Hathaway Bridge on Hwys 231 and 77, is **Panama City Mall**, where nearly 100 speciality shops offer fashions, accessories, books, gifts and other goods. Free puppet shows are staged at weekends.

One mile west of Hwy 232, on *W 23rd St*, is a **Manufacturers' Outlet Center**, where current season noted brand name clothing and houseware items can be bought at up to 70 per cent off the usual retail price.

### Sightseeing

From Apr–early Oct trip boats go to uninhabited **Shell Island**, half an hour from *Thomas Dr*, marinas. People go there to sunbathe and look for shells and on the way may watch dolphins sporting around the boat.

Fishing and diving charter boats operate from nine marinas, there are five major dive shops and centres and half a dozen golf courses in the Panama City area. A dozen or more places offer miniature golf. Most mini-golf courses are themed, with jungle and other adventures, pirate ships, dark caverns, waterfalls or treasure hunts.

**St Andrew's State Recreation Area**, *Thomas Dr., three miles east of Panama City Beach, off Hwy 392, tel: (904) 233-5140.* Woodland, marshland, dunes and beaches form the 1,260-acre park, which has nature trails, a boat ramp, saltwater and freshwater fishing, picnic sites and camp sites. Open daily 0730–sunset. Admission: $3.25 per vehicle.

**Gulf World**, *15412 Front Beach Rd, Panama City Beach, tel: (904) 234-5271.* One of the Panhandle's top attractions, this marine park has sealions, sting rays, a

# TALLAHASSEE–PANAMA CITY

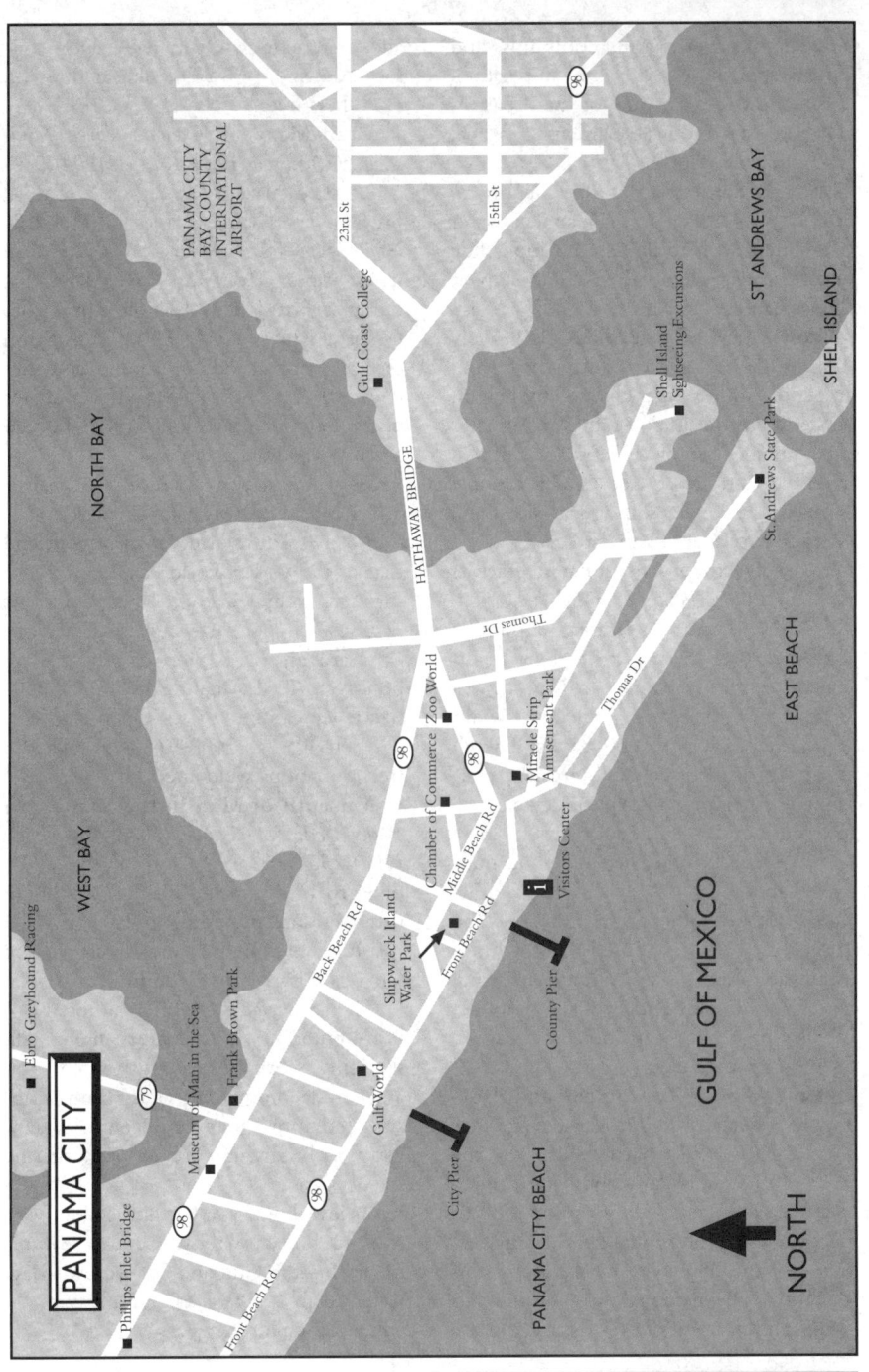

PANAMA CITY MAP

shark tank, performing dolphins and underwater shows with fish and natural coral. Peacocks, flamingos and parrots populate the Tropical Gardens. Seasonal opening from 0900.

**Shipwreck Island**, *12000 Front Beach Rd, tel: (904) 234-0368*. This mega water park offers such thrills as a 35 mph slide and cascades along the Rapid River. Tinies can cool off in the Kid Car Wash or down the Elephant Slide. Open daily 1000–1700 Apr–Labour Day (first Mon in Sept). Admission is charged by height: – $13 for those under 4 ft 2 in, $16 for taller people. Senior citizens: $5, children aged two and under: free. A $25 'Double Park' ticket covers Shipwreck Island and **Miracle Strip** across the street.

**Miracle Strip Amusement Park** is also at *12000 Front Beach Rd, tel: (904) 234-5810*. There are nearly 30 rides to take your breath away at this long-established park. The pitch and toss of the Sea Dragon ride rocks you 70 ft into the air. The roller coaster is 2,000 ft long. There's plenty to do and see, with arcades, continuous entertainment, special events and fast-food outlets. Open Fri 1800–2300, Sat 1300–2300 (mid-Mar–June and mid-Aug–Labour Day), Mon–Fri 1800–2330, Sat 1300–2330, Sun 1500–2330 (June–mid-Aug). Closed in winter. Admission: same as for Shipwreck Island. A $25 'Double Park' ticket provides admission to both attractions and can be used on separate days.

**Zoo World Zoological and Botanical Park**, *9008 Front Beach Rd, tel: (904) 230-0096*, participates in the Species Survival Plan, established by international zoological authorities in 1980 to protect severely-endangered species. Some of the 350 species here are in this category. The gardens are a pleasure to walk in. An aviary and a petting zoo are added attractions. Open daily 0900–sunset. Admission: $8.50, children four–12, $6, others free.

**Gran-Maze**, *at Coconut Creek Mini-Golf, 9807 Front Beach Rd, tel: (904) 234-2625*. The maze is as big as a football pitch. It has a safari theme and the challenge is to found your way out in the fastest time. Coconut Creek also has bumper boats and 18-hole mini-golf. Open daily 0900–2300. Admission charges vary according to the activities chosen – eg, $9 for maze and bumper boats, $10 for maze and golf. Children aged five and under go free.

**Bay County's Junior Museum**, *1731 Jenks Ave, Panama City, tel: (904) 769-6128*. The Florida environment and that of the wider world can be explored through natural history, science and art exhibits. Puppet shows, classes and concerts are given. A pioneer village with poultry to feed, a nature trail and a full-size tepee can be visited. Open Tues–Fri 0900–1630, Sat 1000–1600. Admission: free, donations welcomed.

**Museum of Man in the Sea**, *17314 Back Beach Rd, Panama City Beach, tel: (904) 235-4101*. You don't need to be a diver to be fascinated by the exhibits in this unusual museum, owned by the Institute of Diving and managed by Panama City Marine Institute.

The displays, covering hundreds of years, pinpoint a 17th century diving bell, salvaging work, underwater exploration and archaeology, artefacts from ships wrecked more than two centuries ago, early scuba-diving and modern marine sciences.

A new Toucha-Quarium enables visitors to meet shallow-water creatures inhabiting the Gulf and St Andrew's Bay. Open daily 0900–1700. Admission: $4 adults, $2 children aged six–16.

# PANAMA CITY–PENSACOLA

This has to be one of the easiest drives in the whole of Florida – a gentle saunter along the Gulf Coast for a distance of 109 miles. You can do it in a couple of hours, but why hurry? Tiny communities with superb beaches punctuate most of the journey, and Hwy 98 almost becomes a causeway between Santa Rosa Beach and Fort Walton Beach: Choctawatchee Bay lies on one side and the Gulf of Mexico on the other.

ROUTE: 109 MILES

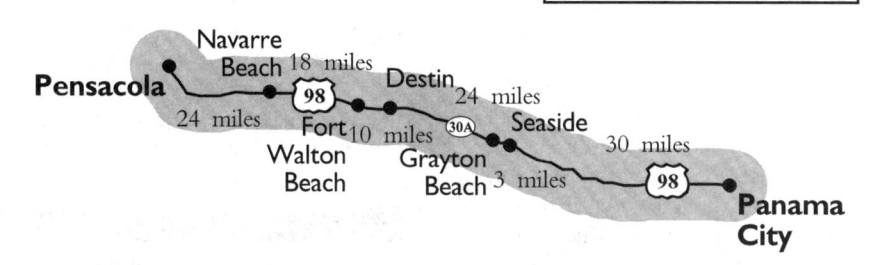

## ROUTE

West of the Hathaway Bridge in Panama City you are faced with a choice. You can continue west on Hwy 98 or take the left fork and travel for a while on Alt 98. It really doesn't matter which route you take since they meet up again at **Sunnyside**, 12 miles along the coast.

It all depends on what kind of scenery you prefer. Alt 98 stays with the shore, passing the condominiums and shopping malls of Panama City Beach. Hwy 98 proper becomes a kind of back road, woodlands shielding it from beachside high-rise blocks to the left, fields and lakes to the right.

The two routes meet again at Sunnyside, two miles beyond laid-back **Laguna Beach**. From Sunnyside, Hwy 98 wends its uninterrupted way towards Pensacola. But for the time being don't take it. Go on Hwy 30A instead. Not much more than a country lane, it hugs the coast for another 16 miles, passing some of the best beaches in Florida, including **Grayton Beach**, declared one of the finest in the US.

Hwy 30A rejoins Hwy 98 at **South Walton**, just beyond **Santa Rosa Beach**. The area between **Seaside** and **Navarre Beach**, a distance of more than 40 miles, is known as the **Emerald Coast**, named for the colour of the sea. From **Destin** you are back in Vacationland, a popular area of condominiums, fast food joints, glitz and ghetto-blasters. It calms down again west of **Fort Walton Beach**.

After passing through **Navarre** and

**Gulf Breeze**, Hwy 98 makes a sharp right turn and heads over Pensacola Bay by way of **Three Mile Bridge**, also known as the World's Longest Fishing Pier. Whatever the weather, there's always a line of hopeful anglers casting their bait upon the waters.

## SEASIDE

If you're looking for somewhere more peaceful than Panama City, you may find it at Seaside. Developed within the past 15 years, Seaside, has half a mile of beach and a beach pavilion. Nevertheless, it has the rocking-chair-on-the-porch ambience of a past, more leisurely, age.

Seaside's well–spaced–out, wood-framed cottages are built in traditional Southern style – off the ground to allow air to circulate underneath, with deep roof overhangs, cross-ventilation in all rooms and large, important porches. Pastel colours prevail. People stroll along brick roads to the shops, restaurants and market.

If Seaside strikes you as just a little bit self-conscious, perhaps it's because of the huge numbers of people from many parts of the world who have come to cast upon it a close professional eye. For this carefully-planned Utopia has received worldwide media interest and won numerous architectural awards. The Prince of Wales has commented on the serious applications the lessons of Seaside could have on UK cities and rural areas.

As you might expect, it's probably the most expensive place to stay in the Panhandle, but its holiday rental cottages are extremely popular. Vacationers can hire catamarans, play tennis and croquet and go for nature walks.

## GRAYTON BEACH

Dozens of mainly underveloped beaches lure visitors to the ribbon of green water and sugar-white sand between Seaside and Pensacola. One of them, Grayton Beach, Seaside's western neighbour, made it to the top ten list in a nation-wide survey. The survey was run by the University of Maryland's Laboratory for Coastal Research, and the evaluation was based on 40 criteria, including water and sand quality, temperature, scenery and accessibility, and nuisances such as crime and mosquitoes.

**Grayton Beach State Recreation Area**, on *Hwy 30A; tel: (904) 231-4210*, is one of the Gulf Coast's oldest townships. It covers 356 acres and offers camping, boating, surf fishing, swimming and nature trails. Open daily 0800–sunset. Admission: $3.25 per vehicle.

## DESTIN

Destin calls itself the World's Luckiest Fishing Village, having notched up five saltwater fishing world records. It has at least 20 tasty game fish species available in any one season.

Filmgoers may find something hauntingly familiar about Destin and Fort Walton Beach. Much of the 1978 movie *Jaws II*, supposedly set in Amity, New England, was shot here.

Sitting neatly between Choctawhatchee Bay and the Gulf of Mexico, Destin boasts Florida's largest charter fishing fleet. Its annual **Fishing Rodeo** lasts through the whole of Oct. **Destin Seafood Festival**, held on the first weekend of Oct, has a dedicated following.

**The Museum of the Sea and Indian**, *4801 Beach Hwy, Destin; tel: (904) 837-6625*, displays Indian artefacts from North and South America and has a small zoo. Admission: $3.75; children 5–16 $2. Open daily 0800–1800 summer, 0800–1700 spring and fall, 0900–1600 winter.

Visiting **Destin Fishing Museum**, *Harbour Walk Plaza; tel: (904) 654-1011*, is like walking under the sea without getting wet. Fish species are viewed as you walk on sand dotted with sponges and shells, lighting and sound adding to the effect. Open Tues–Sun 1100–1600. Admission: free.

## FORT WALTON BEACH

Destin and Fort Walton Beach, 10 miles apart, are promoted together by **Emerald Coast Convention and Visitor Bureau**, *PO Box 609, Fort Walton Beach; tel: (904) 651-7131*. The region has more than 24 miles of beaches, 60 per cent of which are scheduled to be preserved in their natural state.

The Emerald Coast claims an average of 343 sunny days a year. Yet one part of it experiences ice and snow, 100 mph winds and temperatures from -65 deg F to 165 deg F. This is the McKinley Climatic Laboratory, a test chamber at **Eglin Air Force Base** at Fort Walton Beach. Visiting is permitted free – *tel: (904) 882-3393* for information.

Eglin is hailed as the largest air force base in the world, occupying 720 square miles of land and with a vast testing area in the Gulf. The Air Force is responsible for the lovely natural beaches of Okaloosa Island.

Admission is also free at the **US Air Force Armament Museum** at the *Eglin Air Force Base; tel: (904) 882-4062*. Fighter and bomber aircraft from World War I to the 1991 war in the Persian Gulf are displayed. Guns, bombs, missiles, rockets, photographs and war films can be seen. Open daily 0930–1630.

The **Indian Temple Mound Museum**, *139 Miracle Strip Parkway (Hwy 98), Fort Walton Beach; tel: (904) 243-6521*, outlines 10,000 years of Gulf Coast habitation by the Southeastern Indians. The Temple Mound itself, discovered by European explorers 600 years ago, stands beside the museum, which displays 6,000 exhibits, including ceramic artefacts of four Indian tribes.

---

### Keep an Eye on the Sky

The skies over Pensacola and neighbouring Gulf Breeze have been the subject of hundreds of reported sightings of Unidentified Flying Objects in recent years.

'The sheer number of independent witnesses in this area makes these sightings an amazing mystery', says a leaflet issued by the local branch of MUFON, the Mutual UFO Network, and available to tourists.

Several photographs of mysterious craft seen in the area since 1987 are reproduced in the leaflet, which states: 'The UFO photographs have been studied and authenticated by optical experts who agree that there is no evidence of photo trickery'.

The local branch of MUFON, which internationally has more than 60,000 members, meets on the second Sun of every month. Interested visitors are invited to attend a meeting or join members on one of their frequent Skywatch evenings at Shoreline Park South in Gulf Breeze.

For locations and other information *tel: (904) 438-3261*.

## PANAMA CITY–PENSACOLA

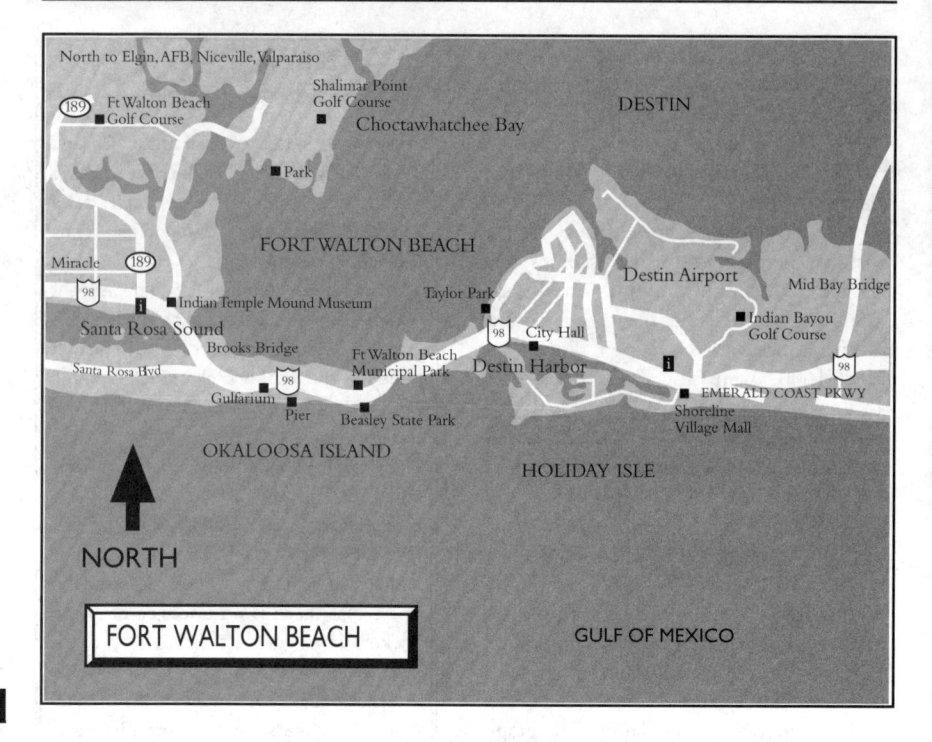

Open Mon–Fri 1100–1600, Sat 0900–1600. Admission: 75 cents; children free.

Opened more than 40 years ago, **The Gulfarium**, *1010 Miracle Strip Parkway; tel: (904) 244-5169*, presents a range of entertaining creatures as well a 'Living Sea' exhibit in which undersea life can be viewed through windows. Performers include dolphins, sealions, penguins, otters, seals and other aquatic creatures. Two-hourly shows take place 1000–1600. Open 0900–1800 spring–summer, 0900–1600 autumn–winter. Admission: $12, children 4–11 $8.

Don't waste time searching Fort Walton Beach for a fort or a beach. It has neither. It was known as Camp Walton when a military outpost was set up there in the Civil War, but never upgraded to fortress status. It is separated from the Gulf's beaches by the Santa Rosa Sound and Okaloosa Island. The 'Fort' and 'Beach' have been added to the name in the last 60 years. The region is noted for its golf courses 225 holes in all – and its shell-collecting at reefs, ledges and sandbars.

The six-day **Billy Bowlegs Festival** held in early June in 'honour' of an 18th-century pirate, involves a parade of hundreds of boats and much costumed merry-making.

## NAVARRE BEACH

With neighbouring Gulf Breeze, Navarre Beach has four miles of beach and dunes, only half of which is developed. Sailing, parasailing, water-skiing, jetskiing, scuba-diving, snorkelling, canoeing and fishing are among the activities.

# PENSACOLA

Pensacola was the first European settlement in North America, but nature took away its claim to be the longest-established.

The Spanish Conquistador, Don Tristan de Luna, landed in Pensacola Bay in 14 Aug 1559 to establish a colony with over 1000 settlers. Unfortunately, a devastating hurricane forced them to abandon the place two years later. St Augustine, was founded four years later in 1565. However, there's no denying that Pensacola has a lot of history, which it wears with pride in its three historic districts.

**Seville Historic District** has been at the forefront of Pensacola's development since the late 18th century. Fishing, shipping and naval provisions were the main enterprises of a community of mixed English, Scottish, French and Spanish descent. Here, traders, trappers and Native Americans haggled and bartered and settlers built homes along the bayfront and in Seville Sq. The district is listed on the US National Register.

The city's present downtown, **Palafox Historic District** was old Pensacola's commercial heart, providing entertainment and services for the kaleidoscopic population of a busy port. A dozen consulates served the needs of foreign travellers. Many historic buildings have been preserved, including a number with New Orleans-style filigree ironwork balconies.

Pensacola's second listing on the National Register, **North Hill Preservation District**, has housed prominent businessmen, politicians and professional people since the late 19th century. It developed between 1870 and the 1930s and contains more than 500 homes in an area of 50 blocks. Architectural styles found in North Hill include Queen Anne, Neoclassical, Tudor Revival, Art Moderne, Mediterranean Revival and Craftsman Bungalow.

With more than 40 miles of sugar-white beachfront and neighbouring resort communities, Pensacola has much to offer.

## TOURIST INFORMATION

**Pensacola Convention and Visitors Information Center (CVIC)**, *1401 E. Gregory St; tel: (904) 434-1234 or (800) 343-4321.* Open daily (except Thanksgiving Day, Christmas Eve, Christmas Day, New Year's Day) 0800–1700. The centre is in an attractive building in a parkland setting with lots of car parking space, overlooking Pensacola Bay at the foot of Three-Mile Bridge, which crosses the bay to Gulf Breeze and Pensacola Beach. Inside, the centre has a relaxed, friendly atmosphere and helpful staff have information, maps and brochures to hand.

**Pensacola Beach Chamber of Commerce VIC**, *735 Pensacola Beach Blvd; tel: (904) 932-1500 or (800) 635-4803*, is conveniently located on a slip road to the right after you have crossed the bridge from Gulf Breeze. Again,

# PENSACOLA

plenty of information available from helpful staff.

**Gulf Breeze and Navarre Beaches Tourist Information Center**, *on Hwy 98 at the foot of the Navarre Beach Bridge; tel: (904) 939-2691 or (800) 480-SAND.* Another centre packed with information.

## Weather

Pensacola enjoys a temperate climate with an average of 343 days of sunshine a year. The temperature throughout the year averages 75°F. Winters are mild, with an average temperature of 54°F.

## ARRIVING AND DEPARTING

### Airport

**Pensacola Regional Airport**, *Airport Blvd at 12th Ave; tel: (904) 435-1745,* is six miles north of downtown on Hwy 289. It is the largest airport in Northwest Florida offering close on 50 departures a day to various parts of the southern US. There are a number of non-stop services to Atlanta, a major gateway about an hour's flight away.

A shuttle service connects the airport with the Pensacola Grand Hotel downtown and the Holiday Inn University Mall at the north end. Taxis are always lined up in front of the terminal.

### By Car

Major highways connect Pensacola with points north, east and west. The major east–west routes are I-10 and Hwys 90 and 98. Hwy 29 and I-110 travel north–south. If you are travelling from the east and heading for Pensacola Beach, make sure you turn left (south) at Gulf Breeze – otherwise you'll find yourself driving across Three Mile Bridge (a $1 toll covers both ways), which really is three miles long.

## GETTING AROUND

The **Escambia County Transit System**, *tel: (904) 436-9383,* provides a local bus service covering more than 280 routes – but not Pensacola Beach. Without your own transport you'll need a taxi to take you there – expect to pay around $10. Bus services to other cities in the Panhandle and nearby Alabama are provided by **Greyhound-Trailways**, with a terminal at *505 W. Burgess Rd, off Hwy 29; tel: (904) 476-4800.* The terminal is about seven miles north of downtown Pensacola, but you can get there and back on bus no. 10.

Downtown Pensacola is a good place for strolling, but a car is necessary if you want to see the area's major sights.

## STAYING IN PENSACOLA

### Accommodation

Not surprisingly, the most expensive accommodation in the area is along those magnificent beaches. Even so, prices are significantly lower than in other parts of Florida – even in peak seasons.

There is a good choice of hotels and motels, but self-catering buffs will find a wide selection of condominiums, townhouses and private villas. Rentals for these are usually handled through the area's many realty agencies, some of which are listed in the *Pensacola Area Visitors' Guide* published by the Pensacola CVIC. Bed and Breakfast inns are to be found in the three historic districts. The cheapest areas for all types of accommodation are downtown, the northern suburbs and near the airport.

Hotel chains near Pensacola include BW, CI, DI, EL, HJ, Hd, QI, Rd, RI.

The area's most famous hotel is the **Pensacola Grand Hotel**, *200 E. Gregory St; tel: (904) 433-3336 or (800)*

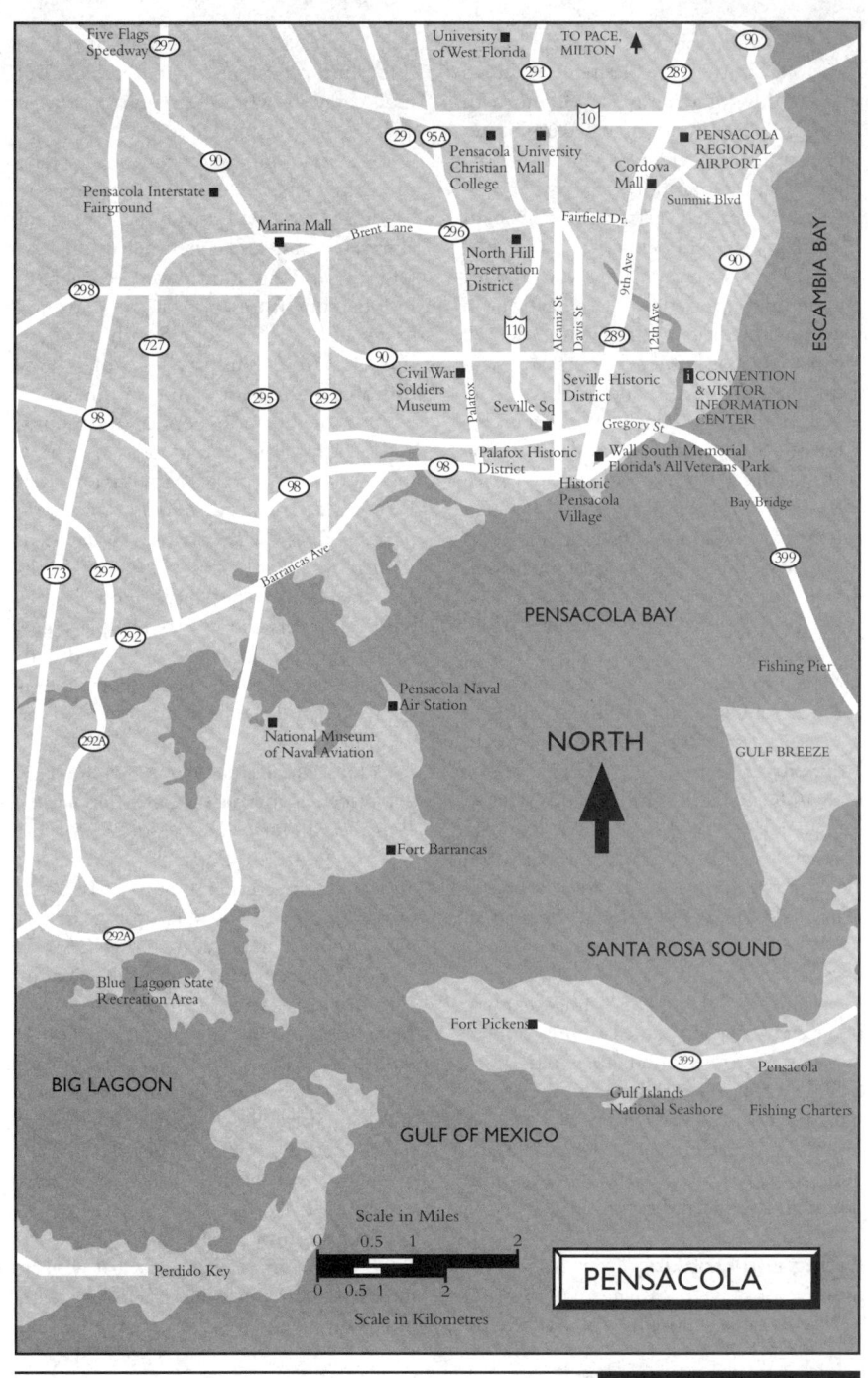

# PENSACOLA

**PENSACOLA BAY MAP**

348-3336. The lobby of this grand hotel is the old Louisville & Nashville Railroad station, now graciously furnished with antiques and period fixtures. Room rates range from moderate–expensive – the higher you are the more you pay.

The moderately priced **New World Landing**, *600 S. Palofax St; tel: (904) 432-4111*, is a 16-room inn with restaurant and pub located near the bayfront in Palofax Historic District. Its themed rooms overlook either a courtyard with fountain or Palofax St and the bay.

On Pensacola Beach, the expensive **Clarion Suites Resort and Convention Center**, *20 Via de Luna Dr.; tel: (904) 932-4300 or (800) 874-5303*, has the look of a quaint old fishing village. Its 86 luxury suites – each with bedroom, living/dining area and kitchenette in a two-storey layout – are moments from the beach.

The area has many campsites with tent and RV pitches. Full facility camping is available at **Big Lagoon State Recreation Area**, *12301 Gulf Beach Hwy (CR 292A*, ten miles south west of Pensacola*); tel: (904) 492-1595*. You can also camp at **Fort Pickens National Park**, *Fort Pickens Rd, Pensacola Beach; tel: (904) 934-2622/3/4*. Newly opened in 1995, **All Star RV Resort**, *13620 Perdido Key Dr.; tel: (904) 492-0041*, is in a beachfront setting with full facilities, including cable TV and laundry. Similar facilities are to be found at the old-established **Navarre Beach Family Campground**, *9201 Navarre Parkway (Hwy 98), Navarre; tel: (904) 939-2188*. The park has nearly 100 pitches with beach and woodland nearby.

### Eating and Drinking

Dining out is a casual affair in the Pensacola area, though it must be said that beach bars aside, the general rule is: 'No shirt, no shoes – no service'. But men certainly won't be required to wear a jacket and tie anywhere.

Beachside and waterfront prices tend to be higher than those at restaurants in town, but you will usually be paying for al fresco dining and a view across the bay. Cuisine in this north-west corner of Florida runs from the grits, biscuits and gravy of the Deep South to the French/Cajun influences of New Orleans, with seafood on every menu.

One of the most popular restaurants, and a tourist attraction in its own right, is the moderate to pricey **McGuire's Irish Pub and Brewery**, *600 E. Gregory St (between Three Mile Bridge and the Civic Center); tel: (904) 433-6789*. Big steaks are the house speciality, with home-brewed porters and stouts. The place gets so frenetic that customers are issued with bleepers to tell them when their table is ready. Open daily, from lunchtime to the small hours.

A local lunchtime favourite is the budget-priced **Norma's Cafe**, *inside the Pensacola Cultural Center, 400 S. Jefferson St; tel: (904) 436-2101*. Located in the atrium of the former Court of Records building, Norma's is noted for its imaginatively filled crêpes and sandwiches.

For a pricey splurge, try **The Yacht Restaurant and Lounge**, *600 S. Barracks St (moored at Pitt Slip); tel: (904) 432-3707*. This vintage 150 ft-long steam yacht is used as a floating restaurant. Seafood, naturally, is a speciality in this stylish setting. Open Tues–Sat 1630–midnight; Sun brunch 1130–1430, dinner 1800–2200.

**Trader John's**, *511 S. Palafox St; tel: (904) 433-7113*, is a legendary bar with an international reputation, a favourite with US Navy flyers since World War II and now on the jetset circuit. Visitors have included Prince Andrew and Bob Hope. Nevertheless, its prices will appeal to the budget purse. Open daily 1200–0300.

Over in Pensacola Beach, the best-known restaurant is **Jubilee Topside**, *Quietwater Beach Boardwalk; tel: (904) 934-3108*. Justifiably pricey, it offers haute cuisine with superb bay views. A hint of Cajun embellishes its imaginatively prepared dishes and the selection of breads are repeatedly proffered by a 'baker's helper'. Open Sun–Thur 1800–midnight, Fri–Sat 1700–midnight; Sun brunch 0900–1500.

For budget satisfaction, try the **Sandshaker Sandwich Shop**, *731 Pensacola Beach Blvd; tel: (904) 932-0023*, Mon–Wed 1100–2100, Thur–Sun 1100–2200. The adjoining **Sandshaker Lounge**; *tel: (904) 932-2211*, is a small but cheerful watering hole noted for the deceptive innocence of its cocktails. The *Bushwacker* is a house specialty.

**Peg Leg Pete's Oyster Bar**, *1010 Fort Pickens Rd, Pensacola Beach; tel: (904) 932-4139*, is an immensely popular waterside lounge and restaurant – a ramshackle building where the service is friendly, the atmosphere casual, the food good and the prices definitely budget.

### ENTERTAINMENT

The best source of information about entertainment and cultural activities is the Pensacola CVIC (see p. 317), but from the visitor's point of view this might be sparse at times. Much of the art and culture is home-grown: the area has a proliferation of associations and societies devoted to the pursuit of a wide range of activities and interests.

Focal point of the performing arts is the **Saenger Theatre**, *118 Palafox Pl; tel: (904) 438-2787*. Located in the Palafox Historic District, the theatre was built in Spanish Baroque style with Renaissance ornamentation and opened in 1925, equipped for both stage and cinema presentations. Its opening night feature was the Cecil B. DeMille epic *The Ten Commandments*.

Today, the Saenger presents performances by the Pensacola Symphony Orchestra, First City Dance, the Choral Society and the Pensacola Opera. The theatre's splendid 1925 Robert Morton pipe organ, installed to accompany silent films, is used for recitals and concerts by prominent organists.

**Pensacola Little Theatre**, based at the *Pensacola Cultural Center, 186 N. Palafox St; tel: (904) 432-2042*, presents a range of performances – musicals, dramas, comedies – throughout the year. The Cultural Center also stages a variety of other events.

### Events

Scarcely a week goes by without some kind of festival or celebration being staged in the Pensacola area. First of the major events of the year is **Springfest**, held downtown in Apr and a riot of jazz, blues, rock and country music by international stars as well as local performers. A **Fine Arts and Masters Show** runs in sedate tandem with the festival. There's more music during the **Pensacola JazzFest**, also staged in Apr.

May sees the annual **British Fair** in *Seville Sq*, a celebration with food, crafts and music of the city's British heritage. A month later in the **Fiesta of Five Flags** the whole city celebrates its development under Spanish, French, British, Confederate and US administrations. The ten-day festival includes a British street party, fishing tournaments, a regatta, a Confederate encampment and concerts.

Independence Day celebrations apart, July festivals include the spectacular **Pensacola Beach Air Show**, with thrilling aerobatics performed by the Blue Angels stunt-flying team. There's also a **Wine Festival** on the Quietwater Beach Boardwalk, when visitors get the chance to taste close on 200 wines from 150 international vineyards.

There's more drink on the cards in Aug – again on the Quietwater Beach Boardwalk – during the **Bushwacker Festival**, a celebration of the local cocktail that looks like a milkshake and acts like a fireworks display.

September sees **Seafood Festivals** at Pensacola Beach and in *Seville Sq*, Pensacola.

Country music lovers rub shoulders with cattle breeders, cereal growers and other country dwellers during the ten-day **Pensacola Interstate Fair**, staged at the Pensacola Fairgrounds on Mobile Hwy during Oct. Admission: $5; children aged three–11, $3, parking $1.

Pensacola's *Seville Sq* is the setting for the **Great Gulf Arts Festival**, staged in Nov. Some 200 artists from the US are chosen and invited to display and sell their work which ranges from ceramics and photography to hand-made jewellery, furniture and musical instruments.

## SHOPPING

Visitors will find Pensacola's specialty shops and stores appealing, but for more down-to-earth shopping there are two malls, 70 shopping centres and a host of boutiques.

The **Bayou Country Store** at the corner of *9th Ave and E. Jackson St, Pensacola; tel: (904) 432-5697*, is a cornucopia of antique Americana – rocking chairs, benches and other porch furniture, as well as kitchenware such as washboards and rolling pins. Open Mon–Sat 1000–1700. For a more eclectic choice of antiques and second-hand articles head for *'T' St, off Fairfield Dr.*, on Pensacola's west side, where you'll find shops selling everything from hub caps to railway memorabilia.

There are more bargain-hunting opportunities at the **Flea Market**, on a massive outdoor site at *5760 Gulf Breeze Parkway, Gulf Breeze; tel: (904) 934-1971*. Open Sat–Sun 0900–1700.

**Cordova Mall**, *9th Ave/Bayou Blvd, Pensacola; tel: (904) 477-5355*, is one of the largest in the south-east US, with more than 140 speciality shops, plus major department stores, four theatres, a food court and year-round entertainment. Open Mon–Sat 1000–2100, Sun 1230–1700.

**University Mall**, *Davis Hwy at I-10; tel: (904) 478-3600*, has more than 70 stores, department stores, theatres and a food court. Open Mon–Sat 1000–2100, Sun 1230–1730.

Shoppers seeking big discounts will have to drive west into Alabama on Hwy 98 to Foley, about an hour from Pensacola. The **Riviera Centre Factory Stores** on *Hwy 59 South; tel: (205) 943-8888*, contains more than 80 factory outlets offering savings of up to 70 per cent on normal retail prices. Open Mon–Sat 0900–2100, Sun 1000–1800.

## SIGHTSEEING

The area's main attractions are undoubtedly its beaches – 40 miles of literally squeaky-clean sand: pure white and so powder-dry it actually squeaks as you walk along it. Located on **Perdido Key**, west of Pensacola, **Pensacola Beach**, **Gulf Breeze** and **Navarre Beach**, they are said to be among the best in the US.

Pensacola's historic districts will keep

history and architecture buffs happy for hours.

A number of houses and commercial buildings in the area bounded by Zaragosa St, Tarragona St, Alcaniz St and Intendencia St have been designated as **Historic Pensacola Village**. The restored buildings, including the **Museum of Industry** and the **Museum of Commerce**, reflect the lifestyles of Gulf Coast Florida's 19th-century residents.

A street of stores and workshops is recreated in the Museum of Commerce, while the Museum of Industry features machinery used during Pensacola's boom years as a timber town and relics of its fishing industry heyday.

Costumed guides conduct visitors on tours of the restored **Lavalle House, Dorr House, Julee Cottage, Lear House, Quina House, Weaver's Cottage** and **Barkley House**. The village is traversed by the **Colonial Archaeology Trail**, a way-marked path that traces sites dating from the city's Spanish and British past.

The village is open Mon–Sat 1000–1630, Sun 1300–1630. Admission: $5.50; seniors and children aged four–16, $4.50. Tickets may be purchased in the central office in the *Tivoli High House, Zaragoza St; tel: (904) 444-8905*, or at the **T. T. Wentworth Jr Florida State Museum**, *Plaza Ferdinand VII*, and are good for seven days.

Technically in Palafox Historic District, and certainly out of the historic village environs, the Wentworth Museum is located in the Old City Hall, built in 1907, and traces the city's history in maps, photographs and artefacts. It has a hands-on Discovery Gallery for children. Open Mon–Sat 1000–1600. Admission: $5 (free if you have a Pensacola Historic Village ticket).

Nearby is the **Pensacola Historical Museum**, *405 S. Adams St; tel: (904) 433-1559*. This time the building is the Old Christ Church, built in 1832 and used by Federal forces during the Civil War as a barracks, prison, hospital and chapel. It now houses a collection of fossils, Indian pottery, maps, Civil War memorabilia, fishing and timber industries equipment and 19th-century domestic artefacts. Open Mon–Sat 0900–1630 (closed public holidays). Admission: $2; children $1.

Further evidence of Pensacola's recycling of old buildings is to be found in the **Museum of Art**, *407 S. Jefferson St; tel: (904) 432-6247*. Here, barred windows and doors hint at the building's original use. It was built in 1906 as the City Jail. Today, its former cell blocks show off collections of local and touring art exhibits. Open Mon–Sat 1000–1630. Admission: donation.

Civil War buffs will certainly want to head for the **Civil War Soldiers Museum**, *108 S. Palafox Pl; tel: (904) 469-1900*. The story of the saddest struggle in the history of the US is told through letters, photographs and artefacts – including a disturbing section on battlefield surgery. Local involvement in the war is highlighted in the Pensacola Room, which features a 20-min video presentation. The museum bookshop has 500 Civil War titles, fact and fiction. Open Mon–Sat 1000–1630. Admission: $4; children aged six–12 $2.

A more recent conflict is recalled in **The Wall South and Veterans' Memorial Park**, *Bayfront Parkway; tel: (904) 433-8200*. This is a three-quarters scale replica of the Vietnam Veterans' Memorial in Washington, DC, with the names of all Americans lost in the war engraved on the wall. Eventually, there will be a memorial for every war from World War I in which the United States took part. Freely accessible.

The **National Museum of Naval Aviation**, *Naval Blvd*, about eight miles south-west of downtown Pensacola; *tel: (904) 452-3604*, is one of the world's three largest air and space museums. It is located in the Pensacola Naval Air Station, established as the nation's first in 1914. Until World War II every pilot in the US Navy was trained here.

The museum houses a growing collection of more than 100 aircraft once flown by the navy, Marine Corps and US Coast Guard. Children especially will enjoy the opportunity to clamber in and out of cockpits, gaining hands-on experience from the pilot's seat. Open daily 0900–1700 (closed Thanksgiving, Christmas Day, New Year's Day). Have some form of identification ready when you enter. Admission: free.

Diverse wildlife is to be found in **Big Lagoon State Recreation Area**, *12301 Gulf Beach Hwy, CR 292A*, about 10 miles south-west of Pensacola; *tel: (904) 492-1595*. The park's sandy beaches and salt marshes fringe the shores of the Intracoastal Waterway and Big Lagoon and provide important habitats for birds and animals. Cardinals, towhees, brown thrashers and nuthatches are commonly seen, as are great blue herons, egrets and other water birds, grey foxes, raccoons, skunks and opossums.

A 40-ft observation tower at East Beach gives a panoramic view of Big Lagoon and Gulf Islands National Seashore (see below). There are facilities for swimming, fishing, boating, camping, picnicking and nature study. Open daily 0800–dusk. Admission: $3.25 per vehicle (up to eight persons) or $1 per person on foot.

**Fort Pickens**, at the western end of Santa Rosa Island, which also encompasses Pensacola Beach, is the imposing ruin of a fort built by slave labour in the early 19th century to protect the area from naval attacks. A small museum tells the story of the fort and there are displays of flora and fauna found in the vicinity. One section tells how the Apache chief Geronimo and 17 of his followers were imprisoned in the fort in 1886. The fort is open daily 0930–1700 Apr–Oct, 0830–1600 Nov–Mar. There are free guided tours Mon–Fri 1100 and 1400 and Sat–Sun 1400. Admission: free.

Fort Pickens is located within the **Gulf Islands National Seashore**, some 150 miles of barrier islands, keys and beaches stretching from Horn Island in Mississippi to Okaloosa Island near Destin, east of Pensacola.

A total of 52 miles of the seashore is in Northwest Florida, including parts of Perdido Key and the **Naval Live Oaks Reservation**, just east of Gulf Breeze, along Hwy 98. This 1400-acre area was set aside by President John Quincy Adams in 1828 to provide timber for building naval vessels. Walk through shady woodlands and visit the headquarters of the Gulf Islands National Seashore. Forestry exhibits and displays of Indian artefacts are on show in the visitor centre. Open daily 0830–1700. Admission: free.

**The Zoo**, *5701 Gulf Breeze Parkway, Gulf Breeze; tel: (904) 932-2229*, contains more than 700 animals – including Bengal tigers and western lowland gorillas – in an area surrounded by botanical gardens. The 'Safari Line' train takes visitors on an excursion through 30 acres of free-roaming animals. Open daily, weather permitting, 0900–1700 (1600 in winter months). Admission: $8.75; seniors, $7.50; children three–11, $5.25.

# PENSACOLA–TALLAHASSEE

There is a choice of routes between Pensacola and Tallahassee, but it boils down to rural scenery with speed, rural scenery without speed or a rural route offering the odd chance to stretch your legs in town.

I-10 covers the distance in the shortest time and crosses much scenic countryside. If you fancy a day of backroads driving, you can head north and take the tangle of rural lanes that snakes back and forth along the Alabama state line, but if you do this make sure you have a full tank of petrol and take food with you – you'll be on the road all day and there are few places where you can fill up either the car or yourself. Hwy 90, running parallel with I-10, at least offers variety in the form of a small town now and then.

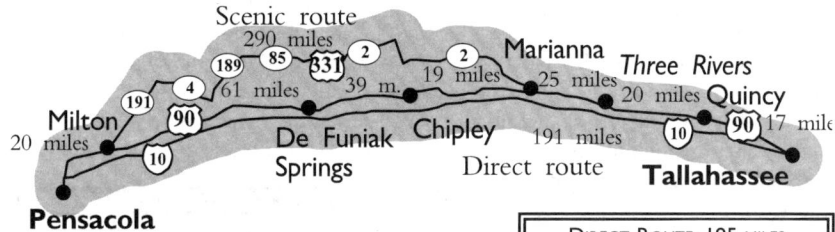

DIRECT ROUTE: 195 MILES

## ROUTES

### DIRECT ROUTE

From downtown Pensacola take I-110 north for 11 miles to its intersection with I-10. Head east on I-10 for 180 miles. At Exit 29, Hwy 27 south leads 3½ miles to the Old State Capitol in downtown Tallahassee. I-10 passes through pretty countryside. There are rest areas every 60 miles or so with toilets, food and drink machines and picnic tables in woodland settings.

### SCENIC ROUTE

This is a route only for those who get a kick out of finding what lies around the next corner, even if it is the same as what lay around the last one. There is the rare novelty (in Florida) of driving up and down hills, and you can experience the heady air of the state's highest point. Communities along the route are few and far between and very, very small with few amenities. You will cover some 290 miles on this route.

From downtown Pensacola take Hwy 291 (Davis Highway) north for 11 miles, then head east on Hwy 90 across a maze of marshes and waterways at the head of Pensacola Bay to **Milton**. Then take Hwy 191 north through the **Blackwater State Forest** to Munson. At Munson head west on Hwy 4 to Baker. Hwy 189 takes you north to Blackman, where you pick up Hwy 2 east.

## PENSACOLA–TALLAHASSEE

You are now in the heart of the mixed farming and forest land that straddles the Florida and Alabama border. Hwy 2 is to be our major route for the next 55 miles or so, but eight miles east of Blackman, we'll make a slight diversion north on Hwy 85. This takes us to **Lakewood**, almost on the state line and as high as you can get in Florida – a dizzying 345 ft above sea level.

From Lakewood head south on Hwy 331 and pick up Hwy 2 east again for 42 miles to **Graceville**. From here Hwy 231 leads south and intersects with Hwy 90 at **Marianna**. Continue east on Hwy 90 for 76 miles to Tallahassee.

### VARIED ROUTE

▐▶ This is probably the best option, covering about 220 miles. Follow Hwy 90 all the way from just north of Pensacola, passing through Milton, **De Funiak Springs, Chipley**, Marianna and **Quincy**. If you feel like a change, you can hop on and off I-10, never more than three or four miles away. From Quincy take a diversion on Hwy 12 to visit historic **Havana**, just 20 minutes from Tallahassee. From there, Hwy 27 south runs you straight to the Old State Capitol.

### MILTON

**Tourist Information: Santa Rosa County Chamber of Commerce**, *501 Stewart St SW; tel: (904) 623-2339.*

Milton is near several scenic rivers where canoeing, camping, picnicking and tubing are popular. The town developed with the lumber business, and many of the fine old homes in what is now **Milton Historic District** were built more than a century ago.

Santa Rosa Historical Society is based in the balconied three-storey **Imogene Theater and Milton Opera House**, which also houses a museum of local history. One of the properties owned by the Historical Society is **Milton Depot**, the railway station which served the area until the 1960s.

**Blackwater River State Park**, with camping, fishing and boating facilities and nature trails, is *off Hwy 90, 15 miles north of Milton; tel: (904) 623-2364.* Open daily 0800-sunset. Admission: $3.25 per vehicle.

Just outside Milton is the headquarters of **Adventures Unlimited,** *Coldwater Creek, Rte 6, off Hwy 87; tel: (904) 623-6197.* From here, people set off on canoeing, kayaking, paddle-boating, rafting or tubing trips. Hiking and biking trails can be followed and cabins and camping are available. Forest hayrides are another option. Open daily 0800–1800, with summer hours extended to 1900 Sun–Thur and to 2000 Fri–Sat.

### DE FUNIAK SPRINGS

If anachronisms intrigue you, pause at De Funiak Springs where an ornate and imposing wooden building overlooks a lake.

A century ago, great theologian orators regularly visited De Funiak Springs to address vast audiences who arrived by train. The building, erected by a zealous religious organisation, has a 4,000-seat auditorium. As the years passed, the organisation lost its vigour and dwindled, but the venue survives.

### CHIPLEY

Chipley is one a sawmill town which has seen better days. It takes its name from railway tycoon W. D. Chipley, whose campaign to extend the railway system to Pensacola succeeded in 1881, bringing tourism to the region as well as benefitting the timber trade.

## PENSACOLA–TALLAHASSEE

**Falling Waters State Recreation Area** is three miles south of Chipley, *off Hwy 77A; tel: (904) 638-6130*. Here you will find something rare in Florida: a waterfall. Although the state has thousands of lakes and rivers, it is too flat to be rich in waterfalls. But here is a 67-footer, complete with observation platform. The waters of a small stream drop into a 100 ft deep, 20 ft wide cylindrical sinkhole. No one knows where the stream goes from there. Falling Waters State Recreation Area, known for its plants and geological formation has nature trails, picnicking and full camping facilities. Open daily 0800–sunset. Admission: $3.25 per vehicle.

### MARIANNA

Tourist Information: Jackson County Chamber of Commerce, *Box 130, Marianna, FL, 32446; tel: (904) 482-8061.*

Geological formations in abundance are a feature of the series of connecting caves in **Florida Caverns State Park**, on *Hwy 167*, three miles north of Marianna; *tel: (904) 482-9598*. Guided tours of the caves take place several times a day. You see stalagmites, stalactites, columns and draperies, all made of calcite, and you learn how the calcite is dissolved from limestone when rainwater containing carbonic acid percolates through the rock into the caverns. Touring the caverns involves stooping and squeezing through narrow apertures.

Dating from prehistoric times, the caves and their curious formations – some beautiful, some grotesque, all fascinating – are very extensive. It is believed Indians lived in them. Most are now closed to the public. Those that are open were exposed soon after the turn of the century when a large tree was blown down in a hurricane.

Canoeing, boating, swimming and full camping facilities are available, and horses can be rented from a local stables. Open daily 0800–sunset. Admission: $3.25 per vehicle.

### THREE RIVERS SRA

For a diversion to see **Lake Seminole** in **Three Rivers State Recreation Area**, take *Hwy 271*, two miles north of Sneads; *tel: (904) 482-9006*. The three rivers are the Chattahoochee, the Flint and the Apalachicola. There's a chance of seeing whitetail deer, grey foxes and a wide variety of birds in this undulating area with its hardwoods and pine forest. Fishing, camping, boating, canoeing and picnicking are other activities.

### QUINCY AND HAVANA

These two villages, both northwest of Tallahassee, developed by cultivating of tobacco and will appeal to visitors interested in historic buildings. The prosperity of Quincy, on Hwy 90, declined after the Civil War, though it has rallied since. It has more than 50 antebellum homes and buildings of the Civil War era.

To visit Havana, leave Quincy by Hwy 12 to the junction with Hwy 157. Havana, too, suffered an economic downswing, but reversed it by switching to the growing of cigar-quality tobacco at a time when the extending railway system provided transport to markets.

Today, Havanna is included in full-day coach excursions from Tallahassee. People enjoy its turn-of-the-century ambience, its two dozen antiques shops, stores selling gifts and collectibles and well as its art galleries and cafés. Its **Civil War Museum** is also of interest.

# TALLAHASSEE–ATLANTA

This route travels from one state capital to another, through the slumbering countryside of the Deep South with its plantations and antebellum mansions – the land of cotton, soya beans and pecan groves. History in the south central region of Georgia means much more than the Civil War. Human activity can be traced over a period of 10,000 years – from primitive palaeolithic hunters to the age of Rock 'n' Roll.

### ROUTE

From the Old Capitol in downtown Tallahassee take Hwy 27 (Monroe St N.) north for 3½ miles, then head east on I-10. Leave the interstate at Exit 29 and take Hwy 319 north to **Thomasville, Georgia**.

The first 18 miles of this attractive highway, between Tallahassee and the Georgia state line, is said to have the highest concentration of plantation mansions in the US. Unfortunately, you can't see them from the road. All are privately owned, still occupied by wealthy families and set well back – sometimes many miles. Nor can you necessarily tell which are the drives that lead to the mansions. Here, there are no wrought iron gates and ornate lodges – it's considered showy to have anything more than a dirt track leading to your colonnaded front porch.

From the Georgia border the highway passes fields of cotton and soya bean plants and regimental rows of pecan trees, reaching Thomasville after a fur-

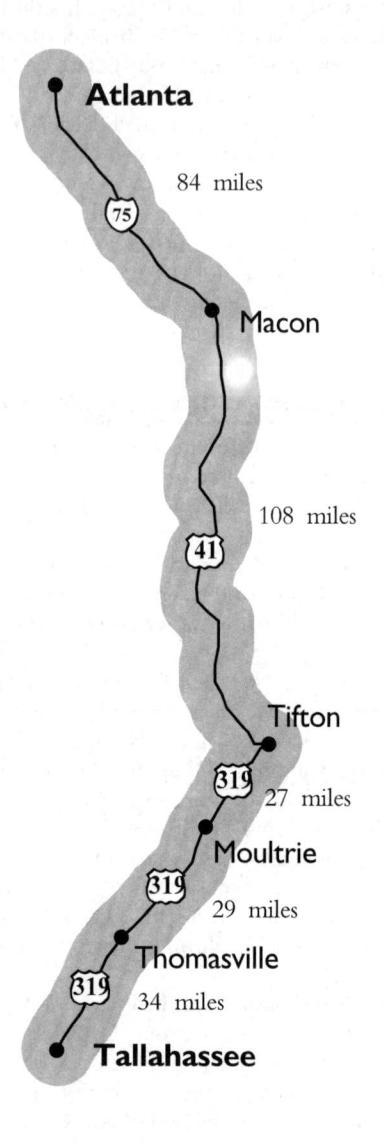

● Atlanta

84 miles
(75)

● Macon

108 miles
(41)

● Tifton
(319)
27 miles

● Moultrie
(319)
29 miles

● Thomasville
(319)
34 miles

● Tallahassee

ROUTE: 305 MILES

ther 13 miles. It passes right through the city centre and continues north to **Moultrie** and **Tifton**.

So far we have been travelling through the area known as Georgia's Plantation Trace region, with vast estates established by gentlemen farmers of the past. From Tifton we follow Hwy 41 north into the Presidential Pathways region, honouring Presidents F.D. Roosevelt and Jimmy Carter who made their homes here.

In this region, our route takes us through the city of **Cordele**, 'Watermelon Capital of the World', where watermelon eating and seed-spitting contests are staged every year in July. Cordele has a **KOA** Campground in a pecan grove on Hwy 300 west, just off Exit 32 of I-75. **Georgia Veterans State Park**, on Hwy 280, nine miles west of Exit 32 on I-75, has cottages as well as sites for RVs and tents.

Hwy 41 travels on into Georgia's Historic Heartland, through **Perry** and on to **Macon**. The highway runs close to and parallel with I-75, so you can always switch to the fast lane if you decide on a change of pace.

Macon is big, but by no means bustling. To get downtown from Hwy 41 turn right on to *Mercer University Dr.*, which becomes *Mercer University Blvd*, then bear left on to *College St* and right on to *Cotton Ave.*

Leave downtown Macon by heading east on *M.L. King Jr Blvd*; cross the Ocmulgee River, then head west on I-16, which intersects with I-75 in two miles. After 79 miles I-75 intersects with I-85 at Exit 88 (Lakewood Freeway, East Point). Follow the combined interstates of I–75/I–85 north and take Exit 93 towards Underground Atlanta and Downtown.

## THOMASVILLE

Tourist Information: Destination Thomasville Tourism Authority, *PO Box 1540, Thomasville, GA, 31799; tel: (912) 225-3919*. The Welcome Center, located at *109 S. Broad St*, has a brochure giving details of a driving tour covering six historic districts with 59 sites dating from the 1830s to the mid-1900s.

Thomasville is a Georgia Main Street City, which means it is committed to a continuous programme of downtown restoration and preservation. A popular winter resort from the 1880s, it continues to attract weekenders from Tallahassee and is rich in bed and breakfast inns, some in vintage houses.

The moderately-priced **Grand Victoria Inn**, *817 S. Hansell St; tel: (912) 226-7460* is in a 100-year-old home handy for downtown shopping.

The **Susina Plantation Inn** offers justifiably expensive accommodation in a splendid antebellum mansion built in 1841 on a 115-acre estate on *Hwy 155, 12 miles south of the city; tel: (912) 377-9644.*

There's also a good range of budget – moderate restaurants. These include the **Market Country Restaurant**, adjoining the Farmers' Market on *Smith Ave; tel: (912) 225-1777*, and **Mom & Dad's**, an Italian restaurant at *1800 Smith Ave; tel: (912) 226-6265.*

The **Waffle House**, *100 Hwy 19 S.; tel: (912) 225-9223*, serves T-bone steaks, chicken and salads as well as breakfast fare and is open 24 hours a day.

Thomasville's best-known sightseeing attraction is **Pebble Hill Plantation**, *Hwy 319, five miles south of Thomasville; tel: (912) 226-2344*. This magnificent mansion, typical of the hunting plantations established in the 19th century by wealthy Northerners, is set among smooth lawns, pines and magnolias. Paintings and sporting prints and a collection of Audubon prints are on show, and there is a large carriage collection in the stables. Open Tues–Sat 1000–1700, Sun 1300–1700 (the last guided tour of the house is at 1600). Pebble Hill is closed from Labour Day (first Mon in Sept) to 1 Oct. Admission – grounds: $2; children under 12, $1. Admission to main house: $5; children, $2.50.

## MOULTRIE

**Tourist Information: Moultrie-Colquitt County Chamber of Commerce**, *329 N. Main St; tel: (912) 985-2131*. A self-guided tour booklet containing maps and directions for five routes is available, as is accommodation and dining information.

For moderately-priced accommodation try the **Moultrie Inn**, *1708 First Ave S.E.; tel: (912) 890-2401*, or **Shoney's Inn**, *1713 First Ave S.E.; tel: (912) 985-2200*. The **Waffle House**, *1900 First Ave S.E.; tel: (912) 985-5050*, serves meals 24 hours a day.

**Colquitt County Jail**, *First Ave S.E.*, described as 'the finest, best architecturally designed jail in Georgia,' when it was built in 1915 is being restored for use as the chamber of commerce offices.

**Colquitt County Historical Museum**, *S. Main St; tel: (912) 985-2131*, has displays featuring local history. Open Wed 1430–1630 or by appointment. Admission: free.

## TIFTON

**Tourist Information: Tifton/Tift County Tourism Association**, *100 N. Central Ave; tel: (912) 386-0216*. The centre has brochures, videos and maps and offers information on attractions, festivals and bed and breakfast locations. The city of Tifton boasts 1,200 motel rooms and 80 restaurants. The moderately-priced **Holiday Inn Tifton** is at the intersection of *Hwy 81 and I-75; tel: (912) 382-6687*.

A Georgia Main St city, Tifton has a revitalised downtown where some 30 shops thrive in a series of restored buildings, including the 1906 **Myon Hotel** complex. Once said to be the finest hotel south of Atlanta, the authentically restored Myon now houses City Hall, a permanent art collection, shops and a bed and breakfast inn.

**Georgia Agirama**, *8th St at I-75; tel: (912) 386-3344*, is a living history museum of late-19th century farm communities where costumed interpreters guide visitors through 35 restored buildings, farms and a small rural town. Open daily. Admission: $6; children, $3.

## MACON

**Tourist Information: Macon-Bibb County Convention and Visitors Bureau**, *200 Cherry St; tel: (912) 743-3401*. The bureau is located in the splendid old railway terminal, built in 1916, that once saw 100 passenger trains a day. Maps, sightseeing brochures and information on accommodation and restaurants are freely available.

### GETTING AROUND

Macon is a fairly large city (pop 106,000) but not too hard on the feet. Visitors should make sure they obtain a copy of *Tour and Enjoy Historic Macon*, an informative brochure detailing three way-marked walking tours. **Sidney's Old South Historic Tours** of the city by minibus start from the bureau Mon–Sat 1000 and 1400.

## Accommodation

The city offers a good range of hotels, motels and bed and breakfast inns. Hotel chains in Macon include *BW, CI, DI, HI, HJ, Ma, Ra, Tl*. *Riverside Dr.*, running along the west bank of the Ocmulgee River, has the greatest concentration of chain hotels and motels.

The best-known of the city's bed and breakfast establishments is the **1842 Inn**, *353 College St; tel: (912) 741-1842*. As its name suggests, the inn was built around 1842, and it is one of the earliest examples of Greek Revival houses in the area. As such, it is a tourist attraction in its own right. Accommodation in the 1842 Inn is provided in spacious rooms in the house and in an adjoining Victorian cottage.

Macon has no shortage of places to eat. Top of the scale is **Beall's 1860 Restaurant**, *315 College St; tel: (912) 745-3663*, a restored Greek Revival mansion with 14 ft ceilings and a colonnaded reception hall.

For a workaday lunch Southern-style, try **Len Berg's Restaurant**, a busy but friendly diner tucked away in the *Old Post Office Alley, off Mulberry St; tel: (912) 742-9255*.

## Sightseeing

Macon has six historic districts on the National Register, including the downtown business area, with dozens of antebellum mansions and streets full of charming cottages.

**The Hay House**, *934 Georgia Ave; tel: (912) 742-8155*, is an 18,000 sq ft Italian Renaissance Revival villa that was built in the 1850s. It has 19 hand-carved marble mantelpieces and some magnificent decorative plasterwork. Recent restorations have revealed beautiful tromp l'oeil decorations. Open Mon–Sat 1000–1700, Sun 1300–1630.

**The Old Cannonball House**, *856 Mulberry St; tel: (912) 745-5982*, was the only home in Macon to be damaged during the Civil War. A cannonball bounced off a front porch column, smashed through the wall and came to rest in the hall. A Confederate museum is at the rear. Open Tues–Fri 1000–1300 and 1400–1600; Sat–Sun 1330–1630.

**Harriet Tubman African American Museum**, *340 Walnut St; tel: (912) 743-8544*, features the city's Black history and culture. In addition to a permanent collection of African–American artefacts and art, there are visiting exhibitions. Open Mon–Sat 0900–1700, Sun 1400–1700.

**Museum of Arts and Sciences**, *4182 Forsyth Rd; tel: (912) 477-3232*. This museum also incorporates the Mark Smith Planetarium. Open Mon–Thurs and Sat 0900–1700, Fri 0900–2100, Sun 1300–1700. Admission: $5, children $3.

**Ocmulgee National Monument**, *1207 Emery Way; tel: (912) 752-8257*, is a massive archaeological site with a number of mounds reminiscent of ceremonial sites in Mexico. Visitors may enter a rebuilt earthlodge. The site's story is illustrated in the visitor centre and museum. Open daily 0900–dusk. Admission: free.

**The Georgia Music Hall of Fame** is scheduled to open at the corner of *M.L. King Jr Blvd* and *Mulberry St* in Mar 1996. The $6.5–million project will focus on Georgia's diverse musical heritage and feature the music and memorabilia of Georgia artists such as Little Richard, Ray Charles and Gladys Knight as well as exhibits about home-grown Macon stars like Lena Horne, Johnny Mercer and Otis Redding.

# JACKSONVILLE–ATLANTA

ROUTE: 336 MILES

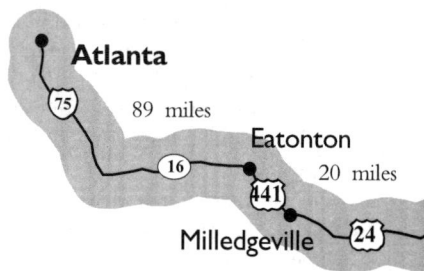

This route offers a variety of landscapes and places — from the coastal marshlands that spread across the eastern borders of Florida and Georgia, to serene farmlands, lakes and forests; from the sophisticated streets of Savannah to the sleepy main streets and squares of tiny towns unchanged since before the Civil War.

## ROUTE

From downtown Jacksonville head north on Main St, then turn left on Beaver St (Hwy 90 west). In one mile take I-95 north, and after 57 miles exit on to Hwy 82 east. After six miles turn left on to Hwy 17, which crosses a neck of St Simon's Sound to reach **Brunswick**, shrimp port and gateway to the **Golden Isles**.

Continue on Hwy 17 north of Brunswick, and after nine miles turn left on to Hwy 99. This intersects with I-95 in one mile, where we head north again. Stay on I-95 as it crosses the wide open beauty of south Georgia's coastal marshlands for another 40 miles, then head east on I-16, which runs into Martin Luther King Jr Blvd in downtown **Savannah**, with the visitors' centre clearly signposted.

Follow the boulevard east and turn left on to W. Bay St, which soon runs into Hwy 80 west. Fifteen miles out of

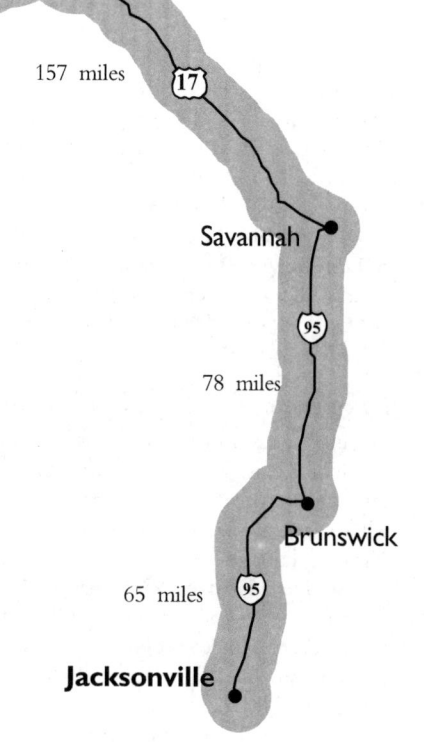

Savannah, turn north on to Hwy 17, which continues north for 114 miles, following the course of the Ogeechee River and the route of the Central Railroad of Georgia for much of the way to the small community of **Louisville**, where we head west on Hwy 24.

After 23 miles, Hwy 24 brings us to Sandersville then on to Milledgeville, a former capital of Georgia, in another 29 miles.

From Milledgeville head north on Hwy 441 for 20 miles to quiet **Eatonton**, home town of two internationally renowned writers, then head west on State Hwy 16 (not to be confused with I-16), passing through the 11,500-acre **Oconee National Forest** for another 20 miles to reach **Monticello**, where the **Forsyth St Historic District** is lined with dogwood and contains antebellum and Victorian homes.

West of Monticello, Hwy 16 continues like an English country lane through forest and cosy farmland to intersect with I-75 after 24 miles. Take I-75 north for 42 miles to where it combines with I-85 then continue to Exit 93 for Underground Atlanta and downtown.

## BRUNSWICK

Tourism Information: Brunswick and Golden Isles of Georgia Visitors Bureau, *4 Glynn Ave; tel: (912) 265-0620.* The bureau offers information on local attractions, activities, accommodation, restaurants and events in the city and in the four beach, resort areas known as the Golden Isles.

Hotel chains in the area include *CI, ES, HI, HJ*. **The Jameson Inn**, part of a Georgia-wide chain, at the intersection of *Hwy 25 and Scranton Dr.; tel: (800)* *541-3268*, has moderately-priced accommodation with complimentary continental breakfast. There are several bed and breakfast inns in the area.

Eating, as usual, should present no problems, with seafood very predominant in a place that calls itself the 'Shrimp Capital of the World'. There are numerous fastfood establishments, including 24-hour **Waffle Houses** at *499 New Jesup Hwy; tel: (912) 262-5917* and at *351 Jesup Hwy; tel: (912) 264-6240.* You can combine drama and dinner at the **Royal Cafe Dinner Theatre**, *1618 Newcastle St; tel: (912) 262-1402.*

**Earth Day Nature Trail**, *1 Conservation Way; tel: (912) 264-7218*, winds across salt marshes, tidal ponds and coastal hammock high ground. An observation deck and tower give views of osprey and eagle nesting platforms. Open daily 0700–1800. Admission: free.

**Howfwyl-Broadfield Plantation State Historic Site**, *5556 Hwy 17 N.; tel: (912) 264-7333*, is an antebellum rice plantation house, built around 1851, with original furnishings. There is also a film museum. Open daily.

**Old Town Brunswick** was laid out in 1771 in a grid pattern of broad streets and parks. Street names still reflect British and German ties.

Brunswick's **Shrimp fleet** may be seen in the docks on Bay St, between Gloucester and Prince streets.

## SAVANNAH

From its early days when Englishman General James Oglethorpe designed it on a grid pattern of 24 leafy squares in 1733, Savannah has been considered a beautiful city. So beautiful that General Sherman could not bring himself to burn it down during the Civil War.

Now the city is being put on the world map by sailing events in the 1996 Olympic Games and a best-selling book, *Midnight in the Garden of Good and Evil*, by New Yorker John Berendt. Tourism to Savannah has soared and everyone wants to see the historic places mentioned in the 'non-fiction novel'.

This riverside city has character beauty, with a pervasive spirit of fun.

## TOURIST INFORMATION

**Savannah Visitors Center**, *301 Martin Luther King Jr Blvd; tel: (912) 944-0461.* Housed in a restored 1860s railway station, this attractive centre has free maps and leaflets on local attractions as well as information on dining and shopping. An audio-visual presentation provides a general picture of Savannah's history, industry and places to visit. There's a complimentary reservations system for accommodation and tours. Open Mon–Fri 0830–1700, Sat–Sun and public holidays 0900–1700.

## GETTING AROUND

Although it is easy and pleasurable to get around the 2.2 sq mile historic district on foot, in the heat of summer you may prefer to take a narrated tour by bus or trolley. **Old Town Trolley Tours**, *601 Cohen St; tel: (912) 233-0083*, leave from the Visitor Center (where you can park free for four hours while sightseeing – obtain a windscreen sticker from the centre). The complete tour is 90 minutes, and you can leave and re-board at designated stops. Daily, half-hourly from 0900. Fare: $14.

**Old Savannah Tours**, *516 Lee Blvd; tel: (912) 354-7913*, has a one-hour ($9) non-stop overview of the Historic District, the squares and River St. A two-hour tour includes stops at two attractions – a museum or historic building – with admission price included in the $14 fare. Passengers with reservations can be picked up at their hotels or inns.

**Carriage Tours of Savannah**, *9 East River St; tel: (912) 236-6756*, has $13 horse-drawn tours and a private **Cobblestone Classic** tour at $60 for two. One of several guided walking tours is **Ghost Talk, Ghost Walk**, based on Margaret Debolt's *Savannah Spectres and Other Strange Tales*. A new walking tour, **By the Book**, visits places featured in John Berendt's novel. A **Negro Heritage Tour**, more bus tours and a choice of river cruises are available.

## ACCOMMODATION

Savannah has a wealth of major hotels and a couple of dozen bed and breakfast inns, mostly of historic interest. **RSVP Reservation Service of Savannah**, *219 W. Bryan St, Savannah, GA, 31401; tel: (912) 232-7787 or 1-800-729-7787*, represents 24 inns and guesthouses in the city. *Savannah Tourist Guide*, a tourist newspaper published every two months, priced at 25 cents, also provides a free hotel reservation service. It has more than 1,500 rooms available in Savannah and neighbouring Tybee Island; *tel: (912) 236-6080*, daily 0900-1800.

Hotel chains in Savannah include *BW, DI, HI, HJ, Hn, Hy, Rd, Sh.*

The expensive **Hyatt Regency**, *2 W. Bay St; tel: (912) 238-1234*, has 346 rooms, some overlooking the Savannah River with a view of South Carolina on the opposite bank. The **Hampton Inn Hotel**, *201 Stephenson Ave; tel: (912) 355-4100*, is moderately priced. At the top end of the price range is the historic 22-room **Ballastone Inn**, *14 E. Oglethorpe Ave; tel: (912) 236-1484.* It has a lounge where you are welcomed with coffee or sherry, and at night you find a glass of brandy has been placed on your bedside table. The **Radisson Plaza**, *100 Gen. McIntosh Blvd; tel: (912) 233-7722*, is a new riverfront property.

## ENTERTAINMENT

**River St** is the place for living it up in Savannah. Container ships and luxury yachts sail by on the river and you hear lively music belting out of the restaurants, taverns and shops in the converted cotton warehouses as you make your way along the cobblestoned street. Some of the restaurants offer entertainment at weekends. Country music fans go to **City Slickers**, *9 W. Bay St; tel: (912) 233-6999. Open Wed–Sat.*

### Events

Festivals with varying themes take place at *Riverfront Plaza* on the first Saturday of every month. *River St* goes Irish in March with a big St Patrick's Day celebration. Private historic homes may be visited, some with meals provided, over the last weekend in Mar when the four-day Tour of Historic Homes and Gardens – a tradition of 60 years – takes place. For reservations contact *18 Abercorn St, Savannah, GA, 31401; tel: (912) 234-8054*. Multi-ethnic foods are served at the Night in Old Savannah festival in mid-May. The Maritime Festival is in early Aug.

## SHOPPING

At least 20 shopping centres and malls are dotted around Savannah. The enchanting specialist shops of the **De Soto Historic District** and the galleries and boutiques of River St's nine blocks provide gifts and mementoes. **The Basket Place**, *305 E. River St*, has baskets from all around the world, including local sweetgrass baskets. **River Street Gallery** has paintings and prints from the Southern states, handmade jewellery and other crafts. **River Street Zoo** is an emporium specialising in childrenswear and toys. The renowned **Shaver's Bookshop**, with 12 rooms of books, is at *326 Bull St*.

## SIGHTSEEING

With more than a dozen museums, two forts, a sprinkling of historic homes and activity on the river, Savannah presents a lot of sights to see. The following is a small selection.

The **City Market** is a renovated four-block sector of the Historic District which features artists working in their lofts and exhibiting their work for sale.

The **Historic Railroad Shops**, *601 W. Harris St; tel: (912) 651-6823*, are acclaimed as the oldest and most complete pre-Civil War railway manufacturing and repair facilities in the US. Open Mon–Sat 1000–1600, Sun noon–1600. Admission charged.

**Juliette Gordon Low Birthplace**, *142 Bull St; tel: (912) 233-4501*. Juliette Gordon Low is revered as the founder in 1912 of the Girl Scouts movement in the US. Her birthplace has been restored to the late 1800s period. It has many of the original family furnishings and is a National Historic Landmark. Open Mon, Tue, Thurs–Sat 1000–1600, Sun 1230–1630. Admission charged.

Next door to the Visitor Center is **Savannah History Museum**, *303 Martin Luther King Jr Blvd; tel: (912) 238-1779*. It unfolds the story of Savannah's cotton industry, its part in the Civil War and its railway age of steam. Open daily 0900–1700. Admission charged.

**Ships of the Sea Maritime**

## JACKSONVILLE–ATLANTA

Museum, *503 E. River St and 504 E. Bay St; tel: (912) 232-1511*, has more than 50 model ships, including Viking warships and the SS *Savannah*, the first steamship to cross the Atlantic. The museum also has a ship-in-the-bottle collection among its exhibits. Open daily 1000–1700. Admission: $3.

### MILLEDGEVILLE

**Tourist Information: Milledgeville/ Baldwin County Convention and Visitors Bureau**, *200 W. Hancock St; tel: (912) 452-4687*. The Welcome Center here offers a complete information service. Two-hour guided trolley tours of the city's Historic Distric start from the centre.

Accommodation in Milledgeville ranges from quaint bed and breakfast inns to more than 400 motel rooms. Two moderately-priced hotels are the **Jameson Inn**, *2251 N. Columbia St; tel: (912) 453-8471*, and **Holiday Inn Milledgeville**, *Hwy 441 N; tel: (912) 452-3502*. The city boasts 65 dining establishments.

Milledgeville was the capital of Georgia from 1803–1868 and is said to be the only surviving example of a complete city of the Federal Period (the period following the War of Independence, noted for the simple elegance of its architectural style and the use of red brick). The best way to see its handsome streets is by taking a trolley tour from the Welcome Centre. The following sights are included in the tour.

**Old State Capital Building**, *201 E. Greene St*, built in 1807 and possibly the oldest Gothic–style public building in the country.

**Old Governor's Mansion**, *120 S. Clark St; tel: (912) 453-4545*, built around 1838 and the home of ten Georgia governors. Open Tues–Sat 1000–1600, Sun 1400–1600.

**Stetson-Sanford House**, *W. Hancock St*, dates from 1825 and is an acclaimed example of Milledgeville Federal architecture.

### EATONTON

**Tourist Information: Eatonton-Putnam Chamber of Commerce**, *105 Sumter St; tel: (706) 485-7701*.

Eatonton has two bed and breakfast inns: **Crockett House**, *671 Madison Ave; tel: (706) 485-2248* and **Rosewood**, *301 N. Madison Ave; tel: (706) 485-9009*. There are campgrounds in the **Lake Oconee Recreation Area**, 12 miles north–east of the town on Hwy 44; *tel: (706) 485-8704*.

The town's most famous offspring are Joel Chandler Harris, creator of *The Tales of Uncle Remus*, and Alice Walker, Pulitzer Prize-winning author of *The Color Purple*.

A statue of Br'er Rabbit stands in front of Putney County Courthouse in the centre of town and there's an **Uncle Remus Museum** in a re-constructed slave cabin three blocks south of the courthouse on Hwy 441; *tel: (706) 485-6856*. Memorabilia and first editions are on show and there are shadow boxes containing delicate wood carvings of 'de Critters'. A large portrait of Uncle Remus and the Little Boy was presented to the museum by Walt Disney. Open Mon–Sat 1000–noon, 1300–1700; Sun 1400–1700 (closed Tues, Sept–May). Admission: 50 cents.

Information on a self-guided **Alice Walker Trail** can be obtained from the Chamber of Commerce. The trail features buildings and locations lived in or known to the author and some which had a bearing on her work.

# ATLANTA

Atlanta, Georgia's capital, has always been at a crossroads. It was born in the 19th century as a crossing of cattle drovers' trails and began its climb to prominence as a railway hub. With lines converging on what is now Five Points in the downtown area, the city was first prosaically named Terminus.

Despite its strong associations with Hollywood's version of Margaret Mitchell's *Gone With the Wind* – which it exploits shamelessly – Atlanta is a modern city, thanks to two major fires. During the Civil War it was practically razed by General Sherman, and a conflagration in 1917 destroyed 2,000 buildings covering 300 acres.

Metropolitan Atlanta is big. With a population of around three million, it covers an area of 5,147 sq miles and is the centre of considerable commercial and political activity.

## TOURIST INFORMATION

**Georgia Dept of Industry, Trade and Tourism**, *Box 1776, Atlanta, GA 30301; tel: (404) 656-3590.* Maps and brochures on tourism throughout the state are available.

**Atlanta Convention and Visitors Bureau** maintains information centres at the following locations: *Suite 2000, Peachtree Center Mall, 233 Peachtree St N.E.; tel: (404) 222-6688.* Open Mon–Fri 1000–1700. *Lenox Sq Mall, 3393 Peachtree Rd NE.* Open Wed–Sat 1100–1800. *Underground Atlanta, 65 Upper Alabama St; tel: (404) 222-6688.* Open Mon–Sat 1000–2100, Sun noon–1730. An information kiosk is also located on *Lower Alabama St* in Underground City. Each centre can assist with reservations and is a treasure house of maps, brochures and leaflets on attractions, tours, accommodation and dining.

**Atlanta Committee for the Olympic Games**, *250 Williams St, Suite 6000, PO Box 1996, Atlanta, GA 30301-1996; tel: (404) 224-1996*, has an information centre and exhibition in Underground Atlanta, adjoining the **Suite Hotel** on *Upper Alabama St*, at *Peachtree St.*

A wealth of information on accommodation, dining, events, entertainment and sightseeing is to be found in *Atlanta Now*, a magazine published six times a year by the Atlanta Convention and Visitors Bureau, and *Where Atlanta*, a monthly magazine.

Both publications are freely available at tourist information centres. *Peachtree*, a monthly newsstand magazine priced at $2.50, publishes restaurant reviews and listings.

## ARRIVING AND DEPARTING

### Airport

**Hartsfield Atlanta International Airport**; *tel: (404) 765-1300*, is ten miles south of downtown Atlanta. One of the busiest airports in the world, handling more than 54 million passengers a year, it has two terminals – North and South – one international concourse and

# ATLANTA CITY MAP

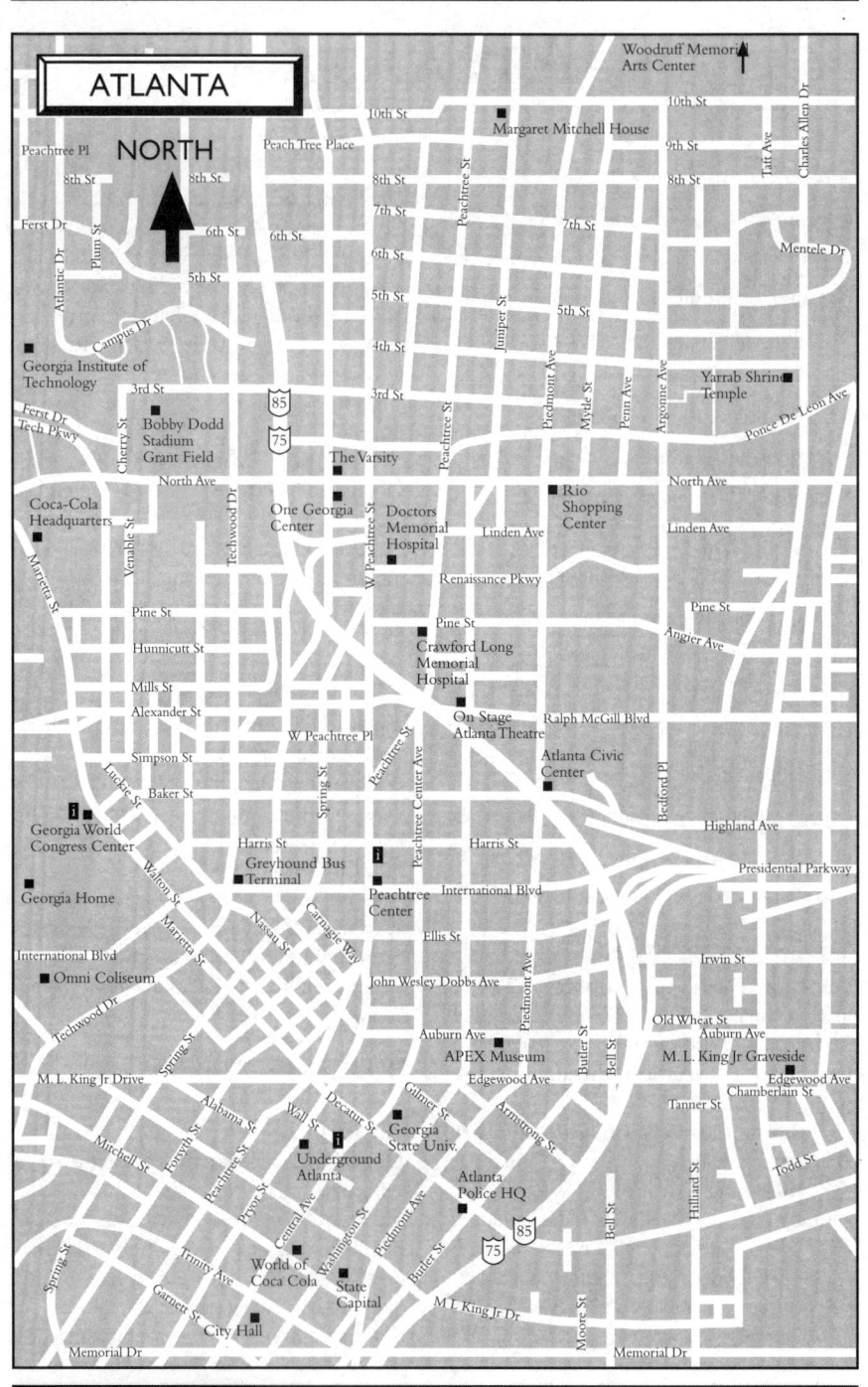

five domestic concourses, which altogether give a total of 182 gates.

The terminals and concourses are connected by a mile-long underground mall, along which travellers can choose to walk, use a moving sidewalk or board an electric train.

The modern, driverless trains operate every 100 seconds, taking passengers to the farthest concourse in less than five minutes at no cost.

Passengers arriving at the international concourse find they have to claim their baggage twice. After passing through US Immigration, passengers are required to hand their baggage in again and to re-claim it at the terminal.

The airport is well served with postal facilities, shops, restaurants and bars. An **Atlanta CVB Visitor Center** is located in the North Terminal. Open Mon–Fri 0900–2100, Sat 0900–1800, Sun noon–1800.

Taxis from the airport to downtown Atlanta cost $15 for one person, $8 each for two persons sharing, $6 each for three or more.

The best deal, however, is MARTA, the rapid transit system (see below). Trains reach downtown in 15 minutes. The fare: $1.25.

## By Car

Atlanta is still a crossroads city, with major highways converging from all directions. I-75 runs to the north from Florida, while I-85 sweeps to the north east from Alabama to North Carolina. I-20 cuts through from east to west. I-285 loops right round the metropolis, intersecting with the other interstates.

Don't think, though, that if you miss your exit all you have to do is go round again. A circuit covers 65 miles.

## Getting Around

As we've already pointed out, Metropolitan Atlanta covers a lot of ground. There are three distinct areas – **Downtown, Midtown** and **Buckhead** – which are as good as separate cities in their own right. Each is connected with the others by MARTA's rail and bus services, but a car is advisable for far-flung sightseeing.

Only the area around Underground Atlanta Downtown is compact enough for walking. And if you find yourself experiencing a feeling of *déja vu* it might be because Atlanta has 32 streets with the name Peachtree.

## Public Transport

Atlanta is blessed with a first-class public transport system. **MARTA** – Metropolitan Atlanta Rapid Transit Authority – runs interlinked rail and bus services. *Tel: (404) 848-4711.*

Fast, comfortable trains run on five major routes – North, Northeast, East, South and West lines – which converge at Five Points station Downtown at Underground Atlanta. The lines cover nearly 39 miles and serve 33 stations, including the airport which is at the South Line's terminus. Trains run daily 0500–0100.

The city has 150 bus routes covering a total of 1,500 miles. A single $1.25 fare covers both rail and bus travel with free transfers between the two systems. There are discounts for multiple purchases of travel tokens and a weekend pass allowing unlimited travel Fri–Sun costs $5.

MARTA publishes an *Attractions Guide* and *What to See and Do on MARTA* (available at stations). Both are free and give details of attractions and how to reach them.

Marietta, a major community in Cobb County, outside the I-285 ring northwest of the city, is served by **Cobb County Transit**; *tel: (404) 427-4444*. Its express services connect with MARTA stations in Buckhead, Midtown and Downtown.

## Taxis

There are some 1,600 registered taxis in Atlanta and cruising cabs may be hailed. They are easy to find at hotels. Fares within the Downtown and Buckhead business districts are fixed at $4 for one passenger, $2 per person for two or more passengers. Elsewhere, the rates are $1.50 for the first sixth of a mile, 20 cents for each additional sixth of a mile and $1 per person for each additional passenger. **Atlanta Taxicab Association**; *tel: (404) 753-7759*. **Checker Cab Company**; *tel: (404) 351-1111*. **Yellow Cabs**; *tel: (404) 521-0200*.

## STAYING IN ATLANTA

### Accommodation

At the last count, Metro Atlanta had more than 55,000 hotel rooms in 340 properties ranging across the price spectrum. The numbers will be considerably increased in time for the Olympic Games, due to open in July 1996.

To ensure fair and reasonable rates during the period of the Games, more than 200 Atlanta and Savannah hotels and motels have made a special arrangement with the Atlanta Committee for the Olympic Games and 80 per cent of available rooms have been reserved for ACOG, which will handle accommodation reservations through a centralised system.

To ease the strain on accommodation, a network of private homes prepared to accept guests has been created – again, ACOG will handle reservations.

**Atlanta Hospitality Bed & Breakfast**, *2472 Lauderdale Dr., Atlanta, GA, 30345; tel: (404) 493-1930*, is a reservation service for more than 60 hosted homes charging budget to moderate rates.

**Bed & Breakfast Atlanta**, *1801 Piedmont Ave, Suite 208, Atlanta, GA, 30324; tel: (404) 875-0525*, arranges lodgings in more than 100 carefully selected and inspected inns, guesthouses and homes throughout the metropolitan area.

Looking farther afield, the **Georgia Bed & Breakfast Council**, *600 W. Peachtree Ave, Suite 1500, Atlanta, GA 30308; tel: (404) 873-4482*, has details of some 200 inns – ranging from antebellum mansions to rustic lodges – throughout the state.

Hotel chains in Atlanta include *BW, CI, DI, ES, HI, Hn, Hy, Ma, QI, Rd, RC*.

The most prominent names among Atlanta's hotels are Renaissance and Stouffer Renaissance. The group has five hotels with nearly 2,200 rooms in the metropolitan area, including the **Stouffer Concourse Hotel**, *1 Hartsfield Centre Parkway, Atlanta, GA 30354; tel: (404) 209 9999*, located just a five-minute complimentary shuttle bus ride from the baggage claim area at Hartsfield International Airport. Many of the expensive hotel's 387 sound-proofed rooms have balconies overlooking the airport runways.

There are two **KOA** campgrounds in the Atlanta area. **KOA Atlanta North**, *2000 Old US Hwy 41, Kennesaw, GA, 30144; tel: (404) 427-2406*, is off I-75 ten miles north of Atlanta – leave at Exit 116, go west two miles to Hwy 41, north for half a mile to traffic lights, then left into campground. **KOA Atlanta South**, *281 Mt Olive Rd, McDonough, GA, 30253; tel: (404) 957-2610*, is off I-75 17 miles south of Atlanta – from Exit 72 go west for 50 yards, then left into Mt Olive Rd. It has tent pitches as well as RV sites.

### Eating and Drinking

Some 200 eating places – everything from sandwich bars to haute cuisine restaurants – plus chains with establishments throughout the area, are listed in *Atlanta Now*. The range of dishes runs from traditional American and Southern Style to almost any ethnic cuisine you can think of.

Southern Style cooking evokes a great deal of nostalgia among expatriate Americans from anywhere south of Philadelphia. It involves much use of fried chicken, fried fish, grilled pork and home-cured ham. Batter tends to be used a lot. Purely Southern peculiarities are turnip tops, corn bread and, of course, grits, a kind of porridge that is made from maize kernels.

**Pittypat's Porch**, *25 International Blvd; tel: (404) 525-8228*, moderate to pricey has been serving Southern Style food downtown for more than 25 years. Open Sun–Thur 1700–2100, Fri–Sat 1700–2200.

Another well-established Southern restaurant – it's been in business more than half a century – is the moderately priced **Mary Mac's Tea Room**, *224 Ponce De Leon Ave; tel: (404) 876-1800*. Located on the Downtown/Midtown cusp, it is open for lunch Sun–Fri 1100–1500, dinner Mon – Sat 1700 – 2100. No credit cards.

Classic American cooking is on the menu at the **Buckhead Diner**, *3073 Piedmont Rd at E. Paces Ferry Rd, Buckhead; tel: (404) 262-3336*. This art deco style restaurant, one of Atlanta's most popular eating places, offers an extensive range of moderately priced dishes. Open Mon–Sat 1100–midnight, Sun 1100–2200. No reservations.

Reservations are recommended for the upscale and pricey **Coach and Six**, *1776 Peachtree St; tel: (404) 872-6666*, which specialises in beef and seafood dishes, especially chops and Maine lobster. Open Mon–Thur 1730–2200, Fri–Sat 1730–2230.

At the opposite end of the scale is **The Varsity**, *617 North Ave; tel: (404) 881-1706*. Better known as 'The V', this cheap and cheerful fast-food place has been an Atlantan institution since 1928. Said to be the largest drive-in restaurant in the world, it covers two blocks, with inside seating for more than 800. It has five television viewing rooms where customers dine at school desks. On football Saturdays, it's claimed 'The V' serves more than 30,000 people.

Underground Atlanta offers nearly 40 assorted eating places, most of them located in the Food Court at the Central Ave end of *Lower Alabama St*.

**Mick's**, *75 Lower Alabama St; tel: (404) 525-2825*, is a large but surprisingly quiet restaurant offering burgers, chicken, pastas and salads in the budget to moderate range.

### Money

**Thomas Cook Foreign Exchange**, *245 Peachtree Center Ave, Marquis One Tower – Gallery Level; tel: (404) 681-9700 or (800) 582-4496*.

### ENTERTAINMENT

Information on the latest entertainment and nightlife scene can be found in the pages of *Atlanta Now* and *Where Atlanta* or you can call **The Arts Hotline**; *tel: (404) 853-3ART*. Tickets, often at discounted prices, can be bought through **Ace Ticket Service**; *tel: (404) 321-3600*, **TicketMaster**; *tel: (404) 249-6400*, or **Tic-X-Press**; *tel: (404) 231-5888*.

Atlanta's major centre for the performing arts is the **Fox Theatre**, *660 Peachtree St; tel: (404) 881-2100*, a 4,518-seat theatre built in Moorish design in 1929. Twinkling stars and clouds decorate the ceiling of the auditorium. Broadway shows and concerts are held here throughout the year.

Other theatres and concert halls include the **Coca-Cola Lakewood Amphitheatre**, *2002 Lakewood Way; tel: (404) 627-9704*, **Georgia Tech Theater for the Arts**, *350 Ferst St; tel: (404) 894-2788*, **Roxy Theatre**, *3110 Ponce De Leon Ave; tel: (404) 233-1062*, **7 Stages**; *1105 Euclid Ave; tel: (404) 522-0911* and **Variety Playhouse**, *1099 Euclid Ave; tel: (404) 524-7354*.

The city's leading film theatres are Buckhead's **Garden Hills Cinema**, *2835 Peachtree Rd; tel: (404) 266-2202*, **Plaza Theatre**, *1049 Ponce De Leon Ave; tel: (404) 873-1939* and **The Screening Room**, *2581 Piedmont Rd; tel: (404) 231-1924*.

The renowned **Atlanta Symphony Orchestra**, plays at the **Woodruff Arts Center**, *1280 Peachtree St; tel: (404) 892-2414*. The **Atlanta Ballet**, *477 Peachtree St N.E.; tel: (404) 892-3303* performs at various theatres.

Nightlife in Atlanta is focussed on Underground Atlanta, Buckhead and Midtown. **Dante's Down The Hatch**, *86 Lower Alabama St; tel: (404) 588-1800*, presents live jazz seven nights a week in its odd sailing ship setting in Underground Atlanta.

**Johnny's Hideaway**, *3771 Roswell Rd; tel: (404) 233-8026*, presents Big Band sounds of the past with nightly dining and dancing.

Those wanting to hear blues music should try **Blind Willie's**, *828 N. Highland Ave; tel: (404) 873-2583*. Rock fans will doubtless want to head for the **Cotton Club**, *1020 Peachtree St; tel: (404) 874-9524*. A wide range of dancing venues is listed in *Atlanta Now* (See page 337).

## Underground Atlanta

Underground Atlanta is a twice 'born-again' city. After Atlanta was largely destroyed by fire in the Civil War, the city was rebuilt, incorporating a series of viaducts and bridges which put it at a higher level.

As time went on, the old town below street level was more or less forgotten, except by vagrants who sought shelter there.

Plans to restore the area were formulated in the 1960s and in 1969 Underground Atlanta opened as a major tourist attraction and city hot spot, with some 70 businesses flourishing.

Then came recession. By 1982 only a couple of dozen enterprises remained. Underground Atlanta was in the doldrums until 1989, when it was again reborn and revitalised.

Today, crowds descend by elevator, escalator or steps to visit the specialty shops, buy from street vendors and relax in the restaurants and bars.

It looks as though it's 'third time lucky' for Underground Atlanta.

## ATLANTA

### Events
More than six dozen events and festivals relating to music, dance, drama, sport, culture and other themes are held in the Atlanta area every year. Gospel, blues, choral and other musical styles are celebrated at Underground Atlanta. Details and a *Calendar of Events* are available from the visitor information centres.

A **Mardi Gras** parade is held in February, and around 17 Mar the **St Patrick's Day Parade** takes to the streets. **Atlanta Jazz Festival** is in May.

The **Arts Festival of Atlanta** is a Sept event, and the **Atlanta Marathon** is held in Nov when *Walt Disney World on Ice* is also staged.

### SHOPPING
Of all Atlanta's shopping malls – and there are more than a dozen – the biggest is **Lenox Sq**, at *3393 Peachtree Rd N.E.; tel: (404) 233-6767*. It's claimed to be the largest between Washington DC and Miami. It has more than 200 shops and restaurants, including big-name stores.

**Phipps Plaza**, *3500 Peachtree Rd at the Buckhead Loop; tel: (404) 261-7910*, is the fashion shopper's delight, with prestigious stores like Saks Fifth Avenue, Tiffany & Co, Gucci and Nike Town. Before the end of 1996 you will be able to add Bloomingdale's to the list.

Superb imported African art, fashions and accessories are intriguing and dramatic. You can see them at **Out of Africa**, *2841 Greenbriar Parkway; tel: (404) 344-7100*, where they also design and tailor-make most of their fashions. **African Pride**, *84 Upper Alabama St, Underground Atlanta; tel: (404) 523-6520*, has hundreds of original, hand-crafted African artefacts on display.

Buckhead is one of the city's trendiest shopping districts, with a number of antique shops among the boutiques and speciality stores. **2300 Peachtree Road** is the name (and address) of a group of European-style antique shops, art galleries and design studios. **Buckhead Marketplace and Antiques**, *2133 Piedmont Rd*, presents 140 antiques and collectibles shops and interior designers' studios in Southern Victorian style.

### SIGHTSEEING
Themed guided tours or general sightseeing with a guide are offered by several companies.

An ethnically-accented heritage tour, the Peachtree city tour and a trip to Stone Mountain are featured by **Atlanta Heritage Tours**; *tel: (404) 262-7660*. **Atlanta Specialty Tours**; *tel: (404) 874-0110*, offers civil rights tours, history tours and African-American tours. **Capital City Excursions**; *tel: (404) 954-7106*, offers daily full- and half-day tours of Atlanta and the surrounding area.

Georgia's largest charter carrier, **American Coach Lines**; *tel: (404) 449-1806*, has video-equipped coaches and mini-buses and transit buses with wheelchair lifts. **Great Historic Tours**; *tel: (404) 228-5197*, has an educational tour covering the King Center and African Market.

Another way to see the city, including the Olympic Village and other landmarks, is to get the overhead view. **Historic Air Tours**; *tel: (404) 457-5217*, provides flights starting at $35.

African art on local African–American history and art works by local and national black artists can be seen at the **African - American Panoramic Experience**

(APEX), *135 Auburn Ave NE, Atlanta; tel: (404) 521-2739.* Open Tues–Sat 1000–1700 (1800 Wed), Sun 1300–1700. Feb and June–Aug only. Admission: $2.

Tropical, desert and endangered plants from around the world are among the attractions at **Atlanta Botanical Garden**, *Piedmont Ave at The Prudo, Atlanta; tel: (404) 876-5858.* Open Tues–Sun 0900–1800, in summer to 2000. Admission: $4.50.

Atlanta's history, the Civil War, the growth of African–American enterprise and Southern folkcrafts are covered at the 32-acre **Atlanta History Center/Buckhead**, *130 West Paces Ferry Rd N.W., Atlanta; tel: (404) 814-4000.* Gardens, two historic homes and an 1840s plantation can also be visited. Open Mon–Sat 1000–1730, Sun 12–1730. Admission $7 (historic homes extra).

**Fernbank Museum of Natural History**, *67 Clifton Rd N.E., Atlanta; tel: (404) 370-0960*, takes you through the chronological development of life on earth. There are interactive light and sound exhibits and IMAX films, a restaurant and shop. Open Mon–Thur and Sat 1000–1700, Fri 1000–2100, Sun noon–1700. Admission: museum only $5.50; IMAX/museum combined: $9.50.

**Fernbank Science Center**, *156 Heaton Pk Dr. N.E., Atlanta; tel: (404) 378-4311*, houses one of the largest planetariums in the US. As well as an exhibit hall it has a 65-acre forest with trails. Open Mon 0830–1700, Tues–Fri 0830-2200, Sat 1000–1700, Sun 1300–1700. Admission: free except to planetarium shows $2.

Built for the 1994 Super Bowl, the **Georgia Dome** is hosting gymnastics and basketball events in the 1996 Olympics. Hosted tours are available Tues–Sat 1000–1600 and Sun noon–1600 on the hour every hour. Admission: $4.

Georgia's **Stone Mountain Park**, off *Hwy 78, Stone Mountain; tel: (404) 498–5600*, is said to be the world's largest granite monolith. A sky–ride, swimming, fishing, tennis and golf can be enjoyed in the 3200–acre park. Open 0600–midnight, attractions open June–Aug 1000–2100, Sept–May 1000–1730. Admission: $5 per vehicle.

A Hall of Flags, a Hall of Fame honouring outstanding Georgians and natural science displays are shown at the 1889 **Georgia State Capitol**, *Capitol Hill, Washington St, Atlanta; tel: (404) 656-2854*. Open Mon–Fri, 0800–1700.

A site where General Sherman's Union troops fought General Joseph Johnston's Confederates in the 1864 battle which led to the fall of Atlanta, **Kennesaw Mountain National Battlefield Park** is set in nearly 3000 acres and includes a small museum. The battle is graphically depicted in a slide presentation. The park, at *Old Highway 41 and Stilesboro Rd, Marietta; tel: (404) 427-4686*, is worth visiting for its beauty and views as well as its historical significance. Open daily 0830–1700. Admission: donations appreciated.

**Martin Luther King Jr Center for Nonviolent Social Change**, *449 Auburn Ave N.E., Atlanta; tel: (404) 524-1956*, includes Dr King's birthplace and grave and Ebenezer Baptist Church where the civil rights leader preached. King Center tours are self-guided. Tours of the birthplace are half-hourly from 1000–1700. Open 0900–1730 (to 2000 in summer).

The art of ancient cultures is featured

# ATLANTA

## An Olympic Legacy

Atlanta's lasting legacy of the 1996 Centennial Olympic Games will be the spacious Centennial Olympic Park under construction close to the major Games events.

Fountains and pools are a feature of the park, landscaped with paths, indigenous greenery and flowers and shady corners with seats.

Many thousands of people have bought themselves a piece of Olympic history by 'adopting' personalised bricks used in structures and paving in the park. The bricks record an anniversary or special event or are simply inscribed with the names of the 'Adopt a Brick' purchasers.

During the Games a temporary amphitheatre seating 8,000 will be used for musical performances in the park. Olympic souvenirs can be purchased at the park's superstore.

A multi-cultural, multi-media expression of Southern life, the Festival of the American South, takes place during the Games, presenting music, dance, crafts and exhibitions.

More than 11 million tickets were issued, costing up to $600 - the cost of a prime seat at the opening and closing ceremonies. Most tickets are priced at $75 or less.

at **Michael C. Carlos Museum**, *571 D Kildo St, Atlanta; tel: (404) 727-4282*. Greek statues, an Egyptian mummy, pre-Columbian pottery and Middle and Far Eastern artefacts are exhibited. Open Mon–Thur 1000– 1700, Fr 1000–2100, Sat 1000–1700, Sun noon–1700. Suggested donation $3.

**SciTrek** – the Science and Technology Center of Atlanta, *395 Piedmont Ave, Atlanta; tel: (404) 522-5500*, is considered one of the nation's top ten science centres. It has more than 100 interactive exhibits, demonstrations, workshops, films and a museum shop. Open Tues–Sat 1000–1700, extended hours in summer, Sun noon–1700. Admission: $6.50.

**Underground Atlanta**, *Peachtree St at Upper Alabama St, Atlanta; tel: (404) 523-2311*, is the city's swinging historic area beneath the city. More than 100 speciality shops, pushcart vendors, novelty spots and restaurants attract thousands of visitors. Open Mon–Sat 1000–2130. Sun noon–1800. (Restaurant and club hours vary). Coca-Cola memorabilia, advertisements through the decades, an entertaining bottling process and a futuristic soda fountain are showcased at the **World of Coca-Cola**, *55 Martin Luther King Jr Dr., Atlanta; tel: (404) 676-5151*. Open Mon–Sat 1000–2130, Sun noon–1800. Admission $2.50.

**Wren's Nest**, *1050 R.D. Abernathy Blvd S.W., Atlanta; tel: (404) 753-8535*, is the Victorian home of Joel Chandler Harris, Georgian author of the Uncle Remus stories. There are guided tours, story-telling programmes and a museum shop with books and Br'er Rabbit memorabilia. Open Tues–Sat 1000–1600, Sun 1300–1600. Admission: $4.

Creatures from Africa and other world locations can be seen at **Zoo Atlanta**, *Grant Park, 800 Cherokee Ave S.E., Atlanta; tel: (404) 624-5600*. Open daily 1000–1630, extended hours on summer weekends. Admission: $7.75.

SIGHTSEEING

# HOTEL CODES
## AND CENTRAL BOOKING NUMBERS

The following abbreviations have been used throughout the book to show which chains are represented in a particular town. Cities and large towns have most except *HI*. Central booking service phone numbers are shown – use these numbers while in the USA to make reservations at any hotel in the chain. Where available, numbers that can be called in your own country are also noted. (AUS = Australia, CAN = Canada, D = Germany, F = France, IRE = Republic of Ireland, NZ = New Zealand, SA = South Africa, UK = United Kingdom, WW = worldwide number.)

*BW* Best Western
AUS (800) 222 422
CAN (800) 528 1234
IRE (800) 709 101
NZ (09) 520 5418
SA(011) 339 4865
UK (800) 393 130
USA(800) 528 1234

*CI* Comfort Inn
(800) 228-5150
AUS (008) 090 600
CAN (800) 221 2222
IRE (800) 500 600
NZ (800) 808 228
UK(800) 444444

*CM* Courtyard by Marriott
(800) 321-2211

*DI* Days Inn
(800) 325-2525
D 069 41 2525;
F 1 44 77 88 03;
UK (01483) 440470

*EL* Econo Lodge
WW (800) 221 2222

*ES* Embassy Suites
(800) 362-2779
AUS 02 959 3922;
CAN 416 626 3974,
403 243 8347, or
604 685 3385;
NZ 09 623 4294;
SA 11 789 6706;
UK 01992 441517

*GT* Golden Tulip
AUS (008) 221 176
CAN (800) 344 1212
IRE (01) 872 3300
NZ (800) 656 666

SA (011) 331 2672
UK (800) 951 000
USA (800) 344 1212

*Hd* Holiday Inn
800) 465-4329
AUS (800) 221 066
CAN (800) 465 4329
IRE (800) 553 155
NZ (800) 442 222
SA (011) 482 3500
UK (800) 897121
USA (800) 465 4329

*HI* Hostelling International
(202) 783-6161
(information only)

*HJ* Howard Johnson (HoJo)
(800) 654-2000
AUS 02 262 4918;
UK (0181) 688 1418)

*Hn* Hilton
(800) 445-8667
AUS (800) 222 255
CAN (800) 445 8667
NZ (800) 448 002
SA (011) 880 3108
UK (0345) 581595
USA (800) 445 8667

*Hy* Hyatt
(800) 233 1234
AUS (800) 131 234

*Ma* Marriott
(800) 228-9290
AUS (800) 251 259
CAN (800) 228 9290
NZ (800) 441 035
UK (800) 221 222
USA (800) 228 9290

*M6* Motel 6

(800) 440-6000

*Ql* Quality Inn
(800) 228-5151

*Rd* Radisson
(800) 333 3333
IRE (800) 557 474
NZ (800) 443 333
UK (800) 191 991

*Rm* Ramada
(800) 228-2828
AUS (800) 222 431
CAN (800) 854 7854
IRE (800) 252 627
NZ (800) 441 111
UK (800) 181737
USA (800) 854 7854

*RI* Residence Inn
(800) 331-3131
AUS (800) 251 259;
IRE (800) 409 929;
NZ (800) 441035;
UK (800) 221222

*Sh* Sheraton
(800) 325-3535
AUS(008) 073 535
IRE (800) 535 353
NZ (800) 443 535

*S8* Super 8
WW (800) 800-8000

*TL* Travelodge
(800) 578-7878
AUS (800) 622240
IRE (800) 409 040;
NZ (800) 801111
SA (011) 442 9201;
UK (0345) 404 040

*VI* Vagabond Inn
(800) 522-1555

# CONVERSION TABLES

| DISTANCE | | | |
|---|---|---|---|
| km | miles | km | miles |
| 1 | 0.62 | 30 | 21.75 |
| 2 | 1.24 | 40 | 24.85 |
| 3 | 1.86 | 45 | 27.96 |
| 4 | 2.49 | 50 | 31.07 |
| 5 | 3.11 | 55 | 34.18 |
| 6 | 3.73 | 60 | 37.28 |
| 7 | 4.35 | 65 | 40.39 |
| 8 | 4.97 | 70 | 43.50 |
| 9 | 5.59 | 75 | 46.60 |
| 10 | 6.21 | 80 | 49.71 |
| 15 | 9.32 | 90 | 55.92 |
| 20 | 12.43 | 100 | 62.14 |
| 25 | 15.53 | 125 | 77.67 |

1 km = 0.6214 miles
1 mile = 1.609 km

| METRES AND FEET | | |
|---|---|---|
| Unit | Metres | Feet |
| 1 | 0.30 | 3.281 |
| 2 | 0.61 | 6.563 |
| 3 | 0.91 | 9.843 |
| 4 | 1.22 | 13.124 |
| 5 | 1.52 | 16.403 |
| 6 | 1.83 | 19.686 |
| 7 | 2.13 | 22.967 |
| 8 | 2.4 | 26.248 |
| 9 | 2.74 | 29.529 |
| 10 | 3.05 | 32.810 |
| 14 | 4.27 | 45.934 |
| 18 | 5.49 | 59.058 |
| 20 | 6.10 | 65.520 |
| 50 | 15.24 | 164.046 |
| 75 | 22.8 | 246.069 |
| 100 | 30.48 | 328.092 |

| WEIGHT | | |
|---|---|---|
| Unit | kg | Pounds |
| 1 | 0.45 | 2.205 |
| 2 | 0.90 | 4.405 |
| 3 | 1.35 | 6.614 |
| 4 | 1.80 | 8.818 |
| 5 | 2.25 | 11.023 |
| 10 | 4.50 | 22.045 |
| 15 | 6.75 | 33.068 |
| 20 | 9.00 | 44.889 |
| 25 | 11.25 | 55.113 |
| 50 | 22.50 | 110.225 |
| 75 | 33.75 | 165.338 |
| 100 | 45.00 | 220.450 |

1 kg = 1000g
100g = 3.5oz
1 oz = 28.35g
1 lb = 453.60g

| FLUID MEASURES | | |
|---|---|---|
| Litres | Imp.gal. | US gal. |
| 5 | 1.1 | 1.3 |
| 10 | 2.2 | 2.6 |
| 15 | 3.3 | 3.9 |
| 20 | 4.4 | 5.2 |
| 25 | 5.5 | 6.5 |
| 30 | 6.6 | 7.8 |
| 35 | 7.7 | 9.1 |
| 40 | 8.8 | 10.4 |
| 45 | 9.9 | 11.7 |
| 50 | 11.0 | 13.0 |

1 litre(l) = 0.88 imp.quarts
1 litre(l) = 1.06 US quarts
1 imp. quart = 1.14 l
1 imp. gallon = 4.55 l
1 US quart = 0.95 l
1 US gallon = 3.81 l

| MENS' SHIRTS | | |
|---|---|---|
| UK | Europe | US |
| 14 | 36 | 14 |
| 15 | 38 | 15 |
| 15.5 | 39 | 15.5 |
| 16 | 41 | 16 |
| 16.5 | 42 | 16.5 |
| 17 | 43 | 17 |

| MENS' SHOES | | |
|---|---|---|
| UK | Europe | US |
| 6 | 40 | 7 |
| 7 | 41 | 8 |
| 8 | 42 | 9 |
| 9 | 43 | 10 |
| 10 | 44 | 11 |
| 11 | 45 | 12 |

| Unit | mm | cm | metres |
|---|---|---|---|
| 1 inch | 25.4 | 2.54 | 0.025 |
| 1 foot | 304.8 | 30.48 | 0.304 |
| 1 yard | 914.4 | 91.44 | 0.914 |

To convert cms to inches, multiply by 0.3937
To convert inches to cms, multiply by 2.54

| MENS' CLOTHES | | |
|---|---|---|
| UK | Europe | US |
| 36 | 46 | 36 |
| 38 | 48 | 38 |
| 40 | 50 | 40 |
| 42 | 52 | 42 |
| 44 | 54 | 44 |
| 46 | 56 | 46 |

| LADIES' SHOES | | |
|---|---|---|
| UK | Europe | US |
| 3 | 36 | 4.5 |
| 4 | 37 | 5.5 |
| 5 | 38 | 6.5 |
| 6 | 39 | 7.5 |
| 7 | 40 | 8.5 |
| 8 | 41 | 9.5 |

| LADIES' CLOTHES | | | | |
|---|---|---|---|---|
| UK | France | Italy | Rest of Europe | US |
| 10 | 36 | 38 | 34 | 8 |
| 12 | 38 | 40 | 36 | 10 |
| 14 | 40 | 42 | 38 | 12 |
| 16 | 42 | 44 | 40 | 14 |
| 18 | 44 | 46 | 42 | 16 |
| 20 | 46 | 48 | 44 | 18 |

| TYPICAL COSTS | |
|---|---|
| Roll of 35 mm print film | $6.50 |
| Can of cola | 75 cents |
| Local morning newspaper | 50 cents |
| Bottle of beer In liquor store | $1.50 |
| Small beer in bar | $2.50 |
| Glass of wine, gin & tonic | $3.00 |
| Glass of whisky | $3.00 |
| Cup of coffee | 85 cents |
| Burger | $4.00 |
| Sandwich | $4.00 |
| Chocolate ('candy') bar | $1.00 |

# INDEX

References are to page numbers. *Italic* numbers are references to maps in the text. **Bold** numbers refer to the colour maps at the end of the book; for instance Amelia Island, **4:B7**, is in grid square B:7 of colour map 4.

## A

Accommodation 16–18 *see also individual towns*
Accidents and Breakdowns 46
Airports 18 *see also individual cities*
Alligators 138
Ambulance 27
Amelia Island 287–289, **4:B7**
Anna Marie Island 193, **6:C1**
Apalachicola 307, **2:D10**
Apalachicola National Forest 307
Atlanta 337–345, *338*, **2:A1**
Aventura 126

## B

Background Florida 55–58
Bal Harbour 125
Bed and Breakfast 17
Belleair 208
Belle Glade 172, **6:D7**
Bicycles 18–19
Big Cypress National Preserve 119, **7:A7**
Big Pine 97–99, **7:D6**
Boca Grande 188, **6:D2**
Boca Raton 142–143, **6:D9**

Books, further reading 44–45
Bradenton 192–193, **6:C2**
Breakdowns 46
Brooksville 227–228, **5:B4**
Brunswick 333, **3:D6**
Busch Gardens 224
Buses 19–20

## C

Caladesi Island 207–208
Camper vans 20–21
Camping 16–17
Cape Canaveral 165, **5:B10**
Cape Coral 184, **6:D3**
Captiva Island 181–184, **6:D2**
Carabelle 306, **2:D9**
Car Hire 46–47
Cassadaga 260
Cedar Key 295–296, **5:A1**
Children 21–22
Chipley 326–327, **2:C7**
Citrus 252
Clearwater 208–211, **6:B1**
Clermont 262, **5:B6**
Clewiston 175–176, **6:D6**
Climate 22–23, 55
Clothing 23
Cocoa Beach 157, **5:B10**
Coconut Grove 85–86
Collier-Seminole State Park 120
Conch Republic 106
Consulates 22
Conversion Tables 347
Coral Gables 81–84, **7:B9**
Corkscrew Swamp Sanctuary 138
Cost of Living 23–24

Crystal River 295, **5:A3**
Currency 24
Customs Allowances 24–25
Customs and Immigration 18

## D

Dania 127
Daytona Beach 267–272, *268*, **4:D8**
Deerfield Beach 141–142, **7:A9**
De Funiak Springs 326, **2:C7**
DeLand 258–260, **5:A7**
Delray Beach 143, **6:D9**
Destin 314–315
Disabled Travellers 25–26
Discounts 26
Drinking 26–27
Driving Distances 14
Driving in Florida 46–54
Driving Terms 54
Driving Times 14
Duval Street, 111

## E

Eastpoint 306–307, **2:D9**
Eatonton 336, **3:A2**
Electricity 27
Embassies, see Consulates
Emergencies 27
Epcot Center 241
Everglades City 118, 120 **7:B5**
Everglades National Park 112–117, *113*, **7:B8**
Expressways 51

# INDEX

## F

Fakahatchee Strand State Preserve 120
Fernandina Beach 286
Fire 26
Flamingo 115–117, **7:C7**
Floods 99
Florida Keys 92
Florida National Scenic Trail 68
Folkston 290, **4:B5**
Food 27–29, 99
Fort Lauderdale 128–135, *129*, **7:A9**
Fort Myers 178–180, *179*, **6:D3**
Fort Myers Beach 180–181, **6:D3**
Fort Pierce 154–155, **6:B8**
Fort Walton Beach 315–316, *316*, **2:B8**
Freeways 51

## G

Gainsville 262–263, *263*, **4:D4**
Gambling 29
Geography 55
Golf 281
Grassy Key, 96–97, **7:D7**
Grayton Beach 314

## H

Hallandale 126
Havana 327, **2:D7**
Health 29–30
Hemingway, Ernest 110
Highways 51
Hiking 30–31
Hitch-Hiking 31
History 55–58
Hobe Sound 152–153, **6:C9**
Holidays 37
Hollywood 126–127, **7:A9**

Holmes Beach 193, **6:C1**
Homestead 89–90, **7:B8**
Honeymoon Island 207
Hospitals 29
Hotel Codes and Central Booking Numbers 346
Hotels 16–17
How To Talk Floridian 34
Hurricanes 31
Hutchinson Island 153–154, **6:B9**

## I

Immigration 19
Insurance 29, 32, 53–54
Interstate Highways 51
Intracoastal Waterway 65
Introduction 7–8
Inverness 228, **5:A4**
Islamorada 95–96, **7:D7**
Itineraries 59–70

## J

Jacksonville 278–285, *279*, **4:B6**
Juno Beach 151, **6:C10**
Jupiter 151–152, **6:C9**

## K

Key Biscayne 86, **7:B9**
Key Largo 90–95, **7:C9**
Key West 100–111, *101*, **7:D4**
Kingsland 289, **4:B6**
Kissimmee 251–255, **5:C7**

## L

La Belle 176, **6:D5**
Lake City 298, **4:C3**
Lakeland 255, **5:C5**
Lake Okeechobee 170–173, *171*, **6:C6**
Lake Seminole 327
Lake Wales 265, **5:C6**
Language 32–33, 34

Leesburg 262, **5:B6**
Live Oak 291, **4:C2**
Long Key, 96, **7:D7**
Loxahatchee 175, **6:D9**
Luggage 33

## M

Macon 330–331, **3:A3**
Madeira Beach 211, **5:D3**
Madison 298, **3:A8**
Maps 33–35
Marathon 97, **7:D7**
Marco Island 121, **7:B4**
Marianna 327, **2:D7**
Melbourne 156–157, **6:A7**
Merritt Island 165–166, **5:B9**
Mexico Beach 308, **2:C9**
Miami 71–87, *73,82–83*, **7:B9**
Miami Beach 86–87, N **7:B9**
Milledgeville 336, **3:B2**
Milton 326, **2:B8**
Monticello 298, **3:A8**
Motels 16–17
Motorcycles 49
Motorhomes 20–21
Moultrie 330, **3:A6**

## N

Naples 121–123, **7:A4**
Navarre Beach 316, **2:B8**
North Fort Myers 185, **6:D3**

## O

Ocala 228–229, **5:A5**
Ochopee 120, **7:B5**
Okeechobee 168, **6:C7**
Okefenokee Swamp 290–291, **4:A4**
Olustee Battlefield 297–298, **4:C3**
Olympic Games 345

**349**

# INDEX

Opening Hours 35
Orlando 230–249, *231, 233*
   **5:B7**

## P

Pahokee 172–173, **6:C8**
Palatka 229, **4:D6**
Palm Beach 144–148, *146*,
   **6:D9**
Panama City 308–311, *312*,
   **2:C8**
Parking 49–50
Parks Information 35–36
Passports and Visas 36, 40
Petrol 50
Pensacola 317–324, *319*,
   **2:A8**
Pine Island 184–185
Pinellas Peninsula 202–212
Police 36, 50
Pompano Beach 140–141,
   **7:A9**
Port Charlotte 187, **6:C3**
Port St Joe 307–308, **2:C9**
Postal Services 36–37
Public Holidays 37
Punta Gorda 187, **6:C3**

## Q

Quincy 327, **2:D7**

## R

Railroad Barons 276–277
Roads 51–52
Road Signs 51
Routes Map 12–13
RVs (recreational vehicles)
   20–21

## S

Safety Harbor 206
St Augustine 272–277, *274*,
   **4:C7**
St John's River 284
St Mary's 289–290, **4:B7**

St Pete Beach 211, **5:D3**
St Petersburg 194–201,
   *195*, **5:D4, 6:B1**
Sales Taxes 37–38
Salvador Dali Museum 199
Sanford 258, **5:A7**
Sanibel 181–184, **6:D3**
Sarasota 189–191, **6:C1**
Savannah 333–336, **3:D4**
Seaside 314
Seat Belts 53
Sebastian 156, **6:B8**
Sebring 168–169, **6:B5**
Security 38–40
Scuba Diving 94
Shark Valley 117, 119
Shopping 40
Siesta Key 191–192, **6:C1**
Singer Island 151, **6:D10**
Smoking 40–41
South Bay 173, **6:D7**
Space Coast 158–166, *159*,
   **5:B9**
Spaceport 160–165, **5:B10**
Space Race 162
Speed City 271
Speed Limits 53
Sponges 294
Sport in Florida 225
Stuart 153, **6:B9**
Sunny Isles 125–126
Surfside 125, **7:B9**
Suwanee 296, **3:A10**

## T

Tallahassee 299–303, *301*,
   **3:A8**
Tampa 216–225, *217*, **5:C4**
Tarpon Springs 293, **5:C3**
Taxes 37–38
Telephones 41–42
Thomasville 329–330, **3:A7**
Three Rivers State
   Recreation Area 327
Tifton 330, **3:A6**

Time Zones 42
Tipping 42
Titusville 158, **5:B9**
Toilets 42–43
Tourism Information 43, *see
   also individual towns*
Trains 43
Travel Essentials 16–45
Treasure Island 211, **5:D3**
Turnpikes 51

## U

Underground Atlanta 342
Unidentified Flying Objects
   315
Universal Studios 245–246
US Astronaut Hall of Fame
   160
Useful Reading 44–45

## V

Venice 189, **6:C2**
Vero Beach 155–156, **6:B8**
Visas 36

## W

Wakulla Springs 296, **3:A8**
Walt Disney World
   241–243, *241*
Weeki Wachee 294–295,
   **5:B3**
Weedon Island 206
Weights and Measures 45,
   347
West Palm Beach 144–148,
   *146*, **6:D9**
White Springs 291, **4:B2**
Winter Gardens 261–262,
   **5:B6**
Winter Haven 255, **5:C6**

## Y

Ybor City 223–224
Youth Hostels 18

# READER SURVEY

If you enjoyed using this book, or even if you didn't, please help us improve future editions by taking part in our reader survey. Every returned form will be acknowledged, and to show our appreciation we will give you £1 off your next purchase of a Thomas Cook guidebook. Just take a few minutes to complete and return this form to us.

When did you buy this book? _____

Where did you buy it? (Please give town/city and if possible name of retailer)
_____

When did you/do you intend to travel in Florida? _____

    For how long (approx.)? _____
    How many people in your party? _____

Which cities, national parks and other locations did you/do you intend mainly to visit?
_____
_____
_____

Did you/will you:
    ☐ Make all your travel arrangements independently?
    ☐ Travel on a fly-drive package?
Please give brief details: _____

Did you/do you intend to use this book:
    ☐ For planning your trip?
    ☐ During the trip itself?
    ☐ Both?

Did you/do you intend also to purchase any of the following travel publications for your trip?
    Thomas Cook Travellers: Florida/Orlando/Miami & Caribbean Cruising
    A road map/atlas (please specify) _____
    Other guidebooks (please specify) _____

Have you used any other Thomas Cook guidebooks in the past? If so, which?
_____

## READER SURVEY

Please rate the following features of On the Road around Florida for their value to you (Circle VU for 'very useful', U for 'useful', NU for 'little or no use'):

|  | | | |
|---|---|---|---|
| The 'Travel Essentials' section on pages 14–43 | VU | U | NU |
| The 'Driving in Florida' section on pages 44–52 | VU | U | NU |
| The 'Touring Itineraries' on pages 57–97 | VU | U | NU |
| The recommended driving routes throughout the book | VU | U | NU |
| Information on towns and cities, National Parks, etc | VU | U | NU |
| The maps of towns and cities, parks, etc | VU | U | NU |
| The colour planning map | VU | U | NU |

Please use this space to tell us about any features that in your opinion could be changed, improved, or added in future editions of the book, or any other comments you would like to make concerning the book:

Your age category: ☐ 21–30  ☐ 31–40  ☐ 41–50  ☐ over 50

Your name: Mr/Mrs/Miss/Ms
(First name or initials)
(Last name)

Your full address: (Please include postal or zip code)

Your daytime telephone number:

**Please detach this page and send it to: The Project Editor, On the Road around Florida, Thomas Cook Publishing, PO Box 227, Peterborough PE3 8BQ, United Kingdom.**

We will be pleased to send you details of how to claim your discount upon receipt of this questionnaire.

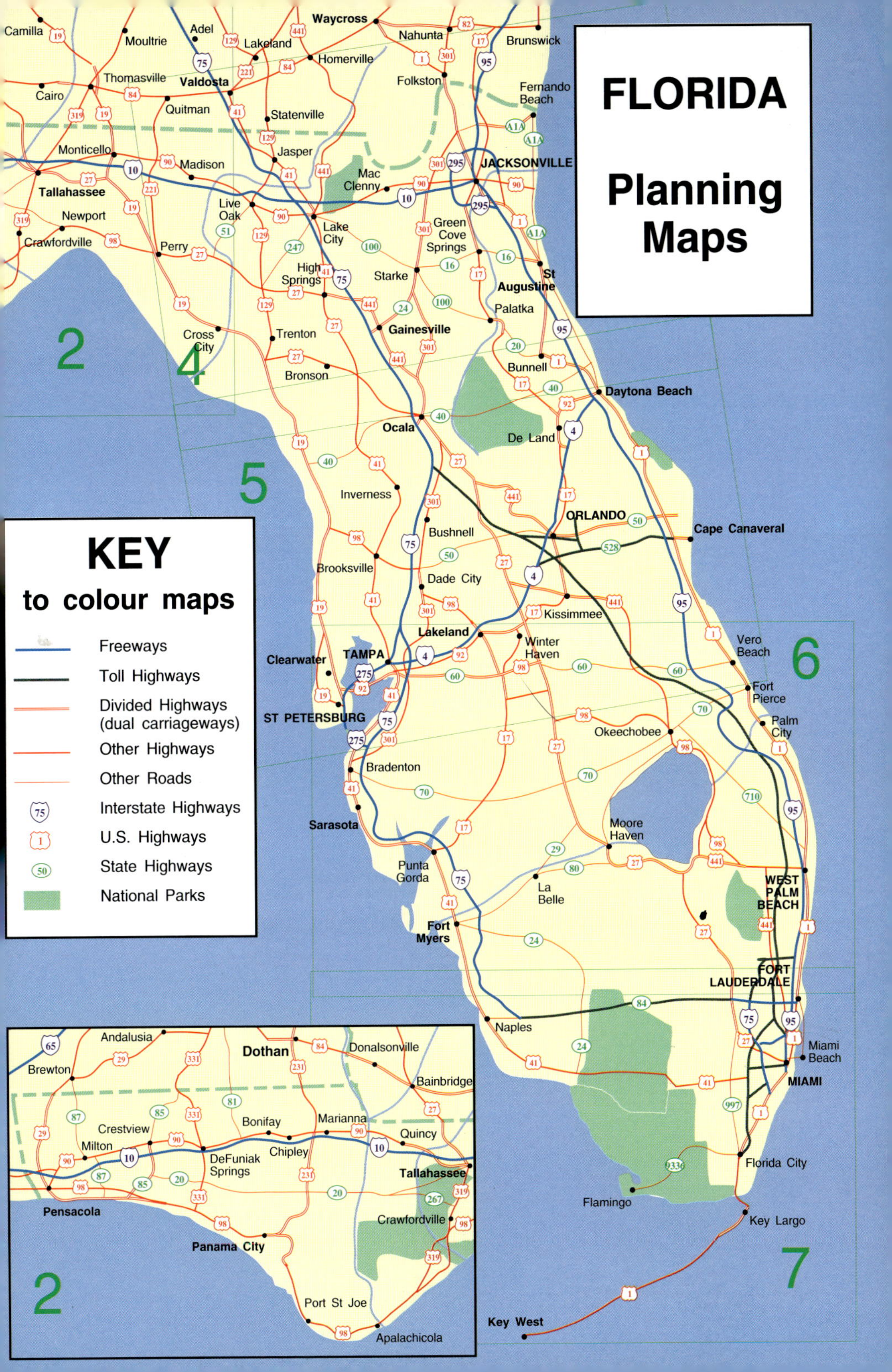
FLORIDA
Planning Maps
KEY
to colour maps
Freeways
Toll Highways
Divided Highways (dual carriageways)
Other Highways
Other Roads
Interstate Highways
U.S. Highways
State Highways
National Parks
Camilla
Moultrie
Adel
Lakeland
Waycross
Nahunta
Brunswick
Homerville
Folkston
Fernando Beach
Thomasville
Valdosta
Cairo
Quitman
Statenville
Jasper
Monticello
Madison
Tallahassee
Mac Clenny
JACKSONVILLE
Newport
Live Oak
Lake City
Green Cove Springs
Crawfordville
Perry
High Springs
Starke
St Augustine
Palatka
Gainesville
Trenton
Cross City
Bronson
Bunnell
Daytona Beach
Ocala
De Land
Inverness
ORLANDO
Cape Canaveral
Bushnell
Brooksville
Dade City
Kissimmee
Lakeland
Winter Haven
Vero Beach
Clearwater
TAMPA
Fort Pierce
ST PETERSBURG
Okeechobee
Palm City
Bradenton
Sarasota
Moore Haven
Punta Gorda
La Belle
WEST PALM BEACH
Fort Myers
FORT LAUDERDALE
Naples
Miami Beach
MIAMI
Florida City
Flamingo
Key Largo
Key West
Andalusia
Dothan
Donalsonville
Brewton
Bainbridge
Crestview
Bonifay
Marianna
Milton
Quincy
DeFuniak Springs
Chipley
Tallahassee
Pensacola
Crawfordville
Panama City
Port St Joe
Apalachicola
2
4
5
6
7
2

2
A
B
C
D
1
2
3
4
5
6
7
8
9
10
ALABAMA
FLO
Jasper
Fayette
Ashville
Anniston
Heflin
Buchanan
Dougla
Carrollton
BIRMINGHAM
Talladega
Harpersville
TALLADEGA NAT. FOREST
Wedowee
Franklin
Sylacauga
Ashland
Roanoke
Greenville
La Grange
Tuscaloosa
Coosa River
Centreville
Clanton
Alexander City
Lafayette
Eutaw
Rockford
Dadeville
Hamilton
TALLADEGA NAT. FOREST
Lake Martin
Greensboro
Mobile River
Marion
Opelika
Phenix City
Columbus
Demopolis
Prattville
Wetumpka
Montgomery
Tuskegee
TUSKEGEE NAT. FOREST
Cusseta
Linden
Selma
Lumpkin
Union Springs
Eufaula
Georgetown
Camden
Greenville
Clayton
Thomasville
Troy
Cuthbert
Chattahoochee River
Luverne
Grove Hill
Fort Gaines
Monroeville
Abbeville
Morgan
Evergreen
Alabama River
Ozark
New Brockton
Blakely
Andalusia
Enterprise
Dothan
CONECUH NAT. FOREST
Colquitt
Brewton
Atmore
Geneva
Bainbridge
Florala
Bay Minette
Century
Blackman
Graceville
Donalsonville
Ponce de Leon
Munson
Escambia River
Chipley
Marianna
De Funiak Springs
Crestview
Chattahoochee
Bonifay
MOBILE
Baker
Havana
Cantonment
Quincy
Milton
Apalachicola River
Valparaiso
Clarksville
Bristol
Freeport
Bloxham
Pensacola
Mary Esther
Blountstown
Shalimar
Gulf Beach
Gulf Breeze
Navarre
Gulf Shores
Pensacola Beach
Fort Walton Beach
Santa Rosa Beach
Lynn Haven
Crawf
Panama City
Laguna Beach
Sopcho
Wewahitchka
Okhlockonee River
APALACHICOLA NAT. FOREST
Carrabelle
Mexico Beach
Port St Joe
East Point
Apalachicola
North
0 25 miles
0 50 kms
© 1995 Thomas Cook Ltd

3
A
B
C
D
GEORGIA
IDA
Athens
Lincolnton
Washington
J Strom Thurmond Reservoir
Edgefield
Modoc
Aiken
Swansea
North
Wagener
Couchtown
Orangeburg
Clearwater
Springfield
Norway
Bowman
Blackville
Denmark
Bamberg
Barnwell
Branchville
Harleyville
Ehrhardt
Ulmer
Savannah River
Allendale
Fairfax
Hampton
Walterboro
Sylvania
Garnett
Yemassee
Ogeechee River
Ridgeland
Beaufort
Statesboro
Springfield
Metter
Claxton
Pembroke
Savannah
Forest Beach
Tybee Island
Hinesville
Ludowici
Jesup
Darien
Brunswick
Conyers
Monroe
Madison
Greensboro
Crawfordville
Warrenton
Thomson
Augusta
McDonough
OCONEE NAT. FOREST
Jackson
Monticello
Eatonton
Sparta
Gibson
Waynesboro
Forsyth
Milledgeville
Louisville
Gray
Barnesville
Sandersville
Millen
Macon
Irwinton
Oconee River
Fort Valley
Jeffersonville
Wrightsville
Swainsboro
Perry
Ocmulgee River
Dublin
Cochran
Oglethorpe
Hawkinsville
Soperton
Eastman
Lyons
Vienna
Cordele
Alamo
Altamaha River
Reidsville
Abbeville
McRae
Ashburn
Hazlehurst
Baxley
Fitzgerald
Ocilla
Albany
Sylvester
Tifton
Alma
Douglas
Pearson
Waycross
Camilla
Moultrie
Nashville
Nahunta
Adel
OKEFENOKEE NAT. WILDERNESS AREA
Woodbine
Lakeland
Homerville
Folkston
Quitman
Valdosta
Statenville
St Marys River
Fargo
Fernandina Beach
Monticello
Jasper
Callahan
Yulee
Amelia City
Greenville
White Springs
Madison
Capps
JACKSONVILLE
Mac Clenny
Live Oaks
Olustee
Baldwin
Atlantic Beach
Jacksonville Beach
Lake City
OSCEOLA NAT. FOREST
Lake Butler
Orange Park
Springs
Perry
Mayo
Branford
Starke
St Johns River
Suwanee River
Alachua
St Augustine
High Springs
Green Cove Springs
Waldo
Crescent Beach
Adams Beach
Old Town
Cross City
Gainesville
Palatka
San Mateo
Marineland
Steinhatchee
Trenton
Archer
Orange Lake
Orange Springs
Flagler Beach
Bunnell
Chiefland
Bronson
Williston
Lake George
Crescent City
Ormond Beach
Suwannee
Oklawaha River
Silver Springs
Seville
Otter Creek
Cedar Key
Ocala
Salt Springs
Daytona Beach

1
2
3
4
5
6
7
8
9
10
A
B
C
D
North
Nashville
Pearson
Waycross
Waynesville
Brunswick
Nahunta
Hoboken
Glenmore
Lakeland
Ray City
Hahira
Homerville
OKEFENOKEE NAT. WILDERNESS
Race Pond
Woodbine
Stockton
Valdosta
Mayday
Folkston
Kingsland
St Marys
Hilliard
Fargo
Twin Lakes
Statenville
St Marys River
Fernandina Beach
Yulee
Oneil
Amelia City
Callahan
Jasper
Belmont
River Suwanee
OSCEOLA NAT. FOREST
Moniac
Kent
Westlake
Genoa
Taylor
Bryceville
Live Oak
White Springs
Jacksonville
Atlantic Beach
Neptune Beach
Jacksonville Beach
Ponte Vedra Beach
Baldwin
Mac Clenny
Sanderson
Wellborn
Lake City
Olustee
Sapp
Orange Park
Durbin
Mayo
Lawtey
Middleburg
Lake Butler
Orangedale
Branford
Fort White
Starke
Green Cove Springs
St Johns River
St Augustine
River Suwanee
Bell
Brooker
Waldo
Keystone Heights
Alachua
High Springs
Grandin
Crescent Beach
Hastings
Marineland
Old Town
Trenton
Newberry
Palatka
San Mateo
Palm Coast
Fanning Spring
Gainesville
Interlachen
Satsuma
Flagler Beach
Archer
Hawthorne
Andalusia
Pomona Park
Micanopy
Orange Springs
Lake Como
Bunnell
Chiefland
Bronson
Orange Lake
Lake George
Crescent City
Ormond Beach
Holly Hill
Lennon
Williston
Ft McCoy
Salt Springs
Seville
Otter Creek
OCALA
Barberville
Daytona

1
2
3
4
5
7
8
9
10
A
B
C
D
0 10 miles
0 20 kms
© 1995 Thomas Cook Ltd
Inglis
Withlacoochee River
Dunnellon
Crystal River
Hernando
Homosassa Springs
Lecanto
Homosassa
Inverness
Floral City
Belleview
OCALA NAT. FOREST
Wildwood
Leesburg
Bushnell
Altoona
Cassia
Grand Island
Eustis
Tavares
Lake Apopka
Apopka
Orlando
Winter Garden
Mascotte
Groveland
Clermont
Lake Monroe
Deltona
Sanford
Geneva
Casselberry
Maitland
Bithlo
Christmas
Scottsmoor
Mims
Titusville
Cape Canaveral
Cocoa
Merritt Island
Cocoa Beach
Satellite Beach
Melbourne
Palm Bay
Grant
Barefoot Bay
Sebastian
Fellsmere
Bayport
Weeki Wachee
Spring Hill
Brooksville
Ridge Manor
Masaryktown
Bayonet Point
Dade City
Port Richey
Land O'Lakes
Holiday
Zephyrsville
Wesley Chapel
Tarpon Springs
Palm Harbor
Ozona
Oldsmar
Dunedin
Clearwater
Belleair
Indian Rocks Beach
Redington
Madeira Beach
Treasure Island
St Petersburg Beach
St Petersburg
Tampa Bay
Tampa
Lutz
Brandon
Kathleen
Plant City
Lakeland
Polk City
Mulberry
Bartow
Bradley
Winter Haven
Dundee
Lake Wales
Haines City
Davenport
Intercession City
Kissimmee
St Cloud
Lake Tohopekaliga
Holopaw
Deer Park
Kenansville
Lake Kissimmee
Nalcrest
Indian Lake Estates
Oasis
Yeehaw Junction
Fort Drum
Frostproof
Fort Meade
Avon Park
Bowling Green
Sebring
Wauchula
Zolfo Springs
Lake Placid
Lorida
Basinger
Sun City
Parrish
Manhattan
Palmetto
Bradenton

6
1
2
3
4
5
6
7
8
9
10
A
B
C
D
Walt Disney World
Bayonet Point
Port Richey
Holiday
Tarpon Springs
Ozona
Clearwater
Tampa
St Petersburg
Tampa Bay
San Antonio
Land O'Lakes
Lutz
Wesley Chapel
Dade City
Zephyrhills
Kathleen
Lakeland
Plant City
Brandon
Mulberry
Sun City
Polk City
Winter Haven
Bartow
Kissimmee
Intercession City
Davenport
Haines City
Dundee
Lake Wales
Nalcrest
Fort Meade
Frostproof
Bowling Green
Avon Park
Wauchula
Zolfo Springs
Sebring
Lake Placid
Arcadia
Fort Ogden
Punta Gorda
Port Charlotte
North Point
Bermont
Palmetto
Anna Maria
Holmes Beach
Bradenton
Longboat Key
Sarasota
Siesta Key
Osprey
Venice
Englewood
Charlotte Harbor
Boca Grande
Bokeelia
Captiva
Cape Coral
North Fort Myers
Fort Myers
Fort Myers Beach
Lehigh Acres
Immokalee
La Belle
Caloosahatchee River
Palmdale
Moore Haven
Lakeport
Clewiston
Devils Garden
Lake Harbor
South Bay
Okeelanta
Belle Glade
Miami Canal
LOXAHATCHEE NAT WILDLIFE REFUGE
Loxahatchee
Pahokee
Canal Point
Port Mayaca
Lake Okeechobee
Buckhead Ridge
Brighton
Okeechobee
Lorida
Basinger
Fort Drum
Kissimmee River
Indian Lake Estates
Oasis
Lake Kissimmee
Lake Tohopekatiga
St Cloud
Holopaw
Deer Park
Yeehaw Junction
Cocoa
Satellite Beach
Melbourne
Melbourne Beach
Palm Bay
Grant
Barefoot Bay
Sebastian
Fellsmere
Indian River
Gifford Shores
Vero Beach
Fort Pierce
Port St Lucie
Hutchinson Island
Stuart
St Lucie Canal
Indiantown
Hobe Sound
Jupiter
Juno Beach
Palm Beach Shores
Singer Island
West Palm Beach
Palm Beach
Lantana
Boynton Beach
Delray Beach

# TYPICAL ROAD SIGNS IN FLORIDA

## INSTRUCTIONS

| Stop | Give way | Wrong way - often together with 'No entry' sign |  No right turn |  No U-turn |

| One-way traffic | Two-way left turn lanes | 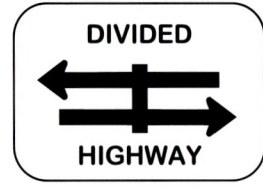 Divided highway (dual carriageway) at junction ahead | Speed limit signs: maximum and maximum/minimum limits |

## WARNINGS

| Crossroads |  Junction | Curve (bend) | Winding road |

| Stop ahead |  Two-way traffic |  Divided highway (dual carriageway) |  Road merges from right | Roadworks ahead |

| Railway crossing |  No-overtaking zone |